W9-AEO-207

ALL THE DOCTRINES OF THE BIBLE

A STUDY AND ANALYSIS OF MAJOR BIBLE DOCTRINES

by
DR. HERBERT LOCKYER, R.S.L., F.R.G.S.

Zondervan Books
Zondervan Publishing House
Grand Rapids, Michigan

Dedicated to
A. H. BOULTON ESQ.,
of Bebington
Who by life and labor, continues by
"sound doctrine both to exhort and
to convince the gainsayers."

ALL THE DOCTRINES OF THE BIBLE
Copyright 1964
Zondervan Publishing House
Grand Rapids, Michigan

Zondervan Books are published by Zondervan
Publishing House, 1415 Lake Drive, S.E.,
Grand Rapids, Michigan 49506

ISBN 0-310-28050-8

Library of Congress Catalog Card No. 64-15558

Printed in the United States of America

85   86   87   88   89   90 / 30   29   28   27   26   25

All the Doctrines
of the Bible

Foreword

The recent revival of evangelism in many parts of the world in our day is something for which Christians of all lands feel very thankful. But with this feeling of thankfulness there ought to go a deep sense of responsibility to those who have been evangelized. When men and women have been converted to a living faith in Christ they need to learn to understand the Christian faith and lead the Christian life in the fellowship of the Christian Church. How can they be helped along the road?

In the Bible they may hear the voice of God speaking to their souls; in the Church they may experience the blessings of the common life in the Body of Christ. Nothing can replace Bible study and church fellowship, but a certain degree of guidance from experienced teachers is most desirable. How should the Bible be studied? How can the Christian faith be worked out in the complicated situations of everyday life? What, in short, does Christianity involve in its most comprehensive aspect?

Dr. Herbert Lockyer, out of his long experience and ripe wisdom, has written a book which will help many to understand the cardinal doctrines of the Christian faith. It will not take the place of the Bible, but prove of greatest use to those who study it along with an open Bible. The Bible, as it recites the mighty and self-revealing acts of God which reach their climax in the coming of Christ, does not arrange the doctrines which it unfolds in an order which we might consider the logical one. The Bible was intended to be much more than a handbook of Divinity. But with minds like ours we can learn the Bible doctrines more readily if someone systematizes them for us in a logical sequence, and this is what Dr. Lockyer has done in these pages.

We should bear in mind, of course, that something is bound to be left out of the most careful and most Scriptural system of doctrine; and no doubt Dr. Lockyer would echo the request of John Knox and his colleagues who drafted the *Scots Confession* of 1560, who begged their readers in the "Introduction" to point out to them any deviation from Biblical truth that might be detected in the *Confession,* so that their reformation of religion according to the Word of God might be even more complete . . . I am happy to commend Dr. Lockyer's work to readers, and wish it a wide and fruitful circulation.

F. F. Bruce

Preface

David asked the question, "If the foundations be destroyed, what can the righteous do?" (Psalm 11:3). Without doubt, the Psalmist had in mind the attitude of the saint when the foundations of state and society are attacked. Truth, righteousness, justice, law and order form the basis of a nation's social and theocratic fabric. But when the righteousness is perverted, society is corrupt, and the righteous are despised, what are the children of God to do? While unable, in themselves, to remedy the perversion of morals, they can exercise faith in God who, because of His sovereignty, is well able to right all wrongs.

From the time of the apostles, other foundations have been assailed. Apostasy preaches the gospel of destruction. Modernism, in open and secret ways, has ever sought to abolish the pillars of truth. The fundamentals of the Christian faith are still being attacked, being reckoned out of course (Psalm 82:5). What are the righteous to do? First of all, they must exercise a deep and ever-deepening faith in the indestructibility of Holy Writ. Modernists or liberals may try to destroy the foundations of Christianity, but like all the foundations of God, they stand sure (II Timothy 2:19). In spite of the effort of adverse critics to mutilate many of the Bible books and doctrines, we seem to hear all of the sixty-six books forming the "Divine Library" saying, "Do thyself no harm, we are all here." The Scriptures cannot be destroyed or broken. They are settled in heaven.

In the next place, when the Word of God is attacked, the righteous must earnestly contend for the faith, which the Lord enables them to do without becoming contentious. But if the integrity of the Scriptures is to be contended for, and all the faith and doctrine they contain upheld, they must be prayerfully studied and clearly comprehended. It is to be hoped that the simple studies making up this volume on "Biblical Doctrines" will help in this direction. The aim of the writer has not been to set forth an exhaustive treatment of the great doctrines of the Bible, but to offer the Christian worker who seeks to defend the foundations of his faith, simple and satisfying outlines of the august truths which, like their divine Author, cannot be destroyed. Terminology too theological or technical has been avoided.

True believers hold that all Bible doctrines are not of men, but constitute the positive teaching of God Himself. To them, the Scriptures are not an ancient literary curiosity, but the revelation of His mind to the mind of man, and they affirm that unless one is indwelt by the Holy Spirit, who made the revelation possible, its contents cannot be discerned or understood (I Corinthians 2:13,14). It is the height of foolishness or irreverence to reject the fact that "holy men of God spake as they were moved by the Holy Ghost" (II Peter 1:21). If the Spirit of God spoke through the men who wrote the Bible, the least we can do is to study it prayerfully as a God-given revelation. To deny such an affirmation is to brand the writers of Scripture as liars, fraudulent and deceptive. How could they be "holy men" if what they wrote was not given them from above?

All *doctrines* need periodic restatement no matter what their subject matter may be. This is why preachers should plan a course of Bible doctrine. Too many present-day congregations are fed on scraps, and because they fail to receive the strong meat of the Word (Hebrews 5:14), the spiritual life of the people is somewhat anemic. In the "Preface" to his volume on *Christian Doctrines*, Dr. R. W. Dale relates the following experience:

Three or four years after I left college, I met in the streets of Birmingham a Congregational Minister, from whom I had heard several very remarkable sermons. There was fancy in them, and humour and pathos and passion, and, at times, great keenness and originality of thought. He was a Welshman, and his preaching had many of the qualities which have given such extraordinary power to the great Nonconformist preachers of Wales. He had reached middle age and I was still a young man, and he talked to me in a friendly way about my ministry. He said, "I hear that you are preaching Doctrinal Sermons at Carr's Lane; they will not stand it." I answered: "They will have to stand it."

Dr. Dale goes on to say that, in order to avoid the danger of failing to give to any of the great doctrines of the Christian faith an adequate place in his preaching, he would draw up at the beginning of the year a list of the subjects he would preach on during the twelve months ahead. The contents of his renowned book on *Christian Doctrines* contains one of the lists Dr. Dale preached from. What about the congregation? Did they appreciate the heavy diet? Says Dr. Dale, "So far from finding that a congregation will not stand Doctrinal Sermons, my experience is that such sermons, if of moderate length, are of great interest to large numbers of Christian people." Perhaps we would have fuller churches, if only theological students were taught how to prepare and preach the august doctrines of Scripture. Too many preachers shear the sheep, instead of feeding them.

CONTENTS

Foreword   v
Preface vii
I. How to Study Christian Doctrine   1
II. The Doctrine of a Divine Revelation   3
III. The Doctrine of a Divine Inspiration   7
IV. The Doctrine of God 11
V. The Doctrine of Christ 36
VI. The Doctrine of the Holy Spirit 59
VII. The Doctrine of the Trinity 121
VIII. The Doctrine of Angels 127
IX. The Doctrine of Satan and Demons 132
X. The Doctrine of Man 139
XI. The Doctrine of the Covenants 146
XII. The Doctrine of Predestination 151
XIII. The Doctrine of Sin 153
XIV. The Doctrine of Salvation 159
XV. The Doctrine of Grace 163
XVI. The Doctrine of Repentance 169
XVII. The Doctrine of Regeneration 176
XVIII. The Doctrine of Substitution 183
XIX. The Doctrine of Redemption 186
XX. The Doctrine of Reconciliation 191
XXI. The Doctrine of Faith 193
XXII. The Doctrine of Adoption 199
XXIII. The Doctrine of Assurance 204
XXIV. The Doctrine of Righteousness 207
XXV. The Doctrine of Peace 212
XXVI. The Doctrine of Sanctification 217
XXVII. The Doctrine of Christian Ethics 221
XXVIII. The Doctrine of Eternal Security 223
XXIX. The Doctrine of Prayer 225
XXX. The Doctrine of the Church 229
XXXI. The Doctrine of Last Things 267
Bibliography 294
Subject Index 297
Biblical Index 305

I

How To Study Christian Doctrine

By way of introduction it may prove profitable to deal with the study of doctrine as a whole. The word itself is from *doctrina*, which is derived from *docco*, meaning "to teach," and denotes both the act of teaching and the subject taught. *Doctor* is associated with the same word and is equivalent to teacher, as indicated in the Revised Version of Luke 2:46; 5:17; Acts 5:34.

The Biblical usage of the term is interesting to trace. In the Old Testament we have the Hebrew words *Lekah*, meaning "what is received," "the matter or message taught" (Deuteronomy 32:2; Job 11:4; Proverbs 4:2; Isaiah 29:24); *Shemuah*, meaning "what is heard" (Isaiah 28:9); *Musar*, meaning "discipline" (Jeremiah 10:8). "The discipline of unreal gods is wood —is like themselves, destitute of true moral force." In the New Testament we have *Didarkalia*, implying "the art of teaching" (I Timothy 4:13-16; 5:17; II Timothy 3:10-16); and "what is taught" (Matthew 15:9; II Timothy 4:3); *Didache*, which is always translated "teaching" (Romans 16:1; R.V. margin). We have the "act of teaching" (Mark 4:2; Acts 2:42) and "what is taught" (John 7:14-17; Romans 2:24). It would seem as if the meaning of the word varied as the Church developed the content of its experience into a system of thought, and came to regard such as an integral part of saving faith. The teachers of doctrine and what they taught can be classified thus:

1. *Pharisaical*

The doctrines of the Pharisees, upon which they set great value, were a fairly compact and definite body of teaching, and comprised fixed traditions, like the Talmud. Handed down from one generation of teachers to another, these humanly conceived doctrines were revered by the religious rulers of our Lord's day. Christ Himself rejected them (Matthew 15:9; 16:12; Mark 7:7).

2. *Christological*

In contrast with the Pharisaic system, the teaching of Christ was unconventional, occasional, discursive and unsystematic. It derived its power from His personality, character and works, more than from His words. Thus the learned doctors or teachers were astonished at it, and fought it (Matthew 7:28; 22:33; Mark 1:22,27; Luke 4:32). It is profitable to trace through the four gospels, all Jesus taught about the doctrines of the Holy Spirit, faith, prayer, baptism, Satan, sin, etc.

3. *Apostolical*

In the early days of the church, the apostles gathered the salient features of Christ's teaching and proclaimed them abroad. The so-called "apostles' doctrine" (Acts 2:42) consisted of three parts—

That Jesus was the Christ (Acts 3:13-18).
That He rose from the dead (Acts 1:22; 2:24,32).
That salvation was by faith in His name (Acts 2:38; 3:16; 4:12).

These outstanding truths were combined with the Hebrew faith as based upon Old Testament revelation and presented in consecutive fashion by Peter and Stephen (Acts 2:14-26; 5:29-32; 7:2-53). What need there is, in these days of modern thought, to return to the pure, apostolic doctrine which, when preached, had far-reaching results!

It was left to the Apostle Paul, however, to produce a more thorough co-ordination of Christian facts. Types of his doctrinal statements can be found in his speeches at Antioch (Acts 13:16-41), at Lystra (Acts 14:15-17) and at Athens (Acts 17:22-31). These inspired utterances reveal a doctrinal system centering around the Resurrection of Christ, and form the burden of Paul's masterly epistles.

4. *Ecclesiastical*

While Paul systematized various aspects of Christian truth, there was not much effort to impose doctrine by authority, on the Church as a whole. In the pastoral and general epistles, the repeated emphasis is upon "sound" or "healthy" doctrine (I

1

Timothy 1:10; 6:3; II Timothy 1:13; 4:3; Titus 1:9; 2:1), and upon "good doctrine" (I Timothy 4:6). These phrases imply that a body of teaching had emerged which could be generally accepted and serve as a standard of orthodoxy. Thus the faith gradually became a body of truth, "once for all delivered unto the saints" (Jude 3).

The old Roman formula, known as *The Apostles' Creed,* is the oldest Christian creed extant, and is so called because it has been ascribed to the apostles themselves. It is supposed to be a statement of truth representing what Christ and His apostles taught, and reads:

> I believe in God the Father Almighty, Maker of heaven and earth, And in Jesus Christ, His only Son, our Lord, who was conceived by the Holy Ghost, born of the Virgin Mary, suffered under Pontius Pilate, was crucified, dead and buried; He descended into hell; the third day He arose again from the dead; He ascended into heaven, and sitteth on the right hand of God the Father Almighty; from thence He shall come to judge the quick and the dead.
>
> I believe in the Holy Ghost, the holy catholic Church (Note: not the Roman Catholic Church—*catholic* here meaning universal) the communion of saints, the forgiveness of sins; the resurrection of the body, and the life everlasting.

Within the organized church of today there are many formulas of systematized truth, each denomination having its own creed or expression of belief to which members must subscribe. The believer's standard of authority, however, is the Word of God. Concerning all doctrines, the rule of Ridley the Martyr must be our guide—

"In these matters I am so fearful that I dare not speak further, yea, almost none otherwise than the text doth, as it were, lead me by the hand."

We must only hold the truth agreeing with "the law and the testimony."

The importance of doctrinal study cannot be over-emphasized. In these days of developing apostasy and perverted doctrines, it is essential to ponder prayerfully the great doctrines of the Bible. Among necessary rules that must be observed as the student endeavors to systematize truth, mention can be made of the following—

1. *Gather all your necessary material.* Once the subject has been chosen, a com-

prehensive concordance should be used to gather all the Scriptures having to do with it. On this point Angus, in his *Bible Handbook* has this to say: "To gather doctrinal truth from Scripture, we bring all the passages that refer to the same subject; whether they be doctrines, precepts, promises or examples; impartially compare them; restrict the expressions of one passage by those of another; and explain the whole consistently (for example, verses dealing with the word "perfect," Matthew 5:48 by others like I John 1:8). When the proposition which we derive from such complete collection of the passages embodies all they contain, and no more, it may then be regarded as a general Scripture truth."

2. *Trace the progress of doctrine.* Truth should be classified according to the Old and New Testaments. As the Church is not the subject of Old Testament teaching, Christian doctrine must be sought for in the New Testament. The doctrine of the Holy Spirit, for example, while mentioned in the Old Testament, is only there as a partial revelation. Christ never takes the Holy Spirit from any child of His (Psalm 51:11 with John 14:16, 17).

> The New is in the Old concealed;
> The Old is in the New revealed.

3. *Balance one doctrine by another.* One doctrine must be held consistently with another. To neglect this rule means that we become like a cake not turned (Hosea 7:8); overdone on the one side, underdone on the other. The doctrine of election must be balanced by the doctrine of free grace. Repentance, faith and obedience are the gifts of God (John 15:5; Acts 5:31; Ephesians 2:8; Philippians 1:29; 2:13; I Peter 1:2). Does this mean that men are guiltless if they do not repent, believe and obey? The guilt of impenitence is charged upon man (Matthew 11:20,21; Revelation 16:9). Unbelief is declared to be a sin and the ground of condemnation (John 3:18; 16:9). Men are exhorted to repent (Mark 1:15), and believe and obey (Matthew 3:2; Luke 13:3).

4. *State Biblical doctrines in Scripture language.* In describing the august themes of the Bible, all scientific and high-sounding phraseology should be avoided. The Authorized Version of the Bible offers us

the purest English to be found in any literature, and one cannot do better than saturate the memory with its exact language. Consult, however, *The Amplified Bible.*" Modernism would have us adopt softened words for *sin, regeneration, hell.* Such language, we are told, is antiquated. Forcible terms like *blood, grace and salvation* are going out of fashion in some quarters, and "words which man's wisdom teacheth" (I Corinthians 2:13) are being substituted for "the words which the Holy Ghost teacheth."

5. *Combine doctrine with practice.* Right thinking should lead to right living. What is the use of a correct creed without a correct character? Scriptural doctrines should result in scriptural holiness. There is an inseparable connection between doctrine and duty; precept and practice. Discovered truth must be applied to life. It is only thus that a doctrine becomes a dynamic.

6. *General principles to observe.* Make no subject a matter of necessary faith which is not a matter of revelation.

Let there be a suspense of judgment until the Word of God itself decides. Bias, away from Scripture, results in fancy and imagination.

Accept the same relative prominence of a doctrine that the Bible gives it. The Second Advent is the most prominent truth in the New Testament, and should be prominent in our witness.

When a doctrine is important and necessary, Scripture will be found to be full and clear. If a theme is not complete and clear, it is not in itself important, or the full knowledge of it is unattainable in our present state (I Corinthians 13:9-12).

The Bible never contradicts itself. Those who reject it as a divine revelation have much to say about apparent contradictions. But "the law of the Lord is perfect," and what appears to be contradictory, disappears when we "compare spiritual things with spiritual" (I Corinthians 2:13).

With this introduction before us, let us now give ourselves to an understanding of those vital doctrines so precious to the hearts of those who accept the Bible in its totality as the inspired revelation of God to man. The following doctrines are sometimes spoken of as "theology," a term meaning knowledge of God and of divine truths. *Doctrine* is teaching as deduced from Scripture. *Dogma* is the teaching authoritatively laid down by the church, and when contrary to Biblical doctrine, must be rejected.

II

The Doctrine of a Divine Revelation

One's attitude toward the Scriptures determines his ability to understand and appreciate the august doctrines they proclaim. If the divine inspiration and veracity of the Bible are rejected, then any system of truth it contains cannot be relied upon. If "every Scripture" is not "inspired of God" (II Timothy 3:16 R.V.), how can we accept as authoritative the cardinal Christian truths it presents? For example, conversion would be impossible if the Bible were not perfect. "The law of the Lord is perfect," and therefore able to "convert the soul" (Psalm 19:7). Thus every one born anew by the Spirit of God is a fresh evidence of the perfection of Holy Writ. Modernism is destitute of soul-winning, simply because it teaches the imperfection of the Word of God.

Before approaching the majestic truths of the Scriptures, then, it is imperative to understand their claims to divine inspiration, infallibility and integrity. If, as we believe, "all Scripture (not some of it) is given by inspiration of God," and is "profitable for doctrine, for reproof, for correction, for instruction in righteousness," how can we be complete and "throughly furnished unto all good works" (II Timothy 3:16,17), unless we know how to rightly divide the word of truth (II Timothy 2:15)? As we face heresy, speculation and ignorance, we must be sure of our ground.

Ignorance on our part not only spells bondage, but defeat (Isaiah 5:13).

Full dependence upon the Holy Spirit produces clarity of thought enabling us to arrive at well-defined statements of doctrinal truth. In His light, we see light (Proverbs 2:3-6). Divine truth is understood from the divine standpoint. Further, as revealed truth is accepted and obeyed, added light is granted. The mystic connection between revelation and sanctification was realized by Elihu when he prayed:

"That which I see not teach thou me: if I have done iniquity, I will do no more (Job 34:32).

Accepting the Scriptures, then, as the authoritative revelation of the purpose and plan of God, let us consider them as a specific revelation, progressive revelation, inspired revelation and final revelation.

A Specific Revelation

There are those who fail to see anything in the Bible to admire. To their darkened and uninstructed minds, it appears to be nothing short of a heterogeneous mass of written material. Even many who profess to be enlightened severely criticize the Bible because of supposed glaring irregularities, apparent contradictions, useless and unimportant parts, lack of true literary merit. The unity and symmetry of the Bible, however, is clearly evident to the honest mind. Its sixty-six different books are co-related and are unintelligible when isolated. Taken together, they are a perfect whole. Their inner relation makes these books one, and such unity is a proof of divine inspiration.

Before considering the specific contents of such a revelation, it may be advisable to understand the significance of terms constantly appearing in Bible study. Too often we are guilty of using these terms lightly. Their true import is not grasped.

1. *Revelation.* What do we mean by the term, "revelation"? The simple yet adequate explanation of the dictionary is, "A revelation is that which is revealed by God to man."

The word itself means "flinging or drawing back the veil," thus signifying the removal of a veil or other obstruction to complete vision; the display or making known of that which was before concealed from view or from cognizance. A divine revelation, then, is the communication or disclosure by God to man of truths which he could not otherwise know, no matter how trustworthy his source of knowledge. Human search can never find God out. Whatever man desires or needs to know about God (all truth in revelation, must come from God Himself.)

Modern criticism, however, denies this specific revelation, and substitutes, as Professor James Orr points out, "psychology for revelation." Here is a terse and telling statement of his: "Accordingly . . . the Old Testament is a product of special divine revelation. The tendency of the modern mind is to substitute psychology for revelation. Instead of God's word to Isaiah, or John, or Paul, it gives us the thoughts of Isaiah, or John, or Paul, about God." Even where the word "revelation" is used, it is with this purely psychological connotation. This, however, is not the Bible's point of view.

The Bible is not primarily a record of man's thoughts of God, but a record of what God has done and revealed of Himself to man. Its basis is not "Thus and thus man thinks," but "Thus and thus saith Jehovah," or "Thus and thus hath Jehovah done."

2. *Inspiration.* It is absolutely necessary to grasp the meaning of this oft-quoted term, seeing there is a vast difference between "revelation" and "inspiration." Revelation is the subject matter of the message, that is, what God imparts to man; inspiration is the power or method by which man communicates his God-given message to others. We may therefore regard inspiration as a special gift of the Holy Spirit, by which prophets of the Old Testament and the apostles and their companions in the New Testament transmitted the revelation of God as they received it.

These two facts are combined by Peter:

For the prophecy came not in old time by the will of man: but holy men of God spake as they were moved by the Holy Ghost (II Peter 1:21).

Here you have God distinctly revealing Himself to man. This sentence describes the unction or inspiration they received to declare the prophecy.

3. *Illumination.* Clarence Larkin observes that "Spiritual illumination is different either from Bible inspiration or

revelation." It is the work of the Holy Spirit in the believer, by which he has his "spiritual understanding" opened to understand the Scriptures (John 16:12,15).

The "natural man" cannot receive the things of the "Spirit of God," neither can he know them, "for they are spiritually discerned" (I Corinthians 2:11,14). "The work, then, of the Holy Spirit in these days is not to impart some new revelation to men, or to inspire them to write or speak as the prophets and apostles of old, but so to illuminate men's minds and open up their understanding of the Scriptures that their heart will burn within them as they compare Scripture with Scripture, and have revealed to them God's plan and purpose in the ages, as disclosed in His Holy Word."

Moreover, this particular illumination is not confined to a few elect souls, for no prophecy is of private interpretation (II Peter 1:20), which means that no man has a right to say what the Scriptures mean, according to his own opinion. The humblest believer, in simple dependence upon the Holy Spirit, can receive the insight into Holy Scripture that baffles and escapes the scholar who, with all his intellectual endowments, and knowledge of the original languages of the Bible, fails to possess, if he comes to the Word minus the aid of the Spirit.

In that defensive volume of his, *"The Church's One Foundation,* W. Robertson Nicol expresses the matter thus:

> We hope we are not wrong, but it seems to us that in these latter days Christians have taken to believing that it is by the use of the grammar and commentary that they can understand the New Testament. Nothing is understood in the New Testament without direct spiritual illumination.

Therefore the true believer prays, "Open thou mine eyes, that I may behold wondrous things out of thy law" (Psalm 119:18), and experiences the opened understanding necessary for the opened Scriptures (Luke 24:45).

The last prayer of Goēthe was for more light. One condition for receiving more light is that we are faithful and true to the light already given. It is sadly possible for us to ask for more light but be disloyal to the illumination already given. In such a case, it is foolish to think that we shall **receive the gift** we are seeking.

From the eyes of the purely critical, the beauty of the Book, the glory of the Gospel, the wonder of the Word, and the sublimity of the Scriptures, are hid. Certain attractions they may discern, but their vision at the best is only a distorted one for, like some sensitive plant, the Bible closes itself at the touch of adverse criticism.

It is only when we come to the Book as babes, and allow it to criticize us, then learn like Isaiah to "tremble at his word" (Isaiah 66:2,5), that the door is opened as if by a magic hand, and we behold treasures untold, and rejoice over such, as one that findeth great spoil. "If I meditate upon any portion of Holy Writ," said Martin Luther, "it shines and burns in my heart."

We now turn to what the Bible definitely reveals. To many it is a disappointing Book simply because people misunderstand the purpose for which it was written. The scientist turns to it, but fails to find what he expected to discover, namely, some detailed scientific treatise, seeing that it professes to be God's Word, and that God, Himself, is the Author of all life.

Yet, as Dr. D. M. McIntyre points out, that "the Bible is *non-scientific* is apparent to the most indifferent reader, but it by no means follows that it is therefore unscientific."

There is much scientific material within the Bible, and let it be said that its scientific statements are abreast of all modern discoveries. The Scriptures were given, not to tell us how the heavens go, but to teach us how to go to heaven.

Says Dr. A. T. Pierson, "I do not claim to be a scientist, but after many years of study of science and revelation, I do affirm that there is not a single point of conflict as to established facts. Theories of science conflict among themselves, but real science and the Scriptures exhibit a wonderful harmony."

If one thinks of theology, morals, history or any other outstanding topic, they will be disappointed if they expect to find in the pages of this most wonderful of all books those systematic, well-defined treatises or codes.

The Bible is a divine revelation. Naturally, we ask the question, a divine revelation of what? Briefly, the answer is:

Of Four Persons

Of God the Father, whose condescending love is manifested.

Of God the Son, whose abundant sacrifice is revealed.

Of God the Holy Ghost, whose holy ministry is described.

Of Satan, whose diabolical purposes are unmasked.

Of Three Classes of People

The Jews, the nation chosen by God for divine purposes.

The Gentiles, that is, the rest of mankind, apart from the Jews.

The Church of God, composed of both Jews and Gentiles.

Of Three Places

Heaven, the dwelling place of the Trinity, the angelic host and the redeemed.

Earth, the sphere of human souls, sin and sorrow.

Hell, the present abode of the lost.

The following summary, taken from Dr. A. T. Pierson's *Seed Thoughts for Public Speakers,* is another way of answering the above question.

There is a sevenfold completeness which marks the whole plan and scheme of redemption, as revealed in the Word of God; and when all these particulars are embraced in our conception, in proper order and relation, nothing can be added. The perfect entirety of the plan is itself a proof of the origin and source of it.

1. *A Supernatural Creation* whose crown and consummation is *man.*
2. *A Supernatural Revelation,* whose crown and consummation is *the Bible.*
3. *A Supernatural Incarnation,* whose crown and consummation is *Jesus Christ.*
4. *A Supernatural Indwelling,* whose crown and consummation is the *Holy Spirit.*
5. *An Elect People,* separated from all the peoples of the earth.
6. *An Elect Church,* gathered out from all nations.
7. *An Elect Kingdom,* finally to incorporate and assimilate all other kingdoms.
8. *A New Creation,* in which holiness reigns and God is all in all. This is the logical and philosophical order.

The historical order is different:

The Creation
The Elect People
The Revelation
The Incarnation
The Indwelling Spirit
The Elect Church
The Elect Kingdom
The New Creation

A life's ministry might be profitably spent in simply going over and over this program. It would be found to include the entire revelation of Scripture truths, to embrace all the great factors of redemption, of man's spiritual history, and God's spiritual dealing with the race. It contains all the divisions of a perfect theological system, and suggests the whole relation and duty of man toward God's creation.

A Progressive Revelation

To those who come to the Scriptures with an open mind and reliance upon the Holy Spirit for illumination, there comes the ineffaceable conviction that they present not a "heterogeneous jumble," as critics affirm, of ancient history, myths, legends and religious speculations and superstitions, but a gradual unfolding of the plan and purpose of God, a progress of revelation and doctrine.

This fact has been ably set forth in Bernard's *Progress of Doctrine.* In this most helpful book on Bible study many principles applied to the New Testament revelation can be fittingly applied to the whole unveiling of God's will, work and ways.

Therefore, because the Bible is a progressive revelation, we should read it as a whole, comparing one part with another in order to gain a true perspective. Thus, Hebrews gives us the completion of Leviticus; the book of Revelation, of Daniel; the gospels, of Isaiah 53.

People often fall into error simply because they accept or appropriate some partial revelation of a given truth. In his *Knowing the Scriptures,* Dr. Pierson has a very timely word about error. "No investigation of Scripture, in its various parts and separate texts, however important, must impair the sense of the supreme value of its united witness. There is not a form of evil doctrine or practice that may not claim apparent sanction and support from isolated passages; but nothing erroneous or vicious can ever find countenance from the Word of God when the whole united testimony of Scripture is weighed against it. Partial examination will result in partial views of truth which are necessarily imperfect; only careful comparison will show the complete mind of God."

Regarding the progress of revelation contained in the Scriptures, Dr. D. M. McIntyre remarks:

We willingly confess that the doctrine moves forward into fuller light and more measured statement, but it moves along the high level of inspiration from the first, the progress of doctrine of which we speak is a progress that is sensible neither of conflict nor of reconciliation. The first word of Scripture is an utterance of God; the first promise has in it the anticipation of completed redemption; the first act of worship looks fixedly toward Calvary. The promise of the end is in the opening chapters; resonance of the first word vibrates in the last. It is presided over by one mind, and that the mind of Christ. The two elements in the progress are a fuller content of truth and a closer relation to the Person of the Redeemer.

Take, for example, the ministry of the Holy Spirit as unfolded in the Old and the New Testaments. Many good people have stumbled over Psalm 51:11, "Cast me not away from thy presence, and take not thy holy spirit from me," and have fallen into darkness, doubt and despair because they have failed to recognize that the Spirit's work in the Old Testament was outward and intermittent, as is witnessed by the fact that He came upon certain men for special purposes, but when such were accomplished, He left them.

The New Testament revelation is that His ministry is inward, and His presence abiding. ". . . he may abide with you for-ever. . . . he dwelleth with you, and shall be in you" (John 14:16,17).

Thus, to live in constant dread lest we have grieved the Spirit out of our life is alien to the progressive truth of Scripture, as well as grievous to Him who graciously indwells us, but whose holy presence is cruelly doubted. See, further, the chapter on "The Totality of Scripture Testimony" in Dr. Pierson's book, above quoted.

Two other illustrations may suffice to prove the progressiveness of revelation:

The Deity of our Lord Jesus Christ and His Equality with the Father

Such sayings as, "My Father is greater than I," need to be put side by side with, "I and my Father are one," and His utterances as a Servant, during the period of His humiliations, with His language as a Sovereign after His glorification. Compare Hebrews 1:1-4 and Revelation 1-3.

The Sleep of Saints in Death

Many passages give countenance to this idea that not only the body but the soul also sleeps in the grave till the Resurrection. But other passages clearly show that while the body sleeps, the spirit is with Christ.

Compare Luke 20:37,38; 23:42,43; and II Corinthians 5:6-8; Philippians 1:23; Revelation 14:13.

III

The Doctrine of a Divine Inspiration

We now come to the most vital part of our consideration of the Scriptures, the foundation upon which they are built, which, if destroyed, causes the whole fabric to totter in ruin.

The modern tendency is to doubt the inspiration of the Bible, and declare that it is no more inspired than some of the outstanding works in the realm of literature, such as those of John Milton, William Shakespeare, etc. But the divine testimony regarding it is that every part of it is inspired by God.

The Meaning of Inspiration

This particular word is found twice in the Bible itself:

In Job 32:8—"The inspiration of the Almighty giveth them understanding."

Here the word signifies "breath," thus showing that God is the Author of man's intelligence.

In II Timothy 3:16—"All scripture is given by inspiration of God."

The particular word used by Paul means "God-breathed," that is, God Himself or through His Holy Spirit, told the writers of the Bible just the very things to record.

Horne defines inspiration, "It is the imparting of such a degree of divine influence, assistance, or guidance as enabled the authors of several Books of Scripture to communicate religious knowledge to others, without error or mistake."

Dr. Pierson, in an article on "The Inspiration of the Bible," says: "It is inspired. This may be said of every good book or noble work of man, in a sense. 'Paradise Lost' or the steam engine came of the inspiration of genius, but this is a 'God-breathed' inspiration. The figure is taken from that work at creation, where the bodily form became instinct with life when the breath of the Creator entered it. This is the Word of the Lord. Into the form of language came the breath of inspiration and so the element of infallibility, distinguishing the Scriptures from all human writings." The dictionary has it, "The procession of the Holy Ghost."

We are reminded by A. R. Fausset that,

> The Greek term has nothing to say of *in*spiring or *in*spiration; it speaks only of a "spiring" or "spiration." What it says of Scripture is, not that it is "breathed into by God" or is the product of the divine "in-breathing" into its human authors, but that it is breathed out by God, "God-breathed," the product of the creative breath of God. In a word, what is declared by this fundamental passage is simply that the Scriptures are a divine product, without any indication of how God has operated in producing them. . . . When Paul declares, then, that "every Scripture" or "all Scripture" is the product of the divine breath, is "God-breathed," he asserts with as much energy as he could employ that Scripture is the product of a specifically divine operation.

The Extent of Inspiration

The thought now engaging our attention is the oft-presented question, "Is the whole Bible inspired?" That the entire Bible from Genesis to Revelation is inspired and can be received as the direct Word of God, is doubted by some in these apostate days. The Scriptures, we are told, may contain the Word of God, but in their totality are not to be reckoned as such.

We affirm, however, that the Bible not only contains but is, from beginning to end, the Word of God. A broken sword will not suffice for the warrior in the conflict; and

likewise, a mutilated Bible, such as Modernists would place in our hands, is utterly unable to wield any power in or through our lives.

The story is told of a man who had, for ten years, listened to a preacher of "higher criticism," who from time to time struck out this portion of the Word as uninspired, and that portion as untrustworthy. The hearer promptly removed book after book from his Bible until nothing was left but the covers, which he then presented to the preacher, as being all that his criticisms of the Bible had left for his hearer's possession.

Of course, it must be understood that we mean by "the inspiration of the whole Bible," the original documents as they came from the hands of the various authors, now no longer extant. Some mistakes may have been made by those who copied or transcribed the Scriptures, and it is the work of reverent criticism to seek, by careful examination and comparison of all existing documents, any errors of the fallible translators and restore, as far as possible, the Scriptures in their original purity.

Dr. C. I. Scofield points out that, "the labors of competent scholars have brought our English versions to a degree of perfection so remarkable that we may confidently rest upon them as authoritative."

After all, it is personal experience that counts, and if any one has reason to doubt the inspiration of the Bible, the certain yet simple test to apply is to yield oneself to its power, strive faithfully to follow its commands, act as it suggests, and as a result, the conviction will irresistibly grow upon the mind seeking proof in this way, that its claim to be inspired of God is not to be questioned, but reverently received, as just and undeniable.

Our Lord said: "If any man will do . . . he shall know" (John 7:17), and in respect to a spiritual understanding of the Scriptures, we are absolutely dependent upon simple and implicit obedience, not scholastic attainment or intellectual ability.

It was Theodore Monod who declared that "Obedience is the greatest commentary upon the Bible—Do, and thou shalt know."

The Mode of Inspiration

Among schools of thought in respect to the extent to which the fallible human writers were controlled by the Spirit of Truth, there are those who believe in

Plenary Inspiration

Such a mode means simply that while the writers acted under the guidance and control of the Holy Spirit, yet they did not write to mere dictation, but were allowed to express God's words in the way most natural to themselves. Here is a sample of this aspect:

> The Divine method of self-disclosure has always been ministration of "truth through personality." The truths which the sacred writers transmit to us, grew to form in their own lives. The Spirit of inspiration witnessed with their spirits. . . . Then out of their varied experiences, they spoke to us.

Such a view implies that while the divine influence prevented all error in the spiritual truth revealed, it did not guarantee inerrancy in other matters, such as numbers of soldiers in an army, money in a treasury, or exclude the expression of too vindictive feeling toward the foes of the writer, his country or his God. But "how far the Spirit of God actually secured the sacred writers from error is a question, the answer to which must be sought in the self-witness of the writings themselves, and in the covering testimony of the Master."

If a statement like this implies that the writers of the Bible possibly erred, not only in unimportant matters, as we have already shown, but in the presentation of some particular truth, then surely such is dangerous ground upon which to tread, if we believe, with Bishop Horne, that "inspiration implies that the authors of the several Books of Scripture communicated religious knowledge to others, without error or mistake."

Common Inspiration

The generally accepted view of the modern school of theological thought, lowers inspiration to the extent of placing it on the same level as the sanctified genius which enabled Milton to write *Paradise Lost,* or Newton and Cowper to compose the *Olney Hymns.* Needless to say, we utterly repudiate such a mode of inspiration. Read some lines from John Milton to a poor, lost sinner and see how far you get in relieving him of his soul-burden. But such is the value of the Bible that one verse like John 3:16 can lead uncounted multitudes to Christ.

Verbal Inspiration

By this is meant that God not only gave the thoughts, but the very words expressed by the writers of the Bible. Some say, "The thoughts, not the words, are inspired," but we think in words. Words give precision, definiteness of form and color to thought. We are not sure of the thought until it is spoken or put into exact, written words.

Dr. James H. Brookes has been at pains to count the separate testimonies of the written Word, to its divine origin. He informs us that such expressions as "God said," "The Lord spake, saying," "The Word of the Lord," and "The Lord commanded," occur 680 times in the Pentateuch, 418 times in the Historical Books, and 1307 times in the Prophets, not to speak of the reiterated attribution to God of the burden of the Poetical Books, and not including at all the New Testament. Here, one might think, the controversy regarding the inspiration of Scripture should be laid to rest.

This stupendous fact is unexampled in the history of the world. The view that orthodox believers hold is that this divine control was sufficiently exerted to produce verbal inspiration; unerring accuracy in every statement made, and divine wisdom in every word uttered or penned. That the writers spoke and wrote the exact words God gave them is clear from their own statements:

> And Moses said unto the Lord, O my Lord, I am not eloquent, neither heretofore, nor since thou hast spoken unto thy servant: but I am slow of speech, and of a slow tongue. And the Lord said unto him, Who hath made man's mouth . . . have not I the Lord? Now therefore go, and I will be with thy mouth, and teach thee what thou shalt say (Exodus 4:10-12).
>
> Which things also we speak, not in the words which man's wisdom teacheth, but which the Holy Ghost teacheth . . . (I Corinthians 2:13).
>
> For the prophecy came not in old time by the will of man: but holy men of God spake as they were moved by the Holy Ghost (II Peter 1:21).

"The living God still lives, and the living Word is a living Word, and we may depend upon it; we may hang upon any word God ever spoke, or ever caused, by His Holy Spirit, to be written. Forty years ago I believed in the verbal inspiration of the Scriptures. I have proved them for forty years and my belief is stronger now than it was then. I have put the promises to the test. I have been compelled to do so, and have found them true and trustworthy." This was the conclusion of J. Hudson Taylor, founder of the China Inland Mission.

The condensed remarks of Dr. C. I. Scofield are worth noting at this point. "The writers of Scripture invariably affirm, where the subject is mentioned by them at all, that the *words* of their writings are divinely taught . . . I Corinthians 2:9-14 gives the process by which a truth passes from the mind of God to the minds of His people.

   a. The unseen things of God are not discoverable by the natural man, v. 9.

   b. These unseen things God has revealed to chosen men, vs. 10-12.

   c. The revealed things are communicated in Spirit-taught words, v. 13.

   d. These Spirit-taught words, in which the revelation has been expressed, are discerned as to their true spiritual content, only by the spiritual among the believers, vs. 15,16.

The Finality of Revelation

The Bible is God's final revelation to man. Such a mode of divine revelation ceased with the book of Revelation. God has given no new or further revelation since John penned the last part of the Scriptures. His complete will for man and for the ages are unfolded therein, and if one appears with the claim that he has received a new revelation, he can be classed as an imposter.

It should be noted, moreover, that the light and truth break forth *from* the Word. We do not expect a new revelation. We are not looking for some new star to arise in the East. We do not expect that any revelation will ever be given to men which will supersede the Bible. All that a guilty sinner can ever need, all that an aspiring saint can ever anticipate, are hidden away in the Divine Library. But all things are not as plain as they will yet be. We are to follow on to know the Lord. "First the blade, then the ear, then the full corn in the ear."

The following paragraph, under the heading, "The Spirit in the Word," appeared in *The Bible Call*:

God gives to no one today the illumination of the Holy Spirit to originate new truth. God's Bible is complete; but He does give in gracious measure the anointing power to humble and sincere seekers, to enable them to recognize and apprehend more perfectly the determinate and unchangeable truths of His Word. We believe in unlimited progress, but it is progress in the fuller apprehension by man of the height and depth, the length and breadth of the unsearchable and inexhaustible treasures of His Holy Book—the Bible.

Let it be remembered that God the Holy Spirit never progresses outside the written Word. God is always causing fresh truths to break forth from His Word, but He does not add to the "faith once for all delivered to the saints." "*Out* of Thy law," not apart from it, truth flows.

The forcible words with which John closes his book make a fitting conclusion, not only to the revelation he received at Patmos, but to the whole substance of revelation as it is found in the sixty-six books forming the Bible:

For I testify unto every man that heareth the words of the prophecy of this book, If any man shall add unto these things, God shall add unto him the plagues that are written in this book: and if any man shall take away from the words of the book of this prophecy, God shall take away his part out of the book of life, and out of the holy city, and from the things which are written in this book (Revelation 22:18, 19).

The first thought that possesses the mind as we take up the Bible and think of its vastness of outlook is, that if the Scriptures are the final revelation of the will and plan of God concerning the world, from its inception to its consummation, then it is possible for us to wrest from its pages by the inspiration of the Holy Spirit, the correct outlines of the different epochs of the world's history, and an understanding of the weighty doctrines it teaches.

Let us therefore settle this question in our minds. Within the Word of God we have the divine plan of the ages, and this plan can be fully understood by every Spirit-taught believer. All that God would have us know regarding the past, present and future history of the earth and of men has been recorded for us, and ours should be the evergrowing desire to study the Word of Truth, in order that we may be able rightly to divide it as the occasion requires.

To many, the Bible is a strange, mysterious Book, simply because they have failed to discover the keys that unlock its pages, and hence the wonderful treasures of the divine purpose remain sealed or hidden. And how applicable is the Lord's word to Ephraim, "I have written to him the great things of my law, but they were counted as a strange thing" (Hosea 8:12).

We can fully understand why the ungodly find nothing to instruct them in the Scriptures, and discard them as "a strange thing." They are spiritually blind, and therefore cannot behold the beauty of the Bible.

How appalling it is to realize that a great number of professing Christians count God's law as "a strange thing," as did Ephraim. Dr. Graham Scroggie says: "It is to be feared that the sad neglect of the Prophetic Scriptures, on the part of very many, is directly due to a disbelief of their supernatural element, and an unwillingness to recognize that in the Bible is revealed a divine plan of the ages." What awful enemies disbelief and ignorance are to the child of God!

IV

The Doctrine of God

Dealing with "The Science of Old Testament Theology" in his massive volume on *The Theology of the Old Testament,* Professor A. B. Davidson reminds us that there are three branches of Biblical theology, of which Old Testament theology is the earlier division.

There is *natural theology* in which nature is the source of our knowledge.

There is *systematic theology* in which Scripture supplies the knowledge, but some mental scheme, logical or philosophical, is made the mold into which the knowledge is run, so that it comes out bearing the form of this mold.

There is *Biblical theology* which is the knowledge of God's great operation in introducing His kingdom among men, presented to our view exactly as it lies presented in the Bible. This aspect of theology, Davidson goes on to say, is a *development.* Commenced in the Old Testament it is completed in the New Testament.

There is perhaps no truth in the New Testament which does not lie in germ in the Old; and conversely, there is perhaps no truth in the Old Testament which has not been expanded and had new meaning put into it in the New. . . . The difference between the New and the Old is not that the same truths are not found in both, but that in the one the truths are found in a less degree of development than in the other.

While we speak of Old Testament *theology,* this same writer says that we do not find a *theology* in the Old Testament; we find a *religion*—religious conceptions and religious hopes and aspirations. As to the theology or doctrine of God, what we have is not a doctrine of God, but a doctrine of *Jehovah, Israel's God;* and the exhortation that the people must be what *their* God, *Jehovah,* was. In the New Testament the emphasis is on God, as the God and Father of Jesus Christ, and of every regenerated Christian.

Another striking feature is that it never occurred to any prophet or apostle to prove the existence of God, as all writers presupposed God's existence with their writings being the product of His influence. Everywhere in the Bible, the existence of God is assumed as a fact, and "as an element in the thought of all men; as connate with man." Whether man knows this God depends upon his moral condition. Sin temporarily eclipses the vision of Him. "The doctrine of Scripture on the *knowability* of God is much more extensive than its doctrine regarding His existence." Man can only come to a true understanding of himself, as he acknowledges God as the beginning and end of all existence, and as the first and final cause of all that is. Both man and things were created by His decision and through His action (Romans 1:

21; 9:5; 11:36; Psalm 33:6; Hebrews. 11:3).

The study of God as He is revealed in Scripture is supremely important because there is a sense in which every other doctrine refers to Him. What is known as *Christian theology* is "a discourse about God and divine things." It is imperative to believe that God *is,* and that the Bible is His Word, before we can approach its teaching on any other doctrine. The central doctrine of redemption, for example, presupposes the divine existence, divine revelation in Scripture, divine nature and attributes, divine work in creation and providence. No truth stands alone.

In the beginning God! What a majestic introduction to the inspired volume of Holy Writ! Dr. Munro Gibson, in a small yet significant handbook of the foundations of the Christian Faith called *Rock versus Sand,* says that there are three main stages in the development of the doctrine of God, namely:

1. The being of God, dominating Scripture
2. The revelation of God in Christ
3. The record of that revelation by the Holy Spirit in the Sacred Word.

Perhaps the last should be first and the first last, for we open the Bible to learn of Christ, and we study His teachings to know God. The Holy Spirit is the way to the Son, and the Son is the way to the Father.

"Through whom (the Son) we all have access by one Spirit to the Father" (Ephesians 2:18).

But as we are building a foundation we do not invert the order. The existence of God must be a settled matter before we can consider whether He has revealed Himself in Christ. Then we must adduce evidence that Christ was all He claimed to be before we can accept His teachings about the Holy Spirit and the Holy Scriptures.

The Importance of the Study of God

Such a doctrine is one of highest importance, and is the greatest and most wonderful to engage the mind of man. Is it not of the profoundest interest to trace the footprints of God both in His Word and His universe? This doctrine is also one of greatest importance because our concept of God determines our views of the world, sin, life, duty and conduct. Distorted ideas or unscriptural notions of God as to His divine character, inevitably lead to perverted concepts of every other Biblical truth.

The doctrine before us exercises a definite spiritual influence upon character. We cannot grasp all that this august doctrine entails and at the same time live adversely to the mind and character of God. *Belief* results, or should, in *behavior.* Reverently, seriously and prayerfully, then, let us approach our study realizing that the ground we stand on is holy ground. As Munro Gibson expresses it—

> There is one thing more, the unspeakable importance of the spirit in which we approach this subject, whether by way of the evidences or by the way of personal trial. We must come in "the spirit of meekness and fear."
> *First*—in the spirit of meekness. If we are vain in our own conceit, all will be vain. The gate of the Kingdom is humility.
> *Second*—in the spirit of fear. It will be in no light and trifling spirit that we come. It is for our life. Come then, in meekness and fear, seek humbly and earnestly, and you will not seek in vain.

The Sources of the Study of God

Broadly speaking, there are two great lines of study, or sources from which all theological truth is derived, namely, *nature* and *the Bible.* As there are many subdivisions to this general division, however, let us examine the following aspects—

1. *The Material Universe.* In the world God created, His reality and natural attributes are taught by the consummate design and workmanship exhibited in the material universe; and also in the laws which govern it.

"The heavens declare the glory of God; and the firmament sheweth his handywork" (Psalm 19:1).

What an inspired witness the book of nature is! How full it is of manifest demonstrations of a supreme intelligence and Architect, or First Cause. Someone must have been responsible for the rich heavens above, with their glorious constellations and glittering lights; and also for the abundant clothing of the earth with its grass and corn; flowers and forests; multiplied minerals—all of which man and beast require for their sustenance. "Nature," it has been said, "is God's *Braille* for a blind humanity."

But no information can be gleaned from nature as to the depravity of the human heart and its cure; and of the love of God for a fallen humanity revealed in the redemptive work of Christ. Neither can nature tell us anything about eternity, and of the conditions necessary for a blessed future. These deeper revelations can only be found in the only Book revealing God — the Bible! Yet although nature describes the power, wisdom and greatness of God there are not wanting abundant illustrations of His grace, love and healing power. Solomon reminds us that "love covereth all sins" (Proverbs 10:12). Is not the spiritual fact illustrated for us in the material universe in the way of nature healing a wound covering it with new flesh, or in the mantling of a slag hill with grass and wild flowers?

2. *Human History.* Next to our personal study of Scripture, the study of history is most profitable, with biography as the key to history. In dealing with the link between the *historical* and the *ethical*, Dr. A. T. Pierson says that—

> History is God's age-long drama with its grand acts, its many scenes, its countless actors, and the whole universe the stage and theatre; only these are not fictions, but real august transactions. Details may be comparatively unimportant, because they are, like drapery and scenery, mere accessories to the main end—the great lesson God would teach, upon which attention should principally be fixed.

It can be truly said that "history" is HIS-STORY. In a measure, God has revealed Himself in His dealings with the human race. From Adam's day down through the ages, God has not left Himself without witness. Through succeeding generations God's over-ruling Providence has been at work. In conspicuous historical events He is found in the shadows, achieving His purpose.

3. *The Soul of Man.* "Man, rightly and fully studied," wrote Dr. Handley Moule, "is to himself a revelation of the Being of God." An innate recognition of the existence of and responsibility to God dwells in all men. Heathen peoples who have not received the Bible or Christianity yet possess a belief in a chief god or spirit of some kind. While in many cases a number of gods may be worshiped, it is a remarkable fact that one is usually singled out for supreme honor. The ancient Romans worshiped innumerable gods, but *Jupiter* was the greatest ruler of all. Evidence of this inbred recognition of God is found in the inscription Paul describes on the altar at Athens—"To the unknown God" (Acts 17:23).

4. *The Revelation of Scripture.* Nature, history and man only partially reveal the existence of God. It is to the Bible alone we turn for the complete and final revelation of His words, works and ways. Within the sacred volume, His glorious attributes, activities and appearances are displayed. Scripture alone unfolds His dealings with man—

Of his creation in innocence and purity;

Of his lamentable and irretrievable fall;

Of his redemption by the finished work of Christ;

Of his future, for in the Bible the curtain of the unseen is rolled away, and the solemn realities of resurrection, judgment, heaven and hell are brought to his knowledge.

The Bible presents man with a fourfold revelation of God—

In *nature*—a God above him.

In *providence*—a God beyond him.

In *law*—a God against his sin.

In *grace*—a God for him and in him.

Everywhere the Bible speaks in the name and authority of God and assumes that there is a consciousness of God within the human soul that will recognize and respond to His claims. If man does not know God, his ignorance is culpable seeing that ample evidence of His existence is available. They are, to quote Paul, "without excuse" (Romans 1:19, 20). Often ignorance of God is due to some moral shortcoming rather than to any mental difficulty (Romans 2:12-15).

Further, the Bible reveals God, not as an abstraction, nor as some remote and impassive deity, but as *Jehovah*, or as "The Eternal"—the living personal God exercising His sovereign power in every realm; and as the divine Father interested in and caring for His children.

5. *The Lord Jesus Christ.* The full and final revelation of the character and will of God was made known in His beloved Son, the effulgence of His glory. Philip said to Jesus, "Show us the Father, and it sufficeth us." Then we have the calm and

authoritative reply of our Lord, "He that hath seen me, hath seen the Father; and how sayest thou then, Shew us the Father?" (John 14:7-9). Thus, as we shall more fully prove, the complete revelation of God came to man through the Incarnation of the Son, the Christ of God, through His manifested Person, Word and Work.

The Object of the Study of God

The question may arise, If the Bible does not set out to prove the existence of God, why should we adopt such a course? Why not be satisfied to rest, as the Bible does, in the fact that God *is*? First of all, evidences and arguments as to the Being of God are necessary in order to formulate a doctrine, by exegesis and exposition, of all that He is in Himself. There is no science of astronomy in the universe, yet the facts are there on which a science is based. The Bible was not all composed at one time. Between Moses and John there were some 1700 years, and consequently revelation of God was progressive necessitating the bringing together of all facets of such a doctrine.

Then there is the counteraction of doubt and unbelief in respect to God. As we shall presently discuss the various avenues of the rejection of the one true God, a brief word will suffice at this point. How necessary it is to be sure of our theistic position and thereby meet the challenge of those who affirm that there is no God!

The Method of the Study of God

If we would win the unbelieving to faith we must have a firm basis for our own faith. We must consider the various forms and phases of unbelief, and, understanding the nature and force of sceptical objections to the existence of a divine Being, disprove untenable tenets by the positive assertions of Scripture. While the doctrine of God is one of the profoundest subjects for the human mind to ponder, it has elicited differing responses. As Dr. T. Whitelaw so tersely expressed it:

The Atheist asserts there is no God.
The Agnostic says he cannot tell whether there is a God or no.
The Materialist boasts that he does not require a God.
The Worldly Fool wishes there were no God.
The Christian answers that he cannot do without a God.

Let us begin by taking a look at *atheism*. The Church's creed reads, "I believe in God." The fool's creed has it, "There is no God" (Psalm 14:1). The term *atheist* is a compound of two Greek words *a*, meaning "no" and *theos* meaning "God." The phrase Paul uses, "without God," is *Atheos* in the Greek. *Theism* is the belief in the existence of God with or without a belief in His special revelation such as the Bible presents. *Atheism* is the rejection of the existence of God, carrying with it the utter rejection of the Bible as giving the complete revelation of God. *Atheism,* then, is the negation of *theism,* and denies the reality and knowledge of a divine Being. As an atheist of a past generation wrote, "There is no heavenly Father watching tenderly over us, His creatures. He is a baseless shadow of a wistful dream." *Atheism,* of course, assumes many forms.

There is *classical atheism.* In classical literature of a past age an "Atheist" is described as one who denied, not the God the Bible sets forth, but who denied the reality of the god of a particular nation. Thus the Christians were repeatedly charged with "Atheism" in the early days of the church because of their rejection of the gods of heathenism. And because of this rejection they were often subjected to the most cruel and determined persecution.

There is *dogmatic atheism,* which consists of the absolute denial of a supreme Being. In our enlightened age there are those who boast that they are "Atheists." To them there is no God who rules o'er earth and sky. But as Dr. A. T. Pierson puts it:

There is nothing more absurd and unreasonable than atheism. Faith in God is sometimes charged with being credulous, but there is no credulity like that of incredulity . . . Had sin not obscured and biased the mental vision, all infidelity would have been impossible. . . . It is because the nature of man is corrupt, his works abominable, his understanding alienated from God, his whole life filthy that he delights in the inconsistencies and apostasies of disciples and seeks to bring himself to believe that there is no God.

There is *critical atheism,* which denies that any divine Being has been shown to exist. No one can demonstrate His existence. Professor Huxley, who once wrote of himself in a letter to Charles Kingsley as, "exactly what the Christian world called, and, so far as he could judge, was justified in calling him, an atheist and infidel," might be taken as an example of a critical atheist. "I cannot see," Huxley wrote, "one shadow or tittle of evidence that the Great Unknown underlying the phenomena of the universe stands to us in the relation of a Father, loves and cares for us as Christianity asserts."

There is *philosophic atheism,* which finds refuge from the questions of faith in the assertion, "If there be a God we cannot know Him because the human faculties are incapable of verifying His existence." But as Dr. Scott Lidgett states it:

> Christians cannot afford to allow their doctrine of God and the world to be construed for them by so-called natural philosophers or by obsolete political thinkers. The former conceive God as a Cause armed with a sufficient power to execute a material task; the latter as a Governor, whose motives and methods are explained by those of earthly sovereigns. Such doctrines of God are both adequate and misleading. They cannot be stretched to include Christ, the world of spiritual religion, or the whole of the universe of which Christ and religion are the supreme features. Our theology must work from Christ outwards and downwards; not from nature upwards and inwards.

The Bible affirms, as we hope to prove, that God is a Person, a self-conscious Being, One who can be known, loved and obeyed, and not merely some First Cause or Force (Hebrews 11:3).

There is *practical atheism.* The dogmatic atheist is guilty of the atheism of *infidelity,* but the practical atheist is guilty of the atheism of *impiety.* The latter believes there is a God but lives as if He did not exist. Alas, how prevalent is this form of atheism today! (See Isaiah 31:1; Jeremiah 2:13,17,18; 18:13-15). Commenting on the Psalmist's phrase, "The fool hath said in his heart, There is no God" (Psalm 14:1), Dr. Pierson says—

> The moral atheism of impiety is probably what the Holy Spirit is here rebuking. The impious fool hath, in his heart, said, "No God." And it may be understood not as an affirmation but as an exclamation, as though he had said within, "Would there were no God," or "Let there be no God." The inward tendency and drift of all impiety is to get rid of

God. With him who is determined to sin it is an object to banish God from the moral universe.

Whatever phase of atheism we may think of, the same is a system of negation, destroying the faith upon which all human relations are built. If there is no God, then there is neither right or wrong, and human action is neither good or bad. *Atheism* leaves human society without a basis for order and human government without foundation (Romans 1:16-32; Psalms 10:4; 53:1). As to the professed causes of atheism, one could dwell on unanswered prayer, the inequalities of life, the inconsistencies of professing Christians, natural phenomena in which the created is worshiped more than the Creator (Romans 1:25). But this "Creed of Fools" is contrary to reason and devoid of satisfaction and hope. Charles Darwin, father of the unproven theory of evolution, was a committed Christian before he became an avowed influence, and wrote an impressive account of the influence of the Gospel in missionary lands he had visited. He died rejecting faith in a future state. Here is his sad confession before he died—

> Disbelief crept over me at a very slow rate and at last was complete. I am like a man who has become colorblind. Though once capable of wonder, admiration and devotion in the presence of the works of God, now, not even the grandest scene could cause any such convictions and feelings to rise in my mind. For myself I do not believe that there has ever been any revelation.

Atheism is also contrary to our human intuitions. Deep, religious instincts within the human breast cannot be dismissed as deceptive or unreasonable. What a convincing evidence Solomon has given us of the innate desire for God—"He hath set Eternity in their hearts" (Ecclesiastes 3:11 R.V. Margin). Further, atheism fails to account for the origin and order of the universe. Atheistic philosophy has no adequate explanation for design, beauty and provision so evident in nature. The intellectual absurdity of atheism leaves—

Creation without a Creator;

Design with a Designer;

The Universe without a Controller;

Human history without a Ruler;

Morality without any basis of Authority;

Iniquity without any adequate restraint;
Death without any hope hereafter.

Atheism stands condemned by its fruits.
The 1787 French Revolution, the testimonies of avowed atheists like Voltaire,
Paine, Goethe, Hume and others, the blood-
shed and bondage following in the wake of
communism alike testify to the hollowness
and heartlessness of the denial of God's
existence. The eminent physicist, Lord Kelvin, once said—

> I have many times in my published
> writings within the past fifty years ex-
> pressed myself decidedly on purely scien-
> tific grounds, against atheistic and ma-
> terialistic doctrines. . . . If you think
> strongly enough, you will be forced by
> science to believe in God, which is the
> foundation of all religion.

There is no doubt that the evil leaven of
evolution has had much to do with the
bowing of God out of His universe. Infidel
evolutionists brazenly affirm that, "Evolution necessitates an entire recasting of the
foundations. If the doctrine of evolution be
true, not one of the doctrines formerly
taught and believed by the church are
tenable." But as Professor Agassiz, of Har-
vard once expressed it—

"Any man accepting the doctrine of
evolution ceases thereby to be a scientist."

Having briefly considered the nature and
aspects of atheism, which can be looked
upon as the source of infidelity, let us now
consider some of the springs issuing forth
from such a polluted source.

There is Materialism. Materia is the Latin
word for *matter*. Thus anything "material"
is in contrast to that which is "spiritual."
In substance, *materialism* denies the independent existence of spirit, and of the spiritual. There is but one element, namely
matter. A materialist is one who finds in
material forces a complete explanation of
life. To him, there is no guiding principle,
or controlling intelligence presiding over
the affairs of the universe, no sin and no
resurrection. To quote Bachner, a renowned
materialist—

> Not God, but evolution of matter is
> the cause of the order of the world.
> There is no God, no final cause, no im-
> mortality, no freedom, no substance, no
> soul. Mind, life, light, heat, electricity
> or magnetism, or any other physical
> fact is a movement of matter.

Materialism cannot account for the origin
of matter, force and the intelligence that
guided their operations in building the
universe and fashioning man. How could
dead matter produce life? Whence came
the human consciousness? Whence come
our human intuitions and moral obligations?
Dead matter and blind force are powerless
to create. To quote Lord Kelvin again—

All living things depend upon an everlasting Creator and Lord.

There is Rationalism. Ratio means "reason," and so "rationalism" is a system or
doctrine agreeable to reason. A rationalist,
then, is a person who believes he is guided
in his opinion solely by reason, and independent of outside authority, especially
in religious matters. A supernatural revelation of God is rejected. Reason is the sole
and sufficient arbiter of faith, and nature,
the sole and sufficient revelation of God.
Reason dethrones faith. Rationalism rejects
the miraculous, affirming that God has so
bound Himself to the laws of nature as to
be incapable of interfering with them. An
ordinary mechanic has perfect liberty to
adjust or modify the movements of a machine he made, but God is unable to order
His creation as He deems best. How refreshing and stimulating to faith it is to
hold that—

> All the inhabitants of the earth are
> reputed as nothing: and he doeth accord-
> ing to his will in the army of heaven,
> and among the inhabitants of earth: and
> none can stay his hand or say unto him,
> What doest thou? (Daniel 4:35).

There is Agnosticism. How prevalent in
these apostate days is this phase of infi-
fidelity! The term, "Agnosticism," itself
was coined by Professor Huxley in 1869.
How he came to adopt it is best told in
his own words—

> When I reached intellectual maturity
> and asked myself whether I was an atheist,
> theist, pantheist, materialist, idealist, a
> Christian, or a free-thinker, the more I
> learned and reflected the less ready was
> the answer.

Accordingly, Huxley took the phrase from
the altar Paul stood at—*The Unknown
God* (Acts 17:23); and from the word
"unknown," which is *agnostos* in the Greek,
he produced his term "agnostic," which is
directly opposite to "gnostic," meaning one

who professes to know everything. *Gnosticism* says, "I know it all." *Agnosticism* says, "I know nothing." The former is the parent of a proud rationalism, while the latter is the parent of *latitudinarianism,* or the broad, liberal theology of today. *Agnosticism* represents a midway position between faith and unbelief, and is a convenient shelter for those who hide their ignorance or indifference under the semblance of scientific doubt. Huxley's attitude was that he could neither affirm or deny the existence of God; or the immortality of the soul. The prophets and apostles lived in the air of glorious certitude. "I *know* that my Redeemer liveth" (Job 19:25. See the many "I knows" of the epistles). Among the last lines written by Robert G. Ingersoll, America's most famous agnostic, were these—

Is there beyond the silent night
  An endless day?
Is death a door that leads to light?
  We cannot say.
The tongueless secret locked in fate,
We do not know. We hope and wait.

How different is the sure and certain knowledge of the believer! "We *know* that we have passed from death unto life." "We *know* that, when he shall appear we shall be like him" (I John 5:14; 3:2). Bless God, we have a Gospel of certainties to proclaim.

Before we come to the positive Bible views of God, let us examine some of the deistic ideas men have held and still hold, and then place them alongside of the transcendence, superiority and pre-eminence of the only true God. In one of his prayer Psalms, David magnifies both the goodness and greatness of God in a sentence, fittingly summarizing the teaching of the Psalm as a whole—

"Among the gods there is none like
  unto thee, O Lord" (86:8).

Aspects of unbelief just considered are all godless creeds in that no reverence or worship is given to a Deity of any kind. The blatant assertion of the atheist is, "There is no God."

The boast of the materialist is, "I need no God."

The position of the rationalist is, "My reason is all the God I need."

The less dogmatic attitude of the agnostic is, "I do not know if there is a God."

In the deistic conceptions we are now to consider, however, God is recognized to a certain degree, either as being equal or inferior to other so-called gods. There is not the positive denial of a divine Being, nor is the necessity of religion discredited. In alien, religious systems strong religious beliefs are held by their devotees. Various philosophical ideas of God have their counterpart and antecedent in some actual religion.

Take Pantheism. Pantheism is the philosophy of the religious consciousness of India, affirming that there is no God apart from nature, and that everything in nature must be considered as a part, or manifestation of God. *Pan,* means "all" and *"Theos,* "God." *Pantheism,* then, implies "All is God and God is All." *The Pantheon,* built in Rome by Agrippa in 27 B.C., means the temple created for and dedicated to the gods, seeing the gods of the nation were considered as one. Pantheistic philosophy, covering a wide field of speculation, can be classified thus—

There is the *One Substance Pantheism,* originated by Spinoza, 1632-1677, the earliest and most influential propounder of this system in Europe. He taught that God is not only the Creator, but also the original matter of the universe which consists of, and is a development of the attributes of both mind and matter, thought and extension. Somewhat similar to this philosophy is *Materialistic Pantheism* of which Strauss, the German theologian of the eighteenth century became the chief exponent. Strauss ascribed to the one substance only the attribute of matter. "All is God." Hegel, another German theologian, earlier than Strauss, taught *Idealistic Pantheism,* which gives to universal substance the attribute of being only, "God is All."

Pantheism speaks of "the begetting and begotten nature"—the "begetting" being the source from which the different forms of nature arise and into which they sink again; while the "begotten" is the ever varying forms of phenomena in the world. Thus nature is both mother and daughter. But from the diversity and confusion of thought in the aspects of pantheism, all of which rob us of the privilege and joy of addressing God as "Thou," we turn to the Bible wherein God is revealed as the Creator, the wholly free personal Cause of all other existence and wholly sovereign over it. Hegel spoke of our eternal God,

"The Absolute Idea which from endless ages realizes, orders and inspires the whole phenomenal World . . . He is not a personal God for none exists neither did it conceive itself for then it would be self-conscious." How these speculations contradict the clear testimony of Scripture as to the personality of God, and to His being as being separate from His creations. Pantheism, failing to preserve the eternal difference between right and wrong, destroys man's own moral powers. As one writer expressed it, "He who denies the personality of God undermines the foundation of his own house."

Take Polytheism. This further alien philosophy teaches a plurality of finite gods or deities, and a belief in the existence of many invisible agents, more or less co-ordinate. *Polys* is the Greek word for "many," while *Theos*, as we know means God. Thus, *polytheism* means "many gods." This form of belief was held by the ancient empires of the East, and by nearly all peoples outside of Jewish *monotheism*. Israel was monotheistic believing in only one God. *Monos* implies "single" or "alone." A monarchy is a system of government in which one rules alone.

Polytheism, representing a multiplicity of gods, formed a constant danger to the Israelites. Hence the repeated exhortations to put away "strange Gods." In that sublime passage of his, Moses exposed the folly of polytheism—

The LORD your God is God of gods, and Lord of lords, a great God, a mighty, and a terrible, which regardeth not persons, nor taketh reward (Deuteronomy 10:17; See Galatians 4:8).

Among the various aspects of polytheism we have the *anthropomorphis*, attributing human virtues to gods, and the representation of them in the form of man or with bodily parts (Psalm 135:15-17; Acts 14:11,12): The *therianthropic* representing deities in the combined form of man and beast. *Thērion* means "beast," and *anthrōpos*, man: and so *therianthropism* is the representation of superhuman beings in a combination of human and bestial forms, worshiped by man. Among the nations there are gods with human bodies and heads of animals, and *vice versa* for example, *Dagon*, half fish, half man; and *Nytane*, the Roman god of the sea. The *henotheistic—Heno*

meaning *one*, as an aspect of religious belief ascribing supreme power to one of the several gods in turn. *Jupiter* was worshiped by the Romans as the supreme god among other gods.

Like other natural religions, *polytheism* differed in its development among different peoples. As to the origin of this particular religious belief, the desire to deify the forces of nature; the creation of a deity to control a particular nation or locality to whom the people turned for protection; superstitious belief in malign powers whose wrath was manifested in disaster, can be named as being productions of *polytheism*.

The answer to this alien creed is obvious. While there may be inferior agents, there cannot be a plurality of gods. Any limitations to the power or scope of a deity makes him a finite creature and is fatal to the claims of godhead. Over against a plurality of gods, we have the constant exaltation in Scripture of the sovereignty of Jehovah. The living and true God is declared to be—

"Greater than all gods" (Exodus 15:11; 18:11).

"God of gods, and Lord of lords" (Deuteronomy 10:14-17).

"To be feared above all gods" (I Chronicles 16:25).

"King above all gods" (Psalms 95:3; 97:9).

Jeremiah, who gives us a pure and well-defined *monotheism* speaks of all other gods as "not gods." To the prophet, other gods have no existence (2:11; 5:7; 16:20).

The regulations imposed upon Israel were no less emphatic. While the captivities cured Israel of polytheistic tendencies, there is no uncertain sound regarding the obligations of the people—

No other god was to take God's place (Deuteronomy 5:7; Exodus 20:3).

No images were to be made of heathen gods (Exodus 20:4,23; 34:17; Leviticus 19:4).

No mention was to be made of other gods (Exodus 23:13; Joshua 23:7).

These gods were to be destroyed, not worshiped (Exodus 23:27).

They were a snare, and therefore no covenants had to be made with people who worshiped idols (Exodus 23:32; Deuteronomy 6:14; 7:4,25).

A curse from the true God would follow

the least defection from Him to these lifeless gods (Deuteronomy 11:28; 28: 14; 29:17).

These gods were an abomination to God (Deuteronomy 12:31; 20:18; Ezekiel 7:20).

These gods were to be as foreign deities to Israel (I Samuel 7:3; Judges 10: 16).

Take Deism. While both deism and rationalism have much in common and are often considered together, we feel that deism should be treated as a distinct aspect of unscriptural unbelief. The term itself is derived from *Deus* meaning, "a god." A deist, therefore, is one who believes in the existence of a divine Being but not in revealed religion, such as Christianity presents. Dr. Handley Moule says that—

Deism denotes the belief of an almighty, mighty Contriver and Maker of the universe, who is not actively sovereign over it, and is not immanent in it. In particular, it is a belief which declines to admit the fact (whether or no the possibility) of miraculous revelation.

Deism prevailed for centuries as man's attitude to God in China, in Islam, in Judaism before it found expression in a rational theory in the eighteenth century throughout the continent of Europe. Edward Herbert (1583-1648), the English philosopher, historian and diplomat, was known as "The Father of Deism." In his enunciation of this doctrine he laid down five propositions or articles of belief based on what he called "the divinely implanted original and indefeasible intuitions of the human mind." These five propositions which became universally recognized as the theology of the deistic system read—

1. There is one supreme God.
2. He is to be worshiped.
3. This worship consists chiefly of virtue and piety.
4. We must repent of our sins and cease from them.
5. There are rewards and punishments here and hereafter.

While deism is a marked advance on pantheism and polytheism it yet comes far short of the Biblical unfolding of God. That deism is anti-Biblical is evidenced by the fact that it repudiates the doctrines of the Trinity, of the divine authority of Scripture, of the Atonement, of the supernatural or miraculous. Morality, deism teaches, is not founded on the Bible—it rests on man's own innate capacity to appreciate work and to apprehend the beautiful. Deism assumes that God, having created the universe, endowing it with the forces necessary of its own existence, has left it to itself. He is "an absentee God, sitting idle ever since the first Sabbath at the outside of His world, seeing it go." Everything is under the rigid reign of universal law, and God cannot, or does not, interfere with the unvarying order of nature. There is no controlling Providence in the world, no divine intervention in human affairs, no revelation from God of Himself, or of His will.

How right Dr. Moule is when he asserts that deism is "a view of God and the world as discountenanced, not only by Scripture, but by independent observation and inference." The fallacy of the deistical position is seen in that it robs God of His prerogatives and glorious attributes. How blessed and comforting it is to turn from the cold, bleak and barren speculations regarding a distant, absentee, indifferent God—a mere abstraction in the universe—to the marvelous, loving, pitiful God of the Bible—the God of salvation, the God of fallen souls who is the Lord of law as well as the Lord of life, and who can therefore regulate and manipulate all the forces of heaven and earth for the accomplishment of His own beneficent purpose (Romans 8: 28).

Take Dualism. This last aspect of infidelity we are to consider is in some respects one of the most subtle forms of unbelief. *Dual* is from *duo* meaning "two." Dualism then, explains the world by the assumption of two radically and absolute elements—

1. The doctrine of the entire separation of spirit and matter, and thus opposed both to idealism and to materialism.
2. The doctrine of two distinct principles of good and evil, or of two distinct divine beings of these qualities.

The dualistic creed had its origin with Zoroaster, or Zarathastra, a notable Persian teacher, who probably lived about the time of Moses. Zoroaster taught that at the beginning of things there existed two great original spirits, *Ormuzd* and *Ahriman* by name.

Ormuzd was the good spirit, the author of light and life and of all that is noble and pure. Ormuzd was also the name of the chief god of the Persians, the creator and lord of the universe.

Ahriman was the evil spirit, the author of darkness and death, and of all that is foul and wicked—the antithesis of all Ormuzd represented. Evil, therefore, like good existed from the beginning.

Dualism, then, was composed of these two antagonistic spirits or forces, each of whom was surrounded by a court of spiritual beings, kindred to himself, who were his agents or messengers in the world. This Zoroastrian religion declined being fully overthrown by Mohammedanism. Zoroaster's dualistic conception, however, was afterwards revived by *Mani*, a native of Southern Babylon, about A.D. 215-276. Like Zoroaster, he taught that everything sprang from two chief principles, light and darkness, good and evil. To Mani this philosophy could be summarized thus—

Light represented God, radiant with ten virtues—love, faith, fidelity, high-mindedness, wisdom, meekness, knowledge, understanding, mystery and insight.

Satan, or the principle of evil, was represented by mist, heat, the sirocco, darkness, vapor.

These two kingdoms originally touched each other like two spheres but did not blend until Satan, in a fit of fury, invaded the kingdom of light.

This form of dualism became known as *Manicheism,* named after Mani. Augustine, during his period of spiritual conflict, was greatly influenced by this system. In Book VIII of his *Confessions,* Augustine gives a full report of his rejection of the Manicheism heresy.

The answer to Dualism can be briefly stated—

If darkness and light are of equal power and authority, then these opposite qualities representing God and Satan, place them on the same level. But the Bible declares that Christ destroyed the works of the devil (I John 3:8)—an infeasible accomplishment if the two were of equal power. Then dualism robs God of the right and opportunity to exercise that fatherly discipline which, although not pleasant is profitable, yielding thereafter the peaceable fruits of righteousness (Hebrews 12:11). If *all* adversity is of the bad spirit or Satan, then God is deprived of a valuable asset in the fashioning of character. Further, experience condemns dualism because many of God's choicest saints have been, and are, sufferers who attribute their sickness or disease, not to Satan, but to the overruling Providence and blessed will of God. "Though He slay me, yet will I trust Him," was Job's assertion.

That there is a form of dualism taught in the Bible is evident from Romans 6 and 7, in which Paul deals with the two laws, or the double nature of the believer. "When I (the new nature) would do good, evil (the old nature) is with me." The Holy Spirit and the flesh are forever in conflict (Romans 8). Zoroastrianism is right when it affirms that the soul of man is the battlefield upon which the conflict is waged and that victory depends upon the will of man. But, in the believer, the opposing powers are not equal as in Dualism. The blessed Spirit of God is mightier than Satan, or the old nature—relic of the fall. Victory depends upon the will. "If any man will." We can *will* our salvation and sanctification. The question is, In which direction is your will and mine traveling?

Having considered theistic and non-theistic philosophies, we now turn from such a negative aspect of the doctrine before us to the more positive arguments for the existence and sovereignty of God—the most sublime, transcendent theme that could possibly engage the human mind; a theme as exhaustless and incomprehensible as it is blessed and profitable. As previously indicated, the Bible does not attempt to prove God's reality but assumes the fact from its opening announcement (Genesis 1:1). The previous Book, however, does refer us to at least four avenues of revelation whereby we can trace the divine footsteps. There are—

1. The Physical Universe (Psalm 19; Romans 1:19,20)

2. The Human Soul (Romans 2:14,15)

3. The Written Word, The Bible (Psalm 19:7-11; II Timothy 3:16)

4. The Living Word, Christ (John 1:18; Hebrews 1:1.

These are the four lines of evidence producing unanswerable arguments for the fact of God as the One who ordered the universe, constituted one being, gave us the Scriptures and speaks to us through Christ, His beloved Son.

The Physical Universe
(Psalm 19; Romans 1:19,20)

Of this fascinating line of evidence a gifted expositor says that:

> The existence of a divine Being is demonstrable by several arguments. Each of these should be carefully considered, as none of them in itself may be a complete demonstration to some minds, but each becomes an important element in a line of reasoning which is fitted to carry conviction to every candid mind. The proofs by which the truth of the divine Existence are drawn, come from several sources.

THE PROOF OF THE INTELLIGIBILITY OF THE UNIVERSE

The existence of natural objects shows that they must have had a Maker, for there can be no effect without a sufficient cause. A house proves that it must have had a builder, and the universe with all its wonders must have had a Maker. Man, by the powers of reason and observation is able to comprehend the order and structure of things around him. He can perceive how they are formed and grouped, and by what laws they are organized. He can formulate the laws of motion, guiding the heavenly bodies in their orbits—investigate and chart the animal and vegetable kingdom, as well as his own being. This fact of the intelligibility of the universe leads us, logically and inevitably to the conclusion that it must have been fashioned by a mind greater than man's mind. The laws that rule our thinking find expression in the laws and arrangements of heavenly bodies. The universe is as a mirror reflecting man's own powers, proving, thereby, a kinship between the mind of man and the *mind* behind the universe. A modern writer impressed with the force of this argument adds to the axiom, "I think, therefore I am," a further one, namely, "I understand, therefore there is a God."

Among the forcible arguments proving the existence of a divine mind are the following:

1. The Cosmological Argument.

Cosmology is that science or teaching dealing with the universe, which offers itself to view as sky, earth and sea, as an orderly and systematic whole. Observing things around us, we come to think of an orderly universe and reach the conclusion that there must be a cause for what we see. This argument from *causation* has as its basic postulate—"Every effect must have an adequate cause." This cosmological approach is latent in Paul's great statement concerning God as the first *Cause*—

"In whom we live, move, and have our being" (Acts 17:28).

A causeless phenomena is impossible—an uncaused beginning is inconceivable—a mindless world could not produce itself and life in it. Origin implies an originating power, the cause being sufficient to produce the effect. Everywhere, nature reveals marvelous evidence of design or adaptation of means to an end, and as design implies a designer; and since design in nature is far superior to anything man is capable of, the designer of the universe must be someone much greater than man.

Whether we think of time and space, force and matter, dependence of finite parts which are derivative, we are driven to the conclusion that there must have been a Cause outside the universe. Behind all intermediate processes there must have been a Being—causative without being caused, who has existence in Himself. We thus rise by necessity of thought from the finite to the Infinite, from the caused to the Uncaused, from reason evident in the structure of the universe to the eternal and universal Reason which is the ground of all. As one scientist expressed it, *Nature is imbued with intelligent thought.*

The amazing intellectuality inwrought within the conscious material gives the lie to the theory that "nature is the offspring of unconscious mind." If "order is heaven's first law," then nature abounds in proof that God, as a God of order and not disorder, is the One who fashioned the laws of nature. A digest of the argument of the cosmos is—

There is a *power* somewhere because there are effects everywhere.

There is *wisdom* somewhere because wise deeds are accomplished everywhere.

There is *intelligence* somewhere for there are order and arrangement everywhere.

There is *goodness* somewhere for there are beneficent agents and resultant gladness everywhere.

The mental act is prior to the physical, that is, thought precedes action, therefore, there is an intelligence prior to the order of the universe. In this intelligence there must have been a *mind* to devise and a *will* to carry that design into effect, and these are qualities belonging to a person. Thus in the cosmological argument we can trace the footsteps of God the Creator.

When Thy amazing works, O God
  My mental eye surveys,
Transported with the view, I'm lost
  In wonder, love and praise.

2. The Teleological Argument.

This further argument carries us a step further than the previous argument which proceeds upon the evidence of order and the harmony resulting therefrom. The *teleological argument* from *Telos*, meaning "issue," can be defined as the science of ends, or final causes. Nature is before us as "a living arithmetic in its development, a realized geometry in its repose." This present line of evidence can be summarized thus—

Order and useful collocations and arrangements pervading a system imply intelligence and purpose as the cause of that order and collocation. Since order and useful collocation pervade the universe there must exist an intelligence adequate to the production of this order, and will adequate to the directing of this collocation to useful ends.

Nature is a complex whole made up of several sections or powers all interacting yet constituting together one complete system. All these parts or activities are connected with each other, the least with the greatest, but order reigns throughout the entire whole and universal harmony prevails for each part serves the other with admirable reciprocity. These parts are so guided as to conspire to sustain and promote—not convulse and subvert—the whole. The classic illustration of the watch as used by Paley comes to mind at this point. There are many other fascinating illustrations from every department of the material universe and in almost every phase of existent life we would like to use.

For instance, we could elaborate upon the intricate solar system with the central position of the sun, binding the system together by the law of gravitation, and furnishing light and heat necessary for the welfare of each of the planets. The ceaseless, speedy rate of the sun, with all the planets and their attendant satellites per-

forming their varied evolutions with unfailing regularity and marvelous harmony is a striking evidence of design. Then there is the constitute elements forming the atmosphere surrounding the earth, the gases of which are blended with such perfect equipoise as to meet the requirements of plants, animals and men.

Associated with this teleological (sometimes called the *physico-theological*) argument are form and color. What skillful adaptation of natural forces we have, all cooperating toward specific ends. Creative skill, design and beneficence are behind the wondrous beauty of form and color in flowers and forests, lakes and landscapes. What an indubitable and convincing proof of design is the human body with its structure and organs, skin and muscles and nervous system and heart and eyes and members! No wonder the Psalmist exclaimed, "I am fearfully and wonderfully made." We could also elaborate upon animals, birds and fish with their adaptation to environment.

The teleological argument is incontrovertible, for sound reasoning demands that effect must have an adequate cause, and that design and adaptation a superintending intelligence. If an imposing cathedral presupposes an architect and builder, surely the infinitely greater and more complexed structure of the universe demands a Creator whose wisdom designed it for profitable ends. Without doubt, "the world we live in is a fairyland of the exquisite" and "our very existence a miracle in itself." Yet as Lord Avebury goes on to say, "So few of us enjoy as we might, and none of us yet appreciate fully, the beauties and wonders that surround us."

The Human Soul
(Romans 2:14,15)

Paul makes it clear that God has not left Himself without witness in man, the crown of His creative work. Gentiles, who had not the same revelation of God as the Jews, were not exempted from accountability because of their lack of a revealed perceptive code. Gentiles possessed that moral consciousness without which a revealed code itself would be futile. Made in the image of God, man has the mysterious sense which sees, feels and handles moral obligation. He is aware of the fact of duty. Not living up to what he is thus aware of, he is guilty. Paul himself testified that there was something within him responding to an outer law which he recognized as the voice of God (Romans 7:7). Within the human realm there are two invincible arguments for the existence of God.

1. *The Psychological Argument*

Psyche is the Greek term for "soul," or the living principle in man, and *psychology* is therefore the science which classifies and analyzes the phenomena or varying states of the human mind. *The psychological argument* insists that there is a consciousness of God within the soul anterior to reasoned thought or experience. While man acquires a full knowledge of God from His general and special revelation, he has an innate knowledge of Him, and a natural capacity to know Him fully. Man has an intuition or natural consciousness of God. Man's "religious instinct" leads him to acknowledge his dependence upon a superior Being while his "moral instinct," or conscience, reproves him when he does wrong, thereby revealing to him a Lawgiver to whom he is accountable.

That this natural consciousness of God is common to all is evident from the fact that every race of people, down the ages, has had some form of religion, however crude—from the way the most unbelieving usually cry to God if overtaken by sudden calamity—from the way that even infidels acknowledge God when they come to die. The more man thinks of himself, the more he thinks of God. "The descent into the human soul is the ascent to God." Man knows that he exists, and his human personality is a strong evidence of a divine Personality. Not only has man self-consciousness, he likewise possesses self-determination or freedom of will, which reflects the liberty of the Creator or freedom of action to accomplish what He deems best for His creation and creatures.

Then man's freedom of will, or self-determinism, which is his inalienable birthright, as proved by the record of Eden, where man used the gift of choice against the Giver, is a prominent part of man's personality. The argument, then, is this: If man can act as he pleases or chooses, and is separate from what he feels, thinks and knows, his Creator must possess the same traits of personality. The consistent testimony of the Bible is that God stands proved as a personal Creator, independent of His works and not part of them as materialism affirms, or unable to control them as rationalism contends. God has liberty or freedom of action to carry out what He deems best for His creation and creatures. And is it not comforting to know that His will is like Himself, holy—just—loving.

2. *The Ontological Argument*

Ontos is the Greek for "being," and so *Ontology* is the science dealing with the principles of pure being. Teleology is a discourse of ends, or final causes, leading us from effect to cause. Ontology is a discourse on reality, and reasons in the reverse way from cause to effect. This line of argument was originated by Anselm, the scholastic philosopher of the eleventh century, who sought to prove that the idea of God in the mind of man is a satisfactory proof that God exists. Although a fool may say in his heart, "There is no God," he thereby shows himself a fool because he asserts something which is contradictory in itself. He has the idea of God within but denies its reality. Ideas of infinite holiness, righteousness and wisdom are not only ideas, there must be a Being somewhere in whom they are inherent and who is their source.

It cannot be denied the consciousness of God is an ineradicable element of the soul. Man has irrepressible longings and aspirations after God from which spring the desire for the worship of, and fellowship with God. "Deep calls unto deep" (Psalm 42: 7). Further, these intuitions are not the result of education, environment or external Christian influences, but were interwoven in man's nature by his Creator. Man may try to suppress or stifle these instincts Godward, but ever and anon they express themselves.

> Down in the human heart,
> Crushed by the Tempter,
> Feelings lie buried,
> Grace can restore.

The intuitions which, as the touch of God upon the human spirit teach us that we are bound to the Creator of our being by manifold ties as the Saviour Himself reminds us when He calls us to worship God with all our *heart, soul, mind* and *strength* (Mark 12:30). Made for God, man is restless until he finds his rest in God. If our *strength* is our inner conscience, is not this faculty the strongest evidence of all of God's existence? Obedience is due to superiors, but why are we summoned to obey, if there be no superior Being to obey. Conscience, with its irresistible conviction of obligation and responsibility is a weighty argument for the existence of God. We speak about our sense of obligation to live aright, but who are we obligated to, if there be no God? Is there not a higher Law claiming our obedience—a righteous Creator who demands our righteous living? Our intuitions do not make our natures a lie. They proclaim that there is a moral Governor and Judge who is omniscient and can discern infractions of His law, and who has the power to inflict the judgment conscience itself pronounces upon such infractions.

The Written Word
(Psalm 19:7-11; II Timothy 3:16)

We have now reached the fascinating, positive evidence of the existence of God, namely, what the Bible teaches us of all that He is in Himself. What Professor A. B. Davidson says of the personality and spirituality of God as revealed in the Old Testament is true of the Bible as a whole.

Unquestionably the most distinct and strongest conception of God . . . is that of His personality. This appears on every page. A God identical with nature, or involved in nature, and only manifesting Himself through the blind forces of nature, nowhere appears . . . He is always distinct from nature, and personal. In the first chapter of Genesis He stands over against nature, and perceives that it is *good.* He stands over against man, and lays His commands upon him: Of the tree of the knowledge of good and evil thou shalt not eat. He puts Himself as a moral person over against men as moral persons, and enters into covenant of moral conduct with them. Not only is He conscious of men, but He is conscious of Himself (Genesis 12:16; Isaiah 45:23). He is not only conscious of Himself as existing, but of what character He Himself is. He resolves with Himself to make man, and to make him in His own image.

While it is our endeavor to classify the revelation of God in Scripture, it must be understood that because of our finite minds we can only arrive at a partial apprehension of the divine nature and attributes of Him who transcends our highest thoughts.

The divine essence in its infinity lies far beyond our ken and cannot be compressed within any analysis the human mind can frame. If man cannot fully understand himself or know his neighbor, how can he possibly comprehend Him whose ways are past finding out. In so many ways He is a God hiding Himself. Human search cannot discover Him. (Isaiah 45:15).

Yet it is necessary to arrive at a clear and orderly concept of God, not in any speculative way, but by the light afforded us in the Bible which is sufficient, correct and reliable; and likewise ample as the basis of faith and rule of life. Because of our human limitations we invariably argue from finity to infinity, that is, we try to imagine what God is like by comparing and associating Him with what we can see. Our finite minds can only understand God by taking the ideas of perfection gathered from observation and reflection and use them to illustrate God's infinity and incomprehensibility. But God, however, is no aggregation of parts, but an absolute unity. To think and speak of His attributes or perfections, as though He were composed of parts, is only an evidence of the limitation of the mind to fully grasp all God is in Himself: God and all His glorious attributes are one. His manifold virtues are simply the manifestations of His divine Being. He, Himself, is undivided and indivisible in nature (John 5:44; 17:2,3; I Timothy 6:15).

As God's nature and attributes are His chief glory, it is our purpose to discern what the Bible has to say about same. By the *nature* of God we mean what He actually *is,* while by His *attributes* we imply the several beams, or the orient excellencies that He *has.*

1. The Nature of God

How essential it is in these days of distorted views regarding the Godhead to have a Biblical understanding of the nature of God. He is not, as Sell proves in his *Bible Studies,* a God of fate, a machine God, an indifferent God, a revengeful God, or a weak God but a loving God and the pitying Father to all those who trust Him. While it is not possible to fully define God, we are given one or two comparative definitions of His Being.

First of all, God is a pure Spirit of infinite perfections. *God is Spirit* (John 4:24; Deuteronomy 4:15,16,19; Psalm 147:5;

Isaiah 40:25,26). *Spirit* is the highest form of being, and God is essentially and eternally "Spirit." This means that He is not confined to the limitations of matter, and does not possess a human body in any way visible to the physical eye. His is an essence infinitely pure in degree, kind and quality; differing from, and immeasurably superior to, any created being. He is of spiritual substance entirely, and not compounded of body and soul as man.

Although without a body, or *person*, God has yet *personality*. He is addressed as a Person, and possesses all the attributes of personality such as life, intelligence with self-consciousness, self-determination (Exodus 3:14; I Corinthians 2:11; Ephesians 1:9,11). He is no impersonal force or power, but as Spirit is an intelligent and moral Being whom we can trust, love and praise. God is distinct from all His creatures in that He is underived and necessarily free and independent. He exists in, and from, Himself. There is none to control Him (John 5:26). As Spirit, He is not capable of the limitations and imperfections of our humanity. There is no other like Him who is "glorious in holiness, fearful in praises, doing wonders" (Exodus 15:11).

Then, how impressive is the *infinity* of God. He is infinite because no limit can be assigned to His perfections and because He is omnipresent. All created beings are *finite*, meaning they have a limit and an end. They are subject to the limitations of time and space. But God is unrestricted by any bounds, and in the unsearchable grandeur of His nature, fills and transcends, duration and space. Although *infinite* is a negative term, it yet expresses a positive idea and when used of God sets forth the boundlessness of His essential nature and attributes (Ephesians 1:23; Jeremiah 23:24; Job 11:7; 26:14; 36:26). Other definitions such as "God is Love," "God is Light," "God is a consuming Fire," each carry their own significance.

2. The Names of God

As the Creator of man it was necessary for God to acquire a *name* by which man could address Him. Revealing Himself to man, He proclaimed the great name—so awesome to the ancient Jew—*Jehovah*, so merciful and gracious. The origin and meaning of this greatest name of God is expressed by Moses (Exodus 3:14,15). God is always the same (Malachi 3:6),

unchanged and unchangeable in His covenant relationship and ever faithful in the fulfilment of His promises. *Jehovah* means, "I will be that I will be," and represents His constancy, and was the *personal* name of the God of Israel. He is the self-existent One revealing Himself to men. For a fuller study of this sacred name, the reader is referred to the chapter devoted to it in Professor Davidson's *Old Testament Theology*.

There are, however, many other names of God, proving His reality and personality. Louis Berkhof observes—

> When God gives names to persons and things, they are names which have meaning and give an insight into the nature of the persons and things designated. This also applies to the names which God has given Himself. Sometimes the Bible speaks of the name of God in the singular, and in such cases the term is a designation of God in general, especially in relation to His people (Exodus 20:7; Psalm 113:3), or simply stands for God Himself (Proverbs 18:10; Isaiah 50:10). The one general name of God is split up into several special names, which are expressive of His many-sided being. These names are not of human invention but are given by God Himself.

Here are some of the divine names extolling God as the high and exalted One and yet as the One worshiping hearts can love and trust—

El is the oldest name and English form for God, and means, "to be strong, power, might." Expressing the general idea of God, *El* is linked on to other descriptive titles of God, as the following names prove.

Elohim is a "plural, and probably a plural of that sort called the plural of *majesty* or *eminence*, more accurately the plural of *fulness* or *greatness*." It is a term suggesting the Trinity, a plurality of powers such as were responsible for creation (Genesis 1:1, where "God" is *Elohim*). This term, used about 2,500 times in the Old Testament, implies "the might *par excellence*, or the plentitude of might."

El Elijon, "the most high God" (Genesis 14:18), points to God's exalted nature and as the sole Object of our reverence and worship. His prerogative as Possessor of heaven and earth to distribute the earth among the nations as He deems best (Deuteronomy 32:8).

El Hai describes Him as "the living God," *El Alah* as the "faithful God"—*Alah*, meaning to swear, bind oneself by an oath.

El Shaddai, "the Almighty God" (Genesis 17:1), portrays Him as the Strength-Giver, the Satisfier, the All-Sufficient One who enriches and makes fruitful (Genesis 28:3,4; John 15:2; Hebrews 12:10). As the "God of overpowering might," He controls all the powers of nature and makes them serve His purpose. He is "God the Omnipotent."

El Olam, "The everlasting God" (Genesis 21:33). Here we have the thought of the eternal duration of the Being of God. "From everlasting to everlasting, thou art God" (Psalm 90:2). He is also God over everlasting things.

We also have several compound names of God revealing Him as One well able to meet man's every need, and what glorious names these are!

Jehovah-Elohim, "Lord God" (Genesis 2:4,7,15,16). This first of the compound names of Deity emphasizes God's Creator relationship, His relationship to Israel, as well as moral authority over man and His redemptive power (Genesis 2:16,17-24; 3:8-19,21; 24:7; 28:13).

Jehovah-Jireh, "The Lord will provide" (Genesis 22:14). While He is able to provide all that man and beast require, the narrative implies the provision of sacrifice.

Jehovah-Rapha, "The Lord that healeth thee" (Exodus 15:26). While the context speaks of physical healing, the deeper healing of the soul is implied.

Jehovah-Nissi, "The Lord our Banner" (Exodus 17:8-15). He is the mighty Victor of the Amalekites of the flesh. In Him, we are more than conquerors (Galatians 5:17).

Jehovah-Shalom, "The Lord our Peace, or send Peace" (Judges 6:24). The Lord, who became our Peace, provides peace for the guilty sinner (Ephesians 2:4; Colossians 1:20).

Jehovah-Rāah, "The Lord is my Shepherd" (Psalm 23:1). Psalm 22 speaks of peace through the blood of the cross, and in this Shepherd-Psalm, the Saviour shepherds His own bloodwashed ones in a hostile world (John 10:11).

Jehovah-Tsidkenu, "The Lord our Righteousness" (Jeremiah 23:6). Man has no righteousness of his own to plead. Naked he must come to Him who was made righteousness, for dress.

Jehovah-Saboath, "The Lord of Hosts" (I Samuel 1:3; Psalm 24:10, etc.). This frequently employed and expressive designation implies God's power and supremacy in every realm.

Jehovah-Shammah, "The Lord is present" (Ezekiel 48:35). What a precious name this is! It promises God's abiding presence with His people. The Lord of Hosts is ever with His own (Psalms 16:11; 46:7,11; Matthew 28:20; Hebrews 13:5).

Adonai-Jehovah, "Lord God" (Genesis 13:2). Several meanings are associated with this compound name. *Adonai* means, "Master," and God as our divine Master demands our obedience and service. He is the Possessor and Ruler of men (Joshua 7:8-11; John 13:13).

Pater, "Father." This further descriptive title is related to God's relationship with Israel (Deuteronomy 32:6; Isaiah 63:16), and also to all those redeemed by the blood of God's Son (Matthew 6:9; I Corinthians 8:6; Ephesians 3:14).

All of the foregoing divine names and others prove the existence of God, and that He can be known, although only partially, by man. As to what *all* God *is* as revealed by His titles, the same is condensed in the expressive, "The *name* of God." This term embodies all His characteristics—is the summary of what He *is* and *has*. The saints of old knew that behind that majestic name there was might and mercy, power and provision. Hence *the name* is prominent—

"They that know thy *name* (all that Thou art) will put their trust in thee" (Psalm 9:10).

"The *name* of the Lord is a strong tower: the righteous runneth into it, and is safe" (Proverbs 18:10).

Professor A. B. Davidson says that what is taught above God Himself may be found in various forms—chiefly two, namely statements or assumptions regarding God, and *names* applied to God.

It will be found, I think, that all other designations of God, and all other assertions respecting Him, and all other attributes assigned to Him, may be embraced under one or other of the two names given to God in the opening chapters of Genesis. What is taught of God in these chapters is, *first*, that God is the absolute Cause and the absolute Lord of all things—heaven and earth; which terms embrace not only the upper and lower matter, but the superior and inferior spirits. And, *second*, that God is the absolute Personality—over against finite personalities, not absorbing personalities in Himself, nor by His Personality excluding personalities beside Himself.

3. The Attributes of God

The virtues or qualities of God are as numerous as His names. These divine attributes imply:

a. Those inherent qualities or parts of character which God has attributed to Himself as constituting His nature or essence.

b. That the sum of these manifold attributes are not to be conceived as constituting God but are His method of revealing Himself to His creatures. His essence or being is not the aggregate of the attributes, but they arise out of His underlying eternal essence or substance.

c. That God never magnifies one of His attributes at the expense of another. Man, because of his imperfect knowledge of the divine will, may think there are seeming contradictions in God's purpose, as, for example, the contradictory action of His attribute of love when a tragic experience befalls one of His own. But mercy and truth, righteousness and peace are always in complete harmony (Psalm 85:10).

As to the definition of God's glorious attributes, theologians have provided us with a variety of classifications several of which cross and intersect each other at different points. Here are some samples—

Physical—Intellectual—Moral Attributes

Incommunicable attributes which are those emphasizing the absolute distinction between God and His creatures.

Communicable attributes which are those finding some limited resemblance in man.

Natural attributes—those which are essential to His nature, and which do not involve the exercises of His will.

Moral attributes—those qualities of His character involving the exercise of His will.

Affirmative attributes—those expressing some positive perfection.

Negative attributes—those denoting the absence of defect or limitation.

Unrelated attributes—those which apply to God as one independent of creature existence.

Related attributes—those which apply to God as related to His creatures.

The best classification, we feel, is that given by Pope, and is the one we purpose using.

1. Those pertaining to God as an absolute and unrelated Being.

2. Those arising from the relation between the Creator and the creature.

3. Those which are related to moral beings.

Absolute Attributes

By "absolute" is meant those qualities belonging to God in, and of, Himself—those attributes God possesses apart from any relationship He may sustain toward His creatures. These attributes reflect His own inherent excellency.

1. Immensity. This is an attribute expressing more than omnipresence. God's center is everywhere as the Bible declares—

> "Behold, heaven and the heaven of heavens cannot contain thee" (II Chronicles 6:18).

Not only does He fill all space—space is an extension within His immensity; and all space contains, or ever can contain, is pervaded by His august presence. His *center* is everywhere—His *circumference* nowhere. How the immensity of God baffles human imagination and explanation!

2. Eternity. Having neither begining nor end, His is an eternal existence (Genesis 21:33). We divide time into past, present, future, but God, as the eternal *Now*, recognizes no divisions (Psalms 90:2; 102:24). His awful Name, "I am" (Exodus 3:14), is the assertion of pure existence and excludes any measurement of time. As the Everlasting One, He has no commencement, no consummation as all sensitive creatures have who live and die. Further, God is different from those who had a beginning but shall have no end, such as the angels, and the souls of men which are eternal *a parti post* (on the side after). Although they have not existed from all eternity as God, they are yet as Him to abide forever. Without beginning and without ending is proper only to Him in "from everlasting to everlasting" (Psalm 90:2). *Eternity* is His title, the jewel of His crown. He is "the King Eternal" (I Timothy 1:17).

God, then, has existed *from* all eternity and shall exist *to* all eternity. He never began to live, and shall never cease to be. While this awesome truth is beyond our comprehension, the Bible teaches it and we must be content, reverently bowing before Him who is the Alpha and Omega and our Everlasting God (Genesis 21:33; Deuteronomy 33:27; Psalms 90:4; 102:12, 24-27; 145:13; Isaiah 43:10; 44:6; 57:15; Revelation 1:4).

3. Immutability. This further attribute signifies unchangeableness. "Thou art the same" (Hebrews 1:12). In His essence, attributes, counsel and will, God Himself remained unchanged and unchangeable. All His attributes are like Himself, unalterably fixed, enduring forever. His perfections, purposes and promises are ever the same (Numbers 23:19; Psalms 33:11; 102:27; Malachi 3:6; Hebrews 6:17; James 1:17). Man at his best is but a creature of eclipses and changes, fits and starts, ups and downs, high tide and low ebb, but the glory of God shines with a fixed brightness. Many of the angels created as "morning stars" became "falling stars." They were fashioned as holy ones yet mutable so "left their first estate." God, however, is never taken for better or for worse—not for better, then He is not perfect: not for worse, then He would cease to be perfect. God is immutably good and holy: there is no shadow of change in Him (Exodus 3:14; I Samuel 15:25; Isaiah 14:24; 46:9, 10).

Seeming changes in God are due to changes of His creatures. His *promises* and *purposes* never change, though His *actions* necessarily vary according to our conduct. While the Bible speaks of God *repenting* this is only a human way of speaking of God, and simply indicates a change in man's relations to God (Exodus 32:14; Jonah 3:10).

4. Self-sufficiency. Because God is the self-existent One, He is independent of everything about Himself. Necessary self-sufficiency is another of His absolute and unrelated attributes. All created beings are dependent upon Him, but He Himself is unconscious of need. He is self-subsisting within Himself. The Psalmist gives us a vivid description of this aspect of the divine nature in the words: "If I were hungry, I would not tell thee: For the world is mine, and the fulness thereof" (50:12).

5. Unity. The Hebrew word for *one* denotes a compound unity, not a single unity, as the following passages prove (Genesis 2:24; 11:6; I Corinthians 12:13; Galatians 3:28). There is only one Jehovah, eternally existing and manifesting Himself to us in a threefold way—in Himself, by His Son, through the Holy Spirit (Exodus 20:3; Deuteronomy 4:35; 6:4; Psalm 86:10; I Timothy 2:5).

While we are not enumerating *perfection* among God's absolute attributes, the same is naturally implied. All that we have said of Him is eloquent with the thought of absolute perfection; which is testified to so frequently in the Bible. His ways, like Himself are perfect (Psalm 19:7).

Relative Attributes

These specific qualities represent the divine Being in its relationship to creatures or the created universe, and affords a concept of God inspiring faith and confidence in Him. "They that know thy name (the divine nature or character) will put their trust in thee" (Psalm 9:10).

1. Omnipotence. *Omni* means "all," *Potence,* "power," so we have *Almightiness,* or the power to carry into effect whatever God may will. He is the All Powerful One (Jeremiah 32:17, 18). That there are some things God cannot do is evident from many Scriptures. He cannot lie, sin, deny Himself, or act contrary to His nature (Numbers 23:19; I Samuel 15:29; II Timothy 2:13; Hebrews 6:18; James 1:13, 17). But apart from these aspects of divine inability, the word "impossible" is not in God's vocabulary. As the source of power, unlimited power is His which always operates in harmony with His wisdom and goodness. In all His dealings in creation there is the process of a universal plan and the adaptation to personal ends (Jeremiah 32:17,18).

Further, to *do* requires no effort on His part. He creates and sustains all animate and inanimate things without the idea of laboring associated with human activity. "He operates, unspent." He is never weary or tired (Isaiah 40:27-31; Jeremiah 27:2; Nahum 1:3,6).

> All nature is absolutely subject to His will and word (Job 42:2).
>
> All men are absolutely subject to His authority (James 4:12-15; Daniel 4:25).
>
> All angels recognize His sway (Daniel 4:25; Hebrews 1:13,14).
>
> All satanic hosts bow to His Almightiness (Job 1:2; 2:6).

In all things the existence of God's omnipotence is limited by His will (Isaiah 59:1,2).

Resident within the attribute of omnipotence is the idea of *sovereignty,* which includes all things we see and know, such as the extent and details of nature. The works and ways of men—the unfolding and progress of history; all things beyond our comprehension which covers the vast, unseen universe—heaven with all its occupants and glories—eternity, with its past and future implications (Matthew 11:26,27; Romans 11:33-36).

2. Omniscience. This glorious attribute implies infinity in knowledge. *Omni,* "all": *science,* "knowledge." God has intuitive, simultaneous, infallible perceptions of Himself, and all other beings and events. Past, present and future are as an open scroll to Him, and His all-knowledge is not the result of reasoning, as with man, but is intuitive, perfect and eternal. He sees and knows everything.

Omniscience is vitally connected with *omnipotence* seeing that power pre-supposes a knowledge of *how* to do. Unless a man knew how to make a watch it would be impossible for him to produce it. In this sense, "Knowledge is Power." The Bible is permeated with the fact that omniscience is the power of knowing the thoughts and motives of every heart and the perfection and infinite of knowledge. There are no afterthoughts with God.

"Of His understanding there is no number" (Psalm 147:5 margin).

God's knowledge is absolute and unacquired. He has no need of secret agents to bring Him information, or radio to flash Him news of what is transpiring, for He is "a God of knowledges" (I Samuel 2:3), the original plural implying the bright mirror of His own essence (Job 37:16; Exodus 3:19 R.V.; Psalm 139:1,2,4; Proverbs 5:21; Romans 11:33). Such omniscience has its servants everywhere.

3. Omnipresence. God, the Creator and Sustainer of all things is present universally and simultaneously in every part of His wide domain, and is able to put forth His entire power in every place at one and the same time. He is present everywhere all the time. It is said that the Turks built their temples open at the top to show that God cannot be confined in them, but is in all places by His presence. Setting bounds, He Himself is without bounds or limits.

Omnipresence and *immensity* are closely allied, the only difference being—His immensity fills space: His omnipresence fills all creation (Jeremiah 23:24). Upon this attribute of omnipresence, or the more comprehensive one of *immensity* hang all the grandeur and sufficiency of all things in the universe, whether spiritual or material. All the forces and laws of nature, even the prolonged existence of things are maintained because God is in, and through them all (I Kings 8:29; II Chronicles 6:16;

Psalm 139:7-12; Isaiah 6:3; 66:1; Amos 9:2; Acts 17:24-28). How beautifully the lines of Alexander Pope describe this divine quality, which—

Warms in the sun, refreshes in the breeze,
Glows in the stars and blossoms in the trees:
Lives through all life, extends through all extent;
Spreads undivided, operates unspent.

What must be remembered is that not only is God present in all things, but that all things are present to Him. The movements of all orders of being are open before Him, and in His encircling sight "we live, and move and have our being." Is not the thought of His omnipresence comforting to our hearts? Does it not make prayer a glorious possibility and fellowship with Him a constant reality? (Genesis 28:16; Matthew 18:20; Ephesians 3:19). John Oxenham in *Vision Splendid* says—

Blessed are they that have eyes to see,
They shall find God everywhere.
They shall see Him where others see stones.

4. Wisdom. Wisdom, which is an aspect of *divine knowledge* is "the virtue of God which manifests itself in the selection of worthy ends and in the choice of the best means for the realization of those ends." Berkhof goes on to say that, "the final end to which He makes all things subservient is His own glory" (Romans 11:33; I Corinthians 2:7; Ephesians 1:6,12,14; Colossians 1:16). Because this attribute of wisdom combines all other attributes for the sole purpose of doing the best thing, in the best way, at the best time, it has been rightly called "the brightest beam of the Godhead" (Job 32:9; Psalm 104:24). Wisdom is the right use of knowledge, therefore, God never makes a mistake, takes a wrong turn, or is sorry for anything He does. While His perfect wisdom implies omniscience, it yet exceeds it.

Man may have knowledge but little wisdom; and the most wise, little knowledge. For instance, a doctor may understand the laws governing his bodily health yet habitually violates those laws by his excesses. He possesses knowledge but proves himself to be destitute of wisdom in his failure to put knowledge into practice. God as the Infinite One, however, is perfect in His natural attributes and uses them for the best purpose thereby revealing His wisdom. This "intellectual element of God's character includes His perfect and eternal knowledge of all things that may be known, past, present and future and an understanding of how to use that knowledge." He is "the only wise God" (I Timothy 1:17; Hebrews 4:13; Acts 15:18; Psalm 139:6-7). One way in which divine wisdom is manifested is *in creation.*

"The Lord by wisdom hath founded the earth" (Proverbs 3:19; Jeremiah 10:12). Creation is a mirror of God's wisdom, as well as a monument of His power. The marvelous universe is resplendent with evidences of a wisdom, grand in its concepts and wonderfully perfect in all its arrangements and adaptations, so just in its methods and entrancing in its harmony and beauty as to draw forth an adoring wonder. One aspect of divine wisdom in this direction is the appointing of the annual seasons. "Thou hast made summer and winter" (Psalm 74:17). If it had been summer all the time the unrelieved heat would have been disastrous to man and beast: if all winter, the constant cold and storms would have been equally disastrous. We all see divine wisdom revealed in human history.

Does not the same wisdom rule, and overrule, in the development of history, whether personal or universal? God is not baffled by all the perplexities and contradictions of human perversity and wrong. With power to make the wrath of man praise Him, God can find in the fiercest antagonism of a wicked heart a chariot to bring His perfect will and purpose to fruition. He knows how to thwart the counsel of Ahithophel and hang Haman on his own gallows. The humblest saint can rest in the assurance that in God there is a wisdom never baffled by opposition and never taken unawares by sudden crises, directing all things toward a blessed consummation (Romans 8:28; 11:33; Colossians 2:3).

The whole scheme of redemption offers us the masterpiece or the highest expression of divine wisdom. To contrive a way to happiness between the sin of man and the justice of God is an aspect of such wisdom, astonishing both to men and angels (I Peter 1:12; Ephesians 3:10). Great is the mystery of redemption for it was all of God that no flesh should glory in His presence.

'Twas great to call a world from nought,
'Twas greater to redeem.

Divine wisdom was personified in Christ Jesus whom God "made unto us wisdom" (I Corinthians 1:20). Says Scofield of Solomon's reference to Christ as *wisdom* (Proverbs 8:22-36), "That wisdom is more than the personification of an attribute of God, or of the will of God as best for man, but is a distinct adumbration of Christ to the devout mind. This passage with John 1:1-3; Colossians 1:17 can refer to nothing less than the Eternal Son of God." Surely such infinite wisdom, expressing itself in creation and providence; in decrees and administration; in adaptions and sequences—in redemption with its provision for a lost world, leads us to

1. Adoration for a wisdom which is an infinite deep none can reach (Psalm 77:9), and

2. Appropriation. As He waits to impart His wisdom, and is never impoverished by giving way we lay hold of all we have in Him (I Kings 3:9; James 1:5).

5. Goodness. Some theologians see in this attribute a combination of divine love, wisdom and righteousness. That *righteousness* must be a constituent element of goodness, is evident from the fact that goodness could not err in justice or in law. God's benevolence and beneficence can be traced in all His works and ways. He will be good, and only good, to all His creatures. *Good* is the old English word for "God." (Genesis 1:31; Psalm 145:9; Mark 10:18). God's goodness is that "perfection which prompts Him to deal kindly and bountifully with all His creatures" (Psalms 33:6; 104:21; Matthew 5:45; Acts 14:17). How His unfailing, great goodness should lead us to repentance!

6. Freedom. In declaring *freedom* as another divine attribute we only claim for God what is essential to His deity. Without the possession of freedom all other attributes would be more or less invalid. God cannot be confined or crippled by the laws of the universe which He Himself created. He must be free to interpose, alter or abrogate their laws as He deems fit. God is under no obligation to any of His creatures (Daniel 4:35; Romans 9:14-24). We recognize that His freedom is ever conditioned by His nature and that therefore He will never act contrary to His holiness or love. Amid the seeming perplexities and mysteries of life, how we cling to this truth.

Moral Attributes

We now consider those august attributes belonging to God as Governor of the moral universe and which imply moral action on His part. Some writers summarize all of these moral traits under two divisions, namely, *holiness* and *love*. "God is Love" and "God is Light" and in these pregnant sentences we have a comprehensive definition of the divine character.

1. Holiness. As the absolutely holy one God is free from evil and hates and abhors sin (Leviticus 19:2). He is "glorious in holiness" (Exodus 15:11)—holiness being the most sparkling jewel in His crown. As His power makes Him mighty, so His holiness makes Him glorious.

God possesses intrinsic holiness.

He is holy in His nature. As light is the essence of the sun, so holiness is God's very being. Because of His divine perfection, "God is absolutely distinct from all His creatures, and above them in infinite majesty" (Exodus 15:11; Isaiah 57:15). He is holy in all His ways. He cannot act contrary to His nature. As the sun cannot darken, so God cannot act unrighteously. "He is the Holy One" (Job 6:10). Holiness is His inward character—not merely a trait of His Being, but His very essence—not one of a list of virtues but the sum of all excellencies rather than an excellence.

God possesses original holiness.

He is primarily holy. He can present Himself as the pattern of holiness because He is the origin and source of it. From the dateless past, He has been free from all moral impurity and is therefore morally perfect (I Samuel 2:2; Psalms 99:9; 111:9; Revelation 15:4).

> Every thought of Holiness
> Are His alone.

God possesses transcendent holiness.

The holiest angel above, or the holiest man on earth cannot measure the just dimensions of God's holiness. "There is none so holy as the Lord" (I Samuel 2:2). With the angels, holiness is a quality that can be lost for many of them "left their first estate." But because God's holiness is His essence, He can never forfeit it. His is an infinite and unchangeable moral excellence, which He eternally wills and maintains (Isaiah 6:3; Mark 10:18; II Corinthians 7:1; Revelation 4:8).

God possesses efficient holiness.

This facet of the diamond of divine holiness implies that He is the Cause of all that is holy in others. He is both the *Pattern* and *Principle* of holiness. "His spring feeds all our cisterns—every crystal stream is from this Fountain." For instance, is not this feature of the divine character impressed upon material things? Does not holiness breathe in nature? How pure is the light untainted by what it touches. How pure is the snow making dull and gray by comparison, the purest human production. The hallowing solitudes of mountain and glen, of nature in all its aspects and phases exert an influence, speaking to the soul of divine holiness.

Further, God's holiness is the standard of our life and conduct. "Be ye holy, for I am holy" (I Peter 1:16). How conscious man is of his sin when in the presence of this thrice Holy One! (Job 34:10; Habakkuk 1:13). As holiness is the principle ruling God's actions toward His creatures, He demands obedience to, and uniformity with, such a standard. God cannot have one standard for Himself, and another for His creatures. "As He *is*, so are we in this world." As a being of perfect goodness God could have had no other ultimate purpose than the creation of beings capable of reflecting such holiness.

Then there is the dominating factor to consider. Since God is all-holy, He must consequently dominate the universe, opposing and condemning and punishing sin. Wherever sin exists, there must be His uncompromising attitude toward same. He must remain forever the absolute and eternal enemy of sin. From such holiness, there comes *justice* and *righteousness*, which as they are administered, moral order is maintained among His intelligent creatures (Deuteronomy 32:3,4; Psalms 36:6; 115:3; 119:142). Paul provides the link in the phrase, "Righteousness and true holiness" (Ephesians 4:24). Thus God's holiness forms the basis of moral significance within the universe. Holiness is the glory of His creation and the grand ascription of worship. Holy! Holy! Holy! will yet become the anthem of a redeemed universe. The awful lake of fire, the coming wrath of the Almighty, the solemn destruction meted out upon all satanic forces present no difficulties whatever to the heart dominated by the fact of God's absolute holiness.

The question of paramount importance is,

Are we living in the white light of God's holiness? When fierce temptation attacked Joseph it was the consciousness of divine holiness that prevented him from yielding to the cry, and to ask in triumph, "How can I do this great wickedness, and sin against God?" The secret of constant personal victory over all that is alien to His holy will is the abiding consciousness of the holiness of Him before whom the seraphim veil their faces.

2. Love. Although often called "the most central attribute of God," it is doubtful whether it should be regarded as more central than the other perfections of God. This conspicuous attribute differs from *goodness* inasmuch as it expresses direct relation to moral beings. Whereas *goodness* has a universal relation, God is good to His creation, but He loves His creatures. The *holiness* and *love* mutually sustain and complement each other.

Holiness presents God as the moral Governor of the universe. As Light, He dispels all darkness. "God is Light."

Love declares Him to be the gracious Father of all who trust and obey Him. As Love, he diffuses all grace. "God is Love."

Every act of God is the outcome of His love, which has been defined in this way:

God imparting Himself and all the good He possesses to others, and seeking thereby to win response that He may possess men for Himself that thereby they may reach the highest possible good.

That God is a being of boundless goodness and perfect love can be proved in the following ways—

1. In His care in providing for the wants, cares, habits and instincts of every living thing. Even the lower order of animals who cannot reason are nevertheless provided for by the kind hand of their Creator with food and shelter. God's love is also evident in the bestowal upon man of that superb adaptation of the other works of His hand for their benefit. The manifold gifts of life, health, comforts, friends and money, they all speak of His love (James 1:17).

2. In The Provision of Human Love. Human love, in its highest and purest form, is but a faint reflection of God's love for mankind. In human affection two seemingly opposite impulses are harmoniously blended with the desire to give. Love lives for its object, and seeks possession of that object. As it rises to its highest altitude, human love becomes capable of a marvelous expression of self-denial and self-sacrifice. But the most wonderful expression of human love can never rise to the height of divine love. Love for another may be disappointed, quenched, starved, but God ever seeks the response of the object loved. The many waters of rejection can never quench God's love (Song of Solomon 8:6-8; John 15:13). His is a love that will not let us go.

3. In the Provision of Scripture. How divine love permeates the divine Book! Nature is eloquent with the truth of God's wisdom and power, but it is the Bible alone that reveals His loving heart. Love often expresses itself in warm letters, and literature has given us some glowing "love letters." What is the Bible? Is it not God's *love letter* in which He reveals His undying love for a world of sinners lost and ruined by the fall?

4. In The Provision of Christ. God's beloved Son came as the personification of His Father's love which love reached its full-orbed manifestation in the work of redemption. Because God loved—He gave (John 3:16; 4:10; 15:9; I John 4:16). It was God's love that drew salvation's plan in a past eternity, and in Christ, God gave Himself for mankind. His love is measureless and passeth knowledge. It is changeless and knows no end. "Behold what manner of love the Father hath bestowed upon us," (I John 3:1-3). Berkhof says that the unmerited love of God reveals itself in pardoning sin and is called *grace* (Ephesians 1:6,7; 2:7,8; Titus 2:11); and that His love relieving the misery of those who are bearing the consequences of sin is known as His *mercy* or *tender compassion* (Luke 1:54, 72,78; Romans 9:16,18; 15:9; Ephesians 2:4). When the same divine love bears with the sinner failing to heed God's instructions and warning, it is named His *longsuffering* or *forbearance* (Romans 2:4; 9:22; I Peter 3:20; II Peter 3:15).

3. Justice. Although God is absolutely holy and unfailing in His love, yet, in His dealings with rational creatures, He is perfectly just and righteous. He acts fairly and rightly with all men (Deuteronomy 32:4). Divine holiness and love reveal themselves in the administration of divine justice and righteousness with the end of maintaining moral order among intelligent creatures. The terms *righteous* and *just*, or *righteousness* and *justice* are equivalent, implying the same idea. Thus the justice of God is that

attribute leading Him always to do right. "Justice is to give every man his due," and divine justice is the rectitude of God's holy loving nature whereby He is prompted to the accomplishment of that which is right and equal.

Because God is an impartial Judge, never rash or unprincipled in His actions, His justice runs in two channels, namely, the distribution of *rewards* and *punishments*. He is just to reward those who accept salvation on His terms, who honor Him in all their ways and diligently labor in His cause; just to punish the rebellious and impenitent both here and hereafter. Divine justice, then, involves the following principles—

God cannot but be just.

God is perfectly holy and must therefore be perfectly just. His holiness will not suffer Him to do anything but what is righteous. He can no more be unjust than He can be unholy or unloving.

God's will is the supreme rule of justice.

His "sweet, beloved will" is the standard of equity. His will is always wise and good, and He wills nothing but what is just. God ever acts toward men in harmony with the purity of His own nature.

God's justice is voluntary.

God is always *just* out of love for justice. "Thou lovest righteousness" (Hebrews 1:9). Justice flows from His nature, and cannot be bribed, forced or perverted. "Justice," says Aristotle, "comprehends in it all virtues." God's justice, then, is the perfection of His being. To say that He is just is to confess that He is all that is excellent. Perfections meet in Him who is not only just, but justice itself.

God never did, or can do the least wrong.

While His justice has been wronged a million times over, it never did any wrong. With God justice is not a mere policy but "the rendering to all that is fit and due and is a requirement of His holiness." Because of divine mercy, severity is abated. God might inflict heavier penalties, but our mercies are more than we deserve and our punishments less (Ezra 9:13).

God's Justice cannot be argued against.

Who dare expostulate with God and demand a reason for His actions? Has He not *equity*, as well as *authority*, on His side? (Isaiah 28:17). He has no need to give any account of His actions. Man's reason may clash with God's justice, but the plumb line of our reason is too short to fathom the depth of divine justice (Romans 9:20; 11:33). Divine justice must be adored even when we cannot see a reason for it. In this we rest that God knows what is right and that because of His justice, sin which He hates, must be punished sometime, somewhere; and that all life's suffering and seeming inequalities will be rightly adjusted. As Dr. J. B. Tidwell expresses it—

God's Justice demands of all moral beings conformity to moral perfection and visits non-conformity with personal loss or suffering. (Psalm 18:25, 26; Romans 2:5).

The reader should note the manifold aspects of divine justice in the following key passages—

Genesis 18:25; Exodus 9:23,27; Deuteronomy 32:3,4; I Kings 8:32; II Chronicles 12:5,6; Ezra 9:15; Job 8:3; 37:23; Psalms 7:9,10; 11:4; 89:14; 96:11-13; 98:1-3; 105:4; 116:5; 119:142; 145:17; Isaiah 6:3; 45:21; Jeremiah 12:1; Daniel 9:12-14; Zephaniah 3:5; Matthew 25:31-46; John 17:25; Romans 3:25; II Thessalonians 1:6,7; II Timothy 4:8; Hebrews 6:10; I John 1:9; Revelation 16:5,6.

4. Mercy. The heathen styled their god *Jupiter* both "good" and "great," but goodness and greatness in their perfection meet only in God in whom majesty and mercy are inseparable. His goodness or mercy is the result of His greatness. As a merciful God, He is full of pity, slow to punish and ready to pardon. It is because of His mercy that we come to know how He regards in pity the sinful and the suffering. How rich in mercy God is!

It was His mercy that prompted God the Son to undertake the plan of atonement, and for God the Father to accept that plan on our behalf.

It is mercy prompting God the Spirit to strive with sinners, enlightening them as to the nature and consequences of their sin.

It was mercy that inspired the promises of Scripture for the relief of the sorrowing and afflicted among the saints.

It is mercy that bears with the sins and insults of the guilty, withholding deserved judgment. The tree is spared, "This year also." How manifold are the aspects of this divine mercy! We could write of preventing mercy, sparing mercy, supplying mercy, guiding mercy, accepting mercy, quickening mercy, supporting mercy, forgiving mercy, correcting mercy, comforting mercy, delivering mercy, crowning mercy. Among the properties or qualification of God's abundant mercy we note that—

It is free.

Not one of us deserves *mercy*. To present merit is to destroy mercy. If God showed mercy only to such as are worthy, He would show none at all, for the best are unworthy (Romans 3:24; Ephesians 1:4; Titus 3:5).

It is infinite.

Because God is great, every virtue He possesses bears the imprint of His greatness. What tongue can describe the overflowing mercies of God, which are new every morning? "The vial of wrath drops, but the fountain of mercy runs (Psalms 42:8; 51:1; 86:5; Lamentations 3:23; Ephesians 2:4).

It is eternal

As long as He is God, He will be showing mercy. It is a mercy which both overflows and ever-flows. Such a river will never dry up (Exodus 34:6,7; Numbers 14:18; Psalms 100:5; 103:9,17; Micah 7:18: James 5:11). This attribute of mercy must abide for two reasons—

1. God is essentially merciful in Himself. Mercy is not only one of His precious virtues, it is an integral part of His own being.

2. God is always relatively merciful toward mankind. Is this not why the Bible presents Him in the white robe of mercy more often than it does in garments rolled in blood? "Thou art good, and doest good" (Psalm 119:68). This relative mercy is but God's innate desire to pity and succor the needy. Mercy, or goodness, is the principle of God's nature leading Him to communicate the blessings of salvation and life to others. If the reader desires a fuller study of this feature of the divine character all references to "mercy," "merciful," "goodness," "pity" and "loving-kindness" must be considered.

The practical outcome of such a profitable and pleasurable meditation should be the imitation of mercy in one's own life. Having received mercy, we ought to be merciful. Says Ambrose—

The sums and definition of religion is,
Be rich in mercy, be helpful to the bodies and souls of others. Scatter your golden seeds: let the lamp of your profession be filled with the oil of charity. Be merciful in giving and forgiving. "Be ye merciful, as your heavenly Father is merciful."

Privileged, as we are, to *preach* the mercy of God, let us strive to *practice* it in our daily actions.

5. Truth. A Being of perfect holiness, as God is, He must possess essential truthfulness. The Bible declares Him to be, "A God of truth and without iniquity: just and right is He" (Deuteronomy 32:4). God always represents things as they are and always keeps His Word. None can gainsay His veracity. True, in His inner Being, He is true in revelation and in His relation to mankind. As the true God He is placed over against idols who are destitute of the virtue of faithfulness (Numbers 23:19; I Corinthians 1:9; II Timothy 2:13; Hebrews 10:23).

Bible saints affirmed that God made good His promises, and that His words are truth forming, thereby, the only correct and infallible standard of truth for His creatures. All of His promises are as firm as the heavens He created. His is—

The Voice that rolls the stars along,
Speaks all the Promises

A perusal of the author's volume on *All the Promises of the Bible* proves how the Bible is God's "Promise Box," and that His mercy in giving the promises guarantees their fulfillment. "There hath not failed one word of all His good promise" (I Kings 8:56). But while it is true that "He is not a man that He should repent" (I Samuel 15:29), these observations must be made:

1. He sometimes delays fulfillment. But His delays are not denials, as Mary and Martha proved, when Jesus did not hurry to help Lazarus (John 11). Simeon received the promise that he would not die until he had seen the Lord's Christ, but he had to wait long for the fulfillment of this joy (Luke 2:26). Our Lord promised to return for His own, but centuries have come and gone, and the Bridegroom has not come—but He will! (Hebrews 10:37).

2. He sometimes seems to change a promise. Changing, however, is not *breaking*. Oft times, God changed a temporal promise into a spiritual. "The Lord shall give that which is good," is a promise God may fulfil in a temporal sense. But often God permits His children to suffer the lack of

temporal blessings in order that they might possess spiritual blessings. If He does not increase the basket and the store, He does grant increase of faith and of inward peace. If a man promises to pay me in cents but pays me in dollars, he does not break his promise in paying me with better coin.

God cannot lie nor suffer His faithful to fail (Psalm 89: 37). He is "plenteous in truth" (Psalm 86:15), a Being upon whom we can rely without fear. So let us "feed upon His faithfulness" (Psalm 37: 3 American Revised Version). What a feast! (Deuteronomy 32:4; II Samuel 23: 5; Psalms 57:10; 96:13; 146:6; Romans 4: 21; Titus 1:2; II Timothy 2:13; Hebrews 10:23).

6. Providence. Doubtless Shakespeare had the providence of God in mind when he wrote that—

There's a Divinity that shapes our ends,
Rough hew them how we will.

What exactly is meant by the "eternal providence," John Milton asserted justified "the ways of God to men"? Scripture makes it plain that such providence is God's wise and benevolent care of His creatures and creation. "The Lord will provide" (Genesis 22:8). God is good to all and "His tender mercies are over all His works" (Psalm 145:9; Proverbs 16:9,33; Isaiah 45:5-7; Luke 12:22-30; Acts 17:28; Romans 8:28· Philippians 4:6,7,19). Dr. W. J. Townsend in his *Christian Doctrine* explains "providence" as, "That unceasing and efficient government which is carried on by the divine Being throughout the universe, by which the creatures are preserved, their wants supplied, and the purposes of the vast creation are accomplished. This active, all-pervading Providence is a prominent feature of Scripture" (Psalm 145:15, 16; Colossians 1:17; Hebrews 1:3).

As to the various aspects of God's providential dealings with all objects of His concern (Psalm 20:4; Jeremiah 10:23), we have—

General providence inviting the secondary causes in His government of the universe (Psalms 37:1-3; 103:1-22; 121:3).

Special providence refers to His direct and active interference in the personal affairs of His intelligent creatures (Genesis 50:20; Acts 4:27,28).

Preventive providence (Genesis 20:6).

Permissive providence (Psalm 81:12,13).

Determinative providence (I Corinthians 10:13).

Scripture abounds with illustrations of God's providence. Joseph was sold into Egypt in the anguish of his soul, and amidst the lamentations of his father. In Egypt, he endured fierce temptation and imprisonment, yet the whole of his affliction came to be seen as part of the divine plan of preserving his family alive. The "evil" of Joseph's brethren became the divine "good." Is not the providence of God evident when He used the most trifling circumstance to accomplish His will on behalf of the Jews? A sleepless night of the king was overruled to save a people from slaughter (Esther 6:1). The Book of Job likewise displays the providence of God in its inscrutableness and mercy. The saints of succeeding ages have proved that—

Behind a frowning providence,
He hides a smiling face.

Because God is sovereign He is well able to exercise an all-inclusive providence, involving a controlling care of all His creatures. A proverb has it, "Providence provides for the provident," but the Bible and experience teach that divine providence permits evil actions, as well as blessing good actions. To quote Townsend again—

The vastness of the sway of Providence cannot be imagined. It ranges from the archangel to the microbe, from the highest heavens to the humblest anthill, from the forgeous Sirian or solar system to the tiniest speck of star dust, from the loftiest destinies of an immortal spirit to the spots upon an insect's wings: nothing is too large for His grasp, nothing is small enough to elude His notice.

Concluding our study of the divine attributes it is essential to observe that all we have described of God, is equally true of the Lord Jesus and of the Holy Spirit. All three Persons are coequal. This is true in respect to the operations of divine providence which is ascribed to—

The Father (John 5:17; Matthew 6:9; I Corinthians 12:4-6).
The Son (Matthew 11:27; 28:18; Colossians 1:17; Hebrews 1:2,3).
The Holy Spirit (Psalm 104:30).

The Living Word
(John 1:14,18; Hebrews 1:1)

It is *in* and *through* Christ that we have the complete revelation of God. Christ came as the sum of the Father's purpose. In Him, the fullness of the Godhead abides; and in Him the thought of God finds utterance and expression (John 1:1-3). Having been the Father's daily delight before days were fashioned (Proverbs 8:30), God was a glorious reality to Jesus, who revealed the sacred relationship of love existing between them. Because Jesus was *The Truth* (John 14:6), all He declared about God must be true. If we want to know if God exists, and what He is like, all we have to do is to study the words, works and ways of Jesus Christ, who was the express image of His Father.

We trust that our survey of the doctrine of God has proved helpful. Knowing Him, we love and adore Him, and seek to serve Him with all our strength. Boyle, in his volume on *The Style of Scripture* says—

> I use the Scriptures not as an arsenal to be resorted to only for arms and weapons . . . but as a matchless temple, when I delight to contemplate the beauty, the symmetry and the magnificence of the structure; and to increase my awe and excite my devotion to the Deity there preached and adored.

V

The Doctrine of Christ

The late Dr. Clarence E. Macartney, who had an expert knowledge of the history of Napoleon Bonaparte, and who wrote a remarkable biography of the renowned Frenchman, gives us a most interesting comparison of Napoleon and the Lord Jesus Christ. In his volume on *What Jesus Really Taught*, Dr. Macartney says—

> The two characters of history about whom more books have been written and more words spoken than others, are Napoleon and Jesus Christ. But what a contrast between these two men who—more than all others—have engrossed the mind of man! Napoleon shed rivers of blood upon which to float his ambitions. The only blood the other shed was His own, which He poured out upon the cross, for the redemption of mankind.

Dr. Macartney then proceeds to describe the accomplishments of the two—one leaving behind him a ghastly trail of dead; the other leaving behind Him a trail of mercy and compassion and life. "These are two men who have had more words written about them, more opinions uttered concerning them, than any other men." Some men are fascinated by the character of Napoleon, others with the Person and work of Christ. That Napoleon himself was drawn to a Greater than he, is proven by the following generally accepted testimony he gave of Christ—

> I know men, and I tell you, Jesus is not a man. He commands us to believe, and gives no other reason than His awful word, *I am God*. Philosophers try to solve the mysteries of the universe by their empty dissertations: fools: they are like the infant that cries, to have the moon as a plaything. Christ never hesitates. He speaks with authority. His religion is a mystery: but it subsists by its own force. He seeks, and absolutely requires the love of men, the most difficult thing in the world to claim. Alexander, Caesar, Hannibal, conquered the world but they had no friends . . . I founded my empire upon what?—force. Jesus founded His empire on love: and at this hour millions would die for him . . . What an abyss between my misery and the eternal kingdom of Christ, who is proclaimed, loved, adored and which is extending all over the earth. Is this death? I tell you, the death of Christ is the death of a God. I tell you, *Jesus Christ is God*.

No other man, born of woman, has gathered around His claims and character such voluminous literature as Jesus Christ. John says that "the world itself could not contain the books that should be written" about His accomplishments (John 21:24,25). Libraries all over the world contain a mountain of books that have been written of Him who came as—

The promised Messiah and Saviour of the world;

The Founder of Christianity;

The Lord and Head of the Christian Church;

The complete Revelation of God to man.

The doctrine before us is the loftiest and sublimest that can engage the mind of man, and presents a course of study of transcendent importance, of vast and varied range, of unrivaled attraction and fraught with the highest practical issues. Theologians, philosophers and poets have written about Christ, one way or the other, often forgetting that our concept of Him cannot be over-estimated because what He is determines what Christianity is, which stands or falls with Him. In all that He is in Himself is the cornerstone of the Christian faith, the key of the battle between faith and unbelief.

While literature, poetry and art have vied with each other in their tributes to the Saviour, and have been stirred to their highest achievements under the influences of His unrivaled glory, beauty, wisdom and might, it is to the Bible alone we turn for the full and final revelation of Him who came as "the Fairest of all the earth beside." Because the doctrine concerning Him is so vast in its range, it is no easy task to classify it. It may be, however, that thinking of all associated with Christ as a whole, we can examine the facts in this threefold way.

1. His past manifestation, which takes us back to the dim, eternal past—to the Old Testament history—to His entrance into our humanity—to His return to heaven.

2. His present ministry, which bids us dwell upon all that He is accomplishing on His church's behalf in the Father's heavenly abode.

3. His prospective majesty, which covers all the future has for His church, the world, and the eternal ages. What glory is to be His!

His Past Manifestation

Coeternal with the Father, and with the Holy Spirit, the beginning of the revelation of Christ goes back beyond the beginning of creation and of man. "In the beginning—a beginning before Genesis 1:1—was the Word" (John 1:1). Claiming for Himself powers and attributes belonging only to God, Christ asserted His *pre-existence*. When among men, He could claim, "Before Abraham was, I am" (John 8:58). John also reminds us that Jesus dwelt in "the bosom of the Father" (1:18), which, strange though it may seem, declares that Jesus lived before He was born. He, Himself, could say that He "came forth from the Father" (John 16:28). He also prayed, "Father, glorify Thou Me with Thine own self with the glory which I had with Thee *before the world was*" (John 17:5). What a manifestation of His excellent glory the angelic host must have witnessed in that past eternity when their Lord was the brightness of the Father's glory (Hebrews 1:3). Did He not share the Father's attribute of eternity, and come into the world as the Everlasting Father, the King Eternal, the Eternal Son, and as the Ancient of Days? (Isaiah 9:6; 23:7; I Timothy 1:17).

A further mystery is that, in that past eternity, before the present earth was formed with man as its occupant, the omniscient God foresaw that man, after his creation would sin, and require a Saviour, who ultimately came as the Lamb slain *before* the foundation of the world (Revelation 13:8). The true church, composed of redeemed souls was chosen in Him *before* the same foundation (Ephesians 1:4; II Timothy 1:9). Thus, in that dateless past, "Love drew salvation's plan," and in "the fulness of time" Jesus came as the foreordained sacrificial Lamb (Galatians 4:4).

We now come to the Old Testament preparation for the coming of God's eternal Son, who did appear as the goal of Old Testament revelation. The prophecies and promises of the manifestation of Christ as the Redeemer—Messiah are interwoven in Old Testament Scriptures from the first promise of Him given to Adam (Genesis 3:15), right on to the last promise of His ultimate glory as "the Sun of Righteousness" (Malachi 4:2). While in the flesh, Jesus could lay hold of all past predictions and relate them to Himself (John 5:39; Luke 24:27,44,45; Hebrews 10:7).

Then in the centuries before Christ, the Jewish mind was prepared for the manifestation of Him as the One who would come from "the tribe of Judah," in all God's revelations to, and dealings with His chosen people. In the provision of prophet, priest and king there was the foregleam of the Coming One who would combine all three offices in His life and labors as we shall presently see. The forecast of a Messianic kingdom, breaking the bounds of Jewish nationalism, and extending through the whole earth and embracing all peoples likewise prepared the way for the appearance of God's King (Psalms 2; 87; Isaiah 60; Daniel 2:44; 7:27).

The most striking Old Testament preparation for Christ's Advent, however, were those wonderful *theophanic appearances.* These pre-incarnate manifestations of His were designed to prepare the world for Christ's more permanent abode in human flesh. Biblical scholars identify "The angel of the Lord"—"The angel of his presence" —"The angel of the Covenant" (Genesis 22:14; 31:11,13; Exodus 14:19; Isaiah 63: 9; Malachi 3:1), as Christ, the Son of God, in pre-incarnate manifestation. "His Incarnation is the center by reference to which all angelic ministrations are best understood."

These are the *theophanies* in order—

His manifestation in Eden (Genesis 3: 15). The pre-existent Christ as God, spoke of Himself as the coming Seed of the woman. As God He was the *promised;* as the God-Man, He became the *Promise,* (see Genesis 3:22-24; Exodus 6:3,5; Jude 14,15; II Thessalonians 1:7,8).

His manifestation to Hagar (Genesis 16: 7-14). This is the first time *the angel* is named. Four times over we have the title, "The angel of the Lord," or "Jehovah." Here we have Him seeking the miserable outcast—a prophecy of His coming redemptive mission (see John 4:14).

His manifestation to Moses (Exodus 3: 2,6,14; 23:20,21; Acts 7:38). Typical deliverances were wrought by "the angel of his presence," who was no ordinary angel because of His exercise of divine prerogatives, the manifestation of divine perfections, and the claiming of homage due to Deity alone.

His manifestation to Abraham (Genesis 18:1; 22:11-13; 26:2,5,24,25). One of the three heavenly visitants entertained by Abraham repeatedly assumed, and received, the name of *Jehovah* with honor due only to Him. Both Abraham, and his son, Isaac, were the recipients of promises from the Lord of Glory.

His manifestation to Jacob (Genesis 28; 32:24-32; 48:15,16; Hosea 12:4,5). The angel, who redeemed Jacob from all evil was no common celestial messenger, but "the angel of the covenant" Himself who, at different periods of the patriarch's life, visited him with words of assurance.

His manifestation to Joshua (5:13-15). As Joshua succeeded Moses as the leader of Israel, the same mysterious Personage appeared, this time as "the captain of the host of the Lord." Joshua had to learn that he was subordinate to another Leader worthy of adoration and worship.

His manifestation to Manoah (Judges 14:15-23; Isaiah 9:6). As the Omniscient One, the angel appeared to Manoah foretelling the birth and character of an extraordinary son, Samson. Here we have a visible revelation of divine majesty and a foregleam of the character of the coming Messiah.

His manifestation to Isaiah (Isaiah 6:1-13; John 12:39-41; see Ezekiel 1:1-28). In His pre-Incarnation appearances to prophets, Christ came as the Revealer of God. The *words* and *burdens* communicated to Isaiah, and others, came from "The angel of his presence," Israel's Saviour (Isaiah 63:8-10).

His manifestation to Zechariah (1:8-13; 2:8-11; 3:1-10; 6:12-15). The prophet Zechariah describes a glorious Person, intimately acquainted with the counsels of the Most High, and as presiding over world affairs, directing, vindicating and interceding as no ordinary angel could do. This Person exhibited the attributes of omniscience, omnipresence and omnipotence. God's name was *in* Him (Exodus 23:21). Other evidences of Christ's pre-existence are hinted at in Daniel 3:25 Revised Version; John 1:15; 6:22; I Peter 1:10,11; Psalm 110:1; Judges 6:12; I Corinthians 10:4,9; Exodus 14:19; Colossians 1:16).

The promise was that the intermittent appearance of Christ in human form were to give way to a more permanent sojourn in man's flesh, so His tabernacle among men naturally follows His pre-existence. We thus come to His fuller manifestation in the New Testament. The angel of the Redeemer is now—

Arrayed in mortal flesh,
He like an Angel stands,
And holds the promises
And pardon in His hands;
Commissioned from the Father's Throne,
To make His grace to mortals known.

His Wondrous Birth

After over four millenniums, the first promise given to man is fulfilled, and Jesus was born as "the seed of the woman" (Genesis 3:15; Matthew 1:1). Paul was very careful to state that when God sent forth His Son that He was "made of a woman" (Galatians 4:4)—not of *a man and a woman*, but only of a woman. Christ is the only babe the world has ever known who did not have a human father. He was divinely conceived. In this aspect of our meditation we are not principally concerned with the *fact*, *time* or *place* of Christ's birth, but with the *manner* of it. As the doctrine of the virgin birth is one of the most vital of the great doctrines of the Christian faith, it is imperative to consider it somewhat fully. *The Incarnation* is the most stupendous miracle comprehending and involving all other miracles, and because it is a theme both deep and delicate, infinite and incomprehensible, how necessary it is to follow Solomon's advice about "finding out acceptable words" (Ecclesiastes 12:10). The ground we approach is holy calling for the putting off of our shoes (Exodus 3:5).

In the presence of such a holy miracle "there can be no fitting attitude," says G. Campbell Morgan, "of the human intellect save that of acceptance of the truth without any attempt to explain the mystery." God manifest in flesh is one of the great mysteries of godliness (I Timothy 3:16). One writer expressed it—

I will seek to believe rather than to reason,
    to adore rather than to explain;
    to give thanks rather than to penetrate;
    to love rather than to know;
    to humble myself rather than to speak.

Who is there with all his innate and acquired wisdom able to explain the mystery of—
    The Ancient of Days becoming a babe at Bethlehem—
    Him who thunders in the heavens crying in a cradle—
    Him who gives to all their meat in due season, sucking at a mother's breast—
    Him who made all flesh now made of flesh—
    Him who could summon legions of angels, while wrapped in infant's clothes—
    The mighty God now a helpless child—

God and man becoming one Person.

No wonder one of the old divines said, "I can scarce get past His cradle in my wondering to wonder at His cross. The infant Jesus is in some views a greater marvel than Jesus with the purple robe and the crown of thorns."

Human reason rejects the virgin birth as being impossible and as contrary to the natural order of things. But Job could confess, "I know that Thou canst do everything" (42:2). Mary accepted the angel's announcement that apart from natural generation she was to become the mother of our Lord and said, "With God nothing shall be impossible . . . Be it . . . according to Thy Word" (Luke 1:37,38). If we try to explain the virgin birth we lose our reason—If we discredit altogether this initial miracle of Christianity we lose our soul, for no one can be a Christian after the New Testament order who totally rejects Christ's birth of a virgin.

The superb structure of the life and character of our Lord, has, as its immovable and only foundation, His virgin birth. In his great work on *The Virgin Birth of Our Lord*, Dr. James Orr remarks—

Doctrinally it must be repeated that the belief in the virgin birth of Christ is of the highest value for the right apprehension of Christ's unique and sinless personality. Here is One, as Paul brings out in Romans 5:12, who, free from sin Himself, and not involved in the Adamic liabilities of the race, reverses the curse of sin and death brought in by the first Adam, and establishes the reign of righteousness and life. Had Christ been naturally born, not one of these things could be affirmed of Him. As one of Adam's race, not an entrant from a higher sphere, He would have shared in Adam's corruption and doom—would Himself have required to be redeemed. Through God's infinite mercy, He came from above, inherited no guilt, needed no regeneration or sanctification, but became Himself the Redeemer, Regenerator, Sanctifier for all who receive Him.

What, exactly, is meant by a *virgin* birth? It does not mean *immaculate conception* such as the Roman Catholic Church teaches when it affirms that Mary herself was conceived and born without original sin; thus Christ was sinless—nor does it mean a *miraculous birth*, for there is no evidence that the process of Christ's birth itself was in any way exceptional—nor was it a supernatural birth merely, for that was true of Isaac and of John the Baptist. By the virgin birth we are to understand that, contrary to the course of nature, Jesus was divinely conceived in the womb of Mary, the Holy Spirit becoming the love-knot between our Lord's two natures. In such a conception, deity and humanity were fused together and Jesus came forth as the God-Man.

In order to earnestly contend for the fact of the virgin birth, which is a most vital part of the faith once delivered unto the saints, it is absolutely necessary to have a clear grasp of the definite teaching of Scripture regarding it. So—"to the law and to the testimony; if they speak not according to this word (and here is the cause of modern unbelief) it is because there is no light in them" (Isaiah 8:20). We purpose summarizing the witness of the Scriptures thus—

1. The Prophetic Witness

This aspect of the testimony of Scripture is so strong that as Dr. Pierson remarks—

> Take a man of intelligence, a stranger to the Christian religion; place before him the Jewish Scriptures, calling attention to the portrait which they furnish of one whom they call "God's Servant" or "Anointed." Then ask him to note that the Old Testament writers lived more than three centuries before the Christian era, and that we have historic proof that these Jewish Scriptures, in their complete form, were in the hands of the Jews for three hundred years before that era began. Then place before him a copy of the Christian Scriptures and ask him to read the Gospels, and note that they were never in existence till at least four hundred years after the last Old Testament writer laid down his pen. And, without suggesting any divine or supernatural element, either in the writings, or in the person of Christ, leave him to compare the two. With what amazement would he find all the main facts recorded in these Gospel narratives long before anticipated in these writings.

In coming to the prophecies and promises regarding Christ in the Old Testament, there seems to be a gradual revelation, that is, the truth is unfolded by degrees. For example—

(a) The Seed of the Woman.

This oldest of all evangelical promises found in Genesis 3:15 predicts in a wonderful way the virgin birth of our Lord. Let us mark the specific language used— "I will put enmity between thee and the woman, and between thy seed and *her* seed." *Her* seed! "Such a thought," says A. T. Scofield, "as a woman's seed, as stated here, is not found elsewhere. Over a hundred times or more, when we read of the seed and seeds, of Abraham's seed, and so forth, it is always the seed of the man. But the seed of the woman is a unique concept, and can only be interpreted as a foreshadowing of the virgin birth, and most remarkable it is that it should be found here. I submit that if our Lord had not been born of a virgin, it would be Adam who would be addressed, and *his* that would be referred to (Matthew 1:18)." See also Luke 1:55.

(b) The Seed of Abraham.

And then the great evangelical promises of Genesis 12:1-13 and 15:18 find their fulfillment in Christ, as one can prove by turning to passages like John 8:56-58; Galatians 3:16. Yes, and what is one of the purposes of Matthew but to prove that Christ is the One who will fulfill the Abrahamic covenant, and so he commences his genealogy with Abraham!

(c) The Tribe of Judah.

See how the revelation is progressive! Now Christ is to be limited to one particular tribe of Israel. Compare Genesis 49:10 with Hebrews 7:14, Revelation 5:5; Matthew 2:5,6.

(d) The House of David.

Then our Lord is to spring from one family in that tribe. Compare II Samuel 7:12,13 with Matthew 1:1; Romans 1:3.

(e) The Son of a Virgin.

Compare "the great Immanuel Prophecy" of Isaiah 7:14 and 9:7 with Matthew 1:22, 23, etc.

(f) The Place of His Birth.

Compare Micah 5:2 with Luke 2:4,15.

(g) His Name.

Compare Isaiah 7:14 with Matthew 1:23.

(h) The Worship by Gentiles.

Compare Isaiah 60:6 with Matthew 2:11.

(i) His Forerunner.

Compare Isaiah 40:3 with Matthew 3:1-3.

And thus, as the time of fulfillment drew near, there were numerous quiet circles, little godly bands, who nourished their hearts on the promises, e.g. Luke 2:25-38. And it was in these faithful hearts that the stirrings of the prophetic spirits began to make themselves felt anew, preparing for the First Advent of our Lord—Luke 2:27-36.

2. *The Angelic Witness*

Coming now to the clearer testimony of the New Testament, we consider, first of all, the witness of the angels, who were the first heralds of our Lord's virgin birth. There are three angelic appearances recorded in Matthew and Luke; or shall we say, three annunciations?

(a) To Zacharias.

While performing the priestly function of burning incense (Luke 1:9), this holy man (1:6) was visited by an angel (1:11) who not only gives him the assurance that a child is to be born to Elizabeth his wife (1:13), but also that their son will be the forerunner of the Messiah about to be born (1:16,17).

(b) To Mary.

The angel Gabriel, who is possibly the same messenger each time, is sent to Mary with the news that she is to bear a son, and call His name Jesus. See—
1. The angel's commission and benediction —Luke 1:26-28.

Notice that verse 28 is omitted in the Revised Version; therefore, there is no support for the Mariolatry of the Romish Church (Mary's wonder and fear 1:29).
2. The angel's announcement—Luke 1:30-33.

(Mary's natural question—1:36.)
3. The angel's explanation—Luke 1:35-37.

(Mary's willing submission—1:38.)

(c) To Joseph.

Turning to Matthew's gospel we discover that Joseph, the espoused husband of Mary, was also visited in dreams by an angel of the Lord. And such a medium of revelation was necessary owing to Joseph's position and perplexity, for when he became aware of Mary's condition, he was shocked as a just man would be (1:19); and so his first thought is to put Mary away and thus avoid scandal (1:19). With these thoughts in mind, follow the angelic announcements thus—
1. The angel's revelation—1:20-23.

(Joseph's willing response—1:24,25.)
2. The angel's directions—2:13; 2:19,20.

(Joseph's magnanimous response—2:14,15; 2:21-23.)

3. *The Historic Witness*

By the historic witness we mean the evidence of the virgin birth as we have it from the lips of those who knew Joseph and Mary. Here we again turn to Matthew and Luke. What to find? Why, that there is abundant witness to the genuineness of our Lord's wonderful birth. Having touched upon the reliability of these narratives already, let us seek to view them in another light altogether.

How did Matthew and Luke come to know the facts of Mary's conception and Joseph's perplexity? Such facts were surely sacred and secret, and could only come from Mary and Joseph themselves.

Matthew received the account of the birth from Joseph, and this is why Matthew's gospel gives the birth from Joseph's standpoint.

Luke, on the other hand, received his facts from Mary, and being a beloved physician, who understands the extreme propriety of the question, we are not "surprised at the marvelous beauty, reticence and, at the same time, accuracy of description as he tells us every small detail that we need to know, and advancing nothing that does not concern us."

In fact, as Professor Sweet observes— "Both narratives exhibit a profound reverence, a chaste and gracious reserve in the presence of a holy mystery, a simplicity, dignity and self-contained nobility of expression which are the visible marks of truth, if such there are anywhere in human writing." Notice one or two minor points, viz.,

a. The historic witness that our Lord was born of a virgin, and not in wedlock (Matthew 1:18-21,24,25; Luke 1:27-34).

b. The guarded utterances of the biographers.

In studying the particular words in the gospel narratives, one is impressed with the guarded utterances of the writers.

1. Luke 1:13; 1:35

By comparing these two passages one gathers extra proof regarding the verity of the virgin birth. "Thy wife Elisabeth shall bear *thee a son.*" Compare this "thee" of verse 13 with the "thee" of verse 35— "that holy thing which shall be born to *thee.*" The phrase, "bear thee a son," which is a usual one of Scripture is omitted in verse 35.

2. Luke 3:23

Notice the parenthesis in this verse—"Jesus began to be about thirty years of age, being (as was supposed) the son of Joseph." At this point it may be as well to state that "Jesus was customarily spoken of by the people of Nazareth, etc., as 'the son of Joseph.' So He was; and it could not be otherwise. To the people of Nazareth, who knew nothing of the circumstances of His origin, Jesus was simply a child of Joseph's home. Joseph from the first stood *in loco parentis* to Jesus." It is this that accounts for phrases like Luke 2:27—"The parents brought in the child Jesus"; Luke 2:41—"Now his parents" etc.; Luke 2:48—"Thy father and I have sought thee sorrowing"; Matthew 13:55—"Is not this the carpenter's son?"

3. Matthew 1:16

In this reference we have "a roundabout way of describing the birth of Christ which is absolutely without meaning or sense unless Christ was born of a virgin." "Jacob begat Joseph the husband of Mary, of whom was born Jesus." The word "begat" is omitted from Mary's genealogy, and the change is important; it is no longer "who begat," but "Mary, of whom was born Jesus." Jesus was not "begotten" of natural generation, but conceived by the Holy Ghost.

4. Matthew 2:11

In the homage paid by the wise men from the East, it will be noticed that Joseph is entirely absent—"They saw the young child with Mary, His mother," etc.

5. Matthew 2:13

How specific this verse is—"Arise and take the young child and his mother," etc. Why, if Christ was the son of both Mary and Joseph as some would affirm, how is it that an angel, above all, does not give Joseph any recognition as a parent?

c. The silence of Mark and John.

As these two disciples were contemporaries of Matthew and Luke, it may be found helpful to add a word under this historical point regarding their silence in connection with the virgin birth. This silence is a great stumbling block to the modern critics, and yet its explanation is very simple.

The subject was a very delicate one and all that could be said about it had been recorded by Matthew and Luke. And thus the sense of delicacy would naturally tend to reticence, at least during the lifetime of Mary. Repetition was therefore unnecessary for "at the mouth of two witnesses . . . shall the matter be established."

But there is another explanation for the supposed silence of Mark and John, an explanation that critics are often blind to, and that is the bearing in mind of the scope or design of such. Why, it is impossible to study any part of the Bible aright without understanding, first of all, the purpose of the Book before one.

What is the purpose of Mark's gospel? Why, he sets out to relate the events of Christ's public ministry, beginning at the baptism in His thirtieth year. Mark's endeavor is to portray our Lord as "The Servant"—and who is concerned about the birth certificate of a servant, so long as the servant's character is good, and his work of the best? Says W. Kelly—

> A genealogy such as Matthew's and Luke's would be totally out of place here; and the reason is manifest. The subject of Mark is the testimony of Jesus as having taken, though a Son, the place of a servant on the earth. Now, in a servant, no matter from what noble lineage he comes, there is no genealogy requisite. What is wanted in a servant is that the work should be done well, no matter about the genealogy.

But although Mark does not recount the details regarding Christ's birth, yet he is acquainted with all the facts respecting it. And so taking such for granted he begins his gospel abruptly—"The beginning of the gospel of Jesus Christ, the Son of God!" Why the very title, "The Son of God," proves that Mark knew all about the divinity of our Lord's conception!

The beloved disciple of our Lord's also had a definite object in writing his gospel. He sets out to narrate the sublime truth that Christ is God as well as man. To the world at large his message is—"Behold your God!" And he goes back to the past eternity, and shows how the Lord existed, nay, was coequal and coexistent with the Father from the beginning. The genealogy is excluded from John because Christ is presented as being without all genealogy. "He is the source," as W. Kelly states, "of other people's genealogy yea, of the genesis of all things. . . . If we admit any genealogy it must be what is set forth in the preface of John . . . which exhibit the divine, natural and eternal personality of His being."

But although he knew the account of Christ's earthly birth, he does not give any details such as Matthew and Luke do. And yet what can we make of a passage like John 1:14—"The Word was made (R.V. "became," and please mark the different rendering) flesh, and dwelt among us" if there was no such stupendous miracle as the virgin birth?

"And," says Professor Orr, "the whole type of his doctrine in gospel and epistle goes against the supposition that he believed Christ to be 'born of the flesh' as ordinary man, needing regeneration (cf. 3:3,7)." In a footnote, the professor remarks that "an old reading actually applies to Him the language of John 1:13."

4. The Apostolic Witness

The apparent silence of the Apostle Paul regarding the virgin birth is sometimes used by the critics to disprove the truth of it. We are told that he did not base his preaching of his gospel upon private, interior matters, such as the virgin birth narratives give, but upon the broad, public facts of Christ's ministry, death and Resurrection. And yet it must be evident to all honest readers that Paul was fully acquainted with the mystery of our Lord's birth. For example—

(a) He was Luke's Companion

When we remember the loving companionship that existed between Paul and Luke, and that Luke was one of the chief witnesses to the virgin birth, we may be assured that whatever Luke knew regarding our Lord he would communicate to Paul.

(b) His Doctrine

Why, by the truths that the apostle declares, he shows how he not only knew the story of the virgin birth but that he received it as a part of the divine revelation. What do passages like Philippians 2:5-28; Colossians 1:18; 2:9; Galatians 4:4; II Corinthians 5:21; Hebrews 2:14 mean if there was no miracle in the constitution of the Redeemer's Person? Why, to Paul the virgin birth would be the most reasonable and credible of events!

(c) His Peculiar Expressions

One of the most singular facts about Paul's language when describing Christ's earthly origin is that he invariably uses some unusual or roundabout expression, implying thereby something exceptional about our Lord's birth. For example, in using the word "born" in passages like Romans 1:3; Galatians 4:4, he does not use the ordinary word *gennetos* that is used, for instance, of John the Baptist who was also "born of a woman" (Matthew 11:11) but

he adopts the other word *genomenos* signifying "becoming" or "became." The Revised Version margin for Philippians 2:7 gives us the same word "becoming" or the words in the text "being made." In Galatians 4 Paul uses the first word three times in speaking of others, but in writing of Christ in verse 4 he selects the wider and more appropriate term.

5. The Authentic Witness

Although strictly speaking the authentic witness, which is the testimony of the Early Church, does not belong to the Scriptural testimony, yet as it arises out of it, we purpose including it here. And it is very necessary to consider this point because the critics sometimes affirm that the virgin birth does not belong to the earliest tradition, that is, to the period when the facts of the gospels commenced to be preached or published. Of this we are certain:

(a) That the general body of Jewish Christians, save the Ebionites or Gnostics referred to, accepted the virgin birth, and that they defended it as a truth of cardinal importance. "John is attested," for instance, "by his disciple Polycarp (through Irenaeus) to have been the keen antagonist at Ephesus of Cerinthus, the earliest known impugner of the virgin birth."

(b) The virgin birth is a fundamental article in the original form of the *Apostles' Creed* which is the oldest form of Christian creed that exists—"Conceived by the Holy Ghost, born of the virgin Mary" is what it declares.

(c) The virgin birth is also attested to by all the early Fathers such as Ignatius, Justin Martyr, Tatian, etc.

(d) The virgin birth is also indirectly believed in because "it is vouched for as belief of the Church by the attacks made on it by pagans and Jews."

(e) And to come nearer still, what more authentic witness to the virgin birth can you have, when you remember the growth of Christianity, its beneficent influence in the world, the testimony of millions—confirmed by their deeds—that Christ because of His entrance into, and death in, the world had transformed their lives?

This may be a fitting point to discuss what is known as *Kenosis* theory. The first to use the term *Kenosis* in a theological sense was Theodotion of the second century, in his translation of Isaiah's word for "emptiness" (34:11). When Paul spoke of Christ emptying Himself he used the word *kenoō*

(Philippians 2:7). Much controversy has raged over the kenotic theory of the person of Christ. When, at His birth, He took upon Himself the form of a servant, of what did He empty Himself?

Professor Wayne E. Ward asks,

> Exactly *who* is the subject of the verb *emptied?* Is it the pre-existent Son of God who by sovereign choice divested Himself of some of the prerogatives of Deity in order to become incarnate: or is it the incarnate Son, who, in the days of His flesh, was involved in a kind of repeated or continual emptying of Himself in order to fulfil His mission as the Servant of God and submit even to death?

Some of the early Fathers felt that Christ emptied Himself of "the being equal with God." Later on, theologians affirmed that His emptying involved the surrender of some divine attributes such as omnipotence, omniscience and omnipresence. Others felt that although He possessed all divine powers, they were kept under a conscious restraint. Yet others affirmed that Jesus was "unaware of the extent of these powers and therefore lived His incarnate life within the limits imposed upon any creature."

Dealing with Paul's reference to Christ's self-humbling Bishop Lightfoot in his commentary on *Philippians* says, "He emptied, stripped Himself of the insignia of Majesty." Professor E. Moorehead has said, "When occasion demanded He exercised His divine attributes." As the Eternal Word, He could not empty Himself either of His deity or His attributes. What He divested Himself of was the constant, outward and visible manifestation of His Godhead. Christ did not surrender deity—He gained *humanity.* Paul deals, not so much with what the Son gave up, but what He gained, namely, exaltation for humiliation. Assuming the role and name of a servant, He came to possess a name above every name. Dr. Ward quotes the Greek scholar, Dr. William Hersey Davis who suggested that "the word *kenoō* should be understood in the sense of emptying one vessel into another vessel so that it was a matter of pouring the same content into another form: Christ emptied Himself, that is, poured Himself into the form of a servant."

When Jesus left the bosom of the Father, He voluntarily chose the path of humiliation. The sovereign choice of love, as well as man's need of a Saviour, led Him to turn His back upon heaven's glory for a cross of shame. Throughout His life there was the conscious restraint of many of His divine powers, that He might be seen as a true "Man of Sorrows." Although rich, for our sakes He became poor, that through His self-imposed poverty we might be rich (II Corinthians 8:9). This Pauline passage has been described as "the best commentary" on the doctrine of Kenosis (Philippians 2: 5-11). May grace be ours to emulate the supreme example of humility!

His Silent Years

Although legends abound as to our Lord's early life in Egypt and Nazareth, Scripture veils the first thirty years of His life on earth. Only once is the veil lifted, namely, when He was twelve years of age and rebuked His mother for failing to understand the significance of His mission among men: "Wist ye not that I must be about My Father's business?" (Luke 2:49).

In connection with Christ's first visit to Jerusalem, when He was found among the doctors, Dr. James Stalker says—

> Only one flower of anecdote has been thrown over the wall of the hidden garden, and it is so exquisite as to fill us with intense longing to see the garden itself.

What we do know is that there was nothing abnormal or grotesque about His growth from childhood to manhood. Legends of His childhood are fanciful and futile. He was no prodigy of nature, but developed normally and healthily. Luke tells us of His *physical* development—"He grew, and waxed strong"; of His *mental* development —"filled with wisdom"; and of His *spiritual* development—"the grace of God was upon Him" (Luke 2:40-51). His was a childhood in its fairest and finest manifestation. "The incarnation was a true acceptance of humanity, with all its sinless limitations of growth and development." Of those obscure, thirty years during which God was preparing His Son for a brief ministry lasting for just over three years, Jesus would go to a Jewish school as any ordinary village child did. He could read and write (Luke 4:17; John 8:6-8). Leaving school around the age of fifteen, He followed the trade of the home and became a carpenter (Mark 6:3). In Joseph's carpenter shop we have the toil of divinity revealing the divinity of toil.

Strange that He should work with wood and nails—He had them when He died!

Scripture also bears witness to the fact that the gentleness and grace of character of Jesus endeared Him to all who knew Him. His fragrance, like that of a rose, could not be hid (Luke 2:52). As Dr. James Orr so beautifully expresses it—

> No stain of sin clouded His vision of divine things. His after-history shows that His mind was nourished on the Scriptures; nor, as He pondered psalms and prophets, could His soul remain unvisited by presentiments, growing to convictions, that He was the One in whom their predictions were destined to be realized.

His Two Natures

The great mystery of godliness which Paul reminds us of is "God manifested in flesh" (I Timothy 3:16), and throughout the Bible, Christ is represented as a Person having two natures, one divine—the other human. In His incarnation He became the possessor of a true humanity in union with His eternal deity. As God, He did not enter a human body or join Himself to man. He *became* Man, that is, He belonged to the stock of humanity when, as the Word, He became flesh (John 1:14). Of the unity of two natures in one Person, Dr. Louis Berkhof writes—

> Christ has a human nature, but He is not a human person. The Person of the Mediator is the unchangeable Son of God. In the Incarnation He did not change into a human person; neither did He adopt a human person. He simply assumed, in addition to His divine nature, a human nature, which did not develop into an independent personality, but became personal in the Person of the Son of God.

Dr. W. J. Townsend develops a similar thought when he says that—

> The Son of God took to Himself a human nature and gave it subsistence in the divine nature. The divine nature of Christ has a personal existence from all eternity and exists still, and the human nature subsists in it for the accomplishment of the purposes of eternal love. The assumption of human nature involved no change as to the Person of the eternal Son, it added nothing to it: the difference is that the second Person in the Godhead who always possessed divinity took also into Himself humanity.

At His incarnation Christ added to His already existing divine nature a human nature, and became the God-Man. At our regeneration, there was added to our already existing human nature, a divine nature and we thus became partakers of the divine nature (II Peter 1:4). Thus, like Christ, every true Christian is *divine-human*. Part of the mystery we cannot fathom is that He has both a divine and a human consciousness, as well as a human and a divine will. Both are unified in His Person, and it is always "the same Person who speaks, whether the mind that finds utterance be human or divine" (John 10:30; 17:5, as compared with Matthew 27: 46; John 19:28). Human attributes and actions are sometimes ascribed to the Person designated by a divine title (Acts 20:28; I Corinthians 2:8; Colossians 1:13,14) and divine attributes and actions are sometimes ascribed to the Person designated by a human title (John 3:13; 6:62; Romans 9:5).

His Humanity. The human nature Christ assumed was not absorbed by or fused into the divine, and that the divine alone remained. In so many ways His full and perfect humanity is manifested. He was born a babe, and needed infant's clothing and a mother's nursing and care. He spoke of Himself as a man, and was so called by others (Acts 2:22; Romans 5:15; I Corinthians 15:21; John 8:40). Then He had the essential elements of human nature—a body and a soul (Matthew 26:26,38; Luke 24:39; Hebrews 2:14). Further, He was subject to the ordinary laws of human development, and to human wants, emotions and sufferings (Matthew 4:2; 8:24; Luke 2:40, 52; 22:44; John 4:6; 11:35; 12:27; Hebrews 2:10,18; 5:7,8).

> O Saviour Christ, Thou too art Man!
> Thou hast been troubled, tempted tried;
> Thy kind but searching glance can scan
> The very wounds that shame would hide.

His Deity. Both Old and New Testaments offer convincing proof of Christ as "the Mighty God" (Isaiah 9:6; Jeremiah 23:6; Matthew 11:27; John 1:1; Hebrews 1:1-3; Revelation 19:16). The Ebionites of the Early Church, and the Unitarians and Modernists of our time, deny the deity of our Lord. To them, He is only a man—a good, holy, exemplary man, but only a man. Thus, the crown of deity is snatched from His brow. But His deity is proven by all He is in Himself, and is able to accomplish—

There is His self-existence (John 1:4; 5:26; 10:30; 14:10; Philippians 2:6)

His eternal existence (John 1:1-3; 8:58; Colossians 1:16,17; Hebrews 1:8-12; 7:3; 13:8; Revelation 1:8-18)

His immutability (Hebrews 1:10-12; 13:8)

His omnipresence (Matthew 28:26; John 1:48; 3:13).

His omniscience (Matthew 9:4; 12:25; Luke 6:8; 9:47; 11:17; Colossians 2:3)

His omnipotence (Mark 1:27; John 5:19-21; I Peter 3:21,22)

His manifold works. Did He not declare that as the God-Man, *all* power was His? And such power was manifested in different ways—

As the Lord of the Sabbath (Mark 2:28; cf. Genesis 2:2,3; Luke 6:5).

As the Commissioner and Controller of angels (Matthew 13:41; Revelation 1:1; 22:6).

As the Forgiver of sin (Matthew 9:2; Mark 2:5-7,10; Luke 5:20-24; 7:48).

As the Commander of death and Hades (Matthew 9:24; Luke 7:14; John 11:43,44; Revelation 1:18).

As the Creator and Preserver of all things (John 1:3,10; Ephesians 3:9; Colossians 1:16-18; Hebrews 1:2).

As the Judge of all men (Matthew 13:39-43; 16:27; 25:31-33; John 5:22,23; Acts 10:42; II Corinthians 5:10).

A remarkable feature of this twin nature of our Lord is that wherever His deity is mentioned, His humanity lingers in the shadows, and *vice versa*. For instance, as the man He needed sleep, and in the boat slept soundly. But when the storm arose, He arose and as God calmed the angry deep. As the man, He wept with the sorrowing friends of Lazarus because He, too, had lost a companion He loved. But as God, He was able to call Lazarus back from the grave. As man, He knows all about our human needs, and as God He is able to satisfy them all.

Further, in connection with our Lord's dual nature, there are two designations which must be considered. His titles are manifold and meaningful but here are two conspicuous ones—

1. The Son of God. This pre-eminent title, given to Jesus by Nathanael, carrying with it the transcendental associations of John's prologue (1:1,14,18), conveys "the idea of super-human dignity and unique relationship." All the truths of pre-existence, deity and Messiahship are contained in this name (Matthew 11:27; 24:36; 26:63; Luke 1:35; John 5:18; 9:35-37; 10:33,36). It is the name expressing Christ's relationship to God (Matthew 26:24).

2. The Son of Man. This further title indicative of Christ's character as Leader and Representative of the race is ascribed to Him upwards of eighty times. As the true, real typical man, He used this title "The Son of Man" of Himself 55 times in the gospels. How definitely was He related to our humanity! Such an expression, however, was not new to the gospels. It is one occurring frequently in the Old Testament (Psalm 8; Ezekiel 2:1; Daniel 7:9-14; 8:17), and in the majority of cases describes humans with a particular work to do for God. The marvel and magnificence of the Gospel is that the Son of God became the Son of Man, that He might make the sons of men, the Sons of God (I John 3:1-3).

His Baptism

After thirty years of obscurity, Jesus now prepares for His brief but dynamic ministry of some three years. John, His forerunner had declared that the kingdom, in the Person of the King Himself, was at hand. As a voice in the wilderness, John preached *repentance* and that the coming kingdom could be entered only through moral preparation. All those accepting the message of the Baptist were baptized of John at Jordan (Matthew 3:6; John 1:28; 3:23). John's stirring words made a profound impression upon all classes, even upon the Pharisees and Sadducees who attended his baptismal ceremony (Matthew 3:7). One day, Jesus appeared upon the scene and John knew his task was finished. "He must increase, I must decrease" (John 3:30). The forerunner had to give way to the *Fulfiller*. Although Jesus had gathered with others at Jordan on that historic day, John intuitively recognized Jesus as different from the rest. As His herald, John had received a sign by which the Messiah should be recognized (John 1:33), so when Jesus presented Himself, asking *baptism* at John's hands, he immediately knew that this was He who should come.

With true humility, John confessed that as a sinful man he had need to be baptized of One, divinely pure (Matthew 3:14). But Jesus said, "Suffer it to be so now," and John baptized Him in Jordan's waters

(Matthew 3:13-17; Mark 1:9-11; Luke 3:21,23). The question troubling many sincere hearts is, if John's baptism was one of repentance, why did Jesus, who was sinless and therefore had no sin to repent of, seek such a baptism? Jesus Himself answered that question when He put His baptism on the ground of *meetness.* "It becometh us to fulfil all righteousness." It was the most *becoming* thing for Him as the Head to enter by the same gateway as the members to His specific vocation in the service of the Kingdom. Dr. James Orr says that in submitting to baptism—

Jesus formally identified Himself with the expectation of the Kingdom and with its ethical demands; separated Himself from the evil of His nation, doubtless with confession of its sins: and devoted Himself to His life task in bringing in the Messianic salvation. The significance of the rite as marking His consecration to, and entrance upon, His Messianic career, is seen in what follows.

What a manifestation of the unity of the Godhead was displayed that day as God anointed Jesus with the Holy Spirit for His brief years of service (Acts 10:38)! Emerging from the water, while still "praying" (Luke 3:21), the heavens were opened and the Spirit like a dove came upon Him. Baptized in water, He is now baptized with the Spirit. With such a baptism there came the benediction of the Father, "This is My beloved Son, in whom I am well pleased" (Matthew 3:16,17). As Mary's son, He was misunderstood and His motives misconstrued, but as the Father's Son all His ways were pleasing. Whether others present saw the vision and heard the Father's voice we do not know. What transpired was primarily intended for Jesus and John (Matthew 3:16; Mark 1:10; John 1:33). Jordan meant Christ's dedication of Himself to His calling for which He received the spiritual equipment necessary for the accomplishment of a divine task and forward He went with the seal of heaven's acknowledgment upon Him. How tragic it is when men try to serve God without a similar dedication and spiritual dynamic!

His Temptation

We would have thought that after such a mighty unction received at Jordan, Jesus was now ready to launch right in and witness and work in Galilee and elsewhere. But no. After the *dove,* there came the *devil*—After the *benediction,* there came the *battle.* Jesus went from Jordan into the wilderness to be tempted of the devil (Matthew 4:1-11; Mark 1:13,14; Luke 4:1-13). Ere He could deliver the multitudes from the power of the devil, He must experience the full weight and strength of the enemy Himself. It thus came about that He was tempted in all points as we are, yet without sin (Hebrews 4:15).

As Jesus was *alone* in the wilderness with the devil we find ourselves agreeing with Lange in his *Commentary on Matthew,* "The history of the temptation Jesus afterwards communicated to His disciples in the form of a real narrative, clothed in symbolical language." The gospel narrative tells us that the period of intense struggle lasted for forty days, during which Jesus neither ate nor drank; that wild beasts surrounded Him; that the tempter and temptations were real; that there were three stages of satanic approach—"each on its own way a trial of the spirit of obedience" (Matthew 4:2,4,7; Mark 1:13; Luke 4:2,4,12 See Deuteronomy 6:16; 8:3; Psalm 91:11,12). The threefold temptation typifies the whole round of satanic assault on man through body, mind and spirit (Luke 4:13 cf. I John 2:6). During the service that followed, Jesus was to be constantly tempted to—

Spare Himself

Gratify Jewish sign-seekers

Gain power by the sacrifice of the right. In the wilderness, He triumphed gloriously over all three temptations, and went forth the Conqueror over all further hellish designs to thwart His mighty work. By faith, His triumph becomes ours.

An aspect of Christ's temptation that must not be forgotten, however, is the fact that in Him there was nothing the devil could appeal to. He was born *without* sin. We were "born in sin and shapen in iniquity," and because of the possession of an evil nature as the result of original sin, the devil has a foothold in every one born into the world. When Christ enters a life, the devil quite naturally contests every inch of ground surrendered to the One who mastered Him in the wilderness and at Calvary.

His Sinlessness

What a positive declaration that is which the writer of the Hebrews associates with the manifold temptations of Christ—*Yet without sin!* Born holy, He remained holy. Before His birth, Gabriel could speak of Him to Mary as, "That holy thing which shall be born of thee shall be called the Son of God" (Luke 1:35). If His *virgin birth is* rejected, then His *virgin life* cannot be accounted for. Born holy, Christ remained holy because through divine unction He was able to successfully resist every enticement of the devil who had nothing *in* Him to fight out from (John 14:30). More than once He claimed sinless perfectness. "Which of you convinceth me of sin?" was His direct challenge (John 8:46). Always, and in all things, He pleased His Father (John 8:29). In order to redeem man from sin, He had to be free from any evil taint of humanity. Had He committed only one sin, He would have been disqualified as the Redeemer of sinful men. Perfect Himself, Christ professed the highest conceivable standard of character and conduct for His followers, "Be ye therefore perfect."

The Bible, then, is emphatic in its witness to the fact that Christ was perfect in thought and deed. In Him was *no* sin (I John 3:5). He could do nothing amiss (Luke 23:41). Demons, as well as angels, called Him, "The Holy One" (Mark 1:24). Judas confessed to betraying "innocent blood" (Matthew 27:4; See Hebrews 7:26; 9:14; I Peter 2:22; II Corinthians 5:21). Because His was "the white flower of a blameless life," His peerless teaching was the very soul of truth and such a halo of purity breathed through all His actions as to compel the confession:

"We stand in the presence of One so holy as to be pre-eminent among the sons of Adam."

Fierce controversy has raged around the subject, Did His deity render sin impossible, and consequently make His temptations unreal? If, to Him, sin was impossible then His temptation by Satan was a meaningless display, and His victory a mere delusion, and His coronation (Philippians 2:6) a shadow. One answer given to this thorny problem is—

"We may say it was impossible Jesus *would* sin. We dare not say it was impossible He *could* not sin."

To Christ, temptation was stronger and the conflict with sin was more intense than with any other of the human race. His knowledge of the human heart made it harder for Him to have the least sympathy with the least semblance of sin. Further, His unstained holiness gave saving efficacy to the blood He shed for sinners. Sinless, He can save from all sin. Only as the Sinless One could He atone for the sins of others (Psalms 40:7-10; 130:3).

Further, it is because Christ remained the highest embodiment of human character that He is our Great Example. Carlyle said of Him, "Our divinest symbol. Higher has the human thought not yet reached"—and never will, we might add. His own life, so passionately surrendered to the will of God, even although this involved the death of the cross, gives Him the right to make imperative spiritual and ethical demands on those who take up their crosses to follow Him.

His Matchless Words and Works

After the wilderness temptation, Jesus returned to Galilee and the fame of Him spread abroad (Luke 4:14). In the short space of just under three years, He lived and labored in such a way as to deeply impress not only those of His own generation, but succeeding generations. No certain dwelling place was His. Often, He had no place to lay His head. But this we know, He "went about doing good" (Acts 10:38). Where He went can be briefly tabulated. After the first *thirty years of preparation,* we have—

1. The Opening Events of His Ministry, lasting for about three months, from January to April, covering the period from the beginning of John the Baptist's ministry to our Lord's first miracle at Cana.

2. The Early Judaean Ministry, lasting about eight months from April to December, and covering Christ's first cleansing of the Temple and the beginning of His wonderful discourses.

3. The Samaritan Ministry, lasting only a few days in the December of the same year and taken up with what happened at Sychar.

4. The Galilean Ministry, the first period lasting from December to May of the next year. These five months or so bring us to Christ's return to Galilee, His choice of the Twelve, and the healing of the withered hand.

5. The Galilean Ministry, the second period stretching from May to April of the next year. During this one year we have

all the events in our Lord's life and labor from the choosing of the Twelve to His withdrawal into northern Galilee—a period packed with parables and miracles.

6. The Galilean Ministry, the third period lasting about six months from May to October and bringing us to His final departure for Jerusalem. In this period we have further parables and miracles.

7. The Later Judaean Ministry, lasting for about three months, from October to December. Finally departing from Galilee we have in Judea a wonderful record of discourses, parables and miracles.

8. The Peraean Ministry, lasting for about three and a half months covers the period from Christ's withdrawal to Bethany to His Parable of The Pounds. Here again are further discourses, parables and miracles.

9. The Closing Events of His Ministry, lasting for a week, known as *The Passion Week* and including the event from Christ's entry into Jerusalem until His body was laid in the tomb.

10. The Forty Days of Confirmation, lasting from April to May and covering all events and appearances from His resurrection to His ascension and to Pentecost.

For a detailed account of all that is associated with the foregoing periods, the reader is referred to a commendable *Harmony of the Gospels,* or to either of the succeeding events as itemized by Dr. James Orr in *The Inter-National Standard Encyclopedia,* or Dr. W. Graham Scroggie's *Guide to the Gospels.* During His manifestation to the world, Jesus revealed the Father in a fourfold way.

Firstly, there was the influence of His life upon those who came into contact with Him. His *life* was the light of men (John 1:4). His love, patience, unruffled calm, silence in suffering, majestic bearing, prayerfulness, humility and graciousness impelled others to follow His example. Sherwood Eddy in *A Portrait of Jesus,* says—

Jesus left no book, no tract or written page behind him. He bequeathed no system, no philosophy, no theology, no legislation. He raised no armies, organized no institutions, held no office, sought no influence. He was no scholar, and yet he is more quoted than any writer in all history. His sayings at times are on almost every tongue, and his words have literally gone out into all the world. No man ever laid down his life in Asia or in Africa

to translate Plato or Aristotle, Kant or Hegel, Shakespeare or Milton, but hundreds have died to carry Jesus' priceless words to the ends of the earth. Several hundred languages have been reduced to writing in order to transmit his life-giving message. Savage tribes have been uplifted, cannibals civilized, head-hunters converted, schools and colleges founded, and the character and culture of individuals and of peoples have been changed as the result of the influence of his words which are creative spirit and life.

Secondly, there were those remarkable *discourses* of His, almost fifty in all, recorded with considerable fullness and heavy with abiding instruction. From the *Sermon on the Mount* right on to the *Sermon on the Holy Spirit,* these utterances of Christ contain His teaching for the saints of all ages. The substance of His teaching covers a wide variety of themes.

Thirdly, there are His *parables,* distinct from discourses in that natural and local imagery was employed. This was Christ's chief method of instruction by which great moral truths were taught. For a complete study of His parables and parabolic instruction the reader is directed to the author's volume on *All the Parables of the Bible* which includes, not only Christ's parables, but parabolic material from Genesis to Revelation. His method, style and themes in teaching elicited the praise, "Never man spake like this Man." All of His teaching, delivered in all kinds of places, was characterized by simplicity, authority, brevity, vividness and picturesqueness. Two prominent features can be noticed, namely—

1. What Christ claimed for all of His utterances (Matthew 7:24-26, 24:35; Mark 4:21-25; Luke 8:15,18,21; John 8:51; 1:47-50).

2. What impressions were created by His utterance (Matthew 7:28; Mark 10:24; 12:37; Luke 4:22; 5:1,15; 6:17; 15:1; 21:38; 24:19; John 3:2; 7:46).

Fourthly, we have Christ's *miracles.* With His own gathered around Him during His last days before the cross, He summarized the character of His mission in the question—

Believest thou not that I am in the Father? The *words* that I speak unto you I speak not of Myself: but the Father that dwelleth in Me, He doeth the works (John 14:10).

Words and *works*. What a simple yet sublime coverage of a life lived in the center of God's will! Christ taught man by His *miracles* as well as His *parables*. "His parables were miracles in words, and His miracles were parables in deeds." All the miracles He performed are not detailed for us, but the thirty-five or so specified in the gospels reveal Him to be the Son of God with power. For a detailed exposition of His miracles, as well as the miraculous in the Bible as a whole, the reader is asked to consult the volume in our "All The" series on *All the Miracles of the Bible*.

His Death

How loaded with grief and suffering were our Lord's last days before His death at Calvary! The betrayal of Judas—the anguish and bloody sweat in Gethsemane—the denial by Peter—the injustice and indignities of His false accusation and trial—the desertion by His disciples. Such was a load heavy enough to break His heart. Then there came the shame, suffering and sacrifice of the cross itself.

> None of the ransomed ever knew
> How deep were the waters crossed,
> Or how dark the night the Lord passed
>   through
> Ere He found the sheep that was lost.

Among the many doctrines Christ enunciated, there was the doctrine of His death. While all men are born to live, they yet enter the world under the sentence of death. "It is appointed unto man once to die" (Hebrews 9:28). Christ, however, is the only One who came into the world for the purpose of dying. These facts are evident as we sift the teaching of Jesus concerning "His decease at Jerusalem."

He predicted the fact and manner of His death (Matthew 9:15; 16:21; 17:22,23; 20:18,19; 21:33-39; Luke 9:22; 18:31-33).

He taught that His death had a universal significance (John 3:16; 12:32,33).

He affirmed that His death had a definite bearing upon the spirit-world (John 12:31).

He linked His Incarnation and Crucifixion together (John 12:27).

He declared that His death was vicarious and substitutionary (Matthew 26:28; Mark 10:45; Luke 22:19; I Corinthians 11:24; II Corinthians 5:21; Galatians 2:20).

He died by His own volition. His life was not *taken,* but given (Matthew 27:50; John 10:18).

He prayed that His death would glorify God (John 12:27, 28; 13:31; 17:1).

It has been pointed out that the space given in the four gospels to the death of Christ is most striking. Two of the gospels, namely, Mark and John, do not record the birth of Jesus, and one does not relate His temptation, namely, John: two of them have no mention of the Sermon on the Mount, Mark and John: two of them have no account of His Ascension into heaven. But *all* the gospels describe with fullness of detail the fact of His crucifixion. "One-third of Matthew, one-third of Mark, and one-fourth of Luke is devoted to the account of His death, and one-half of John's gospel to the last twenty-four hours of Christ's life. One-third of the material in the four gospels has to do with the events of the last week of His life." The amount of space these four writers allot to the cross is an evidence that all Christ taught regarding it made a deep impression on their minds. The prediction of the part a traitor among the disciples would play in His death must have arrested them (Matthew 17:22,23).

Once the cross became a reality and a stark tragedy to Christ's followers, it appeared as if they had buried all their Messianic hopes in a grave. Their lack of belief in His power to conquer death can be found in the sorrowful conversation on the Emmaus Road. Two of the disciples were homeward bound after seeing Him die. Accosted by the risen Lord whom they took to be a stranger, they replied in answer to His enquiry about their sadness—

> "We thought it had been he who would
> have redeemed Israel" (Luke 24:21).

They pictured His body reposing in Joseph's new tomb where they had helped to place it. Before long, however, they were to learn that He had been dead but was now alive forever more (Revelation 1).

While we may not all agree that "the heart of Britain is London, and the heart of London is Westminster," it is certainly true that the heart of Christianity is the Bible, the heart of the Bible the cross, and the heart of the cross, the very heart of God Himself. "God was in Christ, reconciling the world unto himself" (II Corinthians 5:19).

The good news of Easter is that the divine heart was full of tenderest compassion for a sinning, erring humanity; and that that heart was bruised and broken as it atoned for man's guilt. Dr. James Denny, in his monumental volume, *The Death of Christ*, says, "The forfeiting of His free life has freed our forfeited lives."

The writings of Paul, the greatest exponent of Calvary's evangel, drip with the ruby blood of the Redeemer. Take away Paul's contribution to the death and Resurrection of Christ, and the New Testament remains an incomplete, partial revelation. Glorying in the cross, Paul made it his pre-eminent theme. To the churches he founded, the apostle expounded the full and inescapable implications of Christ's finished work.

To the church at Corinth he wrote—

"I am determined to know nothing among you save Jesus Christ and Him crucified" (I Corinthians 2:2).

To the church at Galatia he sent a letter pulsating with the truth of Calvary—
"Who gave himself for our sins" (1:4).
"The Son of God, who loved me, and gave himself for me (2:20).
"God forbid that I should glory, save in the cross of our Lord Jesus Christ" (6:14).

To the church at Rome he affirmed that—
"In due time Christ died for the ungodly (5:6).

To the church at Thessalonica he affirmed—
"We believe that Jesus died and rose again" (I Thessalonians 4:14).

To the church at Philippi he urged the reminder—
"Ye who sometimes were far off are made nigh by the blood of Christ" (2:13).

To the church at Philippi he urged the saints there to—
"Know him and the power of his resurrection and the fellowship of his sufferings" (3:10).

To the church at Colosse he proclaimed the evangel—
"In whom we have redemption through his blood (1:14).

At all times, then, the silver trumpet was pressed to Paul's lips, and unashamedly he echoed forth the Gospel of Easter. His constant message was, "Who gave Himself a ransom for all" (I Timothy 2:6). To the apostle, the constitute elements of the Gospel were the death, burial and Resurrection of Christ (I Corinthians 15:1-4). While there have been a million martyr deaths,

there was only one cross of Christ; only One good enough to pay the price of sin.

THE REVELATION OF THE CROSS

Paul was not the author, but merely the recipient of the Easter Evangel he was so fond of declaring. "That which also I received" (I Corinthians 15:3). The mystery and the meaning of the cross came to Paul as a distinct revelation from God (Galatians 1:11,12). "By revelation He made known unto me the mystery" (Ephesians 3:3-5). In this, the Gospel differs from other gospels originating in the human mind. While the Gospel of Easter is for earth, it is not earthly in its conception.

The truth of the cross still remains a revelation, seeing all truth is revelation. Until the Holy Spirit reveals to the heart its need of Christ, all the significance and sufficiency of Christ's death and Resurrection remain a mystery. Thrice happy are those, who, in a moment of revelation, grasp the meaning of the cross and are transformed by such a vision.

THE FOUNDATION OF THE CROSS

Although the great fundamental foundation of the Gospel of grace is the cross, there are three pillars supporting the structure making impossible its destruction.

1. *Its Prophetic Witness*

Twice over, Paul uses the phrase, "According to the Scriptures" (I Corinthians 15:3,4), and in it he, like his Master before him, sets his seal to Old Testament Scriptures. Christ treated and revered the Old Testament as the Word of God (Luke 24:27). Beyond the prophetic aspect there is, of course, the eternal purpose of God.

The blood-red highway of the cross can be traced in prophetic Scriptures like Psalms 16:10; 22; Isaiah 53—in prophetic symbols like the Red Sea (Deuteronomy 9:26,27) and Israel's restoration (Hosea 6:2)—in prophetic types such as Moses (Hebrews 9:19) and Jonah (Matthew 12:41)—or prophetic ordinances such as the sacrifices and priesthood (Hebrews 9:12, 14).

2. *Messianic Works*

The first creed of Christendom is made up of three parts, forming a trinity in unity. To remove any part is to destroy the sum and substance of the Gospel.

Christ Died For Our Sins. First of all, there is the fact—"Christ died"—a fact directly mentioned some 175 times in the

New Testament. It is an indisputable fact of history that Jesus "suffered under Pontius Pilate was crucified, dead and buried."

Secondly, there is the purpose of such a death—"For our sins." There are those who accept the fact but dispute the purpose. They contend that Jesus died as a martyr, a model in sacrifice, a hero, or was crucified as the result of a blunder. The incontestable fact of Scripture, however, is that Christ died for one purpose, namely, to provide a perfect salvation for a sinning race (I Timothy 1:15).

Christ Was Buried. "Low in the grave He lay," reveals the depth of Christ's humiliation on our behalf. The Highest in heaven buried in the heart of the earth. Willingly He "made His grave with the wicked and with the rich in His death" (Isaiah 53:9), and "buried He carried my sins far away." Bunyan saw in his dream the burden *Christian* carried loosed from off his back and made to tumble into the sepulcher.

He Rose Again The Third Day. The Resurrection was an evidence that God was satisfied with the death of the cross. It was His seal upon the perfection of Christ's work. The Resurrection was also necessary for man's salvation, for had He remained in the tomb then there would have been no justification (Romans 10:9,10). But Christ arose from the dead and is alive forevermore to make the cross actual in our lives. The declaration is in the perfect tense "He hath been raised"—risen to die no more (Luke 24:5,6).

3. *The Historic Witness*

In his Corinthian letters, Paul is found combating false theories by adding the important link of the chronological order of Christ's appearances after His resurrection. Some 514 in all saw Him. If only one person had seen Him there might have been reason to doubt the reliability of the witness. But 514 could not have been wrong. Paul, the level-headed thinker could say, "He was seen of *me* also," and to him the risen Lord was a glorious reality.

THE DESCRIPTION OF THE CROSS

Paul calls it "The Gospel," a term meaning "a glad announcement, good news," (See Proverbs 25:25). *Gospel* has been given as "God's Spell," *spell* being the Saxon word for "story." The Gospel of Easter, then, is God's story, one that had birth in His own heart. It is a story about God's character, love and grace; and which the death of Christ makes so real.

THE PROCLAMATION OF THE CROSS

Within the context, Paul uses different terms to describe the Gospel we must deliver "clear and plain."

1. It is a pre-eminent message—"First of all," Here was Paul's principal message. The cross was foremost in his preaching and evangelization and should be the primary doctrine of the church—primary because we stand or fall by it. Then is it not "first," seeing the first, indispensable experience of the soul is that of the forgiveness of sins the cross alone makes possible.

2. It is a proclaimed message. "I preached unto you," v. 1. The church at Corinth was founded by such preaching (Acts 18:1-11). To preach, means, "to tell the good news," and the preacher, one who announces glad tidings.

3. It is a persistent message. "I declare." The Calvary message is one that needs reiteration. The word Paul uses here implies an effort to remind and impress the memory —the delight and determination to tell the story o'er and o'er again.

4. It is a proved message. "I delivered what . . . I received." The word *deliver* means "alongside of," and infers that Paul took the Evangel to others. Christ did not send salvation, He brought it (John 1:17). Paul only gave to others what he himself had proved. Having experienced the regenerating and transforming power of the Gospel (I Corinthians 15:8,9), he pressed the acceptance of it upon others. Knowing whom he had believed (II Timothy 1:12), Paul urges others to share his knowledge.

THE APPLICATION OF THE CROSS

A crucial point to emphasize is that the work of the cross is only effectual as it is received. Although Christ died and made salvation possible, it is only our faith that can make that salvation *actual*.

So we have the *reception*—"Ye have received," and our eternal welfare hinges upon a personal reception (John 1:11,12). Then there is *foundation*—"Wherein ye stand." The cross is not only a starting point but a way of life—center and circumference. The cross is not only the fountain opened for uncleanness but a fortress in which to hide. Further, there is *sanctification*—"Ye are being saved." The present tense here implies salvation from the present government of sin as well as salvation from its past guilt. This is the truth we must "keep in memory" or "hold fast." Many, alas! "believe in vain." For them "grace is in vain." A mere belief in the historical Christ will not save. Our hope is built on His blood and righteousness, without which we are lost.

His wondrous cross—the focal point of Biblical history—presents many paradoxes, the most conspicuous being the climax of love and hate. At Calvary, the heart of God is revealed and at the same time man's hate is seen in all its heinous horror. Christ's cruel death was the world's *blackest* hour, yet also its *brightest* hour. "It was the blackest hour because human hate came to its fiercest focus. It was the brightest hour because divine love came to its fullest flower."

Love so amazing, so divine,
Shall have my life, my soul, my all.

His Resurrection

The importance of Christ's victory over death cannot be too strongly stressed. "Christianity is a religion of miracle," says one theologian, "and the miracle of Christ's Resurrection is the living center and object of Christian faith." The doctrine of the Resurrection is of primary value for on it all the doctrines of grace depend. If Christ did not rise again then we are still in our sins. (I Corinthians 15:14,17). If all His body stayed in the grave there would have been no salvation for a sinning race. This is why it is only partially true to say that we are saved from the penalty and power of sin as the result of Christ's death. Paul makes this fact clear when he declares that it is only as we believe in our heart that God raised Jesus from the dead that we can be saved (Romans 10:8,9). The Resurrection was God's receipt for Calvary. Christ died to discharge our heavy debt of sin, and that all claims were fully met is evidenced by His triumph over man's last enemy.

This is one reason why the Resurrection occupied such a prominent place in the earliest apostolic preaching. A successor to Judas Iscariot had to be one who had witnessed the Resurrection of Christ (Acts 1:22). The first recorded sermon in the Acts was conspicuous for its emphasis upon the Resurrection (Acts 2:24-32; 3:15). The preaching of the Resurrection resulted in persecution (Acts 4:2, 5:20), but the apostles could not be silenced in their witness to such a dynamic doctrine. If only modern preaching was dominated by the triumphant message of the Resurrection, as apostolic preaching was, what mighty things would be accomplished. Alas, too many preachers have forgotten—if ever they knew it—that the Resurrection is not only one of the main proofs of the deity of Christ (Romans 1:4), but a divine act providing the keystone of the Christian faith (I Corinthians 15:17, 18).

That the Resurrection is the best established fact in Bible history can be proved by the following aspects—

It was the subject of prophecy (Psalm 16:10,11; Acts 13:31-37).

Christ repeatedly declared it (Matthew 16:21; 17:9-23; Mark 8:31).

John believed it as he saw the empty tomb (John 20:8).

The women at the grave reported it (Luke 24:11; John 20:13,15).

Peter reported that Jesus appeared to Him (Luke 24:34).

Christ repeatedly appeared to His own (John 21; Acts 10:40,41).

He was seen by Paul, and hundreds of others (I Corinthians 15:5-8).

The existence of the Church confirms the Resurrection. If Christ had no resurrection body, then there is no mystical body formed by the Holy Spirit who came as the result of Christ's Resurrection and Ascension. The fact and presence of the Church, then, demonstrates the proof of the Resurrection and every believer is a living proof of such a doctrine.

The Resurrection is not only a *fact*, but was a mighty *factor*. The *doctrine* became a *dynamic*, thus Paul speaks of "the power of His resurrection" (Philippians 3:10). Paul came to experience this divine power and was uplifted in its strength and made the most mighty witness in the Early Church. Risen with Christ, can we say that we are sharers of His risen power? If spiritual inertia is ours, then we need to open the avenues of our being to the tremendous forces liberated by Christ's victory over sin, death and hell.

By His Resurrection Jesus became "the first fruits of them that slept," and "the firstborn of the dead" (I Corinthians 15:20; Colossians 1:18; Revelation 1:5). He is so called because His Resurrection was distinct from all those who had been raised before

Him. Jesus arose with a *spiritual* body (I Corinthians 15:44,45). Body and soul were reunited and restored to their original beauty and strength and raised to the highest level. Louis Berkhof says that the Resurrection of Christ has a threefold significance—

1. It was a declaration of the Father that Christ met all the requirements of the law (Philippians 2:9).

2. It symbolized the justification, regeneration and final resurrection of believers (Romans 6:4,5,9; I Corinthians 6:14; 15:20-22).

3. It was the cause of our justification, regeneration and resurrection (Romans 4:25; 5:10; Ephesians 1:20; Philippians 2:10; I Peter 1:3).

His Ascension

The fifth book of the New Testament is sometimes spoken of as "The Fifth Gospel" or "The Acts of the Holy Spirit through the Apostles." This dramatic book, however, is largely a record of two of the apostles—Peter, apostle to the Jews (1-12); and Paul, apostle to the Gentiles (13-28). The events of the book cover a period of about 34 years.

The Acts opens with the risen Lord giving commandments through the Spirit to His disciples, and the Resurrection itself is the strongest witness to the reality of the Ascension. His presence and ministry for 40 days proved that He was alive from the dead. Our Lord did not disappear with the Spirit, even in His risen form, but declared that He would continue to act and speak through the Spirit, as He had done previous to His death (Matthew 12:28; Luke 4:14-18; Acts 2).

While with His disciples Jesus spoke much of the things pertaining to the kingdom of God. The disciples were eager for the promised restoration of the kingdom to Israel and asked for a date when restoration could be expected. Christ rebuked them, not for their desire to have the kingdom restored, but for wanting to know the time of restoration—a matter shut up in the counsels of God.

While the disciples were feasting upon the presence and ministry of the Lord they loved, suddenly as they lovingly looked at Him, He vanished from their sight. From that wonderful moment on, they lived and labored in the power of their risen, as-cended and returning Lord. They not only accepted the Ascension as an historic fact but as a mighty dynamic for service (Romans 8:34; Ephesians 1:20; 4:8; I Timothy 3:10; Hebrews 1:3; 4:14; 10:12). Fact and figure were combined and the Ascension made prediction of Christ's return in glory (Matthew 25:31; 26:64; Philippians 3:20, I Thessalonians 4:16; I Peter 3:22; Revelation 1:7).

THE EXPECTATION OF THE ASCENSION

Having lived with the Father from the dateless past, Jesus, as He dwelt among men, was so homesick for heaven. How He longed to be back again in the bosom of His Father. How eagerly He anticipated His Ascension! This is why many of His sayings breathe the air of expectancy. He predicted that His disciples would witness His departure to heaven (John 6:62). He could steadfastly set His face toward His cross, knowing that it would be followed by His coronation (Luke 9:51 R.V.M.). He was the Householder about to go into a far country from which He would return to reward His servants (Matthew 21:33). Did He not blend His Crucifixion with His Ascension? (John 12:32). Did he not promise His own that He would go to prepare a place for them in His Father's home? (John 14:3). With all authority, He could pronounce "I go unto My Father" (John 14:12,28). He was only to be a little while with His own, then go back to the One that sent Him (John 7:33). Hear Him, as He says, "I leave the world and go to the Father" (John 16:27,28). Did He not forbid Mary to touch Him seeing that He had not yet ascended? (John 20:17)

Two Old Testament saints knew what it was to ascend from earth to heaven in their human bodies, changed as they ascended, namely, Enoch and Elijah. They were spared the sting of death but Jesus died and in His glorified body, with which He rose from the grave and ascended on high, are the marks of the nails—perpetual witness to His anguish on our behalf.

The Transfiguration of Christ anticipated His glorious Ascension (Luke 9:28-36). Had He wished He could have gone right into heaven from the Mount, for "perfect in creation, perfect in probation, He was now ready to be perfected in glory." But His was the great renunciation. Had He ascended from the Mount in His glorified form, He would have gone alone. Back down the Mount He came and endured the cross so that the joy might be His of having multitudes of the redeemed share His bliss above (Hebrews 12:1,2).

THE EVENT OF THE ASCENSION

It is somewhat surprising what little stress there is on the fact of the Ascension in the gospels. Matthew and John do not mention it. Yet, although the treatment is scant, it is sufficient for faith. After the event, the testimony to the Ascension was strong (Acts 2:33; 3:21; Ephesians 1:20; I Timothy 3:16).

The event happened at the Mount of Olives (Acts 1:12), a place so prominent in Christ's life. It was the place of His solitude (Luke 21:37), but will yet be the seat of His sovereignty (Zechariah 14:4). Here, it is the scene of His Ascension glory.

The event also transpired while Jesus was in the act of blessing His disciples on their return from Jerusalem (Luke 24:50,52). As His hands were lifted up in priestly benediction, even as they were on the mount (Acts 3:26), Jesus vanished out of their sight. As His last words fell with all their celestial melody and significance on the ears of His own, the miracle happened and Jesus was uplifted in bodily form from earth to heaven. How those men of Gallilee must have gazed upon Him in rapt attention as He was taken up from them!

What impressed those disciples was the fact that Jesus ascended in His actual form. *He* was taken up. It was not some shadowy form or apparition but Himself, their veritable Redeemer Lord and Friend. The One who had become dear to their hearts through the three years they had spent together, and the heavenly messengers assured the amazed beholders that this *same* Jesus would return in like manner as He went (Acts 1:10,11).

Further, the disciples gazed spellbound at the ascending Lord, for such an event was most unexpected, even though Christ had told them of it. The language used implies that they were struck with surprise. In a moment they saw His mysterious form ascend and heard the two men from heaven say that His return would be just as sudden.

He also ascended in a mysterious grandeur. "The cloud received Him out of their sight." "He was carried up." What kind of a cloud received Him, and who carried Him up to heaven? True, the ethereal clouds became His chariot, but are not the clouds emblems of grandeur and of the angels of God, who carried Elijah to heaven, and who also convey dying saints to heaven? (Psalm 68:17,18; Luke 16:22). Can it be that myriads of angels bore Jesus triumphantly back to heaven? It was a mystic cloud that guided and guarded Israel through the wilderness pilgrimage. Of the angels, Gregg wrote

They brought His chariot from above,
  To bear Him to His throne;
Spread their triumphant wings, and sang,
  "The glorious work is done."

THE EXPEDIENCY OF THE ASCENSION

Is it not hard to credit the surprising truth that Christ's absence is our great gain? "It is expedient for you that I go away" (John 16:7). What are the advantages accruing to us through His ascension? What blessedness is ours because of His departure?

The evangelical *Heidelberg Catechism* assures us of these three advantages of Christ's Ascension:

1. *That He is my Advocate, in the presence of His Father.*

Christ's last act was that of lifting up His hands in priestly benediction upon His own, a symbol of the perpetual ministry He ascended on high to exercise. "He ever liveth to make intercession for us" (Hebrews 7:26). This, then, is the first great gain as the result of Christ's entrance into heaven. He intercedes for *us*, for the efficacy of His intercession reaches no further than the efficacy of His blood. We now have a Friend in the court of the everlasting King, an Intercessor who ever lives, a Petitioner who never fails. He pleads our cause without fee.

Day and night our Jesus makes no pause,
Pleads His own fulfilment of all laws.
Veils with His perfections mortal flaws,
Clears the culprit, pleads the desperate cause.
Plucks the dead from death's devouring jaws,
    And the worm that gnaws.

2. *That I have my own flesh in heaven, as a sure pledge that He who is the Head will also take me, one of His members, up to Himself.*

This further good treasure and boon resulting from Christ's Ascension was one He promised ere He left the earth. "Where I am, there ye may be also." *My own flesh in heaven!* How true this is! One of the ceaseless wonders of heaven is the presence of humanity's dust, glorified, seated on a throne. Christ is now the only Person in the Trinity with a body.

Fausset comments that, "The transfiguration before His passion shows how His resurrection body could be the same body, yet altered so as it will be more or less recognizable to beholders. The process of His glorification probably began from His Resurrection and culminated in His Ascension." What a blessed hope awaits the child of God who, seeing Him will be fashioned into His likeness! (Philippians 3:21; I John 3:1-3).

3. *That He sends His Spirit, by whose power, I seek those things which are above.*

This is the third benediction, says the ancient Catechism, Christ's Ascension brings us. This supreme Gift of all He received for His own and shed Him down on them. The unction of the Spirit is part of the fruit of Christ's Ascension (John 7:39; I John 2:20).

Christ sent the Spirit as the Comforter (John 14:16), and a drop of His heavenly comfort is enough to sweeten a sea of worldly sorrow. The Spirit also came as "an earnest" (II Corinthians 1:22). He it is who gives us an earnest of heaven in our land.

THE EXALTATION OF THE ASCENSION

As Jesus ascended to His Father, He was highly exalted by Him to a position "above all exaltation" (Philippians 2:9). The name of authority bestowed upon Him was the same one given to Him at His birth, namely, JESUS (Matthew 1:21). Calvary saw the Sun of Righteousness in eclipse, but as the result of the Ascension, He shines in full glory.

Christ was first humiliated, then exalted and we must enter glory as He did. "If we suffer, we shall reign with Him" (II Timothy 2:12). The only way up is down. First a cross, then a crown.

What was the nature of the Father's exaltation of His beloved Son? True, there were the Resurrection, Ascension and position at God's right hand, but Paul reminds us of two aspects we must not lose sight of. First, at His Ascension, he led captivity captive. What does this imply? Who were the captives He liberated and then bound

to Himself with eternal chains and led them in the train of His triumph?

Were they not the saints in that part of paradise known as "Abraham's Bosom"? (Luke 16:23). Before Christ's Ascension, when a saint died, he did not go directly to heaven but to paradise, where all the saints were prisoners of hope. When Jesus ascended to heaven, He emptied this temporary abode of the righteous, and took them with Him to heaven. Absent from the body, he finds himself at home with his Lord.

Secondly, Paul reminds us, the ascended Lord "gave gifts unto men," chiefest among which was the gift of the Spirit (Ephesians 4:8). The variety of gifts mentioned indicate Christ's provision for the enlightenment and edification of His Church.

Christ was also exalted in the titles bestowed upon Him. "The name of the Lord was manifest." He was exalted as the Lord. All power became His over angels and men. To Him, every knee is to bow (Matthew 28:18; Acts 19:17; Philippians 2:10). In His sovereignty He has the authority to use three keys—

The key of the grave with which to open the graves of the redeemed.

The key of heaven with which to open the blest abode to whom He will.

The key of hell with which to imprison the condemned (Revelation 1:18).

He was exalted to be a Prince (Revelation 1:5). The princes of earth hold their crowns by tenure of Him who has the power to set one up and cast down another. He was exalted in order to become a Saviour and Mediator. To save sinners is a star belonging only to His crown (Acts 4:12; 5:31). As He conquered sin and hell for everyone of us, His triumph can now be made ours by faith.

Christ is at God's right hand, which implies the position of dignity and honor. It was the manner of kings in advancing favorites to set them at their right hand. Thus Solomon caused a seat to be set for the queen his mother at his right hand (I Kings 2:19). At the Father's right hand, Christ has the key of government on His shoulders and governs all the affairs of the world for the glory of His Father. *Sitting* at God's right hand implies the finished task of redemption (Hebrews 1:3; 10:12).

Christ's exaltation was our exaltation and our responsibility is to exalt Him in our lives. We must exalt Him in all our ways, making Him renowned among others. We must exalt His truth against error, and His liberty against bondage.

After His Ascension, the disciples returned to Jerusalem with great joy and from that moment the personal, literal, visible return of their Lord became their hope and to a large degree their theme. After the Ascension came a remarkable prayer meeting, when the hearts of about 120 were prepared for the coming of the Holy Spirit, the Saviour's ascension gift to His believing people. May our meditation of the Ascension, result in a fresh enduement of the Spirit and in a quickened desire for Christ's return in power and glory!

His Present Ministry

Christ is *active*, as well as *alive*, for ever more. When He left earth for heaven, His ministry did not cease. It ever continues although in a changed form. In fact, His present ministry is based upon His work on earth and is arriving at the completion of same. What are the offices He exercises in glory? Because of His perfect obedience to God while here below and also in virtue of His sacrificial death additional honors are Christ's (John 13:31,32; Philippians 2:9,10; Revelation 5:12-14).

After His glorious Ascension, there came the restoration of the glory He possessed before the world was (John 17:5). Seated at the right hand of God there came the resumption of the exercise of all His divine attributes. All the self-imposed limitations of humanity ceased when He sat down on high (Matthew 28:18,20; Mark 16:20; Revelation 5:12-14). The expression, "right hand of God," (Hebrews 1:3) is figurative of a position of authority, power and glory.

Part of His present ministry is the preparation of an abode for His Church. "I go to prepare a place for you" (John 14:2). Entering heaven, Jesus immediately redeemed His promise and sent the Holy Spirit to fashion the Church He said He would build (Matthew 16:18; John 16:7; Acts 1:4; 2:1-4). In Christ, we are already set in heavenly places and through His Ascension we have the assurance of a place in heaven with Him (John 17:24; Ephesians 2:6). It is His express wish that we should share His glory. Now, by the Spirit, the Church is the habitation of God. Soon she is to have an habitation in the divine abode.

Further, Christ not only rules and protects His Church, governing the universe on her behalf, He also intercedes for her on the basis of His completed sacrifice. In Him, the Church has her great Intercessor at the throne (Romans 8:34; Hebrews 4:14; 6:20; 7:25; 9:24). While on earth, He offered up prayers saturated with tears (Hebrews 5: 25) and in heaven He continues this effective ministry—but without the tears. It is, therefore, Biblical to sing—

"I have a Saviour, who's pleading in glory"

Christ's state and office in heaven brings us to a consideration of His threefold ministry as Prophet, Priest and King—the three Old Testament offices reaching their perfection in Christ (I Samuel 16:3; I Kings 19:16; Psalm 105:15). In His manhood were imparted without measure all the gifts of the Holy Spirit: and so He possesses in the highest degree the *knowledge* of a Prophet: the *holiness* of a High Priest; and the *power* of a King. This threefold division of Christ's mediatorial work proclaims not only His uniqueness but also His prerogatives (I Timothy 2:5).

1. *Christ As Prophet*

Of old, a *prophet* spoke to men about God: a *priest* spoke to God about men. Prophets of old declared the whole counsel of God, and Christ, as the perfect Prophet not only expounded the Word of God—He was the Embodiment of that Word. In Him, it became *flesh* (John 1:16). The New Testament reveals these facts—

a. He calls Himself a Prophet (Luke 13: 33).

b. He claimed to bring a message from God. He was the inspired Interpreter of the Word and will of God (John 8:26-28; 14: 10-24; 17:8,26).

c. He elicited praise as a true Prophet, or Teacher from God. He ever spoke with authority (Matthew 21:11,46; Luke 7:16; 24:19; John 3:2; 4:19).

d. He continues the eternal revelation of God to the saints in glory (John 16:12-14; I Corinthians 13:12). He will ever remain the divine Expositor of truth (Luke 24:27, 44,45).

2. *Christ As Priest*

The Aaronic priesthood, which typified Christ's priestly ministry, represented a *priest* as one called to represent man before God, by offering sacrifices and making intercession. The analogies and contrasts between Aaron and Christ provide one of the prominent themes of the Epistle to the Hebrews. "As the prophetic word is the word of righteousness, Christ's priestly act is the fulfillment of righteousness under judgment, for the world's salvation."

As the Priest, Jesus suffered in man's stead and satisfied divine holiness and opened the way for God to pardon and restore the guilty. One of the most profound mysteries of Christianity is that He became Priest and Lamb and both Punisher and Punished (Romans 3:25,26; Hebrews 9:12; John 1:25).

As Priest, Jesus was, and is, sinless. Aaron had to offer sacrifices for his own sin, as well as for the sins of others (Hebrews 7: 9,10). In heaven, He pleads His efficacious blood on our behalf (Hebrews 2:17; 3:1).

As the Priest, He secures, on the basis of Atonement, all of our temporal and spiritual blessings (Isaiah 53:12; Luke 22:31,32; 23: 34; John 14:16).

As the Priest, He continues His intercessory ministry for the Church on earth (Hebrews 4:15; 9:11-15; 9:24-28; 10:19-22).

As the Priest, He is a kingly one robed with the full splendor of the throne of God, having the distinctive glory of a finished saving work (Hebrews 10:10-14; Revelation 1:13; 5:6,9,12). The marvel is that He has condescended to call us *priests*. What a neglected truth the priesthood of all believers is!

3. *Christ As King*

Kingship is one of Christ's eternal prerogatives. As "the King Eternal," He was born a King. During His earthly sojourn He asserted His Kingship and men recognized His claim (Matthew 2:2; Acts 17:7). As the "King," He died, and in His Resurrection proved His sovereignty. In heaven, He rules as King for the glory of God and for the fulfilment of His purposes (Matthew 28:18; Hebrews 1:3). As King, He exercises power in upholding and controlling the world (Ephesians 1:22; Colossians 1: 15-19).

Messianic kingship foreshadowed the One who would come as God's perfect King (Psalm 2:6). The prediction is that He is to return in regal power and spendor as the King of the Kings, and Lord of all Lords (Revelation 11:15; 19:16). What a glorious coronation will be His, when many crowns diadem His brow! What glory will be His when His kingdom comes as He reigns supreme over the earth! The wonder is that

we are to reign with Him, assisting Him as *kings* in His governmental control of all things. The question is, Do we honor and obey Him as King of our lives? Have we brought forth the royal diadem and crowned Him Lord of all? Does He reign on the throne of the heart?

His Prospective Majesty

Honor and majesty have ever been ascribed to Him who now sits on the right hand of the Majesty on high (Psalm 96:6; Hebrews 1:3). From the dateless past, Christ has been clothed with majesty (Psalms 93:1; 104:1). When in the bosom of the Father, the angelic host sang of His majesty (John 1:18; Isaiah 24:16; 26:10). At His Incarnation, He did not surrender such august dignity and grandeur but brought them with Him. This is why the three disciples who witnessed His transfiguration on the Mount afterward confessed that they had been "eye-witnesses of His majesty" (Matthew 17:1-8; II Peter 1:16). Such *majesty* was the out-flashing of His inherent glory.

It is to His coming majesty, however, that our attention is directed in this concluding section on *The Doctrine of Christ*. In our last chapter dealing with *The Doctrine of Last Things*, more detailed reference to the glory of Christ's Second Advent and millennial reign can be found. When He returns for His true Church, He is to be "glorified in His saints and admired in all them that believe" (II Thessalonians 1:10). Then they will behold His majesty (Isaiah 26:10), and be clothed with it.

During the great Tribulation, Christ, as the Lamb, will gird His sword upon His thigh and in His majesty ride prosperously because of truth and meekness and righteousness (Psalm 45:3,4). Then the earth will know that "with God is terrible majesty" (Job 37:22). None will be able to gainsay Christ's judicial majesty as His righteous judgment overtakes a guilty earth. No wonder the godless multitudes will cry to be hidden from the face of Him that sitteth on His judicial throne! (Revelation 6:16,17; Isaiah 2:10).

But the full meridian of splendor will not be His until He ushers in His reign as "the prince of the kings of the earth" (Revelation 1:5). Then His voice as He rules the earth, will be full of majesty (Psalm 29:4). What royal grandeur, glory and dominion will be the Saviour's when the crown of glory and honor rests upon the brow once scarred by the crown of thorns! (Hebrews 2:7-10). Then Jude's doxology will be universally sung—

"To the only wise God our Saviour, be glory and majesty, dominion and power, both now and ever. Amen! (Jude 25).

The practical aspect of the doctrine of Christ must not be forgotten. All that He is, and has, are at our disposal. The Holy Spirit is not only with us to take of the things of Christ and reveal them unto us. He is within us in order to conform us to the image of God's dear Son (Ephesians 4:15-17). Because God was in Christ, and He is now at God's right hand, He is able to solve all our problems, meet all our needs and banish all our tears. In *The Death of the Desert,* Browning imagines the death and last words of John, and makes John to say:

I say, the acknowledgement of God in Christ
Accepted by thy reason, solves for thee,
All questions in the earth and out of it.

If He is ours, and we are His then we need no other source of supply and satisfaction, He is our sufficiency in all things.

Be Thou supreme, Lord Jesus Christ,
Thy life transfigure mine;
And through this veil of mortal flesh,
Here may Thy glory shine.

VI

The Doctrine of the Holy Spirit

In his Introduction to Abraham Kuyper's monumental work on *The Holy Spirit,* Professor B. Warfield remarks:

The Holy Spirit—a theme higher than which none can occupy the attention of the Christian . . . only a spiritually-minded church provides a soil in which a literature of the Spirit can grow.

It is because the Church has lost sight of the fact that the Holy Spirit is the Administrator of her affairs in this dispensation of grace that she is so devoid of spiritual power in a world of need. Dr. Joseph Parker, in his study of the Spirit in *The Paraclete,* asks the question—

Is not the presence of the Holy Spirit in the Church less distinct today than in the Apostolic Age? Certainly there is not much appearance of Pentecostal inspiration and enthusiasm in contemporary Christianity. Christianity is nothing if not *spiritual.* Why has not a Church now eighteen hundred (*note*—now over nineteen hundred) years old a fuller realization of the witness of the Holy Spirit than had the Church of the First Century? Has the Church accomplished all the purpose of God and passed forever the zenith of her light and beauty?

What we must not forget is that the fountain of the Spirit was not limited to the Spirit, whose experience of Him was so real. The vast resources of the Spirit are for each and all within the church.

It is a gift which all may share,
From prince to peasant rude;
It glows not more in palace halls,
Than in dark solitude.

The Study of the Spirit

Religious teachers and writers are impressed by the fact that Christians everywhere desire a more comprehensive knowledge of the Person and work of the Holy Spirit. It may be that a sense of need and insufficiency cause many to inquire. They want to understand how the Spirit's fullness can be received and retained.

In many cases, misconception and ignorance are responsible for weakness and ineffectiveness in Christian life and labor. If only the Spirit could come into His own, lives would be rich in fruitfulness and fragrant with the perfume of Christ. Realizing all that the Third Person of the Trinity has for us, means the transformation of facts of promise into factors of power. When Spirit-filled, life is enriched, labor is empowered, and the Lord is enthroned.

Approaching the theme before us, sublime and sacred, profound and precious as it is, we have to confess that no saint can explain fully to himself or to others the gracious operations of the Spirit. Personally, we can experience His power and witness His work in and through other lives, but our reach exceeds our grasp. Thus, any exposition of the Personality and work of the Spirit is more or less imperfect because of our inability to describe our experiences correctly.

All of us are able to know with absolute certainty the facts of His indwelling presence, life-giving energy and sanctifying power, even though our opinions as to the origin and theory of the Spirit's presence within the soul may differ. It is imperative to guard ourselves against uncharitable denunciation of fellow believers, whose explanation differs from our own.

As we enter upon these evangelical studies of the Spirit it is with the confession that the doctrine is, in many respects, mysterious. Because of our finite understanding we can have a true but not complete understanding of it. It is a revealed fact of Holy Writ, and as such is to be received and believed. The truth of the Spirit transcends, but does not contradict reason. The Father, the Son, and the Holy Spirit are one and only one God. Each has some characteristics which the other has not. Neither is God without the others, and each with the others is God. The Father says "I," the Spirit says "I." The Father loves the Son—the Son honors the Father—the Spirit testifies of the Son.

The Need of Study

Students of church history have pointed out that the twin truths of the Holy Spirit and of our Lord's return were lost to the Church for a long period. Although recognized, declared and surely believed by the apostles and early fathers, they were lost to vision during the Dark Ages when the Church was almost entirely Romish.

The Spirit's manifold operations allied with the blessed hope now hold a prominent place in the theology of evangelical believers, thanks to the efforts of spiritually-minded teachers throughout the last 150 years.

And it will be observed that these twin truths rise or fall together. If we deny the one, we discard the other. In his monumen-

tal volume on *Christian Doctrines,* Dr. Dale remarks,

There are some who have not discovered that as the coming of Christ was a new and wonderful thing in the history of our race, the coming of the Holy Spirit was also a new and wonderful thing in the history of our race, and that His coming has made an infinite difference in the life of man.

It is imperative to grasp the truth of the Spirit for many reasons:

1. Because it is a neglected doctrine

Although we have more volumes than ever before expounding the graces and gifts of the Spirit, we fear that such enlightenment is sadly neglected by the vast majority of Christians. A recital of the Creed there may be—"I believe in the Holy Ghost," but where He is unknown, or where the essentials of our faith are tampered with, His presence cannot be realized.

Professor Erdman, in his inspiring book, *The Holy Spirit and Christian Experience* wrote:

The Spirit cannot be where Christ is denied as Redeemer, Life and Lord of all. Christ is "The Truth" and the Spirit is "The Spirit of Truth"; all is personal, not abstract, ideal, and the sum and substance of material wherewith the Spirit works in Christ. . . . In brief, the Spirit must be silent altogether in pulpits and churches where "a different gospel which is not another gospel" is preached, and where unrebuked and unchecked prevail, although in a form of Godliness, "the lust of the flesh, and the lust of the eyes, and the pride of life" and the things which are "not of the Father, but . . . of the world"; things which are not of the new nature and spirit in which the Holy Spirit dwells and through which alone He can work and testify . . . . We should be warned by the history of the apostolic churches, once so full of the Spirit, but which perished from their places long ago. The same denial of Christ, the same worldliness is our danger today. All that can help us is the presence of the Spirit of Christ, and He will not work save with the Truth of Christ; and He only must dwell in the Temple of God, which temple we are.

Bearing in mind that He is referred to some 90 times in the Old Testament with 18 different designations applied to Him; and around 260 times in the New Testament with 39 different names or titles we realize His conspicuous place in this age of grace, which is the dispensation of "the ministration of the Spirit" (II Corinthians 3:8): and that it is spiritually disastrous to neglect what the Bible reveals of His activities. Pre-eminence is given to "church work" —"social work"—"mission work," but the apostles knew only one kind of work, namely the Spirit's work. This is why the Acts is saturated with His presence and presidency, and should be renamed "The Acts of the Holy Spirit through the Apostles."

Of William Arthur's fiery message, "Tongues of Fire," issued in 1856, Dr. Campbell Morgan remarked,

It was a book before its time, yet men read it—our fathers tell us—on their knees. (Here is a sentence or two from this spiritual classic.) In this age of faith in the natural, and disinclination to the supernatural, we want especially to meet the credo—"I believe in the Holy Ghost." May the Spirit enable us to challenge the spirit of the age thus! God forbid that we should live and serve as the Ephesians who had sadly neglected, or who had acted ignorantly of the Spirit, and who, when brought face to face with His claims, declared that they had "not so much as heard whether there be any Holy Ghost" (Acts 19:2).

2. Because it is a misunderstood doctrine

Are we not safe in affirming that there is not another aspect of Biblical truth so misunderstood as that of the ministry of the Spirit? Through a lack of this understanding of His nature and labors endless confusion reigns—confusion resulting in heartache and spiritual disaster.

No one can amass printed material on the Spirit without encountering conflicting theories. And what bitterness is sometimes expressed by one section of believers who cannot endorse the opinion strenuously held by another group. As the late Dr. Campbell Morgan so forcefully expressed it,

The greatest peril which threatens the truth of the Spirit's personal ministry today, arises from the advocacy of the Truth by those who are not careful to discover there have been launched a number of wholly unauthorized systems, which have brought bondage where the Spirit would have brought liberty.

One aspect of misunderstanding is referred to by Dr. Dale who speaks of those

who are still sitting in the upper chamber, waiting, praying, longing for the coming of the Spirit; not knowing that the Spirit came almost nineteen hundred years ago with a mighty rushing wind and tongue of fire: that He has never left the Church: that there is therefore no reason for Him to come again. He is here, for according to the words of Christ, the spirit having come abides with us forever.

Satan has two methods of procedure with regard to truth. First, he seeks to hide the vision. When that is no longer possible, when any truth with its inherent brilliance and beauty drives away the mists, then Satan's method is that of patronage and falsification. He endeavors to take it out of its true proportion and turn it into deadly error.

3. Because it is a perverted doctrine

This aspect arises out of the one just considered, for misunderstanding and perversion are inseparably allied. Just now let us consider one aspect of this perversion.

In his concern, lest the converts in Corinth should be drawn from "the simplicity that is in Christ," Paul indicates for them three characteristic marks of false teaching —another Jesus—another Spirit—another Gospel (II Corinthians 11:4). It may be profitable to examine this trinity of perversion or compendium of error.

Another Jesus. It was clearly evident to Paul and the Corinthian believers that the "Jesus" of the false teachers of Galatia and of Corinth was not the "Jesus" they knew— not the Saviour of a lost world the apostle so vigorously preached. And the "Jesus" of present-day Modernism, beautiful and holy though He may be, is still only the peasant of Galilee, and not the Christ of God invested with all the prerogatives of deity. The "Jesus" of modern, cultured thought is not the "Jesus" of the gospels and the epistles: not the "Jesus" of the Church for well-nigh two millenniums: not the "Jesus" martyrs and covenanters died for: not the "Jesus" we believe Him to be, who died, rose again, ascended into heaven there to intercede for us until He shall appear in great glory for His redeemed ones.

Another Gospel. This different gospel was not the one the Corinthians had received from Paul, namely the gospel of pardon through faith working by love. The perverted gospel he refers to was one based on the old Pharisaic lines of works, ritual, ceremonial and moral precepts.

Alas, the old-fashioned Gospel of the grace of God is not fashionable in some quarters today! The Gospel of redeeming blood, of salvation by faith is treated as worn-out theology. Advancing knowledge has brought us a gospel of ethics, a social gospel, salvation by works. But as Paul warns us, "If any man preach any other gospel unto you than that ye have received, let him be accursed" (Galatians 1:7-9).

Another Spirit. From Ellicott's most illuminating "Commentary" on the Scriptures we have this interpretation—

> The words, "Another Spirit," point to a counterfeit inspiration, perhaps like that of those who had interrupted the praises of the Church with the startling cry, "Anathema to Jesus!" . . . Such as these were the "false prophets" of II Peter 2:1; I John 4:3 simulating the phenomena of inspiration, perhaps thought of by the apostles as really acting under the inspiration of an evil spirit.

Modernism in our age has produced "another Spirit," one who has no gracious personality, no deity, but whose manifold works are simply emanations. To quote the findings of the modernistic school of thought, "what the New Testament denotes by 'Holy Spirit' is the divine dynamic energy, pregnant with all the potencies of 'spiritual' or supernatural life, which passed, as in the nervous system of a human organism from head to body, animating and controlling all the members and constituting the whole mystic or spiritual Messianic organism, humanity indwelt by God." All of which verbosity is a polite way of bowing out the august Person of the Spirit from the Biblical revelation of His real substance and service.

A cry for "another Spirit" of a more diabolical sort, however, fills the air. One sure mark of our Lord's speedy return is a greater manifestation of "seducing spirits" (I Timothy 4:1). And it is the Spirit Himself who expressly warns us against counterfeits of His Person and work.

The "Spirit" at the back of "spiritualism" and all spiritist forces is not the Holy Spirit we love and revere. It is "another spirit," even the Evil Spirit, the satanic antagonist of the Good Spirit.

What we need, therefore, is a closer study of the Spirit of grace, as He is revealed in Scripture! and nothing can save the perverted, God-dishonoring factions laboring under the cloak of Christianity from deeper apostasy apart from a repentant return to the Holy Spirit Himself. Once He assumes Lordship, a true antidote is found for all perversion, error, apostasy and spiritual barrenness. When He is dethroned nothing but chaos can reign.

4. Because it is a Scriptural doctrine

Dr. A. J. Gordon, who has given us one of the most wonderful books ever written on the Spirit's ministry, implied that there is no need to prove His Person and prerogatives when they are so clearly taught by Christ in John 14-16. "The discussion," he says, "of the personality of the Holy Spirit is so unnatural in the light of Christ's last discourse that we studiously avoid it." But while such a position is tenable from the standpoint of orthodox believers, we are exhorted to "prove all things." It is to this, then, that we bend ourselves to the task of outlining what the Bible teaches as to the reality and resources of the Spirit.

Some, there are, who belittle the importance of the study before us through a misconception of what our Lord said of the Spirit in John 16:13—"He shall not speak of himself." Such a description is taken to imply self-effacement. If, in all humility the Spirit never speaks of Himself, then why should we say much about Him? This, of course, is a misinterpretation of the phrase, as the next qualifying statement proves— "Whatsoever he shall hear, that shall he speak." A comparison of one or two translations will help to clarify the matter.

The Revised Version has it, "He shall not speak from himself."

Dr. Weymouth expresses it, "He will not speak as Himself originating what He says, but all that He hears He will speak." Moffat translates the phrase, "He will not speak of his own accord." All of which implies that the Spirit does not act or speak on His own authority or initiative. He does not originate the truth He utters—receiving it from God, He, in turn, communicates it to others.

Our Lord's declaration of the Spirit's subordination is in contrast to the attitude of human teachers, as He indicates in a previous chapter—"He that speaketh of himself (that is, acting on his own authority) seeketh his own glory" (John 7:18). Heaven-sent teachers do not speak on their own authority. "I have given unto them the words which thou gavest me" (17:8).

Believing as we do that the Bible was inspired by the Holy Spirit, it is not surprising to find His own visible marks across its sacred pages from Genesis 1:2 to Revelation 22:17. And it is these marks we are going to trace.

5. Because it is a practical doctrine

Conduct, as we know it, is regulated by creed. It is necessary, therefore, to clearly and fully grasp the truth of the Spirit in order that His purposes and character may be revealed in and through our lives. It is not enough to formulate theories regarding His manifestation. All we discover must have a direct bearing upon our lives.

It is a truism that what we most constantly think about, exercises a transforming power over life. A miser, all unconsciously shows his greed and fascination of gold. The ambitious, unscrupulous man cannot hide the cunning schemes he evolves. Pleasure seekers cannot cover up the voluptuousness of their mind. "As he thinketh in his heart, so is he" (Proverbs 23:7).

Thus our aim should be to know the truth, the whole truth and nothing but the truth of the Spirit in such a way as to produce a life of richer devotion and holiness. The Word must become flesh and go out and dwell among men. And that such a theme is intensely and immensely practical is emphasized by Dr. A. T. Pierson's heart-searching words:

If the Spirit dwells in the body of Christ, and is left free to work His own will, He will quicken the whole body. Members will have a new care one for another, suffering and rejoicing together. There will be a holy jealousy for the welfare and happiness of all who belong to the mystical body, and an earnest and loving co-operation in all holy work. All schism, whether manifest in inward estrangement or in outward separation becomes impossible so far as the Spirit of Truth indwells; and all apathy and inactivity in the face of a dying world will give way to sympathetic activity when and so far as the Spirit of Life thrills the body; even as all ignorance of God and superstitious worship of forms flee like owls of the night when the Spirit of God shines in His divine splendor. In a word, all needs of the Church are met so surely and speedily as the Holy Ghost, who still abides in the Church as God's only earthly temple, resumes by the consent and co-operation of disciples, His normal control, actively guiding into all truth and duty.

Must we not confess that a deficient study of the Third Person of the Trinity has resulted in dryness of spiritual experience, a low level of Christian life, formalism in worship, want of discipline in the Church, lack of zeal in missionary enterprise, indifferences to social improvement, schisms embittered by partisan rivalry?

And, further behind all negligence, perversion and rejection of the Spirit's operations is the hidden hand of Satan, for he fully realizes how detrimental to his satanic plans is a perfect understanding of His work and an entire submission to His sway.

The Spirit of Study

It does not matter what realm of investigation may open to one, the spirit or manner in which it is approached, largely determines the measure of success in the pursuit of required knowledge. The scientist with his problems; the naturalist and his studies; the scholar with his quest for knowledge, all alike realize that the frame of mind with which they face their tasks prepares them in a very definite way for their discoveries. What, then, should be the right spirit to adopt as we study one of the holiest of themes?

1. Devotionally

Has not our Lord a somewhat daring word about casting pearls before swine, and giving that which is holy unto the dogs (Matthew 7:6)? Surely, one evident application of such a drastic declaration is that the Holy Spirit will not unveil His magnificence and power unless we strive to maintain a right heart-attitude as we approach such a meditation as this. As we read the pages of this book we must constantly pray that an ever-growing knowledge may be ours and that immediate and implicit obedience to light received will be given. If such a study does not lead to fuller submission to the will of God, to a complete consecration, to a deeper passion for souls, then our goal will not be reached. Light apart from obedience is apt to become darkness, and how great is this darkness!

2. Dependently

There is no reason to linger here. It is taken for granted that we realize our need of a prayerful, absolute reliance upon the Lord for guidance and tuition. May we be saved from studying the truth of the Spirit without the direct aid of the Spirit of Truth Himself!

Paul exhorts us to remember that spiritual verities are not discoverable by human wisdom, but revealed and taught by the Spirit (I Corinthians 2:9-16). What is hid from the wise, who are proud of their wisdom, is revealed unto babes, and as Dr. R. A. Torrey used to say, "the baby method is the best one for discovering truth."

3. Doctrinally

As we come to analyze the various aspects of the Spirit's work, we must be prepared to lay aside our preconceived notions or theories. Our judgment must not be beclouded. We must be ready and willing to think God's thoughts of the Spirit after Him.

The Berean method of searching the Scriptures daily to see whether "[these] things were so" (Acts 17:11) is one to copy as we grapple with any doctrine. And one result occurring from a prayerful, patient and systematic approach to any phase of Scriptural truth is that it becomes a settled conviction. Further, when confronted by the theories, opinions, speculations of men we instantly receive or reject, by the law and testimony deeply embedded within our own mind.

The Scriptures and the Spirit

A close study of Scripture reveals three great dispensations or ages, in which one Person in the Godhead is prominent.

In the Old Testament we have the dispensation of the Father. In it He is at work for us. His promises are scattered everywhere, and must be realized in experience.

In the gospels we have the dispensation of God the Son, during which He lives with us, promising to send us the Spirit. No one before Pentecost could become a partaker of the life and fullness of the risen Saviour.

In the Acts and the epistles we have the dispensation of God the Spirit, who carries on the work of Christ in and through us. Note the progressive development—God is *for* us: *with* us; *in* us. And the Holy Three are vitally connected. The relation of the dispensation of the Spirit to that of the Father and of the Son is one of fulfillment and promise.

While such a threefold division is clearly distinct, outlining as it does, the time and ministry of each Person of the Trinity, yet because the Bible gives to us, from its opening page right on until its closing chapter, a gradual, progressive revelation or unfolding of the Spirit's Person and power, we deem it necessary to analyze the Advent of the Spirit from the moment when He is first unveiled to vision until we reach His full and final manifestation.

Old Testament Activities

Association in Creation

From the first reference to the Spirit (Genesis 1:2) to the last mention of Him in the Old Testament (Malachi 2:15), we have in 22 books out of the 39 comprising this section of the Bible, a wonderful insight into the power and prerogatives of the Spirit, even though His pre-incarnation is limited in revelation.

Of such a limited manifestation Dr. Downer writes,

> His separate Personality, although indicated, was not clearly set forth. Mankind was not prepared for the intense interest belonging to a new personality in the divine nature. They had not yet learned to know the Father perfectly. Nor again, had there yet appeared the divine Man, in whom alone the blessed Spirit could dwell without measure or hindrance, could put forth His noblest powers, could exhibit and unfold God's purpose, not made known previously to the Incarnation, by means of the Mediator's cross and Resurrection.
>
> The true abode of the Spirit was, and ever must be, the God-Man, crucified, risen, ascended, coming again . . . . In its relation to New Testament days, the Old Testament revelation of the Spirit must be regarded as an earnest, the Pentecostal revelation being the fullness. Yet, the work He did in the souls of men before Christ came, He still continues to do, but more perfectly, inasmuch as it is done now in closest connection with the Son of God, Incarnate, crucified, ascended and glorified.

Turning to the Spirit's initial work in creation, we must bear in mind the comment of Bishop Handley Moule, that He is mysteriously, yet distinctly revealed as the immediate divine Agent in the making and manipulation, so to speak, of material things.

Strange, is it not, that although the Holy Spirit is thus named partly because of the contrast to His substance with that which is material, yet He is so definitely connected with a world of matter? In fact, Biblical writers scarcely took into their thinking the idea of second causes, as many modern writers as they seek to ascertain a rational reason for all that is seen. To holy men of old the phenomena of nature was the result of God's direct action through His Eternal Spirit. Let us then, examine the creative works of this "Veni Creator."

1. He is Co-Creator of the world.

There are at least three key passages proving the Spirit's share in the creation of the universe.

"The Spirit of God moved upon the face of the waters" (Genesis 1:2).
"By His Spirit He hath garnished the heavens" (Job 26:13).
"Thou sendest forth Thy Spirit, they are created" (Psalms 104:30; 147: 14-18).

In the latter passages the Psalmist refers to all aspects of creation.

Recognizing what Dr. A. T. Pierson called "The Law of First Mention," our first glimpse of the Spirit in Scripture is that of a Creator (Genesis 1:2). And this is as it should be, seeing that creative power is a dominant feature of His activities.

Before God said, "Let there be light," He said, "Let there be Spirit," comments Dr. George Matheson. It was the keynote of all His voices to the human soul. It is no use to bring light until you have brought the Spirit. Light will not make the waters of life glad unless the Spirit of joy has already moved them . . . . It is well that the Spirit should come before all His gifts—before the light, before the firmament, before the herb of the field."

Alas, we are guilty of inverting the order of the Spirit's work, and crave for gifts rather than the Giver! What we cry for is light, sun, moon and stars; for the green herb, for the birds of heaven, forgetting that without the Giver Himself there could not be light to charm, grass to grow, birds to sing. As Dr. Matheson prayed, "Without Thee the days of my creation are evenings without mornings: the nightless Sabbath shall have dawned when Thou shalt move upon the waters."

2. He is Co-Creator of man.

The *Nicene Creed* speaks of the Spirit as "The Lord, the Life-Giver," and a combination of further passages describing Him as the direct Agent in the creation of man, just as He is responsible for His re-creation. As "the breath of the Almighty," He imparts life to nature and man. Generation and regeneration are among His activities.

"Let us make man in our image, after our likeness" (Genesis 1:26).
"(He) breathed into his nostrils the breath (spirit) of life" (Genesis 2:7).
"The spirit of God hath made me, and the breath of the Almighty hath given me life" (Job 33:4).

Man likes to have an honorable pedigree. He is proud of a good ancestry, an ancestry whose character was goodness.

We have an ancestry which goes back beyond nature, beyond maternity, beyond the flesh. We have a pedigree which is older than the mountains, older than the stars, older than the universe. We are come from a good stock: we are branches of a high family tree: we are scions of a noble house, a house not made with hands, eternal in the heavens. Nature is the parent of our flesh, but the Divine is the Father of our spirits, the Spirit of God hath made us, and the breath of the Almighty has given us life.

This poetic description of our heritage, taken from Dr. George Matheson's "Voices of the Spirit," proves the divinity of our origin. We did not gradually evolve from lower forms of creation. God the Spirit was responsible for our being.

3. He is Co-Creator of the animal world.

It is no degradation of our nature to declare that the same Spirit responsible for our creation fashioned all that has breath. "To believe that God's Spirit is the missing link between ourselves and the animal world," says one writer, "is to reach a Darwinism where there is nothing to degrade. We did not come from them, but we and they together are the offspring of God."

"Thou sendest forth Thy Spirit, they are created" (Psalm 104:27-30). It is evident from the immediate context that the "all," and the "they," refer to the living creatures of the whole world, and to beasts, birds and fish in particular (104:25, 26; Genesis 1:21).

Two thoughts emerge from this aspect of the Spirit's creative work. First of all, seeing we are bound together with the animal world by one Spirit of creation, we cannot be cruel to those creatures sharing our natural life. Here is the greatest argument in favor of a well-known society "The Prevention of Cruelty to Animals."

In the second place seeing we sit at "the one communion table of nature" (cf. Isaiah 65:24,25) the animal world will also share in the fruits of Christ's redemption, and experience a mighty deliverance when He comes to reign as the Prince of the Kings of the earth (Romans 8:19-22).

4. He is the Co-Creator of beauty

Job tells us that it was the Holy Spirit who garnished or beautified, made splendid, the heavens (Job 26:13). Paul discourses on the respective glory of the sun, moon and stars and staggers us with the thought that "one star differeth from another star in glory" (I Corinthians 15:41). And, truly, "the heavens declare the glory of God" (Psalm 19:1-6).

Matthew Henry, one of the most suggestive of Bible commentators, has this expressive comment:

> The Spirit not only made the heavens, but beautified them: has curiously bespangled them with stars by night, and painted them with the light of the sun by day. God, having made man to look upward (to man he gave an erect countenance) has therefore garnished the heavens, to invite him to look upward, that by pleasing his eye with the dazzling light of the sun, and the sparkling light of the stars, their number, order and various magnitudes, which as so many golden studs, beautify the canopy drawn over our heads, he may be led to admire the greater Creator, the Father and Fountain of Lights, and to say, "If the pavement be so richly inlaid, what must the palace be!" If the visible heavens be so glorious, what are those that are out of sight! From the beauteous garniture of the antechambers, we may infer the precious furniture of the presence-chamber. If stars are so bright, what are angels!

But the Spirit is not only the Creator of all beauty above, He is likewise responsible for beauty all around us in a world "where every prospect pleases." What a wealth of loveliness, richness of variety, color and form nature presents! It is here that we can appreciate Psalm 29, especially when we remember that the creative Voice spoken of therein is the Holy Spirit Himself, whom Ezekiel describes as "the voice of the Almighty" (Ezekiel 10:5).

5. He is Co-Creator of substance.

Few of us realize that the continual harvests of the fields are made possible by the Holy Spirit. Combining, however, the following passages we come to praise the Spirit as our daily Provider and Benefactor.

"Until the Spirit be poured upon us from on high, and the wilderness be a fruitful field, and the fruitful field be counted for a forest" (Isaiah 32:13-16). "These wait all upon Thee; that Thou mayest give them their meat in due season" (Psalms 104:27; cf. 136:25; 145:15,16; 147:9).

And what the blest Spirit is within the realm of nature, He is also within the realm of grace. Spiritual harvests and renewals are dependent upon His gracious visitations. Food for the maintenance of our spiritual lives is likewise derived from such a bountiful Source. He it is who feeds our hungry souls with the Bread of Life.

6. He is the Co-Creator of rest.

What a tender, considerate Holy Spirit we have! Who would ever think of associating the sweet, refreshing sleep of hard wrought animals with the gracious Spirit! Yet it is so, for as the Spirit of Life He renews, reinvigorates both man and beast alike with the priceless boon of rest (Psalm 127:2). "As the cattle that go down into the valley, the Spirit of Jehovah caused them to rest" (Isaiah 63:14, R.V.).

And as the gentle Dove, He can put to sleep those fears, doubts and turbulent forces within our hearts making for disquietude and unrest.

"Thou art motion, Thou art rest."

Such a spiritual application is beautifully emphasized in these unforgettable words taken from Dr. Matheson's cameos of the third Person.

> The Spirit gives us rest by abasing our animal nature, "as the beast goeth down into the valley." The process by which the cattle go down into the valley is not restful; it is the descent of a steep. Their rest is reached by unrest—by movement downward. Even so is it with spiritual rest. It is only in the valley of humiliation that thou canst find it. By nature thou art in the mountains. Thou art standing on the hilltop of vanity: thou seest nothing above thee: thou art low unto thyself . . . God's Spirit must lead thee down as the cattle are led down. Thou must be brought down into a lowly place where thy pride shall die . . . . O glorious shadows that hide me from my own shadow, O gentle valley that divides me from the mountains of my pride, O wondrous evening that shelters me from the burden and heat of my selfish care, O rest of love that means the awakening of all that is noble, it is worth while to be brought down that I may repose in Thee.

7. He is Co-Creator of death.

The Holy Spirit, as the Life Giver, able to make alive and continually quicken the body, is also able to take life away. At the command of God, the Spirit looses "the silver cord," breaks "the golden bowl" (Ecclesiastes 12:6,7). Look at these further Spirit passages: "My Spirit shall not always strive with man, for that he also is flesh" (Genesis 6:3; 7:22). "The grass withereth, the flower fadeth: because the Spirit of the Lord bloweth upon it: surely the people is grass" (Isaiah 40:7; cf. Psalms 104: 29; 147:16,17). Turning to Acts 5:1-4 we find that the same Spirit can also produce sudden death.

8. He is Co-Creator of Christ's human body.

As the Spirit formed the first Adam without natural agency, so He fashioned the body of the last Adam apart from the ordinary course of nature. Christ's birth was miraculous, not in formation of His body within the womb of Mary, but in the manner of its begetting. Our Lord's birth was supernatural in that He was created as the result of a divine creative act apart from natural generation. He was conceived of the Holy Spirit (Matthew 1:20).

Further, it was this direct act of the Spirit within the body of Mary that produced, not only a human body for Christ, but a sinless one (Luke 1:35). Christ's body in which He lived, toiled, suffered and died, was glorified and taken up to heaven. And, as Rabbi Duncan expressed it, "The dust of the earth is on the throne of the Majesty on high."

Such a body, however, was composed of flesh and blood received from Mary, who although a virgin was tainted with original sin. Job asks, "How can he be clean that is born of a woman?"—"Who can bring a clean thing out of an unclean? not one" (Job 14:4). How can we account for Christ's sinlessness? The mystery is solved by the phrase, "The Holy Spirit shall . . . overshadow thee" (R.V.). As the Spirit of Holiness, consecrated and purified that part of the virgin's flesh whereof Christ, according to the flesh, was fashioned. A writer of a past generation put it thus—"As the alchemist extracts and draws away the dross from gold, so the Holy Ghost refines and clarifies that part of the virgin's flesh, separating it from sin. Though Mary herself had sin, yet that part of her flesh, whereof Christ was made, was without sin, otherwise it must have been an impure conception."

Thus, what happened from the divine side, was "a divine, created miracle wrought in the production of this humanity which secured from its earliest germinal beginning, freedom from the slightest taint of sin." No wonder one of the old divines exclaims, "I can scarce get past His cradle in my wondering to wonder at His cross. The infant Jesus is in some views a greater marvel than Jesus with the purple robe and the crown of thorns."

9. He is Co-Creator of the new nature.

Our Lord's birth by the Spirit is a type of our new birth or rebirth. "That which is born of the Spirit" (John 3:6)—"Born . . . of God" (1:13)—"Through the Spirit . . . being born again" (I Peter 1:22,23)—"A new creation" (II Corinthians 5:17 R.V. margin).

The notable difference between the creation of our Lord's physical nature, and the creation of our spiritual nature by the selfsame Spirit can be expressed in this way—At the virgin birth of Christ there added to His already existing divine nature, a human nature, while at our rebirth the Spirit adds to an already existing human nature, a divine nature.

Regeneration does not make a sinner a better man, but brings in a new man. The old nature is not improved. By faith the believing one is made a partaker of the divine nature.

10. He is Co-Creator of the Church.

Pentecost marks the birthday of the Church of Jesus Christ. Previously, the disciples existed as units but through the coming of the Spirit they were fused together into the mystic fabric Paul called "the church of God" (Acts 20:28).

Responsible for the Lord's physical body, the Spirit produces His mystical body of which Christ is the Head. And having brought the Church into being, the Creator-Spirit graciously condescends to indwell such a holy creation, thereby, making it His habitation. (Ephesians 2:19-22).

11. He is Co-Creator of the Scriptures.

While over 40 writers were employed in the compilation of Scripture, it possessed only one divine Author. "Holy men of God spake as they were moved by the Holy [Spirit]" (II Peter 1:21; cf. I Peter 1:10,11; II Timothy 3:16; II Samuel 23:2, 3).

And having inspired the Scriptures, the Spirit alone is able to unfold their treasures to obedient hearts. He it is who guides us into all truth and grants us spiritual discernment (John 16:13-15; I Corinthians 2:10-14). Proud man, exalting his acquired knowledge and culture, endeavors to understand the Word of God by the light of his own natural reason, but remains totally ignorant of its spiritual content. Truth is revelation, and such revelation can only come from the Spirit of wisdom and revelation.

12. He is the Co-Creator of the new creation.

While there are no direct Scriptures linking the Spirit to the new creation as being His express work, yet the inference is that having been commissioned by God to act in a creative capacity, He will have a share in the last creation, magnificent beyond degree. The new heavens and a new earth will form the climax of His creations. They will form His masterpiece (Isaiah 65:17; 66:22; II Peter 3:12,13; Revelation 21:1).

With this aspect of the Spirit's activities before us we can understand the holy joy and exaltation possessing such a Creator as He carried John to a great and high mountain and unfolded to his adoring gaze "that great city, the holy Jerusalem, descending out of heaven from God" (Revelation 1:10; 21:10). And, believing that the holy city is "the Bride, the Lamb's wife," that is, the church in government and millennial splendor, we can detect a beautiful combination in such a fact. The Church is not yet without spot and wrinkle. Here below, although the creation of the Spirit, she has many blemishes, living as she does in a corrupt and hostile world. But when she is glorified and made entirely holy, then she is to have a world akin to her perfect nature. Thus, the last creative act of the Spirit is to prepare an absolutely holy home for an absolutely holy Bride and Bridegroom.

Association with Old Testament Characters

Classifying the manifold operation of the Holy Spirit in, through and upon certain Biblical characters is indeed a most profitable study.

Before attempting such an analysis, however, it must be made clear that in the Old Testament the Spirit is found working in an external way. He came upon different men endowing them for different purposes with different kinds of power.

While it is true that He did enter several individuals (Genesis 41:38; Exodus 31:3; Numbers 27:18; Nehemiah 9:30; Daniel 4:8,9; I Peter 1:10,11), yet His incoming was more of an inworking than an indwelling. Remaining among men, He did not abide with them (cf. Psalm 51:11; Haggai 2:5).

In the New Testament, where we have the fuller and final revelation of the Spirit's activities, His internal work is strongly emphasized. He now comes, not merely upon men, but into their hearts, there to remain until death or translation at Christ's return (John 14:16). His coming in the Old Testament was very intermittent, but in the New Testament the glorified Christ sent Him as the permanent Gift to His own.

And so, as it has been expressed, in the Old Testament we have the Spirit of God coming upon men, and working on them in special times and ways, working from above, without and inward. In the New, we have the Holy Spirit entering them and dwelling within them, working from within, outward and upward. Let us, then, trace His footsteps in Old Testament Scriptures.

1. As seen in rulers and kings

As the Dispenser of blessings, the Spirit, as the Executive of the Godhead bestows administrative, governmental and legislative abilities. He inspired leadership and military efficiency and all functions of government legislation, executive, judicial; the direction of troops and the defense of the country.

Joseph received administrative and governmental power (Genesis 41:39).

By the Spirit, Joseph was given political wisdom and ruled wisely and well for Pharaoh. And many national problems would cease if rulers today would choose Spirit-filled men with administrative ability as Pharaoh did.

Moses and the seventy elders were endued with power of leadership (Numbers 11:17-29). The Spirit shared the burden of the people, Moses had carried above with the chosen elders.

Joshua was prepared by the Spirit as successor of Moses (Numbers 27:18; Deuteronomy 34:9). Filled with the Spirit, as the Spirit of Wisdom, Joshua became famous as the leader and guide of Israel. It is ever good when one Spirit-endowed leader follows another.

Saul was associated with the Spirit in a threefold way.

By the Spirit, he was given another heart in order to prophesy (I Samuel 10: 7-10).

By the Spirit, he manifested holy and righteous anger (I Samuel 11:6).

By the Spirit, he was given over to an evil spirit (I Samuel 16:14).

David was empowered by the Spirit to reign and write.

By the Spirit he was anointed king (I Samuel 16:13-18).

By the Spirit he wrote his last message (II Samuel 23:1-3).

By the Spirit he composed all his Psalms (Matthew 22:43; Acts 1:16; 4:8; Hebrews 3:7; 4:3-7).

Amasai was given physical and moral courage (I Chronicles 12:18). And in these apostate days we certainly need men of Amasai caliber, who can say to Christ, what Amasai said to David: "Thine are we, . . . and on Thy side."

Daniel was empowered as an interpreter and ruler. This prime minister of Babylon was helped by the Spirit in a two-fold way.

He gave him power to interpret dreams (Daniel 4:8-18; 5:11).

He gave him political and administrative wisdom (Daniel 5:14; 6:2,3).

Even heathen rulers recognized the hallmark of the Spirit (cf. Genesis 41:38). Destitute of the Spirit themselves they yet recognized the presence of spiritual endue-ment in those who were Spirit-possessed.

2. As seen in power conferred upon judges

Approaching the Book of Judges for the purpose of outlining the presence and plan of the Spirit we are somewhat amazed to find that He imparted special endowments of power without necessary reference to the moral characters of the recipients. The end in view was not personal, merely to the agent, but concerned the theocratic kingdom and implied the covenant between God and Israel. Thus—

Othniel was blessed to judge and de-liver Israel (Judges 3:10).

Gideon was empowered to conquer his nation's foes (Judges 6:34).

Jephthah, by the Spirit, judged and de-livered Israel (Judges 11:29).

Samson received his herculean strength from the Spirit.

For his journeying (Judges 13:25). To slay a lion (Judges 14:6). To slay 30 Men (Judges 14:19). To slay 1000 Philistines (Judges 15:14,15).

3. As seen in the ministry of prophets

It cannot be gainsaid that the most dis-tinctive and important manifestation of the Spirit's activity in the Old Testament was in the sphere of prophecy. True prophets ascribed their messages directly to Him (Ezekiel 2:2; 8:3; 11:1,24; cf. 13:3; I Peter 1:11; 3:19; II Peter 1:21). He it was who gave them spiritual insight and foresight, and made them both forthtellers and foretellers.

It was thus that Moses and the elders prophesied (Numbers 11:17-29).

It was thus that Balaam proclaimed the glory of Israel (Numbers 24:2).

"The case of Balaam," says Professor E. Mullins, "presents difficulties. He does not seem to have been a genuine prophet; but rather a diviner, although it is declared that the Spirit of God came upon him. Balaam serves, however, to illustrate the Old Testament point of view. The chief interest was the national or theocratic or covenant ideal, not that of the individual." Saul presents a similar example. The prophet was God's messenger speaking God's message by the Spirit. His message was not his own. It came directly from God, and at times, overpowered the prophet with its urgency, as in the case of Jeremiah (Jeremiah 1:4-10).

God sometimes uses bad men and dis-obedient believers (Numbers 20:11-13; 23:5; I Samuel 10:10), not because they are bad or disobedient, but because they are the best material at hand for the ac-complishment of His purpose. Balaam, for example, was unworthy of being used by the Spirit and therefore will receive no reward for his work. May we covet to be used by the Spirit because we are worthy of being used!

In order, we have other prophets associ-ated with the Spirit:

Saul and his messengers (I Samuel 9: 19-24).

Elijah (I Kings 18:12; II Kings 2:16).

Elisha (II Kings 2:15).

Zedekiah (False) (I Kings 22:21,24; II Chronicles 18:23).

Azariah (II Chronicles 15:1).

Isaiah (Acts 28:25).

Jeremiah (Jeremiah 1:9; 30:1,2).

Ezekiel (Ezekiel 2:2; 3:12,14; 8:3; 9:1, 5; 36:26,27; 37:1,14; 39:29).

Daniel (Daniel 4:8,9).

Joel (Joel 2:28; Acts 2:16,17).

Micah (Micah 3:8; cf. 2:7).

All the prophets (Nehemiah 9:20; Proverbs 1:23; Zechariah 7:12; Acts 11:28; I Peter 1:11; 3:19; II Peter 1:21).

4. As seen in the service of priests

Closely allied with the ministry of the prophet was that of the priest—the prophet going out to man from God; the priest, going to God from man. Believers are both prophets and priests.

Samuel exercised both offices, being Israel's prophet-priest while the nation was a theocracy.

Among the priests operating by the Spirit, mention can be made of the following:

Jahziel encouraged those to whom he was sent (II Chronicles 20:14,17).

Zechariah rebuked Israel (II Chronicles 24:20).

Zacharias and Christ (Luke 1:5,67).

Priestly work foreshadowed Calvary (Hebrews 9:6-8).

Association With Institutions

Two prominent institutions were associated with the life of Israel from Moses to Christ, namely the Tabernacle and the Temple, the latter being the most permanent structure for religious exercises. And in the erection of these dwelling places of God, certain individuals possessing natural talent and skill received a special enduement of the Holy Spirit, of a constructive and artistic nature.

1. The Tabernacle

Bezaleel and others received artistic beauty and practical skill to work in all manner of workmanship (Exodus 31:1-6; 35:30-32; cf. 28:3).

The Spirit gave wisdom to make priestly garments (Exodus 28:3; 31:3).

He also inspired the people to give liberally (Exodus 35:21,22).

The same Spirit revealed that the Tabernacle was only temporary and typical (Hebrews 9:8).

2. The Temple

The Spirit was also related to the more glorious permanent shrine prepared for by David, and built by Solomon.

All plans for the building of the Temple came from the Spirit (I Chronicles 28:12).

He also inspired the prophecy of its rebuilding in the latter days (Zechariah 4:6). This promise seems to indicate that where man's power and wisdom will be useless, the Spirit of the Lord would cause the Temple to be rebuilt.

Association With Nations

The first indication in Scripture of the Spirit's ministry in respect to national affairs is in Genesis 6, where it is said that He would not always strive with men. It may be that He was the direct Agent in the destruction overtaking the antediluvians. Noah, we know preached and prophesied to them by the Spirit (I Peter 3:18,19).

In the following outline it will be found that the Spirit was not only associated with Israel as a nation, but through her, with surrounding nations. Israel was chosen by God from among the nations, not that He might regard her as a favorite, but that through the chosen race He might gather a vast multitude unto Himself out of every tribe, tongue and nation. Here, then, is a summary of the Spirit's association with Israel.

He foretold her beauty and order (Numbers 24:1-9).

He was her Companion (Haggai 2:5).

He was her Teacher (Nehemiah 9:20).

He revealed her failure (II Chronicles 24:20).

He was grievously sinned against by her (Isaiah 63:10; Micah 2:7; Acts 7:51).

He witnessed against her (Nehemiah 9:30).

He denied her blessing (Psalm 95:7-11; Hebrews 3:7-19).

He predicts her judgment (Micah 3:8).

He promises fullness to her King (Isaiah 11:1-3; 42:1; 48:16; 61:1).

He proclaims her restored fruitfulness (Isaiah 32:15, 16; 44:3).

He guards her interest (Isaiah 59:19).

He equips her Messiah to establish her (Isaiah 61:1-11).

He prophesies wonderful times for her (Ezekiel 2:2; 3:12-14; 8:3. cf. Joel 2:28,29; Zechariah 12:10).

In some old Bibles the headnotes indicate that all the blessings spoken of in the Old Testament were for the Church, and all the curses for the Jews. It is, of course, superfluous to say that such introductions are not a part of original Scripture, but simply the additions of men. The Church is not revealed in the Old Testament as Paul clearly teaches (Ephesians 3:1-5). Thus, all the blessings are primarily for those to whom they were given, namely Israel.

But while all the above is true, the Church, however, has the "life-rent" of many of the foregoing Spirit-inspired promises given to the Jew. Although given to Israel and partially fulfilled on her behalf, their complete fulfillment is in abeyance owing to her disobedience. And now, owing to the Pentecostal effusion of the Spirit, the Church has every right to enjoy the "life-rent" of such promises. Israel's time of full-possession is coming.

Thus, while all the Bible is for us, it is not all about us. For example, take what the prophet has to say about the enemy coming in like a flood and the Spirit lifting up a standard against him (Isaiah 59:19). Although the promise was given to Israel and refers to her coming, final deliverance, we can yet take it and live upon it. The enemy is the devil, and all his forces—the standard is the cross and Calvary's finished work is ever the Spirit's weapon of victory over all satanic powers.

He is the embodiment of goodness (Nehemiah 9:20; Psalm 143:10).

He inspires fear of the Lord (Isaiah 11:2-5).

He represents judgment and righteousness (Isaiah 32:15-17).

He prompts devotion to the Lord (Isaiah 44:3-5).

He begets hearty obedience and a new heart (Ezekiel 36:26).

He leads the soul to repentance and prayer (Zechariah 12:10-14).

A perusal of the foregoing outlines, then, recognizes the Holy Spirit as the source of inward, moral purity, even though such a work is not so fully revealed or developed as in the New Testament. Already, under remarks on Balaam, we have noted that under the old economy, the Spirit came upon people irrespective of moral character. But in this dispensation of grace, things are totally different. Now He enters and abides within believers, and constantly endeavors to transform them into the holiness God commands—"Be ye holy."

Our possession of the Spirit depends upon our acceptance of Christ as Saviour —while His entire possession of us depends upon entire submission to His control and of the continual application of Christ's blood to our sins.

Such, then, is a glimpse of the varied work of the Spirit in Old Testament Scripture. Among His manifold bestowals we have taken cognizance of physical strength, mental power, practical skill, prophetic foresight, political wisdom, moral courage and spiritual insight. What a mighty Spirit the Third Person of the Trinity is—the Spirit of God!

Yet He is mightier now, for He is not only "the Spirit of God" but "the Spirit of Christ," which means that all included in our Lord's Incarnation, death, Resurrection, Ascension and Intercession is added to His bestowals. And this is the august One who condescends to indwell us. What grace!

As we leave the Spirit's activities in the Old Testament, it may be found profitable to indicate His names of equipment as He prepared certain individuals for their specific tasks. He acted in free sovereignty, coming upon men and even a dumb beast as He willed.

1. The Spirit "comes" upon men.

The word for "come" literally means "clothes Himself with men" and is used in three instances—

Gideon—"The Spirit of the Lord came upon Gideon" (Judges 6:34). The name means, "He that bruises, cuts off iniquity." With Gideon, the Spirit became the mantle of exhortation.

Amasai—"The spirit came upon Amasai" (I Chronicles 12:18). His name signifies, "Burden of the Lord," and with Amasai the Spirit became the mantle of courage.

Zechariah—"The Spirit of God came upon Zechariah" (II Chronicles 24:20). A suggestive name this, it means, "Remembrance" or "man of the Lord." The Spirit came upon Zechariah as the mantle of rebuke.

2. The Spirit "comes mightily upon" men.

The phrase, "comes mightily upon," literally implies that He attacked men. As a greater force He compelled them to accomplish His task. It was thus He came upon—

Samson—"The Spirit of the Lord came mightily upon Him" (Judges 14:6,19; 15:14).

Saul—"The Spirit of God came mightily upon Saul" (cf. I Samuel 10:6,10).

David—"The Spirit of the Lord came upon David" (I Samuel 16:13).

3. The Spirit is "upon" men.

"Was upon" is a milder phrase and expresses a divine enduement for the time being. For illustrations of this action turn to Numbers 11:17; 24:2; Judges 3:10; 11:

29; I Samuel 19:20,23; II Chronicles 15:1; 20:14; Isaiah 59:21; 61:1.

4. The Spirit is "in" men.

Such an incoming was not an indwelling. Entering a person He inspired them to act under His internal promptings.

Joseph—"a man in whom the Spirit of God is" (Genesis 41:38).

Joshua—"a man in whom is the Spirit" (Numbers 27:18).

Daniel—"(a man) in whom is the Spirit" (Daniel 4:8,9).

Prophets—"The Spirit of Christ . . . in them" (I Peter 1:10,11; Nehemiah 9:30).

Israel restored—"I will put a new spirit within you" (Ezekiel 11:19; 36:26).

5. The Spirit "rests" upon men.

"Rests" is a gentle word suggesting the dove-like character of the Holy Spirit. It signifies "to be at rest" as in Isaiah 57:2: "They shall rest in their beds."

Seventy elders—"The spirit rested upon them" (Numbers 11:25,26).

Elisha—"The spirit of Elijah doth rest on Elisha" (II Kings 2:15).

The Messiah—"The spirit of the Lord shall rest upon Him" (Isaiah 11:2).

6. The Spirit "enters" into men.

As the Creator-Spirit (Job 33:4; Psalm 104:30), He has the right of entry into His own creation. He has the prerogative of doing what He likes with His own. "The Spirit entered into me" (Ezekiel 2:2; 3:24).

7. He "moves" men.

The word "moves" can be taken to mean "cause to step," and, let it be said, the Spirit can cause us to "stop" as well as "step." We read that "the Spirit of the Lord began to move Samson at times" (Judges 13:25).

New Testament Activities

In contrast to the Old Testament where the Holy Spirit came upon men independent of their character, here in the New Testament conditions are set forth for the reception of the Spirit. As Scofield puts it: "The indwelling of every believer by the abiding Spirit is a New Testament blessing consequent upon the death and Resurrection of Christ (John 7:39; 16:7; Acts 2:33; Galatians 3:1-4)."

The revelation of the Holy Spirit is a progressive doctrine, and when we come to the teaching of our Lord and His apostles we find a mass of information regarding *who* the Spirit is, and *what* He is in

the world to accomplish. As His personality and deity are fully revealed in the New Testament, let us deal with these two aspects in order.

The Personality of the Spirit

Endeavoring to know the Spirit, even as He is known, we must seek after a right adjustment to this Holy One Himself. A spiritual understanding is dependent upon instant and unfailing surrender to truth revealed.

While, of course, the Scriptures do not stop to prove the Spirit's reality, but plainly state the fact, yet because some are guilty, either from ignorance or thoughtlessness, of applying neuter pronouns to Him, or of speaking of Him simply as an influence, or an emanation, both of which are errors, so unscriptural and paralyzing to the most pungent exhortations based on the believer's new life in Christ, we deem it necessary to correct same.

There are one or two introductory thoughts claiming our attention, ere we come to tangible proofs of the Spirit's personality.

1. He is an essential part of a divine revelation.

Seeing that the Bible is divinely inspired, the Holy Spirit as its Author has had a great deal to say about Himself. Everywhere, His prerogatives are before us. And from what He has revealed of Himself, the Spirit means us to understand His part in the divine economy.

2. He is the direct Agent between heaven and earth in this age.

To the Spirit has been committed the sacred task of applying redemption to believing sinners, and of making believers holy. He it is who convicts of sin, regenerates, sanctifies, teaches, guides and inspires us. We are totally dependent upon Him for all that concerns our life in Christ.

3. He is the Administrator of the Church's affairs.

This aspect of the Spirit's office work is strongly emphasized in the Acts, a book dealing with the internal economy and external obligations of the Church. Why, if churches today were controlled by the Holy Spirit as in apostolic days, their life and work would be entirely revolutionized!

It is, of course, the plan of Satan to belittle the importance of a study of the Spirit's activities, or to keep people in ignorance or error of His gracious ministry, for the devil realizes that there is nothing that can ruin his hold upon us, like a perfect understanding of the power of the Spirit.

Further, imperfect views of His mission on the earth make for spiritual barrenness. Downer, in his enlightening volume, *The Mission and Ministration of the Holy Spirit,* says, "The results of deficient attention to the study and preaching of the Third Person have appeared in dryness of spiritual experience, a low level of Christian life, formalism in worship, want of discipline in the Church, want of zeal in missionary enterprise."

Personal not Impersonal

The error of treating the Spirit in an impersonal way can be traced back to the third century, when the theory was first advanced that the Holy Spirit of God was a mere influence; an exertion of divine energy and power; an emanation from God. And such an error has continued with the Church, and is the position of modernists, as well as a few branches of the Christian church, professedly orthodox.

It is conceded that the present usage of the impersonal pronoun by many is attributable to the American Version rendering of Romans 8:16,26 where the Spirit is mentioned as "it." Such, however, is happily corrected in the Revised Version. Surely, there is nothing more dishonoring and displeasing to the Spirit than lack of recognition.

In passages like John 14:16,17; 15:26; 16;7,8 we have the Spirit revealed to us as *Him* not *it;* as the living and conscious Exerciser of true personal will and love, as truly and fully as the first "Paraclete," the Lord Jesus Christ Himself (I John 2:1).

Although He is not an influence simply or a sum or series of influences, He yet possesses divine influence. As Harriet Auber expresses it in her renowned hymn on the Spirit—

He comes, sweet influence to impart,
A gracious, willing Guest.

Our fellowship, then, as Dr. Jowett reminds us "is not with a 'something' but with a 'Somebody'; not with a 'force' but with a 'Spirit'; not with an 'it' but with 'Him.'" And this leads us to affirm that we must equally honor each of the three equal Persons forming the blessed Trinity.

"They that honour Me I will honour," is applicable to the Spirit as well as to the Father and Son. And so we raise our doxology: "Praise Father, Son and Holy Ghost."

True spiritual worship is dependent upon belief in the Spirit's personality. "It is of the highest importance from the standpoint of worship that we decide whether the Holy Spirit is a divine Person," says Dr. R. A. Torrey, "worthy to receive our adoration, our faith, our love and our entire surrender to Himself, or whether it is simply an influence emanating from God or a power or an illumination God imparts to us. If the Holy Spirit is a Person, and a divine Person, and we do not know Him as such, then we are robbing a divine Being of the worship and the faith and the love and the surrender to Himself which are His due."

Our conception of the Spirit likewise determines our attitude toward Him. If we think of Him merely as an influence then our attitude will be an active one— how can we get more of this power? But if we believe Him to be a Person then our attitude will be a passive one. Yielded, and still, our daily desire will be—How can He have more of us?

The Discussion of Important Terms

Almost 100 times we have the designation "The Holy Spirit." Let us, therefore, examine the words forming this general title.

1. *The.*

This simple word may be deemed unworthy of notice, yet in view of modernistic teaching regarding the Spirit, it is imperative to give some attention to such an unpretentious, definite article. While there are passages where "the" is omitted, there is the tendency to drop it altogether by those denying the Spirit's personality. To state the liberal view, the term, "Spirit of God," is not to be interpreted through later theological usage and identified with the Holy Spirit, more probably it is an expression for the life-giving energy of God.

Such a deduction infers that we are not to call Him who is named as "The Holy Spirit," but "Holy Spirit," that is, a holy influence or energy. It is to be used in the same sense as Roman Catholics speak of "holy water." But although the article is missing in some passages relevant to the Spirit, the fact of His personality is not obliterated. Dealing with the question of the missing article, Dr. Handley G. Moule says, "In the general light of Scripture teaching on divine influence we are abundantly secure in saying that this means nothing less than the divine Person at work."

One is not to be disturbed if they discover some commentators reminding us that the article "The" is not in the original. The Spirit Himself is still meant, although not expressly named. When the article is used attention is focused upon the Person Himself. "They were all filled with *the* Holy Spirit" (Acts 2:4 R.V.). When the article is omitted as in Acts 19:2 attention is drawn to the power of the Person. Thus it is essential to remember that when the Bible speaks of the Spirit under a metaphor or without the article the Spirit's operations rather than His Person are being emphasized.

2. *Holy.*

There must be a reason for the use of this adjective some 100 times. Why is the Spirit thus described?

Here are a few reasons:

He is essentially holy in character. Holiness is not only one of His attributes as a member of the Godhead, it is a part of His being, He *is* holy.

He came from a holy God. And all representatives of such an august, holy One must bear His image (See John 14: 26; 17:11; I Peter 1:12,16).

He is in the world to represent the Holy Saviour, "He shall glorify Me" (John 16: 7-15; Hebrews 7:26).

He strives to transform us into holy people, and advances all holy living through His indwelling and dominion. It is thus that He is called "the spirit of holiness" (Romans 1:4), for He is the One who sanctifies the believer (15:16).

And every virtue we possess
And every victory won
And every thought of holiness
Are His alone.

3. *Spirit.*

The Paraclete is called "Spirit" or "Ghost," the old English word for "Spirit," not because He is the only "Spirit" in the Godhead—"God is . . . Spirit," thereby differing from Christ, who corrected His disciples for imagining Him to be a "Spirit" (Luke 24:37-39). He carries this designation simply as One who does not have a visible body such as Jesus possessed.

Relation with the Father and the Son is expressed by "Spirit."

He is named "The Spirit of God" and "The Spirit of Christ," seeing He proceeds from both. As human breath, which is the word used for "spirit," is an invisible part of man, and represents his vitality, his life and energy, so the Spirit of God and of Christ is so designated because He is "breathed forth" or given by both for the accomplishment of their mutual purpose in and through man. The Spirit is "The Breath of God."

The term also indicated that He is in contrast to that which is material. The Spirit is opposite to all that is of the flesh, and something seen. Alexander Cruden has this illuminating comment,

The Holy Ghost is called "spirit," being as it were, breathed, and proceeding from the Father and the Son, who inspire and move our hearts by Him; or, because He breatheth where He listeth; stirring up spiritual motions in the hearts of believers, purifying and quickening them; or because He is spiritual, visible and incorporeal essence.

Again, "Spirit" indicates the particular work of Him who is the Breath of God.

As the thoughts of my mind are articulated through the action of my breath upon the vocal cords, and are transmitted in the shape of words from the inner world of my being to the outer world, so the Spirit, Wind, Breath of God, takes the thoughts of God, as well as the inexpressible yearnings of the believer, and articulates them (Romans 8:26,27).

And then, as "Spirit" the Third Person is the atmosphere in which we live. He, like the air we breathe, comes into continual and indispensable contact with our inner man, supplying our souls with the life and spirit which were in Christ (Ezekiel 37:5-10). The name "Holy Spirit" carries with it the idea of a holy, moving, vitalizing breath. At Pentecost, this mighty breath came down like a rushing wind, bringing the soul-bracing atmosphere of the very presence of God, in and around the waiting disciples (Acts 2:1-4). He is the One who, as the Wind, makes possible regeneration, and then becomes the atmosphere in which the regenerated one lives, moves and has his being (John 3:8). The Spirit also visits us like the fragrant breath from some beautiful and fruitful garden that causes us to feel the reality of that which is yet unseen, and so through hope satisfies every spiritual sense in the new nature, giving us thereby days of heaven upon earth.

4. *Third Person of the Trinity.*

This oft-quoted expression is not a Biblical one. It comes from an ancient creed. "The Third Person of the Trinity, proceeding from the Father and the Son, of the same substance and equal in power and glory, and is, together with the Father and the Son to be believed in, obeyed and worshipped throughout all ages."

The term "Trinity" is likewise a nonspiritual one. It was first formally used at the Synod of Alexandria in A.D. 317 and was coined to express the doctrine tersely. It signifies "threefoldness," and is not, as sometimes stated, an abbreviation of "Tri-Unity." One must hasten to say that this "threefoldness" of Father, Son and Spirit or the grouping together of the three Persons of the Godhead is clearly taught in Scripture (Genesis 1:26; 11:7; Matthew 28:19).

The Spirit is spoken of as being "third" not in any sense of inferiority, for no one Person in the Trinity is inferior to another. All three are coequal, coeternal as we shall presently see. He is spoken of as being "third" because of His manifestation and work. The relative functions of Father, Son and Spirit can be expressed thus—

God the Father is the original Source of everything (Genesis 1:1).

God the Son follows in the order of revelation (John 5:24-27).

God the Spirit is the Channel through which the blessings of heaven reach us (Ephesians 2:18).

Thus the order of divine performance is, *from* the Father—*through* the Son—*by* the Holy Spirit.

As the flowers or fruit form the last revealed part of the tree, so the Spirit is "third," seeing He is the last revealed personality of the Trinity. "He is 'third' not in order of time, or dignity of nature, but in order and manner of subsisting."

Therefore, "there is but one source of Deity, the Father, from whom the Holy Spirit issues through the Son, whose Image He is, and in whom He rests. The Holy Spirit is the Link between the Father and the Son, and is linked to the Father by the Son."

So God the Father, God the Son,
And God the Spirit we adore,
A sea of life and love unknown
Without a bottom or a shore.

Proofs of Personality

We now come to elaborate the truth already indicated, namely, that the Spirit is not a mere "Something," but a divine "Someone." If He were only a mere influence or force, the scriptural method of describing Him would be contradictory and unintelligible. And not only so, but once the truth of the Spirit's personality and work are realized, there opens up to one a life of blessedness and power. Here is Dr. Handley Moule's testimony:

Never shall I forget the gain to conscious faith and peace which came to my own soul, not long after the first decisive and appropriating view of the crucified Lord as the sinner's Sacrifice of peace, from a more intelligent and conscious hold upon the living and most gracious Personality of that Holy Spirit, through whose mercy the soul had got that blessed view. It was a new development of insight into the love of God.

Of course, it must be confessed as we take up the evidences of the Spirit's reality, that no saint can explain fully to himself or to others the gracious Being and ministry of the Holy Spirit, even though every Christian has experienced to some extent His work in himself, and has witnessed His power in others. A man's reach can exceed his grasp. Even the way of the eagle in the air is beyond him. Hence, his interpretation of who and what the Spirit is, is inadequate because of his inability to read or to describe his own experiences fully.

This is certain, however, every believer may know without any doubt whatever the fact of the Spirit's indwelling presence, life-giving energy and sanctifying power. Opinion may differ as to the origin and theory of the Spirit's presence in the soul— but perfect agreement as to the fact and power of His indwelling.

1. The Spirit possesses the true elements of personality.

As we usually associate personality with a body, it is somewhat difficult to comprehend the Spirit's personality seeing He does not have a material form made up of hands, feet, eyes and mouth. What we are apt to forget is that these parts of the human frame are not characteristics of personality, although they are channels of such; they simply represent corporeity, that is, they belong entirely to the body.

True personality, then, is not the outward building but the tenant within. Personality is made up of distinctive features or elements known as heart, mind and will. "Personality," it has been said, "is capacity for fellowship. The very quality which was most singularly characteristic of Jesus manifests itself in the Spirit, only more universally, more intimately, more surely." Being able to think, feel and will, the Spirit has the capacity for fellowship, which is not possible without personality.

The Heart of the Spirit

The heart is the seat of affection. With it, we love or hate, persons and things. Paul speaks of "the love of the Spirit" (Romans 15:30), and, as we have elsewhere proved, He is indeed the Spirit of love. Without a heart, comfort is not possible. Early saints could walk "in the comfort of the Holy Spirit" (Acts 9:31 R.V.). Grief is also an element of the heart. Where there is no love, there is no grief. The Spirit can be grieved (Ephesians 4:30). And how careful we have to be, lest we cause such a loving heart unnecessary pain!

The Mind of the Spirit

The mind is the source of intelligence, reason, knowledge. With our minds we think, plan, devise, comprehend. That the Spirit has a mind is evident from a study of His manifold activities. There is a beautiful precision, thought, order, plan, intelligence in all His works. The incomparable Scriptures, for example, prove His perfect mind. Paul refers to the "mind of the Spirit" (Romans 8:27), and what a mind He has as "the Spirit of Wisdom!" We speak of a person as having a mind of his own. Well, the Spirit has a mind of His own, indicating thought, purpose, decision (I Corinthians 2:10,11).

The Will of the Spirit

With our wills we act, decide, giving expression thereby to our thoughts and feelings. And true personality consists in preserving the balance between the heart, mind and will.

Turning to Acts it would seem as if the will of the Spirit more than any other phase of His personality is emphasized. For example—

It was the Spirit who commanded and removed Philip (8:29,39).

It was the same Spirit who exercised authority over Peter (10:19,20).

It was this Spirit who restrained and constrained Paul (16:6,7).

It was this Person of sovereign majesty who uses us just as He determines by His own will (I Corinthians 12:11).

Personality, then, is essential to our conception of the Spirit, as it is of those of the Father and the Son. And so, personality, implying the possession of the qualities of reason, will and love, is attributable to the Spirit, seeing He is found acting, feeling, knowing and speaking.

The practical issue of the truth of the Spirit's personality is, that because He is a Person, all relationships are personal. A man is known by the company he keeps. If, then, we live in His company and maintain a personal, unbroken relationship with Him, we shall become like Him in purpose, desires, thoughts, spiritual ideals and ambition.

He has a heart, and loves me. Let me therefore love Him and ever strive to please Him!

He has a mind, and constantly thinks and plans for me.

Let me learn of Him and take His plan for my life!

He has a will, so mighty to carry into effect all His loving plans.

May I never cross His will, but have a personality completely dominated by Him!

1. The Spirit was accepted as a Person by Christ.

Language has no meaning if the Spirit is not a Person, seeing that Jesus repeatedly employed the masculine pronoun when speaking of Him. Thirteen times over, in John 16, for example, He refers to the Spirit as *He, Him, Himself.* As the "Advocate" He holds an office only possible to a Person. "I will send you another Comforter" (John 14:16,17). Here our Lord speaks of another like Himself who would be able to intercede, help and console.

2. The Spirit's mistreatment proves His personality.

The meditation, in another part of my book on "the Sufferings of the Spirit," testifies to His gracious personality. He can be grieved, blasphemed against, insulted, lied to (Isaiah 63:10, R.V.; Ephesians 4:30; Matthew 12:31,32; Hebrews 10:29; Acts 5:3).

If the Spirit of God is simply an influence, then, there is no need to concern ourselves about man's treatment of Him, for influence is incapable of recognition, feeling or action. But, believing Him to be one of the Persons in the Godhead "we must treat Him as a Person," says Thomas Goodwin, "applying ourselves to Him as a Person, glorify Him in our hearts as a Person, dart forth beams of special and peculiar love to, and converse with Him as a Person. Let us fear to grieve Him, and also believe Him as a Person." To which we can add the sentiment of Bishop Handley Moule—

May He, the Lord, the Life Giver, personal, sovereign, loving, mighty, preserve us from unfaithfulness of regard toward His blessed Person, from untruth of view of His Divine work!

3: The Spirit's actions could only be performed by a Person.

In all, there are some 160 passages in the Old and New Testaments bearing upon the actions of the Spirit, and to deny personality to Him is to make these references meaningless and absurd. Here, for example, are some things the Holy Spirit can do—

He can search (I Corinthians 2:10). And what a Searcher! No province is beyond Him. "All things"—the things of God, of Christ, of Scripture, of the human heart He searches, then reveals His discoveries, precious or pernicious, as the case may be.

He can speak (Revelation 2:7; I Timothy 4:1). Seven times over we read, "The Spirit saith unto the churches." And His messages are reduced to the individual— "If any man hear." He is thus depicted as whispering into the ear of the saint.

And His that gentle voice we hear,
Soft as the breath of even.

He can cry (Galatians 4:6). "No language but a cry." It is in this way that He reminds us of a blessed relationship—a relationship made possible through His own regenerating work.

He can pray (Romans 8:26 R.V.). Prayer is only possible to a person. The Spirit, then, must be a Person, seeing He can articulate prayer. He is thus identified with Christ as an Intercessor (Romans 8:34; Hebrews 7:25; I John 2:1).

He can testify (John 15:26,27). It is clearly evident from these passages that if the Spirit is not a Person, neither are we endowed with personality, seeing the same ability to witness is applied to Him and ourselves. The Spirit bears witness to us, then through us, to the world.

He can teach (John 14:26; 16:12-14; Nehemiah 9:20). If the Spirit is only a divine emanation or spiritual influence then how can a mere "it" teach? The teaching of the Spirit is denied the believer and Christ proven a liar, if He is not able to lead us into all truth.

He can lead (Romans 8:14). Impersonal influence has no power of direct guidance. The Spirit, however, can gently lead into the paths of God. He is able to direct our footsteps and must therefore have life.

He can command (Acts 16:6,7 R.V.). "Forbidden of the Holy Spirit." If we accept the theory of Modernism that the Spirit is only "a divine dynamic energy," how can we account for Paul's recognition of the Spirit's administration and authority, in and over the affairs of service? To the apostle, the Spirit was the dominating personality within the Church, and had to be implicitly obeyed. Acts presents the presence and presidency of the Holy Spirit of God. And, in this age, it is only as we recognize, realize, revere, then reckon upon His Person and power that we, too, can know what it is to turn the world upside down.

4. The Spirit's titles are a further evidence of personality as well as deity.

The Scriptures present us with a remarkable array of titles and names applied to the Spirit, and patient perusal of same is a most profitable exercise. Dr. F. E. Marsh, in his *Structure of Scripture*, has given us a valuable exposition of many of these titles.

Perhaps one of the most exhaustive classifications of the Spirit's designation is that to be found in "Things of the Spirit," by C. H. MacGregor, a saintly British scholar of a past generation. Introducing his outline, which we have adapted slightly and here present, Dr. MacGregor says that

In the Scriptures we do not find that distinction between nominal and real, which is so familiar to us in the usage of ordinary life. What anything is in name, that it is in reality. The supreme example of this is found in the name of God. What God calls Himself is a revelation of what He is. Therefore, in the names of the Holy Spirit we have a rich revelation of His character and work.

New Testament Names and Titles

Within this part of Holy Writ there are some 90 direct references to the Spirit, in which He receives 18 different titles, falling into three groups. With the aid of your Bible Concordance trace these references.

A. *Those expressing His relation to God*
1. The Spirit of God—13
2. The Spirit of the Lord—23
3. The Spirit of the Lord God—1
4. The Spirit—14
5. My Spirit—13
6. Thy Spirit—4
7. His Spirit—6

B. *Those expressing His character*
1. Thy Good Spirit—1
2. A Free Spirit—1
3. Thy Holy Spirit—1
4. His Holy Spirit—2
5. A New Spirit—2

C. *Those expressing His operations upon men*
1. The Spirit of Wisdom—3
2. The Spirit that was on Moses—2
3. The Spirit of Understanding—1
4. The Spirit of Counsel and Might—1
5. The Spirit of Knowledge and of the Fear of the Lord—1
6. The Spirit of Grace and Supplication—1
7. The Spirit of Burning—1
8. The Voice of the Almighty—1
9. The Voice of the Lord—1
10. The Breath of the Almighty—1

New Testament Names and Titles

According to the Rev. C. H. MacGregor's classification there are in the New Testament 263 passages in which direct reference is made to Him, and in which 39 different designations are applied to the selfsame Spirit, falling into five separate groups.

A. *Names expressing His relation to God the Father.*
1. The Spirit of God—12
2. The Spirit of the Lord—15
3. My Spirit—3
4. His Spirit—3
5. The Promise of the Father—1
6. The Promise of My Father—1
7. The Gift of God—1
8. The Spirit of Him who Raised up Jesus—1
9. The Spirit which is of God—1
10. The Spirit of our God—1
11. The Spirit of the Living God—1
12. The Holy Spirit of God—1
13. The Spirit which He gave us—1
14. The Spirit of Your Father—1
15. The Power of the Highest—1

B. *Names expressing His relation to God the Son.*
1. The Spirit of Christ—2
2. The Spirit of Jesus (R.V.)—1
3. The Spirit of Jesus Christ—1
4. The Spirit of His Son—1
5. Another Comforter—1

C. *Names expressing His own essential deity.*
1. The Spirit—99
2. The Same Spirit—6
3. The One Spirit—5
4. The Eternal Spirit—1
5. The Seven Spirits—4

D. *Names setting forth His own essential character.*
1. The Holy Spirit—over 100
2. The Holy One—1

E. *Names setting forth His relation to the people of God.*
1. The Spirit of Truth—4
2. The Comforter—3
3. The Spirit of Holiness—1
4. The Spirit of Life—1
5. The Spirit of Adoption—1
6. The Spirit of Faith—1
7. The Spirit of Praise—1
8. The Spirit of Wisdom and Revelation—1
9. The Spirit of Power and Discipline—1
10. The Spirit of Grace—2
11. The Spirit whom He Made to Dwell in Us—1
12. The Spirit of Glory—1
13. The Anointing—2

What a magnificent array of titles and designations! Truly, the Spirit can say of Himself—"In the Volume of the Book it is written of me"; which is as true of Him as of the Christ He glorifies! And if our lives were as full of the Spirit as the Bible is, what different Christians we would be! To trace all the above references, noting the connection of each title with the context is indeed a rich and profitable meditation.

Why is the Spirit given such a variety of designations? Well, each bears its own significance and it takes them all to portray all the resources at our disposal in Him. For example, He is styled—

The Spirit of Grace, since He is the Dispenser of the divine favor to all men.

The Spirit of Supplication, because He teaches us how to pray and for what to pray.

The Spirit of Revelation, because He reveals Christ to the eye of faith.

The Spirit of Wisdom, because He imparts wisdom from above.

The Spirit of Adoption, because He certifies the believer's sonship.

The Spirit of Christ, because He was sent by the Father through the mediation of the Son.

The Spirit of Truth, because He makes the Word of Truth and "The Truth" real to us. "Theology without the Holy Spirit," said Professor Beck of Tübingen, "is not only a cold stone, it is a deadly poison."

The Spirit of the Lord God, because He shares the sovereignty of the Godhead.

The Seven Spirits of God, because of the plenitude of His power and His diversified activity.

The Deity of the Spirit

The Scriptures do not stop to prove either the personality or deity of the Holy Spirit. Everywhere, such truth is clearly expressed and constantly implied that men must be blind to miss or deny it. Quite confidently, Bible writers speak of the Spirit as God, know Him as God, and give Him the position of equality with the Father and the Son.

Paul's description of the Antichrist can be rightfully used of the Holy Spirit, who is, as we are now to see, "as God sitting in the temple of God, shewing Himself that He is God" (II Thessalonians 2:4).

1. The Spirit is acclaimed as God.

Often a combination of passages emphasizes the equality of the Persons within the Godhead. Here, for example, is a combination covering Father, Son and Spirit—

"I heard the voice of the Lord" (Isaiah 6:8-10).

"These things said Esaias, when he saw His glory" (John 12:39-41).

"Well spake the Holy Spirit through Isaiah" (Acts 28:25-27 R.V.)

In the threefold "Holy" of Isaiah 6:3, there is a distinct suggestion of the tri-personality of Jehovah. Plurality is also dominant (v. 8.)

Further evidences of equality can be traced by comparing Jeremiah 31:31-34 with Hebrews 10:15,16; Exodus 16:7 with Hebrews 3:7-9; Exodus 16:7 with II Corinthians 3:17,18, R.V. Where the word LORD is printed in capitals it means "Jehovah" (Leviticus 1:1). In Exodus 17:7 R.V. the people tempted Jehovah saying, "Is Jehovah among us, or not?" This is referred to in Hebrews 3:7-9 with Acts 28:25 the Spirit is Jehovah of Hosts. See also Psalm 78:17, 21 and Acts 7:51.

The Early Church had no doubt regarding the deity of the Spirit. Without hesitation, they applied divine names to Him. Comparing Acts 5:3,4 where Peter faces Ananias and Sapphira with their partial dedication he uses the two phrases, "Lied unto . . . God" and "Lie to the Holy Spirit" (R.V.). And the implication is that Peter believed the Spirit to be God.

2. The Spirit shares the attributes of the Father and the Son.

By "attributes" we mean those qualities and properties so conspicuous to deity. Let us briefly consider a few of these divine possessions.

Eternity. "The Eternal Spirit" (Hebrews 9:14). As the Eternal One He is uncreated, and as uncreated is divine. "Eternal" means without beginning or ending of existence. Thus, "the Spirit proceeds timelessly from the Father and is coeternal with the Father and the Son."

Omnipresence. The prefix "omni" signifies "all." An omnibus is a vehicle for all kinds of persons. This quality indicates that the possessor has power to be present everywhere at the same time. Being human, we can only be in one place at a given time. The Spirit, however, is in all believers everywhere. "Whither shall I go from thy spirit?" (Psalm 139:7-10).

Omniscience. There is nothing in, and about God, that the Spirit cannot know. Only God can search the depths of God. All that pertains to God, Christ, Satan, man, heaven and earth is known to the Spirit. "The Spirit searcheth all things" (I Corinthians 2:10-11; cf. Isaiah 40:13,14; Romans 8:26,27).

Omnipotence. Only God can do all possible things. The power of the Spirit is the power of God, who is the Omnipotent One (Revelation 19:6). Christ cast out demons by the Spirit of God (Matthew 12:28), by "the finger of God" (Luke 11:20). The Arm, Hand, Finger of God are titles descriptive of the Spirit's unlimited power (Micah 3:8; Romans 15:13-19).

Holiness. Holiness, an emphatic mark of deity, is a quality attributed to the Spirit some 100 times in Scripture. "The holy Spirit of God" (Ephesians 4:30). And, as the Holy One, He alone can make us the recipients of divine holiness.

Foreknowledge. Deity only can know the end from the beginning or possess the knowledge of a thing before it happens. And that the Spirit has "foreknowledge" is proved by Peter's declaration, "The Holy Spirit by the mouth of David spake before concerning Judas" (Acts 1:16). Thus, some 1000 years before Judas lived, the Spirit led David to make his prophecy. Another evidence of His foreknowledge, which is a phase of omniscience, is given in Acts 11:27,28.

Sovereignty. By sovereignty, or Lordship, we infer complete power of dictation. The apostles recognized this prerogative of deity that the Spirit manifested. "The Lord the Spirit"—"The Spirit saith" (II Corinthians 3:17,18 R.V.; Revelation 2:7). "The Holy Spirit said, Separate Me Barnabas and Saul for the work whereunto I (the Spirit) have called them" (Acts 13:2-4 R.V.).

3. The Spirit performs tasks only possible to Deity.

Divine works accomplished by the Spirit are of a varied nature. As the Executive of the Godhead, the Spirit is God in action. Among His many works there are—

Creation. Man can make, only God can create. Creative power being a divine prerogative was exercised by the Spirit at creation, when, as a mother bird, He brooded over a chaotic condition and produced this beautiful world of ours (Genesis 1:2). As the result of the Spirit's energy, the beauty of the earth, the glory of the sky, and wonders of oceans came into being. Thus, Cowper in "The Task" expresses it—

One Spirit—His
Who wore the platted thorns with bleeding brow,
Rules universal nature. Not a flower

But shares some touch, in freckle, streak or stain,
Of His unrivaled pencil.

Inscribed upon Ruskin's Memorial at Friar's Crag, Keswick, England, are the words,

The Spirit of God is around you in the air you breathe. His glory in the light that you see, and in the fruitfulness of the earth and joy of His creatures. He has written for you day by day His revelation, as He has granted you day by day your daily bread.

The Spirit created the world (Psalm 33:6; Genesis 1:2)—created man (Job 33:4)—beautified the world (26:13)—brings death upon it (Isaiah 40:7)—brings life into it (Psalm 104:30).

Inspiration. In Biblical usage *inspire* means "one who is instructed by divine influence." Thus, when Bible writers are spoken of as being borne along by the Spirit, we are to understand them as having minds and pens controlled by the Spirit. The word "inspiration" is made up of two Latin words, *in* or "unto," and *spirare*, meaning "to breathe." And so to be inspired by the Spirit indicates one into whom He has breathed the truth He desires him to know and declare.

The Spirit came upon individuals both in the Old and New Testaments, causing them to deliver inspired messages (II Samuel 23:1-3).

The Spirit inspired prophecy in general (I Timothy 4:1).

The Spirit inspired Scriptures as a whole (II Timothy 3:16; II Peter 1:21).

Regeneration. As the Spirit of Life, and able to give life, He generated material and physical life at creation—brought into being the God-Man, a life so unique and marvelous—and now produces spiritual life in all who believe (II Corinthians 3:6; Romans 8:11).

The Holy Spirit is the personal Agent in the new birth, and the instrument He uses is the Word of Truth (John 3:1-8). We enter and see the kingdom of God, not by any material process, not by any ceremonial act, not by any self-determination, but by the power of the Spirit of God (1:13).

After quickening and giving life, He indwells those whom He quickens (I Corinthians 3:16), and then endeavors to indwell them fully (Ephesians 5:18). The Spirit abides in those He regenerates as the Seal and the Earnest of our final redemption and future blessedness. And through His indwelling, the Spirit sanctifies (Romans 15: 16; Titus 3:5; I Peter 1:2).

Resurrection. Man can bury, but only God can resurrect. "God which raiseth the dead" (II Corinthians 1:9). Deity is evident in all acts of resurrection. As the Spirit has a share in the Resurrection of Christ, He must be God, "The Spirit of Him that raised up Jesus from the dead" (Romans 8:11). And the same Spirit will aid in our translation at the translation of the Church. "The Spirit lifted me up between the earth and the heaven" (Ezekiel 8:3) can be linked with the meeting of the Lord in the air (I Thessalonians 4:17).

4. The Spirit is identified with the Father and the Son.

Dr. C. I. Scofield says, "There is no Biblical reason for believing in the Deity and Personality of the Father and the Son, which does not equally establish that of the Spirit." How profitable it is to trace the blessed partnership of the Trinity.

The Work of the Cross. Because it is a divine work, the redemption of the soul is precious (Psalm 49:8). None can redeem his brother (v. 7), therefore, Christ was made unto us redemption (I Corinthians 1: 30). As redemption, then, is the work of God, and not of man, all associated with it must bear the same nature.

It is easy to prove that the Holy Three, Father, Son and Spirit were associated in the work of the cross. One key verse is Hebrews 9:14.

There is the Godward aspect—"Without spot to God."

There is the Christward aspect—"The Blood of Christ."

There is the Spiritward aspect—"Through the Eternal Spirit."

There is the manward aspect—"Purge your conscience from dead works to serve the living God."

The three parables of Luke 15—Lost Son, Lost Sheep, Lost Silver, fittingly illustrate the respective work of the Father, the Son and the Spirit in salvation.

The Baptismal Formula. In our Lord's great commission (Matthew 28:16-20), He instructs His disciples to baptize all who believe in "the name of the Father and of the Son and of the Holy Spirit" (R.V.). *Note*, it is not in the names, but "name." All three, then, are one—one in deity and

accomplishments. The singular here presents one God in three Persons.

The Apostolic Benediction. The much loved benediction of the Church, with which Paul closes his second epistle to the Corinthians, is also eloquent with the truth of the Trinity. Not only does this benediction teach us the invocation and adoration of Father, Son and Spirit, it likewise ascribes to each their outstanding quality.

"The Grace of the Lord Jesus Christ"—Medium of all blessing.

"The Love of God"—Source of all blessing.

"The Fellowship of the Holy Spirit"—Dispenser of all blessing.

The Heavenly Witness. While scholars are agreed that John's word, relative to the threefold heavenly witness, is not authoritative but has crept into the narrative, yet the implied truth is nevertheless precious. "There are three that bear record in heaven, the Father, the Word, and the Holy Spirit: and these three are *one*. And there are three that bear witness in earth, the spirit, and the water, and the blood: and these three agree in one" (I John 5:7,8).

The United Access. In emphasizing that Jews and Gentiles are one body in Christ, Paul unites the Persons of the Trinity. "For through Him (Christ Jesus of verse 13) we both (Jew and Gentile) have access by one Spirit unto the Father" (Ephesians 2:18). Thus, whether it be for salvation or worship, we come to God through the Son and by the Holy Spirit.

Concluding this meditation on the Spirit's deity, in which we have sought to prove His equality with the Father and the Son, it may be necessary to indicate evidences of subordination on His part. While the Scriptures draw the clearest possible distinction between the Father, Son and Spirit, and gives to each their separate personalities, and also outlines their mutual relations as they act upon one another, applying pronouns of the second and third persons to one another, the same Scriptures also teach the Spirit is subordinate to God and to Christ.

One of the mysteries of our faith is that Christ, who thought it not robbery to be equal with God (Philippians 2:6), was yet subordinate to the will of His Father (John 8:29,42; 9:4; 17:8). The subordination of the Spirit to the Son is brought out in that He does not glorify Himself but Christ, even as Christ Himself sought not His own glory,

but His Father's (7:18; cf. 16:13-15).
Thus, as Bengel expresses it—"The Son
glorifies the Father, the Spirit glorifies the
Son." And, if any addition is allowed, the
believer glorifies all Three.

The practical application of the Spirit's
subordination is not far to seek. We must be
as subordinate to His sway, as He Himself
was, and is, to the Father and the Son. And
in our continual subordination to the Spirit,
we are inspired by the example of the Master, who, as it has been stated "is the one
perfect manifestation in history of the complete work of the Holy Spirit in man." As
He is our pattern, and "the firstborn among
many brethren" (I John 2:6; Romans 8:
29), then whatever He realized through the
Spirit is for us to realize in our daily lives.

During a preaching mission in Minne-
apolis, D. L. Moody gave his remarkable
sermon on "The Holy Spirit." At the close
of the service a man came up to the evangelist and said, "Mr. Moody, you speak as
if you had a monopoly on the Holy Spirit."
Moody's reply was, "No, decidedly No! but,
I do trust the Holy Spirit has a monopoly
on me." And He certainly had, for his
marvelous work revealed how truly subordinate he was to the Spirit.

The Symbols of the Spirit

The Bible contains the mind and will of
God communicated to man, in human,
everyday language he can readily understand. By means of symbols and metaphors
it pleases God to reveal Himself to our
hearts. "I have . . . used similitudes, by the
ministry of the prophets" (Hosea 12:10).
And Hosea is full of them!

Types, parables and emblems therefore
abound to illustrate the work of the Father,
Son, and the Spirit, as well as the Bible's
own nature and ministry. And the metaphor
of Scripture is a most fascinating form of
Bible study.

Among the most helpful books dealing
with the symbolized work of the Spirit,
mention can be made of the exhaustive
study, *Emblems of the Spirit,* by Dr. F. E.
Marsh. Summarizing these emblems we can
tabulate them thus—

1. Inanimate nature
Air, water, fire, earth, oil, wine, seed,
earnest, seal
2. Animal nature
Dove, peace, beauty, innocence, patience,
sincerity

3. Human Life
The Finger of God
The Porter of the Flock
The Number Seven
The Paraclete

The Holy Spirit is the secret of all blessing—
1. Breath, wind, secret of vitality—life
Speech—testimony
Motion—activity
2. Dew, water, rain, secret of satisfaction
—thirst
Beauty—verdure, flowers
Fertility—crops, harvests
3. Oil, the secret of joy—cheerfulness
Facility—readiness
Fragrance—unction
4. Fire, the secret of light—knowledge
Heat—love
Power—conquest

Coming to a fuller exposition of these
emblems we classify them under two general heads: (1) Symbols from natural life
and (2) symbols from human life.

Symbols Drawn from Natural Life

How condescending of God it is to convey heavenly truth through the media of
emblems associated with the world we live
in. He speaks to us in language we can understand. And this is the only way infinity
can enlighten finity.

1. Wind. "The wind . . . so . . . the
Spirit" (John 3:8).

The wind is invisible, inscrutable, not
amenable to human control, but manifest in
its effects, and, therefore, a fitting symbol
of the mysterious work of the Spirit in regeneration (Ecclesiastes 11:5). He is not
seen in His operations, but definitely felt.

When the prophet recorded the command of the Lord, "Prophesy unto the
wind . . . breathe upon these slain, that
they may live" (Ezekiel 37:9,10), he had
before him the vivifying principle in nature
and applied it to the life-giving, resurrec-
ting power of the Spirit.

Luke describes the appearance of the
Spirit on the day of Pentecost "as a rushing
mighty wind" (Acts 2:2). "Mighty" speaks
of power, and the Spirit, who came imparting power, is all-powerful in Himself.
"Rushing" suggests the approach, efficacy,
filling. Taken together, the language symbolizes the secret of effective testimony in
service, and speed of accomplishment as
witnesses are borne along by the invigorat-
ing, energizing power of the Spirit.

Wind is a great power, yet it can be

modified. It is varied in its manifestations. Sometimes it comes as a mighty tempest or cyclone and with the resistlessness of a tornado. This was the work of the Spirit which the jailer required (Acts 16:28). At other times, the wind is as gentle as a zephyr, the soft breath of even. And it was as such that the Spirit influenced Lydia, whose heart silently opened to the Lord. Let us be careful never to ape another's experience. If you never had a cyclone conversion, do not criticize the man who had.

Come as the wind! with rushing sound
  And Pentecostal grace!
That all of woman born may see
  The glory of Thy Face.

2. Water

Water is one of the most common of symbols used to describe the varied ministry of God's Spirit. It can assume many forms, all of which are employed to unfold the blessings of the Spirit.

There is water—"Whosoever drinketh of the water" (John 4:14). From the context we have the idea of the clear, clean, refreshing work of the Spirit, who alone can quench the thirst of the human heart. He it is who brings satisfaction for the soul's deep thirst. Cleansing (Ezekiel 36:25-27), life, fertility, beauty (47:1-12), joy (Isaiah 12:3), are all aspects of water's beneficial usefulness.

There are rivers—"Rivers of living water . . . the Spirit" (John 7:37-39). How many mighty rivers there are covering the earth, with no two of them alike! Cast in the plural, our Lord's prophecy indicates the many-sidedness of the Spirit's work. He is not confined to one avenue of expression. Diversity characterizes His activities.

There are floods—"Floods upon the dry ground" (Isaiah 44:3). Even though water comes as an avalanche, it is still water. God flooded the earth with a judgment of water in Noah's day, and is just as able to flood it with blessing (Revelation 21:6). Floods, then, can stand for the fullness, copiousness, superabundance of the Spirit's supply.

There is rain—"He shall come down like rain" (Psalm 72:6). Absence of rain means famine, scarcity, ruin. As rain, the Spirit is the fertilizing, life-giving power of God. He can transform the desert, causing it to blossom as the rose (Joel 2:23).

There are springs—"A well of water springing up" (John 4:14). "All my springs are in Thee" (Psalm 87:7). Under this figure we have the Spirit as the perennial source of supply. Within, He is the Creator of all spirituality.

There is dew—"I will be as the dew" (Hosea 14:5). Here we have represented the secret, unnoticed, yet effectual work of the Spirit, He is the early dew of morning.

Come as the dew—and sweetly bless
  This consecrated hour;
May barrenness rejoice to own
  Thy fertilizing power.

3. Fire

In Scripture, "fire" is used in many ways. It is the consistent symbol of the holy presence and character of God (Deuteronomy 4:24; Hebrews 12:29). Various times it is applied to the Spirit (Isaiah 4:4; Acts 2:3): "Cloven tongues like as of fire" (See also Luke 12:49; Revelation 4:5).

And used of the Spirit's operations it is a most expressive figure, for fire gives warmth and light. It consumes what is combustible and tests that which is not so, it cleanses that which neither air nor water can cleanse. Its action is life-giving, as is the warmth of the mother bird while she broods upon her nest.

Fire gives light and therefore indicates the knowledge, the illumination the Holy Spirit imparts. "The eyes of your understanding being enlightened" (Ephesians 1:17,18; Hebrews 6:4).

Fire gives heat—warms cold things and persons and thus symbolizes the Spirit's power to warm cold hearts (Romans 5:5).

Fire gives power, generates steam, driving force and so represents the energizing influence of the Spirit (Acts 2:3,4; cf. Leviticus 9:24; 10:2; Malachi 3:2; I Corinthians 3:13,14 for other actions of fire.)

4. Salt

Another reason why the Bible abounds in symbols is the fact that it was written in the East where language is picturesque, hence our Lord's constant use of common objects. The parables and symbols He used bear the stamp of His thirty odd years of association with the ordinary, simple, everyday life of the people. Salt, for example, was taken to express the influence of the saint's spiritually in a corrupt world. "Ye are the salt of the earth" (Matthew 5:13). "Salted with fire (Mark 9:49,50).

It is the Holy Spirit alone who can preserve our character from deadly insipidity, and give it savor and pungency. How tragic it is when, as salt, we lose our power to arrest the evident decay all around us!

To be "salted with fire" implies the twofold influence of the Spirit. First, as "fire" He cleanses the life of the believer, consuming all uncleanness and putrefaction.

Then as "salt" He keeps the believer clean, preserving him day by day from sin's corruption.

Let us guard against losing our saltness, that is, our Spirit-created spirituality. When this goes, Jesus said, "[We are] good for nothing" (Matthew 5:13; Colossians 4:6).

5. Oil

The use of oil in Bible times makes a profitable study. For example, it played a large part in Old Testament days.

Oil was associated with food. "Fine flour mingled with oil" (Leviticus 2:4,5). Here Christ—Fine flour, and the Holy Spirit—Oil, are brought together. As the Spirit-anointed One, Jesus was food for both God and man to feed upon.

Oil supplied illumination. In the service of the Tabernacle, "pure olive oil" was provided (cf. Exodus 25:6; Matthew 5:16; 25:4). And it is the Spirit's indwelling that enables the believer to shine, and the Church to maintain her testimony in the world. We are the lamps, and the Spirit is the Oil. Light, therefore, comes from within, and is contrary to what is known as "the light of reason." The Spirit alone can give us understanding according to God's Word (Psalm 119:18). One duty of Aaron was to keep the lamps dressed (Exodus 30:7,8). How we need the continual dressing of the lamp of witness!

Oil was supplied for various anointings. Anointing oil is beautifully symbolic of the manifold action of the Spirit. There is, for instance, His healing ministry as He pours oil and wine into our bruised hearts.

Prophets, priests, kings, lepers, diseased and dead are all alike connected with oil-anointing. Christ came as the Messiah; the Anointed One (Acts 4:27; 10:38; Hebrews 9:11). And the Christian likewise is an anointed one (II Corinthians 1:21; I John 2:20). May ours be the experience of a fresh, daily anointing for the Lord's service!

Thou the anointing Spirit art
Who doest Thy sevenfold gifts impart!
Anoint and cheer our soiled face
With the abundance of Thy grace.

6. Wine

This striking symbol represents the refreshing, stimulating, gladdening influence produced by the Spirit in the lives of believers. "Wine maketh merry" (Psalm 104:15; Ecclesiastes 10:19). Are we the Lord's merry men? On the day of Pentecost spiritual exhilaration and joy were mistaken for the effects of wine (Acts 2:13-15). The Spirit-possessed disciples became God-intoxicated men. Christ Himself, Spirit-filled, was taken for a winebibber (Matthew 11:19; cf. Luke 10:21). Paul would have us avoid all fleshly excitement produced by the excess of wine (Ephesians 5:18). We can never drink of God's wine to excess.

7. Seed

As an emblem, "seed" is applied to Christ (Galatians 3:16), the Scriptures (Luke 8:5), and the Spirit: "His seed remaineth in him" (I John 3:9). "His seed" is the remaining Spirit (John 14:16). John's declaration perplexes many hearts. They argue, "Well, I am born of God, yet I commit sin." But all difficulty vanishes when we remember that the Holy Spirit is the Seed, and that the new nature He imparts cannot sin. Are we allowing Him, as the Seed, to grow and reach full fruitage?

Plant and root, and fix in me
All the mind that was in Thee.

8. Seal

Like his Master before him, Paul knew how to use what was around him to illustrate divine truth. Ephesus was a maritime city having an extensive timber trade. Great logs and planks would be brought in and then sealed with burnt-in marks, indicating ownership. Thus he reminded the Ephesian believers of their sealing with the Spirit (Ephesians 1:13; 4:30; cf. II Corinthians 1:22; II Timothy 2:19).

A seal was also used to convey to wax the design of the seal. Such monograms often implied a finished transaction when applied to documents. "Him hath God the Father sealed" (John 6:27). Jesus was the perfect reflection of God—"The express image of His Person" (Hebrews 1:3). Are we carrying the correct impression? Is the Holy Spirit as the Seal, stamping our life with divine holiness? Perhaps the wax of our hearts is too hard—it is not soft enough to receive divine impressions.

9. Earnest

An "earnest" was a deposit paid by a purchaser to give validity to a contract. In

Scotch transaction they have an "arle." One farmer buying land from another would be handed a bag full of the earth bought, a part of his full purchased possession, an "arle." And it is in this sense Paul uses the symbol of "the earnest," in reference to the Spirit, "Who hath . . . given (us) the earnest of the Spirit in our hearts" (II Corinthians 1:22; 5:5; Ephesians 1:13,14).

The gift of the Spirit is the pledge, deposit of our complete inheritance. What God has already given in part, He will bestow at last in perfection. In the Spirit, we have a little piece of heaven to go to heaven with. Presently, we have the firstfruits of the Spirit, but the present enjoyment of Him is a pledge of future glory. And—

If here it is so blessed
What will it be up there?

10. Clothing
"Clothing" as a verb is frequently used in a figurative sense. In connection with the Spirit's enpowerment it can be likened unto an act of clothing. "The Spirit of the Lord clothed himself with Gideon" (cf. Judges 6:34, marg.). "Tarry ye . . . until ye be endued" (Clothed with power from on high"—Luke 24:49; cf. Isaiah 61:10).

11. Seven
Representing perfection, "Seven" is symbolic of the Spirit as the perfection of Deity, and the perfection of His work. Having "seven eyes" (Zechariah 3:9; 4:10; Revelation 5:6), He possesses *perfect insight.* Having "seven horns" (Revelation 5:6), He possesses *perfect power.* As "Seven Spirits" (1:4), He possesses *perfect obedience.* As "seven lamps of fire" (4:5), He possesses *perfect holiness.*

We sing of Him as "the Sevenfold Spirit," and so He is, seeing that light, life, holiness, power, joy, love, hope spring from Him.

As the sevenfold Spirit He is related to the Seven Churches (Revelation 1:3,4), suggesting the beautiful truth of a separate aspect of His ministry for each separate church. He is not the same to all, but gives Himself to each as specifically as a mother gives her whole self to each of the seven children she may have borne.

There are at least five symbols having life, Scripture uses to emphasize the Spirit's omnipotent operation in our daily walk and work.

1. Dove
Charles Wesley taught the church to sing—

Expand Thy wings, celestial Dove
Brood o'er our nature's night,
On our disordered spirits move
And let there now be light.

And such an expressive emblem speaks of the Spirit's nature and office.

"The Holy Ghost descended in a bodily shape like a dove upon Him (Luke 3:22; Genesis 1:2). Such a type speaks of the Spirit's nature—loving; of the Saviour's mission—peaceful and sacrifice; of the saint's character—innocent and harmless. It is profitable to note the sixfold characteristics of the dove as given in the Bible.

It is swift in flight—"Wings like a dove" (Psalm 55:6).

It is beautiful in plumage—"Wings of a dove covered with silver" (Psalm 68:13).

It is constant in love—"The eyes of doves" (Song of Solomon 5:12).

It is mournful in note—"Mourn sore like doves" (Isaiah 59:11).

It is gentle in manner—"Harmless as doves" (Matthew 10:16).

It is particular in food—"The dove found no rest for the sole of her foot" (Genesis 8:9).

And all these qualities are marks of the Spirit. Would that each of us could aspire to the dovelike life!

2. Porter
The word as used by our Lord in John 10:3, "To him the porter openeth," carries a double meaning, *e.g.,* (cf. Mark 13:34; John 18:16,17): "A doorkeeper," from *porta,* one who waits at a door to receive a message. The Psalmist was content to be a doorkeeper (Psalm 84:10). "A burden bearer," from *portare,* to carry. One akin to a station porter.

Christ is before us as the Shepherd, and the Holy Spirit is the Porter, and as such it is His work to open and keep open doors for the Saviour. It may be that John the Baptist was in our Lord's mind when He spoke of a Porter. The Holy Spirit, however, is ever the divine Forerunner of Jesus.

He it is who opens up the door of the heart, preparing the soul for the entrance and reception of Christ (John 16:8-11; Acts 16:14).

He it is who opens up the door of the world at large. The progress of missionary effort is due to the Spirit's promptings, as the book of Acts clearly proves, where He is found shutting a door into Asia, and opening another into Europe (Acts 16:6-11).

Not only does the Spirit open doors, He

also guards them so that strangers and hire-lings cannot pass through. And we have the blessed privilege of assisting Him as the Porter. But are we opening doors for Jesus? As underporters, are we in full sympathy with this doorwork of God's Spirit?

3. Paraclete

It would appear as if this was our Lord's favorite designation of the Spirit, for at least four times over, He is spoken of as the "Comforter." In John 14:16, He is Christ-like and abiding. In verse 26, He comes as the Gift of the Father. In 15:26 He is repre-sented as the Gift of the Son. In 16:7 Christ's Ascension is the basis of such a Gift.

As the Greek is such a pliable language, a word is capable of many meanings. Thus, we have three words for the English one, *e.g.* Christ in His sermon on "The Spirit."

(a) *Comforter*—"Walking . . . in the com-fort of the Holy Spirit" (Acts 9:31 R.V.; cf. margin). And as Augustine expressed it: "He is our sweetest Comforter." As such He is connected with our sufferings.

(b) *Advocate*—"Spirit [Himself] maketh intercession" (Romans 8:26,27). The same word is used of Jesus in I John 2:1, "We have an Advocate." Such a term implies a pleader who comes forward in favor of, and as the representative of, another. Thus, we have two Advocates or Paracletes—The Holy Spirit within us that we may not sin—Jesus with the Father to plead His efficacious blood if we do sin. Here, the Spirit is re-lated to our sins.

(c) *Helper*—"The Spirit also helpeth our infirmities" (Romans 8:26). Scofield has it, "One called alongside to help." God has laid help upon this One who is mighty (Psalm 89:19; Acts 26:22; Hebrews 4:16). Do we require help? Then why turn to human sources for succor when you have such a willing, all-powerful Helper as the Spirit? He is ever the "Help of the helpless."

4. Witness

Doddridge has it—

Cheered by a Witness so Divine,
  Unwavering I believe;
And Abba Father, humbly cry;
  Nor can the sign deceive.

Paul refers to the Spirit in this telling fash-ion. "The Spirit Himself beareth witness" (Romans 8:16 R.V.). "My conscience also bearing me witness in the Holy Spirit" (9:1). Who and what is a "witness"? The word itself is from *witan,* meaning "to know." A witness, then, is one who sees and knows. A witness in court is brought there because of his knowledge of a case before the court.

As a Witness, the Holy Spirit witnesses in, and to, the believer in three ways—

First of all, there is pardon (Romans 5:1; 8:1). Here we are as sinners in the court of divine justice, guilty of crime. But they plead the atoning work of the Saviour, and they are forgiven for the criminality. And the Spirit enters as the Witness of pardon. He gives the assurance that there is now no condemnation.

Then, there is adoption (Romans 8:14-17; Galatians 4:6). Here we are as sons. From a court, we go to a home where we find ourselves brought into a divine family, with the Spirit as the Witness of our adop-tion. His indwelling makes us perfectly at home.

Last of all, there is sanctification (I John 4:13). The pardoned one in court becomes a son in the Father's house and then enters a holier sphere, even the Temple. Here we are as saints. As the Sanctifier, the Spirit witnesses to our sanctification. He it is who prompts us to dedicate all we are and have to the Lord, not that we might become His, but because we are His already. And the consciousness of the presence of the un-grieved Spirit within is a witness of our growing likeness to Jesus.

5. Finger

The Early Fathers spoke of "The Holy Spirit" as "The Finger of the Hand Divine," and the oft-repeated phrase, *Finger of God,* like, *Hand of God,* is synonymous with power or omnipotence, sometimes with the additional meaning of the infallible evi-dence of divine authorship, visible in all God's works.

Combining our Lord's words as recorded by Matthew and Luke we discover that the Spirit is the Finger of God. "I cast out devils by the Spirit of God" (Matthew 12:28); "I with the finger of God cast out devils" (Luke 11:20).

References to the Spirit as the "Finger of God" describe Him as the indispensable Agent accomplishing the purpose of the divine will.

(a) *The Law of God.* "Two tables . . . written with the finger of God" (Exodus 31:18; Deuteronomy 9:10). The Holy Spirit was associated with the Father in the framing and writing of the Word of God. Certainly human fingers actually penned the Scriptures, but they were ever under the control of the divine Finger (Proverbs 22: 20,21; II Peter 1:21).

(b) *The Judgment of God.* When the magicians with their enchantments no longer could produce the same plagues with which God smote Egypt they confessed to Pharaoh, "This is the finger of God" (Exodus 8: 19). Belshazzar saw those fingers as of a man's hand (Daniel 5:5). The sinner is met on his own level and the divine fingers wrote in language humanity could understand.

(c) *The Power of God.* David considered God's heavens as the work of His Spirit, "Thy heavens, the work of thy fingers" (Psalm 8:3), and the Scriptures offer abundant evidence that the Third Person is the Creator-Spirit. The work "firmament" is a wide extent of space, and such expanse is the production of the Executive of the Godhead, the Holy Spirit. And He it is who ever strives after a wider expanse in our hearts for the glory of God to be revealed in some new measure through us.

(d) *The Saint of God.* To Orientals, fingers were essential in conversation as they indicated what mouths dare not utter, namely, concern or grave insult (Proverbs 6:13; Isaiah 58:9).

Paul uses the figure of the "Finger" in describing the Spirit's fashioning of the saint of God—"The epistle of Christ . . . written not with ink, but with the Spirit of the living God" (II Corinthians 3:3; Hebrews 8:10; 10:16). Do we permit this blessed Writer to pen something fresh upon our life as day follows day?

Write Thy new name upon my heart
Thy new, best name of love.

The Saviour and the Spirit

Because of the generally accepted uninspired character of "The Apocrypha," we are not troubling to trace the movements of the Spirit within such dubious literature. It echoes no new and living voices. As for the Inter-Testament Period, known as "the 400 silent years," the Spirit is as a stream flowing underground, only to emerge in the fullness of our Lord's teaching.

Studying the New Testament's fuller revelation of the Spirit we are impressed with the clearer view of His Person, and of His relations, essential and economical, with the other Persons of the Trinity. We cannot escape the ever-expanding exposition of His functions and operations. And an intense personal interest attaches to all we learn of Him and His relations with Christ and His perpetual indwelling in the Church. He is revealed as being infinitely nearer to us. And gradually we see in Him the One who slowly but certainly brings back a lapsed world under the divine sway, thereby realizing the end of that creation in which He appeared as the foremost Agent.

Moreover, it is only as we take the New Testament in our hands and diligently pursue our journey through its sacred pages that we realize how full it is of "the things of the Spirit." Dr. Elder Cumming, whose work, *Through the Eternal Spirit,* is one of the most helpful studies on the Third Person, affirms that "there are in all 261 passages in which the Holy Spirit is specially and directly mentioned. A few of these no doubt may be questioned, but these can make little difference.

> The Gospels—56 passages
> The Acts of the Apostles—57 passages
> Paul's Epistles—112 passages
> Other Books—36 passages

Philemon and the second and third epistles of John are the only books in which the Spirit is not named.

That the blessed Spirit was known and believed in at the dawn of the New Testament era is evident by the fact that those to whom He came clearly understood His words and works. Along with John the Baptist, the Holy Spirit can be counted as a Forerunner, for while John prepared the way for Jesus, it was the Spirit who prepared the way for both John and Jesus.

Pre-Messianic Operations

By the Pre-Messianic operations of the Spirit we mean His movements preliminary to Christ's appearance. As our Lord was about to enter the world, the Spirit began to stir devout souls who had been waiting for the consolation of Israel, and who felt new and strange influences directing their thoughts toward the Coming One.

1. Zacharias and Elizabeth. These two priestly souls, "both righteous before God, walking in all the commandments and ordinances of the Lord blameless," had a unique experience of the Spirit's miraculous creative power.

Zacharias learned that John, his coming son, was to be filled with the Holy Spirit from the womb (Luke 1:15). Elizabeth was filled with the Spirit as John was about to be born (Luke 1:41). Zacharias was filled with the Spirit to declare the prophecy regarding the mission of the Baptist (Luke 1:17,67).

2. Joseph and Mary. With Mary, the virgin, and her espoused, Joseph, who was a just man, the Holy Spirit had delicate, sacred associations. Analyzing the "birth" narratives of our Lord we have this summary—

Joseph was informed that Mary's child would be conceived by the Holy Spirit (Matthew 1:20). Mary's pregnant condition, disturbing to Joseph, was fully explained by revelation (Matthew 1:18,19). Mary receives the secret of our Lord's conception apart from human agency, and her elevation as one blessed above all women as the mother of the Messiah (Luke 1:35).

3. Simeon. This aged saint of Jerusalem, "just and devout," lived in constant expectation of Christ's coming. He waited "for the consolation of Israel," and was given the assurance that he would live to see the Messiah. Simeon's name means "one who hears and obeys" as knowing the voice of the Spirit we find—

The Spirit was upon him (Luke 2:25).

The Spirit revealed unto him the fulfillment of his desire (Luke 2:26).

The Spirit led him into the Temple to see Jesus, when He was brought to the Temple to be given to Jehovah as the firstborn and to be redeemed by payment of a ransom (Exodus 13:12; Luke 2:23,26,27).

4. John the Baptist. Our Lord's forerunner was likewise subject to the manifold operations of the Spirit of God. For example—

John's birth, naturally impossible, is brought about by the Spirit (Luke 1:13-25).

John was filled with the Spirit from his birth (Luke 1:15). John was born of a Spirit-filled mother (Luke 1:41). John exercised his ministry in the power of the Spirit (Luke 1:17; Mark 6:20).

John prophesied the baptism with the Spirit (Matthew 3:11; Mark 1:8; Luke 3:16; John 1:33).

John witnessed the descent of the Spirit upon Christ. See above passages.

Although it is not expressly mentioned, yet we are at liberty to infer that the self-same Spirit, acting upon the foregoing, was

also associated with the search and joy of the wise men from the East, and with the adoration and testimony of the shepherds. Thus, the Spirit bridged the transition period between the two Testaments by permeating the lives of those godly souls grouped around our Lord's entrance into our humanity, with His own holy presence and power.

Messianic Ministrations

We have now come to one of the most profitable aspects of our study, namely, the blessed and wonderful relationship existing between the Holy Son and the Holy Spirit. Peter informs us that our Lord left us an example that we should follow His steps (I Peter 2:21), and in His association with the Spirit we have an example it is imperative to follow, if we would be victorious in life and fruitful in service.

Jesus declared that "the disciple is not above his master, nor the servant above his Lord" (Matthew 10:24), and, surely, one application of such a declaration is that if He had needs which the Holy Spirit could meet, and which He brought to the Spirit in humble dependence to meet them like Christ, we too, as disciples and servants, must be as equally dependent upon the Third Person.

We can gather material on the theme before us thus—

The Spirit in our Lord's teaching and types, and

The Spirit in our Lord's life and labors.

The Spirit in our Lord's Teaching and Types

The teaching of Christ on the Spirit is full and varied, specially near the close of His earthly ministry. And, as we are to prove, He never referred to the "Paraclete" in any impersonal way.

As Scripture presents a progressive unfolding of the work of the Spirit, we expect to find as we reach our Lord's teaching a clearer and fuller revelation of the Spirit's Person and work, than the Old Testament contains, which of course, is what we do. While wonderful expansions of the truth of the Spirit can be traced after our Lord's Ascension, it must be borne in mind that with all the full blaze of a noonday revelation, such as the Acts and the epistles contain of the Spirit's operations, that after

Christ's testimony, no new truth appears. All that the apostles taught regarding the Spirit can be found in germ within Christ's teaching.

Concerning the work of the Spirit as revealed in the New Testament, we can classify the truth thus, Who the Spirit is and what He does is unfolded—

Historically in the *gospels*,
Experimentally in the *Acts*,
Doctrinally in the *epistles*,
Governmentally in the *Revelation*.

The Spirit Was Prayed for by Christ

Several salient features of Christ's revelation of the Spirit are inescapable as we ponder the four gospels. The first is that the Spirit came in answer to Christ's prayer, "I will pray the Father, and He shall give you another Comforter" (John 14:16). And the experiences of the apostles throughout Acts constitute an answer to Christ's prayer.

Christ also enjoined His disciples to pray for the Spirit—"How much more shall your heavenly Father give the Holy Spirit to them that ask him?" (Luke 11:13). And such a request forms the burden of His high-priestly petition of John 17, seeing it is only through the gift of the Spirit that His desires for His own can be fully realized.

As believers, then, we have the Spirit through the joint prayers of the Lord and ourselves.

The Spirit Was Prophesied by Christ

On the last day, that great day of the holiest and greatest of all feasts, the Feast of Tabernacles (Leviticus 23:39), Jesus gave a telescopic view of the Spirit's ministry. Out from within His own, rivers of water were to flow (John 7:37-39). And this word "flow," occurring nowhere else in the New Testament, implies the continual movement of the Spirit. Flowing into the believer, He flows through, then flows out, bringing spiritual refreshment to the dry barren wilderness around.

And the Spirit here symbolized as "rivers of water" was not yet given, for Jesus had not yet been glorified. Such a fact was true *dispensationally*. The Holy Spirit could not come as the Gift of Christ until His entrance into heaven. Thus, the present presence of the Spirit is an evidence of the ascended, glorified Lord. It is likewise true *experimentally*. No believer can realize the fullness of the Spirit in life and service unless he is willing to glorify Jesus. As the Spirit loves to glorify the Lord, He cannot bless and use those who are self-confident, boastful and self-glorifying.

The Spirit Was Given by Christ

As Christ is God's Love-gift to "a world of sinners lost and ruined by the Fall," so the Spirit is Christ's Love-Gift to His blood-bought ones. It is clearly evident, however, that the Gift of the Spirit was a donation that neither the Father nor the Son could give alone—so the procession of the Spirit is from the Father through the Son. The bestowal of this blessed Gift can be set forth in a threefold fashion—

1. The Spirit was given by the Father (John 14:16,26; Acts 1:4).

As Christ is God's Gift (Romans 6:23), who, as the absolute Possessor of all things, possesses Christ (I Corinthians 3:23), so the Spirit is God's Gift, and therefore, His possession (Genesis 6:3; Zechariah 4:6).

2. The Spirit was given by Christ (John 15:26).

In response to Christ's own express declaration to send the Spirit, He came upon the disciples on the day of Pentecost as the promised, empowering Gift of the ascended Lord.

3. The Spirit came on His own initiative. "When He . . . is come" (John 16:13). Behind this affirmation is the willing, voluntary service the Third Person gave and gives. God and Christ had no need to press Him into the ministry He represents. All His operations, like the Incarnation and death of the Saviour, are willing and without coercion.

The Father was willing to give His Son as the sinner's Substitute.

The Son was willing to die in the sinner's stead.

The Spirit was willing to enter and remain in the world from Pentecost until the translation of the Church, and by His long ministry, complete such a Church, which is the Lord's Body.

The Spirit Was Prepared For by Christ

As our Lord was about to ascend on high "He breathed on His disciples, and saith unto them, Receive ye the Holy Spirit" (John 20:22 R.V.). The question arises,

Did the disciples actually receive the Spirit at this time or later on at Pentecost? It would seem as if the experience was prophetic—a foretaste of Pentecost.

By the acted parable of breathing audibly, Christ created an atmosphere, preparing His own to receive the Spirit. Knowing that a right attitude and atmosphere are necessary for the definite reception of the Spirit, Christ seems to be saying, "Get ready to receive the Spirit." Bishop Handley Moule, discussing whether the Spirit was given in "act" or "prospect" at this point says, "The risen Lord's action of breathing was the Sacrament, so to speak . . . of a coming gift of the Spirit."

What we must not lose sight of is the fact that there must ever be the active receptivity on our part of the Spirit whom the Lord out-breathes.

The Spirit Was Received by Christ For Us

Both Peter and Paul emphasize this aspect of our theme. "Having received of the Father the promise of the Holy Spirit, He hath shed forth this, which ye now see and hear" (Acts 2:33). Paul reminds us that on His Ascension, Christ "gave gifts unto men" (Ephesians 4:8).

As the Spirit indwelt our Lord's human body, so the Father gives the Spirit to us in order that He might indwell us as those forming the Lord's mystical Body, exhibiting in and through each believer those spiritual gifts necessary for "the perfecting of the saints, for the work of the ministry, for the edifying of the body of Christ" (Ephesians 4:12).

The Spirit Witnessed Christ's Exaltation

The disciples saw Christ ascend from the earth, but we are possessed by One who witnessed His arrival in heaven (Acts 5:30-32; John 7:39; 16:7). As Jesus, gloriously exalted, sat down on the right hand of the Majesty on High, the Holy Spirit descended to undertake His advocacy of the Lord's people.

And the Spirit being amongst us is not only an evidence of Christ's enthronement, but is the proof of His Resurrection. If His body was stolen, or dissolved into gases, then there could have been no manifestation to the disciples as recorded. If the Resurrection of Christ is a myth, then there was no Ascension after forty days, and, consequently no descent of the Spirit as promised by Christ upon His return to Glory. But the Spirit being here declares Jesus to be alive forevermore.

The Spirit Testifies of Christ

Referring to the ministry of the Spirit, Jesus said, "The Spirit of truth . . . shall testify of Me" (John 15:26). Note the title used here—"The Spirit of truth." As Christ Himself is "the truth" (14:6), it is imperative to have One sharing His nature to bear testimony to Him.

And the Spirit loves to make much of Christ. How He leads us to the Master and keeps Him warm in our heart. The central point of our evangelical faith is that Christ with His infinite resources, with all His love and grace, is near to the individual believer, and made part of His very being by the gift of the indwelling Spirit. Without the Spirit we have practically no Christ.

There is, of course, the twofold witness as indicated by Peter (Acts 5:32). The Spirit's testimony and our own (John 15:26). We give what we get—reflect what we receive. The Spirit testifies to us—we testify unto the world. No man is Spirit-taught, if he fails to preach and exalt Christ.

The Spirit Glorifies Christ

Bengel's pregnant phrase has it, "The Son glorifies the Father, the Spirit glorifies the Son." And the blessed work of the Spirit is to make Christ grander in our estimation. "He shall glorify Me" (John 16:14). Christ's virtues as the God-Man, Saviour, Friend, Companion and Lord are extolled by the Spirit.

Bishop Moule expresses it,

There is no separate gospel of the Holy Spirit. The plan of God assuredly is not to teach us about Christ, as a first lesson, and then, as a more advanced lesson, to lead us on into truth about the Holy Spirit, apart from Christ. We do indeed, and to the last, need teaching about the blessed Spirit. But the more we learn about Him the more surely we shall learn this from Him, that His chosen and beloved work is just this—to glorify the Lord Jesus Christ . . . . He sheds an illuminating glory upon a heart, a face, an embrace— the beloved Jesus Christ, our Lord.

And such a chosen and beloved work is accomplished, be it remembered, both in the character and through the confession of those who are the Lord's (John 17:1,5, 10).

The Spirit Convicts the World About Christ

The time mission of the Spirit began at Pentecost and will continue until the Church is complete. With the translation of the Church at the return of Christ, the Spirit's association with the world in the sense in which He came at Pentecost will cease. Presently, His work is in and with the world, and in, with, and through the Church.

In His sermon dealing with the Spirit's activities, Christ declares His first action is world-wide conviction in a threefold realm, namely, in sin, righteousness and judgment (John 16:8). As the world is dead or spiritually insensible (16:3), it is in dire need of this prevenient or preparative ministry of the Spirit. The tragedy is that such a work is so resisted as to frustrate the saving purpose of God, or received in vain, for change of mind is not always followed by that godly sorrow which carries out the work begun by repentance to its completion in the acceptance of salvation (II Corinthians 7:10). Let us examine the threefold conviction the Spirit strives to produce—

1. Sin. "Of sin, because they believe not on Me" (John 16:9).

The world has come to deal with sin as if it had no real existence. In some quarters sin is treated simply as an offense against law or against the natural conscience, but not against God. Left to himself, man can never know truly and fully what the nature of sin is. The Spirit alone can reveal sin, as He does in many ways. By the Law is the knowledge of sin (Romans 7:7). The character of sin, however, is best seen in the light of the holy life and the self-sacrificing love of the crucified Saviour. In the light of the cross unbelief becomes the sin of sins. Unbelief is the very germ and root of all evil. Notice how conviction of sin was wrought in the minds and hearts of the hearers of Peter through the Word of the cross (Acts 2:36).

2. Righteousness. "Of righteousness, because I go to My Father, and ye see Me no more" (John 16:10).

Revealing Christ as the only Saviour for a condemned world, self-righteousness stands condemned. Christ is God's Righteousness, the Spirit proclaims, and man's only covering for sin.

The world looked upon Christ as a blasphemer, numbering Him among transgressors, ultimately nailing Him to the cross as One accursed (Galatians 3:13). He was rejected as being the Righteous One, but because of what Christ had been, borne, and had done, God raised and highly exalted Him. By accepting Christ as Righteous, God reversed the judgment of man.

3. Judgment. "Of judgment, because the prince of this world is judged" (John 16:11).

By the term "world" we understand human society apart from, and in opposition to, God. It is the God-hating and Christ-rejecting world animated by the spirit of disobedience, even Satan, the prince of this world and god of this age. Since the days of Adam and Eve, by his craft and power, the devil has led men in hostility to God.

Calvary, however, was Satan's Waterloo. Because of sin he had the power of death (Hebrews 2:14), but by dying, Christ slew death. And His Resurrection and Ascension proves that Satan was defeated. Now the Spirit upholds the authority and power of Christ and denounces Satan as a usurper. Through the Word the Spirit assures the fully awakened sinner that the work of Calvary is perfect and final. The devil is a defeated foe, and all who accept the Crucified One are no longer under condemnation (Romans 8:1).

The prince, and kingdom of darkness, in which the world lies, are still evident. But the day is coming when the kingdom of this world shall become in fact what it is by right, the kingdom of our God and of Christ (Revelation 11:15).

Thus, the Holy Spirit convicts in a threefold way—

Man in the realm of sin.
Christ in the realm of righteousness.
Satan in the realm of judgment.

The Spirit Transforms Men Into Christ's Image

Another precious phase of the Spirit's work is the production of the image of the Master within willing, obedient lives. "The glory of the Lord . . . transformed into the same image . . . even as from the Lord the Spirit" (II Corinthians 3:18 R.V.). As we possess four gospels, presenting four different aspects of the one divine Person, so the continuous ministry of the Spirit is to fill the world with men and women reproducing Christ.

In St. Peter's, Cologne, there are two pictures side by side, both of the crucifixion of the Apostle Peter. In the eighteenth century there was only one picture, but Napoleon took it to Paris when he conquered the city. In the absence of the original, an artist painted a copy of it, which was put in its place in the church. When the original was restored, and the two pictures were placed side by side, even experts failed to detect any difference between them. In the absence of the original, the artist had painted a perfect copy.

And this is the glorious work on which the Spirit of God, that Master Artist, is engaged, and however unworthy the canvas may be, His skill is such that He can make a perfect copy on earth of the original who has passed into the heavens. The Spirit is producing Christ in countless lives, and His work shall one day be crowned when the original, who lived His life on earth by the Spirit, is glorified in those who, by the same Spirit, have been changed into the same image, and who, in heaven, shall forever show forth the praises of Him who redeemed them.

What we must be careful to observe is that Paul is speaking of "transformation," and not "imitation." Thomas à Kempis wrote his *Imitation of Christ,* a priceless book of devotion, but the life pleasing to God is not the one in which the ways of Christ are copied or imitated, as suggested by Sheldon in that popular religious novel, *What Would Jesus Do?* It is easy to sing, "Be like Jesus this my song," but imitation is the effort of the flesh, it is the ways of Christ we seek to produce.

Transformation, however, is the unique work of the Spirit seeing that He alone "possesses" the power to reproduce Christ in the lives yielded to His control. Paul could travail in birth until Christ was formed in those Galatian believers he desired to see sanctified in life (Galatians 4:19).

The Spirit Was Named in Different Ways by Christ

As our Lord typifies the Spirit in various ways, as one can see by referring to the chapter in this volume dealing with the "Symbols of the Spirit," so there are distinct titles given to the Spirit by Christ. As all fullness dwells in Christ, and God has summed up all things in His Son (Colossians 1:19), so all the deep things of the Spirit come from the same Source of all knowledge.

1. The Spirit (John 3:5,6,8)

This simplest and shortest name often used by Christ and others is of deep significance. It indicates the Spirit's spiritual, invisible, incorporeal essence. Coming to work within the spirit of man He bears the name similar to His sphere of operation. As "The Spirit" He is in contrast to that which is material. The term "Spirit" is the same translated "wind" (John 3:8), and implies the invisible force of God.

2. The Spirit of the Father (Matthew 10: 20).

Here we have an expressive title referring to the tender, filial relationship, the Spirit Himself brings about through regeneration. And because we are God's children, the Spirit is able to administer grace in times of need.

3. The Spirit of God (Matthew 12:28)

In this first title given the Spirit in the Bible (Genesis 1:2), we have the revelation of His origin. He is thus named because He is one with God in His nature. Coming from God, He functions for God. And having a divine origin and nature, the Spirit exerts divine power and exists to fulfil the divine will. "God" or *Elohim,* meaning "the Strong One," is the creation name and covers the Trinity. (Genesis 1: 26).

4. The Holy Spirit (Luke 11:13)

This frequently used title emphasizes the Spirit's essential, moral character. He not only comes from a Holy God, inspired Holy Scripture, creates our holiness, but is Holy in Himself. "Every thought of holiness is His alone." And, as the "Holy" Spirit, He cannot condone anything in our lives alien to His holy mind and will.

5. The Spirit of the Lord (Luke 4:18)

The word here used for "Lord" is "Jehovah," the Covenant-keeping One. As the Spirit-anointed One, Jesus acts in His official capacity as God's Representative, and as the Fulfiller of all Old Testament predictions.

6. The Spirit of Truth (John 14:17; 15:26)

As "The Truth," Christ must have One who is akin to Him in this respect. And as "the Spirit of Truth," the Spirit is associated with Truth in a threefold way—

He inspires the Truth (Matthew 22:43; Mark 12:36; I Peter 1:11).

He works with the Truth (John 3:5; Ephesians 6:17)

He imparts the Truth (John 16:13).

Riding most triumphantly in His own chariot, the Spirit will only work alongside of, or through, the Truth. Lectures, essays, sermons, so-called, on a variety of subjects, interesting and profitable in themselves, can be conceived and delivered without the least aid of the Spirit. But if the Truth is to be preached and taught, it is imperative to have the illumination and power of the Spirit if the message is to be quick and powerful, sharper than a two-edged sword.

7. The Comforter (John 14:16,26;16:7).

As Jesus was so named by the angel before His birth (Matthew 1:21), so the Spirit was named "Comforter" by Christ before His Advent. The title implies "one called to another to take his part," and is the same word used of Christ in I John 2:1, namely, "Advocate." Thus we have a "stand-by" within our hearts, and another in heaven. And, with such a blessed double advocacy how shameful defeat is in the life of a believer! If we desire to save Christ the sorrow of clearing us up in heaven when we do sin, let us learn to obey the Spirit within our hearts as He prompts us not to sin. "Walk in the Spirit, and ye shall not fulfil the lust of the flesh" (Galatians 5:16).

The Spirit's Tasks Were
Outlined by Christ

The varied ministry of the Spirit, as outlined by our Lord, was of an anticipatory nature. From His revelation of the Spirit we are told who He would be, and what He would do after His coming at Pentecost. The tasks of the Spirit, as we have shown in other portions of this study, cover Christ's earthly life, the world, the Church and the believer.

The New Testament reveals a holy intimacy existing between the Holy Son and the Holy Spirit. A mystic union characterized them. Jesus could say, "I and my Father are one" (John 10:30). It was likewise true that Christ and the Spirit were one. "I . . . by the Spirit of God" (Matthew 12:28), covers our Lord's every action, as well as the casting out of demons.

There are one or two preliminary thoughts claiming our attention ere we come to the absorbing theme before us.

1. The gospels mark the transitional period of the Spirit.

The four gospels, with their life and teaching of Christ, form the bridge between the Old Testament and the Acts and the epistles. The rivers of the Old Testament run into Christ; gather greater volume in His life, than flow out after His Ascension, with a more wonderful fullness.

Already we have thought of the varied operations of the Spirit in the Old Testament. He made possible for certain men, political wisdom, power of leadership, physical strength, practical skill and artistic beauty, prophetic foresight, spiritual insight, moral courage; but all these virtues were never found in one person. All gifts however, meet in Christ, for all the past rivers of the Spirit run into the sea of Christ (Ecclesiastes 1:7). Upon Him came the promises of the sevenfold Spirit (Isaiah 11:2).

Samson had the power of the Spirit, but not His purity. Moses had the wisdom of the Spirit to lead, but not the skill to build. As then, so now, the Spirit distributes His gifts severally as He will. Christ, however, possessed the Spirit in His entirety and through the Lord, the Spirit manifested His manifold gifts.

2. The Holy Spirit exclusively occupied Christ.

Up until Christ's day, the Spirit had not yet a permanent abode in human nature. Now we have something different. The Spirit indwelt a human body for over thirty-three years. A somewhat striking feature of Christ's relationship with the Spirit is that after His birth by the Spirit there is no record of His being associated with any other individual until He came at Pentecost as heaven's Love-gift for all. There had to come a man who was both able and willing to receive the fullness of the Spirit ere that fullness could be bestowed upon others, and for the first time the Man, able and willing, was Christ.

In Old Testament days it was one measure of the Spirit for one man, but God gave not the Spirit by measure unto His Son (John 3:34). The Spirit was not yet (7:39), which means, He had not come to others. During our Lord's sojourn, the Spirit concentrated all His energies about Him, making Him the channel of constant blessing (Acts 10:38). Christ lived and labored in the Spirit. Do we?

3. The exact gift of Pentecost.

What really constituted Christ's ascension gift of the Spirit? Christ in His condescension became "the God-Man." Within the womb of Mary, the Spirit fused deity and humanity into one, thus Christ appeared as God manifest in flesh. Therefore, because of His production and possession of the God-Man, the Holy Spirit came as the Spirit of both God and man. He understands everything from the divine and human standpoints. Indwelling the Man Christ Jesus for so long. He knows all about human needs and emotions and is able to succor accordingly.

Let us look at some of the titles expressing the Spirit's relationship with the Son of God—

"The Spirit of Christ"

Paul's description of the Third Person of the Trinity (Romans 8:9), does not mean a Christlike spirit, but the Spirit Himself who possessed Christ. He is so-called, because He came as Christ's Gift, strives to reveal Christ to us and form Christ within us. And as "The Spirit of Christ," it is not an earthly Christ He glorifies as much as the Christ reinvested with all glory and power.

"The Spirit of Jesus"

"The Spirit (of Jesus) suffered them not" (Acts 16:6,7). Jesus is the earthly name, and is connected with all He endured in the days of His flesh. And does it not enhance our love for the Spirit as we realize that He had heart-fellowship with Jesus as He willingly allowed Himself to be tempted or tested in all points as we are?

"The Spirit of Jesus Christ"

The combination of names here represents Christ as the human One, anointed and raised on high. Paul speaks of "the supply of the Spirit of Jesus Christ (Philippians 1:19). Alas, many of us seem to exist on a meager supply! Yet there is no gauge checking the supply of the Spirit. All He has is at the disposal of the humblest saint.

4. The self-abnegation of Christ.

One of the mysteries of our faith is that of Christ's death to self. Although equal to God, yet as He came among men He elected to become subordinate to the will of the Father and dependent upon the Holy Spirit. "Not My will, but Thine, be done," and "I by the Spirit of God" are the twin desires of Christ.

And in this double way the Master is our Pattern and Exemplar. Says Pascal, "It is one of the great principles of Christianity that whatever happened to Jesus Christ should come to pass in the soul and body of every believer." If it was imperative for Him to depend upon the Spirit as He did, then how great must our need be of the same holy Energizer?

The evident fact that Christ's earthly life became effectual as the result of His obedience to the will of God and through the ministry of the Spirit within Him, and not alone through the inherent virtue and power He brought with Him from His pre-existent state, is one that arrests us. Somehow, such a fact has become one of the commonplaces of theology. We do not realize its true import, and cultivate that humility and dependence of soul, which should distinguish us if our Lord's self-abnegation was ever in view.

Our personal need of a life possessed by the Spirit, even as Christ's life was, is set forth in type in the anointing of Aaron and his sons (Exodus 30:30). Upon both, the oil came. Thus, all the Spirit accomplished for and through Christ, He is willing to accomplish for and through us. Every step of our pilgrim journey we can claim and use the Spirit's fullness, even as the Master did before us.

Reverently, then, let us trace the various aspects of the mystic-union existing between Christ and the Spirit. As our Meal Offering, Christ was the "fine flour unleavened, mingled with oil" (Leviticus 2:5). To change the figure, if Christ was the Vine, the Holy Spirit was the Sap permeating every phase of His life and work. As we meditate upon the inseparable, unbroken separation between these Holy Two, there is beautiful blending, merging, incorporation so soul-inspiring to behold.

Christ Was Prophesied by the Spirit

Concerning the whole of Old Testament Scripture, Christ could declare that such Scripture presented His character and ministry. "In the volume of the book it is written of Me" (Hebrews 10:7; Luke 24:26, 27). And, as Peter reminds us that it was the Holy Spirit who was in the prophets of old inspiring them to testify beforehand the sufferings of Christ and the glory that should follow (I Peter 1:11), the Spirit is before us in the role of Christ's divine Forerunner. In prophecy, type and symbol, the Spirit prepared the way for Christ.

As the time drew near for the prophesied Christ to appear, the Spirit became specially active, prompting devout minds who waited for the consolation of Israel to proclaim the fulfillment of God's promise to send His Son. Zacharias and his wife, as well as John the Baptist, were all alike filled with the Spirit and spake of the coming Christ. The Spirit also comforted Simeon with the assurance that he should live to see the Lord's Christ, and by the same Spirit, he recognized Christ as the salvation of God when He was brought into the Temple as the first-born to be redeemed by payment of a ransom (Luke 1:15,41,67; 2:23,26; Exodus 13:12).

And, as in those far-off days when the Spirit prepared the way for the First Advent, so in these last days He is preparing Christ's own and the world for the Second Advent. It is this fact, we think, that accounts for the unusual interest in prophecy.

Christ Was Born of the Spirit

The consistent revelation of the New Testament is that the Spirit was the Agent of the Father in the Incarnation of the Son. Prophesied that, as the Seed of the woman, He would become the Saviour of man, in the fullness of time He was born of a virgin (Genesis 3:15; Isaiah 9:6; Matthew 1:18).

Matthew's explicit statement reads, "Mary . . . was found with child of the Holy Spirit (Matthew 1:18, R.V.). The Spirit of Life, then, was the Completer of the union of God and man. He was the Love-knot between deity and humanity, producing the God-Man. Within Mary, the Spirit added to Christ's already existing divine nature a human nature, thus He came as the Man Christ Jesus. In our new birth the reverse takes place. The Spirit adds to our already existing human nature a divine nature, making us partakers of the divine nature (II Peter 1:4).

Mysterious indeed is the fact that Jesus was born of a woman, and of a woman who recognized her need of a Saviour, for Mary sang, "My spirit hath rejoiced in God my Saviour" (Luke 1:47), yet He was clean. The questions of Job are, "How can he be clean that is born of a woman?" "Who can bring a clean thing out of an unclean? not one" (Job 14:4; 25:4). Christ was born of a woman, and of a woman, like all women, born in sin and shapen in iniquity, yet out of the unclean the "clean thing" came, for said Gabriel in his announcement to Mary, "Therefore also that holy thing which shall be born of thee shall be called the Son of God" (Luke 1:35).

Apart from the action of the Spirit at the conception we cannot account for our Lord's sinlessness. The miracle and mystery of the Spirit's work are seen in that He was able to lay hold of the virgin's flesh out of which the body of Jesus was to be formed, and purify it, making possible thereby the One who came among men "holy, harmless, undefiled, separate from sinners." As the Spirit of holiness He overshadowed Mary, and apart from natural generation produced a perfectly holy Being. The Spirit touched the springs of motherhood in the most blessed of women, and brooded in the germ cell out of which sprang an incomparably holy life.

And Christ's birth by the Spirit offers a twofold type.

1. Christ was born of the Spirit, and we can only enter the world of grace through the same Agency.

The virgin birth of Christ, and our new birth, are alike in that neither can be explained by human reason. Both these works of the Spirit have to be received by faith.

2. It is a type of our sanctification (Galatians 4:19).

Paul used a delicate and daring simile when he told the Galatian believers that he was as a travailing mother until Christ was formed in them. What is the application of Paul's mystic phrase? Why, as Mary surrendered her body to the Spirit saying, "Be it unto me according to Thy Word," and willingly suffered Him to form Jesus within her, so we are to surrender our bodies to the same Spirit, allowing Him to fashion Christ within our hearts and lives. "Christ liveth in me" (Galatians 2:20; Romans 12:1,2). It is thus we pray—

O Jesus Christ, grow Thou in me,
And all things else recede
My heart be daily freed from sin,
And closer drawn to Thee!

Christ Was Justified by the Spirit

It has been affirmed that there is no direct reference to the Spirit in our Lord's life from His birth to His baptism, and if we confine ourselves to the gospels such an affirmation may be true. The manifestation of remarkable wisdom, however, at the early age of twelve, and the mark of humility in Christ's subjection to Joseph and Mary infer the work of the Spirit in Christ as prophesied by Isaiah (Luke 2:20,47, 51,52 R.V.; Isaiah 11:1,2).

Paul reminds us that Christ was "justified," or vindicated "by the Spirit," which is a phase of the Spirit's action covering not only the three and one-half years of ministry, but the first thirty silent years. In His humble home at Nazareth, Jesus found Himself misunderstood by those around. His brothers did not believe in Him. He was a stranger unto His brethren, and an alien unto His mother's children (Psalm 69:8). But through all those years of rejection, Jesus had the constant attention of the Spirit. To all His claims to divine Sonship, the Spirit could say, "Amen!" As Mary's son, He did not occasion much pleasure, but turning aside from Nazareth and entering His brief, but dynamic ministry there came the benediction, "This is My beloved Son, in whom I am well pleased" (Matthew 3:17; Acts 4:27,30).

And, as Christ's followers, we should know what it is to be dead to self-vindication, awaiting at all times the Spirit's vindication, which, sooner or later is given, much to the confusion of those who misjudge us. Christ cared not about His reputation. He flung it to the winds, making Himself of no reputation (Philippians 2:7). He was ever careful, though, regarding His character. And, as D. L. Moody put it, character is what a man is in the dark.

Christ Was Anointed With the Spirit

At the inauguration of Christ's official life, the Holy Spirit was again active. In the form of a dove, a living symbol, the Spirit comes upon Jesus as He emerges from His retirement for His mediatorial work as Prophet, Priest and King. As it has been stated, "At last the time had arrived when the bud should break into flower."

Basic passages, taken up with this special ministry of the Spirit, are Matthew 3:16; 12:18; Acts 4:27,30; 10:38. And the divine unction, thus indicated, was a necessary preparation for Christ's work. Heavy tasks were ahead. He must go out to seek and save the lost—to die for the world's redemption, and so is endowed marvelously and immeasurably with the Spirit.

It does not say that Christ was baptized with the Spirit, but anointed with His power. Since the baptism of the Spirit, or better still "The Baptism *with* the Spirit" (He is never the Baptizer), results in making us members of the Body of Christ (I Corinthians 12:13), it is evident that Christ did not need this aspect of the Spirit's ministry, seeing He could not be joined to His own body.

1. Christ's anointing with the Spirit was an evidence of His claim.

How were the people to know that this obscure Man of Nazareth was God's Chosen? The Father's benediction and the Spirit's descent upon Christ indicated that He was indeed the Sent-one (Isaiah 48:16; John 6:27). One of the most instructive writers on Hebrew ritual and worship reminds us that it was the custom for the priest, to whom the service of presenting offerings pertained, to inspect with minutest scrutiny, a selected lamb. If without any physical defect, he would then seal it with the Temple seal, thus signifying that it was fit for sacrifice and food.

At Jordan, the Lamb of God presented Himself for inspection, and under the Father's omniscient scrutiny was found to be without blemish. Well pleased with His Son, God anointed Him with the Spirit, who in turn became the Seal of Christ's separation unto sacrifice and service (Matthew 3:16,17; Mark 1:10,11; Luke 3:21,22; John 1:32,33).

2. Christ's anointing with the Spirit was for testing.

Immediately after the double attestation at Jordan there came the conflict in the wilderness. "Then was Jesus led up of the Spirit . . . to be tempted of the devil" (Matthew 4:1). And so the newly anointed Prophet passes into the arena to meet the satanic foe. And it was the Holy Spirit who led Jesus to such a critical conflict, comforting, equipping and building Him by the way. Angels might minister to His lower natural life when the conflict was over, but it must be the Spirit's unshared ministry to bring afresh into view those deep things of God by which His higher life might be sustained. The forces of evil, although far from infinite, are mighty in themselves, and appalling in their resources, and Christ can only venture to meet them by the Spirit.

And what fools we are if, like Peter, we face the Tempter in the spirit of pride and self-sufficiency, in a spirit of reckless-ness and presumption, madly defying the power of the enemy and lacking the unction of the Spirit. Jordan and the wilderness go together. First the Dove—then the devil! And God pity us if we meet the devil without first meeting the Dove. For a vic-torious wilderness, we must have a Jordan experience.

Further, as the natures of the Dove and the devil differ, so do their purposes. The One blesses, the other blasts. Some are all Dove and no devil. Sin, they tell us, has been eradicated and they are now sin-less. Others are all devil. These are hope-lessly defeated. Sin reigns within their lives. The true spiritual progressive life, however, is the one in which both the Dove and the devil are to be found, with the Dove continually keeping the devil at bay. The question is, Do we deliberately help the Spirit in His struggle against the flesh?

Two thoughts suggest themselves as we think of our Lord's temptation, the first being that the wilderness came before His ministry. The first, direct outcome of the Spirit's anointing was not to cast out de-mons, but to defeat the devil himself, both for His sake and ours. He had to exper-ience the full strength of the foe, ere He could deliver those who were bound. The second thought is, Christ's testing followed a deep, spiritual experience. After the wa-ters, the wilderness—After heaven's voice, hell's venom—After the benediction, the battle—After the Dove, the devil. And this is ever the order. Pentecost was quickly fol-lowed by persecution (Acts 2:4). What we fail to realize is that our most critical mo-ments are those immediately following some deep, spiritual experience. After some moun-tain-top revelation we find ourselves assailed most bitterly by the enemy, so much so that we are tempted to doubt the validity of our Jordan. How essential it is to realize in such hours that Satan is out to reclaim all terri-tory lost to the Spirit—that the devil is endeavoring to displace the Dove.

3. Christ's anointing was for service.

What a divine sequence Christ's rela-tion with the Spirit affords! The Dove—the devil—the dynamic. Luke reminds us that "when the devil had ended all the temptation . . . Jesus returned in the power of the Spirit into Galilee" (Luke 4:14,18). Jordan—wilderness—Galilee, these three, and their order is never reversed.

The dovelike form of the Spirit implying peace, tenderness, holy and gentle fellow-ship suggests the nature of the One thus anointed for service. The name "Galilee," means "circle," and Jesus now goes into every circle of need in the Spirit's power to diffuse all that the nature of the Dove portrays.

God's Spirit had no need to come to God's obedient, undefiled Son as scorching fire. The blessed Third Person came with new anointings, discernments and preroga-tives to the humanity of Christ. He came as a fresh vehicle of fresh visions, fresh powers, fresh aptitudes, fresh vocations, which mighty things were by and by to pass from the risen Head to the members of His body.

Fame goes from Christ, and glory re-turned to Him in various ways as He exer-cised that dynamic ministry of His.

(a) *He had power over demons.* It was all in vain that Satan tried to induce Jesus to work in His own strength, in the power of His inherent Godhead, tempting Him to reverse thereby, the self-renouncing hu-mility of His incarnation. Christ stoutly affirmed that demons were expelled by the Spirit of God (Matthew 12:28; Acts 10:38).

(b) *He had power over disease and death.* Another specific result of the anoint-ing with the Spirit was the action of Christ in healing all who were oppressed of the devil. Having gained a decisive victory over the source of all evil and suffering, Christ is now able to deal with the results of same. As the Spirit of Life, the Ener-gizer enabled Jesus to quicken the diseased and pain-stricken bodies and minds of men, and also raise those whom death had claimed.

(c) *He had power to preach and teach.* Recognizing Himself as the Sent-one of God, the perfect Anti-type of all Old Testa-ment types, symbols and ordinances, Christ definitely declared His divine commission to proclaim a divine message. "The Spirit of the Lord is upon Me, because He hath anointed Me to preach . . . to preach . . . to preach" (Luke 4:18,19). And as the result of this equipment the people "wondered at the gracious words which proceeded out of His mouth" (4:22). Surely this is evidence enough that the ministry of Christ was the product of His implicit dependence on the inward Counselor. The Father gave the Word—gave it by the continuous elucidation of the Spirit who indwelt Christ.

This also must be acknowledged, Christ came to His oral ministry because He was divinely called to it, and divinely anointed for it. The usual Rabbinical training He lacked. "How knoweth this man letters, having never learned?" (John 7:14-16). He possessed, however, thé greatest of all equipment for His witness, namely, an intimate knowledge of Scriptures and the fullness of the Spirit. And, lacking these two most vital and essential requisites, all the academical training gathered at cultural centers is but futile and useless.

Christ Was Gladdened by the Spirit

As the hour of Christ's rejection drew near, Luke tells us that He "rejoiced in the Holy Spirit" (Luke 10:21 R.V.). Weymouth translates the passage, "He was filled by the Holy Spirit with rapturous joy." Another rendering has it, "He thrilled with joy at that hour in the Holy Spirit." Thus, the Spirit was the Source of our Lord's joy, enabling Him to triumph over His circumstances and to glory even in His tribulations. Anointed with the oil of gladness, He possessed an inward peace and joy independent of all outward experiences and happenings (Hebrews 1:9).

Have you ever noticed the somewhat unmistakable connection between the Spirit and joy? On the day of Pentecost, the waiting disciples were anointed with the Spirit in such a way as to make them God-intoxicated men. "These men are full of new wine." Theirs was a gladness, a hilarity others could not miss. Later on, when persecution came to these same men, we read that they were filled with joy and with the Spirit (Acts 13:52). Paul speaks of "joy in the Holy Spirit" (R.V.), and of joy "as the fruit of the Spirit" (Romans 14:17; Galatians 5:22; Colossians 1:11; I Thessalonians 1:6).

There is false rejoicing, a superficial, effervescent ecstatic feeling worked up by those who resort to a purely fleshly, psychic appeal. Jesus spoke of His own sharing His joy (John 15:11), and such a brand

of joy can come only through the Spirit, and is a joy independent of all circumstances. This was the joy Paul and Silas experienced, when suffering in a prison cell, which could in spite of much physical pain and discomfort, make them forget sleep and sing praises unto God at a midnight hour.

What do we know of this joy unspeakable and full of glory? Are we sharing Christ's joy? Is ours the right foundation of joy (Luke 10:20)? "There is a river, the streams whereof shall make glad the city of God" (Psalm 46:4). And this gladdening River is the Holy Spirit (John 7:37-39). The city of God is a symbol of the church John saw here coming down from heaven as "The Holy City" (Revelation 21:2). The Spirit in these days of the church's need and challenge is the Source of her abiding, captivating joy, exuberance and radiancy.

Christ Died by the Spirit

The writer to the Hebrews informs us that it was "through the Eternal Spirit," that Jesus offered Himself to God as the sinless Substitute for sinners (Hebrews 9:14). The same Spirit who had formed Christ's human body at the Incarnation enabled Him to become strong, wise and gracious (Luke 2:40), guided and empowered Him, prepared Him for sacrifice and sustained Him as He died. "It was through the Eternal Spirit," says one expositor, "that His sacred will conquered its aversion to death and for love to His Father and His people made Him a Sacrifice for sin, without blemish as a perfect offering. The Prophet now becomes the Victim, and is shortly to be the Priest."

The cross is eternally efficacious, not only because Christ as the perfect, sinless One was thereon, but because all the members of the Godhead were involved in our redemption. God was in Christ and also the Spirit, reconciling earth to heaven.

The Spirit was present at Calvary as a witness of the act of eternal redemption, and is the only living Witness in the world to the sufferings of Christ. Speaking of the cruel death of the Saviour, Peter declared the apostles had been witnesses of such a bitter end, and went on to say, "so is the Holy Spirit" (Acts 5:32 R.V.). The first generation of witnesses have been dead for almost 1900 years, but the divine Witness remains (I Peter 5:1; Hebrews 10:14,15). As Dr. Elden Cumming states it,

> There were human witnesses of the outward tragedy, but the Spirit who had been the lifelong companion of Christ's deepest and most secret thoughts, was the one solitary Witness of the infinite and eternal virtue which enforced and informed the sacrifice . . . Just as an attendant waited upon the steps of the sacrificing priest, who scrutinized the victim to be placed upon the altar, and was a sponsor for its unblemished health, so the Spirit who had watched with unresting jealousy and vigilance over the life of the Son, mediated in His last offering, and as earth and Heaven became the sponsor for its spotlessness and soul-cleansing power.*

What a sublime truth! Wonderful indeed to realize that it was through the faithful influences of this holy and unseen Companion that the work of salvation wrought out by Jesus Christ was crowned. In the darkest and most troubled moments of His earthly life, the Spirit had vouchsafed communications of His Father's love, and by this inward ministry of revelation the Son had been kept unchangeably true to the Father and the Father's appointed work.

And it is because of the Spirit's association with the cross, that He ever blesses "the preaching of the cross." He can illuminate such a truth and visualize the facts of Christ's death. Therefore, let us exalt and magnify the finished work of Christ in absolute dependence upon the blessed Spirit who witnessed its completion. And coupled with our witness, may there come the full offering of ourselves for whatever service He may appoint, without spot of self-interest or self-glory. With a crucified Saviour and a crucified saint, what untold wonders the Holy Spirit can accomplish in a world of sin!

Christ Was Raised by the Spirit

With united voice, the New Testament affirms that the Spirit was "the efficient cause" of our Lord's Resurrection: "The Spirit of Him that raised up Jesus from the dead" (Romans 1:4; 8:11); "Put to death in the flesh, but quickened by the Spirit" (I Peter 3:18). As the Spirit of life, the Spirit of the conception, He was likewise the Spirit of the Resurrection. The Power giving the antenatal life and bringing it to birth was the same who

* *The Eternal Spirit* p. 353.

quickened that body in the tomb and helped to bring it forth as "the first begotten of the dead."

The Resurrection, then, was the supreme effort of the Giver of life, "By it He gave life to the dead body of Christ, but reunited the human spirit to its proper dwelling, not as a mere tenement, but as a home, insusceptible of further death."

Where do you think the Holy Spirit was, while the body of Jesus rested in the tomb? Surely, it is not fanciful to imagine that the Spirit was in the tomb guarding that sacred tabernacle of flesh He had possessed, led and strengthened through all its earthly pilgrimage? The Roman authorities had their seal on the outside of the tomb declaring that Jesus would not rise again—God had His Seal, the Spirit is the Seal, inside proclaiming that His Son would rise again. And rise again He did, on the third day robed with life forevermore. Thus, as in the virgin womb of Mary, the Spirit fashioned the physical body of Jesus, so now in the virgin tomb of Joseph He prepares the glorified body of Jesus. It was the Spirit, then, who quickened into life that holy body which the Psalmist prophesied should not see corruption (Psalm 16:10).

And it is the selfsame Spirit within the believer who is the pledge of his final resurrection (Romans 8:23; Ephesians 1:13,14; 4:30). As the "Earnest," the Spirit is the guarantee of our victory over death. Presently, He is able to quicken us spiritually, physically and mentally. "The Spirit of Him that raised up Jesus from the dead . . . shall also quicken your mortal bodies" (Romans 8:11). An ancient creed refers to the Spirit as "The Lord, the Life-Giver," and as such He can impart to us the resurrection life of the Lord Christ Himself.

Christ Gave Commandments by the Spirit

Out-soaring the limitations and humiliations of His earthly lot, Christ, even in His resurrection form, was still related to the Spirit—"Through the Holy Spirit He gave commandments unto His disciples" (cf. Acts 1:2). By the inspiration of the Spirit, the risen Lord instructed His immediate followers as to the continuance of His work and the committal of the Gospel to others. And the book of Acts proves how those Spirit-filled men preached the Word received from Christ, with mighty power

(Matthew 28:19; Acts 1:8; 2:41; I Thessalonians 4:2).

Coming to ourselves, we realize that our preaching and teaching can only be effective as we communicate to others what we are taught of the Spirit. If Christ, in His risen life, was Spirit-inspired to instruct His disciples, how deep must our need be of the Spirit's teaching ministry (John 14:16; 15:26).

At Pentecost, the ascended Lord sent His Spirit to His previously instructed disciples in order that they might bear testimony to the fullness of their Lord. Henceforth, they are to understand the Saviour's work and worth, and in reliance upon the Spirit's unction convey the saving message to Jews and Gentiles alike.

It is somewhat significant that in the final revelation given to the churches, Christ and the Spirit are still together. The mystic union abides. In Revelation 2 and 3, for example, each letter sent to the churches begins with a glorious title of Christ and invariably ends with, "Hear what the Spirit saith unto the churches." Well might we pray—

> Make Thou the blessed motto of my life to be ever thus, In the Name of the Lord Jesus and by the Spirit of our God, joining Him and Thee together in one secret of power and peace. O Spirit, glorify Christ to me, that Christ may be glorified, in some measure through me.

One final word of appeal. Our gracious Lord realized and enjoyed the Spirit's indwelling and fullness. His own forceful word was so true of His own life and experience—"Out of Him . . . shall flow rivers of living water." Christ submitted to the sway of the Spirit, and now commands all His followers to be filled with the Spirit (Ephesians 5:18).

John reminds us that we are to walk even as Jesus walked (I John 2:6). How did Jesus walk? He walked in the Spirit, and we must go and do likewise (Galatians 5:16).

We are apt to forget that the same resources of the Spirit appropriated by Christ in the days of His flesh, are at our disposal, with this notable addition, namely, all the virtue and efficacy of a crucified, risen, glorified, interceding Lord. What a vast heritage is ours! No gift of the Spirit bestowed upon Christ is denied to His followers if only they seek what the Spirit

has for Christ's glory, and as loyal and uncompromising servants of the divine counsels. As the Spirit was not given by measure unto Christ, so the same unstinted munificence awaits our appropriation. Our heavenly Father ungrudgingly gives the Spirit to those whose needs are deep, pressing and manifold (Luke 11:13).

May our lives then reveal the permeation of the Spirit! He waits to dominate and control our thoughts, words, feelings, actions, pleasures and pursuits, making us, even as Christ before us, "fine flour mingled with oil." To know what it is to be Spirit-possessed we must claim the promise of Acts 1:8—forsake all that is alien to the mind of the Holy Spirit—respond immediately to the least whisper of His voice.

The Saints and the Spirit

Regarding the association between the Holy Spirit and the Church as a collective body of saints, these aspects can be noted. Before we think of His work with us individually, we must dwell upon it as a whole—

1. *The Spirit brought the Church into being.*

Pentecost has been spoken of as *the birthday of the Church*, and it was then by the Spirit that she commenced historically. Hitherto, believers were as units, independent one of another but through the Spirit's agency they were all fused into the mystic body, "The Church of the Living God." They were baptized into one body (Ephesians 2:5,6; 5:23; I Corinthians 12:13-27; Acts 2:47). Since then the true Church has been composed of regenerated men and women united together by a living and indissoluble bond through the Spirit.

2. *The Spirit is the Source of Church Unity.*

There is only one Church of which Christ is the Head, and all true believers form "one man in Christ Jesus" (Galatians 3:27, 28). Those forming the Church are urged to "keep the unity of the Spirit" who, Himself is *one* (Ephesians 4:3,4). But while we are all one in Christ, such unity does not mean uniformity, but unity with diversity with each member of the body fulfilling his own particular purpose (I Corinthians 12:12-26).

3. *The Spirit fashions the Church into His Temple.*

What a solemn truth it is that the Holy

Spirit looks upon the Church as His Temple, as "the habitation of God"! (I Corinthians 6:19; II Corinthians 6:16). Each individual believer is like a Temple of the Spirit, a living stone built into a spiritual house (I Peter 2:5).

4. *The Spirit bestows His gifts upon the Church.*

As the members of the human body are so placed that each of them may exercise their proper function, so in the Body of Christ, each believer has a particular gift of the Spirit's choosing. No believer is without a gift of some sort to be used to the limit in the service of God (I Corinthians 12:11; Ephesians 4:11,12).

5. *The Spirit governs and controls the Church.*

The book of Acts, demonstrating the establishment and expansion of the Church, reveals not only the presence of the Spirit but His *presidency.* He calls the apostles to serve God (Acts 13:2; 20:28)—guides and sustains them in their ministry (Acts 13:4,8,9; 16:6,7)—inspires their decisions (Acts 15:28)—communicates to the Church divine messages (Revelation 2, 3).

6. *The Spirit supplies all that is necessary for the Church's growth.*

Brought into being by His power, the Church is dependent upon the Spirit for all that is necessary for her life (Acts 9:31). He it is who gives the increase.

7. *The Spirit ever magnifies Christ as the Head of the Church.*

Part of His great office is to glorify Christ (John 16:13,14) who, with His own blood bought the church (Ephesians 1:22,23; 5:25). It is the gracious Spirit who is preparing the Church as a Bride to meet the Bridegroom when He returns to claim His own.

Let us now examine the individual aspect of the Spirit's work, and discover just what He accomplishes when He makes the believing one a member of Christ's Body.

The last century has witnessed a revival of interest in the truth of the Spirit's personality and work. Never have we had such a wealth of printed material dealing with such a theme. At an ever-growing number of Bible Conferences, too, this truth is given prominence, causing multitudes of believers to realize that they have by no means exhausted the riches treasured up in Christ.

With many, a sense of defeat drove them to the New Testament to discover what it had to say about the blessed victory the Holy Spirit makes possible through the crucified, ascended and glorified Saviour. And, if all the facts and promises of holiness and holy living through the Spirit are not in the Bible to mock us, but are capable of realization, then, surely, it ought to be our desire to understand and experience such promises of victorious living.

The Truth Outlined

Owing to conflicting ideas regarding the Spirit's ministry in the life and work of the believer, we deem it necessary to closely examine New Testament teaching on the same. Too often this truth is neglected owing to error and confusion as to the functions of the Spirit. Our prayer therefore, is for divine guidance, as we endeavor to rightly divide the Word of Truth.

"I am amazed at a man like you going to these Conferences where you hear a lot about the Holy Spirit," said a critic to a pastor. "What new thing can these Conference speakers tell you? It is all in the New Testament." Replied the seeker for truth, "Yes, that is the trouble. We have left this truth in the New Testament. Whereas we want to get it out of the New Testament into our hearts and lives."

1. *His Ministry of Incorporation*

The great work of the Spirit's incorporation operates in a twofold way, and it is essential to distinguish between the *fulness* and the *filling* of the Spirit. Such terms describe, as we hope to prove, the different actions of the Spirit as He seeks to incorporate Himself within the lives of those who are obedient to His sway.

The filling.

Several are referred to as having received "the filling of the Spirit" (cf. Luke 1:15,41, 67; Acts 2:4; 4:8,31; 9:17; 13:9,52). "Filled" as a participle refers to an occasional experience, a more abundant blessing for the time being than "fullness." This "filling" denotes a special inspiration, a momentary action or impulse of the Holy Spirit for particular purposes.

Those who are habitually full of the Spirit need to be filled to meet a particular need. And in times of peculiar difficulty or trial we can count upon the additional supply of the Spirit's grace and wisdom. Extraordinary enduements for special needs and emergencies can be looked for. Thus, the formula condenses the truth. "One baptism of the Spirit—many fillings."

The fullness.

"Fullness" is an adjective, and suggests a permanent position, a habitual abiding condition. Barnabas and Stephen are spoken of as being "full of the Holy Spirit" (Acts 7:55; 11:24 R.V.). Christ also, was full of the Spirit (Luke 4:1). He received the Spirit without measure (John 3:34).

Although habitually full, there was a need of a filling for specific needs. "Full" was the normal experience. "Filled," the abnormal. What believers should seek and claim as their privilege is the habitual condition—always full of the Spirit. And this abiding condition, being full of the Spirit, should characterize every believer at all times and under all circumstances. This normal experience can be best illustrated by a vessel filled with water to the brim.

Such a spiritual fullness, however, does not render the believer independent of any further supply of the Spirit's power, nor make him self-satisfied. On the contrary, the fuller one is, the more conscious he becomes of his own insufficiency, and of the necessity of the Spirit's sustaining and renewing grace moment by moment.

One who is "full" will find that as special difficulties or calls arise that there are always special fillings for witness, and triumph, and that these fillings come just when God sees they are needed. It is His responsibility to send them, and ours to receive them.

"Fillings" come in the path of service according to need. Therefore, we must not be anxious to receive momentary supplies, the Lord will bestow according to His riches in glory. In this chapter it is rather the "fullness" of the Spirit, the believer's normal life we desire to emphasize.

2. *His Blessed Incoming*

The fullness of the Spirit rests upon the basis of His presence in the life. We cannot be filled with anything we do not possess. Regeneration brings the Holy Spirit into the believing sinner. "If any man have not the Spirit of Christ, he is none of His" (Romans 8:9). "None of His." How emphatic! Such a serious statement demands attention. Where the vital bond does not exist between the soul and Christ, the divine Spirit is not to be found. Whatever virtues a person may possess, or whatever attractions and qualities may adorn his character, if unsaved, he is destitute of the Spirit. One, therefore, must make sure of the initial work of the Spirit, otherwise, it is useless to cry

for His fullness seeing the infilling is based upon regeneration. It is the Holy Spirit who unites us to Christ, making us thereby, accepted in the Beloved. We are joined unto the Lord by one Spirit (I Corinthians 6: 17).

And so, the first pulsation of divine life is due to the divine Spirit. What the soul is to the body, the Spirit is to the soul of the believer.

What are our works but sin and death
Till Thou the Quickening Spirit breathe.

The Holy Spirit then, is the "spot" of God's children. "Their spot is not the spot of His children" (Deuteronomy 32:5). The presence of the Spirit in the life is the divine mark or "spot," by which the child of God is distinguished from a child of the devil.

Then on each He setteth,
  His own secret sign,
They who have My Spirit,
  These, saith He, are mine.

What we must hasten to make clear is the fact that as far as God is concerned there is no reason why the fullness of the Spirit should not take place at regeneration. There need be no intervening period in the life, no gaps. One can blossom almost immediately into life more abundant. Only three days elapsed between Paul's conversion and the fullness of the Spirit. Alas, with the vast majority of believers, it is otherwise! Ignorance of the truth of the Spirit, lack of a full, complete surrender at the moment of the new birth robs them of the Spirit's fullness. Thus, as they journey on they come to yield to the Spirit's infilling, and experience a blessing as distinct and definite as that of His initial work in regeneration. Such an experience is sometimes referred to as "the second blessing." Really, it is the other half of the first blessing, the fuller realization of the presence and power of the Blesser who entered once and for all.

3. *His Permanent Indwelling*

Many are kept back from the realization of the Spirit's indwelling through mistaking it with the reception of miraculous gifts. The Spirit's indwelling, however, is distinct from His fullness and infilling. We can possess the Spirit, yet not be possessed by Him. It is said that "Egypt always has the Nile, but Egypt waits every year for its overflow." Having the Nile is one thing, rejoicing in the overflow is another. The Nile's overflow is Egypt's salvation. But to overflow, the river must first be full. And the overflow from our lives is the world's salvation. But in order to overflow we must first experience the fullness of the blessing of the Gospel of Christ.

(a) This indwelling is personal.

There is a sense in which the Spirit is related to every man, seeing He is the Co-Creator of the unregenerated, who have not yet received the Spirit. And even the unsaved are dependent upon the Spirit. The physical life they enjoy, and their intelligence by which they are gifted, are due to the unknown Spirit. But His wondrous indwelling is an altogether distinct aspect of the Spirit's gracious ministry. "He shall be in you." He possesses each and every one accepting Christ as Saviour. There may be outstanding gifts of the Spirit for a few, but "The Gift of the Spirit" is for every believer, no matter how simple and ordinary.

One of Satan's lies is that such a heritage is not for us. But he knows only too well that the Spirit is the birthright of every believer, his birthright in virtue of the new birth. He also knows what it means to his evil sway when a believer lives in enjoyment of the Spirit's fullness. The question is, Are we living this moment in the realization of this birthright, or like Esau are we despising our birthright? Are we possessing our possessions?

The Early Church was dynamic in witness, simply because all the witnesses were filled with the Holy Spirit (Acts 2:4,33). It is for all, at all times. It is not the luxury of a few. Whether a week or a century old in the faith, we can claim all there is of the Spirit, if His incoming is a realized fact.

(b) This indwelling is permanent.

When the Spirit enters, He enters to remain. His indwelling is permanent (II Corinthians 13:9). He abides with us forever (John 14:16). As the Holy Inhabitant, He remains with us until death. He dwells in our hearts, that is, settles down, never to be driven out (Ephesians 3:16). His is an abiding presence. Grieve Him we may, and do, but we can never grieve Him out of our lives. Our spirit becomes the permanent nest for God's holy Dove. And it is necessary to maintain this attitude until it becomes a settled habit.

As we open our window each morning to welcome and breathe in the fresh air, so let us address the Spirit as each new day commences, welcoming Him as the Inmate of our being, the Fountain of peace and joy, the Strength of our heart, the Director of our life. And as the day proceeds let us count upon Him, who came as the Helper of the redeemed.

4. *His Gracious Infilling*

The work of the Spirit within the believer's life is progressive. As the Well, He longs to rise and fill every part of the inner life and then flow out to influence other lives. So we come to Paul's great word about being filled with the Spirit, a fuller treatment of which is given under "Marks of Infilling."

Saints are referred to as being filled with God (Ephesians 3:19). Christ fills all things (4:10). Coneybeare and Howson translate Paul's command in Ephesians 5:18, "Be filled with the indwelling of the Spirit." And if our lives are to function aright as "the mysterious cabinet of the Trinity," we must be filled with the Spirit in the sense of a pitcher sunk in a well and filled in the well. We are to be in the Spirit and fully filled with Him. Bishop Moule expresses the truth thus—"Let in the holy atmosphere to your inner self, to your whole will and soul. Let the divine Spirit pervade your being as water fills the sponge."

Paul urged upon the Ephesian believers the Spirit's infilling as a habitual condition. In the Acts, this filling was necessary for daily need in service. For witness before kings and rulers, the apostles were filled with the Spirit, exercising thereby the power of reply and defense as occasion arose. It was the Spirit who gave them the mouth of wisdom, so that with simplicity and directness they could answer all questions.

At this point, we can pause to indicate the threefold aspect of the apostolic call to a life filled with the Spirit—

(a) It is a call to receive Someone.

The voice is *passive* not *active*. Thus, the call is not to do anything but permit something to be done in and for us. Such an infilling of the Spirit is, of course, dependent upon the consent of the will, and a right attitude before God. We must be willing to open the avenues of our inner being for the inrush of the living waters.

(b) It is a call to a distinct duty.

We enjoy many privileges in our Christian life, but the Spirit's infilling is not one of them. It is not a privilege, or distinction or honor to be filled with the Spirit, it is our duty. The language Paul uses indicates an imperative necessity; something each of us ought to be and have.

Banks have what are called "unclaimed deposits." Often these were owned by people who lived and died in poverty. Can it be that we have a vast unclaimed deposit in God's treasury? Do we live in spiritual penury, a hand to mouth existence, and yet have such wealth at our disposal? May grace be ours to possess all we have through the Spirit!

(c) It is a call to a positive command.

Later on, we hope to enlarge on this aspect of our theme. Briefly, Paul is giving us an inspired, authoritative command. The Spirit's infilling is not optional, something to please ourselves about. If this is not our normal experience, then we live in disobedience. The Spirit, of course, cannot fill the life if it is full of something else. If full of pride, self, preconceived ideas, prejudice, or the world, we cannot be full of the Spirit.

Willingness must be ours to let Him saturate every part of our life expelling thereby, everything alien to His will. And the Spirit ever fills by displacement.

> Oh, ye that are thirsting for fullness
> Make room by forsaking all sin,
> Surrender to Him your whole nature
> By faith let the Spirit come in.

One may ask, How can the fullness be obtained? The answer is, Be cleansed, consecrated, then claim.

There is, of course, a difference between asking and claiming. If you have money in the bank you do not have to plead with the cashier to give you ten dollars on your account. You present your check and claim what is your own. But suppose your account is overdrawn and you need ten dollars to tide you over a difficulty? Then you have to ask the favor of a loan.

In virtue of our regeneration, we have received the Holy Spirit, therefore we have not to plead—Give, give, give—but claim all we have in Him. The two key words helping to make appropriation possible are "desire" and "receive."

Desire. "If any man thirst" (John 7:37-39).

Do we really desire to be filled, experiencing thereby a life of victory over beset-

ting sins? Without desire, we can never be delivered from a dry and thirsty land where no water is. All prayer for the Spirit is formal and unreal if desire is lacking. "Blessed are they which do hunger and thirst . . . they shall be filled."

Can we truly confess that we have been brought to know our parched and barren condition—the utter folly of all worldly compromise—the necessity of a full and complete surrender to God? If the language of our inner soul is, "As the hart panteth after the water brooks, so panteth my soul after Thee," then we are halfway on the road to blessing.

To be brought to the place of self-despair, shrinking not from the willingness to go all out for God, fearing not the loss of worldly treasures, then the flood tide of the Spirit can be expected. If we desire to be filled, God is determined to fill us.

Receive. "Receive (ye) the Holy Spirit" (Acts 8:15 R.V.).

At Samaria, Peter and John prayed that believers there might receive the Spirit. The fullness of the Spirit, therefore, is not a promise to plead, but a command to obey and a blessing to receive. If some are hindered from appropriation through want of desire, others are destitute of the fullness through lack of reception.

It will, of course, be understood that we do not receive more of the Spirit. Yielding ourselves more completely to His sway, He receives more of us. Through believing reception He permeates every part of our life. If we receive someone into our home, yet only give them the possession of one room, even though it is the best room, they still do not occupy the whole house. If, however, we allow them to take one room after another until they have full control of every part of the house, then and only then can it be called their own. What takes place is not more and more of a man coming into the house, but more and more of the house becoming his possession. Thus it is with the reception of the Spirit's fullness. Our entire life is brought more completely under His control and power.

In connection with such a reception there are two phases to distinguish. First of all, we *receive by resting*. Already we have noted that there is no need to wait or tarry for a special gift as the disciples had to. It is the Spirit who waits to bless.

But soul-rest is necessary in order that we may be ready to receive all the Spirit is willing to bestow. And such an attitude is an essential condition in all spiritual progress. We wait *on* the Lord rather than *for* the Lord. By waiting, or resting, we cease from self, from carrying our own cares, anxieties and burdens. All is submitted unreservedly into the hands of God. We become as clay in the hand of the Potter. Soul-rest produces adjustment of the whole inner being to the divine will.

Secondly, we *receive by faith*. The fullness of the blessing is one of the blessings of the Spirit it is our privilege to claim by the simple act of faith. "Receive the promise of the Spirit through faith" (Galatians 3: 13,14; John 7:37-39). We have not to wait for feeling, for an experience of overflowing joy, but accept by faith. Faith acts as if we felt. If we are conscious that all hindrances have been yielded to the Blood, then we can claim our birthright by faith believing that we do so, the Spirit takes full possession.

As we keep believing, God keeps us filled with the Holy Spirit, who, as the Spirit of faith, makes our faith possible. It has been said that "we must take God's checks by faith and cash them by obedience." By faith, we must reckon we are filled, then daily act as if we are.

The Sufficiency of The Spirit

By the Spirit's plentitude we imply that fullness, completeness characterizing all His manifold works and ways. Four times over we read of Him as "the seven Spirits of God" (Revelation 1:4; 3:1; 4:5; 5:6), a phrase describing the perfection of the Spirit. There are not seven Spirits, only One, who has a sevenfold manifestation.

The Hebrew significance of "seven" suggests, "to become satisfied, satiated or filled." Thus, the primary idea is that of abundance, and is descriptive of nature's perfection with its seven-colored lights and seven notes of music.

The divine significance of "seven" carries the similar thought of perfection, whether of good or evil. There were the seven days of creation. We are to forgive seventy times seven. There were the seven sayings of the cross. Seven other spirits, speak of the completion of satanic possession. Seven also played a prominent part in Levitical requirements.

Spiritually, "seven" speaks of the plenitude of the Holy Spirit's power, and of His diversified activity. As the "seven devils," or "seven other [evil] spirits" (Luke 8:2; 11:26), indicate perfection of evil, so the Spirit, as "the seven Spirits of God," refers to the abundance, perfection of all that is good. "Seven was the expression of the highest power, the greatest conceivable fullness of force and therefore, was early pressed into service of religion," and it is thus we come to apply it to the Spirit's ministry. Such a fullness is evident in a fourfold way—

1. In Himself.

John in his Revelation applies "seven" to the Spirit thus—"The seven Spirits of God" (Revelation 1:4; 3:1; 4:5; 5:6). All His fullness and perfection are derived from God.

"Seven lamps of fire burning before the throne" (Revelation 4:5). To the Spirit is granted the perfection of governmental action.

"Seven horns" (Revelation 5:6). As the "horn" is the symbol of power, we here have the Spirit's fullness of power to execute judgment.

"Seven eyes" (Revelation 5:6). As the "eye" is the symbol of understanding, we understand by "seven eyes," perfect vision, intelligence. As eyes, the Spirit penetrates; as lamps, He reveals, exposes; as horns, He destroys, overcomes.

Amidst all the Spirit's diversity, however, there is an inescapable unity. Though His work was and is various, He is yet "One Spirit."

In the *Old Testament* we have His manifold operation as a physical and material Power.

In the *gospels*, all His grace and energy were concentrated upon one Person, the Lord Jesus Christ. Into Him, the Spirit poured His abundance (John 3:34).

In the *Acts*, we witness the plenitude of His power in the establishment and extension of the Church.

In the *epistles*, He is brought before us as the Source of all spiritual gifts among the members of Christ's Body, the Church.

In *Revelation*, the Spirit is seen acting governmentally from heaven on earth.

It will also be noted that in the economy of God, one member of the Godhead is present on the earth at one time. For example, during the Old Testament dispensation, the Tabernacle, and then the Temple, localized the presence of God. And His "Shekinah Glory" was real to men. The gospels present us with God tabernacling among men in the person of His Son. There He was not in a cloud, but in a Man. Now, in this Church Age, the Spirit tabernacles within saved men and women.

2. In Christ.

Already under "Messianic Activities" we have traced the Spirit's abundance in the life and labors of our Lord. He was fully possessed and energized by the blessed Third Person.

Christ was anointed by the sevenfold Spirit in a sevenfold way, namely as—

The Spirit of the Lord
The Spirit of wisdom
The Spirit of understanding
The Spirit of counsel
The Spirit of might
The Spirit of knowledge
The Spirit of the fear of the Lord (Isaiah 11:2).

As a prism can reflect the seven different colors forming light, so our Lord manifested all the diverse, yet unified operating of the Spirit.

Christ received, by the Spirit, His sevenfold name as—

Child
Son
Governor
Wonderful Counsellor
Mighty Lord
Father of Eternity
Prince of Peace (Isaiah 9:6 R.V.).

Christ was energized by the sevenfold Spirit to perform the sevenfold ministry prophesied of old—

To preach good tidings unto the meek
To bind up the brokenhearted
To proclaim liberty to the captive
To open the prison to them that are bound
To proclaim the acceptable year of the Lord
To declare the day of vengeance of our God
To comfort all that mourn (Isaiah 61: 1,2).

Luke mentions only six aspects of Christ's ministry and omits the sixth from the list, "the day of vengeance," synchronizing with "the day of the Lord," a period covering Revelation 4 through 22. This is man's day, and "six" is man's number, but God's day is coming, and when here, will be one of judgment.

3. In the Church.

When Paul outlines the gifts of the Spirit (I Corinthians 12:4-11), he proves that in spite of the diversity of His gifts there is a unity binding them together. He refers, does he not, to "the unity of the Spirit" (Ephesians 4:3-6). And seven unities are to be kept—seven strands in the cable of Christian unity.

One Body—The true, invisible Church, the mystical body of Christ.

One Spirit—The One, forming, indwelling, sustaining the Body.

One Hope—The completion and translation of the Church.

One Lord—The Christ, the Head of the Body.

One Faith—The full revelation of God in the Gospel.

One Baptism—The work of the Spirit, whereby we are incorporated within the Body.

One God and Father—The Fountainhead of all supply.

He is Father of all—Possession.
He is above all—Pre-eminence.
He is through all—Providence.
He is in you all—Presence.

4. In the believer.

There are seven terms associating the Spirit with the believer, and confusion, bondage and darkness abound if the difference existing between the Spirit's seven operations are not distinguished. Some of these operations are initial and final—others initial and continuous.

Initial and Final Operations

Under this leading we place the Baptism, the Gift, the Sealing, the Earnest of the Spirit. Let us briefly summarize these aspects. For a fuller treatment of all the seven words used to set forth the mission and ministry of the Spirit in relation to the believer, one is referred to Dr. W. Graham Scroggie's excellent tract, "The Fullness of the Holy Spirit," published by the Moody Press. As Dr. Scroggie points out, we must not regard the seven words as synonymous, but as flashes from the diamond of truth, indicating some of its many facets.

1. Baptism with the Spirit.

The Bible nowhere speaks of "the baptism of the Holy Spirit." It is always "with" or "in" the Spirit, for He is not the Baptizer, but the Element in which we are baptized. There are seven passages in all mentioning this particular baptism, five pointing to Pentecost, and two passages going back to Pentecost. Originally and fundamentally, therefore, the baptism with the Spirit is that coming of the Spirit whereby the Church was instituted, and is equivalent in our experience to regeneration, when we are baptized into, or incorporated within the mystic fabric of the Church. "Through one Spirit we have been baptized into one body" (I Corinthians 12:13).

We are cognizant of the fact that both the baptism, and the filling, are treated as interchangeable terms, but the writer holds that these two aspects of the Spirit's mission are to be distinguished. We are not urged to be baptized of the Spirit. The Scripture does command us to be filled with the Spirit.

Some teachers, like the late Dr. R. A. Torrey, affirm that the Spirit's baptism is a definite experience to be sought by every believer. This renowned student taught that the baptism, filling, enduement cover the one and the same experience. "One may have the regenerating work of the Holy Ghost and yet not have the baptism with the Holy Spirit." We believe, however, the baptism with the Spirit is the initial work accomplished in the moment of regeneration, and not any after blessing to be sought. Whether we speak of the baptism or the filling, doubtless we are all after the same spiritual experience. Yet, surely, it is more God-honoring to seek a Biblical blessing, using Biblical language.

2. The Gift of the Spirit.

Once bestowed, the Spirit, as the Gift of the ascended Lord to His believing people, is never withdrawn. Peter makes it clear that this Gift is received when one is regenerated. "Repent, and be baptized every one of you in the name of Jesus Christ for the remission of sins, and ye shall receive the gift of the Holy Ghost" (Acts 2:38).

This coming of the Spirit into a life is both initial and final. It is therefore an insult to ask God to give us what He has already bestowed. Of course, the realization of such a Gift as the Spirit may be akin to the joy of receiving the Gift, but the fact remains that He came as the Gift of the Father and of the Son at Pentecost, and that He is the possession and Possessor of all believers (Romans 8:9,15).

3. The sealing with the Spirit.

Under "The Symbols of the Spirit" we have considered the Spirit as the Seal. The sealing of the believer with the Spirit of God is another initial and final work, accomplished as the soul accepts Christ as Saviour, when he is sealed as God's (II Timothy 2:19). The possession of, and by, the Spirit indicates that we have been purchased, and are now owned by one Purchaser.

And such a seal can never be destroyed nor withdrawn. The Spirit within is the pledge of our full and final redemption. As dirt and rubbish may obscure a signature sealed upon wax, so sin and disobedience in a life can prevent the manifestation of the Spirit's presence and power in and through such a life.

4. The earnest of the Spirit.

The Third Person of the Trinity is a foretaste of all the Lord has stored up for His own. As Dr. Scroggie reminds us, "The grapes brought into the wilderness from Canaan showed the quality of the fruit which the Israelites might enjoy to the full in the land, so the Spirit is the foretaste of heavenly fullness." As the earnest, the Spirit was another initial and final blessing from God (II Corinthians 1:22).

Initial and Continuous Operations

Because of a deficient understanding of the continuous work of the Spirit, the lives of so many Christians are devoid of fragrance and fruitfulness. Truly, there is One among, and in them, whom they know not!

What a different testimony many of us would have if only we realize that there are blessings of the Spirit which are complete, and the permanent portion of all believers; but that there are other operations, progressive and various in their nature, extent, and efficiency, according to individual faith, obedience and spiritual understanding.

The progressive operations of the Spirit in the soul vary. Through His continuous inworking the believer is led into fuller knowledge of the Truth, into closer fellowship with the Father, into richer and deeper experiences of the sustaining, satisfying and sanctifying graces of Christ.

1. The indwelling of the Spirit.

Nothing a believer can do affects this indwelling. Once He enters, the Spirit, as St. Augustine put it, becomes "our perpetual Comforter and our eternal Inhabitant." As Dr. Weymouth translates John 14:17, "He remains by your side and is in you." Dwelling within (I Corinthians 3:16), He fashions the body of the believer into His temple.

2. The anointing with the Spirit.

Such an anointing, necessary in view of service, is not a blessing, gift or grace but the blessed Spirit Himself in all His fullness, resting upon us. Jesus, as He faced His ministry, received this anointing (Acts 10: 38). How tragic it is if we are not equipped and endued for service in the same way. Let us not forget that this anointing must be claimed, not only for special ministry, but for every fresh act of service (Psalm 92: 10; I John 2:27).

3. The filling of the Spirit.

The apostles, although baptized with the Spirit at Pentecost, were filled again and again. Thus as Dr. C. I. Scofield expresses it, "One baptism, many fillings," or infillings.

By the baptism, we are put into the divine element.

By the filling, the divine element fully possesses us.

Two words are used to describe this aspect of the Spirit's work, and recognition of the distinction between the two will save us from confusion. The words are "filled" and "full."

"Filled" with the Spirit. Here the verb suggests an intermittent experience—an aspect of the Spirit's ministry commensurate with need, *e.g.* Bezaleel, Mary, the apostles.

"Full" of the Spirit. Here the adjective implies a normal habitual experience. Christ, Stephen and Barnabas are spoken of as being "full of the Spirit."

We are commanded to be "filled with the Spirit" (Ephesians 5:18), and at least two thoughts emerge as we think of the study of this express command. First, it is a definite act, for the present tense is used. At this moment, one must humbly yield to the Spirit, allowing Him to rise as the well and permeate the life. Second, it is a continuous attitude. Crisis leads to process— act becomes an attitude.

Several years ago a man was stricken ill on the street and was rushed to a near-by hospital, where he died within a few minutes. At his inquest, it was discovered that he was comparatively rich. Yet he had lived in a miserable hovel—dressed in rags— picked up crumbs—looked over eighty, but was only sixty. The verdict of the jury was —"Died of self-starvation, when he had ample funds in his possession and a banking account." Can it be that this is our tragedy, spiritually—living as paupers when

such wealth is at our disposal? May grace be ours to possess our possessions!

The Supplication of the Spirit.

It is to be feared that the majority of Christians fail to realize how dependent they are upon the varied ministry of God's Spirit. The Scriptures, for example, teach that He is the Spirit of supplications (Zechariah 12:10) and, therefore, the One who becomes at once the Sphere and Atmosphere of all true prayer.

When the Spirit takes possession of a soul, He becomes essentially the Spirit of intercession. Yearning for heart-communion with God, yet unable to express ourselves aright, the Spirit is at hand to help us in such an infirmity. He is our aid in prayer, and inspires every outgoing of the mind toward God whether in the nature of supplication, confession, thanksgiving or intercession.

Without the Holy Spirit our prayers are as lifeless as a body without a soul, as ineffective as an arrow without a bow. In his most illuminating and helpful work, *His in a Life of Prayer*, Dr. Norman B. Harrison writes,

> As the telephone is dead and impotent without the electric current, so is prayer apart from the Spirit. He supplies the sending power, He secures the access; He forms the contact, He molds the pray-er into the mind and will of God. The Spirit is at once the Guide of prayer and the Guarantor of its success.

Martin Luther once confessed, "If I fail to spend two hours in prayer each morning the devil gets the victory through the day." Luther's motto was, "He that has prayed well, has studied well." From this we learn it is only by the Spirit that we can pray and live effectually.

As we approach the outstanding features of the mystic truth of "Prayer in the Spirit," it may be found helpful to group together the different passages associated with such a theme.

"Likewise the Spirit also helpeth our infirmities: for we know not what we should pray for as we ought: but the Spirit itself maketh intercession for us with groanings which cannot be uttered. And He that searcheth the hearts knoweth what is the mind of the Spirit, because He maketh intercession for the saints according to the will of God" (Romans 8:26,27).

"And because ye are sons, God hath sent

forth the Spirit of His Son into your hearts, crying, Abba, Father" (Galatians 4:6).

"For through Him we both have access by one Spirit unto the Father" (Ephesians 2:18).

"Praying always with all prayer and supplication in the Spirit, and watching thereunto with all perseverance and supplication for all saints (Ephesians 6:18).

"For we are the circumcision, which worship God in the Spirit, . . . and have no confidence in the flesh" (Philippians 3:3).

"But ye, beloved, building up yourselves on your most holy faith, praying in the Holy Ghost" (Jude 20).

1. The Spirit is the Inspirer of all true prayer.

Responsive prayer is impossible except as we are enabled to pray, and this ability is conferred upon us by the divine Spirit. First of all, He brings the soul into right relationship with God. Being born of God, we have the privilege of sons and as sons we can pray (Galatians 4:6). Spiritual sonship, then, is the true starting point of all access to God. Fear, with its enslaving influence, is driven out, and spiritual adoption takes its place. Contact with God rests upon the basis of regeneration. Prayers are not accepted and are not acceptable unless the praying one is truly saved. The Holy Spirit is not able to pray in and through a life He does not possess, and which has not been adopted into the family of God. It is the Holy Spirit who becomes the filial Spirit, whereby we cry, "Abba, Father."

There are three elements associated with all mighty praying.

Prayer is impossible without an *act of memory*. There must be the recall of all we desire to present to God. Whether it be God's mercies, our sins or needs, or the needs of others, the Spirit must bring to our remembrance all we desire to pray about.

Prayer is impossible without an *act of mind*. As the Spirit of wisdom, He can cause us to use acceptable words as we express our adoration, supplication and petitions. And it is only by His power that we can be delivered from distractions and develop that necessary concentration prayer demands.

Prayer is impossible without an *act of love*. As the Spirit of love, shedding abroad in our hearts the love of God, He is able to lead us to present, sympathetically, the needs of others. Intercession, whether divine or human, rises on the wings of love.

It is the Spirit, then, who quickens the mind and the emotions, and imparts the ability to continue in prayer. This mighty, heavenly Intercessor prepares and possesses and prompts our minds. We easily tire, for true prayer is exacting. We ought always to pray and not to faint. Alas, however, we are better at the fainting than the praying. To pray without ceasing comes hard to the flesh (Luke 18:1; I Thessalonians 5:17). But it is here that the Spirit helps such an infirmity. We can only pray always with all prayer and supplications *in the Spirit* (Ephesians 6:18). To quote Dr. Norman Harrison again:

Were we left to ourselves and our own effort in prayer, we could not be heard. We would be as impotent as a radio set or a telephone without electric current. As electricity gives carrying power to the human voice, projecting it for thousands of miles, so the Holy Spirit performs a like service in winging our worship, petitions and aspirations "unto the Father." We may be well assured that "praying . . . in the Spirit," they do not fall short of His throne of Heavenly Grace. . . . That which enables us to "reach" the Father, giving us "access" to Him, is the Spirit-quality.

2. The Spirit arouses within the soul a sense of need.

Prayer can never attain true perfection unless it is transacted "in the Spirit." It is only through His illuminating grace and personal promptings that we can come to know the hidden consciousness of our own needs.

It is the Holy Spirit who opens to our spiritual vision a new world of purity and power by revealing the contrast between the old world of the natural life and the glorious world of victory and spirituality. And, until we are right with Him on the matter of personal and practical sanctification, we cannot expect His help in prayer. Allowing the Spirit to awaken desires to which we have been strangers, and then adjust us to those spiritual desires, we thereby fit ourselves to pray with all prayer and supplication in the Spirit.

Further, the Spirit knows what we do not know, and thus works in the heart of the believer, begetting earnest longings and groanings after those things He knows to be good and according to the will of God for us. As Dr. A. R. Fausset expresses it, "God as the Searcher of hearts, watches the surging emotions of them in prayer, and knows perfectly what the Spirit means by the groanings which He draws forth within us, because that blessed Intercessor pleads by them only for what God Himself designs to bestow."

But Paul's thought of the Spirit's intercessory ministry goes down to the depths, and includes more than those ordinary and coherent expressions before God, and those desires and feelings emerging from a clarity of apprehension through the Spirit's illuminating work. Within man there is an unfathomed depth in which there are feelings so vast and mysterious that the human mind cannot give definite form to nor articulate in fitting words.

Deep down within human personality, from which our yearnings come, the Spirit moves with perfect familiarity; and sympathizing with these mysterious longings for which we have no language, but a sigh, and a cry, lays hold of the inarticulate groanings and gives them fitting and definite meaning before God. "He that searcheth the hearts knoweth what is the mind of the Spirit." And as we are constantly beset with imperfection, weakness and ignorance, this peculiar office of the Spirit will be necessary and complimentary until we need to pray no more. It would seem as if the depth and ripeness of our spiritual experience produce a deeper sense of our requirements of the Spirit's aid as Interpreter and Intercessor.

3. The Spirit intercedes for us.

As God's free Spirit, He mingles with our spirit and makes our prayers His own, or rather creates the prayers we should pray. As the Spirit of Intercession, He exercises His function within us even as Christ exercises His intercessory work in heaven for us. "Who is he that condemneth? It is Christ that died, yea rather, that is risen again, who is even at the right hand of God, who also maketh intercession for us" (Romans 8:34). "But this man, because He continueth ever, hath an unchangeable Priesthood" (Hebrews 7:24). The Holy Spirit prays in and with and for us. He is our Paraclete on earth, as Christ is in heaven.

The object of the Spirit's petitions is the laying bare before God all the deep and hidden needs of saints. The glorified Christ intercedes in heaven for us, obtaining thereby the full fruits of His sacrifice for all the needs revealed and voiced by the Spirit.

There are two features of this unheard and mysterious groaning to be observed. Such unutterable groanings are known and understood by the Father. And they are also presented in accordance with the will of God. Human needs and divine requirements are thus harmoniously blended.

Another thought emerging from a full realization of our need of dependence upon the Spirit's ministry in prayer is deliverance from all bondage in praying. Instead of saying prayers, we pray—we follow inward guidance and promptings rather than outward, mechanical forms. And with such a mighty Intercessor there is no reason for prayerlessness.

Pray, always pray, the Holy Spirit pleads;
Within thee all thy daily, hourly needs.

4. The Spirit bestows full assurance of faith.

Because we are exhorted to draw near to God with a true heart and full assurance of faith (Hebrews 10:22), it is necessary to have such an atmosphere created for us. It is the Spirit alone who enables us to pray believingly. He creates faith in the promises and ability of God, thus making our prayers, prayers of faith.

And this Spirit-begotten assurance produces a clear recognition of God as the divine source of all supply (James 1:17). It also unfolds to faith, His power and willingness to bestow all that is necessary through Jesus Christ (Ephesians 2:18). Whether it be within the realm of nature or of grace, He is able to answer all true spiritual prayer prompted by the Spirit.

The Sufferings of the Spirit

Having proved the personality and deity of the Spirit, it is clearly evident that He is capable of being wrongfully treated. Because of who and what He is, any kind of sin committed against Him is grievous and condemnatory. The dignity of a person aggravates any crime perpetrated against him. Insulting a prince brings more punishment than the mistreatment of a nameless pauper.

Equality among the Persons of the Godhead means that there is equality of suffering. What One feels, the Others feel. Let us, therefore, classify the various sufferings personally endured by the Spirit. They can be classified thus—

Sufferings—self-imposed.
Sufferings—caused by sinners.
Sufferings—caused by sinners and saints.

Sufferings—caused by saints.

1. Sufferings self-imposed

Like the Saviour, the Spirit also had sufferings self-imposed. Groanings are His (Romans 8:26). He also is touched with the feelings of our infirmities. As the eternal Spirit, He suffered in Christ's sufferings (Hebrews 9:14). Have you ever thought of it like this? Jesus lived on earth for just over thirty-three years, but while He endured so much anguish, particularly during the last three years of His life, His sufferings ended with His Resurrection and Ascension. The Holy Spirit came to earth, as the Gift of heaven, on the day of Pentecost some 1900 years ago, and has been enduring all kinds of insults since then. Willingly He remains among men, and from the multitudes, in succeeding generations since His advent, has suffered much at the hands of both saints and sinners.

2. Sufferings caused by sinners

As this is "the dispensation of the Spirit of grace," and He is definitely related to all who are out of Christ, there are at least three aspects of unworthy treatment meted out to the Spirit by such sinners. For example—

He is blasphemed. "The blasphemy against the Holy Spirit" (Matthew 12:31, R.V.). This declaration of the Master's proves the great importance of the Spirit's ministry in this age of grace. The Holy Spirit is God's ultimatum, His last Witness to men, therefore if they treat Him as they treated the Saviour, then their doom is sealed. This "blasphemy" has become known as "the Unpardonable Sin," and consists in the willful, conscious, final rejection of the Spirit's revelation of Christ.

He is spurned. The Holy Spirit saith, "To-day if ye shall hear His voice (Spirit's voice—Revelation 2:7), harden not your hearts" (Hebrews 3:7 R.V.). As the direct Agent between the Saviour and sinners, it is His work to convince and convict the lost of their need (John 16:8). But there are multitudes all around who are continually convicted of their sinful condition, but who constantly say "No!" to the Spirit. He warns of peril ahead, but all His entreaties are refused. And as refusal follows refusal, links are added to the chain, binding the soul forever.

He is insulted. "Hath done despite unto the Spirit of grace" (Hebrews 10:29). "Has insulted the Spirit from whom comes grace." The word "despite" actually means "to shamefully intreat." It was thus that Simon Magus treated the Spirit (Acts 8:20).

Any sinner insults the Spirit when he refuses to obey His voice. As He says, "Today," to reply, "No, not today, there is plenty of time," is to despise His entreaty.

Further, as the Spirit testifies to the deity of Christ, and the necessity of the cross, to deny these fundamental truths is to insult the Spirit.

3. Sufferings caused by sinners and saints

There are certain Spirit-passages capable of a double application, and some are herewith set forth.

He can be angered. "They disobeyed and made angry the Spirit of God" (cf. Psalm 78:40). The Spirit's sudden descent upon Saul roused his anger and action. "The Spirit of God came upon Saul . . . and his anger was kindled greatly" (I Samuel 11: 6). The Jews made angry the Holy Spirit (Isaiah 63:10). And, it is indeed terrible to have the Spirit as an enemy.

Thus there is "the wrath of the Spirit," as well as "the wrath of the Lamb." Divine anger, however, is different from human anger. Divine anger, speaking of a wounded heart, cries out for atonement—human anger, expressive of wounded pride, cries out for revenge.

The sinners of Noah's day were guilty of arousing the wrath of the Spirit, so that He ceased to strive with them (Genesis 6:3). Saints, although redeemed, can rebel (Isaiah 63:10). When the Spirit reveals unexpected ugliness within, the proud heart acts in a way displeasing to the Spirit.

He can be resisted. Stephen condemns the nation, of which he formed part, of resisting the Holy Spirit. "Ye do always resist the Holy Spirit: as your fathers did" (Acts 7:51 R.V.)

Sinners resist Him when they fail to respond to His promptings. His pleading voice is heard but the heart is kept fast closed. Walls of excuses are built, bulwarks of indifferences are thrown up, resulting in active resistance to His gentle persuasion.

Saints resist the Spirit when they doubt the Word and power of God. Prejudice, the result of Sectarianism, sometimes leads one to resist the Spirit as He prompts us to obey specific commands.

He can be lied against. In the tragedy overtaking Ananias and Sapphira, Peter ascribes deity to the Holy Spirit. "Lie to the Holy Spirit"—"Lied unto . . . God" (Acts

5:3,4 R.V.). The implication here is that
the Spirit was God. This tragic pair were
guilty of acting a lie. False pretentions were
theirs. They represented themselves to be
what they were not. And how we have to
guard ourselves against secret falsehoods of
the heart and deceptive appearances!

Sinners lie against the Spirit when they
pretend to be converted, or when they
make a superficial profession for some ulterior motive.

Saints lie against the Spirit when they
profess to have all on the altar but keep
back part of the price. What wholesale
death there would be in our churches today
if the selfsame Spirit dealt with us as He
did with Ananias and Sapphira! God save us
from pretending to be wholly devoted to
Him, while guilty of indulgence in things
He hates.

He can be tempted. Peter refers to Ananias and Sapphira as agreeing "to tempt the
Spirit of the Lord" (Acts 5:9). Dean Alford's comment on this passage is, "To test
the Omniscience of the Spirit, then visibly
dwelling in the apostles and the Church,
which was in the highest sense to tempt
the Spirit of God." Weymouth has it, "How
was it . . . that you two agreed to try and
experiment upon the Spirit of the Lord?"

We speak of "tempting Providence," and
this is what these two disciples were guilty
of doing. They thought the Spirit was either
ignorant of their deed, or that He would
wink at their duplicity. They forgot that
He was full of eyes.

Have you never read of arrogant sinners
who, denying the reality of God, have
blatantly said, "If there is a God, let Him
strike me dead?" Mercifully, He does not
manifest His power toward those who try
to deny His existence. Asking for signs is
a form of tempting God.

4. Sufferings caused by saints

One way by which we can discover the
treatment saints mete out to the Spirit is to
patiently study what the Bible says of the
Spirit. It is more profitable to read what the
Scriptures say about His activities than a
multitude of good books on the subject.
Satan knows only too well, that, so long as
truth regarding treatment of the Spirit is
forgotten or neglected, saints make slow
progress in spiritual matters.

He is ignored. "Did ye receive the Holy
Spirit when ye believed?" (Acts 19:2 R.V.).
Rebuked by Paul for the lack of spiritual
power in their lives, the Ephesian disciples
confessed, "We have not so much as heard
whether there be any Holy Ghost." Alas,
there are still multitudes who are ignorant
of His personality! "There standeth One
among you, whom ye know not." Ignorance
of His Person and presence is responsible
for spiritual barrenness.

The New Testament ideal for the Christian life is the constant recognition of the
Spirit's reality, and His daily enthronement
over every part of the life.

Ignorance, then, is the sin of the saved,
and affects the progress of spiritual experience, and proves a lack of knowledge.

He is grieved. "Grieve not the Holy
Spirit" (Ephesians 4:30). "Grieve" is a
Gethsemane word. It means "to afflict with
sorrow." Of Jesus we read that, "He began
to be sorrowful" (Matthew 26:37). The implication is that we can give the Spirit His
Gethsemane.

This grieving is the sin of sealed ones, but
can never affect the sealing which is "unto
the day of redemption," that is, the day of
the redemption of the body.

Things pleasing or painful to the Spirit
are outlined in the narrative. Grieving the
Spirit is the sin of the saved as saints, and
is related to holiness of life, inward, outward and upward. The reader is referred to
fuller treatment of this aspect under "The
Grief of the Spirit."

He is quenched. "Quench not the Spirit"
(I Thessalonians 5:19). The word "quench"
means to "put out the fire" and carries a
double significance. We can quench the fire
in other hearts. By criticism, jealousy, un-
kindness, lack of understanding, prejudice
against a message of the Truth, we can
dampen the faith of those we thus treat.

We can quench the fire in our own heart.
By sin, disobedience, worldly desires, we
extinguish His flame. Quenching is the sin
of the saved as servants and is connected
with service, either personal or general. See
fuller treatment under "Quenching The
Spirit."

The Signature of the Spirit

Paul, in affirming that he bore in his body
the *marks* of the Lord Jesus, had in mind
the scars covering his body, his insignia of
sufferings for Christ's sake. And he was as
proud of these scars as a soldier is of his
medals and decorations. There are also the
distinguishing *marks* of the Spirit, evidences
of His possession of us, and of our full sur-

render to His sway. Life in the Holy Spirit means a cross—not a vicarious cross like the Saviour's; but one that is sore and sharp to the natural mind. The flesh, our old darling sins, our pride, our self-life have no welcome for the Spirit, for He is out to pierce and slay them all until we bear branded on every part of our life the very stigmata of Jesus.

I. Marks of Spirituality

While the word "spiritual" occurs only once in the Old Testament, it is found 30 times in the New, and is vitally connected with the Spirit in the life of the believer.

The Spiritual Man—What He Is and Has

Mankind as a whole has been described by Paul in a threefold way.

First of all, there is *the natural man*.

"The natural man receiveth not the things of the Spirit of God (I Corinthians 2:14). Such a man is under the influence of human nature, learned, eloquent, cultured and even religious, but unrenewed by the Spirit, and therefore incapable of understanding the spiritual content of Scripture. He may be educated with all man's wisdom, having "the wisdom of this world," but being unregenerated, counts spiritual things as foolishness.

Secondly, there is *the carnal man*. "Carnal, even as unto babes in Christ (I Corinthians 3:1).

This second man is an improvement on the first, seeing he has the Spirit. In one sense he is spiritual, having spiritual gifts it may be, but not spiritual graces. He walks in the flesh, not in the Spirit, walks as a man guided by principles belonging to men, and not of the Spirit. And, owing to his carnality he cannot take strong meat —the deep things of the Word. Babes need to be fed with simple food—they cannot feed themselves.

Thirdly, there is *the spiritual man*. "As unto spiritual" (I Corinthians 3:1). The spiritual man is the man of the Spirit, the renewed man; spirit-filled and in full communion with God. Such a distinguished name is his on account of what is most prominent in life and character. Spirit-controlled, he is able to comprehend the sublime revelation of God.

The seven marks of carnality, and the seven of spirituality have been classified thus—

The Carnal Man

Carnally minded (Romans 8:5,7).
Carnally limited (I Corinthians 3:1).
Carnally weak (I Corinthians 3:2).
Carnally bound, enslaved (Romans 7:14).
Carnally opposed (Romans 8:7).
Carnally doomed (Galatians 6:8).
Carnally despised (I Corinthians 3:3,4).

The Spiritual Man

Spiritually born (John 3:6).
Spiritually led (I Corinthians 2:11,12).
Spiritually minded (Romans 8:5,6).
Spiritually renewed (Ephesians 4:2,3).
Spiritually sealed (Ephesians 1:13).
Spiritually filled (Ephesians 5:18).
Spiritually freed (Romans 8:2).

Two great spiritual changes are possible within these three classes forming the human race. First, there is the change from the "natural" to the "carnal." This is divinely accomplished by the Spirit, when by faith, Christ is received as the personal Saviour. Secondly, the change from the "carnal" to the "spiritual", which is produced when there is complete adjustment to the Spirit, in life and service. And the spiritual man is the divine ideal.

Examining the spiritual man more closely we find him to be—

1. A man of the Spirit.

He is altogether distinct from the unrenewed, natural man, who is a man of the flesh, and of the world. He has the Spirit, whereas the natural man is destitute of the Spirit (Jude 19).

2. He belongs to the Spirit.

He is in subjection to and under the rule of the Spirit. The repeated phrase, "in the Spirit," implies perfect agreement with Him in all His wishes and work.

3. Endowed with the Spirit's attributes.

As spiritual, he is infused with all the graces of the Spirit. And the manifestation of these graces is measured by obedience and yieldedness to the Spirit.

If the question is asked, How does one become spiritual? the answer would be— Believe it to be possible; realize it is necessary; be willing to be given up to the Spirit; yield unreservedly to His claims. Expressing it more fully, the spiritual man is—

One who has been baptized by the Spirit into the Body of Christ.

One who has received the gift of the Spirit, once and forever.

One who has been sealed as God's possession through Christ.

One who has received the earnest of the Spirit as God's pledge of complete redemption.

One who has the indwelling of the Spirit as the evidence of salvation and sonship.

One who has the anointing of the Spirit for service.

One who realizes the constant infilling of the Spirit.

Thus, as one writer expresses it, "In the New Testament, and general use, 'spiritual' indicates man regenerated, indwelt, enlightened, endued, empowered, guided by the Holy Spirit; informed to the will of God, having the mind of the Spirit, living in and led by the Spirit."

And being in the realm of the "spiritual," all associated with him bears the same character. Tracing the usage of the word we find that he—

(a) *Feeds upon spiritual food*

"Eat . . . spiritual meat . . . drink . . . spiritual drink" (I Corinthians 10:3,4). In the narrative Paul refers to nourishment miraculously supplied in the wilderness, namely, manna and water out of the rock, typical of the spiritual food we require for our sustenance. We are what we eat. Man grows by what he feeds on. And as actual meat and drink form the body, spiritual food produces spiritual physique.

The four ingredients of our spiritual diet are—

The Christ of God—John 6:48-58—bread.

The Will of God—John 4:32-34—obedience.

The Truth of God—Hebrews 5:12-14; Matthew 4:4—bread.

The Things of God—I Corinthians 3:1,2—milk.

If the prodigal is a type of the wayward son of God, then his disgust over hog's food and his confession that there was bread enough and to spare in his father's house carry a pointed message for many. Why feed on husks—selfish, sinful indulgences and trashy novels, and literature when the Father has an unlimited supply of heavenly bread?

(b) *Exercises spiritual gifts*

"Impart . . . some spiritual gift, to the end . . . established" (Romans 1:11).

"Concerning spiritual gifts . . . would not have you ignorant" (I Corinthians 12:1).

"Desire spiritual gifts" (I Corinthians 14:1).

"Zealous of spiritual gifts" (I Corinthians 14:12).

Passages like these indicate that the Holy Spirit bestows various gifts upon believers, equipping them thereby to serve the Lord. To each believer, no matter how humble, there is given some spiritual enablement or capacity for specific service. No child of God is destitute of a gift. Having received the Spirit as the Gift of God, a gift was received from the Spirit to exercise to the limit "To every man severally as He will" (I Corinthians 12:11 cf. Ephesians 4:7,8; I Peter 4:10,11).

Our obligation, then, is to discover our particular gift and, empowered by the Spirit, employ our talent to gain other talents. And as Paul reminds us, each personal gift is necessary for the edification of believers as a whole (Ephesians 4:12,13).

(c) *Sows spiritual things*

"The Gentiles have been made partakers of their spiritual things" (Romans 15:27).

"If we have sown unto you spiritual things" (I Corinthians 9:11). By these "spiritual things," we are to understand those possessions proceeding from the Spirit, and pertaining to man's spiritual life, worship and ministry. Paul, it would seem, is discoursing upon these benefits accompanying our salvation, such as faith, hope, love, justification, sanctification and peace—in fact, all the fruits and blessings and aids of the regenerated life.

As believers, we do not sow merely carnal things for the body, such as food, raiment and money. Philanthropic work is good and necessary, but the greatest benefits we can bestow upon a needy world is to sow spiritual things. Sowing to the Spirit, we reap life everlasting (Galatians 6:8).

(d) *Enjoys spiritual blessings*

"Blessed . . . with all spiritual blessings" (Ephesians 1:3). Such a phrase can be translated, "Blessings of the Spirit," which evangelical blessings are enumerated for us in verses 1-14 of this chapter. Of course, the phrase can represent any blessing ministered to us in the realm of the Spirit. His greatest blessing is His introduction of us into the heavenlies.

How necessary it is to guard ourselves from being taken up with blessings to the exclusion of the Blesser! Satan is subtle enough to know that even a gift can obscure the Giver.

Once it was the blessing,
Now it is the Lord.

(e) *Sings spiritual songs*

"Speaking to yourselves in . . . spiritual songs" (Ephesians 5:19). "Admonishing one another in . . . spiritual songs" (Colossians 3:16). To remember that we are spiritual, and must sing spiritual songs excludes a good deal of worldly trash from our repertoire. These particular songs are those inspired by the Spirit and employed in the joyful and devotional expression of our spiritual life. There are some who declare that the Psalms are alone inspired, and to be used as songs, but Paul's reference to "psalms, and hymns and spiritual songs" excludes a narrow compass.

Many of our modern hymns and choruses are not worth the paper they are printed on. They are purely doggerel, and nothing divine about them whatever. (Note the songs of Revelation 5:9; 14:3; 15:3).

(f) *Part of a spiritual house*

"Ye also, as lively stones, are built up a spiritual house" (I Peter 2:5). This "spiritual house" is not only the Church as a whole, but any body of believers constituting a local church, where the Spirit and power of God are manifested—any company of saints, where His glory dwells. For various applications of the term see Matthew 21:13; John 14:1,2; Hebrews 2:3; Ephesians 2:19-22; I Corinthians 3:16; 6:9.

(g) *Offers up spiritual sacrifices*

"To offer up spiritual sacrifices, acceptable to God" (I Peter 2:5). Peter is here using a figure taken from the Tabernacle sacrifices of old when a lamb was slain and placed upon the altar, signifying the complete and acceptable offering of a self-dedicated spirit. As believers are spiritual, so all associated with them bear the same nature, even their sacrifices. By a spiritual sacrifice we can understand any self-dedicatory act of the inner man yielded to God. And the Word leaves us in no doubt as to the nature of these sacrifices.

There is Christian benevolence (Philippians 4:18; Hebrews 13:16).

These sacrifices are inward (Hosea 6:6).

They include a broken spirit (Psalm 51:17).

They cover our praises (Hebrews 13:15,16).

They represent the surrender of all we are and have (Romans 12:1,2).

(h) *Fights spiritual foes*

"We wrestle . . . against spiritual hosts" (Ephesians 6:12 R.V.). Our actual foes are not clothed in flesh and blood—they are invisible, not visible, wicked spirits in heavenly places. Too often we are taken up with flesh and blood if antagonism comes from such a quarter. Paul, however, takes us behind the curtain and shows us the invisible inspiring the visible. And if only we can gain the victory over hidden, satanic forces, then flesh and blood will not trouble us very much.

> Principalities and powers,
> Mustering their unseen array,
> Wait for thy unguarded hours,
> Watch and pray.

(i) *Awaits a spiritual resurrection*

"It is raised a spiritual body" (I Corinthians 15:44; cf. verse 46). Our resurrection body will be filled to the wants and capacities of our spirit in the celestial world. Here and now, our natural body requires food and raiment and is subject to weakness, pain and sickness. But our new body will be a wonderful organism similar to Christ's glorified body. And all believers await this redemption of the body (Romans 8:23; Ephesians 4:30). Presently our spiritual life is hampered by a natural body, but the promise is "We shall all be changed" (I Corinthians 15:51). The inner is to correspond to the outer. Spiritual life is to have a spiritual body. Love is to perfect what it has begun. The Holy Spirit is to complete His spiritual work and make us wholly spiritual. What a glorious consummation!

The Spiritual Man—How He is Known

Examining another set of passages where the term "spiritual" is found, we find at least six distinguishing marks by which we can know the spiritual man. During the Tribulation era none will be able to buy or sell save those who carry the mark of the beast (Revelation 13:16,17), and in the spiritual realm unless we have the mark of the Spirit we cannot traffic in holy things. Let us look at some of these marks.

1. Misunderstanding

"The prophet is a fool, the spiritual man is mad" (Hosea 9:7). The only reference to "spiritual" in the Old Testament can be translated, "Crazed is the prophet, mad the inspired one." Here a prophet is described who has been driven mad, distracted by the persecution he was subjected to. But is not the spiritual man today looked upon as a fool by Mr. Worldly

Wise? "He himself is discerned (or understood) by no man" (I Corinthians 2:15). Often he does things that appear to be against reason.

The cleaner, more spiritual, and the more marked our separation unto God, the greater the misunderstanding we create. But if there is no cause, no mad actions on our part, causing folks to think us crazy then we are not responsible for what they call us. To many, Christ was a winebibber. God will take care of those who, because of their distorted vision of the nature of the spiritual life, misjudge us.

What we have to guard against, if we claim to be spiritual, is self-created misunderstanding. Unwise, misguided actions, acting without the Spirit's aid and guidance may occasion the just ridicule of the world. If we walk in the Spirit we shall receive enough contempt without adding to it unnecessarily. While it is true that we are to be fools for Christ's sake, we must not make ourselves foolish.

2. Development

"I . . . could not speak unto you as unto spiritual" (I Corinthians 3:1).

"He that is spiritual" (I Corinthians 2: 15). This should be the normal designation of every believer who, although he did not grow into grace, must certainly grow in it. Paul reminded those Corinthian believers that there was a higher state than that of spiritual babyhood. A beautiful baby is a wonderful sight to behold, but a baby remaining a baby all its days is a monstrosity.

Are we spiritual, which means, are we daily growing in grace? The renewed are like a mirror, and the all-important matter is, which way is the mirror turned? If downward it will reflect only earthly things, the mire, filth, dirt of earth. This turning down of the mirror produces carnality. And if in the flesh, we cannot please God. If the mirror is turned upward then it will reflect the heavens with all their glory of sun, moon and stars. And spirituality is simply the spiritual mind reflecting the things of God.

3. Fundamental

"If any man think himself to be . . . spiritual, let him acknowledge that the things that I write unto you are the commandments of the Lord" (I Corinthians 14:37).

All who are born and taught of the Spirit are ever true to the divine revelation. It is impossible to find a spiritual man doubting the infallibility of the Scriptures. And not only so, but a man's spirituality can be judged by the way he handles God's inspired Word. Why do some men criticize the Bible, reject its great fundamental truths, and appear ignorant of spiritual things although they appear to be learned in the wisdom of the world, and reverential? There is only one answer—they are not spiritual, that is, they have not the Spirit, are not truly born again. Reason, and not revelation, is their starting point.

There is a world of difference between mere cleverness and spiritual discernment. One is worldly acumen, the other is heavenly wisdom. A Spirit-taught mind is the first requisite rather than the certain quality of intellect modernists dote upon. It is the spiritual mood and not a learned mind which gives the soul its initial posture for discovering the deep things of God.

4. Discernment

"He that is spiritual discerneth all things" (I Corinthians 2:15; 3:2). This mark of the spiritual man is really a development of the one we have just considered. If we live in the Spirit, then there is no limitation to our understanding of divine Truth. We find ourselves in the attitude to freely receive, and glory in, holy truths, the natural man cannot comprehend. The natural man counts spiritual things dull, stupid, and is therefore, one in whom truth does not produce its proper effect. To him truth is insipid, tasteless, distasteful. He cannot discern its proper nature, cannot conceive of truth as being true, beautiful and good. And his difficulty is not so much in the will, as in the inward state, for truth can only be spiritually discerned, that is, by and through the Spirit. All truth is revelation, but one who is spiritually blind has not the inward condition necessary to the reception of a divine revelation. And spirituality, as we shall now see, covers the entire range of a spiritual man's faculties, namely, his heart, mind and will.

Take the mind. The curse of today is the divorce of the intellectual from the spiritual—Wisdom of words versus words which the Holy Spirit teacheth (I Corinthians 1:17). The spiritual, however, is never divorced from the spiritual, for a spiritual man's intellect is touched, inspired by the divine Spirit. Some of the greatest saints have been the deepest thinkers.

Almost the first result of the adjustment of a regenerated life to the Holy Spirit is the adjustment of human reason to divine reason. Now the believer no longer argues about a divine revelation, he accepts it by faith, and is enabled thereby to think God's thoughts after Him and to clearly discern His purposes. "Filled with the knowledge of His will in all wisdom and spiritual understanding" (Colossians 1:9), he revels in spiritual sublimities.

Take the heart. The spiritual man does not receive truth in a cold, formal way. With a heart pulsating with warm love, he is enabled to lovingly receive all the Spirit reveals to his intellect. There is love for the truth of God, seeing there is first of all love for the God of truth.

Spirituality, then, in the realm of the affections is that state of soul in which the heart with all its holiest love, is centered upon God as revealed in Christ. And this is the specific work of the Spirit, for He it is who sheds love abroad within the soul (Romans 5:5).

Can we say that all our emotions are under the regulating sway of God's Spirit? Such Spirit-love has a keen insight, and is blind to all else save the will of God.

Take the will. George Matheson has taught us to sing—"My will is not my own, Till Thou hast made it Thine"—and unless our will is harmonized with the will of God there cannot be the enjoyment of His favor. To be spiritually minded is to have the mind of the Spirit, and a willing assent to all He desires of us. We cannot be vessels unto honor unless we constantly act under the guidance and dominion of the Spirit.

Thus "when intellect, heart and will focus their energies reverently and affectionately upon Him, love, a passionate, ever-present, ever-dominant love—is the result. This is the true sphere of the Holy Spirit's indwelling and activity, and the character of such a God-centered and Spirit-filled life is described by the exalted word "spirituality."

To be spiritual, then, means to—

Discern the deep things of God with our minds,
Love these deep things with our hearts,
Submit to them with our wills.

5. Compassion

"Ye which are spiritual, restore . . ." (Galatians 6:1).

The spiritual man is also one who, in all humility, endeavors to win back to the Lord a fallen brother. But the question arises, Are we spiritual enough for the Lord to use in this way?

It is only the spiritual who are fitted to undertake this work of restoration. Being in touch with the Spirit, they receive spiritual insight as to the need of the lapsed one, and the message to apply.

Further, we must be spiritual if we are to lift others above their own level. Yes, and all restoration is undertaken considering ourselves. We have nothing to brag about, even if we are without fault, seeing it is the grace of the Spirit that keeps us where we are.

6. Victory

"To be spiritually minded is life and peace" (Romans 8:6). The margin has it, "To have the mind of the Spirit," and as a study in contrast, for Paul speaks of others who have "the mind of the flesh" (Revised Version).

If not spiritually minded, our joys, exercises, objects, motives, are "not subject to the Law of God," "cannot please God," "is enmity against God" (Romans 8:6-9).

"Life" is one outcome of such a mind—death belongs to the carnal mind. Have we this life indeed? Do we by the Spirit, bring to the place of death the deeds of the body, and thereby live the full, abundant life?

"Peace" is another result of having "the mind of the Spirit" (Revised Version). This is not the initial peace—peace from God, but peace in God. It is a deep settled peace, passing all understanding, and misunderstanding also. We are no longer at "enmity against God," but at peace with Him. No matter how adverse our circumstances may be, being spiritual we carry a sweet, undisturbed peace.

II. Marks of Love

The love of the Spirit is a forgotten or neglected truth in the thoughts of believers. There is a tendency to dwell on the love of the Father and of the Son, to the exclusion of the love of the Spirit. Have you ever heard a sermon on such a theme? If the Spirit is, and does love, is it not shameful not to know it, and delight in it?

Believing as we do in the equality existing among the Persons of the Godhead, then we must be equally loved by the

Spirit, as well as the Father and the Son. God loves us and is not satisfied until we rejoice and rest in His love. Christ loves us, and poured out His Lifeblood for us at Calvary, and lives again to plead our cause above. The Spirit loves us, and is content to abide in us until we are as pure as Christ is pure.

Dr. R. A. Torrey states the truth in this forcible way—

> We kneel down in the presence of God the Father and look up into His face and say, "I thank Thee, Father, for Thy great love that led Thee to give Thine only begotten Son to die upon the Cross of Calvary for me."
>
> Each day of our lives we also look up into the face of our Lord and Saviour, Jesus Christ, and say, "Oh, Thou glorious Lord and Saviour, Jesus Thou Son of God. I thank Thee for Thy great love that led Thee not to count it a thing to be grasped to be on equality with God, but to empty Thyself and forsaking all the glory of heaven, come down to earth with all its shame and to take my sins upon Thyself and die in my place upon the cross."
>
> But how often do we kneel and say to the Holy Spirit, "Oh, Thou eternal and infinite Spirit of God, I thank Thee for Thy great love that led Thee to come into this world of sin and darkness and to seek me out and see my utter ruin and need of a Saviour and to reveal to me my Lord and Saviour, Jesus Christ, as just the Saviour whom I need"? Yet we owe our salvation just as truly to the love of the Spirit, as we do to the love of the Father and the love of the Son.

Well, now, let us give ourselves to the study of "the love of the Spirit," a heart-warming theme taught directly and indirectly in the Scriptures.

The Bible proves that the Spirit is Love, that is, love is one of His own inherent, transcendent attributes; and that love is also a quality He bestows.

Direct Evidences

Several passages make it clear that the Spirit is Love, just as God is Love. Let the following citations suffice.

"Grieve not the Holy Spirit of God" (Ephesians 4:30).

"Grief" is a deeper word than "sorrow." Herod was sorry over the request of Salome for the head of John the Baptist, and the king's sorrow came because of his respect for John. Grief, however, springs from a relationship of love. Grief is an element of the heart. The deeper the love, the more poignant and distressing the grief.

Because, then, the Spirit can be grieved, we know what a loving heart He possesses. And Paul leaves us in no doubt as to those sins stabbing the heart of the Spirit. Oh, to live with an ungrieved Spirit!

"The fruit of the Spirit is love" (Galatians 5:22).

Dr. Weymouth translates the phrase, "The Spirit . . . brings a harvest of love." Fruit is ever the same nature as the tree. An apple tree, for example, cannot bear grapes. Therefore, if the Spirit produces love, He Himself must be Love. The fruit must correspond to the root.

And such love is the fountainhead of all other virtues, for the eight succeeding graces are a development of the first.

Joy is love exulting.
Peace is love reposing.
Long-suffering is love enduring.
Gentleness is love in refinement.
Meekness is love with bowed head.
Goodness is love in action.
Temperance is love obeying.
Faith is love confiding.
"The love of the Spirit" (Romans 15:30).

Such a Pauline phrase declares not only the love the Holy Spirit produces or inspires, but His personal love. He cannot lift us above His own level, thus having love in Himself He is able to beget the same in our hearts. And "the love that the Spirit inspires," as another translates the above phrase, is a love pure in content.

"By kindness, by the Holy Spirit, by love unfeigned" (II Corinthians 6:6).

Here we have a trinity in unity, and we are only attested as witnesses when our lives manifest these three graces (II Corinthians 6:4). When the Spirit has the central place in life, kindness and love flow out in all directions. Union with the loving Spirit reveals itself in our loving attitude toward others. "Seeing ye have purified your souls in obeying the truth through the Spirit unto unfeigned love of the brethren, see that ye love one another with a pure heart fervently" (I Peter 1:22).

"Who hath declared unto us your love in the Spirit" (Colossians 1:8).

In an epistle pre-eminently given over

to the theme of the fullness and glory of Christ, this is the only reference to the third Person. Weymouth translates the phrase—"Your love, which is inspired by the Spirit." We often say that we become like those with whom we live. Well, if we live in full harmony with the will of the Spirit, there is bound to be the reflection of His character. His love flowing into us, will flow through and then out, to bless and cheer a loveless world.

Holy Spirit, Love Divine
O'er life's path Thy radiance shine!
Purify my every thought
Help me love Thee as I ought.

Indirect Evidences

Considering various aspects of the Spirit's nature and ministry we cannot escape the conclusion that He is the Spirit of love. Here are five indirect evidences of His undying love.

1. He is likened unto a dove (Matthew 3: 16).
The dove is the lovebird, the bird without gall, and therefore a fitting symbol of the peaceful, loving nature of the Spirit. Solomon speaks of the Beloved as having "the eyes of doves by the rivers of waters," and divine eyes are ever filled with tears of compassion.
Charles Wesley has taught us to sing—

Heavenly—all alluring Dove
Shed Thy overshadowing love
Love, the sealing grace impart
Dwell within a single heart.

2. He was promised as a Comforter (John 14:16).
The Early Church walked in the comfort of the Holy Spirit (Acts 9:31). Comfort is a heart feeling, an outlet of love. God promised to comfort His own as a mother comforts her children (Isaiah 66:13). As a mother comforts her child, because she loves him, so the Spirit consoles us because of the love He bears for us. Jesus loved His own (John 13:1), and the Spirit is another like Jesus—Jesus' other self.

Our blest Redeemer ere He breathed
His tender, last farewell,
A Guide, a Comforter bequeathed
With us to dwell.

3. He dispenses God's love (Romans 5:5).
Natural love is an instinct and passion, and is behind every romance. The love, however, the Spirit floods our hearts with, is a new creation, is the imparted fruit of the supernatural life. Further, natural love is based upon attractive qualities in its object. This is why we find it hard to love the unlovable, and the unlovely. But the love the Spirit dispenses is not human, but divine, and consequently is not exclusive. It has no favorites, it can love the most unattractive. It was while we were yet sinners that God commended His love toward us and Christ died for us.
It is the Spirit, then, who perfumes the life with love. Through us He seeks to love sinners out of their sin. And the more He has of us, the more we are able to exhibit of the love of heaven for all men.

4. He bestows love as a gift.
Taking I Corinthians 12 and 13 together, and they should never be disassociated, we find that the gifts of the Spirit are only effectual as they are ministered in love. We are to covet earnestly the best gifts, and the greatest, says Paul, is love. Particular gifts there may be for certain saints to exercise, but love is the Spirit's gift for all. And His most effective gift, let it be said, is not that of tongues, but of a loving heart. And how the Church needs a baptism of the Spirit's love!
Bickersteth, in his "Bridal of the Lamb" prays—

Spirit of love,
Hear me, who humbly supplicate Thine aid;
That which is gross in me, etherealize
That which in me is carnal, spiritualize;
That which is earthly, elevate to heaven;
The weak enable, and the dark illume,
Till love, which is of God, abide in me
And I abide in God, for God is Love.

5. He is pictured as a jealous Lover.
Jealousy is a part of the divine nature, "I the Lord thy God am a jealous God" (Deuteronomy 5:9). James reminds us that the Holy Spirit indwelling us "loveth us to jealousy" (4:5 Revised Version).
There are, of course, two brands of jealousy—
Divine jealousy—"I am jealous over you with godly jealousy" (II Corinthians 11:2). This is the jealousy of a true lover who will not brook a rival. And the Spirit is a possessive Lover, He wants us all for God, and is jealous to maintain His rights.
Devilish jealousy—"Jealousy is the rage of a man" (Proverbs 6:34).

It is also as "cruel as the grave." Alas, there is too much of this wrong kind of jealousy among Christians! How grievous to the loving Spirit it must be when one believer is so conspicuously jealous of another! True jealousy guards what is its own—Envy covets what is not its own.

The Divine Association

We now approach a strong, irresistible proof of the Spirit's love. What the Father and Son possess, the Spirit likewise shares. Equality characterizes the attributes of the Persons forming the Godhead. The whole doctrine of faith is a most fascinating one. At this point we might be permitted to digress and indicate a comforting and observable fact given by a saintly scholar of a past generation, Dr. Daniel Steele.

The three Persons in the Trinity are never brought together in the Bible without a result of blessing. We have instances in which each Person standing by Himself, is in an aspect of fear. The Father we have seen clothed with the thunders of Sinai; the Son, as "the falling stone that grinds to powder"; and "The sin against the Holy Ghost shall never be forgiven." But there is not an instance upon record in which the three Persons stand together without an intention of grace. And it is a magnificent thought, that the completeness of Deity, in all essence and all operation reveals that all three Persons stand together in "love." The third Person is "the Spirit of God" and as "God is Love" Matthew 3:16; I John 4:8, 16), therefore the Spirit is Love. He is also called "The Spirit of Christ" and Christ is Love (Romans 8:9; Galatians 2:20). The Spirit, then, shares Christ's nature. In fact, each loved the other. A study of the New Testament reveals a blessed partnership between the Holy Son and the Holy Spirit. Jesus was full of the Spirit, and the Spirit is ever full of Jesus. Jesus sends us to the Spirit, and the Spirit points us to Jesus.*

The association bathed in love is of a twofold nature—

The Divine Benediction

Any passage of Holy Writ suggesting the Trinity, proves that the Holy Spirit is indeed "the sacred Being who is the love knot in the Trinity."

The great benediction of the Church universal proves the love of the Trinity.

* *The Gospel of the Comforter*

"The grace of the Lord Jesus Christ, and the love of God, and the communion of the Holy Spirit" (II Corinthians 13:14 Revised Version). "Communion" here, can be translated "fellowship," and there cannot be true fellowship unless there are true fellows. Such an association springs from the same love characterizing God, and the grace Christ brought and personified.

The Divine Sacrifice

Because of His connection with the redemptive work of Calvary, the third Person must have a heart of love. "Christ, who through the eternal Spirit offered Himself without spot to God" (Hebrews 9:14). This great Trinity passage clearly teaches the Spirit's share in the cross. He enabled Jesus to die, and was a Witness of His sufferings (Acts 5:32). And now the Spirit is the heavenly Eliezer seeking a Bride for the heavenly Isaac. And one day He will bring the beautiful Rebekah home and witness the blissful union (Revelation 22:17).

The Spirit's present love-ministry is to lift up Christ, extol His love and sacrifice, quicken the sinner's conscience, lead to Christ, impart faith and impart the assurance of salvation.

Too often we forget the Holy Spirit's own sacrifice. The sacrifice of the Father and of the Son was indeed great, yet think of the length of the Spirit's sacrifice. Willingly Jesus tarried in the world with all its corruption for just over 33 years. He dwelt among men as untainted as a sunbeam. But the Holy Spirit has been in the world for over 1900 years. What a voluntary sacrifice!

Yes, and He not only dwells among men but within them. Mary Slessor of Calabar tells of the horror she felt when she was forced to live in the vile atmosphere of a harem. How must the Spirit abiding in our hearts feel, for alas, we are so unlike Him, so disappointing, disobedient and sinful! Such sacrifice has been fittingly expressed in these words—

What a tenement He has condescended to enter, and what a glorious work He is pleased to be bearing forward there! He found it dark as night, and foul as the very grave. From a den so filthy, from a cage so full of unclean birds, He might well have turned away. But the Spirit of grace, He unbarred the gate, and entered in. And what a change He has wrought! Where darkness long brooded, light now shines; where Satan held sway, Jesus now sits enthroned; where enmity long burned, love now glows; where death—the worst of deaths—the death of sin—long prevailed, life now reigns—life—with its beauty and the bliss of holiness.

And this Holy Spirit will not leave the bosom He enters. Grieved He may be, ten thousand times, yet despite unnumbered provocations to depart, He remains—remains to finish the work He began, till at length He presents us faultless before the throne of God and of the Lamb. Truly, such pursuing love is without compare!

The practical import of this blessed meditation can be found in the apostle's exhortation—"I beseech you . . . by the love of the Spirit" (American Standard Version). What an incentive this presents to holy loving and living! If men are to know that we are filled with the Spirit, we must be filled with love (John 13:35). We must reflect His loving nature. As Andrew Murray put it, "Oh, do let us learn the lesson and pray God fervently to teach it to His people, that a church or a Christian professing to have the Holy Spirit must prove it by the exhibition of Christlike love."

But what unlovely traits are ours, and how unlovable we are! Unconquered temper, prevailing selfishness, harsh judgments, unkind words, unlovely ways, impatience all alike proclaim the absence of the Spirit's love. Well might we pray with Horatius Bonar—

> Love of the living God,
> Of Father and of Son;
> Love of the Holy Ghost
> Fill Thou each needy one.

VII

The Doctrine of the Trinity

A perfect understanding of this infinite and wonderful theme is not possible to man in his present, finite state. The modes of the existence and operations of divine beings can never be fully apprehended by human beings. The sacred mystery of the Trinity is one which the light within man could never have discovered. That such a revealed truth is beyond the full comprehension of the creature is readily granted. Yet although natural reason may not be able to grasp and explain the Trinitarian conception, this precious doctrine is a part of the divine revelation the Bible presents.

Because the Three-In-One God is beyond our understanding, the truth should not be doubted on account of its mysteriousness. God is infinitely greater than man, and therefore there is much about Him that our searching cannot reveal. Yet, while there is truth regarding Him beyond our reason, it is not contrary to our reason. Are we not surrounded by mysteries? Who is there with all his accumulated wisdom able to explain life, consciousness, sleep and other realities? Thus is it with a perfect meaning or definition of the words, distinctions, or subsistence used to distinguish between the Father, the Son and the Holy Spirit. As two natures in Christ yet but one Person is a wonder, so three Persons yet but one Godhead cannot be perfectly defined. So as Professor J. Kenneth Grider put it in his article on "The Holy Trinity" in *Christianity Today*—

> "Off with our shoes, please, for the Holy Trinity is holy ground. Away with figured syllogisms and ordinary arithmetic: here, logic and mathematics do not suffice. The need is rather for a listening ear, an obedient heart (John 7:17), rapt adoration, a careful engagement with the Holy Scriptures.

Daniel Webster was once asked, "How can you reconcile the doctrine of the Trinity with reason?" The statesman of giant intellect replied, "Do *you* expect to understand the arithmetic of heaven?"

While, however, no complete understanding can be attained of the manner in which the three personal distinctions in the God-head subsist, yet the fact is clearly affirmed that in the unsearchable nature of deity, the threefold distinction exists and that the one God in three Persons is "an audacious conception." Here is indeed a great deep—the Father-God, the Son-God, the Holy Ghost-God, yet not three Gods but only one God yet three Persons in essence. This is a divine riddle where one makes three and three makes one. Truly, our narrow thoughts can no more comprehend the Trinity in Unity than a nutshell can hold all the water in the sea!

The fact and features of the Godhead composed of three Persons coeternal, co-equal; and the same in substance but distinct in subsistence permeates the Bible. Granted that there is not presented a for-mulated definition of the Trinity, yet the gathering together of allusions of such a three-foldedness prove it to be a scriptural doctrine as certain as any other. While the term *Trinity* is not found in the Bible, the truth of it is strewn across its sacred pages.

It is affirmed that the word *Trinity* it-self was first formally used at the synod held at Alexandria, in A.D. 317, and took its place in the language of Christian the-ology for the first time in a Biblical work of Theophilus, Bishop of Antioch, in Syria, from A.D. 168 to 183. But that the holy mystery of the Trinity was a common article of Christian confession before this, is seen by the passage from Lucian, great-est Greek writer of the Christian Era, and the "Voltaire" of antiquity, about A.D. 160. In his *Philopatris,* the Christian is made to confess to—

"The exalted God . . . Son of the Father, Spirit proceeding from the Father, One of Three, and Three of One."

The word "Trinity" itself is derived from the Latin, *Trinitas,* from the adjective *Tri-nus* meaning "threefold," or "three in one." Doubtless the terms arose from the need of a word to express the doctrine tersely. So it properly means "threefoldedness," that is, God's threefold manifestation, and is not, as sometimes stated, an abbreviation of *Tri-unity* which is a term belonging to the realm of metaphysics.

The Godhead is a Trinity in Unity seeing there are three inner distinctions but a single divine life. The three Persons are equal but one Essence (John 14:11,16,17; 15:26; II Corinthians 3:17; Galatians 4:6).

Attempts have been made to find analogies to the Trinity. Man, for example, is a tri-partite being, composed of spirit, soul and body (I Thessalonians 5:23), but no three persons are structurally one. In nature, the universe presents itself to view as earth, sky and sea. Atmosphere is made up of light, heat and air. Matter itself is solids, liquids and gases. Water is found as snow, ice and liquid. From the sun we have light, heat and chemical effects. Saint Patrick used the illustration of the three green leaves of the *shamrock* to con-vey to his Irish congregation an intelligent conception of the three Persons in the God-head. Triads of divinities can be found in many religions, *three* being recognized as a sacred number, but in the Christian doc-trine of the Trinity there is nothing in com-mon with the threes of mythology.

While the above comparisons are faint and suggestive, it is impossible to describe by means of material things, the profound-est truth concerning the three Persons form-ing the Godhead. Being essentially unique, the Trinity is therefore lifted far above the possibility of perfect comparison or illus-tration. We cannot find a perfect analogy of the theological tenet we are presently considering.

The Trinity is a subject that has engaged the greatest minds during the centuries of the Christian Era, but even Christian phil-osophers have utterly failed to explore its profound depths. Augustine gave the study of this mystery of the Trinity the best powers of his great mind. It is related of him that walking along the seashore one day, absorbed in deep contemplation, he came across a lad digging a trench. Asking the lad what he meant to do, he told Au-gustine that he wanted to empty the sea into his trench. Whereupon Augustine said to himself—

Am I not trying to do the same thing as this child in seeking to exhaust with my reason the infinity of God and to collect it within the limits of my own mind?"

Councils and theologians who have grap-pled with the ineffable mystery of the three foldness of the Godhead have left us helpful definitions of such a profound and vital doctrine without which Chris-tianity could have no existence.

Irenaeus, in his treatise against heresies, demands—

Complete faith in one God Almighty—of Whom are all things, and in the Son of God, Jesus Christ our Lord, by whom are all things and His dispensation by which the Son of God became Man, also a firm trust in the Spirit of God Who hath set forth the dispensations of the Father and the Son, dealing with each successive race of men as the Father willed.

In the *Nicene Creed* of A.D. 325 we have a Trinitarianism in which the three Persons are divine and are of one substance. The *Athanasian Creed* which came centuries later spells out both the oneness and the threeness much as an anthem conveys and re-conveys its message. Think of this formula—

"So the Father is God; the Son is God; and the Holy Ghost is God. And yet there are not three Gods but one God . . . Neither confounding the Persons, nor dividing the substance."

One of the early articles of the Church of England gives us this summary—

"In the unity of this Godhead there be three Persons, of one substance, power and eternity—the Father, the Son and the Holy Ghost."

From R. Watson, the eminent theologian, we have the doctrine defined thus—

"The divine Nature exists under the personal distinctions of the Father, the Son and the Holy Ghost."

W. P. Pope, another renowned theologian gave us the following summary of the Trinity—

"One divine Essence exists in a Trinity of co-equal personal subsistences, related as the Father, the Eternal Son of the Father, and the Holy Ghost eternally proceeding from the Father."

As the Bible alone unfolds the doctrine of the Trinity, we must accept its teaching regarding same. An unbiased study of what the Bible says about "Trinitarianism" confirms one in the conviction that while the mystery of the Trinity transcends reason, it does not contradict it. This sacred doctrine is above reason. Erudite philosophers who give themselves to an understanding of the causes of things, cannot by deepest search unravel the mystery of the Trinity. The same is of divine revelation and must be adored by those who humbly and believingly accept it. The Trinity is an object of faith. The plumb line of reason is far too short to fathom this mystery. But where reason cannot wade, there faith may swim. There are some aspects of our Christian faith that may be demonstrated by reason, namely, that there is a God, but the Trinity of divine Persons in the Unity of Essence is wholly supernatural, and must be accepted by faith.

This doctrine is a scriptural revelation, being taught exclusively in the Bible. While a basis for the Trinity has been sought in the laws of being and of thought, it is to the Bible alone that we are indebted for the revelation of the Godhead as consisting of—

The Father, the Great Upholder and Purpose of all things.

The Son, the One and Only Redeemer of Mankind.

The Holy Spirit, the Indispensable Sanctifier and Enlightener.

Each having their own distinct spheres of operation yet found acting together in perfect unison.

Old Testament Gleams

Although the mystery of the Trinity is not fully revealed in Old Testament Scriptures it certainly underlies the teaching of the Old Testament. The gradual unfolding of this doctrine is an instance of a progressive revelation. Each step in the development of a truth is made clear before another step is taken. In the Old Testament there are no dogmatic announcements of the Trinity but hints, apparent gleams or foreshadowing of it which gather more definiteness with the completion of the divine Revelation, the Bible as a whole is. Expressions are not lacking of the operations of the three Persons of the Trinity. Among these the following can be considered.

Elohim, the divine term used of God at the beginning of the Bible (Genesis 1:1), is a plural noun used some 500 times by Moses and some 5,000 times in the New Testament accompanied continually by a verb in the singular. This is a term revealing the oneness of Deity and the plurality of Persons in the Godhead. Further, this proper noun in the plural number, meaning more than one, is associated with creation. God said, "Let *us* make man after *our* image, and after *our* likeness" (Genesis 1:26). Then we read, "So God created man in His own image," which compared with Paul's statement concerning Christ— "Through whom also He made the worlds" (Hebrews 1:2), reveals a unity of operation. Plural pronouns and plural verbs abound, proving that the Old Testament does not present a vague or obscure intimation of the Trinity. As Professor A. B. Davidson expresses it, "If God, who speaks in these passages, uses the word *us* of Himself, there is a perfectly clear statement to the effect that the Godhead is a plurality—whether that plurality be a duality, or a trinity, or some other number is spoken of. When the divine Speaker uses *us* of Himself, He includes His heavenly council along with Him" (See Isaiah 6:8; 61:1; 63:9,12; Haggai 2:5,6).

The same plural form is used after the Fall of Adam, "The man is become one of *us*" (Genesis 3:22), and at Babel when God confounded the language of the people, "Let *us* go down" (Genesis 11:7; cf. 20:13; 35:7). Then there are certain repetitions of the name of God which seem to distinguish between God and *God* (Genesis 19:28; Psalms 45:7; 110:1; Hosea 1:7). The account of Jacob's wrestling also suggests a plurality of Persons in the Godhead (cf. Genesis 32:24,30; Hosea 11:3). The threefold benediction of the High Priest was accepted by ancient Jews as a foregleam of the Trinity (Numbers 6:24-26), as were the liturgical formulas of Deuteronomy 6:4 and Isaiah 6:3. God, His Word, His Spirit are brought together and co-causes of effects are adduced (Psalm 33:6).

Attention can be drawn to the several manifestations of God in the Old Testament in which He is described as Himself, His Messenger or Angel. God appears at once as Sender and sent. The remarkable phenomena connected with the appearances of the Angel of Jehovah indicate a plurality of Persons in the Godhead (See Genesis 16:2-13; 22:11,16; 31:11-13; 48:15,16; Exodus 3:2,4,5; Judges 13:6,21; Jeremiah 23:6; Malachi 3:1).

New Testament Unfolding

Charles W. Lowry in *The Trinity in Christian Devotion* says of the concept of such a doctrine that it is "at once the ultimate in the supreme glory of the Christian faith." Any doctrine *latent* in the Old Testament is *patent* in the New Testament. Suggested by the prophets of old, the Trinity is revealed with greater distinctness and emphasis by our Lord and His apostles—a fact which proves the continuity and progress of the divine revelation. Thus, as Grider expresses it in connection with the Trinity—

> After the nature of God was floodlighted by the New Testament revelation, Christians began to see that in the Old Testament there are numerous lesser lights thrown upon God which point to His tri-personality.

The conspicuous names of *Father, Son* and *Spirit*, are used both separately and conjointly. Further, there is the declaration that the Father is *God*, that the Son is *God*, that the Holy Spirit is *God* (John 8:54; John 1:1; Acts 5:3,4). The New Testament emphasizes the Unity of God (John 17:3; I Corinthians 8:4; I Timothy 2:5), and also teaches that the Godhead consists of three Persons. The Triune God whom the apostles worshiped was the *Elohim* of the Old Testament. To them, the concept of the threefoldness of God was no novelty, no new concept of God but simply the expansion of the testimony of holy men of old.

We cannot study those groups of passages manifesting the operations of Father, Son and Spirit without coming to the conclusion that the New Testament is *Trinitarian* to the core and that "all its teaching is built on the assumption of the Trinity; and its allusions to the Trinity are frequent, cursory, easy and confident." Benjamin B. Warfield, in his masterful summary of this doctrine set forth in *The International Standard Bible Encyclopedia*, writes—

> The doctrine of the Trinity is not so much heard as overheard in the statements of Scripture. It does not appear in the New Testament in the making but as already made. We do not have a record of development or assimilation. Everywhere it is presupposed that the doctrine was the fixed possession of the Christian community; and the process by which it became the possession of the community lies behind the New Testament.

Is it not wonderful in the unfolding of this truth as an old German writer suggests how this doctrine in a silent and imperceptible way took its place without struggle—and without controversy—among accepted Christian doctrines? As the following references prove everywhere God the Father, the Lord Jesus Christ, and the Holy Spirit appear as "the joint objects of all religious adoration and the constant source of all divine operations." Divine names and titles are given to each of the three Persons; divine works are accomplished by each; divine worship is given and commanded to be given to each; divine attributes are ascribed to each.

While the Bible does not supply us with any definition of the Trinity, church councils and theologians have endeavored to describe its nature, as we have already indicated. What the Bible does say is that each Person in the Trinity is really and truly God, and is to be worshiped as such. The Three are coeternal, and coequal in power and glory. God, in His Fatherhood, is supreme; the Son was begotten of the Father; the Holy Spirit proceeded from the Father and the Son. The Holy Spirit is referred to as "The Third Person of the Blessed Trinity," and is thus called "not in order of time, or dignity of nature, but in order and manner of subsisting." A verse of one of the Salvation Army songs reads—

> Blessed and glorious King!
> To Thee our praise we bring,
> For this glad hour.
> Thou God of peace and love,
> Thou Christ enthroned above,
> Spirit whose fruit is love,
> Display Thy Power.

At our Lord's birth we have an unequivocal testimony to the association of Father, Son and Holy Spirit.

"With *God* nothing shall be impossible."
"That holy thing which shall be born of thee shall be called *the Son of God.*"
"*The Holy Ghost* shall come upon thee, and the *Power of the Highest* shall overshadow thee" (Luke 1:35-37).

At our Lord's baptism, the Holy Spirit descended upon the Son, and at the same moment the Father's benediction came from heaven (Matthew 3:13-17). At Jordan, each of the Trinity is presented as a distinct Person (See also Mark 1:10,11; Luke 3:21,22; John 1:32-34). "The Three Persons are thrown up to sight in a dramatic picture of which the Deity of each is strongly emphasized."

Further, all the teachings of Jesus are Trinitarian in nature. He often dwelt upon, not only His own work, but His Father's work, and the work of the Holy Spirit. He claimed to be the Son of God and the Spirit-empowered One (Luke 10:22; 12:12; 22:70; Matthew 12:28). The Father sent the Son, and both the Father and the Son sent the Spirit. Perhaps the most striking illustration of the grouping of the three Persons of the Trinity as equals is that to be found in our Lord's teaching on the promise of the Spirit (John 14:16-26).

"But the Comforter, which is the Holy Spirit (Third Person) whom the Father (First Person) will send in My name (Second Person). He shall teach you all things and bring all things to your remembrance, whatsoever I have said unto you."

As we meditate upon the manifold teachings of the Master "we are kept in continual contact with Three Persons who act, each as a distinct person, and yet who are in a deep, underlying sense, one," as Warfield reminds us. "There is but one God—there is never any question of that—and yet this Son who has been sent into the world by God not only represents God but is God, and this Spirit whom the Son has in turn sent into the world is also Himself God."

In the baptismal formula our Lord gave His disciples, we have the nearest approach to a formal announcement of the Trinity in the gospels. The unity of the Godhead is recognized in the use of the *singular*—"In the *name* of the Father, and of the Son and of the Holy Ghost." It does not say in the "names of," but only one name for all three as if we had merely three designations of one Person. Father, Son and Spirit "all unite in some profound sense in the common participation of one Name," that glorious, fearful Name, so sacred to godly Jews (Isaiah 30:27; 59:19). By the use of "the name" the disciples came to realize that the mighty Jehovah of old was now to be known as the Father, Son and Holy Spirit. To quote Warfield again as he deals with the significance and genuineness of the baptismal formula (Matthew 28:19).

What we are witnessing is the authoritative announcement of the Trinity as the God of Christianity by its Founder, in one of the most solemn of His recorded utterances. Israel had worshipped the one only true God under the name of Jehovah;

Christians are to worship the same one only and true God under the Name of "the Father, the Son and the Holy Ghost." This is the distinguishing feature of Christians; and that is as much as to say that the doctrine of the Trinity is, according to our Lord's own apprehension of it, the distinctive mark of the religion which He founded.

Coming to the chief exponent in the Early Church of the doctrines enunciated by our Lord, we discover how the truth of the Trinity is woven into the fabric of Paul's epistles, all of which are rich in their witness to the Trinitarian concept of God. "Everywhere, throughout their pages, God the Father, the Lord Jesus Christ, and the Holy Spirit appear as the joint objects of all religious adoration, and the conjunct source of all divine operations." All three Persons are brought together as Co-Sources of all saving blessings which are the heritage of all believers in Christ. To list all the passages bearing evidence of the Trinity would require more space than we can allow. References such as Romans 1:7; 3:30; I Corinthians 1:3; 8:4; II Corinthians 1:2; Galatians 1:3; 3:20; Ephesians 1:2; 4:6; Philippians 1:2; II Thessalonians 1:2; I Timothy 1:2; II Timothy 1:2; Titus 3:4-6 can be followed with interest. Particular attention is drawn to the gifts and administrations of the Church, ascribed to God, Christ and the Holy Spirit (I Corinthians 12:4-6). Then among other conjunctions of the three Persons (See Revelation 8:9; I Thessalonians 1:2-5; II Thessalonians 2:13,14; II Timothy 1:3,13,14; Titus 3:4-6) there is the great apostolic benediction (II Corinthians 13:14).

"The grace of the Lord Jesus Christ, and the love of God, and the communion of the Holy Spirit be with you all."

In this usual benediction, employed in the dismissal of a religious gathering, "the three highest redemptive blessings are brought together and attached distributively to the three Persons of the Triune God." Is it not a comforting fact that all three Persons of the Trinity are never brought together in the Bible without resultant blessing? Dr. Winnington Ingram reminds us that—

We have instances in which each Person, standing by Himself is an aspect of fear. The Father we see clothed with thunders on Sinai; the Son as the falling stone that grinds to powder; and the sin against the Holy Ghost shall never be forgiven. But there is not an instance upon record in which the Three Persons stand together without an intention of Grace. And it is a magnificent thought, that the completeness of the Deity, in all His essence and in all His operation is never mentioned but for mercy.*

Attention must also be drawn to the way in which Paul saturates his Ephesian letter with his concept of the Trinity. Each chapter carries its own evidence.

"Blessed be the *God* and Father of our *Lord Jesus Christ,* Who hath blessed us with all the blessings of the *Spirit*" (Ephesians 1:3).

Prayer for spiritual knowledge and power is linked to God, Christ and the Spirit (Ephesians 1:15-18), as is access to a throne of grace (Ephesians 2:18), and intercession for inner fulness (Ephesians 3:14-21). The upbuilding of the Church is ascribed to the co-operation of the three Persons forming the Godhead (Ephesians 4:4-16). For his walk and warfare, the resources of the Trinity are at the disposal of the believer (Ephesians 5:18-20; 6:10-18). The doctrine of the Trinity and all that is associated with a redeemed sinner stand or fall together.

Other New Testament writers affirm that the redemptive activities of God rest on a threefold source in God the Father, God the Son and God the Holy Spirit. Thus these "Three Persons repeatedly come forward together in the expression of Christian hope or the aspiration of Christian devotion." Instances of Trinitarianism can be found in Hebrews 2:3,4; 6:4-6; 10:19-31; I Peter 1:2; 2:3-12; 4:13-19; I John 5:4-8; Jude 20,21; Revelation 1:4-6.

For an understanding of heresies regarding the Trinity, the reader is referred to the excellent summary given by Dr. W. J. Townsend in his *Handbook on Christian Doctrines.* Summarizing the repeated expressions of the Trinity assumed in the Bible we can set forth the most perfect Unity making the three Persons one in holiness, love, wisdom, power and eternal nature thus—

The Father is first in mode of operation, the Original Source of all things. "In the beginning God" (Genesis 1:1). He is the Fountain Head of grace. He is the Father

* *The Love of the Trinity*

of the Lord Jesus Christ (Ephesians 3:14); and the Father of all men, as the Source of their being; and particularly the loving Father of all those redeemed by the blood of His Son (I Corinthians 6:17,18; 8:6; Ephesians 4:6; Luke 12:30,32).

The Son is second in the process of manifestation, and the Medium of all things, even Judgment (John 5:22). He came as grace personified. He appeared and died as the Redeemer of mankind. It was through Him that God manifested Himself outwardly to all men (Acts 5:31; 13:38, 39).

The Spirit is third, seeing His is the last revealed personality, and the One who came as the Agent transferring the blessings of the Father and the Son upon the redeemed (Ephesians 2:18). He shares the attributes ascribed to God and Christ (Psalm 139:7; I Corinthians 2:10,11; Isaiah 40:13,14) and is especially the Helper and Sanctifier of the saved (I Corinthians 6:11; Galatians 5:16). As the Channel, the Spirit communicates, applies and seals. The order of divine performance appears to be—From the Father; Through the Son; By the Holy Spirit

> So God the Father, God the Son
> And God the Spirit we adore,
> A sea of life and love unknown,
> Without a bottom or a shore.

What must not be forgotten is the value of the doctrine of the Trinity in relation to life and practice. The warning of the saintly mystic, Thomas à Kempis, should be heeded by all who are the Lord's—
"What will it profit thee to be able to discourse profoundly on the Trinity if thou art wanting in humility and so art displeasing to the Trinity?"

As there is one God subsisting in three Persons, may we be found giving equal reverence, love and obedience to all three. Let us—

Obey God the Father, even as His own beloved Son did (John 4:34).

Obey the Son, giving to Him the kiss of obedience (Psalm 2:12).

Obey the Holy Spirit upon whom we are dependent (Acts 5:1-5; 26:19).

Man himself is a Trinity being composed of spirit, soul and body.

Man is assailed by a Trinity—the world around, the flesh within, the devil below.

Man is guilty of a sinful Trinity—lust of the flesh, lust of the eyes, pride of life.

Man can only be saved and sanctified by the heavenly Trinity, the Father, the Son, the Holy Spirit.

While we may not be able to penetrate the mystery of the Godhead, of Father, Son and Spirit undivided in essence, and coequal in power and glory, yet although there may appear to be insuperable difficulties in the traditional definitions of the Trinity then as Dr. R. W. Dale expresses it—

If you love and obey and trust and worship the Lord Jesus Christ as a divine person; If you shrink from sin lest you should "grieve" the Holy Spirit, if His care for you and His patience with you fill your heart with courage and gratitude; and if you believe, at the same time, that the Son and the Spirit are one with the Eternal Father, your life is rooted in the facts which the doctrine of the Trinity is intended to express, although you may be unable to accept the Trinitarian creed.

VIII

The Doctrine of Angels

It is to be regretted that this most profitable and practical doctrine is so seldom preached upon to twentieth century congregations. In a previous volume—*The Mystery and Ministry of Angels*—I endeavored to condense what the Bible has to say regarding the creation, number, nature, ranks, attributes, fall, appearances, mission and the Lord of Angels. Independent of the above study this entrancing theme is herewith differently approached.

The Rejection of Angels

How is it that the doctrine of angelic

reality and agency, laden with so much comfort and instruction, is largely neglected amongst us? Modern liberal theology has, for the most part, discarded the belief in such spiritual beings as angels, as well as other aspects of the invisible world. The Sadducees, with their materialistic outlook, denied the Resurrection of Christ, and regarded angels merely as symbolical expressions of God's actions. Modernists are closely associated with the Sadducees in their rejection of the miraculous and of the reality of the spirit-world. Then there are those who argue, "As so little has been revealed, we must not be wise above what is written!" or, "It is the part of humility not to pry into subjects so much above us!" But surely these are excuses to cover up idleness or justify indifference. If the Bible has anything to say about angels, surely it is not true humility to ignore or neglect what God has disclosed? While we must not be wise *above* what is written, we must be wise as to *what* has been written. Is it not our solemn responsibility and part of true wisdom to investigate prayerfully, and understand clearly, all the Holy Spirit has been pleased to reveal on Angelology, and on every other doctrine?

Another argument advanced against the study of angels is that of Rome's worship of them, and the transforming of these sympathizing, heavenly friends into unwilling objects of shameless idolatry. "Thinking about Angels may lead to their adoration as witness the Church of Rome," is no reason for indifference to an understanding of angelic agency. Is it not a false premise to renounce a privilege because some have abused it? Should we grope willingly in darkness because Satan sometimes transforms himself into an angel of light?

Further, there are many spiritually-minded believers who have no doubt about the existence of angels who seem to take up the position that their visible activity has come to an end, because of the cessation of their mediating work. In this age of grace, God deals directly with man through Christ and by the Spirit, and therefore angelic aid is not necessary. But this position is likewise false, seeing the Bible affirms that angels ever function as "ministering spirits" on behalf of the redeemed, and continue to ascend and descend for their good.

The Reality of Angels

Believing as we do that the Bible alone offers us the divine revelation on any specified doctrine or theme, ours must be the effort to discover all the Bible has to say about God's curious workmanship displayed in His angels. Has He not willed such an order of celestial beings, not only as His messengers, but as our trusty friends now and our loving companions hereafter? That the angels fly to and fro through the entire Bible is evidenced by the fact that in its 66 books there are almost 300 references to the appearances and activities of the angels. So, as one expositor puts it—

What is written—shall be our study—
Thus it is written—shall be our weapon."

We are not left to our own wisdom or imagination or conjecture on this absorbing subject. Scripture does not seek to convince us of the existence of angels, but taking the fact for granted presents to our view the world of unseen spirits having differing ranks, stations, attributes, enjoyments and employments. What cannot be denied is the way in which the Bible abounds in angelic appearances and ministrations. We meet the angels at every turn of the way. Are they not associated with some of the most remarkable histories, events and persons? Let us, therefore, try to classify what Scripture reveals regarding those great and glorious beings who ever bless the Lord, excel in strength, obey God, and hearken unto His word (Psalm 103:20); and who occupy an intermediate sphere between the heaven and earth.

While with many of the great doctrines of the Bible a progressive revelation can be traced, with Angelology it is different. Such a doctrine is not gradually developed. Angels, with their particular functions and features, meet us at the beginning of the Bible, at its close and almost everywhere in between. One writer affirms that by the time of the Babylonian captivity, "the consciousness of sin had grown more intense in the Jewish mind, and God had receded to an immeasurable distance; the angels helped to fill the gap between God and man." But earlier references to angelic ministry clearly indicates that the Jews were intimately related to angels. Everywhere in the Old Testament the existence of angels is assumed, and are introduced to our notice as being related to the beginning of the world.

Their Appearances

Angels were present at the creation of the world (Job 38:7). Their own creation is referred to in Psalm 148:2,5; Colossians 1:6. Filled with wonder and gladness over the display of God's creative power, the angels "shouted for joy."

Angels were present at the Fall of Adam. With the pronouncement of the curse, Paradise could no longer be the abode of the guilty pair, so they were expelled. Two angelic beings were placed at the gate of Eden with "a flaming sword which turned every way, to keep the way of the tree of life" (Genesis 3:24).

Angels came down and consorted with the daughters of men and produced a corrupt condition of society necessitating the terrible flood (Genesis 6:1-4; II Peter 2:4; Jude 6). This aspect of angelic rebellion is enlarged upon under the section dealing with *The Doctrine of Satan and Demons.*

Angels comforted Hagar, the fleeing, weeping bondwoman. It was an angel who sent back Hagar to her tent with the promise that she would become the mother of a son whose seed should not be "numbered for multitude" (Genesis 16:10). Again, when a fugitive with her boy and dying with thirst, an heavenly messenger opened Hagar's eyes to discover a well of water for her preservation, and to hear afresh the promise that "a great nation" would spring from her son (Genesis 21:17).

Angels, in the guise of men, appeared to Abraham in the plains of Mamre, as he sat in the tent door. One of the angelic trio foretold the birth of Isaac and the approaching judgment upon the cities of the plain (Genesis 18:2). It was likewise an angel who prevented Abraham sacrificing his son, and revealed to him the ram caught in the thicket (Genesis 22:11, 15).

Angels appeared to Lot, and in spite of his reluctance to leave the doomed city, compelled him to do so (Genesis 19).

Angels came to Jacob at Bethel where, with the ground for his bed and a stone for his pillow, he had a dream of the mystic ladder reaching from earth to heaven, which was traversed by the bright and beautiful messengers of God (Genesis 28:11). Angels—a troop of them— met Jacob at Mahanaim before his meeting with Esau after his return from Padan-aram (33:11).

It was a unique angel—the Angel of the Covenant—that wrested with Jacob at Peniel (Genesis 32:1).

Angels were associated with the Israelites in so many ways. It was "the angel of the Lord" who appeared in the burning bush (Exodus 3:2) and who went before the chosen people as they left Egypt for Canaan (Exodus 23:20; 32:34). An angel stood in Balaam's way as an adversary against him. The ass saw the angel, but not the hireling prophet (Numbers 22:20-35). It was the illustrious angel who revealed himself as "The Captain of the host of the Lord" to Joshua at Jericho (Joshua 5:13-15). An angel reviewed the Israelitish invasion of Canaan to Joshua's death (Judges 2). An angel interpreted Gideon's dream of the Median victory (Judges 7:14,15). An angel gladdened the hearts of Manoah and his wife by the promise of Samson's birth (Judges 13:3-5, 9-21). The angel of the Lord meted out the judgment David's sin brought about (II Samuel 24:10-25; I Chronicles 21).

Angels had an intimate association with Elijah the Tishbite (I Kings 9:5-7; II Kings 1:3,15).

An angel slew the vast Assyrian army (II Kings 19:35; Isaiah 37:36). It is interesting to note that angels came with denunciations of wrath, as well as heralds of mercy. An angel slew the firstborn in Egypt in punishment of Pharaoh's pride— brought pestilence upon Jerusalem for David's error in numbering Israel—destroyed 185,000 Assyrians, and struck Herod with a loathsome disease for his blasphemous flattery. Angels were God's ministers in His providential government of our lower world.

Angels preserved the Hebrew youths from destruction in the fiery furnace (Daniel 3:25-28), and guarded Daniel who, when falsely accused, was thrown into the lions' den (6:22: See also 8:16; 9:21; 10:5-21; 12:5-7).

Angels likewise played a great part in the amazing prophecy Zechariah declared (Zechariah 1:8-10; 2:3; 3:1-6; 4:1-5; 5:5-10; 6:4,5; 12:8).

Coming to the New Testament, it seemed but natural that when the eternal Son, the Lord of angels, left heaven and took upon Himself the likeness of our flesh that the angels should attend Him through each stage of His earthly sojourn. The angel Gabriel announced to Mary that she was to be the mother of the world's Redeemer. Angels proclaimed to the shepherds the birth of Christ, and filled the night air with their praises. Joseph was enlightened and warned by an angel. Zacharias was instructed by an angel. Angels appeared to the lowly shepherds (Luke 1:16-38; 2: 9-14; Matthew 1:20; 2:13,19). As angels were specially active in the beginning of the Old Testament, so they appear frequently in the New Testament. Angels appeared to strengthen Jesus after His long exhausting fast, and intense struggle with Satan (Matthew 4:11). Toward the close of His life of sorrow and toil, the angels came to succor Him as He knelt in an agony in the garden (Luke 22:43).

Jesus spoke of having "twelve legions of angels" standing ready to protect Him. With a word He could have commanded these shining squadrons and they would have delivered Him from His foes (Matthew 26:53). Angels were present at, and assisted in, His Resurrection. An angel rolled away the stone of the tomb, and angels appeared to the sorrowing women (Matthew 28:2; Luke 24:23; John 20:12). The angels, we may be sure, were those who carried the King of Glory back to heaven (Luke 24:51).

Angels displayed miraculous power on behalf of some of the apostles. Peter and John (Acts 5:19), Philip (Acts 8:26), Cornelius (Acts 10:3,30-32), Peter (Acts 12:7-11), Paul (Acts 27:23).

Angels are to be judged by the saints (I Corinthians 6:3). Their worship is forbidden (Colossians 2:18; Revelation 22:8). Angels watch all human affairs with deep interest and minister to the saints (I Corinthians 11:10; Hebrews 1:14). Christ has the supremacy over all angelic beings (I Peter 3:22).

Angels are prominent in the Book of Revelation where we see them constantly employed by the Redeemer as ministers of His will. Through them He exercises His governmental control of the earth. The angels are His agents restraining persecution—sounding the judgment trumpets—pouring out vials of wrath upon the godless—raising shouts of triumph over the fall of Babylon—accompanying the Saviour as He comes to reap the harvest (Revelation 1: 20; 5:11,12; 7:1; 12:7; 14:18; 16:5; 19: 17).

From a consideration of the aforegoing appearances one or two facts emerge, the most important being that Christ who came as "a temporary preincarnation of the Second Person in the Trinity" in the Old Testament being known as, "The Angel of Jehovah," or "The Angel of His presence" (See Genesis 22:11; 24:7-40; 32:24), had no doubt whatever about the reality of angels, both good and bad. Sifting our Lord's teaching we find Him speaking of—

The angels in heaven (Matthew 22:30)

The devil and his angels (Matthew 25: 41)

The angels as holy ones (Mark 8:38)

The angels without sex or sensuous desires (Matthew 22:30)

The high, let limited intelligence of angels (Matthew 24:36)

The angels as bearers of the saved to heaven (Luke 16:22)

The angels ready to obey their Lord (Matthew 26:53), to accompany Him at His return (Matthew 25:31), to assist in judgment (Matthew 13:41, 49)

The angels joy over repentant sinners (Luke 15:10. cf. I Corinthians 4:9; Ephesians 3:10; I Peter 1:12)

The angels as witnesses of Christ's confession (Luke 12:8).

The angels are specially interested in God's little ones (Matthew 18:10)

For the Christian, the whole weight of the question regarding the existence, reality and activity of angels hinges upon what Christ believed. Did He merely adapt Himself to the rabbinical conception of Angelology, more or less fanciful although beautiful? As *The Truth* (John 14:6), He could not, and dare not, adjust Himself to popular belief which was not true. Thus, all He said about angels came as to those who heard His Words as a divine revelation. "So we find ourselves restricted to the conclusion that we have the guarantee of Christ's word for the existence of Angels, for most Christians that will settle the question."

Further, from angelic appearance we learn a good deal about these glorious beings who, at present, have nobler powers and mightier capacities than we have. For example, they are—

Vast and countless in number (II Kings 6:17; Psalm 68:17; Daniel 7:9,10; Matthew 26:53; Hebrews 12:22).

They are spirits with delegated power to become visible in the semblance of human form (Psalm 104:4; Hebrews 1:14; Genesis 19:1,5).

Their power is inconceivable (II Kings 19:35; Psalm 103:20; Revelation 18:1,21).

They are conspicuous for *great wisdom* (II Samuel 14:20; 19:27; Matthew 24:36; Ephesians 3:10), *patience* (Numbers 22:22-35), *meekness* (II Peter 2:11; Jude 9), *modesty* (I Corinthians 11:10), *holiness* (Mark 8:38), *obedience* (Psalm 103:20; Matthew 6:10), *knowledge* (Mark 13:32; I Peter 1:12), *will power* (Isaiah 14:12-14), *linguistic ability* (I Corinthians 13:1), *glory* (Luke 9:26), *immortality* (Luke 20:36), *needing no rest* (Revelation 4:8), *operating in material realms* (Genesis 18-19:22; II Kings 19:35), *travelling at great speed* (Ezekiel 1; Revelation 8:13; 9:1), *ascending and descending* (Genesis 28:12; John 1:51), *wearing garments* (John 20:12), *being subject to God, standing before Him* (Matthew 22:30; II Chronicles 18:18; Revelation 12:12; 13:6), *appearing unawares* (Hebrew 13:2), *being inferior to Christ* (Hebrews 1:5; 2:6).

They are immortal, they cannot die (Luke 20:34-36).

Then it would appear as if there are different ranks and orders among the angels of God. The word *angel* itself simply means "messenger" and is used of the angelic host (Psalm 104:4), of men (Revelation 1:1,20), and of Christ (I Corinthians 10:4,9; 11:3) who came as the Messenger of God to mankind (Exodus 23:23; 32:34). Only three out of the vast host of angels are named—

Michael, one of the chief princes, the Prince of Israel (Daniel 10:13,21; 12:1; I Thessalonians 4:16; Jude 9; Revelation 12:7-9).

Gabriel, who stands before God and who announced Christ's birth (Daniel 8:16-19; 9:20-23; 10:8-11; Luke 1:19,26).

Lucifer, the original ruler of God's created world, but who became Satan (Isaiah 14:12-14; Ezekiel 28:11-17; Matthew 4:1-11; Ephesians 2:2).

We also have the unnamed Princes of Persia and Grecia (Daniel 10:13-11:1; Revelation 11:7; 17:8).

Among the divisions of angels mention can be made of—

The Seraphim (Isaiah 6:1-7)

The Cherubim (Genesis 3:24; Ezekiel 1:5-28; 8:1-4; 10:1-22),

The Archangels, or chief angels (Colossians 1:15-18; I Thessalonians 4:16; Jude 9).

Paul cites four kinds of angels among those who rebelled with Satan against God—

Principalities—chief rulers, those of highest rank in the Satanic kingdom (Colossians 2:10; Ephesians 1:1; 6:12).

Authorities, fallen angels whose power is derived from Satan and who execute the will of their chief ruler (Ephesians 1:21; 6:21; Colossians 2:10).

World rulers of darkness, spirit world rulers who assist in the plans of the god of this world (Daniel 10:13-21; (Ephesians 1:21; 6:12; Colossians 1:16-18).

Spiritual wicked spirits, operating from the heavenlies, where Satan has his seat of operations (Ephesians 1:21; 6:21; Colossians 1:16-18).

Good angels are referred to as *Watchers* (Daniel 4:13-23), *Sons of the Mighty* (Psalm 89:6), *Sons of God* (Genesis 6:1-4; Job 1:6; 2:1; 38:7), *Congregation of the Mighty* (Psalm 82:1), *Saints* (Psalm 89:7), *Hosts* (Psalms 33:6; 103:21; Luke 2:13), *Spirits* (Hebrews 1:14), *The Elect* (I Timothy 5:1).

The Responsibilities of Angels

From the appearances of angels and the collected references to them in the Bible, we find that the activities cover a wide field. Their varied work could only be possible as those specially created and endowed of God. With joy and alacrity they do His pleasure (Psalm 103:21). Their mission and ministry are generally related to guardianship and government. Able to fight boldly, they are capable of operation in the material and earthly plane (Revelation 12:7). Amazed at the divine plan, the angels yet help to execute it (I Peter 1:12). Usually described as being in *white* (Revelation 4:4) speaks of the righteousness of their mission. Here is the list of the varied activities of these celestial beings Finis J. Dake gives in his *Notes on Psalms:*

They drive spirit horses (II Kings 2:12; 6:13-17; Zechariah 1:7-11; 6:1-6).

They guard gates (Revelation 21:12; cf. Genesis 3:24).

They wage war in actual bodily combat (Revelation 12:7-9; II Thessalonians 1:7-10).

They execute judgments (Genesis 19; II Samuel 24; II Kings 19:35; II Chronicles 32:21; Psalm 78:49; Matthew 13:41,42; Acts 12:23; Revelation 8:1-9,21; 15:1-16:2).

They minister to saints (I Kings 19:5-7; Daniel 6:22; Matthew 4:11; Acts 10; Hebrews 1:14).

They rule nations (Daniel 10:13-21; 12:1).

They help each individual (Matthew 18:10).

They sing, praise and worship God (Luke 2:13; Psalms 103:20; 148:2; Revelation 5:11).

They strengthen in trial (Matthew 4:11; Luke 22:43).

They lead sinners to gospel workers (Acts 10:3).

They direct preachers (Acts 8:26).

They appear in dreams (Matthew 1:20-24; 2:13-19).

They minister before God (Revelation 8:2; 14:15-19).

They bind Satan and guard his abyss (Revelation 9:1; 20:1-3).

They regather Israel (Matthew 24:31).

They protect saints (Psalms 34:7; 91:11; Acts 12:7-10).

They separate the good from the bad (Matthew 13:19-41). They accompany Christ to earth (Matthew 16:27; 25:31; II Thessalonians 1:7-10).

They witness confessions (Luke 15:8,9).

They receive departed spirits (Luke 16:22).

They give laws and revelations (Acts 7:33; Hebrews 2:2; II Kings 1:15; Daniel 8:19; 9:21-23; 10:10-20).

They impart God's will (Acts 5:19,20; 10:1-6).

They bring answers to prayer (Daniel 9:21-23; 10:12,13; Acts 10).

They are present in the Church (I Corinthians 11:10; Ephesians 3:10; I Timothy 5:21).

As the angels, then, occupy an intermediate sphere between heaven and earth, God and man, is it not incumbent upon us to give ourselves to an understanding of the doctrine concerning their relationship to the saved and unsaved alike? Because they are constantly employed by God as ministers of His will in the Church to her Rapture, and in the government of the world, should we not be found meditating more than we have been doing upon these guardian and attendant spirits (Acts 13:15)? As Canon C. Bell expresses it in his volume on *Angelic Beings—Their Nature and Ministry—*

It may indeed be urged that there is One greater than angels who is our Friend— One as full of pity, as He is our power, and who is "about our path, and about our bed, and spieth out all our ways." Yet doth He act providentially towards us by the agency of creatures, whether angelic or human. And the angels, we must remember, are bound up with us in the unity of our blessed family in Christ. . . . Amongst other blessed companionships, "Ye are come to an innumerable company of angels."

IX

The Doctrine of Satan and Demons

A distinguishing feature of the Bible is its faithfulness in recording the life and character of all beings, whether human or angelic, saintly or evil. Within the sacred volume we not only have the biography of man, but also the history of those beings who occupy the foremost rank of created intelligencies. In the foregoing study we considered the doctrine of those "elect" or

"chosen" angels, confirmed by God in their holy position.

The Bible, however, unveils the record of those angels who "left their first estate," and are still in a state of rebellion against their Creator. Sad though it is, yet there is the revelation of those angelic rebels, outcasts from the favor of God and the bliss of heaven. Here within the Bible their origin and original happiness, their sad declension, their evil influence upon men, their present destructive work, and their future terrible doom are brought before us as themes for trembling interest and for solemn warning.

We are to consider Satan and the demons as one doctrine because they were one in their rejection of God's claim, and have remained one since their deposition from heaven in their diabolical purpose to thwart God's benign purposes on man's behalf. Had Lucifer not become Satan, there would have been no demons. Our Lord spoke of "The devil and *his* angels," thereby identifying them as *one* evil brood. Of the religious leaders, who blindly rejected His claims, our Lord could say, "Ye are of your father, the devil," and he is the father of all who despise Christ as "The Truth"; and also of those evil spirits responsible for prompting despisers in their rejection of the Saviour.

First of all, then, let us gather together what the Bible says about the origin, history, work and doom of Satan. A conception of the nature of this evil parent will prepare us for an understanding of his offspring. At the outset let it be stated that the Bible makes no apology in giving the world the biography of the devil. God, Christ, prophets, apostles and Satan-bound souls had no doubts as to the reality of this enemy of man. It is a cunning device of Satan's, however, to try and convince man that he does not really exist.

How shocked all true evangelical Anglicans and believers in other denominations were to read that Dr. Ramsey, when Archbishop of Canterbury, answered Cambridge undergraduates' questions about Satan, he said—

> I do not draw from the Bible the inference that there is an individual monarch of evil. I think it is too dogmatic to say that evil spirits have had the best of it.

One wonders from what kind of Bible the genial Archbishop reads. It must be one from which all references to a personal devil and hosts of evil spirits have been expurgated. As we shall see, the devil was the real monarch of evil to Christ. Was He not manifested to destroy the works of the devil? If there is no devil, then we would like to know who is carrying on his devilish work. The Rev. John Pearce-Higgins, chairman of the Modern Churchmen's Union, a group of clergymen who seek to proclaim the Christian Gospel in the light of modern knowledge, says—

> If when I die, I am met by someone with horns and tail calling himself the devil I hope I shall not be frightened but reassured, knowing that I am having my leg pulled and there is humor in the hereafter.

The modern churchman tends less and less to dogmatism, but he says pretty firmly: "There is no devil." He regards Satan as he regards Adam and Eve—a mythological part of man's growing up.

As to the Archbishop's belief that "evil spirits have not had the best of it," how does he account for the appalling moral condition of society within a radius of fifty miles of his London palace? Vice and crime of all kinds have reached alarming proportions. Prisons are crowded to capacity—and the churches distressingly empty. Then, looking out upon the nations as a whole, and thinking of their bloody conflicts and of the threat of a catastrophic nuclear war, it seems as if "evil spirits" are having the best of it. The Bible declares that the devil is "the god of this world," and because he is, what else can we expect but a devilish world in which its evil host carries out his plans among nations and men?

There are those who deny the existence of a personal devil who yet speak of the existence and reality of evil forces. But how can there be evil forces without a figure behind them, responsible for their activity? Behind all evil powers there must be a personality directing them. The sin of the world must have a source. Principles are not self-propagating. Rejecting, then, all caricatures of the devil as a being with hoofs, horns, tail, holding a pronged scepter as he presides over the doomed in the Lake of Fire, let us classify the teaching of the Bible concerning him who was "the first sinner, the first rebel, and the first to consecrate himself to self-gratification and to wage war against society."

His Origin

It has been asked, "Where the devil did the devil come from?" God is the Creator of all, even of angelic beings. Therefore, God created the Lucifer, the highest of the order of the Seraphim. God did not create him a devil. The devil made himself a devil. By his own free act he lost his original supremacy and dignity and turned himself into a fiend. His great wisdom, corrupted by pride, developed into craftiness and wickedness. Originally *Lucifer*, meaning "Son of the Morning, The Light-Bearer," through his folly became "The Prince of Darkness."

There are several hints that Satan was originally created along with other beings, principalities and powers in heaven (Job 38:6; Colossians 1:15-18). Two great portions of Scripture contain valuable material regarding Satan's early history. First of all, there is this one in the prophecy of Ezekiel--

> Moreover the word of the Lord came unto me, saying, Son of man, take up a lamentation upon the king of Tyrus, and say unto him, Thus saith the Lord GOD; Thou sealest up the sum, full of wisdom, and perfect in beauty. Thou hast been in Eden the garden of God; every precious stone was thy covering, the sardius, topaz, and the diamond, the beryl, the onyx, and the jasper, the sapphire, the emerald, and the carbuncle, and gold: the workmanship of thy tabrets and of thy pipes was prepared in thee in the day that thou wast created. Thou art the anointed cherub that covereth; and I have set thee so: thou wast upon the holy mountain of God; thou hast walked up and down in the midst of the stones of fire. Thou wast perfect in thy ways from the day that thou wast created, till iniquity was found in thee. By the multitude of thy merchandise they have filled the midst of thee with violence, and thou hast sinned: therefore I will cast thee as profane out of the mountain of God: and I will destroy thee, O covering cherub, from the midst of the stones of fire. Thine heart was lifted up because of thy beauty; thou hast corrupted thy wisdom by reason of thy brightness: I will cast thee to the ground, I will lay thee before kings, that they may behold thee. Thou hast defiled thy sanctuaries by the multitude of thine iniquities, by the iniquity of thy traffic; therefore will I bring forth a fire from the midst of thee, it shall devour thee, and I will bring thee to ashes upon the earth in the sight of all them that behold thee. All they that know thee among the people shall be astonished at thee: thou shalt be a terror, and never shalt thou be any more (28:11-19).

Scofield's comment is apt at this point--

> Here, as in Isaiah 14:12, the language goes beyond the King of Tyre to Satan, inspirer and unseen ruler of all such pomp and pride as that of Tyre. The unfallen state of Satan is here described; his fall

in Isaiah 14:12-14. But more is here. The vision is not of Satan in his own person, but of Satan fulfilling himself in and through an earthly king who arrogates to himself divine honors, so that the Prince of Tyrus foreshadows the Beast (Daniel 7:8; Revelation 19:20).

While the prophecy or statements of this passage are addressed to the person named, they appear to go beyond an earthly monarch and can only apply to a supernatural being of some kind. Ezekiel, talking of contemporaneous events goes beyond them, and using them as a type, goes from a reference to the King of Tyre to Satan, of whom the King is a type. Before he sinned, or iniquity was found in him, Satan was known as *Lucifer*.

"Thou wast perfect in thy ways from the day that thou wast created." Here is the simple explanation of the true origin of the angelic being who became the devil. He was created by God with these original characteristics--

"Full of wisdom, and perfect in beauty" (Ezekiel 28:12).

"Thou art the anointed cherub that covereth; I have set thee so: thou wast upon the holy mountain of God; thou hast walked up and down in the midst of stones of fire" (28:14).

"Thou wast perfect in thy ways . . . till iniquity was found in thee" (28:15).

As the anointed cherub, he covered God's throne, that is, he guarded it. But instead of covering it, he *coveted it* and so fell. His sphere of activity also included the mountain of God, or God's special dwelling place. Does this imply his control of God's original creation? Our Lord referred to Satan as the God, and also the Prince of this world (John 12:31; 14:30; 16:11). During the Temptation, he offered Jesus the kingdoms of this world (Matthew 4). Were they his to give? Did he originally represent God in His creation (Genesis 1:1), and does he now, by rebellion, hold the kingdoms of this world? (See Isaiah 14:12; Jeremiah 4:23-26; Luke 10:18; II Peter 3:4-8).

This we do know, there are several plain Scriptures declaring that Lucifer fell from his high and privileged position. His beauty caused his heart to be lifted up in pride—and his brightness brought about his corruption (Ezekiel 28:11-17; I Timothy 3:6). Additional information about this fall of Lucifer is given by Isaiah—

How art thou fallen from heaven, O Lucifer, son of the morning! how art thou cut down to the ground, which didst weaken the nations! For thou hast said in thine heart, I will ascend into heaven, I will exalt my throne above the stars of God: I will sit also upon the mount of the congregation, in the sides of the north: I will ascend above the heights of the clouds; I will be like the Most High (14: 12-14).

Lucifer became Satan when he tried to make himself not only equal with God, but as one *above* God. Note the fivefold personal pronoun *I*. Covetous, he would not be satisfied with anything short of the very highest position in God's original creation. Pride preceded his overthrow (Proverbs 16:18). The middle letter of *pride* is *I*, just as it is in *sin*, and it was the the big *I* that brought about the fall of the divinely created anointed cherub. He sinned against divine sovereignty and was thus cast out of heaven (Isaiah 14:13,14; II Thessalonians 2:4,9). And, as we shall see, when we consider *the demons*, he was not alone in his sin and fall. Many of the angels likewise revolted against God and aspired to divine authority, and followed Lucifer as their recognized head (Matthew 9:34; 25:41; Ephesians 2: 2).

If Satan, when Lucifer, was the first ruler under God of His original creation before the appearance of man on the earth, then perhaps his fall was related to the destructive upheaval in the created world between Genesis 1:1 and Genesis 1:2. The first verse of the Bible speaks of a definite, perfect condition accomplished in the dateless past, but verse two describes a disordered, disfigured condition that overtook that creation. What we speak of as creation was actually the refashioning of what God had previously created. (cf. Genesis 1:3-2:25 with Jeremiah 4:23-26; Isaiah 24:1). Was this overthrow of the primal order a divine curse upon creation because of Satan's usurpation of dominion?

His History and Character

The Bible offers no evidence that Satan was ever merciful, good, loving, kind, gentle, pitiful and patient. Although still an angelic being, He has never manifested any of those angelic graces and qualities characterizing unfallen angels. From the moment of his fall Satan labored with superhuman power, along with his evil hosts, to destroy the beneficial work of God on behalf of man. Who and what Satan is can be gathered from the following glimpses of him. First of all, as to his reality—

The Bible presents him as a real being (I Chronicles 21:1; Job 1:6-12; 2:1-7; Psalm 109:6; Zechariah 3:1,2; I Peter 5:8,9; Revelation 12:7-12).

Christ dealt with him as a real being (Matthew 4:1-11; Luke 4:1-13), and waged war with him as a real person (Luke 10:18; 13:16; See Acts 10:38; I John 3:8; Revelation 12:7-12; 13:1-4; 20:1-10).

The apostles thought of and encountered Satan as a real being, and constantly warned the saints against the wiles of this personal devil (Ephesians 4:27; 6:10-18; I Thessalonians 2:18; I Peter 5:8,9; James 4:7).

Personal singular pronouns are made of him, and he is credited with personal statements (Job 1:6-12; Isaiah 14:12-14; Ezekiel 28:11-17; Zechariah 3:1; Matthew 4:1-10; Jude 9).

Descriptions, name and titles given of him likewise indicate personality and what he became when deposed by God. Each of these designations carries its own significance—

Lucifer (Isaiah 14:12-14), *Devil and Satan* (Revelation 12:9), *Beelzebub* (Matthew 10:25; 12:24), *Belial* (II Corinthians 6:15), *Adversary* (I Peter 5:8,9), *Dragon* (Revelation 12:3-12; 13:1-4; 20:1-3), *Serpent* (II Corinthians 11:3; Revelation 12:9), *God of this world* (II Corinthians 4:4), *Prince of this world* (John 12:31), *Prince of the power of the air* (Ephesians 2:1-3), *Accuser of the brethren* (Revelation 12:10), *Enemy* (Matthew 13:39), *Tempter* (Matthew 4:3), *The wicked one* (Matthew 13: 19,38; I John 5:18), *Fowler* (Psalm 91:3), *Wolf* (John 10:12), *Destroyer* (John 10: 10), *Roaring Lion* (I Peter 5:8,9), *Thief* (John 10:10), *Father of lies* (John 8:44), *Murderer* (John 8:44), *Sower of discord* (Matthew 13:39). How Satan's diabolical character is revealed in these various descriptions! Yet the Archbishop of Canterbury, ecclesiastical head of the Church of England, cannot find the devil in his Bible!

The Bible is no less explicit when it comes to the record of Satan's history and activities which like his names are manifold. Ponder these formidable facts—

He was a sinner from the beginning (I John 3:8).

He was condemned for his pride of heart (I Timothy 3:6).

He goes from place to place (Job 1:6-12; 2:1-7; Matthew 4:10,11; Mark 4:15).

He is a celestial and territorial ruler (Ephesians 2:2; 6:10-18; II Corinthians 4: 4; John 12:31).

He has a realm divided into organized principalities and is the head of all the powers of darkness and ignorance (Daniel 10:12–11:1; Matthew 12:24-30; Ephesians 6:10-12).

He controls fallen angels and fallen men (Matthew 25:41; John 8:44; James 2:19; I John 3:8-10; Revelation 12:7-12).

He is active in some religions and religious affairs (II Corinthians 11:14; Revelation 2:9; 3:9).

He sows tares among the wheat, and is the enemy and accuser of the Church (I Peter 5:8; Revelation 12:5).

He is the author of persecution and tribulation, and afflicts the bodies of men (Luke 13:16; Acts 10:38; I Corinthians 5:5; II Corinthians 12:1-8; I Timothy 1:20; Revelation 2:10).

He attacks with cunning snares and with fiery darts, and suggests evil thought (John 13:2; Acts 5:3; I Corinthians 7:5; II Corinthians 2:11; 11:14; Ephesians 4:27; I Timothy 3:7; 6:7; II Timothy 2:26; Ephesians 6:16).

He has power over man extending to death, but not beyond it (Hebrews 2:14).

He was overcome by Christ (Luke 10:18; Acts 26:18; Hebrews 2:14; I John 3:8), and can be successfully resisted by the Christian (Romans 16:20; Ephesians 6:11; James 4:7; I Peter 5:9; I John 2:13; 5:18; Revelation 12:11).

He will share the eternal doom of all those whom he has seduced (Revelation 20:1-3,7-15).

With such a diabolical fiend operating as he has from the beginning of human history, unceasingly active in the destruction of the redemptive purpose of God, and the peace of man, the question arises, Why does God permit the devil to continue his devilish work? Why was he not bound with chains and cast into everlasting darkness when many of his angelic dupes were (Jude 6)? Here are some reasons why God continues to suffer His saints to be buffeted by Satan's wiles and machinations—

One wise and holy end of Satan's temptations is to try us. He tempts that he may deceive and destroy. But God permits him to tempt us to try us. "Temptation is a touchstone to try what is in the heart." Job's sincerity was tried by temptation. Satan told God that Job was a hypocrite and only served Him for what he could get out of it. God permitted Satan to tempt Job, but Job did not curse God to His face. Job remained holy and worshiped God. Temptations for Job were the touchstone of sincerity (1:11, 20,21).

Another purpose God has in permitting satanic temptation is that our love and courage might be tried. Satan's darts may be most fiery but our love to God is a strong protection. Temptation met and triumphed results in the development of character and faith (James 1:12; I Peter 1:7-10; 5:8,9; II Peter 1:4-9; Jude 20-24).

Further, God often suffers His children to be tempted that they may be kept humble. For Paul, the thorn in the flesh—the messenger of Satan was designed to prick the bladder of pride which it did (II Corinthians 12:7).

Then temptation is also permitted to enable us to comfort others and to speak a word in due season to those who are weary through satanic conflict. Victorious, we are able to succor those beset by Satan's stratagems (II Corinthians 2:11).

A further reason for temptation is to provide a conflict for saints that they may be rewarded through overcoming. Tempted, they are brought to repentance and made to experience the power of God over Satan's power (Mark 16:17-20; I Corinthians 4:9; 5:1-6; II Corinthians 2:5-11; Ephesians 2: 7; 3:16; I John 2:13; 4:1-6; Revelation 2: 7-28; 3:5,12,21; Job 33:14-30).

In all our temptations we are encouraged and sustained by the fact that Christ was tempted in all points such as we are. He sympathizes with us, and succors us as we face Satan in the wilderness (Hebrews 2: 18; 4:15), and preserves us as the apple of His eye (Zechariah 2:8). The word *succor* means "to run speedily to one's help," which is what Jesus does. He knows that Satan is fierce and mighty, and that we are so weak and frail. But He who is Almighty, is at hand to succor the tempted (Hebrews 2: 18).

Our responsibility regarding Satan is clear—

We must be sober and watch, lest he devours us (I Peter 5:8,9).

We must give him no foothold whatever (Ephesians 4:27).

We must resist him in virtue of the cross (James 4:7; I Peter 5:8,9).

We must put on the whole armor of God (Ephesians 6:11-18).

We must not be ignorant of his crafty devices (II Corinthians 2:11).

We must overcome him by the victorious Word (Matthew 4:1-11; I John 2:14).

We must triumph over him in Christ's name (Ephesians 1:19-22; 2:6; II Corinthians 2:15).

We must overcome him by regeneration and faith (I John 2:29; 3:9; 5:1-4,18).

We must overcome him by the Holy Spirit (Romans 8:1-13; Galatians 5:15-26).

We must overcome him by the blood of Christ and our testimony (Revelation 12:11).

Satan is a defeated foe. Calvary was his *Waterloo*. Therefore it is our solemn responsibility to constantly claim victory on the ground of the cross. By faith we must appropriate all Christ secured for us when He destroyed the works of the devil and follow Him in the train of His triumph. Last of all, let it never be forgotten that Satan cannot go any further than divine permission in tempting us (Job 2:5). When God says to Satan, "No further!" then he must stay his attacks. God, knowing each one of us, knows how much we can bear of satanic assault, and is nigh to deliver.

We now come to consider the doctrine of demons, bound up as it is with the doctrine of Satan. Evil spirits pervade Scripture, just as their tyrannical master does. While their particular, original sin is not revealed, it is assumed that inspired by Satan when he revolted against God, they too, defied divine authority (II Thessalonians 2:4,9). Although like Satan they were created good, sinning with Satan, they became angelic fiends bent on the destruction of the gracious purposes of God.

These subordinates of the great spirit of evil and his active coadjutors in his diabolical designs are divided into two distinct classes. All, of course, are evil and seducing spirits—demons and spirits being convertible terms in the New Testament (Luke 10:17,20; Mark 9:20-26; 7:25,29)—but separated into those who are bound, and the others who are free to roam.

The Fettered.

All of the fallen angels, along with the devil who, because he is the personification of wickedness, is called *"the* evil one," come within Jude's category of those "which kept not their first estate, but left their own habitation" (Jude 6). But those Jude describes were immediately chained and cast into darkness as soon as they fell. Deposed, they were bound, and since then have been inoperative as wicked spirits and beyond the bidding of their satanic lord.

Because of their immediate transference to the realms of darkness, it would seem as if their revolt must have been deeper and more heinously criminal than the demons who are free. Cast down into hell, to suffer millenniums of terrible bondage (II Peter 2:4), was the divine condemnation upon their sin. What sin is associated with leaving their "first estate" is not stated. Many Bible expositors link the above references from Peter and Jude to Genesis 6:2, and affirm that leaving their first estate implies the failure to retain their position as angels. Through their intercourse with women, they forsook their own principality, and for this abominable sin, God consigned those lustful angels to perpetual darkness and doom.

Apocryphal literature and mythology reflect the same view that powerful giants were born of illicit unions. Was it to these angelic perverts Christ preached in their fearful prison (II Peter 2:4,5)? Did He proclaim to these imprisoned spirits not only the message of a bloodbought victory over all satanic powers for the sons of men, but the ultimate eternal judgment of the devil and all his angels? For a fuller treatment of this phase of the doctrines of demons, the reader is referred to the writer's volume already mentioned, on *The Mystery and Ministry of Angels.*

The Free.

Scripture and experience offer abundant evidence that there is a vast number of evil spirits who, like their devilish leader, are free to roam the heavenly places and over the earth. With the devil they, too, fell into condemnation through pride and since then have been the adversaries of both God and man. These are the *demons* prominent in heathen mythology, and referred to by the Psalmist thus, "The gods of the heathen are demons" (Psalm 95:5 LXX). Paul, writing of the Gentiles of his time, speaks of them as sacrificing "to demons and not to God" (I Corinthians 10:20).

The word *demon* itself is not found in the Bible. What it implies, namely "evil spirits" or "devil," pervades Scripture from Genesis to Revelation. *Devil*, meaning "an adversary, false accuser, one who throws down, a slanderer," is used of Satan himself, of all evil spirits, called *devils*, and also of men who are false accusers and slanderers (Matthew 9:34; 12:24; John 6:70; I Timothy 3:11; II Timothy 3:3; Titus 2:3). Other designations of the demons, or devils, are *familiar spirits, unclean spirits, evil spirits, seducing spirits* (Leviticus 20:6; Mark 1:27; Luke 7:21; I Timothy 4:1). The Bible is emphatic on the point that traffic with demon spirits is forbidden (Leviticus 19:31; 20:6; Deuteronomy 18:10; Acts 16:16; II Peter 2:1-3).

As to the nature of demons, Scripture makes it plain that they are intelligent and wise angelic beings (I Kings 22:22-24; Acts 16:16)—powerful but not almighty (Mark 5:1-18), disembodied evil spirits (Judges 9:23; Revelation 16:13-16), inhuman yet seeking human possession (Matthew 10:7; Mark 16:17), have knowledge but not omniscience (Matthew 8:29; Luke 4:41; Acts 19:15), have faith (James 2:9) and feelings (Matthew 8:29; Mark 5:7), have wills, emotions and desires (Matthew 8:28-31; 12:43-45; Acts 8:7), have their own doctrines (I Timothy 4:1). In the great Tribulation, miraculous powers will be theirs (Revelation 16:13-16). They are likewise fierce and wrathful (Matthew 8:28; Revelation 12:12).

The manifold activities of these demons occupy considerable space in the Bible, as I have shown in the volume of mine mentioned above. Briefly stated, evil spirits—

Possess people and cause diseases, dumbness, deafness and blindness (Matthew 4:23,24; 9:32,33; 12:22; Mark 9:25).

Cause grievous vexation, suicide, lunacy and mania (Matthew 4:23,24; 17:14-21; Mark 5:1-8; 9:20).

Disseminate uncleanness (Luke 4:36. Some 21 times they are called *unclean spirits*). They are also the source of *lusts* (John 8:44; Ephesians 2:1-3; I John 2:15-17).

They manifest supernatural strength (Mark 5:18), and seek counterfeit worship (Leviticus 17:7; Deuteronomy 32:17; II Chronicles 11:15; Psalm 106:37; I Corinthians 10:20; Revelation 9:20).

They are guilty of error, deceptions,

lying, witchcraft, heresies and false teachings and prophecies (I Timothy 4:1,2; I John 4:1-6; I Kings 22:21-24; II Chronicles 33:6; I Samuel 18:8-10).

They can oppress, be jealous, steal, fight, tell fortunes, possess men at will, travel, imitate the departed dead (Acts 10:38; I Samuel 16:14; 18:8-10; I Timothy 4:1; Matthew 12:43-45; 13:19; Luke 8:12; Ephesians 4:27; 6:10-18; I Peter 5:8; Leviticus 20:27; Acts 16:16; I Samuel 28:3-9; I Chronicles 10:13; Isaiah 8:19; Deuteronomy 18:11).

Thousands of them can possess a man at the same time, being disembodied they can enter and control both men and beasts (Mark 5:1-18; Matthew 12:43-45).

They wage war on saints, influence men, have unbelievers in league with them, inflict physical maladies on those they possess (Ephesians 2:1-3; 6:10-18; I Timothy 4:1-5; II Peter 2:10-12; Matthew 12:22; 17:15-18).

What must be the attitude of the Christian toward these evil agents of Satan who unceasingly operate in so many ways against God, the saints and men in general?

First and foremost, believers must realize that demons can be made subject to them, even as they were subject to Christ. Through the victory of Christ over Satan and his host, and death, and in the mighty name of Christ and by the Holy Spirit, freedom can become the possession of the child of God from all satanic purposes (Matthew 8:16,17; 12:28; Mark 16:17; Luke 10:17; Acts 19:15).

These demons must be discerned, tested, resisted and rejected by believers (I Corinthians 12:10; Ephesians 4:27; 6:10-18; I Peter 5:8, 9; I John 4:1-6). They recognize those who have power over them (Acts 19:13-17).

Fearing the God they rebelled against (James 2:19), they are cognizant of their deserved eternal fate (James 2:19; Matthew 8:31,32; Luke 8:33; Revelation 9:1-21).

Our only resources against these hosts of wickedness are watchfulness, prayer and appropriation of the whole panoply of God (Matthew 7:21; Ephesians 6:10-18). Abundant provision has been made for us and by the grace and power of Christ we are invincible (II Timothy 2:1; I John 5:

8). Has not Isaac Watts taught us to sing?—

> Should all the hosts of death,
> And powers of hell unknown,

> Put their most dreadful forms
> Of rage and mischief on,
> I shall be safe; for Christ displays
> Superior power, and guardian grace!

X

The Doctrine of Man

How necessary it is to consider the doctrine of man, seeing that all the doctrines of grace are definitely related to him. After all the disappointment and sorrow man has occasioned his Creator by his sin and disobedience, is it not a wonder that He has any good intentions toward His self-marred handiwork? It was God's bountiful provision for His sinning creatures that led David to ask, "What is man, that thou art mindful of him? or the son of man, that thou visitest him" (Psalm 8: 4). It would have been a far darker world than it is, if God had abandoned man to outer darkness forever. Man, God's masterpiece of creation, has brought untold misery into the world, yet God has been so merciful toward him, as can be proven by the doctrines of grace.

To understand aright what God has provided for man, it is important to have a knowledge of man's nature and need. It is not our purpose to go fully into the doctrine of anthropology, as have done theologians like Dr. A. H. Strong in his monumental work—*Systematic Theology*. In simple language we want to outline the salient features of man's origin, history and destiny. In his most valuable commentary on *Genesis*, Dr. G. Campbell Morgan summarizes the teaching of the book under three key words: GENERATION, DEGENERATION, REGENERATION. Borrowing these expressive words, let us use them to cover the story of man.

His Generation

A seventh century writer, James Thomas, wrote of

"Majestic man,
A secret world of wonders in thyself."

Purpose, it has been said, is the autograph of the mind, and such an autograph is seen in all the works of God, especially man, who takes the highest place in God's creation. Man, as the crowning work of God, has faculties no other creation of God possesses. Man alone has the ability of—

1. Seeing God in His Work—
   "Because that which may be known of God is manifest in them; for God hath shewed it unto them. For the invisible things of him from the creation of the world are clearly seen, being understood by the things that are made, even his eternal Godhead . . ." (Romans 1:19,20).
2. Tracing evidences of His wisdom—
   "O LORD, how manifold are thy works! in wisdom hast thou made them all: the earth is full of thy riches" (Psalm 104:24).
3. Marveling at His power—
   "Praise ye the LORD . . . praise him in the firmament of his power" (Psalm 150:1).
4. Appreciating His goodness—
   "He loveth righteousness and judgment: the earth is full of the goodness of the LORD" (Psalm 33:5).

Man is not "Nature's sole mistake," but as old Francis Quarles expresses it, "Man is heaven's masterpiece." John Milton, the blind poet, wrote thus of man:

> All these His wondrous works, but
> chiefly man.

The privileges and power of man have been beautifully expressed by Dr. F. B. Meyer as follows:

> Man was placed in the world like a king in a palace stored with all to please him, monarch and sovereign of the lower orders of creation. The sun to labor for him like a very Hercules; the moon to light his nights, or lead the waters of the earth in tides, cleansing its shores: elements of nature to be his slaves and messengers: flowers to scent his pathway: fruit to please his taste: birds to sing for him: beasts to toil for him and carry him: and man himself, amidst all this luxury, God's representative, His vice-regent. This is man as God made him.

But what man has made of himself is another story, as we shall presently see.

Man was fashioned with deliberation and counsel for the record says, "Let us make man" (Genesis 1:26). In creation, God began with things less noble and excellent, then came to man, the most exquisite piece in creation. "Every man is a little world." But because man was to be the masterpiece of the visible world, a solemn council of the sacred Persons of the Trinity was called to decide on the making of so rare a piece. "Let *us* make man." Thus man bore the stamp of the divine, and was made partaker of many divine qualities.

Several untenable theories of the method of man's creation have been propounded. With one of these theories we have no sympathy whatever, namely, that of spontaneous generation which teaches that there was no creator of man. He simply came into being without a cause or "out of the nowhere, into the here." But man is too much of a miracle just to happen.

The evolution of man is another concept of man's origin we totally reject. Many college and history books still teach that through a series of natural developments and aggregation of matter through the centuries, man by chance or by law appeared. In the name of science, *evolution* assumes man to be the offspring of animals, "immediately from the ape, and secondarily from a long series of vertebrates." The evolutionist boldly declares that there is no clear boundary line between man and the animals from whom he sprang, either in his physical, mental or moral structure.

But there is no concrete evidence to support the unbridled imagination that man originally was a protoplasm, and that he gradually evolved into an ape, and then in some mysterious way became a man. What the evolutionist has failed to do is to bridge the gap between the ape and man. The missing link is ever a source of trouble to those who hold the theory of evolution, which is flatly contradicted by Scripture and the known facts of history.

The distinction between man and animals in respect of mental and moral nature is one of kind, not merely of degree. If, as the evolutionist would have us believe, there came a gradual improvement in the types of life developed until at last the progression rose from the protoplasm to the zoophyte, that is, a simple animal with a superficial resemblance to plants, then from the zoophyte to the fish, from the fish to the bird, from the bird to the quadruped, from the quadruped to the ape, from the ape to the man, how came the subtle but unmistakable difference between man and animal? Man can be educated; the beast cannot go beyond a very low level. It is impossible to teach apes what men are capable of comprehending. A few circus tricks monkeys perform are a very poor substitute for the noble ways of man. What monkey possesses the human attributes of man? Plato's definition of man as a "two-legged animal without feathers" was ridiculed, and rightly so, by Diogenes, who produced a plucked cock, saying, "Here is Plato's man."

Think, first of all, of the size of the brain. Man's brain is out of all proportion to the mental needs of the highest of the animal creation below him. The weight of the largest brain of a gorilla is considerably less than half that of the average man, and only one-third that of the best developed of the human race. In his reasoning powers, man is separated from the lower creation by an impassable gulf. Man's intellectual capacity belongs to a different order altogether. Romanes, the eminent Oxford scientist, after collecting the manifestations of intelligent reasoning from every known species of the lower animals, found that they only equalled, altogether, the intelligence of a child 15 months old. Thus, man's superiority is seen in his faculty of reasoning, and in his power to acquire indefinite increase of knowledge, and of making deductions from knowledge gained, leading to practical results.

Man has been defined as a "tool-using animal," as Boswell expresses it in his "Life of Johnson." But what animal can use a tool intelligently, much less make the tool to use? Yet the lowest races of men show great ingenuity in making tools. The rudest flint implements bear indubitable evidence of a power to adapt means to an end, which places their maker in a category of his own.

Aristotle wrote of man as being by nature "a civic animal"; while Charles Lamb called man "a gaming animal." What beasts are able to conceive and observe correct customs and to devise and enjoy sports like men? Man has also been described as "a fire-using animal." In his lowest stages man knows how to make fire at his will. So great is this accomplishment that the ancient Greeks looked upon fire as a gift from heaven. But what animal is able to make a fire? Monkeys may gather around a fire when it has been made, but are unable to provide a fire around which to gather.

One of the most marked distinctions between man and beast is the gift of expressing thought in articulate speech. Certain animals and birds may have the faculty to imitate the human voice and mimic a few words, but they cannot create words. It is for this reason that man has been spoken of as "a speaking animal," seeing that he alone has the gift of language. Man has not only the power of speech— he can also transcribe his thoughts. How absurd it would be to try and educate an ape to understand and translate the original manuscripts of Scripture!

Seneca wrote of man as "a social animal." A Latin proverb has it, "Where there are men, there are manners." While some animals can be bribed to obey, where are there those able to emulate the graces, charm and attractive qualities of a well-groomed man? Animals are still on all fours, and cannot walk upright with the bearing of man.

Because man is able to respond to and profit by religious impulses and influences, he has been designated as "a religious animal." Man alone has spiritual concepts and the ability to worship God. Said Edmund Burke, "Man is by his constitution a religious animal." Ovid, the Latin philosopher wrote, "God gave man a countenance exalted and made him to contemplate the heaven." Where is the ape with a concept of spiritual intelligence able to arrive at ideas of right and wrong? Man is the only creature of God with moral qualities to discern the difference between right and wrong. Who would ever think of trying to improve the nature of animals by beginning to preach the Gospel to them, or distribute Bibles among them? Yet the Bible, a Book composed of every kind of literature, and containing the highest flights of poetry and eloquence ever written, presenting the sublimest concepts of God and of the future life ever entertained, has been translated into all languages, and has found in these languages the appropriate figures of speech for the effective presentation of the ideas contained in the Book. Further, the declaration of these ideas even among the most primitive of men, has elicited praise, worship, adoration and love toward the Creator.

Having the power to decide issues, man acts upon the revelation of God and is blessed thereby. Tennyson reminds us that, "Man is man, and master of his fate." Man is master of the fate of animals. Shakespeare in *Julius Caesar* expresses the same idea—

Men, at some time, are masters of their
   fates:
The fault, dear Brutus, is not in our stars,
But in ourselves, that we are underlings.

All animals are dumb before the great, solemn crises and issues of life. Animals may have instinct, but man has intellect to guide him in important decisions.

It was once held that there was no difference between the blood of an ape and that of a man. Exhaustive tests, however, have proved the blood of monkeys to be most inferior to the blood of a man. It is safe to assume that no surgeon would be as foolhardy as to transfuse a quantity of an ape's blood into the veins of a man, which brings us to the great, fundamental truth of creation, namely, that God made everything after its *own* kind.

And God created great whales, and every living creature that moveth, which the waters brought forth abundantly, after their kind, and every winged fowl after his kind. And God said, let the earth bring forth the living creature after his kind, cattle, and creeping things, and beast of the earth after his kind: . . . and God made the beast of the earth after his kind, and cattle after their kind, and every thing that creepeth upon the earth after his kind: and God saw that it was good (Genesis 1:21,24,25).

The Bible opposes the claim that man and animals have a common origin, and reveals how impossible it is to reconcile the Genesis account of creation with the theory of evolution. To those who think that evolution does not oppose the Bible account of the origin of man, we ask an answer to the following questions:

1. At what point in the ascending scale do moral questions emerge, or where does irresponsible animal passion pass into moral obligation?

2. At what point does a spiritual nature, carrying the gift of immortality, appear?

3. At what particular stage in the development of a semi-animal, semi-savage creature, can we apply the words, "Made in the image of God"?

4. How does the theory affect the Person of Christ, and how far back along the process of development does His redemptive work take effect?

Approaching the positive side of man's origin, there are three aspects to distinguish. Man was—

1. *Created by a divine, direct and definite act of God*

To "create" means to make something out of nothing, which is practically what God did when, out of a few grains of dust, He formed the body of man. The trilogy, or anthem over the creation of man is given in the key word *created*, thrice repeated. Accepting the almightiness of God as we do, we see no reason why He was not able in a moment of time to fashion the perfect, physical body of Adam. The body is the offspring of the dust. Christ declared that God was able to raise up children unto Abraham out of stones, which are solidified dust. ". . . for I say unto you that God is able of these stones to raise up children unto Abraham" (Luke 3:8; cf. Genesis 1:27; 5:1; Ecclesiastes 7:29; Acts 17:26). The first chapter of Genesis records the fact of man's creation (1:27); the second chapter describes the mode (2:7).

We are children of splendor and fame,
Of shuddering, also, and tears:
Magnificent, out of the dust we came,
And abject from the spheres.

At death, the body travels back by quick stages to its natural element, "Unto dust shalt thou return" (Genesis 3:19). He who brings the body to the dust because of sin can also raise it from the dust in resurrection glory (Daniel 12:2; Philippians 3:21). Man, then, is of the earth, earthy (Genesis 2:7). His body is not a house of *clay*, but fashioned out of the finest materials of earth, and functions as the house of the inner man (Job 4:19; II Corinthians 5:1-4). The same elements are to be found in a human body that are in the earth upon which man walks.

Why did God form the body of man out of the dust of the earth? Was it not that he might use the earth for his needs and replenish the earth with a new order? (Genesis 1:28; 3:20). God created man as a necessary complement of His plan. The tilling of the earth God had made was evidently a work the Creator wanted man to do. "There is not a man to till the ground" (Genesis 2:5,15). God made the earth for man, then made man for the earth. Thus work, originally, was not of necessity and a curse, seeing labor was introduced before the curse was pronounced. By setting man to work on the earth God created, He indicated thereby that He was becoming dependent upon human instrumentality. Work, when well directed, is good (Ephesians 4:28), angelic (Hebrews 1:14), and divine (John 5:17; 9:4).

2. *Created in the Divine Image*

While there are striking resemblances between God and man, there are also many disparities. "Man is like God, as shadow is like substance." Sin defaced the divine image, and estranged man from the holiness of God. Christ came as the perfect Man, "the express image of God" (Hebrews 1:3). But as we shall presently see, restoration to the full likeness of God awaits redeemed men (II Corinthians 3:18). In the new creation, they are to gain more than that possessed by unfallen men in the old creation (Ephesians 4:24).

Man's present condition and position has been aptly described by Alexander Pope in *An Essay on Man*—

Chaos of thought and passion, all confused,
Still by himself abused, or disabused:
Created half to rise, and half to fall;
Great lord of all things, yet prey to all;
Sole judge of truth, in endless error hurled,
The glory, pest and riddle of the world.

What exactly is implied by the recorded truth that man was created in the divine image and likeness (Genesis 1:26,27; 9-6; I Corinthians 11:7; James 3:9)? Is there a distinction to be drawn between "image" and "likeness"? There are expositors who affirm that "image" refers to bodily form, and "likeness" to the spirit. It would seem, however, that "image" refers to constitution, and includes the gift of personality, mental and moral capacity, free will, free agency. This first term implies that man in his sphere becomes a self-guiding cause, even as God is in His.

"Likeness" is associated with moral and spiritual resemblance to God, which it was possible for man to develop, but which, alas, he quickly lost.

1. Physical resemblance

While it is true that God is Spirit (John 4:24), and invisible (Colossians 1:15), He yet has a form in which He manifests Himself to the eye (Psalm 17:15 R.V.; Isaiah 6:1; John 5:37 R.V.; Philippians 2:6, 7). Adam's creation prefigured the image of Christ. "Who is the *figure* of Him that was to come" (Romans 5:14).

2. Moral resemblance

God made man upright as Himself. Man is still the only erect being among living creatures. He alone can look up naturally and without effort. But he lost his birthright when he looked at what was on a level with his eyes, and occupied himself only with what was on the plane of his own existence. By sinning, he lost the God-like innocence with which he was created. This moral likeness, lost by the fall, is restored by grace (Ephesians 4:23; Colossians 3:10; Romans 8:29; II Corinthians 3:18; Psalm 17:15 R.V.).

3. Created with a three fold constitution

Man is a tripartite being, made up of spirit, soul and body. There are those expositors who reject this trinity-in-unity possession, and accept the dual nature of man. Soul and spirit are treated as being identical and not separate and distinct elements. While it is a fact that spirit and soul are sometimes used as interchangeable terms, in the majority of cases they are employed as contrasted terms (Hebrews 4:12; I Thessalonians 5:23). Man's body was formed from the lower elements—the divine Spirit was inbreathed—a living soul resulted from the union of the first two. Justin Martyr spoke of the man's trinity

in this way, "As the body is the house of the soul, so the soul is the house of the spirit."

BODY. "The Lord God formed man (that is, his body) of the dust of the earth" (Genesis 2:7). Here we have the external, visible part of man, representing everything that is done without. The body, being made up of the five senses of hearing, seeing, smelling, tasting and feeling, connects us with the world without and around us. The body, therefore, represents *world-consciousness*. The body is to the spirit and soul the medium of expression and impression. Thomas Watson in his "Body of Divinity" speaks of the parts of man's body thus—

> *The Head,* the most excellent architectural part, is the fountain of spirits and the seat of reason. In nature the head is the best piece, but in grace the heart excels.
>
> *The Ear* is the conduit-pipe through which knowledge is conveyed. Better lose our seeing than our hearing, for "faith cometh by hearing" (Romans 10:17). To have an ear open to God is the best jewel on the ear.
>
> *The Eye* is the beauty of the face; it shines and sparkles like a lesser sun in the body. The eye occasions much sin and therefore may well have tears in it.
>
> *The Tongue.* David called the tongue his glory because it is an instrument to set forth the glory of God. The soul at first was a viol in tune to praise God, and the tongue made the music. God has given us two ears, but one tongue, to show that we should be swift to hear, but slow to speak. God has set a double fence before the tongue—the teeth and the lips—to teach us to be wary that we offend not with our tongue.

It may be that God made the body out of dust, and the dust out of nothing, to keep down man's pride. David speaks of the body as being "curiously wrought." Being "curiously wrought" makes us grateful to God, but being taken out of the dust makes us humble.

> Thy body is but air and dust mingled together, and the dust will drop into the dust. If thou hast beauty, it is but well-colored earth. When God told the judges they were as gods, lest they should become proud, he reminded them that they would die as men (Psalm 82:6,7).

SOUL. "Man became a living soul" (Genesis 2:7; I Corinthians 15:45). The beasts of the field have bodies, but not souls, after the order of man's living soul. Other aspects of God's created world are possessed of life. There is *organic life,* life in grass and trees, and *sentient life* in fish, fowls and beasts, which are able to move (Genesis 1:20). Man, however, is endowed with a higher reach in the scale of life. Beasts may distinguish one from another (Isaiah 1:3) but man has the faculty of reasoning with God (Isaiah 1:18). Cattle "nourish a blind life" but man has a perceptive faculty and can follow the footprints of Deity (Romans 1:20). At his creation, Adam had perfect intuitive knowledge (Genesis 2:20). He was not an "adult infant."

The soul is the seat and source of varying emotions and appetites (Genesis 42:21; Deuteronomy 12:15; I Samuel 2:16; Isaiah 61:10). The soul is "the man of the man—the diamond in the ring—a spark of celestial brightness." The soul is derived from the union of the body and the spirit, and in turn is that which unifies them. Man has a body and a spirit, but he *is* a soul. He "became a living soul." The infusion of the immaterial spirit into the material frame produced the third possession, a soul, and it is reasonable to suppose that with the separation of the body from the spirit, that which depended upon their union ceases to be. Spirit can exist apart from body, and body can exist apart from spirit, but the soul cannot exist while spirit and body are apart.

The soul is the central part of man, the hub of his little universe. Within the soul, there are all the powers that go to make up what we call personality. The soul is a trinity in unity, possessing heart, mind and will. My soul is myself, and represents *self-consciousness,* just as the body stands for *world-consciousness.* Within the soul, there is the mind, the source of knowledge and intelligence (I Corinthians 2:11). With the mind we think. Animals do not possess this faculty (Psalm 32:9). There is also the heart, which is not merely a muscle of the body, but the source of love, affection, as well as consciousness (Hebrews 10:22). Because Adam was endowed with intelligence, he had the ability to give names to the living creation over which he was to have dominion (Genesis 2:19,20). Then there is the will, giving man the capacity to choose, act or decide. Man's power to choose is both an end, and the means to attain it. The tragedy of sin is that man used the gift of will against the Giver. Sin

entered the world by man's conscious and voluntary choice. Tennyson gives us these lines—

> Our wills are ours, we know not why;
> Our wills are ours, to make them Thine.

Within man's inner self there is also conscience, the echo of God's voice. Robert Browning describes conscience as "the great beacon light God sets in all." Wordsworth speaks of it as "the daughter of the voice of God." Conscience has been seared by sin (I Timothy 4:2; Hebrews 13:18).

The centrality of the soul gives it a position of importance. Being in the center, it can swing the balance in either direction. It is also acted upon by two sets of attractions. There are the attractions of the world around, reaching the soul through the body, and the attractions of heaven above, reaching the soul through the medium of the spirit.

SPIRIT. God breathed into the nostrils of Adam "the breath (spirit) of life," (Genesis 2:7). We now come to the deepest, eternal part of man. God is spoken of as "the Father of spirits" (Hebrews 12:9). Within the spirit, there are the faculties for worship, communion, adoration and praise. Fellowship with God is possible through the spirit, and can stand for *God-consciousness.* In his physical creation, man is linked to the animal creation, and hence is capable of grossest debasement, as we shall see when we come to his degeneration. In his spiritual nature, man is akin to God, and therefore has infinite possibilities of spiritual development. The spirit is the essential part of man's nature, the heart of all human life. God is Spirit, man is spirit, and therefore greater than the material universe. The spirit is immaterial being, eluding the test of the biologist or chemist. "Imponderable—it cannot be weighed; intangible—cannot be handled; invisible—it cannot be seen."

When God deals with the creation of man, He begins with the body, as it should be. "First that which is natural" (I Corinthians 15:46), but when He comes to the sanctification of man, He reverses the order, journeying from the center to the circumference (I Thessalonians 5:23). Man's work of reformation is outward— God's work begins within. The ancients had a fitting way of illustrating the threefold possession of man. They likened the body to the material framework of a chariot—the soul, with all its powers, to the horses driving the chariot along—the spirit, to the charioteer, whose firm hands held the reins and whose keen eyes determined the course. If the spirit-part of man is inoperative, or under the control of evil spirits, as in the case of Spiritism, or Demonism, then there is chaos, tragedy and death, for God meant the body to be the servant of the soul, and the soul, the servant of the spirit: and spirit, soul, and body all servants of His and avenues along which He can journey to a lost world.

His Degeneration

Constituted to live in perfect accord with his Creator, and to be at peace within himself and in harmony with his environment, man forfeited his holy and blessed position through sin. Evolutionists speak of "The Fall" as "a fall upward," whereby man is gradually shedding the animal. The stirring of passion we call "sin," is merely the strain of man's ferocious animal ancestry in his blood. But Scripture testifies otherwise (Romans 5:12-19; I Corinthians 15:45-49; I Timothy 2:13,14). By reason of sin, man has lost much of his original dignity (Ecclesiastes 7:29). He was made to have dominion over the works of God (Psalm 8:4), a distinction he still retains to a remarkable degree. The tragedy of sin is that he is less subservient to the purpose of his being than the brutes he controls (Isaiah 1:3). Sin has weakened his power to dominate nature. Christ remained the perfect Man, and therefore had full control over nature (I Corinthians 15:24; Hebrews 2:8; see His miracles). During the millennial reign, man will be restored to the full dignity he had in Eden, as the Psalmist foreshadows. "The upright shall have dominion . . . in the morning" (Psalm 49:14).

The Fall of man, then, is not an old Babylonian fable, but the pitiable history of man, as Scripture testifies (Romans 5: 12). Man's

crown is rolled in the dust and tarnished. His sovereignty is strongly disputed by the lower orders of creation. The earth supplies him with food only after arduous toil. The beasts serve him only after they have been laboriously tamed and trained, while vast numbers roam the forests, setting him at defiance. So degraded has man become

through sin, that he has bowed before the objects that he was to command, and has prostrated his royal form at shrines dedicated to the birds and to four-footed beasts and creeping things.

In such a description of what man has become through sin, Dr. F. B. Meyer must have had Romans 1:21-32 in mind.

The Fall resulted in the total depravity of man, which means that although he is not altogether bad, every part of his nature became tainted by sin. Robert Louis Stevenson in *The Wrecker*, remarks, "Every man has a sane spot somewhere." Man's whole being is corrupted—his spirit is darkened (Ephesians 4:17,18; I Corinthians 2:14); his soul is debased (Jeremiah 17:9; Ephesians 4:19); his body is diseased and death-ridden (Romans 7:24); his will is weakened (Romans 7); his conscience is blunted (I Timothy 4:2). Sin brought a schism into man's nature, the lower dominating the higher. Man, apart from grace, has "the mind of the flesh" (Romans 8:7, 8 R.V.) and a heart that is deceitful (Genesis 6:5-12; Romans 1:17-24). He is spiritually dead (Ephesians 2:1); under wrath and judgment (John 5:28,29; Psalm 130:3; Romans 2:5-12; Ephesians 2:3; II Thessalonians 1:6-9; Revelation 20:15; 21:8); utterly lost (Luke 19:10); a guilty sinner before God (Psalm 14:2,3; Isaiah 53:6; Romans 3:9-23); a child of the devil, and under the control of Satan (Ephesians 2:2).

The extent of man's fall is graphically described by John Milton in *Paradise Lost*—

Of man's first disobedience and the fruit
Of that forbidden tree, whose mortal taste
Brought death into the world, and all our
    woe, with loss of Eden.

Yes, the results of Adam's sin are terrible to contemplate. Sin became universal (Romans 5:12,19); it meant the loss of communion with God (Isaiah 59:2; Genesis 3:24); it brought the condemnation of God (Galatians 3:10; Colossians 1:21); it resulted in earthly sorrow (Lamentations 5:16,17); it produced spiritual death (Genesis 3:17); and ends in eternal punishment (Matthew 25:41).

Dr. R. A. Torrey lists five steps in the Fall of man as given in Genesis 3:1-6. Adam was guilty of—

1. Listening to slanders against God.
2. Doubting God's Word and His love.
3. Looking at what God had forbidden.

4. Lusting for what God had prohibited (I John 2:16).

5. Disobeying God's commandment.

The many-sided sin of Adam has also been expressed in the following way—

It was willful sin, for Adam was not deceived as Eve (I Timothy 2:14).

It was rebellion against the rule of God (Lamentations 1:18).

It was a reflection upon the goodness of God (Romans 2:14).

It was a breach of the law of God (I John 3:4).

It was an act of spiritual suicide (Romans 5:12).

It brought evil upon others (Romans 5:12).

His Regeneration

The rest of our study of the cardinal truths of our Christian faith is devoted to an understanding of all God has provided for the sinning sons and daughters of Adam's race. Having lost the image of God through sin, sinners should never rest until that image is restored. Now they have the devil's image in pride, malice, envy. God's image, however, consisting of knowledge and righteousness, can be recovered (Colossians 3:10). If Paradise has been lost, it can be regained.

1. *Present Recovery*

God alone is able to repair the damaged image of Himself. Having once made us, He can make us anew. Sin has defaced the image, but it can be drawn again by the pencil of the Holy Spirit (John 3:6,7; Romans 8:29; I Corinthians 6:9-11; II Corinthians 3:18; 5:1). Such a restoration

was made possible when Christ, the true Image of the invisible God (Hebrews 1:3; Colossians 1:15), took upon Himself our human nature and our liabilities, and redeemed us from the consequences of the Fall. Adam was lost because he took the fruit from a tree, and now lost men are saved through the Sin-Bearer who died on the tree (Galatians 3:12; I Peter 2:24, 25). In Adam we die, in Christ we are made alive (I Corinthians 15:22).

The present position of those who have put off the old man and have put on the new is one of sonship as our study on "adoption" will clearly prove (Galatians 4:7; I John 3:2). The believer is also a partaker of the divine nature (II Peter 1:4), and is sealed by the Spirit unto the day of final redemption (Ephesians 1:13,14; 4:30).

2. *Prospective Reign*

In the future, there are not only the glorious blessings of resurrection (John 5:24-29); eternal life (John 6:47); eternal glory (I Peter 5:10); immortality (I Corinthians 15:53); manifestation with Christ (Romans 8:18; I John 3:2), but a restoration of the dominion we lost through sin. The inspired writer of the Hebrews teaches us that when Christ returns to earth, He will exercise all the power over His creation lost through sin (Hebrews 2:5-10 cf. Psalm 8:4-8). The miracle of grace is that all who are no longer in Adam, but in Christ, are to assist and share in His glorious reign. They are to reign with Him, aiding Him in His governmental control of all things (Luke 22:28,29). Sharers of His throne (Matthew 19:28; II Timothy 2:12; Revelation 5:10), will possess dominion Adam could never have known, had he remained innocent all his days.

XI

The Doctrine of the Covenants

The most common uses of the word *covenant* in the Bible are for covenants between God and His people. The term, along with the kindred ones of *agree* and *agreement* occur about 250 times in Scripture. Webster, explaining that a *covenant* is "an agreement between persons or parties," or

"to enter into a formal agreement" says that in theology, *covenant* covers "the promises of God as revealed in the Scripture." Generally speaking, the covenants were originated by God for man's good to condition life on the earth. From His side these covenants cannot be broken. Man may make covenants and break them—as he often does, but God's Word, or promise, or covenant cannot fail.

"My covenant will I not break, nor alter the thing that is gone out of My lips" (Psalm 89:34).

Herbert M. Carson, in his study on "The Covenant of Grace" in *Christianity Today* (September 15, 1961), said—

A covenant is essentially a pledged and defined relationship. There are three main elements in it—the parties contracting together, the promises involved, and the conditions imposed. It is clearly possible to have a covenant between equals, or one which is imposed unilaterally by a superior. It is obvious, however, that any covenant between God and man can never be as between equals, but must be imposed from above.

Professor Davidson draws attention to the fact that originally the idea of a covenant was not a religious agreement, and applying only to things of religion. "It was a concept transferred from ordinary life into the religious sphere." The word *covenant* itself was associated with a term meaning "to cut," implying any agreement entered into under the solemn ceremonies of sacrifice (Jeremiah 35). So "to cut an agreement" suggested the slaying of victims in the forming of an agreement, with the sacrifice sealing the agreement.

Anything agreed upon by two nations or two persons was a covenant. Often, into these covenants or contracts, God came as a third Party—the Guardian of the contract. "Men swore by God, or offered a sacrifice, part of which was given to Him, the rest being eaten by the contracting parties. Thus all three were drawn into the bond and bound by it." Examples of the Lord upholding the right of a contract can be seen in the following—

When Laban left his daughters to Jacob, a covenant was made and a cairn raised in witness of the contract (Genesis 31:49).

When Sarah, enraged by Hagar, her maid, said to her husband, "The Lord judge between me and thee" (Genesis 16:5), there was the same idea of God as the Guardian of a contract. Instances of covenant-making abound in Scripture.

Two tribes that agree to live at amity, to intermarry or trade together, made a covenant often with a sacrifice eaten in common.

When a king was elected, there came a covenant between him and his people.

When two were married, the marriage became a covenant.

When David and Jonathan confessed their brotherly relation of affection, they made a covenant.

When Job determined to live at peace with the beasts of the field, and to keep his eyes from looking sinfully upon a woman, he made a covenant (5:23; 31:1).

When victors returned from battle they made a covenant with the vanquished to give him quarter and spare him.

When Abraham and Abimelech declared themselves equal they made a covenant (Genesis 21:31). The covenant between Joshua and the Gibeonites was one between parties who were unequal (Joshua 9:15).

When one invoked the superior power of another, as when Asa bribed Benhadad, a covenant was entered into (I Kings 15:19).

Coming to the covenants God made, which are sometimes treated as *dispensations* or *ages*, it is important to note that they were made with people as a whole, and not with individuals. "The people were regarded as a whole and individuals share the benefit of the covenant as members of the nation." The study of these divine covenants is not only vital to an understanding of God's purpose for Israel, the Church and all mankind. They also provide great assurance to the soul, intensifying faith in Him who is the covenant-keeping God.

The Covenant With Adam

(Genesis 1:28-30)

This primeval covenant which Matthew Henry calls "The Covenant of Innocence" God made with Adam before the Fall, was fundamentally an alliance of friendship, and promised continued life and favor on condition of obedience. Many aspects of this first covenant extend throughout human history. God charged Adam to be "fruitful and multiply" and to "subdue the earth." Such a covenant of blessing revealed the heart of the benevolent Creator. But God's original plan for Adam to be lord over the earth was frustrated, for he disobeyed God and lost thereby much of the power promised him in the covenant. A complete and glorious fulfillment of the covenant, however, will be experienced when Christ sets up His millennial kingdom (Psalm 2:5-8; Hebrews 2:6-8).

After Adam's fall, there came what can be called the *Adamic Covenant* (Genesis 3: 14-19,21-24). To prevent man in his fallen state from becoming utterly corrupt, God established a covenant, placing restraints and limitations on man, the serpent and physical creation. The serpent was cursed, and received the prediction of his final doom; the woman heard of the sorrow motherhood would bring her, and of the position of headship man would have; man heard how his sin resulted in the earth he was to govern, being cursed, and how with hard labor he would have to wrest his living from the earth. Yet, at the back of this judgment the Creator had a benevolent object in mind. Constant occupation would serve as a restraint to the evil tendencies of man's now fallen nature. A foregleam of the covenant of grace can be seen in the "coats of skin" God provided for the nakedness of Adam and Eve (Genesis 3:21). Through Christ's sacrifice believing sinners are clothed with the garment of salvation (II Corinthians 5:21; 8:9).

"Naked come to Thee for dress."

The Covenant With Noah

(Genesis 6:18; 9:8-17; Isaiah 54:9;
Jeremiah 33:20-25)

At the heart of this divine agreement was the promise that never again would God flood the earth. Here God guaranteed the stability of natural law. Still, as the moral Governor of men, God expressed the sacredness of natural human life—the consciousness of man as belonging to God. Conditions of this covenant were the abstention from blood, the preciousness of life, and the token in the clouds which would appear as the symbol of the new light of God's face. *The Noahic Covenant* was everlasting, and for all generations. It carried the promise of the orderly cycle of the seasons and of day and night as long as the earth remains. "As a codicil of the Covenant the ethnic divisions of the race are established (9:24-27). *Ham* is to have a servile posterity. God especially identifies Himself with *Shem*, from whom the Messiah came. *Japheth* was to be enlarged in a material way."

The Covenant With Abraham

(Genesis 12:1-3; 13:14-17; 15:1-7; 17:
1-14; 22:15-24; 26:1-5; 28:10-15;
Galatians 3)

This covenant which God made with Abraham and his seed was for individuals as well as for the nation as a whole. It is referred to as *The Old Covenant* or *The Old Dispensation,* and was confirmed with Isaac and Jacob (Exodus 2:24; Leviticus 26:42), and ensured a blessing through Israel to all nations. The rite of circumcision and symbol of a putting off the natural and entering upon a new spiritual life, was adopted as the token of the covenant (Acts 7:8). Here we have a covenant of grace, of spiritual life, for we now pass from "the region of nature to that of grace; from the wide area of Creation and of Natural Human Life, to the Moral Region and to the Redeemed life. The conditions of this Covenant were the Promises." God covenanted with Abraham to be his God and demanded on his part faith in Himself as the God of the covenant.

The terms of the *Abrahamic Covenant* are most fascinating to study. A natural seed, Israel; a spiritual seed, believers of all subsequent generations (Galatians 3:7); personal blessing and greatness for Abraham himself, and the promise of the Promised Land as an eternal possession—The promise that through the *seed,* that is, through Christ (Genesis 3:15), God would bestow all spiritual blessings for time and eternity. Beginning with Abraham, God created His chosen people, Israel, from which came the Scriptures and the Saviour of the world.

The Covenant With Moses

(Exodus 19:20; 34:10,27; Leviticus 26:9; Deuteronomy 5:2; 7:11-25; 8:
1,19,20; Galatians 3:17-24)

Made with Israel at Mount Sinai, with Moses as the mediator, this covenant is called the *first* in contrast with the everlasting *new* covenant (Hebrews 8:6-8). This covenant, renewed on the plains of Moab (Deuteronomy 29:1) and frequently referred to in the Old Testament is a covenant of great significance. "It was really a constitution given to Israel by God, with appointed promise and penalty, duly inscribed on the tables of the Covenant (Deuteronomy 9:9,11,15), which were deposited in the Ark (Deuteronomy 10:2,5). Whilst the Sinaitic Covenant is rightly regarded as the Charter of the Jewish Dispensation, the establishment by God of a new constitution was contemplated by the Prophets" (Jeremiah 31:31,33; 32:40; 50:5; Isaiah 55:3; Ezekiel 20:37; 34:25).

With this covenant, Jehovah became the God of the nation, the motive behind the formation of such a covenant being His love. The basis of the covenant was Israel's deliverance from Egypt (Exodus 19:4), which was actually the outcome of God's covenant with Abraham. It was because God had pledged Himself to be Israel's God that He delivered them (Exodus 2:24; 3:16,17). This covenant of law also revealed the holiness of God and the sin of the people and reminded them that the law only condemned. It could not save but was the *schoolmaster* or "child-leader" to Christ (Galatians 3:24). In ancient times, the "child-leader" was the servant, taking the children to and from school. While the law leads to Christ, the believer is no longer under the law, but under grace, or *in-lawed* to Christ (Romans 6:14; 8:4; II Corinthians 3; Galatians 2:16; 3:4; John 1:17).

The Covenant With Israel

(Deuteronomy 28:29,30; 30:1-10;
Leviticus 26:1-13)

The covenant made at Sinai witnessed the era of Israel's birth as a nation. It was then that God created them as a people for His own possession (Malachi 2:10). Henceforth, there was to be a close relationship between God and His people. The covenant before us is known as *The Palestinian Covenant*, and was entered into on the Plains of Moab, just before Israel crossed Jordan for the Promised Land. The purpose of this covenant was to set forth conditions regulating possession of the land, and to assure the people of their national conversion to Christ and final restoration to the land which has ever been theirs by divine right and gift.

In this covenant, linked on to *The Abrahamic Covenant* (Deuteronomy 30:1-10), God emphasizes His special relationship to His redeemed people. Because they are His very own, and He is their God, they must obey Him. Lovingly He warned them of coming chastisement and temporary dislodgement from their land, but assured them of judgment upon their oppressors (Deuteronomy 28:15-68; 29:22-28; Leviticus 26:14-39).

Attention can be drawn to the covenant with Phinehas which contained the promise of the establishment of an everlasting priesthood in his line (Numbers 25:11). then we have the covenant between Joshua and the people, when the latter contracted to serve Jehovah only (Joshua 24:25); a similar covenant between Jehoiada and the people (II Kings 11:17)—between Hezekiah and the people, with the solemn agreement to reform the worship of the sanctuary (II Chronicles 29)—between Josiah and Ezra and the people for the strict observance of the law (II Kings 23:3; Ezra 10:3).

The Covenant With David

(II Samuel 7:8-17; Psalm 89:3,20-27;
Jeremiah 33:21; Luke 1:27-33.)

The covenant between God and David and his seed has at its center the establishment of an everlasting kingdom. The prophetic aspect of the divine promises made to the Davidic House should have the closest study of all Bible lovers. With the everlasting Davidic dynasty there came the promise of Christ's glorious earthly kingdom. As the "Seed of David" there was given to Christ "the throne of His father David" (Luke 1:32). The final and ultimate fulfillment of the Davidic Covenant will be experienced during our Lord's millennial reign (Psalm 89:27).

While, however, this covenant is eternal, there is a proviso regarding chastisement for those of the Davidic line guilty of sin (II Samuel 7:14,15; Psalm 89:30-33). The sin of the house of David in rejecting his seed, the Messiah, has been severely chastised (Acts 15:16). But although the Tabernacle of David has fallen down, the prediction is that David's Greater Son will build again upon the ruins of the Tabernacle (Acts 15:16).

The coming of Christ to the world in order to save man is the subject of three of the Old Testament covenants which are actually divine promises concerning the redemption of mankind to be accomplished as the result of the Incarnation and Crucifixion of the Son of God. For instance—

In the Adamic Covenant (Genesis 3:15), Christ is predicted as *the Seed of the woman* winning a supreme victory over the enemy of mankind. At Calvary, the serpent's head was crushed.

In the Abrahamic Covenant (Genesis 22:18), Christ is foretold as *the Seed of Abraham*, who would deliver mankind from the reign of sin and death, and bless all the nations of the earth.

In the Davidic Covenant (II Samuel 7:13), Christ is presented as *the Seed of David*, the Builder of God's House and the Eternal King, whose reign will know no end.

The Covenant of Grace

(II Corinthians 3:6; Hebrews 6:13-20;
8:6-13; 9:16; 10:12-18; 13:20)

This everlasting covenant is spoken of as "The New Covenant" or "The New Testament," and was an agreement ratified by the shed blood of the Redeemer. It is referred to as a "Better Covenant" because it is one of *grace*. The Old Testament centered around the covenant of the *law*. The covenant of grace is a spiritual covenant of God in Christ, covering all who are regenerated by the Spirit. There is a sense in which this covenant is the culmination of all previous ones. The *better thing* (Hebrews 11:40) God has provided for us is the new covenant and its realities of which the old covenant sacrifices and rituals were shadows. In Christ, Old Testament promises were fulfilled (Jeremiah 33:31; Luke 1:72). The law, once written on stone, is now written on the heart. Animal sacrifices are no longer necessary for the blood of God's Son provided a perfect redemption, with Christ Himself as the heart and Mediator of this covenant of redemption (Matthew 26:28; Mark 14:24; I Corinthians 11:25). Now, in the full blaze of revelation, the believer lives by faith and not by works, although, as James reminds us, his faith must be an active one.

Further, this covenant of grace which God confirmed with an oath (Hebrews 6:13-20), and which leads to a perfect and eternal work (John 6:40; Philippians 1:6), has as its center the great work of *justification*, which means "to make just, or righteous." This is the act of God whereby He not only forgives the sinner on the merit of Christ's death but also imputes to the believing sinner the perfect righteousness of Christ. The word *impute* means "to reckon to the account of." Man's own righteousnesses are as filthy rags (Isaiah 64:6), but the miracle of grace is that all past sins are blotted out and the sinner forgiven and robed in a righteousness divinely provided (Isaiah 44:22; I Corinthians 1:30; Colossians 2:9,10; I John 1:7). *Justification* is by faith which, in turn, manifests itself in good works (Romans 3:28; 4:5; Ephesians 2:8-10; James 2:14-26). How blessed we are if sheltered by "the blood of the everlasting covenant" (Hebrews 13:20), and in the enjoyment of all the benefits of this new covenant of grace (Psalm 50:5; Isaiah 55:

3). Are you in covenant-relationship with God? (John 6:35-40).

The Covenant With Death and Hell

A word is necessary in that this shameful covenant on the part of God's covenant people is necessary (Romans 9:4). In his study on *The Major Covenants Of Scripture* Dr. F. J. Meldau says—

Many of the major covenants of Scripture are between God and Israel. But this covenant (of temporary duration?) is between Israel and antichrist. During the great Tribulation, after the Rapture of the Church, Israel will rebuild their temple in Jerusalem. They will then plumb the depths of their apostasy and unbelief by resuming the sacrifices of animals on the temple altar (Daniel 9:27), again nationally repudiating the sacrifice of Christ on Calvary. Eventually, in this agreement with hell, Israel will set up the worship of the Beast and his image (Revelation 13) in the holy place of their temple. This worship of the Beast and his image is called "the abomination that maketh desolate," or "the abomination of desolation" (See Daniel 12:11; 9:27; Matthew 24:15; cf. II Thessalonians 2:3,4; Revelation 13:11-18).

During the great Tribulation, Israel will make this covenant with the "Roman prince," head of the revived Roman empire, and the first "beast" of Revelation 13. We give here a paraphrase of Daniel 9:27, which we trust will make clear to the reader the essential terms of this covenant with hell. "And he (the Roman prince, head of the coming revived Roman empire) shall confirm the covenant with many (of the people of Israel) for one week (seven years): and in the midst of the week (at the end of the first three and a half years) he shall cause the sacrifice and the oblation to cease (the resumed temple offerings), and for the overspreading of abominations he shall make it desolate (the blasphemy of putting the image of the Beast in the temple, to be worshipped by men), even until the consummation (until the end of the great Tribulation Period), and that determined shall be poured upon the desolate (the "beast" of Revelation 13)."

This "firm covenant" (Daniel 9:27 R.V.) between many Jews and the Beast (the coming Antichrist) is "a covenant with death and with hell," in which the people will do as they have so often done in the past—ignore the Lord their God and turn to false gods—in this case, the Antichrist himself (Isaiah 28:15,18). Because of their terrible apostasy and sin, Israel will suffer special judgments during the great Tribulation; in fact, that period is called "the time of Jacob's trouble" (Jeremiah 30:6, 7). But through the judgments which will fall on Israel during that time the nation, decimated and refined, will turn to Christ in repentance and will be saved! (See Zechariah 12:10-14; Zechariah 13:1; Romans 11:25,26).

In conclusion, there are several *covenant* phrases calling for consideration. First of all, Paul speaks of

Covenant breakers (Romans 1:31). These are those who feel that they are not morally bound to any agreement. In these modern times there are many who are not dependable. They are treacherous to covenants, faithless to promises and false to trusts. Hosea refers to covenant breakers from Adam, down (Hosea 6:7; 8:1).

The Messenger of the Covenant (Malachi 3:1). The Messianic Servant of the covenant of the people (Isaiah 42:6), is none other than Jesus Christ who came not only as the *Messenger* but also the Mediator of the new covenant (Luke 1:20).

The Book of the Covenant, and *The Little Book of the Covenant* (Exodus 20:22, 23; 34:11-26), referring to the oldest code of Hebrew law which they contained. Promises are attached to the keeping of this covenant (Exodus 23:20-32).

A Covenant of Salt, or *The Salt of the Covenant* (Numbers 18:19; Leviticus 2:13; II Chronicles 13:5), convey the same primary idea, namely, a perpetual covenant, in the sealing or ratification of which salt was used. The eating of salt was a token of friendship, sealed by sacred hospitality. The use of salt constituted an inviolable bond. The term *covenant* is used by various religious groups to denote the agreement entered into by the members of the churches in question, and often follows the confession of faith as, for example, the *Christian Endeavor Society.* Scotland is proud of her illustrious "Covenanters."

XII

The Doctrine of Predestination

All Bible lovers come up against apparent problems in their quest for fuller knowledge. Peter found it hard to understand some of the truths Paul wrote about (II Peter 3:16). While we rejoice in all of the simplicity of the Word, we readily concede the presence of deep sayings requiring prayerful and patient study. How true is the saying of one of the Early Fathers, "If there are shallows in the Bible where a little child may wade, there are depths where a giant must swim."

One of these seemingly problematic truths is *predestination*—a theme upon which volumes have been written, but also one which has separated many of God's dear children. Wrested out of its Biblical setting, this doctrine has been given a prominence out of all proportion to related truth.

It would seem as if there is a triad of words closely associated with God's sovereignty, namely, *foreknowledge, election* and *predestination.* Taken together, they present a trinity in unity. Dr. C. I. Scofield's comment on their relationship is terse and most enlightening. Here is the way that eminent teacher of the Word describes this triplet of divine attributes—

The divine order is foreknowledge, election, predestination. That foreknowledge determines the election or choice is clear from I Peter 1:2, and predestination is the bringing to pass of the election. Election looks back to foreknowledge: predestination forward to the destiny. But Scripture nowhere declares what it is in the divine foreknowledge which determines the divine election and predestination. The foreknown are elected, and the elect are predestined, and this election is certain to every believer by the mere fact that he believes (I Thessalonians 1:4,5).

We may find it profitable to take these weighty terms separately, and examine their content and context.

Foreknowledge

"Fore" or "before" simply means that God knows beforehand what the future holds. Because of His omniscience, He knows the end from the beginning. Nothing is hid from Him, who knows what things we have need of *before* we ask Him. Perfection of prescience belongs to God alone, for as the Almighty, He has a clear and full knowledge of events before they occur (I Peter 1:2; Romans 8:29). There is, of course, no contradiction between God's foreknowledge and man's freedom of choice. But God knows in advance how man will act.

Foreknowledge, then, means to define and determine beforehand, to mark out boundaries in advance. All the details of our salvation were arranged in a past eternity before time commenced. "All" implies every possible blessing for time and for eternity, which the Holy Spirit has to bestow, even the entire sanctification of the believer (Romans 8:28,29). In his exposition of Paul's declaration, "Whom He did foreknow" (Romans 8:29), Walter Scott says,

> God's absolute foreknowledge of persons, of things, of events, small and great, is necessarily a divine attribute. With God all is one ever present. The eternal God *is*. A past and future are relative ideas. But what a strength and consolation to God's tried saints that *they* individually were known to God in eternal ages, their life-history, the most trivial circumstances concerning them, every detail of life and character lay open to Him. All were and ever are before Him. The text of Romans 8 refers to individuals. We, and each personally, before Him in absolute knowledge of *what* and *where* we were, before Him in our sin and ruin, yet He chose us for blessing.

"For whom He did foreknow, He also did predestinate to be conformed to the image of His Son" in glory. Thus, it is with deep-seated joy that saints can sing—

> In every hour in perfect peace
> I'll sing, He knows, He knows.

Paul's reference to God's *purpose* and *counsel* (Ephesians 1:11) is associated with his *fore*knowledge. His *purpose* refers to the blessed fact that God, in Himself, in the exercise of His divine, sovereign will, in the dateless past devised a system of government and glory to be displayed in coming ages. His *counsel* intimates the way, the means and method of realizing to the full His purpose.

Election

This second scriptural term represents the *sovereign* and *eternal* choice of persons (Ephesians 1:4), infallibly secures all God's election, and is a fact which believers *now* know (I Thessalonians 1:4). All those divinely chosen cannot perish, for they were chosen in Christ before sin entered or the course of human responsibility commenced. Thus elected, neither the state of the one elected nor his doing can destroy God's eternal purpose. All who are saved are the "vessels of mercy which He had afore prepared unto glory" (Romans 9:23). "Sovereign election where all are guilty, is our only ground of hope. Who dare arraign the purpose of God in choosing same? His right to do so is unquestionable."

Two phases of divine choice can be discerned, *corporate* and *individual*. The first aspect is seen in the election of Israel as a nation (Isaiah 45:4), and the Church as a spiritual institution (Ephesians 1:4). Then, as Dr. C. I. Scofield reminds us, there are various aspects of the nature of God's choice.

1. Election is according to God's foreknowledge (I Peter 1:2).
2. Election is wholly of grace, apart from human merit (Romans 9:11; 11:5,6).
3. Election proceeds from divine volition (John 15:16).
4. Election is the sovereign act of God, whereby certain are chosen from among mankind for Himself (John 15:19).
5. Election is God's sovereign act whereby certain elect persons are chosen for His distinctive service (Luke 6:13; Acts 9:15; I Corinthians 1:17,18).

With God, election is always inclusive, never exclusive. He chooses a few in order that all may be blessed (I Timothy 2:1-7).

Predestination

Because of who and what He is, God is free to do as He likes. He is a Being of infinite wisdom, acting with a plan. His providences are ordered and ordained in everything relating to our lot and life. "Predestination is that effective exercise of the will of God by which things before determined by Him are brought to pass" (See Ephesians 1:5).

Predestination is linked to God's love, therefore, He can never be guilty of anything capricious. He never acts contrary to His own nature. Predestination is the exercise of divine sovereignty in the accomplishment of God's ultimate purpose or decree. God purposes in Himself. He is never influenced by any external consequences. The whole reason for our redemption sprang from within God. It was His love that drew salvation's plan. The Church existed in God's mind, eternally, before it existed in time.

A fact to remember is that the Scriptures present the union of divine sovereignty and human responsibility (John 6:37-40). There is no contradiction between the two. Walter Scott reminds us that "*Predestina-tion* refers to that special character of blessing to which we are set apart. Thus *predestinated* to adoption (Ephesians 1:5), to have part in Christ's glorious inheritance, (verse 11); and to be perfectly conformed to God's Son (Romans 8:29,30)."

What must be borne in mind is the fact that *predestination* is not God's predetermining from past ages who should and who should not be saved. Scripture does not teach this view. What it does teach is that this doctrine of predestination concerns the future of believers. Predestination is the divine determining the glorious consummation of all who through faith, and surrender become the Lord's. He has determined beforehand that each child of His will reach *adoption,* or "the son-placing" at his resurrection when Christ returns. It has been determined beforehand that all who are truly Christ's shall be conformed to His image (Romans 8:29; Ephesians 1:5).

XIII

The Doctrine of Sin

There is no fact as evident and no subject so important as that of *sin,* which is as old as man, nay, older still, since it originated in the mind of Satan before the creation of man. Satan became the first sinner, when lifted up with pride, he desired equality with God (Isaiah 14:12-14). Since sin's entrance into the world it has become universal. "All have sinned" (Romans 5:12). A right concept of sin is therefore imperative for if man errs here, he errs everywhere. If he does not have scriptural views of sin's nature, he will not have scriptural views of sin's efficacious remedy. Man's estimation of sin differs considerably. What is sin to one is not sin to another. But to accept the Bible's verdict on "sin" is to accept the Bible's provision of salvation from sin by the Saviour.

At the outset of our study, we cannot emphasize too strongly the necessity of understanding the mind of God, as revealed in the words of God. In these apostate days there is an insistence upon a change of evangelical phraseology. Ruin by the Fall, redemption by the blood, are deemed to be out of date. Terms like "sin," being "lost," "hell-bound," "saved by the blood," are no longer intelligible to the modern, cultured mind. Such language is antiquated. Old truths must be given a modern dress. But no matter how we try to camouflage sin, it is still SIN.

If we honestly desire to know the mind of God regarding any truth, we must examine the words He uses to describe it. This method, of course, brings us to the acceptance of verbal inspiration or the inspiration of the Holy Spirit affecting the very words, as well as the matter of Scripture. Of this we are absolutely certain, that God was very careful in leading men to express sublime truths in the most correct words, even though we now have many translations endeavoring to interpret those words.

Coming to the Bible's estimation of sin, there is no study so illuminating. And our obligation is to study such a theme, not from the moral standards of society, but from God's standpoint. Sin occupies a most conspicuous place in the Word. In fact, one is both surprised and appalled at the space given to such an intrusion into God's universe. Under the divine searchlight of the Word, the ramifications of evil in the human heart are revealed as being varied and intricate. It is only as we discover the heinous nature of sin that we can rightly extol Him who came to save us from its curse and condemnation.

The Nature of Sin

The teaching of the Old Testament on this subject is both solemn and searching. Sin originated with the devil, before he became a devil, and entered the world through Adam, and became universal (Romans 5:12), resulting in physical and spiritual death (Genesis 2:17; Romans 6:23). Man is born to sin (Psalm 51:5); but not born *a slave to sin*. He becomes the latter by voluntarily yielding to sin (Romans 6:16). Man is a sinner by birth, but is not responsible for this. When he becomes a sinner by practice, then he is responsible to God and others for sins committed.

Sin is the transgression of a divine command.

Hosea (6:7) gives us the word *abar* for sin—a term applied to Adam's transgression —and it means to "pass over." It is akin to "Hebrew" (Genesis 14:13). "Passing over a boundary" is at the heart of the term "transgression." It signifies the breaking of a known command, going beyond assigned limits, thus, to trespass or transgress. An illustration of this aspect greets us when we are about to wander over prohibited land. "Trespassers will be prosecuted." It is this aspect of sin presented by Genesis 3. Adam, when he fell, overstepped certain limits set by divine command, and the same view of sin is consistently maintained throughout Scripture. The very principle of sin is unbelief in the divine word and denial of the divine will. Thus sin can be summarized in the threefold way Dr. C. I. Scofield indicates:

It is an *act*, the violation of, or want of obedience to the revealed Word of God.

It is a *state*, the absence of righteousness.

It is a *nature*, enmity toward God.

Man in root, branch and fruit is incurably sinful, hence the necessity of the new birth so imperatively insisted upon by Christ if the sinner desires to enter heaven (John 3:1-8).

Sin is the denial of the divine right to command.

Another word used for sin is *Pāsha,* and means "to break away from," representing lawlessness or spiritual anarchy (I Timothy 1:9). Man began his downward career when he overstepped divine limits, and went on to deny the right of God to impose such limits. Rebellion led to rejection, and the sinner found himself at enmity with God.

Yet supremacy, absolute and unconditional, is an integral part of the idea of God's sovereignty. If we deny God His supremacy, we deny His right to be. "If He is not Lord of all, He is not Lord at all," as Hudson Taylor used to express it.

Sin is the failure to attain to the divine standard.

The most common word the Bible uses for "sin" is *Chāta,* meaning "missing the mark," or coming short of the glory of God (Romans 3:23; I John 3:4 R.V.). Behind the term is the illustration of the archer, releasing the arrow, but failing to hit the bull's-eye. Sin, then, is man's failure to reach his true end. Where *chāta* is employed, it signifies deviation from the divine will, and indicates that man has missed his true center, proving that having deliberately overstepped the divine boundary, he has become unable to attain the divine standard.

Man's act of transgression produced a condition of shortcoming. Adam having sinned against God, came short of God's glory. Thus his fall brought ruin to himself and to his race. Now the question to bear in mind is that it is impossible for man, with the root principle of sin within his heart, to reach the divine standard. We hear a great deal about the "divine" in man, or the possession of a "divine spark" needing only to be fanned into a flame. But the sinner is unable to evolve out of himself a standard pleasing to God. The best of men are sinners and must begin at a new center, which is the regenerating work of the Holy Spirit within the life.

Gathering together scriptural descriptions of sin, it is not too difficult to delineate its subtle inner working and complex nature. Sin separated man from God, turned him adrift from a heavenly Father, and filled his heart with hate and rage. What has sin given him in exchange? Because sin is rebellion, it issues in chaos and disaster. What is this "sin" man lives in and for, and clings most tenaciously to? Bible answers to such a question are extraordinarily full and illuminating.

(1) Sin Is a Lie.

It started in the Garden with the question of divine veracity—Hath God said? Sin is thus false, seeing it had its origin in the father of lies, even Satan, whom Christ called a liar. Sin entered the world through a blasphemous lie and maintains its hold upon men by asking them to believe a lie. Several terms are used by the Holy Spirit to expose the essential falseness of sin. Under the term deceit there are at least ten different primary roots used to denote the seducing, deceiving, misleading nature of sin. So we have *agōb*, in Jeremiah 17:9; *kāzāb* in Isaiah 28:15; *shāgār* in I Samuel 15:30. Our Lord confirms the lying nature of sin when He speaks of the devil as one who is a stranger to truth (John 8:44).

(2) Sin Is a Delusion.

As sin is naturally treacherous, it is full of guile and that by which man is cruelly betrayed. This is taught in the use of the word, *mirmāh*, the root meaning of which implies cunningness and craftiness in deluding people. "In whose spirit there is no guile" (Psalm 32:2). Looking within sin's fair promises there can be heard the hiss of the serpent. Sin is ever deceptive. What it affirms is fictitious! It is full of make believe.

> Sin unto thy hive may bring
> A little honey—
> But expect the sting.

Sin offers much pleasure, but only the pleasure of which Robert Louis Stevenson writes: "pleasure with a thousand faces, and none of them perfect; with a thousand tongues, and all of them broken; with a thousand hands, and all with scratching nails." Sin offers itself as a friend, then becomes a fiend.

(3) Sin Is Darkness.

The darkness of sin represents fundamental and final ignorance of God, who is Light (John 1:5; I John 1:5). This phase of sin is taught in the word *bāyād*, implying, to cover up, and is before us in Proverbs 13:15. Sin comes from the darkness, lives in and loves the darkness. It shuns the true light lest its true nature should be discovered (John 3:20). Satan is referred to as the prince of darkness (Ephesians 5:11). He it is who inspires works of darkness, and his end is the blackness of darkness forever (Jude 13).

(4) Sin Is Separation.

Sin separates man from God, and man from man (Isaiah 59:2). Those smitten with the plague of leprosy had to dwell alone because of the contagious character of the disease. Moral leprosy also results in spiritual isolation. The sinner is not only separated from God here and now, but dying in sin, is eternally separated from God (Revelation 20:15).

(5) Sin Is Perversion.

That sin is crooked, a perverse, distorted thing, is taught by the term *āvōn*, translated "iniquity" (as in Isaiah 64:6). Sin perverts man's thoughts of God and His law, and is contrary to equity. At the same time it works for the destruction of the human soul. Sin not only perverts, but pollutes. Loose thinking leads to loose living. The Spirit's work is to reveal to our minds the loathsomeness of sin.

(6) Sin Is Servitude.

It is most impressive to note how the Bible takes pains to teach us that indulgence in sin means grievous toil and bondage, in labor of the most wearying kind. Words like *otsēb* (Psalm 139:24) and *amēl* (Job 20:22) speak of the bitter, hard servitude and utterly unsatisfactory wages the devil offers his dupes (Romans 6:23). The tragedy is that the majority around prefer to be slaves of Satan rather than servants of God.

(7) Sin Is Emptiness.

There are two other words proving that sin is vanity, something without profit, a thing of nought. We have *āven* (Psalm 66:18), meaning emptiness or hollowness: *belizaal* (Psalm 101:3), meaning the very negation of value. A man who serves sin gets nothing for it. The apples of sin are the apples of ashes. Failure, defeat, disgust and disappointment are written over the life of a sinner. "I was born, indeed, in your dominion," said *Christian* to *Appollyon*, "but your service was hard and your wages such as a man could not live on, for the wages of sin is death." The rewards of sin are confusion and dissatisfaction.

(8) Sin Is a Mistake.

A further sin term, *shāgāh*, is a pathetic word, bringing tears to the eyes of those who clearly understand it, for it means "to wander," "to go astray" (Isaiah 53:6). All who sin become like shepherdless sheep—a prey to enemies. All who sin discover, sooner or later, that they have made a mistake, tragic and fatal. John Bunyan, in his *Pilgrim's Progress*, depicts "one who took the way called 'Danger' which led him into a great wood, and the other took directly up the way to 'Destruction,' which led him into a wide field, full of dark mountains, where he stumbled, and fell and rose no more."

What the Bible teaches regarding the effects of sin is clear and unmistakable. There are a few Hebrew words describing the ruinous affects of sin. If we weaken or ignore scriptural definitions of sin, we depart from what Christianity really is. Surely it is important to know God's thoughts regarding the abominable thing He abhors.

(9) Sin Renders the Soul Guilty Before God.

This result of sin is taught in the word *Asham*, found in Proverbs 14:9. The guilty are deserving of and liable to punishment. "The soul that sinneth, it shall die." Disobedience carries with it a curse (Galatians 3:10). While the sinner may seek to deny that sin renders him guilty, and brings him into danger, yet guilt means exposure to the wrath of God and is the first and the worst effect of sin. Guilt is a judicial term, implying that the guilty one is deserving of judicial punishment.

(10) Sin Produces a State of Wickedness

There is a word *rāsha*, ordinarily translated "wicked" or "bad." It is an expressive term implying that the sinner is actuated by an evil principle, and therefore becomes desperately wicked (Psalm 9:17). Alas, what low, vile depths the sinner often reaches!

(11) Sin Ruins Life and Hope.

The small word *ra*, so often used for "wicked" or "evil," means the ruin of a soul by breaking it in pieces. Because of sin, the potter's vessel, made to be fitted moment by moment with the glory of God, is dashed to the ground and lies broken. It is in this sense that the word for "sin" before us is used in Proverbs 15:26. It is somewhat remarkable that while in the word "holiness" there is the suggestion of wholeness or completeness—in the word for "wickedness" there resides the idea of ruin, brokenness, destruction.

(12) Sin Results in Distortion.

The word already considered, *āvon*, speaks of a crooked or perverse attitude and illustrates the terrible twist within human nature as the result of sin. Such a twist remains in the regenerate person. "The good that I would do I do not, and the evil I would not, that I do" (Romans 7:19,20). Sin bends man's nature toward all that is alien to God, and blinds him to the peril of indulgence. This aspect of sin is presented in Psalm 32:3. Refusing the way of life, the sinner ends up in the way of death (Matthew 7:13).

(13) Sin Defiles the soul.

Defilement or moral and ceremonial uncleanness is the fruit of sin. "Woe is me . . . I am unclean." This defiling influence of sin is brought out in the word *mûm*, meaning to cover with blots and blemishes (Isaiah 1:6). When the soul is guilty of practiced sin, it becomes like a white sheet of paper on which ink has been spilt, or as pure snow trodden underfoot. Virginity of soul is lost.

(14) Sin Corrupts the soul.

One of the strongest words used in the Bible for sin is *shāchath*, implying loathsomeness, a condition of rot. It is found in Genesis 6:12, and describes the vile condition which the sin of the antediluvians brought into the world. It is found again in Psalm 14:1, and shows that those who reject God are corrupt. The force of such a word is terrific, for it proves that sin destroys the soul, rendering it rotten, loathsome, unclean. When God is dethroned in national or personal life, the corrupt forces of sin hold sway. The clearer our conception of divine holiness, the deeper our consciousness of the exceeding sinfulness of sin.

(15) Sin Ensnares the soul.

This is a further word to study, namely, *kāshal*, which reminds us that sin not only implies a fall, but involves the sinner in utter ruin (Ezekiel 18:20). Sin blinds, deludes, deceives, defiles, then destroys. If unforsaken, sin results in irretrievable ruin. It is here that we can understand the unspeakable terror resident in the fatal words of the Master, "Depart from Me, for I never knew you." If the sinner despises divine warnings, and dies in his sin, he is cast into outer darkness, where the worm dieth not.

The Remedy for Sin

Man's concept of sin has a direct bearing

and influence upon his understanding of the need and nature of salvation. Low thoughts never produce high thoughts of God. The Biblical concept of sin is a kind of rule by which we measure the necessity for a Saviour. The revelation of the loathsomeness of the abominable thing God hates, brings with it a realization of a divine deliverance. And such is the rich and full provision for sin God has made, that its power can be nullified. The Holy Spirit makes it so clear that Christ alone is able to counteract the evil of the old nature by the implantation of a new nature.

Redemption is a work of undoing and in nothing does the glory of our Saviour appear more manifest than in the way He deals with the havoc wrought by sin (I John 3:8). Where sin abounds—grace much more abounds. By His finished work Christ overcomes all the effects of sin. God the Son alone can deal with the sin of man. Christ came into the world to save sinners. He died for our sins, according to the Scripture.

He Bore Our Curse

Sin brought a curse upon the sinner (Genesis 3:17). At Calvary, the guilt of sin was dealt with and forever canceled by the merit of Christ's atoning work. Upon the cross, He became a curse for us (Galatians 3:13). Willingly He became the propitiation for our sins (I John 2:2).

O Christ, what burdens bowed Thy head,
Our curse was laid on Thee.

When the Psalmist spoke of transgression being forgiven (Psalm 32:1) he used the word *nāsā*, which literally means "borne away" (John 1:29). Dealing, then, with our transgression, Christ takes up His abode within us and keeps us right with God. He it is who strengthens us to do all things right, enabling us to stand perfect and complete in all the will of God. Impelled by the Spirit, we keep within the boundary of every divine command.

He Provides Our Cleansing

Sin defiles, but through His shed blood, Christ is able to make the vilest clean. He alone can make the black heart of a sinner whiter than snow. He washes, justifies and sanctifies the sin-smirched life. Not only does He cleanse from sin, He also keeps the cleansed one clean (I John 1:9; I Thessalonians 5:23).

He Is Our Healer

Corruption and loathsomeness are associated with sin, and this is why the leper is a fitting type of the sinner. But Christ can make us, as moral lepers, whole. All vileness is expelled through the power of a new life from Him. Thereafter, walking in the Spirit, the healed one fulfills the lusts of the flesh no more. "Ransomed, healed, restored, forgiven," the saved one experiences spiritual health—and often, physical health as well.

He Is Our Deliverer

We have seen that sin enslaves, binds the soul, but Christ emancipates the ensnared sinner (Revelation 1:5 R.V.). "He sets the prisoner free." The once sin-bound soul is saved with an everlasting salvation (John 10:28). At every point the devil is defeated and the power of sin is overthrown, the disturbing bondage of sin annulled by the presence of the Holy Spirit within. As the Gift of the ascended Lord, the Spirit sets us free from the law of sin and death (Romans 8:2). Although the crooked, perverse old nature remains, the impartation of a new nature delivers us from adding to sin's perversity.

He Remakes Us

Sin results in the destruction of the divine Potter's work. The intrusion of sin marred God's handiwork and ruined His plan for man. Through grace, the believing sinner is remade (Jeremiah 18:1-4). But by His power, God refashions the sin-marred vessel into a vessel unto honor (II Timothy 2:21). Broken vessels become pleasant vessels. "He makes the rebel a priest and a king." There is no limit to His transformation of a soul, once its transgression has been thoroughly dealt with. As the result of the cross, Christ can take sinners from the dunghill and place them among the princes.

He Produces Goodness

Sin makes us bad in every way. But Jesus died to make us good. And such goodness is all of grace. We cannot manufacture it. Regeneration is not the patching up of the old nature, or its improvement in any way. Christ does not evolve the new life out of the old life, but imparts a new man altogether (Ephesians 4:22). In Him, we become new creatures.

He Is the Truth

Sin is a lie, and is responsible for lying

abominations. Satan is a liar and the father of lies, but Christ came as the Truth (John 14:6). To those under the dominion of falsehood, doubt and ignorance, Christ presents Himself as the Truth about God. The ministry of the Holy Spirit is to enlighten the eyes of our understanding in order to discover that the truth is in Jesus (Ephesians 4:21). Then He leads us into all truth (John 16:13). Thereafter the heart of God is gladdened as His children walk in the truth (III John 4).

He Is Light

"The whole world was lost in the darkness of sin." The sorrow is that men love such darkness, rather than light, because their deeds are evil (John 1:5; 3:19). But to those in total spiritual darkness, as natural men are, Christ offers Himself as the Light of the World (John 1:9; 9:5). And all receiving Him cease to walk in darkness, seeing they have the Light of life. Children of darkness become children of light, and as lights in the world, seek to bring others out of darkness into the kingdom of God's dear son (Colossians 1:13).

He Is Guileless

Sin is deceit, producing all that is fictitious and false. The devil is likened unto a serpent because of the cunningness, subtlety and delusion he causes to lurk within sin. Jesus came as the Lamb, innocent, harmless, clear and transparent. There is no delusion or deception about what He offers those who are willing to turn from the lies of the devil. To all those deluded by sin He comes, as He did to the demoniac of old, to clothe them in a right mind.

He Is Rest

The wicked are like the troubled sea, whose waters cannot rest. Sin disturbs the soul, robbing it of peace and tranquility. Hell is eternal restlessness. But to all who are oppressed and depressed by the load of sin, Christ offers Himself as rest (Matthew 11:28).

He Is Satisfaction

Sin brings an emptiness with it into the life. The pleasures it offers are empty bubbles. Sinners spend their strength for nought, and labor for bread that cannot satisfy. Jesus offers the bankrupt sinner the unsearchable riches of His grace. The empty He filleth with good things (Luke 1:53).

How empty the life is without Christ, who came as the Fullness of God!

He Is Our Righteousness

Sin is unrighteousness. When a man sins, he ceases to be right. He becomes crooked and has perverted thoughts of God and His ways. Scripture presents Christ as the one perfect Being, who knew no sin, who was never guilty of crookedness. He was holy, harmless, undefiled and separate from sinners (Hebrews 7:26). He was familiar with every particle of the will of His Father, and implicitly obeyed Him. By faith, He becomes the sinner's righteousness, "The Lord our Righteousness." Sin is the absolute denial of divine righteousness, a breaking away from the divine standard and the divine right to command. But when the sinner turns to God and is saved by grace through faith in Christ, all self-righteousness and unrighteousness are fully dealt with. Naked we come to Him for dress, and are clothed with His righteousness. His sweet will becomes the fixed center of our being.

Christ, then, has made a full provision for the guilt and government of sin. Through His atoning work, He is able to save from the penalty of sin. Alive for evermore, He is able through the Spirit daily to save us from the power of sin. When He returns the second time without sin unto salvation, He will deliver His saved ones from the presence of sin within and around. Hallelujah, what a Saviour!

The Bible describes so many sins for our enlightenment and warning. There are little sins (Song of Solomon 2:15); big sins (Psalm 25:11—a strange plea for mercy); tall sins (Revelation 18:5—colored iniquity); secret sins (Ezekiel 8:7,12—a darkened gallery); open sins (I Samuel 2:23—talk of the town); youthful sins (Job 20:11—malignant germs); middle life sins (Psalm 91:6—prayer book version); old age sins (II Chronicles 16:12—gouty troubles); ignorant sins (Leviticus 4:1,35—a merciful provision); sins against light (John 15:22—a cloakless evil); sins against God (Psalm 51:4—a royal penitent's wail); sins against man (I Corinthians 8:13—abuse of Christian liberty) and sins against the Holy Spirit (Matthew 12:32). Is it not blessed to know that the blood of Jesus Christ is able to cleanse us from *all* sin?

The Biblical concept of sin, therefore, carries with it—

1. A high view of man's nature at the

beginning. Made in God's image, man obeyed the voice of the tempter, and became a sinner thereby. After the act, making Adam a sinner, sin became a state and a disposition.

2. A grave view of the depths to which man fell as the result of the Fall. The terrible destruction of the Flood testifies to the enormity of human iniquity. Man became full of putrefying sores (Isaiah 1).

3. A hopeful view of the glorious redemption from sin Christ made possible when He died and rose again. In Adam we die, but in Christ we become alive and live.

XIV

The Doctrine of Salvation

No evangelical theme is more deserving of prayerful and careful study than that of *salvation*. The pre-eminent reason for a Biblical understanding of this basic doctrine is that it represents the supreme mission of the Master. Why was He, when He was so rich in heaven, willing to become poor on earth? Why did He willingly discard a garment of glory for the robe of our humanity? Paul answers these, and other pertinent questions associated with Christ's incarnation. He came into the world to save sinners (I Timothy 1:15). He did not leave the battlements above, where He was the Prince of Glory, to become a teacher, or a model for our obedience, or as a martyr willing to die for truths and principles He believed. According to His own declaration, He came to seek and to save the lost (Luke 19:10). His saving name was ready for Him as soon as He entered the world to die as its Saviour, "Thou shalt call his name JESUS: for he shall save His people from their sin" (Matthew 1:21). Such a matchless name has carried with it the promise of deliverance from sin's guilt and government.

It is also imperative to know all the Bible teaches about salvation, seeing it contains the only divinely provided remedy for sin. Without such a provision, the sinner is both helpless and hopeless. Accepting this blood-bought salvation so freely offered, the sinner can experience freedom from the past with all its failure; victory in present days from sin's tyranny; and hope of escape from sin's full reward in hell. All who are lost are shut up to God's perfect, peerless salvation. There is no other way out of the gloom and despair of sin. "There is no other name under heaven given among men whereby we may be saved" (Acts 4:12). If this salvation is neglected and finally rejected, there can be no escape from the righteous judgments of God (II Thessalonians 1:9; Hebrews 2:3). All we could ever know about this indispensable salvation is to be found within the covers of the Bible, and what it says about this important theme is all that concerns us. With man's estimation of salvation we are not concerned.

The Greatness of Salvation

The salvation of infinite proportions, the writer of Hebrews warns us against neglecting (Hebrews 2:3), is specifically the salvation related to sin. Throughout the Bible the term is associated with a salvation or deliverance from physical diseases (Luke 7:50), as well as freedom from material wants. The "great salvation" is the greatest manifestation of God's power to deliver, namely, the salvation from satanic bondage which Christ's death and Resurrection made possible.

Such a peerless salvation is well-named "great," for there is nothing greater in all the universe than this inclusive word "gathering into itself all the redemptive acts and processes—as *justification, redemption, grace, propitiation, imputation, forgiveness, sanctification* and *glorification*." "Great is the Lord, and greatly to be praised" (Psalm 48:1), and everything from His heart and hand bears the imprint of His greatness. All of His creative works pale into insignificance alongside His saving grace and power.

Salvation Is Great Because
of Its Divine Author

What a marvelous origin "the salvation of your souls" has (I Peter 1:9)! It antedates creation, being conceived in the mind of God in the dateless past. It came to us according to the eternal purpose of God (Ephesians 3:11; II Timothy 1:9; Titus 1:2). It began with God's foreknowing. It was no immediate, unpremeditated plan to meet a sudden emergency, no after-thought on God's part. "Deep and far in an untrackable Eternity its foundations were laid. It is not a thing of yesterday. It will not pass away with tomorrow. The Father has endorsed it with His own everlastingness." Salvation, then, is great seeing that God is its Source or Origin.

"But God commended His love toward us, in that, while we were yet sinners, Christ died for us" (Romans 5:8).

"According as He hath chosen us in Him before the foundation of the world, that we should be holy and without blame before Him in love" (Ephesians 1:4).

"In hope of eternal life which God, that cannot lie, promised before the world began" (Titus 1:2).

"Who verily was foreordained before the foundation of the world, but was manifest in these last times for you" (I Peter 1:20).

Salvation Is Great Because of the Price Paid to Procure It

Negligence or rejection of this matchless salvation is made more terrible because of all Jesus endured to provide it. By His blood-shedding, death and Resurrection, He secured a perfect salvation for a sinning race. It is therefore a precious salvation, seeing it has come down to us drenched with the precious blood of Christ. He had to give His life as a ransom in order to save us (Matthew 20:28; II Corinthians 5:21; Hebrews 2:14,15; I Peter 1:19).

Creation was a great work of God, but it only cost Him His breath. "He spake, and it was done." But when it came to our salvation, He had to give more than His breath, He had to give His blood. We were purchased by that precious blood (Acts 20:28).

Salvation Is Great Because of Its Agency

It is the Holy Spirit who makes possible the actual work of salvation in the heart of the believing sinner. He it is who applies the efficacious blood.

The terms of salvation are so simple that a child can understand them. "What must I do to be saved? Believe on the Lord Jesus

Christ, and thou shalt be saved" (Acts 16:30,31). Repentance toward God and faith in Christ form the channel of salvation.

"But as many as received Him, to them gave He power to become the sons of God, even to them that believe on His name" (John 1:12).

"Testifying both to the Jews, and also to the Greeks, repentance toward God, and faith toward our Lord Jesus Christ" (Acts 20:21).

How grateful we should be for the simplicity of the Gospel. Here, then, are the key words of salvation: repent, call, receive, believe (Titus 3:5-8).

Salvation Is Great Because of Its Universality

Because God so loved the world, and through the finished work of His Son, provided salvation for all the world, He wills all men to be saved. Alas, however, multitudes will not come to Him that they may have life! Irrespective of nationality, position, condition, age or need, God's salvation is for all (John 3:16; I Timothy 2:4-6; 4:10; I John 2:2; 4:14).

Such a universality does not mean Universalism, a false system of religious teaching that believes all men are to be saved ultimately. Jesus declared that all who fail to accept Him as Saviour must "perish" (John 3:16)—a word meaning not annihilation, but eternal banishment from the presence of a thrice holy God. Our Lord's teaching on the finality of hell also proves the falsity of Universalism (Luke 16:19-31).

Salvation Is Great Because of the Blessings It Bestows

What constitutes this unique salvation which prophets and apostles wrote about? On the *negative* side, it offers emancipation from the bondage of sin, and from all its eternal consequences. Its constituent elements are deliverance from the powers of darkness, from the curse and condemnation of sin. On the *positive* side, salvation provides us with a perfect standing before God through the merits of the Saviour. It brings us into the fellowship of our Deliverer, with whom we are made one forever. Once saved, we cease to be our own. We become His property.

What? Know ye not that your body is the temple of the Holy Ghost which is in you, which ye have of God, and ye are not your own? For ye are bought with a price: therefore glorify God in your body, and in your spirit, which are God's (I Corinthians 6:19,20).

We also receive satisfaction with our salvation, power as well as pardon, joy as well as justification.

Salvation Is Great Because It Is eternal in Its duration

Ours is an eternal salvation in the Lord (Isaiah 45:17; 51:6). It awakens in us a ceaseless wonder and an undying gratitude, seeing that it travels toward a consummate goal. Salvation is not for this life only. It ends in the inheritance incorruptible and undefiled, and that fadeth not away. Christ is the Provider of an unceasing salvation (Hebrews 5:9; 9:12). Through His wondrous grace, the Saviour imparts eternal security to all He saves (John 10:28).

Salvation Is Great Because It Is Incomparable

There is no other way God can clear and deliver the guilty save through the sacrifice and mediation of His beloved Son. The sinner in his need is shut up to God's provision. Did not Jesus Himself say, "No man cometh unto the Father, *but by me*" (John 14:6)? Man's own worth or works are useless as avenues of salvation or of justification in the sight of God. The lost have to come just as they are, without one plea, and depend upon divine mercy for salvation (Ephesians 2:7-10).

Salvation Is Great Because It Came to Us Personified

We are prone to forget that salvation is not *something*, but SOMEONE. "The Lord Jehovah . . . is become my salvation" (Isaiah 12:2; Psalms 27:1; 62:2). If salvation is treated as an intangible something we must struggle in order to keep, then there will be a constant fear that we may lose it. But our salvation is not a mere *it* but HIM, even the Saviour Himself, and it is ludicrous to try and keep Him when He is Saviour and Keeper combined. He is able to keep what He has committed unto us, seeing that what He committed was Himself.

The Grades of Salvation

It is to be feared that not all evangelicals fully comprehend the implications of salvation. Too often it is confined to what takes place in the initial experience of conversion. Christ is accepted as Saviour, and with the guilt and burden of sin removed, the confession is made, "Praise God, I have been saved." And there the matter rests. But the teaching of the New Testament is, "I have been saved: I am being saved: I have yet to be saved." If we fail to recognize these three aspects, tenses or gradations of salvation, then ours is not the realization of the uttermost salvation the Lord has for His own.

> Wherefore He is able also to save unto the uttermost them that come unto God by Him, seeing He ever liveth to make intercession for them (Hebrews 7:25).

God's perfect salvation covers the past, includes the present and embraces the future, as Paul so clearly reveals in his Roman epistle.

1. A Past Salvation

Salvation is a gift we receive the moment we accept Christ as our Saviour. In the moment of our surrender to His claims, we experience His Gospel to be the power of God unto salvation (Romans 1:16). No matter how sinful we were in the past, in a moment of time the red blood of Jesus makes the black heart whiter than the snow.

> Come now and let us reason together, saith the Lord: though your sins be as scarlet, they shall be as white as snow; though they be red like crimson, they shall be as wool (Isaiah 1:18).

Under the curse and condition of sin, we came to know what it was to be saved from the guilt and penalty of our sin (Luke 7:50; I Corinthians 1:18; II Timothy 1:9). And saved, we are *safe*. It is this aspect of salvation we have in mind when we sing:

> My sin! O the bliss of that glorious thought,
> My sin, not in part, but the whole
> Is nailed to His Cross, and I bear it no more,
> Praise the Lord, praise the Lord, O my soul!

As to the nature of this initial grade of salvation, Scripture proclaims it to be—
A Common Salvation (Jude 3).

The word "common" suggests something for all, universal. None are excluded from the pale of mercy, except by their own fault.

God, not willing that any should perish (II Peter 3:9) has provided a salvation adapted to all and needed by all.

A Personal Salvation.

What is universal must also be personal if it is to be of any practical value. Each of us can appropriate this blood-bought salvation and say, "This is *my* salvation" (Psalms 25:5; 35:3; Romans 10:9). Further, no one can act for us in this all-important matter.

A Present Salvation.

Because it is a *personal* salvation, it becomes effective as we recognize it as a *present* salvation (II Corinthians 6:2; Luke 19:9). When God says, "Now," He means "*Now*," or this very moment. It is folly to look upon salvation as a long and laborious process through which we must struggle and then have only a vague hope that we are saved.

A Powerful Salvation

Because God is mighty to save, there is no case He is not able to cope with. The blood of Christ can make the vilest clean (Luke 1:68,69; Romans 1:16).

2. A Present Salvation

Too many who have been saved are ignorant of the fact that their salvation covers the journey between their conversion and death or the return of Christ. Because He continues His ministry in glory, Christ's salvation is unfailing (Hebrews 7:24,25). Paul had this aspect of salvation in mind when he wrote—

For if, when we were enemies, we were reconciled to God by the death of His Son, much more, being reconciled, we *shall be* saved by His life (Romans 5:10).

Here we have a double salvation—one by the *death* of Christ, and the other by His *life.* "Reconciled to God by the death of His Son"—this is past salvation. But Paul said "much more." Is there something more than being saved? The apostle says there is—"being reconciled, we *shall* be saved by His life."

The reference to "his life" does not apply to the earthly life of Christ. There is no salvation through the life He lived among men, even although there are those who teach salvation by imitation. Live like Jesus, imbibe His teachings, emulate His example, and all will be right. But Christ after the flesh is not a Saviour. Paul, then, had in mind the present life of Christ, His

risen, glorified throne-life. He ever liveth to keep us saved, to provide us with a day by day salvation from the power of sin, as well as its penalty: from sin's government as well as its guilt. This is the grade of salvation we are to exhibit (Psalm 96:2), and represents salvation from the habit and the dominion of sin (Romans 6:14; Philippians 2:12,13; II Corinthians 3:18).

The question of paramount importance is, Are we being saved? Have we daily victory over the flesh? Do we reign in life by Christ Jesus? Are we more than conquerors? Is ours the overcoming life? Or can it be that, although we can look back and think of the day we were saved from our guilty past, we are miserably defeated in the present? Ours is an up and down experience. What joy and freedom becomes ours when we can sing—

Moment by moment I'm kept in His love,
Moment by moment I've life from above;
Looking to Jesus, 'till glory doth shine,
Moment by Moment, O Lord, I am Thine!

3. A Prospective Salvation

Paul must have had the future in mind when he gave us this third aspect or tense of salvation.

"Now is our salvation nearer than when we believed" (Romans 13:11).

This is also the grade of salvation of which Peter speaks, as being "ready to be revealed in the last time" (I Peter 1:5). "Nearer than when we believed?" Did we not receive salvation when we believed? Yes! Do we not receive salvation as we keep on believing? Yes! Then what brand of salvation did Paul refer to when he said it is "nearer" than it was in the initial hour of faith? It is a salvation from the *presence* of sin, just as the past salvation delivered us from the *penalty* of sin, and a present salvation delivers us from the *power* of sin. We need salvation from the presence of sin within, and from the presence of sin around us in the world. When will this salvation take place? Why, when Jesus comes. He is our "Salvation," and as such is nearer than when we believed. Returning, He will save us from sin within, giving us an unsinning nature like unto His own.

Behold, what manner of love the Father hath bestowed upon us, that we should be called the sons of God: therefore the world knoweth us not, because it knew Him not. Beloved, now are we the sons of God, and it doth not yet appear what we shall be: but we know that when He shall appear, we shall be like Him, for we shall see Him as He is" (I John 3:1,2).

He will also save us from the presence of sin around, for when caught up to meet Him in the air, we shall be saved to sin no more. With the redemption of the body (Romans 8:23; I Corinthians 15:51-54), the seat, source and seductiveness of sin will be removed. This last aspect of salvation will bring us entire conformity to Christ. At the Rapture, the Church will be saved to sin no more.

XV
The Doctrine of Grace

The importance of a right understanding of this further basic Christian doctrine can be judged by the fact that "grace" and its cognates, "gracious" and "graciously," occur almost 200 times in Scripture. A study of the doctrine of grace is also precious to the saints who seek to share in the riches of grace.

To the praise of the glory of his grace, wherein he hath made us accepted in the beloved. In whom we have redemption through his blood, the forgiveness of sin, according to the riches of his grace (Ephesians 1:6,7).

Salvation from commencement to consummation, service from start to finish, sanctification from beginning to end are all associated with the grace of God. From the first reference to grace in Genesis 6:8, "Noah found grace in the eyes of the Lord," until the last reference in Revelation 22:21, "The grace of the Lord Jesus Christ be with you all," this glorious, evangelical theme dominates the Word. Pascal sang of grace, "To make a man a saint, grace is absolutely necessary and whoever doubts it, does not know what a saint is or what a man is." None of the other fundamentals of the Gospel can be rightly understood, if the Biblical unfolding of divine grace is not fully grasped. Perverted views of grace mean perversion in all areas of divine truth.

Magnanimous in Its Conception.

Grace has been described as "God's riches at Christ's expense"; "Unmerited, undeserved favor"; "A comprehensive word of boundless reach as it carries an infinite depth of significance signifying unlimited favor to the undeserving, all who by reason of transgression have forfeited every claim to divine favor, and have lost all capacity for meritorious action"; "Grace is the benignity of parental love and the ground on which God saves men"; "Grace is free, favor manifest in the gift of God's Son, and the blessings of salvation through His sacrifice on the cross." The Scriptural definition of grace will never be improved upon—

The kindness and love of God our Saviour toward men . . . not of works of righteousness which we have done . . . (Titus 3:4,5).

An examination of the word "grace" shows that there is nothing ungenerous or mean in its provision. Everything about it is enriching and ennobling. In Greek terminology *charis* implied a favor freely done, without claims or expectation of return. Aristotle, defining the term, says that it suggests "something that is conferred freely, with no expectation of return, and finding its only motive in the bounty and free-heartedness of the giver." Used by New Testament writers, *charis* carries a more wonderful, richer and deeper content of meaning. Luke gives us its classical significance, "gracious words" (Luke 4:22). What came from the lips of Christ gave joy to His hearers. Both Luke (17:9) and Paul (Romans 6:17) use *charis* in its Greek meaning of "thankfulness." As used by Peter the word implies "that which is beyond the ordinary course of what can be expected, and therefore commendable" (I

Peter 2:19,20). When used by the Greeks themselves, *charis* expressed favor shown to a *friend*. When the word is applied to Christ dying for sinners (Romans 5:8-10), it takes a leap forward for He expressed His favor toward His *enemies*. Divine grace is therefore more commendable than human grace (I John 3:1). God's grace is infinite, boundless, immense, unspeakable, inconceivable and unsearchable.

Grace is the spring and source of all benefits received from God (Romans 11: 6). He who saves us by His grace brings us into the area of grace, endowing us with all the activities and attributes of grace. Grace is one of His own transcendent attributes.

". . . and it shall come to pass, when he crieth unto me, that I will hear; for I am gracious" (Exodus 22:27).

". . . but thou art a God ready to pardon, gracious and merciful, slow to anger, and of great kindness" (Nehemiah 9:17).

". . . for I knew that thou art a gracious God, and merciful, slow to anger, and of great kindness" (Jonah 4:2).

"But the God of all grace . . ." (I Peter 5:10).

Grace is unmerited favor manifested toward sinners and indicates that the demands of divine justice have been met, seeing that the penalty was placed upon Christ.

Grace introduces us into a new realm. Through it we are taken out of the sphere of death into life (Romans 5:2; Galatians 1:6). By grace we are fully and freely justified. What a glorious doctrine to proclaim!

Grace also signifies the gifts bestowed upon the saved (II Corinthians 8:19); Christian virtues to be manifested (II Corinthians 8:7); Christian benediction to be enjoyed (Ephesians 6:24). God vouchsafes toward us restoring grace as well as life-giving grace. Edmund Spenser, a writer of long ago, exclaimed:

But O! the exceeding grace
Of highest God that loves His creatures so,
And all His works, with mercy, doth embrace.

Such grace is unlimited in its resources. God is described as abounding in grace (Romans 5:20). The word Paul uses here for "abound" means "to exist in super-

abundance and then more grace added to this superabundance." God's grace is also abundantly given (Romans 5:15; II Corinthians 4:15; 9:8). This abundance is proven by the calling of sinners and workers alike (Galatians 1:15); in placing those who are redeemed, forgiven, accepted, in the heavenlies and in providing them with everlasting consolation and good hope (Romans 3:24; Ephesians 1:6,7; 2:5-8; II Thessalonians 2:16).

The covenant of grace differs considerably from Old Testament covenants. Under the old economy, law blessed the good, but grace saves the bad (Exodus 19:5; Ephesians 2:1-9). The law said, "Pay me that thou owest, even to the uttermost farthing." Grace says, "You have nothing to pay your debt with. I freely forgive all." The Law curses—grace blesses. The law evicts, as a landlord evicts a tenant who cannot or will not pay rent—grace steps in, cancels the bond and relieves the debtor. The law reveals a sinful condition and condemns the sinners to death—grace provides a righteousness the sinner could never attain (John 1:17; Romans 6:14).

This dispensation, or day of grace (Hebrews 3:7), began with the death and Resurrection of Christ and will end with His return to the air for His own (Romans 3:24-26; 4:24,25; Hebrews 4:7). This age of grace is soon to end, and all who die with hearts destitute of divine grace must face the judgment of the Great White Throne (Revelation 20:11-15). Edmund Spenser has given us these lines in Old English—

Her gracious, graceful, gracious Grace,
Ay me, how many perils do enfold
The righteous man, to make him daily fall,
Were not that heavenly grace doth him uphold,
And stedfast Truth acquite him out of all.

Magnificent in Its Simplicity and Sufficiency.

What grandeur, majesty and glory surround the gracious acts of God! His grace is as magnificent as Himself. An ancient proverb has it, "Divine grace was never slow." The marvel of God's grace is that it hastens to the aid of the graceless. The greatness of divine grace is also evidenced by the channels of its operation.

Grace comes to us from God. He is its Rise and Spring (Psalm 84:11; I Peter 5:10; James 4:6). Grace flows from the glorious and transcendent nature of God. It is one of His infinite attributes, and is the result of the eternal counsel and purpose of His will (Ephesians 1:2; II Timothy 1:9). Grace is an act, not only a favor, a gift revealing the divine character. Grace reveals what God *is* as well as what He *does*.

Grace comes to us through Christ (John 1:17; I Timothy 1:14). The prophets declared that grace would be manifested and personified in Christ (I Peter 1:10). Grace came to us in His Person (John 1:14; Luke 2:40; Romans 5:18; Titus 2:11). His life was a platform upon which grace was displayed and His lips were eloquent with its message (Psalm 45:2; Luke 4:22). Through His death grace for all mankind became possible (Hebrews 2:9).

Grace is characteristic of the Christian Gospel (Acts 20:24,32). Through the Gospel of grace manifold blessings are brought to the soul. This Gospel does not say, "Try to reach these blessings." That is the teaching of the law. Grace comes down to the lost one with God's best. The Gospel declares to all unbelievers that grace is free, the gift of God.

Grace is applied to the believing sinner by the Holy Spirit, who is the "spirit of grace" (Zechariah 12:10). To reject the cleansing blood of Christ is to do despite unto the Spirit of grace (Hebrews 10:29) and thereby seal one's doom.

A perusal of the constituent elements of grace convinces one of its all-sufficiency. What a vast storehouse of spiritual wealth is open to us! Here are some of the riches of His grace:

1. The free and undeserved love and favor of God, and the inexhaustible benefits flowing therefrom (Romans 11:6; II Timothy 1:9). Under grace, God freely gives to the sinner eternal life (Romans 6:23) and accounts to him a perfect righteousness (Romans 3:21,22), and accords him a perfect position (Ephesians 2:19-22). This free and unmerited love of God was the original motive in the provision of salvation, which is bestowed apart from any merit of the recipient. His love and mercy provides for all (John 3:16).

2. Grace embraces Christ's meritorious undertaking whereby all true believers become righteous in the sight of a righteous God (Romans 5:19). They are also made the recipients of the free favor and bounty of Christ (II Corinthians 8:9).

3. A further provision of grace is the excellent and blessed state of reconciliation and fellowship the regenerated soul experiences (Romans 5:2). "At peace with God —how great the blessing."

4. Then there follows the work of the Spirit, renewing those who are saved after the image of God, and continually guiding and empowering them to know and obey the divine will. The Spirit also enables the believer to resist, mortify and overcome sin (Romans 6:14). He also makes possible spiritual instruction and edification (Ephesians 4:11-13). Grace likewise qualifies the believer to exercise the gifts of the Spirit (Ephesians 3:8; Philippians 1:7).

5. Grace is associated with the development of faith and patience, enabling us to bear up under suffering until we receive the final installment of our salvation at the return of Christ (I Peter 1:13). As we linger amid the shadows we are to wear the ornament of grace (Proverbs 4:9), and find grace both in the sight of God and man (Genesis 39:4). Access into grace is by faith (Romans 5:2).

6. Another aspect of the magnificence of grace is its power to make spiritual things a relish to the child of God. All the means of grace become a delight to him. Dr. C. I. Scofield remarks, "Grace is not only the method of divine dealing in salvation, but is also the method of God in the believer's life and service. As saved, he is 'not under the law, but under grace'" (Romans 6:14). Having, by grace, brought the believer to the highest conceivable position (Ephesians 1:6), God ceaselessly works through grace to impart to and perfect in him corresponding graces (Galatians 5:22,23).

This area of grace covers *prayer*, whereby we have boldness to enter the holiest of all (Hebrews 4:16). The throne of grace is sweet to the believer, but has no savor to graceless persons. Christianity has been referred to as the "religion of access." The law thunders, "Stand afar off"—but grace invites us to "draw near." Grace provides access to God (Romans 5:1,2).

The Word of God also has a relish to those who are saved by grace (Psalm 19:10; Jeremiah 15:16). How sweet to their taste are the promises of God inherited through grace (Romans 4:16).

Grace feeds on meditation upon the three *Persons of the Blessed Trinity*. How pleasant and savory is it to dwell upon the virtues of the Father, the Son and the Spirit (Psalm 104:34)!

The Book of Common Prayer speaks of baptism as "an outward and visible sign of an inward and spiritual grace."

The recipients of grace enjoy converse with each other. The *"fellowship of kindred minds* is like to that above!" (Malachi 3:16; Luke 24:32).

Joy in liberality is another evidence of grace. A heart possessed of grace becomes a liberal heart. Grace begets a charitable disposition (II Corinthians 4:15; 8:1,2,7-16; 9:14). The grace of God results in the grace of giving, as well as getting.

Grace can make something distasteful, savory. Afflictions are not bitter nor irksome. Imparted strength to bear sorrow is a gift of grace (II Corinthians 12:9). "It was good for me that I had been afflicted."

Graciousness naturally springs from grace, and is required by grace (Titus 2: 11,12). Behavior and deportment before others should reveal the residence of grace within. The lightness and the looseness of the graceless are foreign to those who desire to manifest "the grace of life" (I Peter 3:7) in all of the relationships of life. Alas, there is not always the radiation of graciousness on the part of those who are saved! Grace they may have, but sweetness of spirit and graciousness are conspicuous by their absence. Grace should teach us how to behave as children of God (II Corinthians 1:12).

Lord Byron, in his description of Don Juan, has the lines—

> Though modest, on his unembarrassed brow
> Nature had written "gentleman"; he said
> Little, but to the purpose; and his manners
> Flung hovering graces o'er him like a banner.

Grace seasons the tongue, until it is as true of the saint as it is of the Saviour, "Grace is poured into thy lips." The Bible has much to say about the grace of speech (Proverbs 10:20; Luke 4:22; Colossians 4:6). A biting, critical, cynical, complaining tongue is foreign to the nature of grace. Grace always thrives in an air of kindness (Ephesians 4:3,32).

Grace kills all that would torment the conscience. It is a sovereign remedy against all sin. It keeps the believer in victory (II Thessalonians 1:11,12), and makes him more than a conqueror.

Grace is not only a gift, but a trust to keep. So we have the stewardship of grace (I Peter 4:10). Business transactions are clear and transparent. Crookedness and dishonesty are abhorred.

The consummation of grace is glory. Paul glowingly extols the transcendent riches of divine grace, speaking of glory as an attribute of grace (Ephesians 1:6). The steps of grace are easily discernable.

1. Transferred from death to life by grace (John 5:24).
2. Transfigured by the Spirit by believing in Christ (II Corinthians 3:18 R.V.)
3. Translated by the power of God at Christ's return (Hebrews 11:5).
4. Transformed by the Saviour and made like Him (Philippians 3:20,21).

It is profitable to trace the blessings of grace in Ephesians, the epistle of grace. This characteristic keyword is used 13 times. Paul, the apostle of grace, reminds us that through grace, we have—

Acceptance—"To the praise of the glory of His grace, whereby he hath made us accepted in the beloved" (1:6).

Forgiveness—"In whom we have redemption through his blood, the forgiveness of sins according to the riches of his grace" (1:7).

Salvation—"Even when we were dead in sins, hath quickened us together with Christ Jesus: that in the ages to come hath raised us up together, and made us sit together in heavenly places in Christ Jesus: that in the ages to come he might shew the exceeding riches of his grace in his kindness toward us through Christ Jesus; for by grace are ye saved through faith; and that not of yourselves, it is the gift of God" (2:5-8).

Display as trophies—"That in the ages to come he might shew the exceeding riches of his grace in his kindness toward us through Christ Jesus (2:7).

Witness—"For we are his workmanship, created in Christ Jesus unto good works . . ." (2:10).

Avenue of Service—"Let no corrupt communication proceed out of your mouth, but that which is good to the use of edifying, that it may minister unto the hearers" (4:29).

Benediction of Love—"Grace be with all them that love our Lord Jesus Christ in sincerity" (6:24).

Old William Langland, who lived in the 13th century, wrote—

But Lord, amende us all
And give us grace, Good God, Charité to folwe.

Measureless in Its Scope

In his "Pleasures of Hope," Thomas Campbell, the seventeenth century poet, wrote—

Who hath not owned, with rapture-smitten frame,
The power of grace, the magic of a name?

Let us now dwell upon the range of grace, and its divine power, and the magic of the divine name manifesting such limitless grace. Truly, there is no determined extent of provision in God's amazing grace. It is for "all men" (Titus 2:11). If you take the "g" from *grace*, you are left with *race*, and grace is for all within the race of men upon one common ground, namely, that of being sinners. Grace levels the moral condition of men and comes only to those who realize their need of it (Luke 5:31,32).

Further, grace does not imply the thought that God passes by the sin of any person. Grace supposes sin to be so horribly base and bad a thing that God in His holiness cannot tolerate it. If any man in his unrighteousness and evil condition could patch up his ways and stand before God, there would be no need of grace. But God sees the sinner utterly ruined, hopeless and helpless, and the triumph of grace is seen at Calvary, where "Heaven's love and Heaven's justice meet." Christ bore the load and curse of human sin, and with God's hatred against sin vindicated on the basis of His grace, He can now forgive the sinner.

The recipients of grace are identified as:

1. Those who formed the Early Church (Acts 4:33).
2. Paul, who testified that his power was due to the undeserved favor of God (Romans 15:15).
3. The apostle, as a wise church-builder, was dependent upon grace (I Corinthians 3:10).
4. He traced his abundant labors to grace (I Corinthians 15:10).
5. His ministry to the Gentiles was all of grace (Ephesians 3:8).
6. The whole of his life was a glowing tribute to grace (I Timothy 1:13,14).
7. He urged the apostolic churches to manifest grace (II Corinthians 9:8; Philippians 1:7 R.V.; Ephesians 4:7).

God's grace knows no barrier of race, age or sex. All have sinned and come short of God's glory, and all who are willing to be saved can bathe in the ocean of grace. Grace is extended to all in succeeding generations. Once a soul experiences salvation by grace, there is a growing understanding of its relation to service, as well as salvation. For example:

Election through grace is accepted by faith (Romans 11:5,6).

Salvation as an act of grace is rejoiced in (Acts 15:11; Ephesians 2:8; Titus 2:11).

Justification resulting from grace is fully realized (Ephesians 1:7,8).

Faith, as the appropriating hand of grace, is maintained (Acts 18:27; Ephesians 2:8,9).

Grace is God's part—faith is ours. Faith never makes what is in the heart its object, but God's revelation of Himself in grace.

The call to live and labor for Christ is of grace, (Galatians 1:15,16) and the exercise of spiritual gifts in service streams from the same grace (I Peter 1:10). It is better to grow in grace than to grow in gifts. Gifts edify others—grace is for our own development. Grace alone is the basis of service (Romans 12:6).

Daily strength in the hour of need is also of grace (II Corinthians 12:9; II Thessalonians 2:16). There is ever need of grace, and grace for every need.

Grace likewise prompts generosity toward others (II Corinthians 8:6,7,9), and is quick to perceive grace in others (Galatians 2:9).

Peace is welcomed as the sister of grace (Philippians 4:1-9). Grace is the fountain, and peace the refreshing water issuing from it.

There is perpetual gratitude for the revelation of divine grace (II Corinthians 4:15).

Amazing grace, how sweet the sound!
That saved a wretch lie me;
I once was lost, but now am found,
Was blind, but now I see.

Those who come to know what it is to be saved by grace are not long in discovering that they cannot remain static. Grace is found to be related to Christian growth

(II Corinthians 1:12; Ephesians 4:29). We cannot grow *into* grace but once grace becomes a possession by faith, we grow *in* it. Once we are made the sharers of divine grace, then it becomes a progressive force in life (II Peter 3:18). There is grace upon grace (John 1:16). We pass from one degree of grace to another degree (Psalm 84:7; Philippians 1:9; Romans 1:17). Grace is not a seed in the heart that cannot grow, but a blade, an ear, then the full corn in the ear. Once we are made the recipients of grace we are not like Hezekiah's sun dial that went backward, nor Joshua's sun that stood still, but are ever increasing in holiness. There is a continuous unfelt progression as we journey on from the first measure of grace to the riches of grace. As the roots spread, the tree grows (Colossians 2:7).

Growth in grace is the best evidence of its possession. If we are not growing in grace, then there is something lacking in one's faith (I Thessalonians 3:10). Loss of spiritual appetite is a sure sign of spiritual decline. Lack of affection for the provision of grace indicates a static position in grace. Alexander Maclaren reminds us that "our churches are full of monsters, specimens of arrested growth."

How can we grow in grace? By using all the available means for such a growth. We must exercise ourselves unto godliness (I Timothy 4:7). As with the body, so with the soul—it grows stronger by exercise. Goëthe wrote, "Grace makes a man irresistible." Doubtless the ancient philosopher had in mind acquired graces, lending charm to character. Such a pronouncement is true when applied to the activities of divine grace within a saved person.

Growing in grace we grow less in our own eyes. Growing Christians are humble Christians (I Peter 5:5,6). Through grace we grow out of all self-conceit (Psalm 22:6). Grace subdues self (I Corinthians 15:10).

Growing in grace means that all graces grow proportionately. In physical growth all parts of the body develop proportionately. Thus it is in the spiritual realm. Knowledge increases (II Peter 1:5). We grow in meekness and brotherly love. Grace results in graciousness. Alas, however, not all who are saved by grace are as gracious as they should be in their dealing with others. We likewise grow in peace. Grace is the image of God, and as we grow up into the full stature of Christ, His tranquility becomes ours.

As we grow in grace, the growth of corruption is hindered. The flowers of grace prevent the weeds of sin from spreading. When grace rules within, the whole being is brought into subjection to Christ, and the Spirit transforms us into His holiness.

> O to grace how great a debtor
> Daily I'm constrained to be;
> Let Thy goodness, like a fetter,
> Blind my wandering heart to Thee.

Grace is the beauty of holiness (Psalm 29:2), and such growth is the beauty of the believer. As physical health is reflected in complexion, so spiritual health (health and holiness are related terms) provides the growing Christian with a spiritual complexion clearly apparent to those who contact us. Filled with the fruits of righteousness, we manifest a practical righteousness. Growth in grace means a more spiritual frame of heart, and a desire to become more spiritual in activities as well as in affections.

While it is possible for a believer to fall *from* grace (Galatians 5:1), he can never fall *out* of grace. Paul's phrase can be translated, "fall away from grace." We may fall *on* the Rock, but we cannot fall *off* of it. Christ is our Rock, and has promised our eternal security (John 10:28,29). Our vision of sovereign grace becomes dim when we trust in anything else besides the all-sufficiency of Christ's provision and power. His grace is our coverage for time and eternity.

How melodious, then, is the Gospel of grace to the ear and heart of the believer! Grace plants a new song within (Psalm 40:3), and then creates for us a happy attitude and demeanor. Thus we come to know what it is to sing with grace (Colossians 3:16). Grace becomes a charming sound, harmonious to the ear.

"The grace of the Lord Jesus Christ be with you all."

XVI

The Doctrine of Repentance

We live in a superficial age, and nowhere is superficiality more evident than in the religious realm. Generally people do not want their conscience disturbed, so the message of repentance is seldom preached. Militant conservatives and destructive liberals alike are guilty of the abandonment of any truth distasteful to the ears of the self-satisfied, or that which is difficult to enforce.

It is contended that our forefathers placed too much emphasis on poignancy of grief as a necessary element in true repentance, in so far as they permitted any idea of merit to attach to the experience. Yet surely they were right in insisting on a deep and genuine upturning of the soul. In our age we have swung to the other direction. We seldom hear the old prophetic cry, "Break up your fallow ground, sow not among thorns" (Jeremiah 4:3). This generation, with all its religion, has lost the sense of sin and pays preachers to "Prophesy smooth things." Repentance is robbed of its true significance. The plow of conviction is never driven deep into the human soil. So-called "revivals" and "evangelistic efforts" produce shallow results because of the shallow repentance preached. Deep mourning for sin, hot, scalding tears of repentance, souls writhing in agony because of their burden are not common as they used to be. Saved and unsaved alike are not over-awed by the august holiness of God, and the filthiness of their own evil nature. The sob of anguish, "Woe is me, for I am undone," is seldom heard in a religious service today. Instead, young people and others walk down our aisles to make a decision for Christ with a giggle on their faces. Statistically-minded, the church counts numbers. God give her numbers that count! We go out for quantity. God seeks quality.

Wherever true repentance is preached and insisted upon, however, solid results accrue. Those saved under such preaching usually make robust Christians. While, of course, faith in Christ is *the* great characteristic in gospel preaching, repentance toward God must also be strongly pressed.

All who proclaim the truth must pray and labor for the Spirit's convicting work in the conscience. If sin is slurred over and repentance belittled, there cannot be depth or stability. The more thoroughly conscience is disturbed and stung on account of sin, the more solid and enduring the results when the Gospel is preached. It must be shown that repentance is indispensable to salvation (Luke 13:3). The prodigal must return in sorrow if he is to be reinstated—the rebel must submit before clemency can be exercised and favor bestowed—the sinner must repent before relations with an offended God can be restored. This is why, as we are to see, the call to repentance rings out in resonant tones from the pages of Scripture.

George Lyttleton has the line, "Without any snivelling signs of contrition and repentance." When the Spirit is active in convicting men of sin, there is never anything "snivelling" about the tears He produces. Would we could see more holy water of this kind, for as Alexander Pope puts it, "A noble mind disdains not to repent." John Fletcher, philosopher of the sixteenth century, proudly wrote—

I ne'er repented anything yet in my life,
And scorn to begin now.

He must have been a very perfect man indeed if he had no sin or failure to repent of. Only One has appeared who had no need of repentance, the One who could ask, "Which of you convinceth Me of sin?" The rest of us, *all* of us, have need of repentance. What a different world this would be if the repentance of Nineveh could be repeated, when all, from the Ruler down, were covered with sackcloth and cried mightily unto God (Jonah 3)!

There are those who cry repentance down, calling it a *legal* doctrine, but the Bible is full of this basic doctrine. Christ preached it! At His farewell, when He was about to ascend to heaven, He commanded that repentance should be preached in His name (Luke 24:47). Repentance may be a bitter, drastic pill for our sin-sick generation to take, but it is necessary if the needed spiritual healing is to be experienced. May God raise up fearless witnesses who will preach repentance until men repent and turn to the Saviour!

Seeing then that repentance is imperative, let us seek to outline what the Bible has to say on such an important theme.

Its Scriptural Basis

The Bible unhesitatingly and emphatically declares that repentance is the first step in the soul's return to God: that it is not arbitrary, but necessary, seeing no soul can be saved without it. Thus the summons to repent is the dominant note in God's call to men in both Old and New Testaments: and the preacher whose witness lacks the urgent, vibrant note is neither in the prophetic line nor in the Apostolic succession. Because repentance is indispensable it is imperative that we understand what it means and implies. It is clearly evident that defective and counterfeit views are prevalent. Men try to persuade themselves that something else, or something less, can pass for repentance (Jeremiah 25:5; Ezekiel 14:6; Joel 2:13, 14; Acts 5:6-11).

The Old Testament prophets knew how to address and arouse the conscience and produce deep repentance. What contrition David manifested when he was stung by Nathan's pointed condemnation, "Thou art the man!" Repentance also occupied a prominent place in apostolic preaching, in spite of the fact that John's gospel, using *believe* about a hundred times, never uses *repentance* once. It will be found that Romans, designed to show how sinners are justified, only mentions the word once. Galatians, written to protest the spirit of legalism—Ephesians, presenting Christ as the measure of the saint's standing—Philippians, exhibiting Christ as the saint's life pattern, object, strength—Colossians, revealing our completeness in Christ—I Thessalonians, teaching the coming of Christ as the joy of the believer—II Thessalonians, showing Christ as the Coming One for the judgment of unbelievers—James, reminding us of our walk and work in the world— never once speak of repentance. Yet in spite of this silence, the truth permeates the Acts, where we have the historical foundation of the Church (Luke 24:47; Acts 2:38; 3:19; 8:22; 20:21; 26:20). Both John the Baptist and Christ Himself

gave emphasis to the message of repentance, overlooked in modern-day preaching. The New Testament opens with John's stern summons (Matthew 3:2-8), which was taken up by our Lord, and became the recurring note in His ministry (Mark 1:15; Matthew 4:17; 11:20-24). And, as we have seen above, the apostles understood His charge to preach repentance.

The present age, desiring to be left undisturbed in its sins, must be aroused. Saturated with worldliness and indifference, the multitudes must come to know the urgency of the call, "Repent for the Kingdom of God is at hand." The pungent preaching of the prophets, and the direct approach of Christ and His apostles produced results. Surely we cannot improve upon their message and method! If, as Thomas Chalmers said, "Repentance is that deep and radical change whereby a sinner turns from his idols of sin and self unto God, and devotes every movement of the inner and outer man to the captivity of His obedience," then away with the popular ideas, and give us the preaching producing Holy Ghost conviction and conversions.

Its Significance

The word "repent" in its various forms occurs 45 times in the Old Testament, and carries the underlying thought of *contrition*. Two words are translated "repent." The one means to *sigh or groan*, then to *lament or groan*. This word is used about 40 times, and in most cases refers to God. The other word means to *turn or return*. It is given as "repent" but three times (I Kings 8:47; Ezekiel 14:6; 18:30, see R.V.), and is translated as "turn," "turn away," "return," and similar terms, nearly 600 times. In the New Testament, the word occurs 61 times, with the meaning of thinking differently, that is, to change one's mind. The character of the experience described by the words used varies in the estimate of different individuals according to their concept of the nature of sin. H. S. Miller, in *The Christian Worker's Manual*, tells us that there are two words in the New Testament translated repent. The one means "to care afterwards," or a sorrow or remorseful regret. It may lead to turning (Matthew 21:29; Hebrews 12:17), or it may not (Matthew 21:32), as in the case of Judas, whose repentance was merely regret (Matthew 27:3). It occurs six times, and is twice translated in the R.V. "regret" (II Corinthians 7:8).

The other word is the stronger and the far more common word, used in all the commands and teaching concerning repentance. It occurs in the noun and verb forms 57 times. It means to *change one's mind for the better, to have another mind.* As the word for "mind" includes the feelings, judgments, desires and purposes, repentance means a reversal of man's nature, intellectual, affectional and moral.

The general scriptural significance of repentance, then, is *to turn, right about face.* The Psalmist summarizes it, thus:

"I thought on my ways"—Halt!
"I turned my feet unto Thy testimonies" —Right about turn!
"I made haste and delayed not to keep Thy commandments"—Quick march! (Psalm 119:59,60).

Repentance, applied to man, means "to go the opposite way and to do the opposite thing, based upon deep sorrow and remorse for and abhorrence of sin"—and such remorse and abhorrence usually come from a sight of God and His holiness.

There are three Greek words for "repentance" to be distinguished—

Metanoeō. This word means to change one's mind, always for the better, and morally. It is a change of mind leading to a change of life. Archbishop Trench says that it "expresses that mighty change of the mind, heart and life wrought by the Spirit of God." This may be the reason why this word is used in the *imperative* (Matthew 3:2; 4:17; Acts 2:36-38; 3:19). Here we have, not a mere forsaking of sin, but a change of one's apprehension regarding it. Occurring 34 times, the term before us is akin to the Latin *resipisco,* meaning to recover one's senses, to come to oneself as the Prodigal Son did. It is an *after-mind.* John the Baptist preached to the Jews that this change of mind or after-mind was necessary to their reception of the Messiah (Matthew 3:1-3). Jesus preached that the same change of mind was necessary if He was to be accepted as the Messiah (Mark 1:14,15). Peter preached this change of mind if Christ was to be received as Saviour and Lord (Acts 2:36-38).

Repentance after this sort is not mere sorrow for sin, nor reformation of life, nor faith, nor godly sorrow—it refers to a moral judgment of self in the presence of the goodness and holiness of God. It is a thorough awakening of the conscience to the reality of sin, and abandonment of it, a deep, soul-searching process. How lacking this aspect is today, when conscience is so feebly addressed!

Metamelomai—This further word implies "regret," "to have after-care," or "annoyance at the *consequences* of sin rather than a deep regret at the *cause* from want of knowing better." This "after-sorrow" word, occurring five times, expresses regret with little reference to sin (II Corinthians 7:8). With Judas it was deep remorse (Matthew 27:3,4), a sorrow of the world working death. Such remorse, however, is not a saving repentance (II Corinthians 7:9,10). It is this word that is used of God, and signifies a change of action or dealing. The New Testament use of the word declares *unchangeableness* of His action (Romans 11:29; Hebrews 7:21). The Corinthians, although carnal Christians, repented because they did not want to be a continual reproach to Christ. It is impossible for an unsaved person to exercise godly sorrow. He is ungodly and nothing godly can come out of ungodliness.

Metanoia—Here we have a word signifying a real change of mind and attitude toward sin itself, and the cause of it— not merely the consequence of it—which affects the whole life and not merely a single act. It has been defined as "a change in our principle of action from what is, by nature, the exact opposite." It appears some 24 times (except in Hebrews 12:17) and expresses a real and genuine repentance toward God. It is associated with the Holy Spirit and is connected with the remission of sins and the promises of salvation.

The Hebrew word rendered "repent," translated 40 times in the Old Testament, is given as "comfort" some 65 times. When a sinner repents, turns to God through Christ, he is sure to be comforted by the touch of the divine hand. The Chinese proverb has it, "Repentance is the May of virtues." When men repent in the Biblical way, a brighter and fairer day dawns.

Its Substance

Enlarging upon the foregoing meanings of the words used in Scripture for *repentance,* it may be profitable to consider false and true views of such a basic doctrine. Because right thinking is essential to right living, let us go to the heart of the matter.

This negative approach brings us to what a man is prone to think repentance is. Satan, who seeks to counterfeit any Bible truth, has certainly succeeded in creating a false estimation of the one we are presently considering.

Repentance is not the mere presence of tears. Some people have a natural softness and tenderness of heart. It is easy for them to weep. Their liquid grief flows over the least thing. They weep easily over another's misery, but never over their own sinful condition. The story of the cross appeals to their pity, and they shed drops of grief —not because it was their sin that nailed Christ to the cross, but simply because He suffered so. Their tears are not of the repenting kind.

Further, superficial tears are of no avail. When afflicted, many cry, "Lord, have mercy on me!" Ahab rent his clothes, but not his heart (I Kings 21:27). His eye was watery, but his heart was like flint! How many there are who are made sensible of their sin and who shed copious tears, but who, after the tempest of conscience is past, have dry eyes! Walter Scott, in *Rob Roy* has the line, "But with morning cool repentance came."

Good notions are not repentance. We know only too well that bad notions can be stirred up in the godly, and good notions in the ungodly. Herod had good thoughts and inclinations as he listened to John's preaching, but never truly repented. He murdered the Baptist, and lived on in his sin.

Solemn vows and resolutions are likewise substituted for repentance. In times of adversity, promises are made to God, but as quickly forgotten as made, when brighter days dawn. How many there are who, upon a bed of sickness, covenanted with the Lord to follow and serve Him if only He would raise them up! Graciously He restored them, but their part of the bargain was not kept, and they walk about as a living lie.

Repentance is not necessarily the leaving off of sins. True repentance, of course, results in the abandonment of all that is alien to God's holy will. Too often, however, people exchange one sin for another. There may come reformation in one direction, but degeneration in another. All counterfeit repentance, then, must be shunned. If a broken bone sets wrong,

the surgeon must break it again and set it right. All who desire to be born anew must be deeply convicted of sin in the divinely prescribed way. Seneca says that, "He who repents, having sinned, is almost innocent." But repentance is not salvation nor innocency. Repentance cannot save. Christ alone can blot out the sin of a guilty past.

Sir John Vanbrugh, in *The Relapse*, has the couplet:

Repentence for past crimes is just and easy,
But Sin-no-more's a task too hard for mortals.

Repentance after God's order is always just but never easy. To sin no more is indeed a task too hard for mortals, but through grace they can sing, "Thanks be unto God, who giveth us the victory!"

What It Is!

Several ingredients make up genuine repentance. First of all, there is *humiliation* (Leviticus 26:41), revealed in "attrition," that is, the breaking of the heart as when a rock is broken; God's word as a hammer functions in this way (Jeremiah 23:9). Then there is *contrition,* or that brokenness of heart referred to as the smiting of the breast (Luke 18:13); plucking of the hair (Ezra 9:3); watering the couch with tears (Psalm 6:6). The Word of God, as fire, melts the heart, as heat melts ice into water. All humiliation, however, does not end in deep contrition. There must be a sincere *grieving* for sin because of its dishonor to God, as well as its defilement of the soul (Jeremiah 31:18,19). "The seal is set upon the wax when it melts; God seals His pardon upon melting hearts."

If, in repentance, sin is only regarded as a failure of duty to one's self, or one's neighbors, due to natural infirmity, then repentance for wrong doing will not be accompanied by deep conviction. But if sin is seen to be against God—an infraction of His will, a challenge to His authority, a reflection on His wisdom, a doing despite to His love—then a true repentance will be wrung from the soul, and in the throes of penitence, it will be abased before God. Too many are sorry simply because their sin has been discovered; the shame of exposure hurts their pride. Others are disturbed by reason of the temporal loss or suffering sin entails. Few seem to be moved to contrition by a sight of the vileness of sin, and by the fact that it is evil toward a good and holy God. Sin defiles the soul's glory; it is a plague, a sore; it changes glory into shame (Joshua 7:11; I Kings 8: 38), and must be repented of. Such unrepented sin has the devil for its father; shame for its companion; death for its wages (Romans 6:23). Without this repentance, there is final damnation.

There is no sacrifice so pleasing to God as a broken spirit—broken because of the sight of the heinousness of sin (Psalm 51: 17). Repenting tears of this sort are the joy of God and of angels (Luke 15:7-10). Mary brought her tears and ointment to the feet of Jesus (Luke 7:38). Of the two, the tears were more precious to Him. There is also sweetness in repenting tears. "Weeping days become festival days." The Hebrew word for "repent," *nicham*, means "to take comfort." Sorrow is turned to joy (John 16:20). Christ turns the water of tears into wine. Through a Spirit-produced repentance, although bitter at first, comes true sweetness. God comforts those who mourn for sin committed against Him (Isaiah 57:18). One of old cried, "Lord, wash my tears in Thy blood." When "we drop sin with our tears, we need Christ's blood to wash them."

Matthew Henry's comment is—

> Repentance is a daily duty: He that repents every day for the sins of every day, when he comes to die will have the sins of only one day to repent of. Short reckonings make long friends.

With "contrition" there is "confession" and "conversion," or a turning to God. "We have sinned"—this is confession; "They put away their strange gods" (Judges 10: 15,16)—this is conversion. The repentant confession of sin is not for the ears of a priest or a man, but God only (Psalm 51: 4). Such confession should never be more public than the sin confessed. Confession of this sort shuts the mouth of hell and opens the gates of Paradise (Psalm 32:5). Negative and positive sides are herewith combined. We confess our sin, and turn from it to God. This is "repentance toward God" (Acts 20:21), and results in remission. Such a repentance, however, is a condition, not the cause of salvation. Christ alone can save, and once He blots out our confessed sin, sin must be forsaken. "If we hide one rebel, then we are traitor to the crown."

Transformation follows, seeing that a genuine repentance works a change in the whole man. After the recognition of wrongness and wrongdoing (Joshua 7:6; I Samuel 7:6; 15:24; Luke 15:18; I John 1:19), and the putting away of same, a change is recognized in many directions. For instance, there is a change of mind (Matthew 21:29; II Timothy 2:25). As we have already seen, one Greek word for repent means "after-wisdom." Realizing how corrupt and deformed we were, and how damnable our sin was, our mind is changed concerning its nature. We become penitent. Repentance brings a change of judgment (Jonah 2:9; Acts 26:9; cf. Philippians 1:8). Feelings are reversed (Job 42:6; II Chronicles 33:12). Action and attitude are changed (Ezekiel 18:28; I Thessalonians 1:9,10). Affections are transformed. We come to hate what we once loved (Psalm 119:104). Instead of rejoicing in sin, there is sorrow for it. Life as a whole is completely revolutionized, seeing that God begins with the heart. Mary Magdalene, who kissed her loves lustfully, came to kiss Christ's feet in worship. The break with sin must be through. All sin, whether secret, habitual or public, must be shunned, not out of fear, but because of a disgust for sin produced by a vision of divine holiness and sacrifice for sin (Daniel 4:27). Repentance toward God must mean a spiritual divorce lasting until death. It is not enough to repent for our sin, we must leave it and become lost in God's service. The repenting Prodigal not only came to himself; he came to his father. Leaving the harlots and the swine, he was reinstated in the joys and privileges of sonship. When repentance is true, then the heart turns directly to God as the needle of the compass to the north pole, and the fruit and works worthy of repentance follow (Matthew 3:8; Luke 3:8-14; Acts 26:20 R.V.).

Its Source

From what does genuine repentance spring? How is it produced? What are the forces responsible for its upsurge within the soul? At the outset it must be made clear that repentance is not penance. No one can be saved without repentance. None are ever saved on account of their repentance. Human nature is prone to gather merit out of something it can do or feel. Salvation, however, does not come through some penitential act or meritorious work, but only as a gift, a free gift, from God.

Strange though it may seem, repentance is produced, not by the threats of divine wrath and judgment, but by the goodness of God (Romans 2:4; Jonah 4:2). Repentance is the gift of God, and not the work of an unbelieving man, which he must perform; neither is it a burden he must bear in order to move the pity of God. It comes as the gift of the risen Saviour (Acts 5:31; 11:18), and of God (Acts 11:18; II Timothy 2:25). It is wrapped up in the scheme of saving grace (Romans 7:23; Ephesians 2:8,9). Repentance is a pure Gospel of grace, and is wrought out through the Gospel as it sets the Crucified One before our eyes.

If repentance could aid the sinner in procuring the favor of God, then it would be a work of which he could boast. But salvation and all leading to it is entirely of grace. Man may look at his depravity and vile sin for a hundred years and never repent, but when he sees Christ dying for his sins, then he sees in God the posture of a broken-hearted Father beseeching a wayward son to be reconciled (Jeremiah 31:18-30; II Corinthians 5:20,21). Repentance, then, is God's sovereign gift, is produced by His goodness, and is unto life (Acts 11:18).

Further, repentance is always connected with faith. The repentance is toward God, while faith is toward our Lord Jesus Christ (Acts 20:21). Both repentance and faith are necessary to salvation, and both are simultaneous acts in the sinner convicted of his sin. Repentance and faith are inseparable. As there can be no faith without repentance, so there can be no valid repentance without faith (Mark 1:15; Luke 16:30,31). The convicted sinner must be careful not to be occupied with his repentance, but rather with Christ. He must not look within and watch his repentance but look out at Christ. If the truth of His saving grace is not understood, then all the groans and moans the sinner is capable of will never save. If Christ has been accepted by faith, then a Biblical repentance has been experienced (Hebrews 11:6).

Dryden suggests that repentance is "the virtue of weak minds" which agrees with Byron's assertion that "the weak alone repent." But repentance is not of man. It is God-produced. The Spirit is the One convicting men of their need. Repentance is

much more than sorrow or anguish of spirit, although some is present (II Corinthians 7:10). Too often such sorrow is compounded with repentance. Esau found no repentance in spite of his tears (Hebrews 12:17). Tears in themselves, are no evidence of a genuine repentance. Unless the sinner sees himself as being utterly worthless, he will never turn to God and accept the gift of His grace. Repentance toward God is essential to salvation. When repentance unto life is exercised and experienced, the sinner turns from resting upon anything self may do to resting entirely in Christ (Luke 13:3,5; II Peter 2:9). The best way to preach repentance, then, is to believe on Christ (John 6:29). The manifestation of His grace ever imparts a true sense of unworthiness and need. "Repentance is the tear faith drops when Christ is received for sins."

Its Subjects

Repentance is God's command to all men, and everywhere (Acts 17:29,30).

Sinners Must Repent

Irrespective of nationality, position or condition, sinners are called to repentance (Acts 5:31; 20:21; 26:20; Matthew 9:13; Luke 15:17,19; 24:47; II Peter 3:9). Saving repentance is the sinner's forsaking of his own ways, the giving up of his own thoughts, and his full surrender to Christ. Repentance is not something the sinner must do to win God's compassion. It is no protracted agony of soul, but a repentance to the acknowledging of the truth (II Timothy 2:24,25). Repentance ushers in pardon for the sinner—it makes way for God's pardoning grace (Acts 5:31). When David was humbled and broken because of his sin, Nathan said, "The Lord hath put away thy sin" (II Samuel 12:13). Pardon is the richest of blessings for the repentant, believing sinner. "Pardoning mercy is the sauce that makes all other mercies taste the sweeter; it sweetens our health, riches and honor."

No matter how black a person's sins may be, God's pardon is the basis of repentance. "If thy sins are as rock, yet upon thy repentance, the sea of mercy can drown them" (Isaiah 1:16-18). When the head is as a fountain to weep for sin, Christ's side is seen as a fountain to wash away that sin. It is not the greatness of sin that destroys, but the lack of genuine, saving repentance. Such repentance results in humility, obedience and practical righteousness (Luke 3:8-18; 24:47; Acts 3:19-21; II Corinthians 7:10).

The time for the sinner's repentance is *now*. While he has opportunity and desire, he should repent of his sins and accept Christ (Acts 17:30; Revelation 9:20,21; 16:9-11). Too many wait until they are about to die before repenting. "Death-bed repentance seldom reaches to restitution." A late repentance may be unable to make restitution for past sin, but it can result in salvation. The dying thief who repented and believed had no time to make restitution for his crimes, yet he was saved on the stroke of twelve. But how mean and contemptible it is to delay one's salvation to a death-bed repentance. Sinners should be urged to repent and give God a life He can use in His service.

Saints Have Need of Repentance

The Book of Revelation presents us with a direct call from Christ to His Church to repent. As the seven churches described in Revelation 2 and 3 present different phases of church history from Pentecost to the Rapture, how apt is the message of repentance when applied to those bearing His name.

Ephesus left her first love, and had to repent and return to her first works, or lose the privilege of witness (Revelation 2:4,5).

Pergamos, forgetting her spiritual calling, became guilty of sensuality and priesthood, and had to choose between repentance or judgment (Revelation 2:16).

Thyatira tried to undo the adultery and abominable practices of Jezebel, and had to repent or suffer tribulation (Revelation 2:21,22).

Sardis, like so many today, had a name to live, but was dead. Repentance or retribution was left to her choice (Revelation 3:3).

Laodicea, type of the organized, apostate church of today, was taken up with her own possessions. Her greatest Possession had been crowded out, and left on the doorstep. Repentance is her only road to spiritual recovery (Revelation 3:19).

The repentance of an erring *saint* is before us in Luke 22:61,62, and that of a failed and failing assembly in II Corinthians 7:8-11. Each of us, if the Lord's, have sins and failures calling for repentance. Portius Cato said that he had only three things of which he repented, namely,

"When he revealed a secret to his wife;
When he had passed a day in idleness;
When he had journeyed by sea to any place accessible by land."

The second reason for repentance is common to us all. The best of us fail to redeem the time. Killing time is a murder all of us must account for. Shakespeare refers to repentance in *Hamlet*: "Repent what's past; avoid what is to come." To which we can add the Greek proverb, "Forethought is better than repentance."

The question arises, Should repentance be particular or general? Whether we think of the repentant sinner or saint, the answer is, both.

Particular. Specific sins that weigh on the conscience should be confessed and forsaken, and forgiveness sought. "*My* sin is ever before me" (Psalm 51:3,4). If others have been injured by a particular sin, confession and reparation may also be due them.

General. Often repentance is ineffectual because it is too general. Yet, because there are times when the sense of innate sinfulness overshadows the recollection of individual acts of transgression, we can but pray, "God be merciful to me, a sinner" (Luke 18:13). What we *do* is the fruit of what we *are*. Too often we forget that "there is more guilt in the sinfulness of our nature than in all our actual transgressions." We repent over the *fruit*, but not over the *root*. Tears flow for *sins* but we neglect to repent over *sin*—the polluted source of the tainted stream.

Christ and His Baptism Unto Repentance

"Holy, harmless and undefiled, and separate from sinners," Jesus had no need of repentance. As the Sinless One, He never had a guilty conscience. Yet the Bible does not explain why, needing no repentance, Christ submitted to a rite signifiying confession of sins (Matthew 3:6). John's "baptism" was unto repentance (Matthew 3:11), meaning that the water-burial was an outward sign of an inward work of God. Repenting of their sins, those who responded to the preaching of John confessed they were sinners and turned to God. Submission to baptism testified to the world around that a spiritual and moral change had taken place. But Christ had no need to bring forth fruits meet to repentance. He never deviated one hair's breadth from the will of God. Why, then, did He submit to a rite associated with repentance? His own explanation is given in the command, "Suffer it to be so now: for thus it becometh us to fulfil all righteousness (Matthew 3:15). Dr. C. I. Scofield's suggestive comment on this verse is worthy of consideration:

> John's baptism was the voice of God to Israel, and the believing remnant responded (v. 3). It was an act of righteousness on the part of Him who had become, as to the flesh, an Israelite, to take His place with the believing remnant. Christ's baptism was a presentation of His identification with the sinners He had come to save. Knowing no sin, He was yet made sin for us.

God Sometimes Repents

It mystifies some minds to read that God repents. This we know, that whatever the nature of the divine repentance, it cannot be like that required of us. "The strength of Israel will not lie nor repent, for He is not a man that He should repent." H. S. Miller, answering the question, Does God Repent? says, "No, and Yes."

First of all, God does not repent. Some of His statements are absolutely unconditioned. When Saul disobeyed and rebelled against God's command in regard to the slaying of the Amalekites, God absolutely and finally rejected him as king, and no amount of acknowledgment of sin and pleading for pardon could cause Him to repent, or turn from His purpose (I Samuel 15:23-29). But He did not repent from making Saul king and sent Samuel to anoint David (I Samuel 15:35; 16:1). He declared Christ to be a Priest after the order of Melchizedek, and He will not repent (Psalm 110:4; Jeremiah 4:27,28; Hebrews 7:21).

In the second place, there are times when God does repent, but with this difference. Man's repentance implies a change of mind, leading to a change of life—God's repentance is a change of circumstances and relations. Many of God's promises are conditional, and when people repent of their evil, He repents, or turns from punishment and realizes for the penitent the blessings of His promises. This principle is before us in Jeremiah 18:5-10; Exodus 32:10-14. Usually repentance, when used of God, signifies not only a change of action or dealing, but the unchangeableness of His actions (Romans 11:19; Hebrews 7:21). "God's repentance is the unmovedness of Himself," says Edersheim, "while others move and change. The divine finger ever points to the same spot; but man has moved from it to the opposite pole. As in all repentance there is sorrow, so, reverently let it be said that is true of God. It is God's sorrow of love as, Himself unchanged and unchanging, He looks at the sinner who has turned from Him." What a stay for our hearts is the truth of God's unchangeableness! "I am the Lord, I change not" (Malachi 3:6).

XVII

The Doctrine of Regeneration

In Christian circles, *conversion* and *regeneration* are treated as being the one and same experience. They are used as interchangeable terms. But although the two events are closely related and cannot exist apart from each other, there is yet a clearly marked doctrinal distinction between them proving that a closer study should not be ignored. An evidence of the difference between *conversion* and *regeneration* can be found in Christ's forewarning of Peter.

Our Lord predicted the denial by His disciples, and also spoke of Peter's repentance and return in the words, "When thou art *converted*, strengthen thy brethren" (Luke 22:32). In this declaration of future usefulness after Peter's restoration, Jesus did not imply that Peter was not one of His. Peter had been a true disciple for over three years. The word *converted* simply means *turned again*.

Peter was about to shamefully deny his

Master and reach the depths of despair. In effect, Jesus is saying, "Peter, you are about to grieve and fail Me, but when you realize your sin and repent and return to Me in humble surrender, I will make you a greater channel of blessing than you ever were in the past." And Peter *turned back*, and became the apostle to the Jews. Like Peter, then, a person may backslide and yet in penitence turn back to God.

Tracing the Biblical usage of *conversion*, we find it mentioned five times in the Old Testament (Psalm 19:7; 51:13; Ihaiah 1:27; 6:10; 60:5) and then times in the New Testament (Matthew 13:15; 18:3; Mark 4:12; Luke 22:32; John 12:40; Acts 3:19; 15:3; 28:27; James 5:19,20). Two ideas seem to underlie the employment of the term, namely—

1. The act of turning to God
2. The act is a human one, rather than a divine act.

Conversion is set forth as the act of an individual turning to God. In the Revised Version, the verb is changed from the passive to the active voice. Thus, "lest they be converted" reads "lest they turn." In a study of this theme the Revised Version should always be consulted, seeing it enables one to fix the precise meaning of the terms and also define its relation to *regeneration*. Suffice it to say at this point that regeneration and conversion are distinct yet indissolubly connected.

Regeneration is God's act in the soul, and once accomplished, can never be repeated. "What God doeth is forever."

Conversion is the act of the individual in which he turns to God. Being a human act, it can be repeated many times.

Regeneration is the introduction of a new life.

Conversion is the first exercise in such a direction.

Regeneration is the inward expression of which *Conversion* should be the outward expression.

A good deal of what we know as "backsliding" is attributable to a deficient understanding of the difference between conversion and regeneration. In many so-called "revivals," scores are "converted" but not "regenerated." A person cannot be regenerated without being converted, but he can be converted without being regenerated. Under the impact of the preached Word, consciences are stirred and the

God and the sinner actually met? Often the lack of separation from the old life, the absence of desire for the things of God so necessary to spiritual growth, prove that there was a profession without possession— a conversion without regeneration. Deep emotional feelings and a movement toward God there might have been, but absence of any change in life indicates that those concerned were not born of the Spirit, so they are called "backsliders." But are we justified in speaking of them in this way? A Bible backslider is one who has had an experience of God's grace within the soul, but who allowed his testimony to be eclipsed for awhile by sin. Peter was a backslider, but he knew the Lord. Although there was the temporary denial of Christ, yet Peter had had three wonderful years with the One whose deity he had declared (Matthew 16:18). The look Jesus gave Peter brought him to a realization of his sin, and he wept bitterly. Turning again to the Master he had denied, fully restored, Peter declared his undying love for Jesus (John 21); and became a mighty soul-winner (Acts 2); and also a strengthener of the brethren (I, II Peter).

The Necessity of Regeneration

Although it was to Nicodemus, a man highly educated and deeply religious, Jesus said, "Ye *must* be born again," yet this is an imperative every soul must face. One of the most complete studies on "The New Birth" which we have encountered is that by Alfred Gibbs, published by the Walterick Publishing Company, Fort Dodge, Iowa. All who preach the Gospel should read, mark and inwardly digest this unique brochure costing only 50 cents. In his "Introduction," Alfred Gibbs says that there are three things each person *must* do— . . . . . .

He must die. The confession of all humanity is found in II Samuel 14:14, "We must needs die," which agrees with Hebrews 9:27, "It is appointed unto men once to die . . ."

He must meet God. Sinners will have to face God with disastrous consequences to themselves. "Every one of us shall give an account of himself to God" (Romans 14:12).

He must be born again. The subject of the new birth should have the sober and earnest consideration of all men, seeing that apart from it, there is no hope whatever of eternal blessedness (John 3:3,7). All who assume to be spiritual leaders must understand this doctrine and have undergone the fundamental change themselves.

The theme before us is of vital importance, seeing that a rebirth is the only gateway into the kingdom. "Except a man be born again, he cannot see . . . he cannot enter into the kingdom of God." Yet there is no New Testament doctrine so grossly misunderstood as the new birth. As the unsaved hear it preached, their minds are confused as Nicodemus' was, when he said, "How can a man be born when he is old?" Too many people in our churches who are religious but not regenerated, find preaching about the necessity of being born anew is in phraseology beyond their comprehension. To them, regeneration is an enigma. Therefore, for the benefit of Christian workers, let us try to express this basic truth as clearly and simply as possible.

1. The Terms Used

The word *regeneration* occurs only twice in Scripture, and, in each case, signifies a *new beginning*, or the act of a new birth. In Titus 3:5, the term is associated with the spiritual rebirth of the individual, or more exactly, with the believer's *new* and outward place on earth, into which baptism has introduced him, hence the phrase, "the washing of regeneration." *Regeneration*, in Matthew 19:28, refers to that *new* and outward change of things on earth which Peter describes as "the restitution of all things," that is, the Millennium (Acts 3:21). Fausset reminds us that "Besides his natural birthday, the believer has a spiritual birthday in this life, and a birthday to glory in the life to come."

The one *regeneration* involves the other. The divine process beginning with the individual, "the new man" (Ephesians 4:24) widens out to the utmost range of creation. "I make all things new" (Revelation 21:5). While we have come to speak of a regenerated person as one born of the Spirit, yet the terms "new birth" and "regenerated" are not as interchangeable as we think, even although both are true of the individual. Walter Scott puts it,

Regeneration is an *objective* state or condition, while the new birth is the expression of an inward or *subjective* one. "The washing of regeneration" can only

be witnessed by the eye of God as it indicates an internal condition. We may here remark that "the renewing of the Holy Spirit" is not the same as new birth by the Spirit. The former is a process, a "renewing," and the latter is an act effected at once, finally, and in its nature incapable of repetition.

Kindred terms are "born again" (John 3:3,7; I Peter 1:3,23); "born (or begotten —same word in original) of God" and "born of Him" (John 1:13; I John 2:29; 3:9; 4:7; 5:1,18); "born of the Spirit" (John 3:5,6,8). First John is conspicuous as the epistle of the new birth. The words "born" and "begotten" occur ten times.

2. The Necessity of the New Birth

The third chapter of John presents us with one of the conversational sermons of Jesus. Some of the greatest truths He uttered were given to individuals. The fourth chapter is a further proof of this fact, when Jesus speaks to the woman at the well of the necessity of spiritual worship.

Nicodemus was the high churchman, yet totally ignorant of spiritual truth. He was a cultured, courtly, educated, thoughtful and even religious man, but he had a heart destitute of grace. He needed to be born anew, or born from above (John 3:6), and our Lord's declaration places the necessity of the new birth beyond all possibility of doubt and religious misapprehension. His language leaves no room for argument, neither can caviling modify its force, "Ye must be born again."

Two things create this necessity, namely, the nature of the human heart, and the nature of heaven.

The Nature of the Human Heart

Man is born in sin (Psalm 51:5) and needs to be born again. By reason of sin, the sinner is spiritually dead and cannot receive the impartation of new life (Romans 8:6; Ephesians 2:1; I Timothy 5:6; Revelation 3:1). Apart from God, he cannot perceive or understand the things of God (I Corinthians 2:14), and must be reborn, if he is to "see" and "enter" the presence of God (John 3:35). Being unregenerate, he lacks eyes to see the kingdom and the power to enter. He also has no affinity with the Spirit and capacity for spiritual things. Without the Spirit, the sinner is "a child of the devil" (John 8:44; I John 3:10). When born again, he becomes a child of God (John 1:12). The false teaching abroad today that all men are the children of God needs to be opposed strenuously. The unregenerated are children of their father, the devil (John 8:44).

The imperativeness of the new birth then rests upon a perfectly logical and reasonable basis. The need for such an essential experience should awake no wonder. This was why Jesus said, "Marvel not" (John 3:7). The reason for this divine birth is clear. At his first birth, the sinner received a *physical* life and a human nature. Through the new or second birth he receives a spiritual life and is made a partaker of the divine nature.

The Nature of Heaven

If the unregenerated person could go to heaven, he would be the most miserable person there, seeing he would not have a heavenly nature to enjoy the people and the provisions of heaven. Of course, without a new nature, none can enter heaven, but if entrance was possible, such a person would be most out of place. All who are destitute of the Spirit are in the flesh (Jude 19) and, if in the flesh, cannot please God or see Him (Romans 8:8). In regeneration, the Holy Spirit supplies one with a heavenly nature to go to heaven with.

O ye who would enter the glorious rest,
And sing with the ransomed the song of the blest,
The life everlasting, if ye would obtain,
Ye must be born again.

3. The Nature of the New Birth

It may be found profitable to discuss the negative and positive sides of this foundational truth. Because of misunderstanding regarding the exact composition of regeneration, even in religious circles, let us emphasize firstly—

What It Is Not

Regeneration is not the improvement of the old nature, but the impartation of a new nature. God will have nothing to do with the old Adamic nature with which we were "born into the wrong family." It stands forever condemned (Romans 6:6). God does not waste time whitewashing a filthy pump giving unclean water. Regeneration is not a mere outward reformation, or the turning over of a new leaf, but

the bringing in of a new life—a life that can never be developed or earned. There is a feeling in some circles that the new birth is a gradual process. Man has a germ of divine life within him, with which all are born, and all that is necessary is to cultivate the spiritual germ until it blossoms into a full Christian life. But the Bible declares the sinner to be spiritually dead and altogether destitute of life (I John 5:10-13). How, then, can a person develop what he does not possess? Spiritual life cannot be evolved—it is imparted by the Spirit.

The new birth, then, is a divine transformation, and comes as the gift of God (Romans 6:23). One's morality, good deeds, noble character, or even religiosity, cannot win them eternal life. Nicodemus came to know this. Alfred Gibbs says, "Reformation may be likened to a new *suit* for a man, but the new birth is a new *man* for the suit. The difference between reformation and regeneration is the difference that exists between whitewashing and washing white . . . Reformation deals with exterior things, but regeneration with *interior* realities. Reformation alters a person's manner; but regeneration alters the man himself." Lindsell and Woodbridge, in their most valuable volume, *A Handbook of Christian Truth*, speak of the average unregenerated person as "utilizing the wood of character and the nails of conduct, to construct a ladder to reach the gates of glory. His effort originates below, in his own will and purpose, and it cannot succeed. Life eternal originates above in the loving heart of God, and comes through regeneration."

Three negative and unavailing efforts are cited by John (1:13).

(a) Not of blood, or bloods.

Regeneration cannot be inherited, it is not hereditary. No sinner has an inborn, divine spark he or she can fan into a flame. Virtues and vices are transferred to us in physical birth, but no one can inherit the new birth from parents, even though they may be the saintliest who ever breathed. Regeneration is a personal necessity and a personal responsibility.

(b) Not of the will of the flesh.

The new birth does not come by way of self-effort or self-determination. We were not born, physically, by any desire or decision on our part. Just as our earthly parents were responsible for our entrance into the world, so God, by His Spirit, is responsible for our new birth and entrance into a spiritual realm.

(c) Not of the will of man.

No human influence or agency can produce a regenerated person. Many agencies exist for the reformation of a man. But law-keeping, good works, charitable activities, church associations, christening or baptism, culture or education cannot bring a dead soul to life. The prerogative of imparting life belongs to the Life-Giver above.

What It Is

Having seen what the new birth is not, let us find out what it actually is. H. S. Miller in *The Christian Worker's Manual* summarizes the positive side thus—

1. It is new or second birth (John 1:13; 3:3).
2. It is a cleansing process (John 3:5; Titus 3:5; Ezekiel 36:25).
3. It is a life-giving process (Ephesians 2:1,5,7).
4. It is God's piece of work, a creation in Christ Jesus (Ephesians 2:1,10).
5. It is a new creation (II Corinthians 5:17; Galatians 6:15).
6. It is a spiritual resurrection into a new life (Romans 6:4-6).
7. It is an exchange of hearts (Jeremiah 17:9; cf. Ezekiel 36:26).

Regeneration, as the word implies, involves a radical change of the profoundest character. It is not merely a change of opinion, habit or mode of life, but the impartation of a new disposition, aim and outlook. It is a condition of becoming "alive from the dead" (Romans 6:13); being "renewed in the spirit of your minds" (Ephesians 4:23); "putting on the new man" (Colossians 3:10). It is a transference to a new state "from the power of Satan to God" (Acts 26:18; Colossians 1:13).

One should hasten to say that the new birth does not represent the incoming of a new life principle, which the born again one can henceforth hold and use of himself. He is "quickened" and united to the risen Christ (Ephesians 2:5; Romans 6:4,5; 7:4; Colossians 3:3,4). There comes, through the creative act of the Holy Spirit, a participation in the life of Christ (John 14:19), membership in the body of which He is the Head (I Corinthians 12:12,13), union with the Vine (John 15:5). Regen-

erated, one can truly say, "I live: yet no longer I, but Christ liveth in me" (John 17:23; Galatians 2:20).

4. *The Agents in the New Birth*

Nicodemus asked two questions: "How can a man be born when he is old?" (John 3:4). Perplexed over Christ's teaching about being born again, the man of the Pharisees confused physical and spiritual birth. He could not understand the nature of such a birth. His second question, based upon a clearer comprehension of regeneration, was taken up with its method: "How can these things be?" (John 3:9). The narrative proves that there are divine and human agents working together in the rebirth of a soul.

The Divine Side

All three Persons of the Godhead are bound together in the regeneration of the soul. The basis of this divine work is the finished work of Christ. When Nicodemus asked, "How can these things be?" Jesus went on to say, "The Son of Man must be lifted up." Through redemption we have regeneration.

Born . . . of God (John 1:13).

The transaction giving regeneration, going deeply into the spirit-part of man, can only be effected by God the Spirit. All human agencies are unavailing, for God alone can bring about the new birth. No other but He can communicate a spiritual nature to those brought into His family by means of a spiritual birth.

(a) Born of the Spirit (John 3:6,8).

The Holy Spirit is the most active Agent in regeneration. As the Spirit of life, that which is born of Him is spirit and life. He it is who convicts of sin, applies the efficacious blood and turns from the guilt and government of sin to God. The Spirit cleanses, quickens, renews (Titus 3:5). Alfred Gibbs says we should be thankful for the Holy Spirit for

He *wounds*, that He may *heal; exposes* our sin, that it might be *put away; convicts* us of our need, that He might *supply* that need by His regenerating power; produces *unrest*, that He might lead to the One who *gives rest;* shows us our guilt, that we might be guilty and receive God's pardon; shows us our dreadful *disease*, that we might be brought to know the Great Physician and be cured; makes us *miserable* and anxious about our state before God, that He might bring us to know the *joy* and peace of God's salvation.

As one of the divine Agents in the new birth, the Spirit is mysterious in operation. None can penetrate His secret work or diagnose His movements with the soul (John 3:8).

> I know not how the Spirit moves,
>   Convincing men of sin—
> Revealing Jesus through the Word,
>   Creating faith in Him.

(b) Born of Water (John 3:5).

Divergent views have arisen as to the exact meaning of being "born of water." We certainly reject what is known as "baptismal regeneration." There are those who utterly refuse any reference to water baptism, yet may we suggest that there must have been present to the mind of Christ the classic Old Testament promise of New Testament blessing, "I will sprinkle clean water . . . a new heart also will I give . . . I will put my Spirit within you" (Ezekiel 36:25-27), and that He here intimates that this promise was to be realized. To this fact must be added the echoes of the Baptist's call to the baptism of repentance, still vibrating in the minds of the people. This is why many interpret the words to signify that the new birth was a process of divine cleansing and spiritual renewal, and that this inward change was to be accompanied by water baptism as the outward symbol of admission into the kingdom.

Other writers see in the "water" a symbol of the Word of God, just as Jesus used "wind" as a symbol of the Spirit's operation. That the Scriptures are another divine agent in regeneration is clear from passages like John 15:3; Ephesians 5:26; I Peter 1:23; James 1:18; Psalm 119:9. One of the early saints said that the Holy Spirit rides best in His own chariot, the Bible.

The Human Side

While the Holy Spirit alone can regenerate, He never regenerates alone. On man's side, there are conditions to be observed. There is *repentance* over the sinful condition the Spirit revealed (Mark 1:15; Acts 20:21). There is also *faith*, which becomes operative as the Spirit presents Christ as Saviour (John 1:12; 3:14; I John 5:1). The moment faith receives Christ, the miracle of regeneration takes place.

With the human, objective side of the

new birth, our Lord used the illustration of Moses (John 3:14). The bitten Israelites had to look at the brazen serpent if they were to be healed and live. So the sinner looks to Jesus and by the act of faith yields to Him, and the Holy Spirit entering within the act of surrender, completes His work of re-creation.

A person had nothing to do with his first birth. He did not will it, or enter the world on his own volition. But with the new birth it is totally different, for a person wills his own salvation or damnation. God never forces the human will (John 7:17). Without the fulfilment of conditions on the sinner's part, God cannot accomplish His part in the impartation of a new life.

5. *The Results of the New Birth*

The spiritual benefits accruing from the work of regeneration in a soul are manifold. Let us outline a few of the privileges accompanying the new birth.

(a) The reception of a new Name.

Once saved, the sinner becomes a saint. He is no longer known as a child of the devil, but a child of God. Described as an "alien" he is now a "citizen" (Ephesians 2:12).

(b) The reception of a new Life.

Unregenerated, the sinner is dead (Ephesians 2:5). Alive physically, mentally, socially, he is yet dead in sins—dead while he lives. But the acceptance of Christ as Saviour brought life forevermore. "In *Him* (and only in Him) is life." *Spiritual* and *eternal* life are in Him who is alive forevermore (I John 5:12; Revelation 1:18).

(c) The reception of a new Relationship.

As our physical birth brings us into an earthly family relationship, so our spiritual birth ushers us into a heavenly relationship. God becomes our Father, and all who love Him become our brothers and sisters (Galatians 3:26; Romans 8:16,17).

(d) The reception of a new Creation.

All in Christ are a new creation—God's masterpiece in His role as Creator. Angels, the starry heavens and the wonderful earth, all works of His hands cannot compare with the fashioning of a saint (II Corinthians 5:17; Galatians 6:15; Ephesians 2:10). There is a blessed exchange of old things for new.

(e) The reception of a new Nature.

In regeneration, God does not take away the old Adamic nature with which we were born. This "old man" or "the man of old" remains within until our death or rapture at Christ's return. What happens is something unique, namely, the communication of a new nature of divine origin (II Peter 1:4). The new birth makes us new men (Ephesians 4:24; Colossians 3:10).

(f) The reception of a new Victory.

In the old life there is nothing but defeat. Sin is the master, and we are its slaves. But with the incoming of the Spirit, there is, in Him, victory over the world, flesh and devil. Born again one can exultingly sing, "Thanks be unto God who giveth us the victory!" By the blood of the Lamb we become overcomers (I John 3:9; 5:4,18; Revelation 12:11).

(g) The reception of a new Mind.

The word Paul uses for "mind" (Romans 12:2) covers thoughts, affections, purposes, desires. All inclinations for the things of the old life are taken away. This new "mind" is so effective seeing it is the mind of Christ, and the mind of the Spirit (Philippians 2:5). The carnal mind has little sympathy with divine things (Romans 8:7).

(h) The reception of a new Standing.

In our lost estate we had no "standing" with God. If we say that a person has no "social standing" we mean that he has not the financial and social fitness to meet the requirements social circles demand. By the believer's standing we mean his ability through grace to meet the holy requirements God demands. Regeneration makes us "accepted in the beloved" (Ephesians 1:6). In Christ, we are complete, and so near to God, that nearer we cannot be.

(i) The reception of a new Destiny.

As sinners, eternal death and destruction faced us. We were "without hope." But by the new birth all is changed. Now we have "the blessed hope" and the glorious assurance that when absent from the body, we shall be at home with the Lord (Philippians 1:6; II Corinthians 5:6-8; Philippians 1:23; I Thessalonians 4:16,17).

6. The evidences of the new Birth

As soon as a baby enters the world, there are many tokens of its arrival in a home. From its first cry, all around are aware of the coming of a new life. In like manner we, and others, quickly discover that the new birth is a reality. "We *know* that we have passed from death into life" (I John 3:14). The Spirit's incoming and indwelling are evidenced in many ways. The evidences are twofold.

Internal Evidences

The newly born may not be able to explain all that happened in their regeneration, yet with the man born blind, they can say, "One thing I know, that whereas I was blind, now I see" (John 9:25). Inner evidences are, at least, twofold—

(a) The Consciousness of a New Life.

Just as a living man has the consciousness of natural life, and cannot be argued out of the assurance this consciousness gives him, so the man made spiritually alive has the consciousness of a new and higher life, manifesting itself in the glow and throb of new affections, aims and outlook. An inner appetite for prayer and meditation upon Scripture is also begotten.

(b) The Witness of the Spirit.

Once the Spirit takes up His abode in a soul, He imparts to the believer the pledge and assurance that, being reborn, he is now a child of God (Romans 8:16; Galatians 4:6), with all the privileges of sonship. Regeneration restores to man all Adam had before his fall, with added blessings.

External Evidences

Outer marks of the new birth are new characteristics. Old things pass away. The fruits of the Spirit quickly manifest themselves in the outward life. Physical force is one evidence of physical life; thought and reason furnish evidence of intellectual life; so the fruits of the Spirit and the new spiritual activities of the transformed life prove the new birth. Other evidences are a change of companions, of pleasures, of interests. "All things become new." What was previously loved, is now hated. Sins hitherto relished are now abhorred. Regeneration brings with it a new set of values. The outer change may be more conspicuous in some lives than in others. A person brought up in a Christian atmosphere, who has never journeyed into deep and horrible sins, but who was religious in his ways, will not, when he turns to Christ, exhibit the same transformation of life as a man who was degraded and debauched in life. But whether moral or immoral makes little difference. Once the new birth takes place in a person, good or bad, there are changes evident to all around.

In conclusion, a word may be necessary as to the exact time of the new birth. The precise moment of our physical birth is known, for we have a birth certificate declaring when we were born. It is so with the spiritual birth of many. They know the very time and place where the transaction happened and they were born anew by the Spirit. "I was there when it happened," as the old Scotch fisherman put it when asked how he knew that he was saved. But there are others who do not know the precise hour of their new birth. Born into and brought up within a Christian home, they somehow grew up in the faith without an exact time of their regeneration. Yet because all who love the Lord have been regenerated, the miracle must have happened, if not as consciously as in the case of others. The matter of primary importance is not the record of the happy day that fixed our choice, but the inner assurance of salvation and the Spirit's constant witness to sonship.

XVIII

The Doctrine of Substitution

The familiar word "substitute" simply means "a person or thing put in place of another," or "to exchange." It was quite a military term when a friend could enlist for military service in the place of a conscript or a drafted man. Many years ago in the war between France and Germany, a summons went out to Germans residing in England to take their place with the troops at Paris. At that time a man was walking along the streets of London, when he met a German friend. Surprised to see him there, he asked why he was not in France.

"Oh, I am dead!" was his answer.

"Dead! What do you mean?" asked his friend.

"Let me explain," said the German. "My name was called among others and I thought I should have to leave England; but I had no wish to do so and I set to work to find some way by which I might escape. The command was stringent, so that it was impossible to evade it, but at length I found a substitute, willing for a sum of money to take my place. I gladly paid the sum, and am thankful that I was free to remain in England. My substitute, however, had not been many days with the German Army when a French shell burst close to where he was standing, and he was killed. He was there for me, his death was counted as mine, so in the eye of the law, I am dead, and the German nation has no further claim upon me."

Substitution, then, means one man taking the place of another and answering for him, giving his life to fight and die in the other man's stead.

Turning to Christ, we believe His substitutionary work to be the heart of the Gospel. In fact, it is a glorious Gospel in itself. While many theories of the cross have been advanced, the simplest unfolding of it is the truth of Christ dying in our room and stead. C. H. Spurgeon was fond of saying that his theology could be summarized in the four words, "He died for me." Christ dying as our Substitute alone answers the question of God remaining just and yet becoming the Justifier of those who believe in Him. (Romans 3:26).

Ancient Types of Substitution

Israelites of old clearly understood the import of substitution. It was the basis of many of the Tabernacle offerings. The creatures acceptable for sacrifice were the bullock or ox; the sheep or lamb; the goat; the turtle dove or pigeon, but running through all the sacrifices was the idea of substitution. "It shall be accepted for Him (in his stead) to make an atonement for him" (Leviticus 1:4). In a most impressive way the sweet-savor offerings typify the substitutionary character of Christ's work at Calvary.

The offerer had to identify himself with his offering. "He shall put his hand upon the head of the burnt-offering" (Leviticus 1:4). By so doing there was the transference of the offerer's guilt to the lamb, and also the transference of the virtues of the lamb to the offerer. When the sinner lays the hand of faith upon the dear head of the Lamb of

God, and accepts Christ as his Sin-Offering, his Substitute, then identification takes place and the same double transference is realized. Trusting Him to remove our guilt, the Substitute makes us the recipients of His grace.

In the yearly return of that solemn and deeply impressive atonement day (Leviticus 16), two goats were presented before the Lord, the one was Jehovah's lot, while the other was for the people. One goat was killed and its blood carried within the veil and sprinkled *once upon* the Mercy-Seat and *seven times before it*. The other goat was presented alive before the Lord, and the sins of the people confessed over it by the high priest. Here we have portrayed the two parts of Christ's work—glorifying God by the shed and sprinkled blood, and bearing away the sins of the people—when regarded as a whole, constitutes atonement. Propitiation and substitution are inseparable. *Propitiation* answers to the blessed work done within the veil and before the eyes of God; *substitution* refers to the transference of sins to the head of the scapegoat and its dismissal to a land not inhabited.

The offering of the two birds alive and clean (Leviticus 14:4) by a leper tells the same story. One bird was slain and the live bird then dipped in the blood of the slain bird, and released, illustrating for us the two blessed aspects of our salvation. Christ "delivered for our offences and raised again for our justification" (Romans 4:25).

For the most striking type of Christ's substitutionary work, we have to turn back to Abraham and his son Isaac on Mount Moriah (Genesis 22). In obedience to divine command, Isaac was bound and placed upon the altar. Abraham, with raised knife ready to slay his son of promise, was halted by the angel of the Lord, and beheld a ram caught in a thicket by his thorns. Abraham took the ram and offered him up for a burnt offering *in the stead of* his son (Genesis 22: 13). We speak of Isaac as a type of Christ, who as God's only begotten Son, was obedient unto death, and so He is. But Christ is also seen in the ram offered up as Isaac's substitute. As the consecrated Ram, Christ the Substitute was offered up in our stead.

> Wherefore when he cometh into the world, he saith, Sacrifice and offering thou wouldst not, but a body hast thou prepared me; in burnt offerings and sacrifices for sin thou hast had no pleasure. Then said I, Lo, I come (in the volume of the

book it is written of me) to do thy will, O God. Above when he said, Sacrifice and offering and burnt offerings and offering for sin thou wouldest not, neither hadst pleasure therein; which are offered by the law; Then said he, Lo, I come to do thy will, O God. He taketh away the first, that he may establish the second. By the which will we are sanctified through the offering of the body of Jesus Christ once for all (Hebrews 10:5-10).

Caiaphas, the high priest, surely had an insight into Christ's substitutionary work when he said that it was "expedient that one man should die for the people" (John 18:14).

Attested Truth of Substitution

The cardinal doctrine of substitution is woven into the texture of the Scriptures. Both Testaments are eloquent with the truth that several things happened to Christ which should have overtaken us. Now, with Him as our personal Substitute, we are altogether free from guilt. Having no debt of His own to pay, He voluntarily paid our debt. The many claims of God against us, Christ offered to make His own, and now by His finished work we are fully, freely, and finally justified from all that was against us (Acts 13:38,39).

The simple word "for" used so often in connection with Christ and ourselves means "in behalf of." In what ways did Jesus take our place? Well, as H. S. Miller reminds us, the brazen altar placed in the outer court of the Tabernacle represents the substitutionary work of our Lord. The altar was foursquare (Exodus 27:1), and God has at least four charges against the sinner, and by His death Christ met and settled every one of them. The handwriting against us has been blotted out, and now with Christ as our Saviour-Substitute we are free.

We were sinners.

None are excluded from the category for "all have sinned." Irrespective of who or what we were, the Scripture concluded us all under sin (Galatians 3:22). But the glory of the Gospel is that Christ died for our sins. He "suffered for sins, the just for (instead of) the unjust, that He might bring us to God" (I Peter 3:18). He was made sin (not a sinner) for (insead of) us (II Corinthians 5:21). At the cross, we see

Jesus as the Lamb of God bearing away the sin of the world. He agonized upon the accursed tree in our room and stead. He bore God's displeasure against sin, instead of us. He paid the wages of sin (Hebrews 9:25).

We were under sentence of death.

Among God's specific statements as to sin and its results, there is this one that the sinning soul shall die (Ezekiel 18:4). Sin's wages is death—spiritual, physical and eternal death. Christ, however, *died* for (instead of) the ungodly. He tasted death for every man (Romans 5:6-8; 6:23; Hebrews 2:9,14,15). We stood before the bar of God condemned justly for our sins, and awaiting the execution of the sentence of death. But Christ, our Passover, was sacrificed for us and because He died for us and is alive for evermore, we share His life. "Because I live, ye shall live also" (John 14:19).

We were under a curse.

Inherent and persistent disobedience of God's law brought us under a curse. But as our Substitute, Christ became a curse for us (Galatians 3:13). This is why the cross is referred to as "the accursed tree." Offending even in one point of the law, we were guilty of all. Christ, however, was the obedient Son. He met every demand of God's holy and just law. He magnified it, became the end of it, and was alone able to become our Substitute in curse-bearing. By His cross, Christ has turned the curse into a blessing.

We were under wrath.

Sin occasioned the righteous wrath of God, and all sinners were under His wrath (Romans 1:18; Ephesians 2:3). What we too often forget is the solem truth that unsaved men and women are still under divine wrath (John 3:36). But Christ in His death became our propitiation, or wrath-offering. We have been saved from past and coming wrath (I Thessalonians 1:10). He bore the wrath due to our sins (Romans 3:25; 5:9; I Corinthians 5:7; cf. Exodus 12:3-14). In sight of God we have been punished for our sins, in the punishment His Son willingly endured.

Redeemed, we are now the special objects of the Father's love. Christ gave Himself for us (Galatians 2:20), and as one with Him we know that we have been crucified in the person of our Substitute. Ours was the sin—His the penalty. His was the

shame, ours the glory. His was the cross, ours the crown. When assailed by the devil for the past, we cry to our Substitute, "Answer for me, O Lord, our Righteousness!" In our place Christ stood condemned, outcast, forsaken of man and of God. Death and the curse were in our cup, but He drained it, and for us it is empty now. "That bitter cup, Love drank it up." But by His stripes and passion we are now healed.

There are other benefits accruing from Christ's substitutionary work at Calvary. Because He is our Substitute, we have—

1. His present, prevailing intercession in heaven (Romans 8:34; Hebrews 7:25)
2. The effective intercession of the Holy Spirit (Romans 8:26)
3. The constant protection of God from all foes (Romans 8:31)
4. Jesus within the Veil, pleading the efficacy of His blood (Hebrew 6:20; 9:24)
5. An eternal redemption (Hebrews 9:12)
6. Immediate access into the presence of God (Hebrews 10:19,20)
7. A compensating glory for earth's afflictions (Corinthians 4:17)

Apostolic Teaching of Substitution

Pentecost interpreted Calvary for the disciples. While Christ was among His own He had to tell them that there were many things they could not understand, but that when the Spirit came, He would shew them all things. "What I do thou knowest not, now, but thou shalt know hereafter." One of the great truths the Spirit illuminated for the apostles was the inner significance of Christ's ministry as the Substitute. Peter's message was vibrant with the truth that Christ "His own self bare our sins in His own body on the tree" (I Peter 2:24). "Christ also hath once suffered for sin" (I Peter 3:18). John also caught and taught this aspect of Christ's death. God "sent His Son to be the propitiation for our sin" (I John 4:10). Christ died as the Saviour of the world (John 3:16; I John 4:14). It would seem, however, that to Paul, more than to any other apostle, was given the most complete unfolding of all that was involved in Christ's voluntary death on our behalf. "Christ died for our sins" (I Corinthians 15:3). "He was made sin for (instead of) us" (II Corinthians 5:21). "He gave Himself for us" (Galatians 2:20).

"Christ died for the ungodly" (Romans 5:6).

Considering the teaching of the apostles, the question may arise, whose Substitute is Christ—the sinner's or the Christian's? Walter Scott remarks that "Universal bearing *of* sins by Christ necessarily involves the monstrous thought of universal salvation *by* Christ." In declaring the gospel of substitution, we must guard against Universalism and the denial of the justice of God. Christ is the Substitute of the believer, and becomes the sinner's Substitute once He is received as Saviour. Comparing the teaching of Peter and Paul, it would seem as if dying for sins and bearing sins are believers' truths. Substitution is the actual bearing of the sins of all believers (I Corinthians 15:3; I Peter 2:24).

Further, substitution is not *in* another, but *instead of* another. While we use the phrase, "We died *in* the Person of our Substitute," actually we did not die in Christ, else we must have shared in God's judgment on Christ on the cross. Because we are *in Christ*, we share in the benefits resulting from such a union. The condition of the Head of the race determines that of each member of it. Thus we are dead with Him to sin and to the law (Romans 6:7). We have been quickened, raised and seated with Him (Ephesians 2:5,6; Colossians 3:1). "It shall be accepted for him," not accepted *in*, but the reverse, "it for him" (Leviticus 1: 4). So we must "*preach* propitiation to sinners—the blood on the mercy seat, and God in righteousness and grace freely receiving all who will but come. *Teach* substitution to believers—their sins confessed and borne by Christ and never to be remembered."

It is not Biblical to urge sinners to lay their sins on Jesus. God accomplished this when He laid on Christ the iniquity of us all (Isaiah 51:6). Faith appropriates all that He accomplished. Strange though it may seem, the clearest and most appealing picture of Christ as our Substitute is found in the Old Testament, namely, in Isaiah 53, the chapter Philip used to lead the eunuch to accept Christ as his Substitute (Acts 8: 32-35). Isaiah presented Christ as—

A Bearing Substitute—"He hath borne our griefs" (53:4)

A Crushed Substitute – "Wounded" – "Bruised" (53:5)

A God-punished Substitute—"God laid on Him the iniquity of us all" (53:6)

A Silent Substitute—"He opened not His mouth" (53:7)

A Sinner's Substitute—"He was numbered with the transgressors" (53:12)

A Sin-made Substitute—"He was made an offering for sin" (53:10)

A Rewarded Substitute—"He shall see of the travail of His soul and be satisfied" (53:11).

XIX

The Doctrine of Redemption

Among the cardinal truths of our Christian faith, none demands our prayerful and intelligent consideration as that of redemption. Not only is it chief among the doctrines of grace—it permeates them all! It is from the spring of redemption that all the rivers of grace flow, for redemption is a most comprehensive term, being associated with regeneration, justification, adoption, sanctification and resurrection.

Thinking of the Bible as a whole, what would you say are the two inescapable truths forcing themselves upon our attention? Are they not *man's departure from God* and *God's deliverance of man?* Ruin and redemption can fittingly summarize the teaching of Scripture. In its broadest sense, redemption covers the entire work of God in Christ, delivering man from the guilt and government, penalty and presence of sin.

Approaching, then, this soul-thrilling theme of redemption, let us endeavor by the Spirit to answer a few questions.

What is the True Significance of Redemption?

It will be found most profitable to gather together the different words used by the Holy Spirit to express the truth of our deliverance from sin's condemnation and captivity, through the finished work of the Redeemer. Believing, as we do, in the verbal inspiration of Scripture, we know that its very words are worthy of our devout and careful study, seeing the Spirit never used a word without a special reason for its selction. How true this is in respect to the various terms employed to describe our Saviour's glorious redemption.

LUTROO

This word means "to loose by a price"; "the price paid for freeing a captive"; "to release by a ransom." It is used in this way in I Peter 1:18, "Forasmuch as ye know that ye were not redeemed with corruptible things, as silver and gold, from your vain conversation, received by tradition from your fathers"; and in Luke 1:68; Titus 2:14; Hebrews 9:12. With the prefixed preposition *from*, it is found in Luke 21:28; Romans 7:24; Ephesians 1:7,14; 4:30; Colossians 1:16. The thought resident in this term is that of release from bondage or captivity by the judgment of a ransom, the ransom being the precious blood of Christ. He is the One who, by His sacrifice, liberates the sinner from the control of sinful and foolish self by a most costly price to Himself. By "the expulsive power of a new affection," He substitutes His redeeming love as the governing principle, instead of the sinful selfishness hitherto degrading and disgracing the sinner. We were slaves of Satan, sold under sin, and utterly unable to ransom ourselves because of the absolute obedience due to God. No act of ours could satisfy for the least offense. But Christ became our Ransom (Matthew 20:28; I Timothy 2:6).

EXAGORAZO

Here is another "redemptive" word meaning "to purchase out"; "to buy up out of the possession of any one." Young, in his *Analytical Concordance*, renders it "to acquire out a forum," and it is the word used in Galatians 3:13; 4:4,5; Ephesians 5:16. A court of justice is represented by this word, with Christ claiming what He had bought. Having paid the ransom demanded by the law, Christ brings the sinner out from any further claims upon him, and leads him forth to liberty. Our Redeemer not only went into the market place to buy us, but brought us out of our captivity and set us free. Now Christ exhibits the ransom He paid, which perfectly met all the demands of the broken law of God.

"Now we are free, there's no condemnation." Paul makes it clear that Christ, by His ransom, redeemed us once for all and completely, so much so that there is now no condemnation burdening us (Romans 8:1).

PAD-dah

This third word, meaning "to set free, to let go," is translated "redeem" some 250 times (Deuteronomy 21:8; Psalm 34:22; Jeremiah 15:21; Hosea 7:13). When God liberated His oppressed people in Old Testament days, He set them free by the substitution of a spotless lamb to bear the merited stroke of death in their place and stead.

PAN-rak

This further Old Testament word means "to break off, to tear away, rescue, deliver" (Psalm 136:24). As used by the Psalmist, the verb denotes "a violent action," which is always characteristic of the Redeemer's delivering power. The Messianic aspect of this Psalm must not be lost sight of. When Christ returns to earth He will snatch His own away from their enemies. When He appears at the Judgment of the nations gathered against Jerusalem, His action will be swift and effective.

P'dooth

The word *division* used in Exodus 8:23, "I will put a *division* between my people and thy people," is the bloodword *redemption*, as the margin states it. The division made by the sprinkled blood of the spotless lamb was a redemption. The same word is found in Psalms 111:9; 130:7. If we have been redeemed by the precious blood of Christ, then there should be a division between us and the unbelieving world around.

GAH-al

This further Hebrew word implies not only "to redeem, ransom, recover," but also "to avenge," and brings into view the office of one who at once was kinsman, deliverer, redeemer, husband and avenger. It is found in Jacob's dying blessing (Genesis 48:16–to be free by avenging); in God's promise to Israel (Exodus 6:6); in Job's noble confession (19:25); in the Psalmist's song (Psalm 103:4); in Isaiah's prophecy (Isaiah 59:20); in God's word of cheer to Hosea (13:4). Such an application of this particular "redemption" term is full of promise for God's ancient people who have suffered much at the hands of godless rulers. When Christ returns, He will avenge His chosen people speedily. Christ will also, as our Kinsman-Redeemer, avenge us from the wrongs we have suffered at the hands of the world, death and the devil.

AGORAZO

Akin to the second word we considered (*exagorazo*), this carries a similar meaning, "to buy or purchase," and is found but three times in the Word, and then only in the book of Revelation (5:9; 14:3,4). This last word takes us up into heaven itself, when the Redeemer takes possession of His bought ones in the presence and amidst the glory of God. What a Redeemer He is! From the lowest degradation to the loftiest sublimity of bliss, He is our blessed Redeemer. His redemption will not cease until we are forever delivered from all iniquity. While Christ's redemption in all its fullness and power and everlasting efficacy is applied to us the moment we receive Him as our Saviour, yet completion will not be ours until we see Him face to face.

How Was Redemption Secured?

The Bible is a crimson Book. Repugnant though it may be to the modern, cultivated yet unregenerate mind, the fact remains that the Bible is a blood-drenched Book. From the hour God made coats of animal skins for fallen Adam and Eve, down to the millennial day, blood is seen as the purchase price of access to God. The saints can sing no other song than "Thou wast slain and hast redeemed us to God by Thy blood" (Revelation 5:9). Acquittal can only be claimed on the ground of a satisfied law. Christ bore the law's curse and suffered its condemnation of death. Apart from man's reception of Christ as Redeemer, there can be no acquittal.

Paul reminds us that we have been "bought with a price" (I Corinthians 6:20; 7:23). And what a price! Our English word for "redemption" means the act of bringing back from slavery, captivity, or death by the judgment of a price (Leviticus 25:51, 52), which price is called a "ransom." In paying our ransom, Christ became our Substitute (Exodus 13:13; I Peter 1:18,19), and because He paid the price, God will not demand a second judgment. Facts to remember are:

God sent His Son to redeem (I Corinthians 1:30; Galatians 4:4,5) Christ gave Himself as the Ransom (Romans 3:24; Galatians 3:13; Titus 2:14).

Redemption was purchased with Christ's own blood in contrast to silver and gold commonly used for human ransom (Ephesians 1:7; I Peter 1:18; Revelation 5:9).

The purchased redemption is eternal in nature (Hebrews 9:12).

The blood representing the price paid, namely, the outpoured life of Christ, was the blood of Deity (Leviticus 17: 11-14; Genesis 9:4; Acts 20:28; Hebrews 9:12).

Back of the redeeming work of Christ are many factors. First of all, there is the mighty power of God (Nehemiah 1:10; Deuteronomy 7:8; Isaiah 50:2). *Jehovah* is the redemptive and covenant-keeping name of God. In the second place, away back in the dateless past it was God's love that planned our redemption (Isaiah 52:3). Christ came as the Lamb slain from before the foundation of the world. Further, the love and pity of God are at the back of our redemption (Isaiah 63:9).

The *right* to redeem is founded upon the blood of the Lamb, and the *power* to effect it is the glorious power of the Redeemer Himself.

Another aspect we must not overlook is that God came to the aid of captives because of their utter inability to deliver themselves (Psalm 49:7,8). Apart from redeeming grace, the sinner is both helpless and hopeless. Then further still, because the redemption of the soul is precious, corruptible things such as silver and gold could not purchase redemption (I Peter 1:18,19). Nothing but the precious blood of Christ can avail on the sinner's behalf. Fully to understand the purchase price of our deliverance from sin and death, we must think of all that was involved in Christ's voluntary humiliation; His rejection by men; His agonies, bloody sweat, tears, cruel mocking and brutal death. When we remember all that it meant to God to give His Son, and for that Holy Son who knew no sin, to be made sin for us, what else can we do but hate the sin for which He died.

But none of the ransomed ever knew,
How deep were the waters crossed,
Or how dark the night when the Lord
passed through,
Ere He found the sheep that was lost.

Under the Old Dispensation, the *Goel* or kinsman-redeemer played many important parts, all of which offer a fitting type of Christ, our Redeemer. One sold in captivity could be redeemed by one of his brothers (Leviticus 25:48). Christ became Man so that, as our elder Brother, He could redeem us (Hebrews 2:14-18). The Old Testament *Goel* or redeemer had three rights under ancient law.

1. He could purchase back the forfeited inheritance for an Israelite who through poverty had to sell his land. Man, heir of all things, bartered his magnificent birthright for vanity. But Christ, assuming manhood, became our *Goel* and saves us from being disinherited forever (Hebrews 2:9-15).

2. The *Goel* ransomed his kinsman from bondage to the foreigner (Leviticus 25:47-49). Man sold himself to Satan and bondage. Christ with the price of His own blood, ransomed the lawful captive (Isaiah 49:24).

3. The *Goel* avenged the death of his slain kinsman as a point of honor. Christ, through death, destroyed man's murderer, as Satan is described (John 8:44). He had the power of death (Hebrews 2:14,15), but now man can be delivered from everlasting bondage to him (Hosea 13:14).

At this juncture, it might be fitting to describe the distinction between *purchase* and *redemption*, seeing these terms are constantly confounded in current theology. Purchase implies a change of masters—Redemption signifies a change of state and condition. The Church has been purchased by the blood of God's Son (Acts 20:28); even false teachers, spreading their damnable heresies, have been bought by the Lord (II Peter 2:1), and their judgment will be all the more swift and sure. Christ tasted death for everything, as the Greek of Hebrews 2:9 implies. Christ bought the world God loved—the world of things and persons. The field is the *world* (Matthew 13:38-44; John 3:16; Hebrews 2:9).

Redemption, however, is a very different matter from purchase for, as we have seen, purchase merely intimates a change of master. You may purchase a slave, but that is not deliverance from the state of slavery. We belonged to Satan, and were in slavery to him, doing his will (Ephesians 2:2,3). Now by purchase we belong to God and as His slaves we gladly do His will (Romans 6:22). Redemption gives freedom, an entire change of state, as well as master. The change of *position* and *state*—from Adam to Christ, from the flesh to the Spirit, is true in God's sight, and is so presented as doctrine and truth for the saint to make practically his own, and in this sense he is already redeemed.

The Scriptures, then, intimate the *purchase* of mankind, but never the *redemption* of the race. All persons and things have been purchased, and as such belong to Christ, but believers only now share and enjoy redemption by *blood* (I Peter 1:18; Ephesians 1:7; Revelation 5:9). Creation has been purchased, but its redemption is yet future, and will be effected when it passes from bondage to liberty, from pangs to praises (Romans 8:19-22). The soul of the saint is redeemed, but not his body. The final completion of his redemption is future (Romans 8:23). Redemption in its fullest extent for the Church, for Israel, and for creation is future, and Christ will gather His redemptive rights to the full.

What Are Our Redemption Benefits?

The blessings and benefits of redemption are as varied as they are vast. Simply and solely with His precious blood Christ has redeemed us from the penalty, power and consequences of sin; from the curse, condemnation and rule of the law: from this present evil world and from its prince and god; from ourselves and the world; from the wrath of God and the pangs of hell. The slightest doubt as to the full coverage of our redemption bespeaks a low estimate of the value of the ransom-price Christ paid. It also casts the dishonor of a foul suspicion upon the divine Redeemer Himself.

H. S. Miller in his *Christian Manual* has summarized the expanse of our redemption in this way. We have been redeemed from—

1. All iniquity (Psalm 130:8; Titus 2:14)
2. The curse of the law (Galatians 3:13)
3. The bondage of the law (Galatians 4:5)
4. The power of sin (Romans 6:18,22)
5. The vain manner of life (I Peter 1:18)
6. Bondage (Exodus 6:6; Deuteronomy 15:15; Micah 6:4)
7. All evil (Genesis 48:16)
8. All trouble (Psalm 25:22)
9. All distress (I Kings 1:29)
10. All adversity (II Samuel 4:9)
11. Deceit and violence (Psalm 72:14)
12. Destruction (Psalm 103:4)
13. Death (Job 5:20; Hosea 13:14)
14. Hell (Psalm 49:15 R.V.)
15. The hand of the enemy (Psalms 106:10; 107:2; Jeremiah 15:21)
16. Our enemies (Psalm 136:24; Micah 4:10)

Viewing the manifold results of Christ's

redeeming work upon the cross, we find ourselves loaded with benefits—

1. It brings justification (Romans 3:24).
2. It imparts forgiveness of sins (Ephesians 1:7; Colossians 1:14).
3. It prepares for the adoption or sonplacing (Galatians 4:4,5; Romans 8:23).
4. It purifies a people for God's own possession, zealous of good works (II Samuel 7:23; Titus 2:14; I Peter 2:9).
5. It makes us God's property, not our own (Isaiah 43:1; I Corinthians 6:19, 20).
6. It enables us to sing the new song, the song of redemption (Revelation 5:9).
7. It delivers from fear (Isaiah 41:10-14; 43:1).
8. It brings joy and a holy walk, even as it will bring the same to Israel (Isaiah 35:8-10; 51:11; 62:12).

Because our redemption is so precious (Psalm 49:8), and plenteous (Psalm 130:7), and eternal (Hebrews 9:12), may we be found realizing to the limit all the Lord bought for us when He died as the sinless Substitute for sinners. Redemption rightly understood, covers three realms—past, present and prospective. The first aspect rests immovably upon the finished work of Christ, the second forms part of our daily experiences under the patient leading and testing of the Holy Spirit, the third points forward to all Christ promised us at His return. Thus, in one respect we *are* redeemed; in another we *are being* redeemed; and in another, we *wait for* our redemption.

Redemption—Past

"Christ *hath* redeemed us" (Galatians 3:13). The first tense of our redemption is in passages like Romans 3:24—

"Being justified freely by His grace, through the redemption that is in Christ Jesus,"

where it is linked on to our justification: Ephesians 1:7—

"In whom we have redemption through His blood, the forgiveness of sins according to the riches of His grace,"

where we have the joyful and grateful recognition of the believer of propitiation through faith in Christ's blood; I Peter 1:18,19—

"Forasmuch as ye know that ye were not redeemed with corruptible things, as silver and gold, from your vain conversation, received by tradition from your fathers; but with the precious blood of Christ, as of a lamb without blemish and without spot,"

where redemption as a *purchase* reminds us of the price beyond all compute the Redeemer paid.

Redemption—Present

This second aspect has a glory all its own, as Paul emphasizes in Titus 2:14, where redemption is before us as the basis of the *present* resources of our Redeemer for daily help and deliverance. This progressive redemption proceeds entirely upon the ground of Christ's accomplished redemption. The Holy Spirit, sealing us as God's purchased ones, translates our *standing* into *state*. Christ, as our Redeemer, not only bore our sin upon the tree, His daily grace avails as our living Deliverer to impart victory over the government of sin.

Redemption—Prospective

The redeemed life within is a prisoner of hope, awaiting the redemption of the body (Romans 8:22,23; Philippians 3:20, 21; I Corinthians 15:52). This future redemption we long for with absolute certainty of expectation, will be ours at the return of Christ for His redeemed ones. Here is the final part of our redemption, too glorious to describe. "Until the redemption (future) of the purchased (past) possession" (Ephesians 1:14). Eternal life dwelling within, is pent up in a mortal body of humiliation. We wait, however, for the most glorious display of our redemption, namely, our glorification. Even Job, who lived before the cross, had a revelation of Christ as the coming Redeemer (Job 19:25-27). From his flesh, as from a window, the patriarch knew that a blessed resurrection would be his.

Our present responsibility requires little emphasis. Being redeemed from sin to God, it is our solemn obligation to glorify Him in every phase of life (I Corinthians 6:19,20). Bought with a tremendous price, we must live to the praise of Him who died and rose again on our behalf (Psalms 71:23; 103:1-4; Revelation 5:9), and we must never be ashamed to testify to the wonders of His redeeming grace—"Let the redeemed of the Lord say so" (Psalm 107:2).

> To Thee, our great redeeming Lord,
>   What lasting thanks we owe;
> For raising sinners to such joys,
>   From depths of endless woe.

XX

The Doctrine of Reconciliation

While there is a close affinity between *atonement* and *propitiation* and *reconciliation*, the latter work of grace represents a phase of Christ's death deserving of separate exposition. Nothing could be more positive than the declaration of Paul, "We were reconciled to God by the death of His Son" (Romans 5:10).

The Meaning of the Term

Fausset reminds us that "reconciliation" signifies "the changing of places, coming over from one to the other side." Used of ourselves, the word implies "changing" the judicial status from one of estrangement and condemnation to one of acceptance and justification. Saul had need to be reconciled to David, and take him back to his royal favor (I Samuel 29:4). Being "reconciled to thy brother" means "propitiate him to lay aside his anger and be reconciled to thee" (Matthew 5:24). When Paul says that "God hath reconciled us to Himself by Christ Jesus" (II Corinthians 5:18, 19), he is affirming that God has restored us to His favor, once for all, on the basis of satisfying the claims of His justice against us.

Christ is called "the high priest in things pertaining to God to make reconciliation for the sins of the people" (Hebrews 2:17). Here the term actually means "to propitiate their sins." From the human standpoint God's *justice* was propitiated by Christ's sacrifice. "But as God's *love was side by side* from everlasting with His *justice*, Christ's sacrifice was *never expressly* said to propitiate God." Reconciliation was not necessary from God's side. Man has ever been the offender. His sin estranged him from God, and he has been at enmity with Him. Thus as an enemy, someone had to make possible a reconciliation. Christ, assuming human nature, satisfied divine justice for our sins at Calvary, and through our acceptance of Him as Saviour we are received into favor again with an offended God. He never departed from man, and therefore has no need to be reconciled.

In our presentation of gospel truth we must guard against unbiblical and faulty expressions. Phrases like, "A reconciled God in Christ," "The death of Jesus turned the heart of God to man," deny the truth of the magnificent declaration that before the cross, "God so loved the world that He gave. . ." (John 3:16). God never "gave" in order to "love." He gave because He loved. The cross was not the cause of God's love, but the effect of it. God, then, is *not* reconciled to sinners, for He has ever loved them, and has never been estranged from them. Not He, but *we* needed the reconciliation. He has never been alienated from His sinful, guilty creatures, but they were and are strangers to Him, and need to be made *at one* with Him. Christ is the blessed Reconciler, reconciling enemies to God (Romans 5:10,—margin; Colossians 1:20-22; II Corinthians 5:18-20). He is the Daysman betwixt us (Job 9:35).

The Message of the Truth

Already we have hinted at the soul-satisfying message at the heart of the truth of reconciliation, which means "to change thoroughly from." The Hebrew word signifies "appeasement," while the Greek word means, as we have stated, "the changing of places, coming over from one side to the other side." In our sinful state we were in the place of condemnation, and on the side of enmity against God. But in and through the reconciling work of Christ, condemnation has been exchanged for justification, and enmity for love and friendship.

In his comment on Colossians 1:20, **Dr.** C. I. Scofield says, "Reconciliation looks toward the effect of the death of Christ upon man in propitiation (Romans 3:25) in the Godward aspect, and is the effect of the death of Christ upon the believing sinner which, through divine power, works in him a 'thorough change' toward God from enmity and aversion to love and trust. It is never said that God is reconciled. God is propitiated, the sinner reconciled." (Romans 5:10; 11:15; I Corinthians 7:11; II Corinthians 5:18-21).

Reconciliation, then, is restoration to divine favor. God not only remits our penalty and blots out our guilty past. As justified ones, He places us where we can partake of the promises and rewards of those who are His. Reconciliation, as applied to persons and things, implies the bringing back of them to God. Both persons and things have departed from God; the former willingly, the latter involuntarily (Romans 8:20); hence the need of reconciliation. This double reconciliation is presented as the fruit of the atonement in Leviticus 16. Such a reconciliation changes the attitude of persons and things to God, not God to them.

Believers are already reconciled, the death of God's Son being the ground of their reconciliation (Romans 5:10; II Corinthians 5:16; Colossians 1:22). All things in heaven and on earth await reconciliation which will also come as the result of the shed blood of Christ (Colossians 1:20). "The long-continued alienation of the celestial and terrestrial spheres from each other will cease," says Walter Scott, "and all estrangement from God in these regions —in these only—is to be set aside (Hosea 2:21,22). For the reconciliation of things we wait the second return of our Lord in power." Paul speaks of the universal subjection to Christ of all in heaven, earth and hell (Philippians 2:10). This aspect is wider in range and extent than all things in heaven and earth reconciled. The Philippian epistle teaches the future subjection of heaven, earth and hell's inhabitants to Christ. It must be carefully noted that while "all things" will be brought back to God, not "all *persons*" are to be reconciled. The occupants of the Lake of Fire are forever estranged from God, and will never be reconciled to Him.

The reconciliation of man to God is the blessed character of God's present ministry in the Gospel toward the world, and our solemn obligation as ambassadors for Christ is to beseech men in Christ's stead to be reconciled to God (II Corinthians 5:18-20).

How privileged we are, if reconciled to God ourselves, to preach "the word of reconciliation" to those far off from God (II Corinthians 5:18,19). Although living at immeasurable distance from the Holy One who inhabiteth the praises of eternity, sinners can be assured that the moment they receive Christ as Saviour, the gulf is crossed and they are made nigh by the blood of Christ. It is not the blood and something beside—our repentance, feelings, baptism or the Church, but the blood alone is sufficient for the divine acceptance of the vilest sinner. That shed blood fully satisfies and glorifies God on account of sin, and so is all-sufficient to bring those who are far off, nigh unto God.

Akin to *reconciliation* is *atonement* which means *satisfaction* or *expiation made for wrong*. The great doctrine of atonement displays the moral glory of the Triune God and the central fact of His ways with man. The *Incarnation* divides time; the *Crucifixion* eternity. Christ came as the foreordained Lamb and in the fullness of time died the voluntary, vicarious and propitiatory death for sin. Through such a death man is reconciled to God (I Peter 3:18). The blood alone maketh an atonement for the soul (Leviticus 17:11; John 1:29; 3:14; II Corinthians 5:21; I Peter 2:24). The scope of the atonement is unlimited because Christ's death was a propitiation for the sins of the world (I John 2:2). He was a Ransom for all (I Timothy 2:5,6).

But while there is the *provision* of atonement for all, such a propitiation only becomes *actual* in a person as he or she repents of sin and exercises faith in all Christ accomplished on their behalf (John 3:18; Acts 13:39; Romans 5:1,2; Ephesians 2:8; I Peter 1:5; I John 5:1). What does it mean to *atone*? Break the word into two; and you have the answer. To *atone* means to be *at one*. Are you *at one* with God or at peace with Him? If not, as you read these lines you can acquaint yourself with Him and be at peace with Him.

XXI

The Doctrine of Faith

That faith is a potent force is proven by our Lord's declaration that faith is able to remove mountains. Faith laughs at and triumphs over impossibilities. What triumphs of faith the Westminster Abbey of the Bible (Hebrews 11) presents! By faith, those warriors of the Early Church subdued kingdoms. John encourages us to believe that faith can overcome the world (I John 5:4).

It is fitting to consider *faith* after *repentance*, seeing that true repentance merges into faith as the blossom ripens into fruit. Tears of sincere grief over sin lead to a saving trust in God. Without faith, repentance recedes into indifference, or moves on into helpless remorse. Faith is vital in that it leads the repentant soul to God, first to receive His forgiveness, then to appropriate His resources for daily victory and holiness, and inspiration for effective service.

The importance of faith is also indicated by the fact that all men are dependent upon it as the avenue of access to God. Sinners, convicted of their need, must exercise faith in God as One ready to pardon them, if they are to be saved. Saints, saved by grace through faith in Christ, must keep on believing. "As ye have therefore received Christ Jesus the Lord, so walk ye in Him" (Colossians 2:6). Initial faith made us His—continuous faith keeps us His. Outlining the basic doctrine of *faith*, we have—

Its Definition

While Bible scholars have given us many descriptions of the nature of faith, the Bible itself has one definition only, if you can call it a definition. Often attempts to define faith only tend to make the doctrine more obscure. The writer to the Hebrews says that "Faith is the substance of things hoped for: the evidence of things not seen." Arthur Way's translation is expressive, "Faith which issues in the winning of life. Faith is that attitude of mind which is the foundation-rock on which hope stands, that which satisfies us of the reality of things as yet beyond our ken" (Hebrews 11:1). Noyes gives us this rendering, "Faith is the assurance of things hoped for, and conviction of things not seen." Dean Alford has it, "Faith is the confidence of things hoped for, the evidence of things not seen."

God's Spirit makes known in God's Word certain things not seen, and produces within the believer the conviction that these actually exist. Thus he endures as seeing things invisible. The sum and substance of this solitary Bible definition or statement of faith seems to be that by it the believing one is able to penetrate beyond the veil that marks the limit of sense and enters into the region of unseen things, making them tangible and real. Such faith is not mere human wisdom or sagacity. It has its foundation in a spiritual understanding. It is the receiving of the testimony as true (Hebrews 11:1; Numbers 23:19; Isaiah 7:9; Matthew 8:8-13). This faith comes as the fruit of the Spirit (Galatians 5:22), and enables one to grasp things hoped for, that is, the unseen and unknown future, and gives them actuality. "By faith Isaac blessed Jacob and Esau concerning things to come" (Hebrews 11:20). It was this faith that stretched out its hands into the dim future and came back filled with a blessing that was, in Moses' estimation, of greater value than his flocks and herds. This is a faith that can lay hold of things in the unseen world *now* (Hebrews 11:26,27). With Moses, we, too, can endure as seeing Him who is invisible. To Moses, the unseen treasures made real to his faith by far outweighed the crown and throne and glory of Egypt.

In his monumental work, *What the Bible Teaches*, Dr. R. A. Torrey gives us this definition of faith,

To believe God is to rely upon or have unhesitating assurance of the truth of God's testimony, even though it is unsupported by any other evidence, and to rely upon and have unfaltering assurance of the fulfillment of His promises, even though everything seems against fulfillment.

Its Synonyms

The various synonyms of the Bible for faith help to illustrate its nature and action—

Hear—"Faith cometh by hearing" (Romans 10:17).

"Hear, and your soul shall live" (Isaiah 55:3).

The Spirit-possessed soul listens, is attentive to the divine Word, recognizes its authenticity and responds to it. Dr. Alexander Smellie reminds us that

Faith is the ear, which refuses to be troubled longer by harassing questions and suspicious doubts, but listens in simplicity to what Jesus says. And what melody there is in His voice! Yet the ear does not evoke the chords and strains; it only drinks them in.

Look—"Look unto me and be ye saved" (Isaiah 45:22).

The listening soul looks out and waits till the veil parts and God is fully revealed. Looking, He becomes real, then His Word and His salvation become real. Faith, as the eye, gazes upon the wealth and loveliness of the Saviour. As the eye, faith turns away from the unhealthy scrutiny of self and sin to the examination of Christ's marvelous grace, and the sight the eye beholds is so satisfying and transcendent! Of course the eye does not create the surpassing splendors, it simply grasps them.

Receive—"As many as receive Him . . . even to them that believe on His name" (John 1:12).

Faith is the hand receiving and appropriating the divine Gift, and grasping all His treasures. Even when all is dark, faith does not tremble, seeing the everlasting Hand of the omnipotent Lord holds the frail hand outstretched to Him. It is that, that faith is to the soul, the counterpart of what the senses are to the body, and enables it to have traffic and intercourse with unseen spiritual realities.

Believe—The word translated "believe" is found 247 times in the New Testament, and the kindred term "faith" occurs 244 times, while "faithful," which simply means full of faith, appears 67 times. The Greek word for "believe" means to persuade, to give credit to, to trust or confide in. The Hebrew word for "believe" means to stay, to support, and then, that which forms the stay, its foundation. It is from the Hebrew

word that we derive the English term, *Amen,* signifying "of a truth," or "so be it." So when we read that Abraham believed God, he actually "amened" Him.

The employment of these similar terms reveals the importance of the theme in the mind of the Spirit. All through the New Testament we find "faith" referred to as attending every step of Christian experience, from its commencement to its consummation. At all times and under all circumstances, such faith is essential (Mark 16:16; Romans 14:23; Hebrews 3:19; 11:6; Revelation 21:8), and counts on God to make good His promises, when not one of them is at hand (Luke 5:18-20; John 4:46-53; Hebrews 11:11-13; Isaiah 11:2; 26:3). Spelled out as an acrostic, faith means—

Forsaking
All
I
Trust
Him

This faith we are considering is not a blind, unintelligent act of the mind, nor is it credulity. It rests upon a knowledge of God as revealed in His Word. Ours is not a blind trust, in an unknown stranger. ". . . they that know Thy name will put their trust in Thee" (Psalm 9:10). Faith through knowledge leads to committment. Faith reaches its end in surrender (II Timothy 1:12). A person may know that a bank is sound, and trusts its security, but only when a transfer of funds has taken place has actual business been done.

Its Necessity

Faith is not something we can please ourselves about. The Scriptures declare in plainest terms its imperativeness. "Without faith it is impossible to please Him" (Hebrews 11:6). Condemnation overtook Israel "because they believed not God" (Psalm 78:22; Hebrews 3:19). Faith is absolutely essential to salvation. "He that believeth not shall be damned" (John 3:36; Matthew 13:58). This saving faith relies wholly upon the Saviour and does not seek a mixture of works (Ephesians 2:8-10; Titus 3:5; Romans 4:4). It leads to confession of sin (Romans 10:9; II Corinthians 4:13), and has simple confidence in God to deliver from the curse and dominion of sin, and at last receive us to Himself (II Timothy 1:12; Acts 10:43; Galatians 2:16).

Faith is a humble grace, excluding all glorying in the creature. "Faith fetches all from Christ," says Thomas Watson, "and gives all glory to Christ; it is a most humble grace. Hence it is that God has singled out this grace to be the condition of the covenant. If faith be the condition of the covenant of grace, it excludes desperate, presumptive sinners from the covenant." The reason, then, for faith's necessity is perfectly clear. Apart from the faith God asks for, there can be no access to Him or blessing from Him. Without faith, God stands outside a closed door and His grace and power cannot prevail. The electric current cannot communicate its energy till contact is made. Faith, then, is the switch supplying the spiritual contact. It links the soul to God so that, up to the measure in which all the avenues are opened, the power of God is released. Unbelief sets God aside, enthrones self-will, and becomes the crowning act of sin.

Its Sources

Faith in the invisible things of God is not the natural faith we grow up with, and which we exercise whether saved or unsaved. It comes as the gift of God. It is a faith toward God, seeing it comes from Him (Galatians 2:20; Hebrews 6:1). Faith is a gift of God resulting from His grace. He not only supplies a Saviour, but the faith to believe in Him as such (Acts 15:11; II Timothy 1:12; Ephesians 2:8). God deals to those who are His the measure of faith (Romans 12:3). "It is given in the behalf of Christ . . . to believe on Him" (Philippians 1:29). This faith likewise becomes ours as the fruit of the Spirit (Galatians 5:22).

The full realization of the divine gift of faith is experienced by us as we strive after a deeper knowledge of the Giver Himself (Mark 4:22). The Spirit of faith Himself, part of whose fruit is faith, strengthens our trust and confidence. As He is allowed to have His way in and through the life, He makes the Object of our faith more precious (I Corinthians 12:4,8,9; Acts 1:5,8; 11:24). The gift also increases with the occupation of Jesus, the greatest Example of faith and the *Author* and *Finisher* of our faith (Hebrews 12:1,2). This is true as we constantly meditate upon the historic role of the faithful (Hebrews 11).

Like begets like. Faith has ever been the royal road of others, and as we witness the exhibition of faith in their lives, grace will be ours to manifest the same gift. Think of faith as in the lives of Abraham (Genesis 12:4a; 22:5; Romans 4:17-25); Isaac (Genesis 21-25); Jacob (Genesis 25-29); Jehoshaphat (II Chronicles 20); Hezekiah (II Chronicles 29-32); Nehemiah! We have also the example of George Müller, Hudson Taylor and many other stalwarts of faith.

It must be borne in mind that faith is both a human act and a divine operation. Man has the capacity for faith and is responsible for its use. Daily he exercises faith and acts upon it. It is also a divine operation, inasmuch as it becomes effective only as the Spirit of God moves within the soul (Ephesians 2:8). Faith becomes an anchor in the storms of life, when we look away from all crises and circumstances to Him, who is greater than them all (Acts 27:20-25; Romans 4:17-24; I Corinthians 2:5).

Further, as God bestows His gifts in answer to prayer, intercession for the increase of the gift of faith receives a ready response from God (Mark 9:24; Luke 17:5,6; II Corinthians 10:15). With such a prayer, however, there must be the willingness to abandon all that hinders the development of faith (Hebrews 12:1).

Its Warrant

Faith in God is no delusion. The warrant of faith's accomplishments is the Word of God. All of its promises warrant the soul's approach to and confidence in God. Yet it must be made clear that faith rests ultimately not on itself nor on any inward experience, nor even on the Word, but on Him whom the Word reveals. God in Christ reconciling us unto Himself is the object of faith (Mark 11:22; II Corinthians 5:19). Then there is God's faithfulness guaranteeing us that if we trust in Him we shall never be confounded (I Thessalonians 5:24). All of His promises are Yea and Amen in Christ. When Christ said to the blind man, "Thy faith hath saved thee" (Luke 18:42), He did not imply that there is any intrinsic virtue resident in faith. Its power rests in the fact that it unites the needy soul to the strong and all-sufficient Lord. As Alexander Smellie puts it, "Faith is the foot, which flies to God—Father, Son, Spirit. It makes me at home in His fulness, His nearness, His friendliness. It takes me into what the mystic called 'The Rose-Garden of my Redeemer, Jesus Christ.' But my foot itself has small credit for that inevitable flight to Paradise."

Its Works

Obedience and service are part of the fruit of saving faith and proof of its genuineness (Romans 4:5; 5:2; Ephesians 3:12). James reminds us that faith without works is dead. One has only to study those who proved their faith by their works. Read the following passages and note what each believed for, and what each did as an example of faith:

The Centurion (Matthew 8:5-10,13; Luke 7:2-10)

The Paralytic (Matthew 9:2-8; Mark 2:3-12)

The Woman with the Issue (Matthew 9:20-22; Mark 5:25-34)

The Two Blind Men (Matthew 9:27-30)

The Syrophenician Woman (Matthew 15:21-28; Mark 7:24-29)

Blind Bartimaeus (Mark 10:46-52; Luke 18:35-43)

The Sinful Woman (Luke 7:36-50)

The Leper (Luke 17:12-19)

The Nobleman (John 4:46-52)

The Man at the Beautiful Gate (Acts 3: 2-16)

The Crippled Man (Acts 14:8-10)

Abraham (Romans 4; Galatians 3:6,17; James 2:23)

Faith must be our life if we are to know the life of faith. H. S. Miller reminds us that "not only are we saved by faith, but the Christian life preeminently is a life of faith from beginning to end. We stand by faith (II Corinthians 1:24); walk by faith (II Corinthians 5:7); live by faith (Galatians 3:11). "Without faith it is impossible to please Him" (Hebrews 11:6). No one is pleased if another ever acts as if he doubted his word. There are two persons to whom all things are possible, God, and the believer (Mark 9:23; 10:27), and it is a sin to doubt (Romans 14:23). Unbelief is a hindrance to mighty works (Matthew 13:58; 17:19,20), and Jesus often upbraided His disciples for their unbelief (Mark 4:40; 6:6; 16:14; Luke 8:25). The life of faith is the life that wins (I Thessalonians 1:3; II Corinthians 5:7); that results in spiritual progress and perfection (Ephesians 4:13; 6:16).

Its Power

Faith links us on to the omnipotence of God and makes us more than conquerors (Mark 9:23; Acts 3:16; Hebrews 11:30). All power and blessing accruing from faith are not in faith itself but in the divine Object. A strong faith in a wrong object achieves very little. A weak faith in a right object can accomplish great things. Faith can provide boldness in witness (II Corinthians 4:13); result in good works (Titus 3:8; James 2:14-17); drive away fear (Mark 5:36); appropriate victory (Galatians 2:20; Ephesians 6:16; I John 5:4,5); produce bodily healing (Matthew 9:22,29; James 5:14,15); inherit the promises of God (Luke 1:45; Hebrews 6:12); make real a glorious future (John 11:25; I Thessalonians 4:14; I Peter 1:8,9).

In the lives of many Old Testament saints, faith was the root principle and impelling force in their witness. Abraham was strong in faith and gave glory to God (Romans 4:20). It was the faith of the patriarch that sustained his obedience under all tests, culminating in his great act of self-sacrifice (Hebrews 11:8-17), and also developed within him a character of singular nobility and magnanimity. Nowhere in the Bible is the power of faith so fully illustrated as in the virtues and achievements of the named and unnamed heroes in Hebrews 11. It was faith that gave them lofty pre-eminence in attainment and action.

In the sphere of prayer, the possibilities of achievements are unlimited. God has opened wide the doors of His vast treasury, but somehow the answers to our prayers are meager and fitful (John 14:13, 14; 15:16). What is wrong? James supplies the answer. We do not ask in faith believing (1:6,7). There is much beseeching, but there is the lack of appropriating hands of faith to grasp the promises and bring the blessing back.

Amid the complex experiences of life, the power of faith is also operative. Through the permissive will of God there are disciplinary and educative processes to undergo, but unbelief rises to protest the divine testings and God's purpose in our spiritual development is frustrated. Faith, however, resting in God's good and acceptable will, accepts *dis*appointments as *His*-appointments. Faith sets us free from anxious care regarding temporal concerns (Matthew 6:30-32), and inspires fortitude in the face of seeming disaster (Acts 27:23), and victory over the world's hostility (I John 5:4). The powers of darkness can never stand before the man of faith—God-sent and God-sustained. How courageous, buoyant and invincible he is! (Acts 6:5-8; 11:24; Hebrews 11:33). The conditions of power being recognized, service becomes effective and faithful (Matthew 8:13; 9:2, 29; 17:20). Why is the Church so powerless? Can it be that the lack of faith is responsible for her impotence in the presence of the forces of evil so rampant today? How such a lack brings discredit on the name of her Lord (Matthew 17:19,20)! If only the Church would realize anew the power of faith, and concur with the operation of the Holy Spirit, what a spiritual force she would be in a world of need.

Its Transcendancy

The clash between Modernism and Fundamentalism has brought the issue of faith *versus* reason into prominence. Liberals give reason the ascendancy in the handling of divine truths, and thus the miraculous element of the Bible is denied. What cannot be explained from a rationalistic standpoint is rejected. Conservatives, on the other hand, hold that faith transcends reason. God is infinite, and finite minds are not able to grasp all that God is in Himself. There are aspects of the divine character that faith must accept, although reason cannot explain them. No one is able to understand fully the virgin birth of our Lord, and so the modernist rejects it and offers us One who came by natural generation, withal born out of wedlock. True Christians, however, believing that with God all things are possible, accept the miraculous and are content to walk by faith.

Actually, there should be no conflict between faith and reason, if only each enduement functions appropriately. Reason is a gift of God, the crown of manhood and the principle in man to which God Himself appeals (Isaiah 1:18). Faith is also a gift of God (Ephesians 2:8). So when He endowed man with these dual qualities, He never meant there to be any inherent antagonism between them. They were designed to co-operate and be mutually helpful, but sin has separated them. Reason is the eye of the soul, and faith is the eye of the spirit. "Faith which is irrational is irreligious: reason which is unbelieving is illogical."

Faith does not contradict reason, but rises superior to it. What reason cannot understand, faith accepts. Faith is not subject to reason, seeing it rises into the realms of the unseen where reason cannot follow. Man, with all his God-given reasoning powers, cannot find God out, but faith accepts Him as a living, bright reality. Faith trusts God where reason cannot trace Him. Reason argues from things seen that there must be an unseen realm. Faith enters that unseen world and endures as seeing Him who is invisible. The Christian walks by faith, not by sight (Colossians 2:16; II Corinthians 5:7). "Sight" here means *form, external appearance,* and is the opposite of faith (Hebrews 11:1; Romans 6:24,25), by which "we know," and "we have" (II Corinthians 5:1). "Blessed are they that have not seen, and yet believe" (John 20:29). Reason may ratify the conclusions of faith, but it cannot override them. Reason, baffled in its quest for God, has to utter Job's pathetic confession—

> Behold, I go forward, but he is not there; and backward, but I cannot perceive Him: on the left hand, where he doth work, but I cannot behold him; he hideth himself on the right hand, that I cannot see him; but he knoweth the way that I take; when he hath tried me, I shall come forth as gold (Job 23:8,9).

But faith, grasping the unseen, beholds God and utters its jubilant declaration:

> I have heard of thee by the hearing of the ear; but now mine eye seeth thee (Job 42:5).

Faith, then, rises into the sphere where God is all and in all and in which He moves and rules without the limitation of godless reasoning. Reason is full of "whys" and "wherefores." Faith, on the other hand, asks no questions. It takes God at His Word. In the realm of truth it is not what do reason and experience say, but what does God say, that counts, and faith rests in the assurance that there is nothing too hard for Him.

Its Quality

That there are various aspects and degrees of faith is the clear teaching Paul emphasizes when he speaks of faith leading to more faith (Romans 1:17), and also of "the measure of faith," and of "the proportion of faith" (Romans 12:3-6). But whatever degree of faith we have, Christ is the Author of it all (Hebrews 12:2). The Bible Concordance reveals these degrees of faith. Where does experience place us?

No Faith
". . . Children in whom is no faith" (Deuteronomy 32:20)

". . . How is it that ye have no faith?" (Mark 4:40).

In both cases those addressed belonged to God, yet were destitute of a Spirit-inspired faith in divine ability to meet the crisis of the hour. While faith mentioned in these references is whole-hearted trust and confidence in God, "faith" is used to describe the body of revealed doctrine. Our Lord asked whether He would find "the faith" that is, the sum of truth as found in the Scriptures, when He returns (Luke 18:8). This is "the faith" Paul said many professing to be Christ's would turn from (I Timothy 4:1), and which the saints must earnestly contend for (Jude 3). Is it not tragic that many professors of religion have "no faith' in the respect outlined above?

Little Faith

"O ye of little faith" (Matthew 8:26) "O ye of little faith, wherefore didst thou doubt" (Matthew 14:31)

It is evident from the question of our Lord that little faith is equivalent to lack of faith. Placed over against "doubt" suggests that the disciples were lacking in confidence in Christ's power to undertake for them in an emergency. Faith, even although "little," can be effective if it is directed toward the Almighty One. If the quantity of faith is small, it can be increased. If the quality of faith is of the wrong sort, it can be purged and directed into right channels.

Weak Faith

"Him that is weak in the faith, receive ye . . ." (Romans 14:1).

The context implies the observance of liberty when it comes to matters not expressly forbidden in Scripture. Tolerance is necessary when we encounter those who are weak in the faith, that is, who do not have full spiritual intuition and guidance. Abraham was not weak in faith, but strong in such a virtue (Romans 4:19,20).

Dead Faith

"Faith, if it hath not works, is dead, being alone" (James 2:17). Faith in God should become active in service for God. Works cannot save, but they are the evidence of salvation. A living faith is that which obeys and serves and suffers (Hebrews 11:4-38; James 2:14-18). We have too many in church life who have faith, but it is not the kind that leads to action.

Vain Faith

"Your faith is also vain" (I Corinthians 15:14). Here *vain* means empty, worthless, of no avail. In this great resurrection chapter, Paul lays stress upon the necessity of faith in this cardinal doctrine of Christianity. If Christ is still in the grave, then we have no Saviour, and our faith is void of hope. We have Christian leaders today who deny the Resurrection of Christ. Theirs is an empty faith. It lacks substance and succour.

Great Faith

"I have not found so great faith, no, not in Israel" (Luke 7:9).

In commending the centurion for his remarkable faith, Christ at the same time was rebuking the religious leaders of His race for their absence of trust in Him. This Gentile soldier had a spiritual discernment of Christ's authority and power, the leaders in Israel lacked.

Full of Faith

"Barnabas was full of the Holy Ghost and of faith" (Acts 11:24).

Barnabas was full of faith because he was full of the Spirit. Faith is part of the fruit of the Spirit (Galatians 5:22). How much faith is a man capable of? We cannot say. When he is full to capacity, God enlarges the capacity. This is evident: if one is full of faith there is no vacuum for doubt, mistrust or despair.

Stedfast Faith

"The stedfastness of your faith in Christ" (Colossians 2:5). If faith is to be stedfast, meaning rooted and grounded so that the winds of doubt or trial never will move it, it must be "in Christ." It is by this stedfast faith that we can resist the devil and all his emmisaries (I Peter 5:9). Such a strong, stedfast faith may be tested, but it abides the fiery trial (I Peter 1:7). This is the kind of faith the saints are to manifest during the great Tribulation (Revelation 13:10; 14:12).

Rich Faith

"Rich in faith" (James 2:5). The contrast James uses is striking. He speaks of those who are paupers in material things being millionaires in spiritual things. The greatest benefactors in the world are not necessarily those with unlimited financial resources, but those who are on intimate terms with Him who rules the world.

Unfeigned Faith

"Faith unfeigned" (I Timothy 1:5; II Timothy 1:5). The word "unfeigned" means without counterfeit or hypocrisy. The faith Paul commended was sincere, genuine. There was nothing false about it.

Precious Faith

"Precious faith" (II Peter 1:1). The apostle loved this term "precious." He speaks of tested faith as being more precious than gold (I Peter 1:7); of the precious blood (I Peter 1:19); of the precious Christ (I Peter 2:4,7); of the precious promises (II Peter 1:4). Spirit-inspired faith is doubly precious—to God and to ourselves.

Holy Faith

"Building up yourselves on your most holy faith" (Jude 20). Such a faith is rightly called a "holy faith," seeing it is inspired by the Holy Spirit, reposes in a Holy God, and is taken up with the Holy Son. It is also a "holy faith" because it results in holiness of life.

XXII

The Doctrine of Adoption

As the writer approached this cardinal Christian doctrine, he was surprised to find how little is said in theological books on such an important gospel truth. Much can be gathered on *regeneration,* but its twin truth of *adoption* is dispensed with. Should it be? Is it not a definite part of the whole counsel of God? Prime aspects of a divine revelation are connected with *adoption.*

It may be that this theme is neglected because of the fact that a believer *is* a son of God through the work of the Spirit. Being born, then, into the family of God, how can he be adopted, when co-optation means the entrance into a family of one unrelated? What is the explanation of the Biblical fact that the saints, made sons by the new birth, are also treated as adopted ones? Prayerfully seeking the tuition of Him who is the Spirit of adoption, let us give ourselves to a consideration of the glorious dignity of adoption, bestowed upon all who are the children of God through faith in God's beloved Son who, as the Son of God, became the Son of Man, that the sons of men might become the sons of God.

The Practice of Adoption

One difficulty some have in understanding adoption is that we cannot very well be both born and adopted, according to the modern concept of the latter term. They cannot get beyond the adoption, so common today, whereby the act of making another person's child one's own is recognized by law. Orphans and Children's Homes are visited and children are carefully selected and taken home, to be fed, clothed, educated and cared for in every way as children of the home. They receive the name of the adopted parents, are loved as dearly as if they were natural children, and often are heirs to considerable property. The difference when we come to the relationship existing between God and His children by faith, however, is that He only adopts into His family those who have been born anew. As used in Scripture, *adoption* implies a change of nature and a change of relationship. Sonship precedes adoption.

Behind the New Testament use of adoption lies the Roman law, and the customs associated with such a practice. A recognized authority on Roman law gives us this original significance of *adoption.* A Roman family, from the legal standpoint, consisted of a head or ruler, and of the persons subject to his absolute power. The lawful children of the head of the family were in his power, as also were persons unconnected with him by blood, if they had been brought into his power by the artificial tie of adoption. It might happen that a marriage was fruitless, or that the sons went to the grave before him, and that the head of the family had thus to face the extinction of his family and of his descent to the tomb without posterity to make him blessed. To obviate so dire a misfortune, two alternatives were open to him: either to give himself to adoption and pass into another family, or to adopt someone as a son who should perpetuate his own family. The latter was the course usually followed, and was called *adoptio* or adoption. As used by Paul, then, the term implied a ceremony of conveyance, or an order of a Roman court of justice whereby one was transferred to the family of the adopter. The adopting parent acquired the *potestas* (legal power) over the adopted child exactly as if it were the issue of his own body; while the latter enjoyed, in his new family, the same rights as if he had been born into it. The Greek word for "adoption" is *luiothesia*, a compound of the words "son" and "a placing," meaning not the putting into the place of *child*, but the putting into place of a *son*.

There was another Roman ceremony throwing light on Paul's teaching in Galatians 4:1-3 and Romans 8:19-23 which had to do with a senator's son becoming of age, and heir to his father's possessions. It was known as *Tirocinium Fori*, which commemorated the conclusion of boyhood, when the youth exchanged the garment known as the *Pretexta* for the *Toga veritas* or garment of manhood. It signified that the youth had reached his "majority," which would probably be his sixteenth year, when military service commenced. Evidently the ceremony began with a domestic sacrifice at the altar of the lares, where the youth deposited the *insignia pueritia*. The Romans set great store by this ceremony, and care was taken that the youth appeared in the Forum with becoming pomp. It is somewhat uncertain whether the youth was introduced before the Tribunal of the *Praetor* at this time. After the Forum was visited, the cavalcade proceeded to the Capitol to offer a sacrifice. With the *Titocinium*, entrance into public life began.

With this background of the glorious dignity of adoption before us, we are more prepared to understand the New Testament implication of the term, namely, placement as sons in a position of authority. "Regeneration has to do with son-making —Adoption with son-placing."

The Old Testament offers instances of the modern thought of adoption, that is, taking the child of another and giving him the position and advantages of a son born into the family. Moses was adopted as the son of Pharaoh's daughter (Exodus 2:10). We have Abraham's proposal to Jehovah, because of his childlessness, to adopt his worthy steward, Eliezer of Damascus, as his son and heir (Genesis 15:2). Then we have the willingness of husband and wife jointly to adopt a son and heir, the child of

Hagar (Genesis 16:1-3). The definite adoption by Jacob of the two sons of Joseph as his own sons (Genesis 48:4) is another evidence that adoption, that is the receiving into a family one who does not belong to it by birth, did not originate with the Latin race. Esther became the adopted child of her cousin, Mordecai (Esther 2:7). Israel was grafted into the true olive, and dignified with glorious privileges. "Who are Israelites, to whom pertaineth the adoption and the glory" (Romans 9:4).

Between man's practice of adoption and the Bible's concept of it, there is a difference to observe. A child is adopted because of some attracting interest in him. There are engaging qualities, beauty of person, sweet disposition about the child, and a benevolent spirit on the part of those eager to adopt the child, which results in his adoption. Pity for an orphan, or an unwanted child, leads others to take over parental care and protection. But no matter what motive is behind the adoption of a child, such adoption can never impart the disposition, facial characteristics or nature of the adoptees to the adopted child. With such an adoption there is no natural bond. With God's children, however, it is different. Those born anew by the Spirit and adopted by God experience the impartation of the divine nature. His life enters and as a natural child resembles his parents in many ways, so those who are God's by faith in Christ receive His love, grace and disposition. "As thou art, so were they; each one resembled the children of a King" (Judges 8:18). Filial disposition can only come from a filial relationship. Through the new birth the believer effectually assimilates spiritual disposition and character as natural generation assimilates a child to his parents.

The word *adoption*, then, is used by Paul who, as an accomplished Greek scholar, knew how to translate the Roman word to express the idea of setting a child of God in the relation of a son. "The believer's relation to God as a child results from the new birth (John 1:12,13) whereas adoption is the act of God whereby one already a child is, through redemption from the law, placed in the position of an adult son (Galatians 4:1-5)."

While both *adoption* and *regeneration* imply a transition from a state of spiritual death to one of spiritual life, and both alike represent this translation making us children of God in a sense we were not His children before, yet the terms present different truths.

Regeneration is an internal change wrought in us by the Spirit of God, resulting in a new nature resembling God.

Adoption is the action of God whereby He admits those born anew to the conditions and privileges of children by a sovereign act. This is a position based upon the internal change regeneration produces.

The Privileges of Adoption

The *Westminster Catechism* describes adoption as "an act of God's free grace, whereby we are received into the number and have a right to all the privileges of the sons of God." It is the "reception into a family of one who does not belong to it by birth." What are some of these adoption-privileges? Robert Lee gives us the following bare outlines.

1. We become, because of our adoption, "Fellow citizens with the saints, and of the household of God" (Ephesians 2:19).
2. Deliverance from a servile spirit, from a slavish fear of God (Romans 8:15).
3. Heirship in relation to God (Romans 8:17).
4. The duty of loyal obedience to all His commands (Romans 8:29; 8:5).
5. Freedom from over-anxious care (Matthew 6:25-34; 10:29-31).
6. Parental Correction (Hebrews 12:5-11).
7. An inheritance of future glory (Romans 8:17; I Peter 1:4).
8. An enigma to the world (I John 3:1).
9. Family affinity and unity with fellow-believers (John 13:34).

Among other great and glorious privileges of adopted ones is that of divine guidance. A sure sign of adoption is the unerring leading of the Spirit in all matters (Romans 8:14). Having the Spirit as the Seal of adoption (Romans 8:14, 16; Galatians 4:6), all true believers have a likeness to God marking them out as His in this present evil world. They are God-directed and God-like as His children. Whom God adopts, He anoints; whom He makes sons, He makes saints. We have already seen that when a man adopts another for his son and heir, he may give him his name, but he cannot give him his own disposition and characteristics, but when God adopts He sanctifies. He gives

not only a new name, but a new nature (II Peter 1:4). He turns the lion into a lamb. He works such a change as if another soul dwelt in the same body. It is indeed a privilege to be ennobled with God's name. "I will write on him the name of my God" (Revelation 3:12). All whom God adopts bear the name of Him who adopts them. Such a privilege, of course, is extended to all whether Jews or Gentiles (Romans 9:4; Acts 10:35), and also to both sexes (II Corinthians 6:18). In some countries, females do not enjoy the same privileges as males. But every gracious soul can lay claim to adoption, and have an interest in God as a Father.

Liberty is another privilege of adoption, seeing God adopts us to a state of liberty. Adoption is a state of freedom from the law and sin. Hitherto we were slaves, sold into sin. "Thou art no more a servant but a son" (Galatians 4:7). But the adopted son is not free to do as he likes. Free from the reign of sin, the tyranny of Satan, and the curse of the law, the adopted one is free in the manner of worship. Being indwelt by God's free Spirit, adopted ones become free and faithful in the service of God.

God also adopts us to a state of dignity. Adopted and made heirs of promise, God installs us into honor (Isaiah 43:4). We are made His treasure: His jewels: His first-born (Exodus 19:5; Malachi 3:17; Hebrews 12:23). We are privileged to have angels as our lifeguards (Hebrews 1:14). We are made the blood-royal of heaven (I John 3:9), having remarkable spiritual heraldry. Think of our coat of arms! Sometimes it is the lion for courage (Proverbs 28:1); sometimes the dove for meekness (Song of Solomon 2:14); sometimes the eagle for flight (Isaiah 40:31).

Another privilege accruing to God's adopted ones is protection from evil (Luke 10:19; Psalm 91: 10). He does not say that no affliction shall befall His children, but *no evil.* The hurt and poison of it are taken away. Sorrows overtake them, but the furnace makes the gold purer (Hebrews 12: 10). Condemnation likewise is removed for the adopted (Romans 8:1). So, as old Thomas Watson expresses it,

What a blessed privilege is this, to be freed from the sting of affliction and the curse of the law, to be in such a condition that nothing can hurt us! When the dragon has poisoned the water, the unicorn with his horn extracts and draws the poison out. So Jesus Christ has drawn out the poison of every affliction that it cannot injure the saints.

The greatest privilege of adoption is that of having God as our Father (Galatians 4:5). In pardon, God is viewed as Sovereign; in justification, He is viewed as Judge; in adoption, He is presented to us as Father. As a Judge, God clears us for the sake of His Son, from the charge of sin: as Father, He confers upon us the honor, dignity and privileges of a filial relationship, and is not ashamed to call us His sons and daughters (II Corinthians 6: 18; Hebrews 2:11). Dignity and prerogatives become ours as the sons of God (John 1:12). Christ was the Son of God the Father by eternal generation, a Son before time began. All men have God as Father, but only in the sense of creation (Acts 17: 28). This is no privilege, for men may have God for their Father by creation, and yet have the devil as their father. The Bible does not teach the universal Fatherhood of God. He only becomes the Father of those who experience the new birth and who, through such, are adopted as sons. Man would never adopt his mortal enemy as a son, but such is the wonder of the Father's love that although we were His enemies, He received and pardoned us and made us His heirs. We have been adopted into the family of heaven. Christ is bringing many sons to glory (Hebrews 2:10). Men adopt but one heir, usually, but our Father in heaven is resolved to have a multitude of sons in glory, no man can number.

The wonder of the Father's love in adopting us is evident in many ways. Why should He want to adopt us when He had a Son of His own (Matthew 3:17)? Christ is called God's "dear Son" (Colossians 1:13), and "better than the angels" (Hebrews 1:4), yet God condescends to call us His sons. Certainly we needed Him as a Father, but He did not need sons when He had His only begotten Son. Further, the Father was well-pleased with His Son. Mordecai adopted Esther, because she was fair. A man is not likely to adopt as his heir one who is crooked or ill-favored, but God adopted us, even although we were black with sin, diseased, polluted (Ezekiel 16:6); when He took us we were not bespangled with jewels of holiness nor bedecked with the glory of angels.

God's adopted ones are referred to as *children, sons, heirs. Children* expresses nearness to the Father; *sons,* our position before Him; *heirs,* our future inheritance in Him. Old Testament saints were children, but did not have the dignity of sons. Sonship is a privilege peculiar to believers of *this* dispensation—one of an eternal character as well (Revelation 21:7; Galatians 3:26 R.V.; 4:2-5). Angels are spoken of as "sons" but are not called "children." Every creature owes its being to God, but it is only through the new birth that men become His children and are privileged to call Him "Father." As *children,* we have a filial relationship to God, and have the feeling and nature proper to such a near and blessed relationship because it is founded on the birth-tie. As sons we have a position of great dignity and privilege before God. The Apostle John, both in his gospel and epistles, dwells more fully upon our relationship as children than any other of the sacred writers. He traces it to its source, the sovereign will of God, and expounds the moral characteristics of our nature as God's children (John 1:12; I John 3:1,2; Revelation 21:7).

The act of our adoption goes back to the dateless past, "before the foundation of the world." Is it not wonderful to realize that in the great unmeasured eternity before we were born, before our parents were born, before even the worlds were called into being, God chose us? And having been adopted by a divine act, perfect and complete, such can never be repeated. Adoption is once and for all in time and for eternity. Adoption is associated with the Father's purpose, in His eternal counsels (Ephesians 1:4,5). He has willed many things, but this is "the *good pleasure* of His will" that we should be "predestined to the adoption of children," and "to the praise of the glory of His grace."

The Price of Adoption

Walter Scott reminds us that "Sonship is a blessing peculiar to this dispensation because of the way we become sons (Galatians 3:26 R.V.). No saint prior to the Ascension of Christ could be a son of God, as faith in Christ Jesus was impossible until His death, Resurrection, and Ascension had taken place. Thus sonship was dependent upon the cross and upon Christ's going on high. Adoption then is an act of pure grace, and purchased at a dear price." To make heirs of wrath become heirs of the promise involved the death of God's only begotten Son. When God determined to adopt us, He sealed the deed with the blood of His own Son. Free grace, then, runs through the whole privilege of adoption and brings us a greater mercy than Adam had in Paradise. He was a son by creation—we are sons by adoption.

Faith, based upon the finished work of grace, brings us into the privilege of adoption (Galatians 3:26). As Thomas Watson expresses it, "Before faith is wrought, we are spiritually illegitimate, we have no relation to God as a Father. An unbeliever may call God judge, but not Father. Faith is the affiliating grace; it confers upon us the title of sonship, and gives us the right to inherit." Adoption does not depend upon any worthiness in us, but upon unmerited favor. It is all of grace. Acknowledging our utter unworthiness of such a privilege, seeing we were "enemies" and "aliens" (Ephesians 2:12; 4:18; Colossians 1:21), faith in Christ's sacrifice became the channel of our adoption. Covered with His worthiness, we are accepted as sons, and have an adoption resting upon His oath, His covenant and His blood.

The Purpose of Adoption

The full benefits of adoption are in the future. Dr. C. I. Scofield says that, "The indwelling Spirit gives the realization of this in the believer's present experience (Galatians 4:6); but the full manifestation of the believer's sonship awaits the resurrection, change and translation of saints, which is called 'The redemption of the body' (Romans 8:23; Ephesians 1:14; I Thessalonians 4:14-17; I John 3:2)."

The Spirit of adoption is the Spirit as the pledge and earnest of adoption (Romans 8:15; Ephesians 1:13,14).

We are depicted as waiting for the adoption (Romans 8:23).

As the redeemed, we are to receive the adoption or son-placing (Galatians 4: 5).

Being saints, we are predestinated unto the adoption (Ephesians 1:5).

Our glorious inheritance as *children* (Romans 8:17), and our position as *sons* (Galatians 4:1-5) are assured. What a magnificent future awaits us! God adopts all His sons to an inheritance (Luke 12:32). Adoption is also to end in coronation, for the kingdom God has for His adopted ones is to excel all earthly monarchies (I John 3:2). We are to be joint-heirs with Christ (Romans 8:17; I Corinthians 3:21-23; 4: 15-19; Hebrews 6:17; Revelation 21:7). By *justification* we are freed from condemnation and accepted as righteous in His sight. By *adoption* we are made His children and joint heirs with the Son of His love. What unspeakable honors are to be ours! Our present responsibility as adopted ones is to extol and magnify God's mercy and to live for His pleasure. As His sons, we must bear His likeness. Those who belong to distinguished families do their utmost, by noble living, worthy actions and dignified mien, to uphold the honor and reputation of their forebears, and not in any way disgrace the family's good name. Because of our glorious family connections through wondrous grace, "What manner of persons ought we to be in all holy conversation and godliness?" (II Peter 3:11).

Here let us each Thy mind display,
In all Thy brilliant virtues shine;
And haste that long-expected day
When Thou shalt own that we are Thine.

It is so blessedly true that the day of Christ's manifestation will be ours (Colossians 3:4), and that when we see Him, we are to be like Him, perfectly conformed to His image, and to know what it is to have adoption usher us into the redemption of our body, but there is a present likeness to seek after. Presently the Lord should be admired in all His saints. As adopted ones, our lives must reflect His beauty. It is thus that others are attracted to Him.

XXIII

The Doctrine of Assurance

As *assurance* is the spiritual birthright of every believer, it is their privilege and duty to experience and enjoy such an inner possession. Webster defines "assurance" as meaning a pledge or guarantee: the state of being sure or certain: insure against risk: security, certitude, confidence. In the realm of salvation, the word "assurance," occurring six times in the Bible, means *full of confidence*, and expresses the guarantee the believer has that he is forever secure. As Dr. C. I. Scofield expresses it, "Assurance is the believer's full conviction that, through the work of Christ alone, received by faith, he is in possession of a salvation in which he will be eternally kept. And this assurance rests only upon the Scripture promises to him who believes." The Biblical statement of this vital Bible truth is given by Isaiah—

The *work* of righteousness shall be peace: and the *effect* of righteousness, quietness and confidence forever.

This assurance of salvation is plainly written over the pages of the New Testament. Christ and His apostles lived in the air of certainty. Doubt in a regenerated heart is everywhere condemned. The epistles glow with the truth that we may *know* we possess salvation. They present a tenor of joy in a present experience, but the tragedy is that while all who are saved have the right to assurance, all do not experience it. As a letter can be written, and yet not sealed, so grace may be written within the heart, but faith is not strong enough to set the seal of assurance to the accomplishment of the Holy Spirit. Faith in the heart, however, should appear in the fruit of assurance.

Many lack assurance through dependence upon their feelings. But it is amazing to discover that the Bible maintains a profound silence on feelings. The Concordance shows that the word is used only twice in the Word, and in neither case is it employed in connection with our salvation. In Ephesians 4:19 the word describes a Christ-rejecting and hardened sinner. In Hebrews 4:15 the word denotes Christ's feeling or His power to sympathize. The word "feel" is found in six places, but in no instance is it related to a true Christian experience. Our salvation rests, not upon fluctuating and fitful feelings, but upon the unassailable facts the Scriptures present.

Saving faith directs attention away from self to the Saviour. The Bible does not say, "He that feeleth good, or feeleth bad, shall be saved," but "he that *believeth*." We are not left to pump dry hearts and bring up feelings, but are to have thoughts wholly occupied with Christ and His finished work on our behalf. We must hasten to say that it is not our experience or even our faith that saves, but Christ alone. He, alone, is the ground of our salvation and certainty. Whatever our changing feelings, our minds must be wholly stayed on the Lord. It was Faber who taught us to sing—

These surface troubles come and go,
   Like ruffles of the sea;
The deeper depth is out of reach,
   To all, my God, but Thee.

It cannot be emphasized too strongly that the Bible teaches the truth that all who are regenerated by the Spirit can be absolutely certain of their standing in grace. All who have accepted Christ as Saviour *are* saved, but a few timid souls probe their feelings, practicing psychoanalysis. With them it is, "I hope so"; "maybe"; "Perhaps so," while it should be "I know so"; "Have"; "Is"; "You have." This is a profound assurance, of which John wrote:

These things have I written unto you that believe on the name of the Son of God; that ye may know that ye have eternal life, and that ye may believe on the name of the Son of God (I John 5:13).

There can be no assurance within unless there is the acceptance of the direct testimony of the Word of God. Such an assurance is not a mere mental assent to the veracity of scriptural statements, but an inner light, produced by believing God. Assurance is no vocal or audible voice or the revelation of an angel, but a condition of being secure, the willingness to take God at His word.

Assurance is the mental and spiritual certainty of sins forgiven, of justification before God, of the possession of eternal life. Uncertainty regarding these facts breeds doubt and fear. But when with confidence we can say with Paul, ". . . I know whom I have believed, and am persuaded that he is able to keep that which I have committed unto him against that day" (II Timothy 1:12), all doubt is excluded. Assurance is a birthright we must preserve and never forfeit. We must "hold fast the confidence and the rejoicing of the hope firm unto the end" (Hebrews 3:6,14). Such confidence must never be "cast away" (Hebrews 10:35). When Peter took his eyes off Christ and looked at the waves, he began to sink.

The Source of Assurance

Full assurance rests upon unassailable and unchanging Bible facts. An objective source of our assurance are the unconditional promises of God like John 6:37; 10: 27, 28; Romans 8:31-39. True assurance is built upon a scriptural foundation.

In the first epistle of John, the word translated *know* occurs 42 times, and should be sufficient to stay all doubts as to the certainty of salvation. What peace of mind a doubting, fearing believer forfeits if he is uncertain whether he is a real believer. Assurance comes through the acceptance of divine promises. Jesus declared that all receiving Him as Saviour will *never* perish (John 10:28). To doubt His affirmation is to make Him a liar. Paul says that Christ is able to keep us (II Timothy 1:12); that we *are*—not may be—in Him; that we *have been* forgiven (Colossians 2:13). With all these precious facts and promises, how sad it is to encounter many believers tossed about on the troubled sea of uncertainty and insecurity. What God begins, He will complete (Philippians 1:6). Faith in what the Bible declares produces a harvest of assurance.

Another source of assurance is the completeness of Christ's atoning work. "It is finished" (John 19:30); "Purged our sins" (Hebrews 1:3). Dr. R. A. Torrey once wrote, "It is the blood of Christ that makes us safe; it is the Word of God that makes us sure."

Full assurance also rests upon the intercessory work of Christ, who is "able to succour" and also able to "save to the uttermost" (Hebrews 2:18; 7:25). God's own nature, imparted to the believer in the hour surance. Christ becomes "our Life" (Colossians 3:4). By faith, through grace, we become partakers of a divine nature (II Peter 1:4; I Peter 1:23).

Further, assurance springs from righteousness, not our own, but the Lord's (Isaiah 32:17). Many are confident that all is well because of their own morality. But their assurance is false, seeing all their righteousness is as filthy rags in God's sight. Only divine righteousness can avail on our behalf, and when clothed with it, a blessed assurance becomes ours. Assurance rests not upon what we are in ourselves, but upon what we have become in Christ (Hebrews 12:2, margin).

The inner witness of the Spirit is likewise a contributing factor to our assurance. The Holy Spirit is a voice of divine assurance (I John 4:13). Thus, the sources of assurance are external and internal. The Spirit within us, who inspired the Word, creates assurance in all it declares concerning our relationship to God. While the assurance of salvation is a subjective experience, it results in the inner consciousness and confidence that all is well between the soul and God. Assurance of an eternal salvation is based on understanding (John 20:31; Colossians 2:2; I John 5:13,20). Assurance is an *intellectual process* whereby the mind is enabled by the Spirit to accept revealed truth, resulting in an *emotional state*, or a deep soul satisfaction. John Wesley wrote of assurance as

an inward impression on the soul, whereby the Spirit of God directly witnesses to my spirit that I am a child of God: that Jesus Christ hath loved me and given Himself for me: and that all my sins are blotted out, and I, even I, am reconciled to God.

Assurance, then, comes as the fruit of a Spirit-inspired faith in divine facts. We recognize that many who lack this assurance are as truly saved as those who are confident they are the Lord's. Those who live in *doubting Castle* have faith, but it is a weak faith. We disagree with Martin Luther and John Calvin, both of whom suggested that one lacking personal assurance cannot be regarded as a true believer. Faith may be weak, but it is nevertheless a genuine faith and as it blossoms into the full assurance of faith (Hebrews 10:22), the soul is elevated from the valley of doubt to the plateau of assurance. It is the purpose of God that all believers should possess a strong, lively faith, and it is their privilege and duty to experience same.

The Scope of Assurance

The Scriptures present the following three aspects of the believer's assurance:

Full Assurance of Faith (Hebrews 10: 22). The believer is saved by grace through faith, and such a faith rests upon the eternal Word of the eternal God.

Full Assurance of Understanding (Colossians 2:2). Here we have the mental grasp of all spiritual privileges. The Spirit of understanding (Isaiah 11:2) is responsible for our mental comprehension and apprehension of truth.

Full Assurance of Hope (Hebrews 6:11). This aspect of assurance is related to the confidence and joy resulting from the discovery and appropriation of revealed truth. The hope assurance covers is one making the future bright with the blessed hope (Titus 2:13; I Peter 1:4,5; I John 5:13).

Some of the facts of our faith confidently embraced by assurance are:

Salvation (Isaiah 12:2). The fact of our salvation being not something, but Someone, produces quietness of spirit and an unshakeable confidence.

Adoption (I John 3:2). Assurance of sonship is a most inspiring factor in life and service. As sons, we have the legitimate heritage of all that is in Christ.

Vital Union (II Corinthians 13:5). Our loving, living, lasting union with the risen Head should result in a grateful assurance. His, *forever* His!

Love for Others (I John 3:14; I John 5:1). Love for fellow believers is a striking proof that assurance is well grounded. Jealousy, bitterness and hatred never foster assurance. The absence of brotherly love, the presence of ill-will, cynicism, resentment, blast the fruit of assurance. While it is important to believe correctly if we would have assurance, it is equally important to behave correctly, if assurance is to be enjoyed.

Holiness of Life (I John 5:18). Unconfessed, unforsaken sin can rob one of full assurance. Sympathy with sin destroys confidence. "God never pours the wine of assurance into a foul vessel." We must exercise ourselves unto all godliness (I Timothy 4:7). Holiness is the sap helping to produce the fruit of assurance.

Contentment amidst all circumstances. Paul experienced the fact that a deep-seated assurance is the secret of contentment (II Timothy 1:12; Hebrews 13:5). The apostle wrote of being sorrowful, yet always rejoicing (II Corinthians 6:10). Assurance that we are eternally the Lord's and that He loves, knows and cares, silences all murmurings against His dealings. "Assurance," an old writer has said, "is like the mariner's lantern on the deck, which gives light in a dark night. Assurance enables us to rejoice in tribulation, to discover honey in the lion's carcass, and to take joy in the spoiling of our goods."

Latimer, the martyr, wrote, "When I sit alone, and can have a settled assurance of the state of my soul, and know that God is mine, I can laugh at all troubles and nothing can daunt me."

Peace of Soul (Ephesians 2:13,14). The devil rocks men in the cradle of a false peace (Isaiah 57:21). To be saved and to be sure we are saved creates a peace passing all understanding. True peace is the sister of assurance, and springs from our union with Christ and constant submission to Him. Unfortunately, not all believers experience this deep, settled peace. They have the title to it, and the ground of it in their relation to Christ. Grace made them His, and they have the seed of peace within, but lack of obedience or full understanding of their position prevent the blooming of the flower of peace.

When peaceful assurance is ours, we have God's smile, and mount up with wings as eagles in the exercise of Christian service. "Assurance will be as wings to the bird, as weights to the clock to set all the wheels of obedience running." Such assurance forms the first fruits of Paradise. How can a bride be happy if doubts validate her marriage? Commenting on the Christian graces, Paul speaks of as being the fruit of the Spirit (Galatians 5:22), William Pope says, "The clearer these graces shine forth, and the more abundant they are, the greater will be the measure of assurance which they gender in the heart."

Witness among the Lost (I Thessalonians 1:5). Unless we have complete assurance within, there will not be convincing boldness as we witness for Christ among the unsaved. Paul possessed unwavering faith in his own salvation, hence his dynamic witness (Acts 28:31). If a believer has doubt as to his eternal salvation, how can he recommend it to others? As a gardener improves the quality of his fruit, we can improve the quality of our assurance, by telling others of all we find in Christ, telling the lost how He unlocked for us the secrets of free grace, causing them to yearn for the delights of His love. While Paul possessed the pearl of assurance, he did not boast of it. He thought of himself as being less than the least of all saints (Ephesians 3:8). Indifference to the need of our fellow men prevents assurance from budding (I John 3:17).

The Pauline assurance was not presumption. There are those who affirm that to declare we can know we are saved and safe for heaven is mere assumption. But both Paul and John could say, with all humility, "I know." There is, of course, a distinction between true assurance and presumption. Assurance comes from faith in God's Word, and His accomplishments on our behalf. Presumption is the forbidden fruit of self-confidence in our own possessions and attainments. No man has the jewel of assurance who does not abhor the works of the flesh. Assurance is associated with true humility, while presumption is the other face of pride. Presumption estranges God from the soul. "The jewel of assurance is best kept in the cabinet of a humble heart."

Assurance can be cultivated by believing all God says (I John 2:23; 5:2; 5:14), by Bible study, by prayer, and by desiring all the things of the Spirit. Lack of love for the Word and ignorance of the indwelling presence of the Spirit hinders assurance. Assurance is also strengthened as we scorn the garlic and onions of Egypt, sitting loose to the things of earth, and longing after the joys of heaven. Having assurance of our title to the realms of bliss, we should certainly long to be there.

Too many of the saints of God lack full assurance. They suffer themselves to be chained by fear and doubt. Possibly they are religious, but not regenerated. Theirs has never been the full commitment to the Saviour. No one can know if they are saved, unless they are prepared to be fully saved.

Others lack assurance simply because they are unwilling to carry out the known will of God. Obedience to all He reveals results in an assurance nothing can disturb. The absence of assurance means the presence of doubt. Modernism is responsible for the destruction of faith in the supernatural, and therefore stands condemned as the blatant destroyer of assurance.

There are some timid souls, smitten with an inferiority complex, in whom their failures and shortcomings create a feeling of inferiority and they deem themselves utterly inadequate to witness for Christ. Such an unwholesome attitude damages assurance.

Others allow their trials to produce an eclipse of their assurance. At one time David confessed, "Thy lovingkindness is before mine eyes" (Psalm 26:3). Contrast this with his question, "Lord, where are Thy former lovingkindnesses?" (Psalm 89:49).

God desires His children to have a sky without a sunset, or the uninterrupted assurance of His provision and protection. But if we doubt His providential care, how can we approach Him with confidence ?

Blessed assurance, Jesus is mine!
Oh, what a foretaste of glory divine!
Heir of salvation, purchase of God,
Born of His Spirit, washed in His blood.

XXIV

The Doctrine of Righteousness

Righteousness, divine and human, forms the warp and woof of Scripture. Doctrinal and practical righteousness meet us on almost every page. Such an important truth has been treated as if it is most difficult. Theologians may have made it so, but the Word of God is simple and clear in its teaching on this doctrine of grace. Is it not tragic that a theme so beautifully and blessedly simple has been muddled, confused, tortured, twisted and disputed over through centuries of wrangle and strife.

The imperative need of our day is a right understanding of righteousness because of its association with the soul's relation to God, and also responsibilities to others. Walter Scott says,

Righteousness is the necessary basis of God's dealing with saint and sinner; the ground too, on which grace gloriously sways its sceptre (Romans 5:21), and the super-structure on which all Christian life, progress and service repose. It underlies every position and relation of life. Righteousness is the keystone of the arch of divine revelation.

It may help us as we approach a study of the basic doctrine of "righteousness" to bear in mind that it is a relative term involving our dealings or relations with others. The simple idea resident within the word is that of "doing what is right." While there may be shades of meaning associated with the word, the root idea wherever it is used is a state of *rightness* whether toward God or man. "Righteousness" can be defined as "consistency in every given position and relation which a creature occupies in regard to others." It may make for clarity if we summarize this theme of tremendous importance in the following ways—

1. *God is righteous, and as such, demands righteousness, for without it there can be no possible fellowship between the Creator and His creatures.*

The consistent testimony of Scripture is that two cannot walk together except they be agreed. Righteousness cannot have fellowship with unrighteousness (Deuteronomy 25:16; Psalm 1:5,6; II Corinthians 6:14; Romans 1:18; 2:8,9). But what do we mean by "the righteous act of God"? This phrase, peculiar to and characteristic of Paul's epistles, signifies God's consistency with His own nature and character in freely and perfectly justifying a sinner believing on Jesus. It is the revelation of the righteous ground on which God can and does freely justify a guilty sinner.

God always acts rightly, in perfect harmony with His nature in all His actions. Thus, when divested of the involved theological descriptions of "righteousness," how simple and how profound is its significance. And what a sure repose of soul the truth of divine righteousness also provides. In describing this blessed attribute, Paul uses a verbal difference. "The righteousness of God," that is, God's own inherent nature (Romans 1:17; 3:21-23); "The righteousness which is of God" (Philippians 3:9). In this latter phrase Paul is contrasting two kinds of righteousness, namely, that which is of or *from* the law, he himself rejected; and that which is of or *from* God, which Paul, as a pardoned and justified sinner, rested in.

2. *Man has no righteousness of his own with which he may meet the righteous and inexorable demands of God.*

It cuts clean across our fancied greatness and goodness to be told that all our righteousness is but a filthy rag in God's sight. All we pride ourselves upon is rejected by God. Ignorant of divine righteousness, we try to establish our own (Romans 10:3; Ecclesiastes 7:20; Isaiah 64:6). How futile is our effort to work out, even under the law, a character which God can approve! The human heart is corrupt, deceitful above all things, and desperately wicked (Jeremiah 17:9) and cannot therefore out of rottenness produce righteousness acceptable to God.

If personal and vicarious righteousness by law-keeping or obedience in life could be ours, the justification by blood is a nullity. It was because of our utter inability to satisfy the righteous demands of God that He Himself provided a garment of perfect righteousness. The garment, as a symbol of righteousness, is used in a twofold way. In the bad, ethical sense, it represents our own self-righteousness, which was the brand the Pharisees prided themselves upon (Isaiah 64:9; Luke 18:9; Philippians 3:6-9). In the good sense, the garment represents the righteousness of God, clothing all who believe (Romans 3:1-19). The glory of the Gospel is that law*breakers* and not law*keepers*, believing in Jesus, are accounted righteous by God.

The righteousness of God excludes the righteousness of many Jews and Gentiles alike. By human righteousness no man can be justified (Psalm 143:2; (Romans 1:17; 3:20). The mind of the flesh, even good flesh, is enmity against God (Romans 8:7). How arrogant the proud sinner is then, when having no righteousness of his own, he deliberately and contemptuously rejects Him who is alone qualified to be his righteousness! How dreadful is the end of the rejectors of divine righteousness (I Corinthians 6:9)! If only they would cease resisting the wooings of the Holy Spirit, and turn to and trust in Christ, and have their faith accounted unto them for righteousness (Galatians 3:6), what peace would be theirs.

If the sinner is to have a righteousness acceptable to God, it must be divinely provided. His eyes must turn away from his own ruin and self-righteousness to Christ, who was made unto us righteousness (I Corinthians 1:30; Romans 8:7; Isaiah 45: 8,24; 46:12,13; 54:17). The sinner is altogether lost unless he can sing—

> Had I an angel's righteousness,
> I'd throw away that beauteous dress
> And wrap me up in Christ.

3. *The sinner, through believing, is constituted the righteousness of God in Christ, the sinless, righteous One.*

Christ, on the *cross*, was made sin for us. Now on the *throne* He is the righteousness of God, that is, the perfect expression of it. The phrase, "the righteousness of Christ," is not to be found in Scripture. The substitution of this for "the righteousness of God" has created much misunderstanding. The grandest, fullest witness of righteousness on the part of God is expressed in setting Christ at His own right hand—crowned and glorified as "The Lord our Righteousness." In the exalted One we have a marvelous exhibition of the righteousness of God, and in Him we have become the righteousness of God (I Corinthians 1:30; II Corinthians 5:21 R.V.).

The kernel of the Gospel is that Christ died for our sins and was raised again, manifesting thereby God's work in love and righteousness for sinners (Romans 4:25; I Corinthians 15:3,4). Grace *reigns* through righteousness and the salvation of all who believe on Christ is a righteous salvation. Even the devil cannot call in question the fact that God is "just and the Justifier of him which believeth on Jesus" (Romans 3: 26; Hebrews 2:14; Zechariah 3:2). Thus we are thrice secure and serene if we rest in the confidence that—

> Christ is our Peace—Who can disturb it?
> Christ is our Hope—Who can destroy it?
> Christ is our Righteousness—Who can tarnish it?

In union with Christ by faith, we are, in the sight of God, in the very Son Himself. What a privileged position! In justification, Christ is the embodiment of righteousness imparted unto us. In sanctification, such righteousness is imparted unto us. From Him, as the Head, life flows into the members. Justin Martyr had this truth in mind when he wrote,

What else could cover our sins but His Righteousness. In whom could we transgressors be justified but only in the Son of God. O sweet exchange! O unsearchable contrivance that the transgressions of many should be hidden in one righteous Person and the Righteousness of One should justify many transgressors!

Our righteousness, then, is not *something* but *Someone,* even Him who possessed Lordship (Mark 12:36,37; John 13:13).

At this juncture it might be well to consider the whole matter of *imputation* with which Paul deals in his epistle to the Romans. To impute means to reckon or count to one something which he, himself, is destitute of. "Abraham believed God, and it was *imputed* unto him for righteousness" (James 2:23). Imputation is perfectly illustrated for us in Paul's desire to have Philemon receive Onesimus, the run-away slave, back as himself. "Receive him as myself" or "reckon him to my credit" (Philemon 17). "If he hath wronged thee or oweth thee ought, put that on mine account," or "reckon to me his demerit" (Philemon 18). With God, imputation is His gracious act whereby He accounts righteousness to the believer in Christ, who has borne the believer's sins in vindication of the law.

Attention must be drawn to the fact that righteousness is not *infused* but only imputed to man, and that such a divine act changes the believing sinner's relation to God, legally or forensically. In the first instance, imputation does not change his character. Daniel speaks of the wise turning many to righteousness (Daniel 12:3), which means they are brought to God who alone can justify them.

"Imputed righteousness" is not Biblical language, for divine righteousness is not imputable, neither is it the law-keeping of Jesus. Righteousness in itself has not the character of imputation. Righteousness imputed or reckoned is what the Word teaches. The righteousness of one cannot be put to another's account. If you could transfer one's righteousness to another, then one is left destitute of it. There is a righteousness imputed, but it is not said to be "the righteousness of God" (Romans 4:3,5,6,9, 22-25). Such righteousness is nowhere said to be reckoned or imputed, but righteousness is put to the account of a guilty sinner accepting God's terms of salvation. God is as righteous in justifying as in punishing—

as consistent with the claims of His nature in doing the one as the other. Thus the imputation of God's righteousness is a moral impossibility. It *is* God's and ever will be a part of Himself, displayed in relation to His creatures. God cannot impute that which is essential to Himself, in His dealings with men.

The righteousness of God is that righteousness of which He is the Source and the Owner. It is God's in a real sense, divine in quality and character. It is also toward men as *from* God, reckoned unto man on the ground of Christ's finished work. Further, the righteousness of God is not to be confused with a legal righteousness by the perfect law-keeping or obedience of Christ. Such an understanding affects both the *person* and *sacrifice* of Christ. If "the righteousness of Christ" is put to our account, then it leaves Him without it, or *un*-righteous. If, by the vicarious obedience of Christ to the law we are declared righteous, then clearly His death is in vain (Galatians 2:21). Neither is it a righteousness associated with the law (Romans 3:21). It is irrespective of the law, although witnessed to by the law and the prophets. David describes the blessedness of the man to whom God imputes righteousness (Psalm 32:2).

As a sinner has no righteousness of his own, he must have a righteousness without works. Thus the only righteousness for him is the imputed one of God's in Christ. God alone is able to justify a guilty sinner, and He alone can impute righteousness to one who is destitute of it. But this divine action is not the placing of a quantity of righteousness *in* a man. It is simply holding, or regarding as righteous or just, one who is not so either in nature or practice, as Romans 4 clearly shows. Righteousness imputed supposes that one is destitute of it. Otherwise why reckon it to him? Nowhere is it implied that there is a conferment of an inward righteousness. The message of grace is that a man who in himself is wrong can be counted right through the righteousness of Another.

Before man's bar, the righteousness on account of which he is justified or counted righteous is *his own*. Before God's bar, the righteousness on account of which he is justified is Christ's, who has been made unto us righteousness (II Peter 1:1; I Corinthians 1:30). Pardon accompanies justification before God's bar, but pardon would be scorned by one innocent. Acquittal before

man is not always accompanied with justification. The sinner, however, pardoned before, and by God, is always justified also. It would be an immoral action for a king or magistrate to declare a man right who was wrong. A judge cannot justify or declare practically right a *proved* offender—he may pardon but he cannot justify. Yet God is just and the Justifier of all who believe, and Calvary explains it all. Christ bore the judgment of God upon our offenses, but was raised again for our justification (Romans 4:25). In this great chapter, "righteousness" occurs eight times, but the words "of God" are not added. "The righteousness of God" is nowhere said to be imputed or reckoned unto us, but "righteousness," that is, all Christ accomplished in our stead and behalf is put to our account through acceptance of Him as Saviour.

4. *Divine righteousness can only become ours by faith.*

A sinner can only be justified—
Judicially by God—Romans 8:33
Meritoriously by Christ—Isaiah 53:11; Jeremiah 23:6; Revelation 5:9.
Instrumentally by faith—Romans 5:1-9; 8:1; John 5:24.
Evidentially by works—James 2:14-26.

Righteousness must be accepted as a divine gift (Romans 4:5; 9:30-32; 10:4). Paul cast to the dogs the righteousness of which he was once so proud. Those things he counted gain were willingly reckoned loss that he might be found clothed in his Lord's righteousness (Romans 1:16,17; Galatians 2:16; Philippians 3:6-9). It was so with John Bunyan, whose mind was saturated with the gospel of grace. The believer in Christ is now, by grace, shrouded under so complete and blessed a righteousness that the law from Mount Sinai can find neither fault nor diminution therein. This is that which is called "the righteousness of God by faith" (Romans 3:26; 4:6; II Corinthians 5:21).

Jesus, Thy blood and righteousness
My beauty are, my glorious dress;
'Midst flaming worlds, in these arrayed,
With joy shall I lift up my head.

The noble *Westminster Confession* states that:

Faith, receiving and resting on Christ and His Righteousness, is the *alone instrument of justification,* yet it is not alone in the person justified, but is ever accompanied with all other saving graces.

5. *It is essential to exhibit practical righteousness in everyday life.*

We deceive ourselves if we deem ourselves righteous yet fail to manifest righteousness in life. "Doing" righteousness is the sure fruit and proof of "being" righteous, that is, of having the only principle of true righteousness within and the only means of justification, namely, faith (Romans 4:3-8; Ephesians 2:5,8-10). Noah, the preacher of righteousness, was just or righteous in life (Genesis 6:9). Of course, it is not doing righteousness that makes us righteous. Our standing before God is revealed in our state among men. Positional righteousness has its reflection in practical righteousness (Romans 10:3-10). Right with God, we shall live right before men. Here, then, is a phase of righteousness covering every relation and position in life (Titus 2:12). Doing what is right is the divine claim of righteousness for one and all.

When John urged the saints to do righteousness (I John 3:7), he meant them to live that righteous life ever resulting from salvation. "The righteous man under the law became righteous by doing righteously," says Dr. C. I. Scofield. "Under grace he does righteously because he has been made righteous (Romans 3:22; 10:3). Faithfully and minutely we must fulfill every obligation of life, whether religiously, socially or publicly. We must be righteous as a saint, servant, worshiper of God; as a worker, master, citizen of the world; as a husband, father, wife or child in the circle of social relationship; as a steward as God has bestowed upon us health, time, talents, treasures and influence." To be righteous is simply to *be* right and to *do* right toward God and man.

The word "righteous" means equitable, upright, free from wrong. But where can we learn this practical righteousness, or the full extent of our obligation Godward and manward? How can God supply us with motive and power to act rightly in all things, at all times and in all relations? In these matters, as in all others, we must turn to Scripture for satisfactory answers. Wherever life's duties and responsibilities are unfolded, we are always directed to Christ as the grand and constraining motive. How righteous He was in all His ways. As to the power by which practical righteousness can be effected, we know that the Holy Spirit alone can transform position into practice.

Satan, the enemy of the Righteous One and of righteousness, is determined and wily and an everwatchful foe (Ephesians 6:14). He knows that if practical righteousness is lacking in a saint, he is exposed to satanic attacks. Lack of consistency in any realm of life leaves one weak, powerless and unfruitful in service. Practical righteousness is the keynote of the Sermon on the Mount (Matthew 5:6). It is ever the ground of our appeal in prayer (Psalm 4). The paths of righteousness must be trod by a blood-purchased flock (Psalm 23). One must have the determination to "follow righteousness" (II Timothy 2:22), in all things, in all places, in all relationships. Walter Scott reminds us that the principle, "Of two evils choose the least," is utterly false. "We must have a holy path to tread, a clean place to dwell, a good conscience to exercise. We must never belie the nature of God—sacrifice at the shrine of expediency of numbers, of supposed usefulness, of an ecclesiastical unity the practical righteousness demanded from every saint and service of the Lord Jesus Christ."

6. *The manifold blessings resulting from the acceptance of a divinely provided righteousness.*

The "other saving graces" the *Westminster Confession* speaks of as accompanying our justification are worthy of remembrance.

The righteous are blessed with prosperity.

"Say ye to the righteous, that it shall be well with him: for they shall eat the fruit of their doings" (Isaiah 3:10).

The righteous are surrounded with divine favor.

"For Thou, LORD, wilt bless the righteous; with favor wilt Thou compass him as with a shield" (Psalm 5:12).

The righteous enjoy peace, quietness and assurance.

"And the work of righteousness shall be peace; and the effect of righteousness quietness and assurance forever" (Isaiah 32:17).

The righteous experience deliverance from affliction.

"Many are the afflictions of the righteous, but the LORD delivereth him out of them all" (Psalm 34:19).

The righteous have enlightened minds and glad hearts.

"Light is sown for the righteous, and gladness for the upright in heart" (Psalm 97:11).

The righteous are never forgotten.

". . . the righteous shall be in everlasting remembrance" (Psalm 112:6).

The righteous are constantly guarded.

"For the eyes of the Lord are over the righteous, and His ears are open unto their prayers . . ." (I Peter 3:12).

How amazed we are at the greatness of God's grace! Truly it is too much for us to comprehend and receive, yet not too much for Him to give. The time is coming when the heavens will declare His righteousness, and all peoples are to see His glory (Psalm 97:6). When the Sun of Righteousness appears with healing in His wings (Malachi 4:2) accompanied by all the heavenly saints, what a glorious consummation that will be of His work on our behalf. The ultimate blessing of righteousness by faith is eternity with Him who is our righteousness. This is the glad hope of the righteous (Proverbs 10:29,30; Malachi 3:17,18; Matthew 13:43; 25:46). "We through the Spirit wait for the hope of righteousness by faith" (Galatians 5:5). We do not hope *for* righteousness. By faith we have that now. But hope directs our gaze to the future, and the "hope of righteousness" is the sight of the righteous One Himself, even Him who promised to return for His own (John 14:3).

O let the dead now hear Thy voice;
Now bid Thy banished ones rejoice;
Their beauty this, their glorious dress,
Jesus, Thy blood and righteousness.

XXV
The Doctrine of Peace

In our restless age there is a universal yearning for peace. It is because human nature sighs for tranquility of soul as "the ocean shell, when placed to the ear, seems to sigh for the untroubled depths of its native home," that many books on the subject, such as Dr. Billy Graham's *Peace With God,* enjoy a wide circulation.

Multitudes of fevered, troubled lives seek "the repose of the unruffled waters of a mountain lake." Is there such a peace? Does Christ mock the human heart when He says, "My peace I give unto you"? Is there a balm for the hearts of sinners, described by the prophet as being like the troubled sea that cannot rest, casting up mire and dirt? (Isaiah 57:20). Is there peace for our war-weary, blood-soaked earth? Let it be shouted from the housetops that for nations and men there is a divinely provided peace.

It is enough; earth's struggles soon shall cease,
And Jesus call us to heaven's perfect peace.

The Bible speaks of peace in various ways. There is peace or reconciliation with God: Peace with ourselves or our own conscience: Peace with our foes (Proverbs 16:7); Peace with, and amongst men: Peace amongst saints, or mutual accord and agreement: Peace as opposed to war—cessation of hostilities (II Kings 20:19; Judges 4:17): Peace as opposed to church heresies and schisms (Psalm 122:6; Acts 9:31): Peace as opposed to unrest of mind—a perfect rest and joy nothing can disturb or molest (Isaiah 57:2; II Peter 3:14).

The aspect of peace we desire to present is that peace coming to us through a knowledge of sins forgiven—a peace flowing from the merits and suffering of the Saviour (Ephesians 2:14)—a peace arising from a sense of our reconciliation, which is the gift of Christ and wrought in us by the Spirit (Romans 14:17; Philippians 4:7)—a peace resulting from submission to the will of God (Job 22:21). Among the basic doctrines of our Christian faith none is more satisfying than this "peace, the gift of God's love." And we deem it fitting to summarize this Bible doctrine under the three general heads—

Peace with God, or Peace above us
Peace of God, or Peace within us
Peace from God, or Peace around us.

Peace With God—Peace Above Us

All that the Bible has to say of our reconciliation to God through Christ is condensed for us in the exhortation of Eliphaz,

"Acquaint thyself now with God, and be at peace; thereby good shall come unto thee" (Job 22:21).

Nought but good, both here and hereafter, follows those who are at peace with God. There is no treasure in the world comparable to restored fellowship with Him whose Son came to bestow peace on the earth (Luke 2:14).

At peace with God! How great the blessing
In fellowship with Him to be,
And from all stains of sin set free,
How rich am I such wealth possessing.

At peace with God! No change can harm me,
Whichever way my course may run;
One wish alone, God's will be done,
I seek since I have known His mercy.

What are the constituent elements of this peace of conscience we experience as by faith we accept what Christ accomplished for us at Calvary? First of all, such a perfect peace is divine in its origin, seeing the three Persons of the blessed Trinity are united in its acquisition and application.

God the Father is the God of peace—

"And the very God of peace sanctify you wholly . . ." (I Thessalonians 5:23).

"And the God of peace shall bruise Satan under your feet shortly . . ." (Romans 16:20).

God the Son is the Prince and Personification of peace—

"For unto us a child is born . . . and his name shall be called . . . The Prince of Peace" (Isaiah 9:6).

"For he is our peace . . ." (Ephesians 2:14).

God the Spirit provides the Fruit of peace—

"But the fruit of the Spirit is . . . peace" (Galatians 5:22).

The Father decreed peace: the Son purchased peace: the Spirit applies peace:

The ground of the peace we experience in the hour of initial faith is the precious blood of Jesus, satisfying God and pacifying the conscience (Hebrews 12:24). Calvary is the guarantee of the believing sinner's peace. The shed blood is the only balm to cure a wounded, sin-seared conscience. "Peace" and "pact" are from the same source. Through Christ our Peace we have a pact with God.

"Peace, perfect peace, in this dark world of sin, The blood of Jesus whispers, 'Peace within.' "

The cross reconciles the sinner to God (II Corinthians 5:19,20). Nothing more is requisite save to lay aside fear, suspicion and doubt and accept the blood-bought peace of Calvary which Christ now sweetly and freely offers to all. All obstacles to peace with God have been entirely met and put out of the way. God's holy justice no longer pursues us to seek our death. His justice and righteousness were vindicated in the death of His Son. The broken law has been forever silenced by the obedience and death of the Law-Giver Himself. When the disciples, cowering for fear of the Jews, saw the nail prints in the hands and feet of Jesus, and heard His benediction, "Peace be unto you" (John 20:25,26) their troubled hearts were calmed.

The blood on the lintel secured Israel's peace (Exodus 12:13). Nothing more than the blood was required. It is thus with ourselves in this gospel age. The blood of Christ is the only true ground of peace. The Israelite knew that he was not partly sheltered by the blood, and partly exposed to the sword of the destroyer. He knew he was entirely safe. He did not hope so, or pray to be so. He knew he was safe, because God had said, "When I see the blood, I will pass over you." Peace, then, was the Israelite's by blood *alone*, not his thoughts about it—deep or shallow. His safety had nothing to do with his own thoughts or feelings. God did not say, "When *you* see the blood, I will pass over you." What He said to His people was, "When *I* see the blood." Thus, the people had tranquility of heart because they knew Jehovah's eye was on the blood sprinkled upon their houses.

Peace with God was secured through the shedding of Christ's blood, and this is the very substance of the Gospel (Colossians 1:20). Feeling cannot alter such an unchangeable fact. Such a peace is not a fluctuating feeling, but a permanent state or condition based upon Christ's finished work. How necessary it is for the soul to be firmly established in the truth of peace with or toward God. Often sinners are exhorted to make their peace with God, especially as they come to die. While we recognize the good intentions of those who use this approach, such language is not Biblical. Lost, guilty sinners cannot make peace with God, but through infinite love peace has been made through the blood shed on the cross of Calvary.

Further, this blood-bought peace is not an intangible something, but a Person. "*He is our peace*" (Ephesians 2:12,17). To all in open insurrection to the law of God, Christ came preaching peace (Acts 10:36). Peace with God was made before we were born. All we have to do is to appropriate it by faith. "Being justified by faith we *have* peace with God through our Lord Jesus Christ" (Romans 5:1). A sin-hating God met the sin-bearing Christ at Calvary and there and then made a full settlement of the sin question.

By Christ on the Cross, peace was made;
My debt by His death was all paid;
No other foundation is laid
    For peace, the gift of God's love.

Christ is our Peace not only in His death, but also in His Resurrection. The first word addressed to His own after His victory over the grave was, "Peace be unto you" (John 20:19). He assured His disciples that the enemy had been conquered and the accuser for ever silenced. He is also our Peace in His Ascension (Luke 24: 50-52). At His birth there was the anthem of peace by the angel host—"On earth, peace . . ." (Luke 2:14). He is likewise our Peace in service. The first installment of peace the risen Lord gave His disciples was associated with their service for Him (John 20:21). Out they went into a hostile and unfriendly world, but they went out in peace. Christ is our Peace in trouble (Psalm 29:11). He is our Peace to meet daily needs (John 14:27; 16:33). "Peace is the nurse to plenty" (Psalm 147:14).

Peace, perfect peace, by thronging duties pressed?
To do the will of Jesus, this is rest.

Peace, perfect peace, with sorrows surging round?
On Jesus' bosom naught but calm is found.

Peace, perfect peace, with loved ones far away?
In Jesus' keeping we are safe, and they!

Christ is our Peace in death. The promise His children cling to is so precious,

"Thou shalt be gathered unto thy grave in peace" (II Kings 22:20). In the last hour our thoughts turn away from ordinances, unction, prayers and feeling, to Christ our Peace. The wicked are destitute of this peace in life and death (Isaiah 57: 21).

Peace, perfect peace, death shadowing us and ours?
Jesus has vanquished death and all its powers.

Christ is our Peace in His return. Eight days after His Resurrection He said, for the third time, "Peace be unto you" (John 20:26). Ours is the faith of the believing remnant of Israel when they said, "This man shall be the peace, when the Assyrian shall come into our land . . ." (Micah 5:5). As the shadows of judgment gather around a guilty world, the God of peace stands ready to sanctify His own (I Thessalonians 5:23,24). As we await His coming to a war-weary and blood-soaked earth, we hear Him say, "Peace, be still," and there is a great calm in our hearts.

Peace with God is impossible apart from faith in the Word of God. Peace can only come through believing (Romans 15:13). How many there are who miss God's peace because they are guilty of looking into their hearts to see how they feel! Dependance upon feelings means torture. If we try to seek peace through the media of feelings we will find ourselves on a dead-end road. We must concentrate heart and mind upon the mighty facts and promises of the Word (John 5:24; Acts 13:29-33).

What is it to believe? Does it not signify the handing over of our entire life to Christ, trusting Him according to His Word to save us and keep us saved? While the Bible does not say that feelings are an essential condition to salvation, it does say that joy and peace become ours through believing. There are many timid souls who are not sure whether they have the right kind of faith. Well, there are not many kinds of faith. All faith is *faith*. It is not the amount or the strength of faith that saves, but the Object of faith, even Christ. If we only have faith as a grain of mustard seed, the same is sufficient to save. Peace must inevitably ensue when we are persuaded that God will keep His Word and that He is able to keep all we have committed to Him (II Timothy 1:12).

Ere leaving this aspect of peace, it might

be necessary to add that while the ministry of the Holy Spirit has its rightful and imperative place in our lives, the Spirit did not make peace with God as Christ did. God did not send the Spirit "preaching peace." This was Christ's mission (Ephesians 2:14-17; Colossians 1:20). So we are presently dealing not with the work of the Spirit *in* us, but the work of Christ *for* us, as the ground of our peace. Of course it is the blessed Spirit who reveals Christ, and causes us to know, enjoy and feed upon Christ, but the Spirit Himself is not the Source of our peace, although He helps us to realize it. "The fruit of the Spirit . . . is peace" (Galatians 5:22).

Peace of God—Peace Within Us

We now come to consider the peace of heart flowing from a full, unhindered and unbroken fellowship with Him who is our Peace. It is this experience of peace Christ bestowed as a legacy upon His own, "My peace I give unto you" (John 14:27). Alas, not all who are at peace with God, have peace within! They have the title to it, but fail to enjoy their inheritance. How the devil seeks to rob believers of this inner peace by causing them to dispute their standing in grace and creating doubt within! If he cannot steal our pardon, he will try to ruin our peace.

Peace within flows from purity of heart. Therefore we must walk humbly with God (Galatians 6:16). Further, to retain such peace we must guard against a relapse of faith. We must not return to folly (Psalm 85:8). If we meddle with sin, we forfeit our peace. To preserve ourselves from a lost peace, we must make up our spiritual accounts daily. Concluding each day, we must take stock of matters between God and our own soul (Psalm 77:6). This is a sure way to retain an undisturbed peace. "Often reckonings keep God and conscience friends. We just do with our hearts what we do with our watches, wind them up every morning by prayer and at night examine whether our heart has gone true all the day, whether the wheels of our affections have moved swiftly toward heaven."

In Jesus for peace I abide,
And as I keep close to His side
There's nothing but peace doth betide,
Sweet peace, the gift of God's love.

Paul reminds us that this inner peace passing all understanding (Philippians 4:7) is communicated to us by God the Spirit upon three conditions:

Careful for Nothing

While we are to exercise our minds calmly and judiciously in both spiritual and temporal affairs, we must not allow ourselves to be shaken with fears, vague uncertainties and ceaseless alarms.

Things that once were wild alarms,
Cannot now disturb my peace.

Faith learns to trust the God of peace today and tomorrow. Dr. F. B. Meyer urges us to remember that "if we allow worries, anxieties, careworn questions to brood in our hearts, they will soon break up our peace, as swarms of tiny gnats will make a Paradise uninhabitable."

Prayerful in Everything

What a strong link there is between prayer and peace! What else but believing prayer can correct the feverish restlessness of the heart, bringing us into God's atmosphere of calm. "Prayer counteracts the manifold dangers in which I live," says Dr. Alexander Smellie, "summoning spiritual allies from unseen worlds. Prayer enables me to continue stedfastly in well-doing, giving me back my old energy. Prayer endues me with marvelous influence over others, opening not only the door of the Celestial City, but the door of human hearts, and my King comes in."

Thankful for Anything

Thanks and tranquility—praise and peace are fast friends. Possession of "the peace of God" enables us to believe that "all is right which seems most wrong, if it be His sweet will." In every, and any hour, whether sunshine or sorrow be ours, as we trust in perfect peace, we can sing, "He knows! He knows!" This is the life which is life indeed. The first gift of peace—peace with God—is the legacy of the dying Jesus. This second gift of peace—the peace of God—is the legacy of the living gift. It is His own peace (John 14:27).

Peace From God—Peace Around Us

The salutations of the epistles are fragrant with this peace which, like grace and mercy, is from God (Romans 1:7; I Corinthians 1:3; Galatians 1:3; Ephesians 1:2). In all of these invocations it will be observed that in none of them is the Holy

Spirit invoked. With variations, it is usually "peace from God and the Lord Jesus Christ." There is no slight whatever upon the deity or personality of the Spirit, for Father, Son and Spirit are coequals. The personal Spirit is our abiding Comforter and eternal Inhabitant, ever present inditing our petitions. It has been pointed out that in the book of Revelation, which contains the judgments of God upon apostate Christendom, the Spirit is invoked with the Father and the Son, as the Hinderer of the Antichrist.

Peace from God includes all the blessings of God we need for time and for eternity. The grace of God is the unfailing fountain —The peace from God, the ever-flowing stream. The unmerited favor of God is the source of all the good we could possibly receive. Peace from God is the outgoing of that favor in practical benefits to all who are saved by grace (Romans 15:13).

As to the quality of this peace, there is no doubt. The Bible extols it in many profitable ways. It is a—

Perfect Peace (Isaiah 26:3)

Coming from God, it bears the imprint of His own perfection. This God-like peace is without flaw. Nothing can disturb it. The rabble rout of care cannot invade it, seeing it is the peace that reigns from heaven.

Peace Passing Understanding (Philippians 4:7)

How inexpressible is this peace! It defies analysis. It is beyond compare. "Better felt than telt," as the Scotch put it. Like His love, God's peace passeth knowledge. It passes all *misunderstanding* also. "Great peace have they that love Thy law: and nothing shall offend them" (Psalm 119:165).

Peace as a River (Isaiah 48:18)

God's peace is no trickling stream, but boundless as a mighty, surging river, and like a swelling river, it broadens and deepens and fills up.

> Like a river glorious
> Is God's perfect peace;
> Over all victorious,
> In its bright increase.
> Perfect, yet it floweth
> Fuller ev'ry day;
> Perfect, yet it groweth
> Deeper all the way.

Great Peace (Isaiah 54:13; Psalm 119:165)

Because God is great (Psalm 48:1), everything He provides bears the seal of His greatness. The peace of God is great because it is eternal (Isaiah 57:2; II Peter 3:14). It is great because it is able to fortify our hearts and minds (Philippians 4:7). The word here means "garrison," which speaks of a fortified place where soldiers are quartered. Peace as a sentinel guards us, as a sentry guards a palace. It is also a great peace seeing there is no limit to its increase. "Of the increase of His government and *peace* there shall be no end" (Isaiah 9:7). God's peace has no frontiers. Surely, the prophet's word can be applied to hearts as well as nations. Has He the government of our lives? There can be no peace if there is perpetual, clashing rebellion within. The increase of His peace depends upon the increase of His control over every phase of life. Around there may be tribulation, but in Him—peace. It is likewise a great peace, seeing it enables us to follow peace with all men (Hebrews 12:14). The writer is here using a hunting illustration—"Follow peace, as the hound does the hare." Peace among ourselves prevents Satan in his evil designs. He is ever active, sowing discord among believers, alienating the hearts of Christians one from another. "Have peace one with another" (Mark 9:50). How can the Church be as mighty as an army with banners, if disunity characterizes her! Her power for God in a world of sin and need depends upon her appropriation of the great and glorious peace of God.

XXVI

The Doctrine of Sanctification

A study of the doctrine of *sanctification* is imperative for all Christians who desire to become more Christlike in every phase of life. Another reason for the necessity of a clear Biblical exposition of this truth is the confusion produced by various modern holiness and healing movements. The importance of a right understanding of the fundamental theme before us can be gleaned from the fact that as Christ was about to die, He prayed for the sanctification of His own (John 17:17-19).

Occasionally we meet those to whom "sanctification" is a term of reproach. They feel that the people who speak of being sanctified lay claim to a superior piety, but such is untrue. Writing to the church of God in Corinth, Paul spoke of those who formed it as being sanctified in Christ Jesus (I Corinthians 1:2; 6:11), yet in the list he gives of those thus described, there are no good, pious people (I Corinthians 6:9,10). Approaching the subject in hand, then, let us seek to be governed wholly by the words of God as to its worth and work.

The Substance of Sanctification

The first question to be faced is, *What is sanctification?* Its root meaning suggests a setting apart from that which is common and unclean. The Old Testament uses the term, generally speaking, to describe *things,* while the New Testament employs it to denote *persons.* Sinners can separate themselves unto sin (Isaiah 66:17). Throughout Scripture, both persons and things are spoken of as "holy," that is, set apart for a divine purpose. The reader is directed to Dr. A. B. Davidson's great chapter on *The Holiness of God* for a study of words used. "Sanctify" is one of the words related to "consecrate," and suggests not only a separation *from* but *unto.* Separated from sin unto salvation, from works unto grace, from hell unto heaven. It implies a purging from sin or the old leaven (I Corinthians 5:7) and stands for a renewing (Romans 12:2). Thus a sanctified one is not only washed from sin, but adorned with purity. The priests not only washed at the laver, they

had to be clothed in glorious apparel (Exodus 28:2). Thomas Watson, the Puritan divine, says that "Sanctification is a principle of grace's savingly wrought work, whereby the heart becomes holy and is made after God's own heart."

The Oxford Dictionary defines *sanctification* as "the action of the Holy Spirit in sanctifying or making holy the believer, by implanting within him of the Christian graces, and the destruction of the sinful affections." The Ancient Catechism expresses *sanctification* as "the work of free grace whereby we are renewed in the whole man after the image of God and are enabled more and more to die unto sin and live unto righteousness." Biblical sanctification, then, is the work of God whereby we are separated from the reign of sin unto God for His service.

Counterfeits of God's prescribed "sanctification" abound. The shields of gold become shields of brass (I Kings 14:26,27). Man's developed holiness is a poor imitation of the real. Having already considered what sanctification is, it may be profitable to state what it is not.

It is not moral virtue. A person may cultivate many excellent virtues yet have a heart destitute of God's sanctifying grace. Of course, one cannot be sanctified without exhibiting the highest virtues. Socrates preached and practiced a strict morality, yet was ignorant of Biblical holiness. A moral person may hate sin, and also hate grace just as much as sin, seeing that grace means that God does not recognize human worth and merit. The Stoics who were prominent among moralized heathens were yet the bitterest foes Paul had (Acts 17:18).

Talk we of morals! O Thou bleeding Lamb,
The best morality is love of Thee.

It is not a mere religious practice. Paul writes of those who had a form of godliness, but who were destitute of its power (II Timothy 3:5). They pretend a holiness they do not possess. They have a dazzling profession, but are lamps without oil. A true holiness (Ephesians 4:24) implies there is a feigned brand. Clouds are without rain (Jude 12). A pretended sanctification is a statue without life. Behind holy habits there must be a holy heart.

It is not eradication. The rise of various holiness movements has been responsible for different interpretations of sanctification or divine holiness. The eradication of the old man—sinless perfection—entire sanctification are terms we meet with. Without doubt, we should be more afraid of Christian *imperfection* than Christian *perfection.* The Lord has certainly made possible for His own a constant deliverance from all known, conscious sin. Such an experience, however, does not suggest a condition of sinlessness. "If we say we have no sin, we deceive ourselves"—*but no one else!* There is a world of undiscovered sin within the most holy among us.

> They who fain would serve Thee best
> Are conscious most of wrong within.

Sin does not die within the believer, he dies to sin. When Paul declared, "I die daily," he meant that he had acquired the habit of reckoning himself dead unto sin. There is a difference between sin being in us against our will, and reigning in us with our permission (Romans 6:12). In spite of the affirmation of many that their old nature has been eradicated, it remains until death or until Christ's return. A person who claims he is so sanctified that he cannot sin, actually sins by such an assertion.

From the positive side, sanctification is God's master work in the believer, and can be approached in several ways.

It is a supernatural work. Sanctification is of the Spirit's planning. This is why it is called "the sanctification of the Spirit" (I Peter 1:2). Weeds grow of themselves; flowers are planted. We are inherently sinful, thus it is God's prerogative to cleanse (Leviticus 21:8). Holiness is divinely infused. It is God's perfect work whereby He sets believers aside perfectly and forever for Himself. In systematic theology justification is made to precede sanctification but in Scripture, sanctification precedes justification (I Corinthians 1:2; 6:11).

It is an intrinsic work. Sanctification is akin to the "adorning of the heart" which Peter wrote about (I Peter 3:4). It is not merely an external covering as dew wets grass, but as sap in a root. When the Holy Spirit weans us from sin, His work of holiness is deeply seated in the soul (Psalm 51:6). We do not become holy by adopting clean habits. Holiness must be inwrought by God ere it can manifest itself in holy ways. Sanctimoniousness is not Biblical sanctification.

It is an extensive work. Original sins depraved all of our faculties. No part of our being is sound. The whole head is sick. ". . . from the sole of the foot even unto the head there is no soundness in it" (Isaiah 1:5,6). A divinely provided sanctification covers all of our depraved being, "Spirit, soul and body" (I Thessalonians 5:23). As the result of the Fall, the will was affected and became obstinate. The sanctifying work of the Spirit blends the human will with the will of God, becoming blessedly pliable thereby. The sin of our first parents corrupted the affections until they became misplaced on wrong objects—sanctification turns them into right channels. Thus, as Paul reminds us, sanctification is not partial, but "wholly" (I Thessalonians 5:23). Although we can only be sanctified in part, yet it is in every part.

It is a beautiful work. Sanctification elicits the admiration of heaven (Psalm 110:3). It glorifies God. "Holiness is the most sparkling jewel in the Godhead" (Exodus 15:11). When we strive after holiness, heaven begins in our soul. "Sanctification and glory differ only in degree; sanctification is glory in the seed, and glory is sanctification in the flower." The more saintly we become, the more is our holy Lord admired in us.

It is an abiding work. What God doeth is forever. Our practical sanctification may suffer an eclipse, and the peach lose its bloom, but our positional sanctification can never vary (I John 2:27; 3:9). "Ye *are* sanctified" (I Corinthians 6:11), and in this aspect there can be no improvement or progress. Positional sanctification is the privilege of all who have accepted Christ and who, consequently, have been set apart by and for God. We are sanctified at the moment of our regeneration (Philippians 1:1; Hebrews 1:1). It is the responsibility of all who are saved to have an outward, external life pleasing to God. In this sense, *persons* (I Corinthians 7:14) and *things* (I Timothy 4:4,5) are embraced.

It is a progressive work. Justification does

not admit of degrees, for a believer cannot be more justified than he is. We are sanctified when we are saved. It is not something we hope for as we reach maturity, or after death. Justification is what Christ has already done *for* us—sanctification is what He is doing *in* us. And, practically, this inner work never ceases this side of heaven. With the increase of spiritual knowledge (Colossians 1:10), and of faith (II Corinthians 10:15), there is the increase of sanctification. The morning sun grows brighter until it is seen in full, meridian splendor (II Corinthians 7:1; II Peter 3: 18). As Christians receive the Spirit without measure, holiness in life is progressive. If we are not growing up into the stature of Christ, something alien to its nature is stunting our spiritual growth. Not only *are* we sanctified, but we are *being* sanctified. Position must be translated into practice, and standing into state. This progressive sanctification as taught by Christ (John 17:17) is accomplished not by fleshly efforts or in the suppression of sin, but only by God (I Thessalonians 5:23,24; John 17: 19). The once for all act continues through life and reaches finality at Christ's return (I Thessalonians 3:12,13).

The Secrets of Sanctification

Christ was sanctified by His own act (John 17:19) and for our sakes that He might reveal the extent of His love and purpose (Psalm 4:3). Christ was separated from the world and the measure of His separation should be ours (John 17:15,16). As His sanctification was for our sakes, our daily sanctification should be for His sake (Hebrews 2:11).

We are sanctified by God (I Thessalonians 4:3; 5:23; Hebrews 10:11; Jude 1). It is He who justifies the guilty and sanctifies the unclean. As with all other spiritual blessings, the source of our sanctification is traced to God.

We are sanctified by Christ. As God is the *Source* of our sanctification, so Christ is the *Medium* of it (Hebrews 2:11; 10: 10,14; 13:12). Christ died for our sanctification (Titus 2:14). Christ is both Altar and Laver. He died to save us from the government of sin, as well as from its guilt. As the crucified One, risen on high, He is the *Object* presented to the soul. He is our sanctification (I Corinthians 6:11). Thus sanctification is not *something*, but *Someone*.

In the Lord my Righteousness, I have everything
I need for my pardon;
In the Lord my Sanctification, I have everything
I need for my holiness;
In the Lord the Perfecter of my faith, I have everything
I need for my future.

We are sanctified by the Spirit. He is the active Agent in our holiness, impressing His own sanctity upon our heart, as the seal leaves its impression on the wax (Romans 15:16; II Thessalonians 2:13). He clothes us with His own virtue (I Corinthians 6:11; II Thessalonians 2:13; I Peter 1:2).

We are sanctified by the Word (John 15: 3). The sanctified Christ taught that the Word of God is also instrumental in our sanctification (John 17:17). The Scriptures function as a mirror and a laver (Ephesians 5:26), in that they enlighten the mind and cleanse the heart. What the light reveals, the blood can cleanse.

We are sanctified by faith. Faith purifies. The woman who touched the hem of Christ's garment was healed. Miraculous faith can remove mountains—sanctifying faith can remove mountains of sin and pride (Acts 26:18). This sanctification by faith has two sides, a death side and a life side. On the *death side,* we accept the *possession* of life freely offered by divine grace. On the *life side,* we accept and enter upon a divinely assigned *position* of death and also a resurrection enabling us to walk in newness of life. The *negative side* is the putting off the old man, nullifying the principles of evil (Romans 6:12; Colossians 3:5-8). The *positive side* is the puttng on of the new man (Colossians 3:12-17). Too many of us live in negatives. It is "Don't do this," or "Don't go there." How useless it is to remove the things of the world, unless we substitute for them more positive pleasures and pursuits!

We are sanctified by prayer. It is in answer to unceasing, believing prayer that God can make the unclean, clean (Job 14: 4). The word "create" implies the ability to make something out of nothing (Psalm 51:10). How good God is at this holy task! Are we wearing the jewel of sanctification?

We are sanctified by godly fellowship. We must not only "take time to be holy," but "make friends of God's children" (Proverbs 13:20). Association results in assimilation. Communion of the saints is not only in the ancient creed, but should be the characteristic of the company we keep.

We are sanctified by our own will. Not only as God wills our sanctification, but as we will it, does it come (I Thessalonians 4:3; Romans 6:7; I Corinthians 6:17). God never saves nor sanctifies against the human will. All divine gifts are to be received through the voluntary exercise of the will.

We are sanctified by the blessed hope.

With such a blessed life in view,
We would more holy be.

We cannot live a sinful, evil life if we believe that Jesus is coming again (Titus 2:12,13). His return is a sanctifying hope (Acts 20:32; I John 3:3). The believer's complete sanctification awaits Christ's return (Ephesians 5:27).

We are sanctified by chastisement. We are prone to reject our adversity as a secret of sanctification. But the chastisements of life, if accepted as from the Lord, help to fashion us into His image (Hebrews 12: 6-11; I Peter 1:7). Refined in the fire of trial, we come forth as gold.

The Signs of Sanctification

How are we to know whether we are being sanctified? What are the evident tokens of personal holiness? Are the workings of God by His Spirit through His Word perceptible? Yes! "By this shall all men know that ye are My disciples."

There will be separation from all known sin and enmity to God (James 4:4). This separation is *from* the world *unto* holiness (Colossians 3:1).

There will be the determination not to stand up for our rights, but to trust God as our Defense (Romans 12:19).

There will be the constant effort to guard our hearts against all that is unbecoming in a sanctified life (Ephesians 5: 15-17).

There will be a decorum in dress, pleasing to Him who wore a seamless robe. Costly array is not the only raiment for our perishing bodies (Ephesians 6:11; I Peter 3:4).

There will be a growing resemblance to God. Adam sinned in that he aspired to be like unto God in omniscience. But we aspire to be like Him in holiness (I Peter 1:16). Our immediate goal is conformity

to Christ (Romans 8:28,29). Our ultimate goal is perfect likeness to Him. The partial is to become the perfect (I John 3:2).

There will be the distinguishing breastplate of holiness. Our Christian witness is exposed to reproach if we do not reflect God's holiness. Being sanctified, we wear the double seal—the seal of *positional* sanctification, "the Lord knoweth them that are His"; the seal of *practical* sanctification, ". . . let every one that nameth the name of Christ depart from iniquity" (II Timothy 2:19). It is one thing to be a saint—all the saved are saints—but a different thing to be a sanctified saint. It is possible for a person to leave his sin, yet still love it. The serpent casts its coat, but retains its sting. Sanctified persons not only leave their sin, but loathe it. Do we manifest this holy antipathy against sin? (Psalm 119: 104).

There will be the spiritual performance of all God requires. Desiring holiness of life, we fly on wings of delight. God's will is a constant joy. Study of His Word is never a drudgery, but always a delight (Psalm 1:2,3).

There will be a well-ordered life. If the heart is sanctified, the fragrance will permeate every phase of life (I Peter 1:15). The circumference will correspond to the center. One cannot have a good heart and a vicious life (Proverbs 30:12). If we are "glorious within" our clothing will be all of gold (Psalm 45:13).

There will be stedfast resolution to follow Christ all the way. We may be persecuted, ridiculed, maligned because of our separated life, but the more water poured on the fire, the brighter the flame produced. We prefer sanctity to safety (Job 27:6).

There will be the manifestation of the Spirit's fruit and favor. As the unclean spirit in the unsanctified carries them to all forms of wickedness, so the Holy Spirit works reversely in the sanctified, leading them to do those things pleasing to God (Galatians 5:22-24; Hebrews 13:21).

The Summons to Sanctification

There are several reasons why we must seek after sanctity of life. The appeal to sanctification is presented from many angles.

God demands it. He may not will us to be rich, or famous, but He does will us to be holy. He does not command us to sin, to be unclean, to be proud, but He does command us to be sanctified in life (Ephesians 1:4; I Thessalonians 4:7). God loves holiness. He has two abodes, the holy heaven and a holy heart.

It is a proof of our justification. Out of Christ's side there flowed blood and water. The blood represents justification, the water, sanctification (I John 5:6). Justification and sanctification go together, and what God hath joined, we dare not put asunder (I Corinthians 6:11; Micah 6:8; 7:18).

Without sanctification we have no title to the new covenant. Only the sanctified can plead the benefits of the covenant (Ezekiel 36:26). In law, it is only those named in a will who can claim what the will provides for them. It would be presumption for them to claim that to which they were not entitled. Sanctification is a sign of our election. Election is the *cause* of our salvation—sanctification is the *evidence* of it.

Without sanctification, there can be no vision. Holy hearts alone know the joy of gazing upon the glory of the Holy Lord (Hebrews 12:14). God's presence is not like Noah's ark, into which entered the clean and the unclean beasts. We can only see the Lord reflected in His Word, as we constantly obey the Spirit's call to holiness of life.

XXVII

The Doctrine of Christian Ethics

As we are dealing with Biblical doctrines in this volume we confine ourselves to Biblical ethics. Among philosophical schools of ethics there are those who teach that the greatest good can only come from the happiness of the individual, or by seeking the happiness of the community, the state, or society. The *Epicureans*, named after the Greek philosopher, Epicurus, taught that pleasure is the chief good. "Eat, drink and be merry." *Hedonism* represented by Aristippus and the Cyrensics, stood for physical pleasure and sensual enjoyment. *The Greeks* taught that supreme good came from the perfection of the individual and thus gave prominence to perfection of body and personality, both physical and mental. *Altruism* teaches the happiness of others at the expense of one's own happiness: while *Utilitarianism says* that the highest good is the happiness of the community.

The highest code of ethics, however, is the system of moral teaching inculcated by Christ, and which represents Christianity on its practical side, as carried out in private, social and communal life. In fact, Biblical ethics bring us to the outward manifestation of the inward work of grace. Being made righteous before God, it is imperative for us to live righteously before men. Says Dr. W. J. Townsend, "The moral laws and precepts of Christianity are based on Righteousness, and is their pervading element in all relations" (Isaiah 54:14; Matthew 6:33).

Before examining the nature and absoluteness of the Christian ethic, it may help us to look at some of the terms used. *Ethic* is from a Greek word meaning "character" and is connected with custom or habit. *Moral* is from the Latin *"mores,"* meaning habits or customs. Thus, *moral philosophy* deals with right conduct, ethical duty, virtue. *Right* is from the Latin *"rectus"* implying "straight" or "according to rule." *Summum Bonum,* or "the supreme good," is the supreme end at which we aim. Our actions may be directed toward many ends. Ethics, then, are taken up with the supreme or ultimate end to which our whole lives should be directed.

From the foregoing definitions we find that *ethics* represent the science of the ideal in conduct, or the science of human duty and the principles of right actions, sanctions and ideals of human conduct and character. By *Christian ethics* we mean that the greatest good and highest morality can only come from following the will of God as it is revealed in the Bible. An *ethic* is a standard of character, and God's standard for us is Jesus Christ (Philippians 2:5; II Timothy 3:16, 17; Hebrews 12:2; I Peter 2:21; I John 2:6). God, however, has not only a standard *for* us, He intends Christians *to be standards* (I Timothy 4:12; James 1:22). Think of these manifold requirements.

> We are to be different from the world (II Corinthians 5:17; Romans 6:4; 12:1,2).
>
> We are to shine as lights amidst the world's darkness (Matthew 5:14-16).
>
> We are to walk worthy of God, as His ambassadors (II Corinthians 5:20; Ephesians 5:8).
>
> We are to live pleasing to God (I Thessalonians 4:1; II Thessalonians 1:11-2:17; Colossians 1:10).
>
> We are to be examples to others in all things (I Corinthians 4:13; I Timothy 4:12).
>
> We are to be victorious in temptation and tribulation (Romans 12:12; Colossians 1:11; James 1:2-4).
>
> We are to be conspicuous for our humility (Ephesians 4:12; Colossians 3:13; I Peter 3:3,4).
>
> We must appropriate divine power for the accomplishment of all God wants to make us, and desires us to be (Philippians 2:13; 3:21; II Peter 1:3).

Although some of the ordinary systems of *moral philosophy* may seem to run parallel to a certain extent with Biblical ethics, "the latter supply the defects of the former, and carry the springs and motives of conduct into a higher region than non-Christian philosophers, past and present, know." The moral concepts from prophets, Christ and the apostles, in Jewish and Christian writings are superior to the tenets of moral teachers who affirm that the highest good in life is "the furtherance of human interests"—"the acquisition of happiness"—"the pursuit of pleasure"—"the attainment of the useful." Christ is the perfect One from whom issues the life of highest order. He it was who "translated virtue into holiness, duty into privilege, and opened out a goal of perfect bliss through self-sacrifice."

In the Old Testament, morals and worship are inextricably entangled. Morality is enjoined and carried with it the token of God's favor (Exodus 40:20; Deuteronomy 10:5), and when Christ appeared among men He reaffirmed such teaching (Matthew 5:17; Romans 3:31).

"Whatsoever things were valuable, Christ conserved, unified and developed. The old doctrine acquired wings, and sang a nobler, sweeter song (John 1:17). But the glad and noble life which Jesus came to produce could come only from close attention to man's actual condition."

Our Lord took cognizance of sin, and of man's guilty state, and of satanic forces arrayed against him. He knew that goodness could not be lived out unless moral evil was renounced by a penitent heart. The fountain of conduct had to be cleansed. Thus, the One possessing goodness, righteousness, and mercy called upon men to settle, first of all, the sin question and then manifest those attributes which were God's own peculiar glory (Exodus 33:18,19; 34:4,7). The character of Christ, then, is the standard of Christian ethics. As the Head and Representative of the human race, He enacted laws amidst human conditions, and in Himself revealed how these laws could be adapted to the needs of man. He lived perfectly for God and man. Subjecting Himself to divine and human laws, in obedience to them He fulfilled all righteousness (Hebrews 5:8).

As Christ's life was completely filial and fraternal it stands out as the pattern life for us to follow.

> Although sorely tempted, He overcame the Evil One (Matthew 4:1-11; John 16:33).
>
> In spite of demons and men, He completed His life's task (John 17:4).
>
> His was a life without sin (John 8:42; II Corinthians 5:21; Hebrews 4:15).
>
> He laid down love to Himself as the principle of obedience to His law (John 14:23; 15:10-12).
>
> He granted His Spirit to foster loyal devotion (John 14:16,17).
>
> To the loving and obedient, He imparts His peace as the highest blessedness (Psalm 119:165).
>
> His law embodied the moral law contained in the Ten Commandments, with addition (Exodus 20:2-17; Matthew 7:12; John 13:34).
>
> He regenerates man by His Spirit, takes him in union with Himself and bestows power to reach the lofty standard of holiness (John 3:6; Romans 8:2,9,29; Galatians 5:22,23).
>
> His ethical instructions are incomparable, and rest upon His immediate authority (John 13:34).

Throughout all of the *epistles* are scattered rules and directions, covering the whole ground of private and social life. The apostles taught that as a man *believes*, so must he *behave*. Creed should be reflected in conduct. *Virtues* must be acquired (Galatians 5:22,23; Colossians 3:12-17; II Peter 1:5-7; Titus 2:12), and *vices* shunned (Galatians 5:19,20,21; Colossians 3:5-9). Love, as the parent of all virtue, must be fostered (Romans 5:1,2,7,8; I Corinthians 13; II Corinthians 5:19; Hebrews 11). Christ's image must be reflected in the lives of those He saves (Romans 8:37-39; I Corinthians 15:49-58; II Corinthians 5:8; Philippians 3:8-14).

Truly, ours is a high and holy calling. Belonging to Christ, we must behave accordingly. Having accepted Christ we must *live* Christ, which is not a mere fleshy imitation of Him but the outworking of His own life within. If His law is written upon our heart (Hebrews 8:10), and His Spirit enlightens our conscience (John 16:13); this, with a will harmonized to the Lord's will (Psalm 143:10), and affections set on heavenly things (Colossians 3:1), there will be no contradiction between profession and practice. What we believe will influence behavior, and creed will harmonize with conduct and character.

XXVIII
The Doctrine of Eternal Security

What rest of faith is ours if we know that we are not only saved but *safe!* Alas, there are a good many who are so fearful because they feel that although they were saved at some time or another, they are not yet secure! They seem to think that although saved one day they may be lost the next. Thus, they must strive and struggle to keep their salvation. But because salvation is not *something* but Someone and that One, Christ Himself, it is ludicrous for sheep to try and keep the Shepherd. Did He not say that the keeping is His responsibility? "Those whom Thou hast given Me, I have kept" (John 17:12).

The doctrine of eternal security, sometimes associated with *the perseverance of the saints,* is referred to as a *Calvinistic* doctrine. John Calvin taught that this doctrine stands proven, not only by its association with other doctrines like those of election, atonement, the intercession and mediatorial dominion of Christ, imputed righteousnes and regeneration, but from those Scriptures declaring that *eternal life* is always connected with believing, and other Scriptures encouraging the believer to depend upon the love, faithfulness and omnipotence of God.

Over against this Calvinistic interpretation, which we believe to be the right one, there is *Arminianism,* so named after its founder Arminius (A.D. 1560-1609), who taught, among other things, in his "Five Articles," that although God had, from eternity, decreed to eternal life those who would persevere in their faith, and to eternal death those who should die impenitent, yet that His eternal decrees were determined by His eternal foreknowledge as to the perseverance or impenitence to death of each particular person to be saved or lost. Whether those united to Christ can fall away and be lost is a question we have no answer for in the Bible.

Arminianism continues today in those who teach that the final triumph of the Christian is dependent upon his own stedfastness and diligence; that although a child of God he can yet forfeit the gift of life by backsliding and apostasy. It is affirmed that God makes the continuance of His favor contingent upon man's faithfulness, and I Chronicles 28:9; I Samuel 25:1-44; Ezekiel 3:20; 33:12, are quoted in favor of same. Advocates of Arminianism also teach that Christ makes salvation dependent upon fellowship with Himself, and cite the following as proof passages—Matthew 7:24,25; 25:1-46; John 15:2-6; 17:12.

In Great Britain, as the work of George Whitefield and John Wesley developed, Whitefield became the father of *Calvinistic* Methodists, and Wesley of the *Arminian* Methodists. The many off-shoots of Methodism hold the latter theory, and teach the epistles use language of caution and warning concerning Christians which is utterly incompatible with the doctrine of final perseverance. These warnings against backsliding and apostasy would not have been made if believers *could not* fall away, become castaways, or make shipwreck of their faith. Nor would the Bible close with the threat that the unfaithful should have their names erased from the book of life, if there were no intention in it. Then these Scriptures are used in support of their theory—I Corinthians 9:27; 10:12; I Timothy 1:19; Hebrews 4:1; 6:4,5; 10:23,29; I Peter 5:8.

But while these warnings and exhortations may seem to assume the possibility of being lost after an experience of salvation, the fact is that they only go to prove that God works mediately and wants men to cooperate in the work of perseverance, which is more the work of God than an activity of the believer. "The assurance of man's salvation lies in the fact that God perseveres." There is no proof that the apostates cited in the above passages were born-anew believers (See Romans 9:6; I John 2:19; Revelation 3:1). Louis Berkhof remarks that—

"Perseverance may be defined as that continuous operation of the Holy Spirit in the believer, by which the work of divine grace that is begun in the heart, is continued and brought to completion" (John 10:28,29; Romans 11:29; Philippians 1:6; II Thessalonians 3:3; II Timothy 1:12; 4:18).

An argument used against eternal security is that such teaching makes men careless concerning separation from the world and of personal holiness and that there can be no confidence, therefore, of final salvation unless there is a present and increasing holiness. Thus, true final perseverence comes through holding on to the end by clinging to faith (Romans 2:7; Hebrews 3:14). But how impossible it is for the believer to achieve such an end. First of all, both Calvinists and Arminianists agree that salvation from the guilt and power of sin is a divine work. If this be so then it can never be repeated.

I know that, Whatsoever God doeth, it shall be *for ever*; nothing can be put to it, nor anything taken from it: and God doeth it, that men should fear before Him (Ecclesiastes 3:14).

Through believing *eternal* life, *eternal* salvation, and *eternal* redemption are received (John 3:15; Isaiah 45:17; Hebrews 5:9; 9:12). But how can these possessions be *eternal* in nature if we can have them today and lose them tomorrow?

Further, is not *regeneration* a divine act

that can never be repeated? Once born into the family of God, the believer can never un-born himself, to coin a phrase. Because of countenanced sin in the life *communion* with the Author of eternal salvation may be ruptured, but *union* with Him can never be severed (John 1:11-13; 3:7,16).

Then there is Christ's own declaration that His sheep have eternal life and therefore cannot perish (John 10:27-30). *Shall not perish!* What an assuring promise this is! Our Lord further said that no one can pluck a child of His out of His hand, nor out of His Father's hand for both the Father and the Son are one in their purpose to preserve their own. *Pluck* here means "to take by force"—"to catch away"—"to pull away" (John 6:15; Acts 8:39; Jude 23). The Father and the Son are greater than all the united forces of hell and of evil men, and are thus able to care for the sheep.

The question is raised by those rejecting the eternal security of the believer: Can God keep us contrary to His will? He never kept the devil and his angels who left their first estate, nor kept Adam and Eve from sinning in the Garden. But when Christ said that no child of His could possibly perish, He never said, "Shall not perish if certain conditions are kept." His declaration is positive enough and stands alone, "Shall *not* perish." By *perishing* is meant to be lost, here and hereafter. All who are Christ's are bound to Him by an indissoluble union.

The believer's security is guaranteed because of the following, abundant provision—

1. Through the Redemption of the Cross

Because of all Christ accomplished by His death and Resurrection, the believer is pardoned (Ephesians 1:7; Colossians 1:14) —his sins have been put out of reach, and sight and mind (Psalm 103:12; Isaiah 38:17; Hebrews 10:17)—they have been completely blotted out (Isaiah 44:22; I John 1:7).

2. Through Christ's Advocacy Above

Because of His ministry at the right hand of God in heaven, the believer is *preserved* (Hebrews 7:25; Jude 1). Christ's ceaseless intercessory work as the great High Priest and Advocate guarantees the believer's security (Hebrews 2:17; 4:14; 8:1; 10:21; Luke 22:21,22). As the great High Priest He succors, sympathizes and delivers (Hebrews 2:17; 4:15; 7:25,26). As the Advocate He pleads our cause before the Father when we sin. It does not say, "If any *confess*," but "if any man *sin*" (I John 2:1). His advocacy is put into effect the moment the believer sins, thus maintaining his position before the Father's face. Frank and prompt confession of sin on the part of the believer, restores fellowship and communion (I John 1:9).

3. Through the Agency of the Indwelling Spirit

The believer is blessed with two Advocates—One within, the Holy Spirit, that he might not sin: The Other above if he should sin (Ephesians 1:13,14; 4:30; I Corinthians 3:17; II Corinthians 9:8).

4. Through Christ's Revelation at His Return

When He returns for His own—all of them—He will present them *faultless* before the Father (I Corinthians 1:7, margin; Ephesians 5:7; I Peter 1:13; Jude 24). Then Christ's desire as expressed in His high priestly prayer will be fulfilled (John 17:24; cf. I Thessalonians 4:17; John 14:3). Thus the Lord Jesus Christ is Himself the believer's security for the past, present and future.

> I am His, and He is mine
> For ever and for ever.

XXIX

The Doctrine of Prayer

If, as James Montgomery has taught us to sing—

> Prayer is the Christian's vital breath,
> The Christian's native air

then surely it is incumbent upon us to know all we can about such vitalizing air. As in the physical realm our life depends upon the air we inhale and exhale, so in the spiritual sphere the development of our Christian life is dependent upon the recognition of the importance of prayer. Communion with God must be the element in which we live, move and have our being.

Prayer is not only a privilege, it is a necessity, for without its exercise we are cut off from the Source of life, light and love. No one can read the gospels and fail to recognize that Christ constantly urged His followers to make it the chief business of their lives to pray. From His own example we learn the necessity of prayer. When He left the glory above and wrapped Himself around with the robe of humanity, He died to self-sufficiency in that He became the God-dependent Man. His life and labors reveal an entire absence of self-dependence. "I can of mine own self do nothing."

The Revelation of Prayer

The Bible is the believer's prayer-guide. It unfolds the nature and necessity of prayer, and is eloquent with praise as to its privilege and power. Within the covers of such a sublime Book is all we need to know of the many aspects of our approach to God, through Christ, by the Holy Spirit. With the aid of Dr. C. I. Scofield's Bible references, go through all of the Bible prayers and note how men and women prayed and for what they prayed. Reference can be made to my volume on *All the Prayers of the Bible*. Give attention to all the exhortations and examples of Jesus in the holy art of prayer, and you will discover that the secret of all true blessedness is to be found in the Christian life, in prayer. You will also come to agree with the old Jewish mystic who said of prayer that, "it was the moment when earth kissed heaven."

Scripture reveals that when God made man, He did not leave Himself without witness. Within the spirit of man God implanted a desire for Himself. This is one reason why even godless men instinctively pray when some trouble or sore trial overtakes them. Plants in a dark dungeon bend toward a crack of light.

There are four blessed truths to keep before us as, by faith, we approach the mercy seat where Jesus answers prayer—

1. Not only do we venture nigh through the blood of Him who died for our sins. By virtue of His finished work we are united to Christ, and having nothing of our own, seeing all we have was bought with a price, we yet "possess all things in Christ." It is this

identification with Christ which forms the ground of our appeal and approach.

2. God in His mercy has given us a name above every name to present as we enter His presence. God delights to honor the name of Jesus, the name which has come to mean so much to multitudes all down the ages. God cannot refuse us when we plead the name of His well-beloved Son.

3. Although we have been made "temples of the Holy Spirit," we are still subject to frailty and ignorance. Because of this fact we know not how to pray as we ought. The Holy Spirit, however, "helpeth our infirmities" (Romans 8:26,27). What a comfort to our hearts to realize that "He that searcheth the heart knoweth what is the mind of the Spirit, because He maketh intercession for the saints according to the will of God."

4. Christ, who was essentially the Praying One on earth, continues His intercessory ministry on our behalf at God's right hand (Hebrews 7:25). This is one reason why we can come boldly to the throne of grace, and find grace to help in time of need.

The Reality of Prayer

It is no vain thing to wait upon God. A vast amount of provision and power is opened by prayer. Prayer occupies a most serious and important place in Scripture. It stands next to the atonement in value before God. The Bible abounds in illustrations of the reality of prayer. The prayers of saints are treasured up in heaven. Not one is forgotten by God. Long after the death of saints, the prayers they prayed on earth, apparently unanswered, are answered (Luke 18:7; Romans 8:4). The prayers of saints and the merits of the Lamb seem to mingle together before the throne, and cause future glories to shine forth (Revelation 5).

Although it is centuries since heaven received Elijah, the prophet is still remembered by his dynamic prayers. They continue to remind us that the supplication of a righteous man availeth much in their working (James 5:16 R.V.). The fiery prophet's prayers seem to say—

Pray, pray, pray—no help but prayer,
A breath that fleets beyond this iron world,
And touches Him that made it.

Elijah had no doubt regarding the reality and efficacy of prayer. This is why he brought definite requests to God. He was specific. He had particular petitions to place and plead before the Lord, and what he asked for, he received (Luke 11:5-12). Although we believe in the provision of prayer, our prayers are "shot like arrows into the wide and vague expanse of the air: there is no mark set before them to which they are winged; they ask for nothing practical." Aimless prayers never reach their goal. How can we expect to receive anything from God, if we ask amiss?

Church history likewise proves the reality of prayer. It would take volumes to record how renowned saints of God have stormed heaven with their prayers and become mighty through God to the pulling down of strongholds. Hudson Taylor and his great missionary activities in China: George Müller and the care of his much loved orphans: David Brainerd and his passion to convert the Indians, all testify to the reality and blessedness of "a correspondence fixed with heaven," as Robert Burns described prayer.

The Realm of Prayer

Bible saints made entreaty about temporal, spiritual and national matters. Some of Elijah's prayers were related to sunshine and storm (James 5:17,18). There are those who would have us believe that prayer in connection with personal, material matters are useless and unscientific, and that the world is governed by iron laws which our prayers are unable to modify. But surely the God who hears and answers prayer is "mightier than the laws of His enacting and the forces of His guiding."

Many Bible prayers teach us to pray for others rather than for ourselves. We are not to confine our petitions to the realm of our own necessities. Too often our prayers are tainted with selfishness. We do not have large hearts. The God to whom we pray "giveth to all men liberally," and we should learn how to practice His liberality in our prayers. In private and public, our petitions avail much when they are concerned with others. F. E. Marsh tells the story of two young people, a boy and girl aged six and eight, who were being put to bed by their mother, and she saw, like a good mother, that they prayed before they got into bed. Just before she had taken them to the bedroom, the boy had provoked his mother, and she had spoken to him reprovingly. When the lad was saying his prayers, he said, "O Lord, bless Mamma, and save her from getting cross." When the girl prayed, she was more consistent. She implored the Lord to "Bless Mamma, and save us from making her cross."

When we come to pray for others, it is necessary to observe balance in prayer. Our prayers may be biased in such a way as to reflect upon others. It is better to pray that we may be right in our attitude toward others and be a blessing to them. In this matter the Bible leads the way in right praying for others:

We must pray like Epaphras, that we "may stand perfect and complete in the will of God" (Colossians 4:12). When we are right with God, prayer is effective in any realm.

We must pray as did Paul for the Thessalonians, that "all the saints may be sanctified wholly" (I Thessalonians 5:23). We must emulate the apostle's example when he prayed for the elders and church at Ephesus, that they might be kept from error and evil, and kept in the grace of God (Acts 20:36).

We must pray as the apostles did when it came to the election of deacons, that they might be qualified by the Holy Spirit for the service of the Lord (Acts 6:6).

We must pray as the Church did for Peter, that he might escape from his prison (Acts 12:5). Our prayers can liberate many from their prison-house of difficulties.

We must pray as Peter and John did for the believers at Ephesus, that they might receive the Holy Spirit (Acts 8:15), and as the Church at Antioch did for Paul and Barnabas, that they might be blessed of the Lord (Acts 13:3).

We find, as we study our Lord's prayer habits, that He prayed *before* and *after* the great events of His life. He prayed before He made the choice of those who were to become His disciples and perpetuate His teaching. Christ also prayed after some of the crises of His life. He prayed after His great works were accomplished in order that their spiritual values might be assured and fixed. For instance, after feeding the five thousand, he went up into the mountain to pray. After the healing of the sick, as the throngs surged around Him, Christ withdrew to pray.

The circumference of Spirit-inspired prayer is boundless. More things are wrought by prayer in any sphere you care to name, than this world dreams of. When we turn aside to pray, we converse with One whose domain covers every phase of life.

The Rules of Prayer

Christ never labored to prove that prayer is real, and that our need of prayer is real and imperative. He knew that man is a "praying animal," as he has been described. But Christ did teach the conditions upon which prayer is answerable and successful. His directions as to how prayer is to be offered are clear and specific.

He taught that prayer must
be accompanied by faith.

"Jesus . . . said unto them, Verily I say unto you, If ye have faith, and doubt not, ye shall . . . say unto the mountain, Be thou removed, and be thou cast into the sea; it shall be done. And all things, whatsoever ye shall ask in prayer, believing, ye shall receive" (Matthew 21:21,22). How can prayer be effective if it is not founded upon faith in God's power and willingness to answer ?

He taught that prayer must
be offered in His Name.

" . . . Verily I say unto you, Whatsoever ye shall ask the Father in My name, He will give it you" (John 16:23). The name of a person represents his character, his merit. The value of a check lies in its signature. The amount specified gives it no value at all, without a trustworthy signature. When we pray in the name above every name, we are assured of an answer, seeing that we plead the merit of Christ, of His perfect propitiation for sin.

He taught us to pray simply.

We must remember that God does not answer prayer according to our intelligence, but according to His own.

"But thou, when thou prayest, enter into thy closet, and when thou hast shut thy door, pray to thy Father which is in secret; and thy Father which seeth in secret shall reward thee openly" (Matthew 6:6). The simpler we are in prayer, the more blessed the exercise becomes. We are not heard for our volume of words.

He taught us to pray in secret.

" . . . pray to thy Father which is in secret . . . " (Matthew 6:6). Behind closed doors, alone with God, the world shut out, prayer can become both a battle and a benediction. Dr. J. Stuart Holden, commenting upon this verse, remarks, "This is not mere ritual. Shut the door, for none must invade the holy intimacy between you and God. Shut the door, for you are engaged in the greatest enterprise of your life. Shut the door, for only so can you call in wandering thoughts. This is why we find it most helpful to pray with eyes closed, lest the mind become distracted, and drawn off from the great central purpose of this tryst with God."

He taught us to pray persistently.

"Ask, and it shall be given you; seek, and ye shall find; knock, and it shall be opened" (Luke 11:9; cf. Luke 11:5-8). Intensity and earnestness of purpose are expressed in such persistency. Of course we are not to adduce from the Parable of the Loaves that God is unwilling to bless and that He must be coerced into granting us what we ask Him, for He is more willing to give than we are to receive, to bless than we are to be blessed. The saints of old knew how to storm heaven with their prayers. We too easily tire and retire.

He taught us to pray in all humility
(Luke 18:9-14).

The prayer of the Pharisee never rose above the ceiling of the Temple, simply because he prayed with himself. His prayer was an expression of his pride, of heart and religion. But the prayer of the publican, short in comparison, was accompanied with humility and penitence, and was graciously answered by the Lord who blessed the sinner with justification.

He taught us to pray, conscious that
we are right with others.

"But if ye forgive men their trespasses, your heavenly Father will also forgive you; but if ye forgive not men their trespasses, neither will your Father forgive your trespasses" (Matthew 6:14,15). A wrong relationship with a fellow believer hinders effective prayer, even although we may have a right relationship with God. To pray successfully there must be subsequent acts of reconciliation with those with whom we may be at cross purposes. For God to answer prayer on our behalf, there must be on our part a steady, maintained attitude of forgiveness. By exhortation and example, Christ urges us to pray for our enemies.

When we turn aside to prayer, it is of immense importance to harness our prayers to the promises of God. The mightiest prayers are those that arise from holy hearts

saturated with the Word of God. As we pray, God is only able to quicken us according to His word (Psalm 119:25). We must cultivate the art of turning a promise into petition, instruction into intercession. One of the greatest of all prayer secrets is to pray in the realm of Bible truth and language.

The Refusals of Prayer

Where is the believer who has not been perplexed at some time or another, with the problem of unanswered prayer?

The Bible teaches that the answers to some prayers are delayed, but God's delays are not denials, as Mary and Martha had to learn (John 11:6). The needy woman prayed and prayed, until she got what she wanted (Matthew 15:21-29; I Peter 1:7). Moses prayed to enter the land of promise (Deuteronomy 3:23-29), but had to wait fifteen years for the answer (Matthew 17: 1-4). David prayed much about the erection of a temple, but his prayers had to wait for Solomon's day.

The Bible is also explicit on the matter of prayers God cannot answer. Prayers in accordance with His will and for His glory are always answered. Prayers alien to His holy mind and purpose, find no echo, for "our prayers must be as clean as our hearts." Prayer goes unanswered—

When it is substituted for necessary action (Exodus 14:15; Joshua 7:7-15).

When it seeks to change God's declared decrees. God cannot act contrary to Himself (Deuteronomy 3:23-27).

When it ascends from an unclean heart. The holier the heart, the purer its prayers (Psalm 66:18; Lamentations 3:8,40-44).

When it seeks to avert deserved and necessary chastisement (II Samuel 12: 16-18; II Corinthians 12:7-9).

When it totally disregards the known, revealed will of God (I Samuel 8:9,10).

When it is offered in arrogance and foolish pride. Pharisaism in prayer is an abomination to God (Proverbs 8:13).

When it is prompted by selfish, ulterior motives (Matthew 6:5; James 4:2,3).

When it arises out of a heart full of ill will and hatred toward others (Matthew 5:24).

When it simply expresses meaningless and repetitious phrases (Matthew 6:7).

When it lacks sincerity and faith (Mat-

thew 6:5,7; Hebrews 11:6; James 1:
6,7).

When it is inspired by carnal motives,
and not by the Spirit (James 4:2,3).

When it is unaccompanied by confessed,
conscious sin (I John 1:8-10).

When it seeks the recall of lost opportuni-
ties (Luke 13:25-28). Once doors are
closed from the divine side, it is useless to pray for their opening.

The essence of true, effective prayer is
found in a right relationship with God.
Where such a relationship is lacking, God
is under no obligation to answer our prayers.
Yet to the best of saints, there are times
when the heavens seem as brass. Faith,
however, must not waver when divine silence greets our petitions. At daybreak,
when the mysteries of life are unraveled, we
will praise Him for our unanswered, as well
as our answered prayers.

In that immortal classic, *The Pilgrim's
Progress,* Mr. Badman's wife was deeply
concerned over the lost estate of her husband, but John Bunyan makes her say, "Are
my prayers lost? Are they forgotten?
Are they thrown over the bar? No! They are
hanged upon the horns of the Golden Altar
and I must have the benefit of them myself,
that moment that I shall enter the gate at
which the righteous nation that keepeth
truth shall enter. My prayers are not lost.
My tears are yet in God's bottle." As we
linger amidst the shadows, we must "pray
without ceasing."

XXX

The Doctrine of the Church

Because Roman Catholics and Protestants
differ as to the essential nature of the
Church, it is imperative to discover from the
Bible what is its actual composition. Ro-
manism thinks of the Church as an external
and visible organization only, consisting
primarily of cardinals, archbishop, bishop
and priests under the authority of the Pope.
Protestants, or Christian believers, hold that
the Church of Jesus Christ is an invisible
and spiritual communion of saints, with the
Lord only as the Head.

Paul divided for us humanity as a whole
when he wrote of the Jews, the Gentiles and
the Church of God (I Corinthians 10:32).
The latter section is the greatest of the
three seeing it is composed of regenerated
Jews and Gentiles. Approaching the *Doctrine of the Church,* there are one or two
preliminary aspects worthy of consideration.

First of all, the subject of the true nature
of the Church is important in these degener-
ate days when there are so many opposing
groups all claiming allegiance to the New
Testament standards of church life and
government. The worldling, outside the
Church, wonders who is right as he thinks
of the numerous religious denominations and
sects, all claiming to exist for the same end
although so diverse in theology, church
service and government. Without doubt,
there are many honest seekers, zealous to
follow the Lord who find themselves in
doubt as to what church is actually nearest
the New Testament ideal. They pause, and
ask, "Which church shall I join?" An understanding of the first form of church life and
government in apostolic days should help
them answer their own question.

Another necessary factor to bear in mind
in our quest for truth in any direction, is
that of having no bias as we endeavor to
master a doctrine. No aspect of scriptural
truth will yield its divine significance if we
bring it to preconceived ideas, traditional
trappings and self-instituted explanations.

No matter what denomination or unde-
moninational denomination we may favor,
we must come to the Word with open
minds, teachable spirits and a willingness to
follow the Holy Spirit as He unfolds truth
from the divine standpoint. As light is
granted, it must be obeyed. Obedience in
following the Spirit in the matter of church
fellowship may prove to be somewhat costly.
Ideas, long and dearly held, may have to be
parted with—a more marked separation
unto the Lord Himself may follow—antagonism from those more anxious to defend

creed and tradition rather than follow Christ may ensue.

Mary, Queen of Scots, asked John Knox—the only man who could make her weep—"Who shall I obey then, *you* or the Pope of Rome?" Knox replied, "Neither, madame, ye shall obey God as He speaks in His Word, for the Holy Spirit is never contrarious unto Himself." Should this not be our attitude, no matter what phase of knowledge we desire? "Ye shall obey God as He speaks in His Word." Taking up our present theme, then, let us consider in the first place—

The Church—Her Origin

Archbishop Trench in his *Study of Words* says that vast harvests of historic lore can be often garnered from single words; that the important facts they declare and preserve have survived nowhere else but in them. How much history is wrapped up in the word—*church!* How did such a word come into being, and what are its implications?

Trench sees no sufficient reason to dissent from those who derive the word *church* from the Greek term *curiake,* meaning, "that which pertains to the Lord," or "the house of the Lord." Other scholars connect the word with *circus*—a word from which we get the Scotch word *Kirk* meaning "a circle" because the oldest temples, like those of the Druids, were circular in form.

In Old Testament usage, *church* was not originally a specifically religious word. Its root idea is that of "a body of called out ones," and was translated by the Latin term *Ecclesia,* from two Greek words, *ek,* meaning "out" and *kalein,* "to call." Although *Ecclesia* is now used in a distinctively Christian sense yet it is found scattered throughout the Old Testament in many forms. Its Hebrew equivalent *Kahal* is found no less than 123 times and was used to describe a congregation, assembly, multitude or company of any kind.

The first occurrence of the word is found in the blessing of Jacob by Isaac, "Be a *multitude* of people" (Genesis 28:3). It is seen again in Nehemiah's pronouncement "The Moabites should not come into the *congregation* of God for ever" (13:1). The Greek translation of the Hebrew Old Testament, the Septuagint, generally used *Ecclesia.* Thus, wherever the word is found, it signifies a group of certain people selected from among others for a particular purpose, not necessarily religious. The gathering of rioters at Ephesus is referred to as the *Ecclesia* (Acts 19:32). When used in respect to Israel, however, it has a religious aspect; denoting that the Israelites were a people selected, called out by God, for God. Thus Stephen describes Moses as being with "the church (congregation R.V.M.) in the wilderness" (Acts 7:38).

Although not originally a Christian term, *church* came into Christian history invested with significance for Jew and Gentile alike. To the Jew, *church* meant a theocratic society whose numbers were the subjects of the heavenly King. To the Gentile, *church* would suggest a self-governing democratic society. That the pre-Christian history of the word had a direct bearing upon its Christian implication is evident from the fact that the *Ecclesia* of the New Testament is likewise viewed as being a theocratic democracy; that is, a society of those who are free, but *who* are always conscious that this freedom springs from obedience to their King. *Church* occurs over 100 times in the New Testament.

It was Jesus Himself who became the Head of the Church, who first applied the word to a Christian society: "I will build my church" (Matthew 16:18). Knowing that His rejection by the Jewish people was imminent, and that His disciples must move on independent lines, He turns from the term *Kingdom* and sanctifies the ancient word for *church,* using it to designate the new body, He was about to create. When Christ said to Peter, "Upon this rock I will build my church," He did not mean, as the Roman Catholic Church erroneously teaches, that Peter himself was to be the foundation of the Church. The Church was to be built, not upon Peter, but what Peter confessed, namely, the deity of Christ, or Christ Himself: "Thou art the Christ, the Son of the living God." Immediately Jesus said, "Upon this rock, upon all you have said of Me, I will build my church." Those who deny the essential truth of the deity of Christ cannot be a part of His Church. Later on, Christ uses the term again. Twice over *Ecclesia* is employed in reference to the Jewish synagogue (R.V.M. synagogue), rather than to the Christian Church (Matthew 18:17). Doubtless the principles Christ unfolded are applicable to both. If, however, the *Ecclesia* of 18:17 is the same of 16:18 then the former passage reveals the fact that Christ thought of a church as a society, possessing powers of self-government, in which church questions of discipline were to be decided by the collective judgment of the members. As one church historian puts it—

> Very early in the ministry of Jesus Christ we observe indications that He intended to found a Society, based upon principles of the kingdom of God, in which the members should be held together by outward and visible ties of fellowship in addition to a common belief and the observance of certain sacraments. The Society is the Church, or assembly.*

Throughout the Greek world, down to apostolic days *Ecclesia* was the regular description for a regular assembly of the whole of the citizens in a free state, who had been "called out" by a herald for the discussion and decision of public business (Acts 19: 32-41). The apostles took the word and Christianized it and thereafter used it as the word describing the society of men and women united to Jesus Christ by a living faith.

Fausett remarks that—

> *Ecclesia* is never used in the New Testament of the building or house of assembly for church buildings never appeared until long after the apostolic age. It means an organized body, whose unity does not depend on its being met together in one place; not an assemblage of atoms, but members in their several places united to One Head, Christ, and forming one organic whole.

This is a point of importance, especially in these days when so much is made of particular buildings, religious in character. The nearest approach to the later idea of the church as a building is suggested by Paul when dealing with the matter of *tongues* (I Corinthians 14:19,28,35). We must get it out of our minds that in the first century a *church* consisted of bricks and mortar. What the apostles meant by a church was not an edifice with pulpit, chancel and pews, but a congregation or society of regenerated people built together like living stones and content to meet in some upper room in private dwellings like that of Mary, mother of John Mark.

As for the preaching side of their minis-

try, the apostles largely used the open air. Paul, for example, preached wherever he could get a hearing—in a synagogue, by the riverside, on Mars' Hill, on the steps of the citadel, or in a hired house under the shadow of Caesar's throne. He never wasted his energy on building material shrines.

Used in a local sense, then, *Ecclesia* denoted a body of believers meeting in a particular place. At Jerusalem (Acts 5:11; 8: 1)—Antioch (Acts 13:1; 15:22)—Caesarea (Acts 18:22)—Thessalonica (I Thessalonians 1:1)—Corinth (I Corinthians 1:2; II Corinthians 1:1). See Revelation 2 and 3 for seven other spheres. Paul localized the word to represent a single household, or small group assembling in private homes for worship and fellowship (Romans 16:5; I Corinthians 16:19; Colossians 4:15; Philemon 3). Used comprehensively, the Church describes the whole body of believers, whether in heaven or on earth (Ephesians 1:22; 3:16,21; 5:23; Colossians 1:18,24). Paul employed the term to denote the sum total of existing churches as forming one body (Acts 9:31 R.V.; I Corinthians 10:28, 32). Then the apostle used it to describe the Church as ideally and positionally the body of which Christ is the Head (Ephesians 1:22; 3:7,11,21; 5:25; Colossians 1: 18-24). This spiritual or ideal concept of the Church dominates Ephesians. Bishop Handley Moule reminds us that—

> All other meanings of the word *church* are derived and modified from this, and this must not be modified by them. The true doctrine of the church may be summarized, "Where Christ is, there is the Church."

As Christ is in every born-again believer there is the Church. Paul had this in mind when he used *church* of an individual believer (Romans 16:5,23).

Although church is the usual description of those who belong to Christ, other precious terms are used to express the relationship existing between the Head and the Body. How one would like to linger over the following similes, explaining the significance of each!

1. The Body of Christ—Ephesians 1:22, 23; Colossians 1:24.
2. The Bride of Christ—Ephesians 5:31-33; II Corinthians 11:2,3; Revelation 19:7; 21:9.
3. The Glory of Christ—Ephesians 3:21; II Corinthians 8:23.
4. The House of Christ—Hebrews 3:6.

---

* Wm. Stewart, *History of the Christian Church*.

5. The House of God—I Timothy 3:15; Hebrews 10:21.
6. The Habitation of God—Ephesians 2: 19-22; I Peter 2:4,5.
7. The Temple of God—I Corinthians 3: 16,17.
8. The Temple of the Living God—II Corinthians 6:16.
9. God's Building—I Corinthians 3:9.
10. God's Husbandry—I Corinthians 3:9.
11. God's Heritage—I Peter 5:3.
12. The Church of God—Acts 20:28.
13. The Church of the Living God—I Timothy 3:15.
14. The Church of the First Born—Hebrews 12:23.
15. The Israel of God—Galatians 6:16.
16. The Flock of God—I Peter 5:2.
17. The City of the Living God—Hebrews 12:22.
18. Mount Zion—Hebrews 12:22.
19. New Jerusalem—Revelation 21:2.
20. Heavenly Jerusalem—Galatians 4:26; Hebrews 12:22.
21. Spiritual House—I Peter 2:5.
22. The Pillar and Ground of Truth—I Timothy 3:15.
23. The Family in Heaven and Earth—Ephesians 3:15.
24. A Mystery—Ephesians 3:9; 5:32; Colossians 1:25,26.
25. The Light of the World—Matthew 5: 14.
26. The Golden Candlesticks—Revelation 1:20.
27. The Salt of the Earth—Matthew 5:13.
28. One Bread—I Corinthians 10:17.
29. An Elect Race . . . Royal Priesthood . . . Holy Nation—I Peter 2:9.

Joseph Angus, in *The Bible Handbook*, remarks that we can gather from the Acts and the epistles the character and order of the first churches of Christ. As the apostles gained converts, they taught them statedly in Christ's name, on the first day of the week, instructed them in Christian ordinances and appointed suitable ministers to feed and guard the flock (Acts 2:42; 6:1-6; 14:23; 20:7,18,28-32). The Church is a divine institution and combines the advantages of every form of society into which we have been gathered.

It is not a *caste*, for it despises none, and rejects none; yet like caste, it preserves amidst human change a sacred order; *all* kings and priests unto God.

It is not a *secret society*, for it makes no reserve, and yet its members have a hidden life, and a joy which the stranger intermeddleth not.

It is not a *nation*, for it selects individual persons from among each of the nations; yet it is clearly defined though more extensive.

It is not a *family*, and yet its bonds are equally tender, only they are incomparably more expansive. One design of the Gospel was to reveal Christ; another design no less marked, was to form a people for His praise. Both designs illustrate the wisdom and love of God.

Having discussed the meaning of the term *church* itself, we now come to a consideration of how the Church of Christ herself came into being. Apparently she had three beginnings, or three different phases of her one origin.

It is customary to speak of Pentecost as the Church's *birthday* because the company of believers in Christ were then, for the first time, constituted a spiritual body through the baptism and by the indwelling of the Holy Spirit: and while such is true, yet as we shall see the Church is older than Pentecost, older than the Bible, older than the World. The Church originated—

ETERNALLY WITH GOD

It is here that we enter the realm of mystery. For the exact commencement of the Church we have to travel back to the past eternity: it was there that its constitution was conceived, and is, therefore, older than Israel in respect to her election, and previous to the creation of man and the world. There are great portions of Scripture that emphasize the Church's eternal origin like Ephesians 1:4-14; I Corinthians 2:1-8; II Timothy 1:9; Titus 1:2; I Peter 1:2,20; Revelation 16:25, and which claim the closest study of all those who love the Church. Suffice it to say that such eternal election implies, as Dr. Scofield points out—

1. The sovereign act of God in grace whereby certain are chosen from among mankind, for Himself (John 15:19).
2. The sovereign act of God whereby certain elect persons are chosen for distinctive service for Him (Luke 6:13; Acts 9:15; I Corinthians 1:27,28).

Both thoughts are true in respect to the divine choice of the Church.

In the mysterious will of God all that form the true Church have been and are being chosen from amongst mankind first of all, for Himself; and the Church as one united body has been elected to a distinctive piece of service, which Paul informs us to be a life of separation—"Holy and without blame before Him, in love."

Moreover, it is this wonderful thought of God's eternal choice regarding the Church which causes it to differ from Israel. That Israel and the Church are distinct and separate and cannot be blended, is clear from the fact that their "election" was made at different dates, and that the "election" of the Church antedates the "election" of Israel, for Israel was chosen in Abraham from the foundation of the world (Matthew 25: 34), while the Church was chosen in Him (Jesus) *before* the foundation of the world (Ephesians 1:4-6).

Thus the Church is not of human creation, nor the outcome of any merely natural tendency on the part of men to form a society which will give expression and effect to their faith; it is of divine origin, being fashioned above.

"It is God's Church (Galatians 1:13), and as such it is doubly dependent on Him. It was originated by Him. It is a building which He has reared (I Corinthians 3:9). It is also dependent upon Him for support. This is expressed by the figure which represents believers as God's tillage—His arable field (I Corinthians 3:9). He cultivates it and augments its fertility."

Further, because it is begotten of God, nothing of earth can destroy it, no weapon formed against it ever prospers. Whoever touches it, touches the apple of His eye, for it is His dearest treasure, and His choicest gift to the world.

> Crowns and thrones may perish,
> Kingdoms rise and wane;
> But the Church of Jesus constant will remain;
> Gates of hell can never 'gainst that Church prevail;
> We have Christ's own promise, and that cannot fail.

It is this fact that makes her as mighty as an army with banners. She sprang from the heart of the Eternal One, and therefore, like Him is eternal. Let us have courage, then, for "like a mighty army moves the Church of God."

FOUNDATIONALLY WITH CHRIST

The first glimpse that we have of the Church in time, is in the words of the Lord Jesus Christ already referred to in Matthew 16:18, and possibly 18:17. As I have pointed out, the Church is not predicted in the Old Testament although, doubtless, it is beautifully typified therein. The apostle tells us that the revelation of this mystery was kept secret from the beginning of the world (Romans 16:25; Ephesians 3:1-11). There are two pivots upon which this aspect of the Church's origin swings.

1. *His Deity*

For this, we turn again to Matthew 16: 18, where our Lord is giving us a description of His future purpose, and not His then present activity,—"I will build my church." This was a prophetic utterance. Dr. W. Graham Scroggie remarks, "Here, for the first time directly, there comes into view the divine work which was to be accomplished between the sufferings and the glories, and which, as we now know, was to extend across a period of nearly 2,000 years.

Nothing is said in this passage of the character and constitution of the Church, which, in the nature of the case, would not be revealed before the Crucifixion, Resurrection and Ascension of Jesus Christ, for, as it has been said,

> A church before *Christ's death* would have been *an unredeemed church;* before *His Resurrection,* it would have been *without the indwelling Spirit;* and before *His Ascension,* it would have been *a headless body.*

It can be a matter of no surprise that so little is said of the Church by our Lord, for facts always precede doctrines, and it was not until years after the Church had become a fact that the doctrine of it was enumerated."

From the time of these two utterances our Lord set about the training of the Twelve, by doing needful preparatory work, laying the foundation of His Church by His ministry of truth, and in due time becoming its Foundation by His death of expiation, and His triumphant Resurrection. When this preliminary work was thus completed, the Church was visibly established on the day of Pentecost, through the operation of the Holy Spirit.

His deity, then, is the first pivotal point of the Church's foundation—"On this rock." What rock? On Peter? No, not on Peter, but on Himself as the God-Man, as Peter himself is careful to tell us in I Peter 2:4-9. Further, as we have already hinted, whenever the visible Church departs from the fact of Christ's deity she ceases to be His Church.

2. *His Death and Resurrection*

While it is perfectly true that Christ Himself is the Founder, and the Foundation of His Church as Acts 4:5-12; I Corinthians 3:11; I Peter 2:3-8 clearly show, yet it was very clear to all the New Testament writers that the death of Christ was that by which the institution of the Church was made possible. She is the Church of God, which He purchased with His own blood (Acts 20:28).

In this great verse the deity and the death are combined. It is the Church of "God," not of man, but of God; and the impenetrable mystery of the Church's existence is that she has been purchased with the blood, not of man merely, but of God. It is indeed strange that these two truths should stand or fall together. If we have distorted views of Christ's deity, we shall underrate the meaning and necessity of the cross. Alas! such is the attempt of Satan in these apostate days. The Church's Head and Lord was not God, but merely a Palestinian Jew: and His death was not the birth-throes of the Church, but merely the martyrdom of a good man who suffered for a cause dear to His heart,—such is the gospel of many today. But we are still loyal enough to believe that—

The Church's one foundation is Jesus Christ her Lord:
She is His new Creation by water and by word:
From heaven He came and sought her, to be His holy Bride,
With His own blood He bought her, and for her life He died.

Such, then, is the second aspect of the Church's origin, and let us never retreat from it, but ever declare that Christ loved the Church, and gave Himself for it (Ephesians 5:2,25; I Corinthians 5:7; 11:25).

HISTORICALLY WITH THE HOLY SPIRIT

Although the Church was originated eternally by God, and by the coming of His well-beloved Son, who after thirty-three years of human sojourn died upon the cross, thus laying the impregnable foundation of such a spiritual super-structure, yet in reality the Church did not exist as a united body until after Christ's Ascension. This is why

"Pentecost" is fitly termed *the birthday of the Church*.

Before Pentecost, the disciples of our Lord existed as separate units, but through the coming of the Spirit they were baptized into one body (I Corinthians 12:12,13)— which baptism really constituted the Church. The Church, historically, began with the disciples gathered together in that upper room when the Holy Spirit descended, and with the 3,000 or so converted on that momentous day. This mystic fabric quickly grew in those mighty days, for following the 3,000 in Acts 2:41, we have the number increased to 5,000 in Acts 4:4; while in 5:14 the description given for the increase is multitudes, and in 6:7 a great number increased to 5,000 in Acts 4:4; faith. Thereafter, you find the Church broadening out to receive the Gentiles as in 15:14-17, while in 15:14 you have the explicit purpose of God for this age declared, namely, the calling out age, the *Ecclesia* epoch, "to take out of them a people for His name."

If some are taken out, then others must be left; therefore from this we gather that world-wide conversion is not the divine plan. As the Church commenced historically with Pentecost, the saints of the Old Testament are thus excluded. Certain it is that they were quickened by the Spirit, and were united to God by holy ties, but the fact remains that they were not united to the risen Head in heaven, as such a risen One was not manifested until after their day.

The personal aspect of this fact regarding the Church's origin which it is imperative to face and settle, is—Has the Church commenced in us? Great though the three phases above are, the personal origin is of vast importance. Therefore let us have the certainty that we are part of "the general assembly and Church of the first-born, which are written in heaven" (Hebrews 12:23), and that we are building upon the indestructible foundation of Christ's deity and death "for other foundation can no man lay than that is laid, which is Jesus Christ."

The Church—As an Organ

If an organ is "an instrument or means by which anything is done," then we can discern in the institution of the Church, the purpose that its Founder had in founding it, namely, to express Himself through its instrumentality to an unregenerate world. Perhaps one or two helpful definitions of the ends for which our Lord founded His Church may serve as a fitting introduction to this aspect of our study.

The Evangelical Free Church Catechism. In this very useful manual, the question is asked—"For what ends did our Lord found His Church?" And the answer given is—"He united His people into this visible brotherhood for the worship of God and the ministry of the Word and the Sacraments; for mutual edification, the administration of discipline, and the advancement of His Kingdom."

The Church of England. In Article 19 of this church's creed there is the following definition of the Church which is truly scriptural—"A congregation of faithful men in which the pure Word of God is preached, and the sacraments be duly ministered according to Christ's ordinance in all those things that of necessity are requisite to the same."

Cruden. Under the subject of "Church" in his valuable *Concordance*, Cruden gives this description of the Church—"A religious assembly selected and called out of the world by the doctrines of the Gospel, to worship the true God in Christ, according to His Word."

Rev. Thomas Arnold. "The true and grand idea of a church is a society for the purpose of making men like Christ, earth like heaven, the kingdoms of the world the kingdom of Christ."

Such quotations are sufficient to reveal the purpose of the Church's foundation. There are two words, however, that call for distinction and discussion at this point, two words which describe the twofold aspect of this section which we are now considering, namely, the Church as an *organism*, and the Church as an *organization*.

By the use of these two terms—organism and organization—we are not merely playing with words, but emphasizing a sadly neglected truth. Sufficient distinction is not made between the true Church, and the professing Church; between the outward and the invisible; between the Body and the building; or between the Church organized, and the Church organic.

1. AN ORGANISM HAS LIFE, AN ORGANIZATION NONE

Let us try to illustrate the difference between these two phrases. First of all, what is an organism? Well, my body is an organism, it is an organic structure manifesting in many ways the activity of life. But an organization is something which, although an orderly whole, having its different parts and functions, yet lacks the vital principle of life. Here again, let us illustrate our point. Take a church in which we are worshiping on the Lord's Day. There are distinct units like the doors, windows, roof, floors, seats and rooms or halls. Operational activities and organized aspects of a church's work also form the organization; but all born-again believers, who labor with all sincerity in this organization, form the organism.

An organization can be removed and replaced by new parts without destroying the integrity of the building. Doors and windows could be impaired, and new ones replaced; or some parts could be taken away altogether and alterations carried out and yet the place still remain perfect in respect to utility. But this cannot be done with an organism. Reverting to the human body again one cannot remove an eye, or ear, or arm, or foot without destroying the integrity of the body and causing a mutilation. False members may be attached like a false arm, etc., but that does not make the body whole again. The Church of God is an organism, for it is called "the Body of Christ." Can this body lose any of its members or, to use language more understandable, can a Christian fall away and be lost? No, for if he could, then the Body of Christ would be forever mutilated, and therefore never perfect.

With such distinctions in mind let us endeavor to trace the difference between "churches" and "the Church." Churches, that is buildings with all that they contain and use are *organizations*, but the living men and women within and without those churches, who are truly born again, form the *organism*.

The true Church, or the invisible Church, or the organism, is a Church "whose existence does not depend on forms, ceremonies, cathedrals, churches, chapels, pulpits, fonts, vestments, organs, endowments, money, kings, governments, magistrates, or any act of favor whatsoever from the hand of man. It has often lived on and continued when all these things have been taken from it; it has often been driven into the wilderness or into dens or caves of the earth, by those who ought to have been its friends. Its existence depends on nothing but the presence of God and His Spirit; and they being ever with it, the Church cannot die." This excellent quotation from Bishop Ryle simply implies that, although the Church may be robbed of its outward organization, striped of all through which it expresses itself, it nevertheless remains an organism.

2. AN ORGANISM HAS ONE HEAD, AN ORGANIZATION MANY HEADS

The outward Church, which is called Christendom, is nothing short of great amalgamations of assemblies, which in the commercial world are called combines, arranged under systems and governments as varied and diverse as the mind of man can invent, held together by creeds, articles, ordinances and commandments, admittedly "of men," many of them making no distinction between regenerate and unregenerate. The head of one of these great systems, the Romish Church, is blasphemously called "The Vicar of Christ"; and "the claim of the Papal Church is to be, in her own words, 'the holy Catholic and Apostolic Roman Church, Mother and Mistress of all Churches.'" While her attitude regarding all those who fail to submit to her authority is given in her Trent Confession of Faith— "The True Catholic Faith, outside which no man can be saved." What arrogancy! What perversion of Scripture!

The State Church of England acknowledges the reigning sovereign as its head, and is governed by a constitution given to it by act of Parliament.

In the Presbyterian Church it is the moderator who presides as the official head, whether generally, as at assemblies, or locally, as at synods.

In other sections of the non-conformist bodies the recognized head is styled as president or chairman.

Now while it is readily granted that many of the sections of the organized Church recognize the supreme Headship of our Lord, although they may have their underheads; and while we do not deny that many who remain in these systems, "hold the Head," and gather to the Name of their Lord and ours, yet the organism or the true Church recognizes and acknowledges only one Head (Ephesians 1:22,23; Colossians 1:18).

No man is called Master, and for all spiritual authority, this mystical body is entirely dependent upon her living Head.

She is a "Church which is dependent upon no ministers upon earth, however much it values those who preach the Gospel to its members. The life of its members does not hang upon church membership and baptism, and the Lord's Supper—although they highly value these things, when they are to be had. But it has only one great Head—one Shepherd, one Chief Bishop— and that is Jesus Christ" (Ryle.)

Cruden, in his second definition of the Church, calls it—"All the elect of God, of what nation soever, from the beginning of the world to its end (we say from Pentecost to the Translation), who make but one body, whereof Jesus Christ is Head." Therefore, let these four thoughts summarize the attitude of all the members of this body:

1. We should confess no Head but our Lord Jesus Christ; who is "over all God blessed for ever. Amen."
2. We should know no "Church," but that of all believers, who together form His body.
3. We should gather to no other Name than His.
4. We should acknowledge no authority, but the Word of God, as taught by the Spirit.

Ere passing from this entrancing section, let it be said that the utmost sympathy exists between the Head and the members of the body called the Church of God. Just as my head feels immediately anything happening to my hand, the nerves therein conveying both the news and the feeling to the head, so our blessed Head feels, knows and understands all that concerns our lives as individual members of His body. Moreover, the aptness of the figure as treated by Paul in Colossians 2: 19; I Corinthians 12 is easily seen as one considers one's own body; how every member is in vital touch with, and guided by, the head, and all working harmoniously together under its sole direction. John Newton, speaking of the persecution of the Church by Saul of Tarsus, says: "He hurt the body on earth, and the Head complained from heaven, 'Saul, Saul, why persecutest thou Me?'"

3. IMPERATIVE DISTINCTIONS BETWEEN THE TWO

It must not be thought for one moment that we are guilty of tautology, or that we are merely splitting hairs over terms, when we insist upon necessary distinctions between "churches" and "the Church," between the organization and the organism of this organ known as the Church. The subject is far too sacred and momentous for such an attitude, as the discovery between the two may be a question of life or death for many.

Listen to these weighty words of the late Bishop Moule—"The Church as an organized society, open to human observations, is to be distinguished from the Church as a spiritual organism, living with a life whose secret and limits are fully known only to God, and whose manifestations is by Faith, Hope and Love." Further on he remarks—"If this be true,—and it lies in the nature of the case,—the greatest care is needed in the use of the word Church, lest claims should be made for the outward organization, even in its original and truest form, which ought to be made only for the spiritually living organism."

The Personal Question

The question to settle is—To which do I really belong? To the organism or the organization? To quote Moule again—"That we may belong to a Church, or the Church, as organized within human observation, and not to the Church in the supreme sense, is plain from e.g.

Acts 8:21. 'Thou hast neither part nor lot in this matter: for thy heart is not right in the sight of God.'

Romans 8:9. 'Now if any man have not the Spirit of Christ, he is none of His.'

II Corinthians 13:5. 'Examine yourselves, whether ye be in the faith.'"

A person may be in the organization, as alas! many are, who are not within the organism: they are in some building, called a church, their names are on the roll of that church, but not written in heaven; they have a creed but no Christ, profession but not possession, a name that they live but are dead. On the other hand, one can be in the organism and not in the organization, for after all salvation depends upon one's connection with Christ and not any particular church. It would seem as if our Lord Himself is outside of the Church as an organization if we take the Laodicean Church of Revelation 3:16-22 as descriptive of these present days. His message to that Church was: "Behold, I stand at the door" that is, outside.

What a sad attitude for the Christ! And yet it is His attitude today.

The following lines condense in a terse way the nature of those who compose the true Church, and our conscience will quickly testify, if we are but honest, if we are included among such—

What is a Church? Let truth and reason speak,
They would reply, "The faithful, pure and meek
From Christian folds—the one selected race
Of all professions, and of every place."

Our question to men and women should be—Do you belong to Christ? and not—To what church do you belong? If they are within the Church or without, saved and consistent, our union with them should be because they belong to Christ (Mark 9:1) and not to any sect.

The Entrance Question

Another aspect that distinguishes the true Church from the professing church is the important question of entrance or admittance into fellowship. It is just here that we can detect the unscripturalness of the methods adopted by various sects in respect to church membership. In the visible Church, the entrance is broad and inclusive. Often all that is required is a mere mental assent to a set of questions relative to the Church's creed or doctrines; while in other cases prestige, position or possessions are a sufficient guarantee and reason for admittance into the organized Church. The desire on the part of the Church's representatives is to get people connected with a system rather than to a Saviour; or into a mere organization and not into an organism.

But the pathway leading into the true Church is very narrow, and through it men and women must pass, as through a turnstile, one by one. Distinction of race, position and culture are unknown, the condition of membership being the same to all, black or white, rich or poor, learned or ignorant, prince or pauper. And such a solitary yet imperative condition is found in our Lord's words to Nicodemus—"Ye must be born again" (John 3:7).

Bishop Moule says that Pearson (of the Creed) cautiously but clearly distinguishes in the Church those who are "efficaciously called, justified and sanctified," and says of others that they have no "true internal communion with the members and Head of the Church," the congregation of those persons here on earth which shall hereafter meet in heaven.

In the early Christian Church participation in the worship of the Church as a member depended upon the recognition and acceptance of three essentials:—

a. Repentance of sin.

b. Faith in Christ.

c. Confession by baptism.

Acts 2:38-41; 3:19; 4:12.

Is it not true that the dearth of spirituality in the Church's life today can be traced to the setting aside of these essentials? Joining a church means nothing, aye only adds to one's condemnation and remorse in hell, unless the inner life has been regenerated.

The Union Question

Again, in the outward organized Church there is, and always has been schism, division, and the lack of harmony and agreement—

> With a scornful wonder
> Men see her sore oppressed,
> By schisms rent asunder,
> By heresies distressed.

Certainly there is a strong effort—now known as the *Ecumenical Movement*—to close up the ranks, unite forces, sink all differences and present to the world one great united Church; and such a union there will be but it will never become the union of an organism, for Scripture proclaims that as in the days of Nebuchadnezzar, so in the days of the Anti-christ, there will be the unification of all religious sects with one controlling head, who will not be the Lord Jesus, but the False Prophet. Such a united Church will become thoroughly apostate, as is seen by her symbol of an unchaste woman, sodden with the greed and luxury of commercialism (Revelation 17:1-6; 18:3,11-20).

The true Church, on the other hand, has no need to plead for union because she has never been dislocated, or broken by disunion. The unity of this vital organism has been made by the Holy Spirit, and it has never been broken. Although the members of such a holy union may or may not be within the organized Church, yet if they are in any branch of the outward Church, then, irrespective of sect, denomination or creed, they are all one in Christ Jesus. As one has put it—"It is One Church." In no true sense can Christ be said to have churches, nor is the word ever used in the plural where the general body of believers is concerned. True and essential Oneness is not destroyed among believers by denominational distinctions.

"Many denominations have been forced into a separate existence by their loyalty to the truth, and have stood as witnesses for sound doctrine or righteous principle, which has been neglected or rejected by other Communions. But, nevertheless, vital unity has been preserved among believers (Ephesians 4:3-6). Christ has been the central hope and joy, and all true saints have had communion in Him."

The English Keswick Convention is a fitting illustration of the mystical union that exists between all believers, for in spite of the multitudinous sects represented, yet the motto of the movement is so descriptive of its character—"All one in Christ Jesus."

It is in the highest sense that the words of that hymn we often sing can be applied to the Body of Christ; the Church of God:

> We are not divided,
> All one body we,
> One in hope and doctrine,
> One in Charity.

It would seem from the apostle's words in Ephesians 4:3-6, where he enjoins the Ephesian believers to keep the unity of the Spirit in the bond of peace, that there are seven perfect strands in the living cord binding believers to each other, and to their one Lord and Head. Let us enumerate them:—

1. *There is One Body*, v. 4. Here the "one" is highly emphatic. The Lord does not recognize our denominations, but only believers in living union with Himself, called His "Body."

2. *One Spirit*, v. 4. The Holy Spirit is the immediate Agent in regeneration, uniting each regenerate individual to the Head, and, as the Sanctifier, maintaining the union.

3. *One Hope of your Calling*, v. 4. And what is the blessed hope of the Church but the coming of its Head? The community of blissful prospect, binds faster the communion of sympathy and affection.

4. *One Lord*, v. 5. Jesus Christ, the object of the sinner's faith, Possessor and Prince of all His people equally.

5. *One Faith*, v. 5. That is—one and the same way of access to, and union with, the one Lord. It is saving faith, or the trustful acceptance of Christ.

6. *One Baptism*, v. 5. The baptism with

the Holy Spirit, by which the sinner becomes the Lord's. There are those who connect this with the rite of baptism, but if such had been meant, Paul would surely have made some reference to the Lord's Supper.

7. *One God and* FATHER OF ALL, *who is above all, and through all, and in you all,* v. 6. The new relationship of Fatherhood is expressed here, as well as Him who is the ultimate source of spiritual unity.

The Apostasy Question

Last of all, the organization is to end in failure, apostasy and disaster, as we have already indicated. Rank apostasy, the Word tells us, is to mark its termination (Luke 18: 9; II Thessalonians 2:1,2; II Timothy 3: 1-8; I Peter 4:17; Revelation 3:15,16). And alas! like Israel under the old economy, so with the Church under the dispensation of grace, the glory has already departed, for with its modernism, formalism, worldliness and denominational price, its substitution of Churchianity for Christianity, it has long ago earned the judgment of being spued out of Christ's mouth.

Now it is just here that we must mark the distinction between the organization and the organism, both of which are covered by that one sacred word—Church. For example, when it is affirmed that the Church is dead, or apostate, we must understand that the visible or organized Church is meant, because it is utterly impossible for the invisible, true Church, to become dead or apostate, seeing she is bound to the Living Lord.

We do distinguish between the *visible* and the *invisible* Church as she exists on earth. She is *invisible* as far as her spiritual nature and bond are concerned, so that it is impossible to determine precisely who do, and who do not belong to her. She becomes *visible* in the profession and contents of her members, in the ministry of the Word and the sacraments; and in her external organization and government. *Invisible,* the Church can be defined as "the company of the elect who are called by the Spirit," or simply, "the communion of believers." *Visibly* the Church may be defined as the community of those who publicly profess their faith.

The outward Church ends in apostasy, but how different is the end of the Body of Christ, the Church of the First-born. Her end is one of glory not gloom. For her, it is the Advent, not apostasy, as the Word declares (Matthew 13:36-43; Ephesians 5:25-27; I Thessalonians 4:14-17).

The individual responsibility of every believer must be urged in these dark apostate days, namely, that of closer attachment to the Lord, and of more complete detachment from the world and its ways, as well as from the false corrupt systems of men. The signs of the times point to the completion and translation of the Church invisible, when she will be caught up and changed, having no spot or wrinkle nor any such thing. What a glorious consummation!

> With such a blessed hope in view
> We would more holy be,
> More like our Risen Glorious Lord,
> Whose face we soon shall see.

If we claim to be members of the body of Christ, then let our hearts be filled with rapture at the prospect awaiting us, and let such a glorious hope fill us with an ever-deepening desire to help our Lord to complete His Church. His present purpose is to gather out those who are willing to be placed as living stones in the sacred building called His body, and He will labor on until He sees the travail of His soul and is satisfied.

Since the building of His Church has commenced it is reasonable to suppose that it will be completed. "Finished"—why, this is one of the Lord's great words; a word describing His power to accomplish all that He undertakes, for He is not like the man who began to build but was not able to finish (Luke 14:29,30).

When creation received its final touch it is said—"Thus the heavens and the earth were finished" (Genesis 2:1). And perfect are all His works.

When Moses completed the Tabernacle, which he fashioned according to the divine pattern, it is affirmed—"So Moses finished the work" (Exodus 40:33).

When at a later period the Temple took the place of the Tabernacle, and was reared in all its grandeur by King Solomon, the word used describing its completion is—"Thus Solomon finished the house of the Lord" (II Chronicles 7:11).

When our blessed Lord came to redeem a lost world from sin, and lay the foundation of His Church, a Church composed of those who would appropriate that redemption He did not rest until in anguish He cried—"It is finished" (John 19:30).

The day is fast dawning when the last one will be saved, and added to His mystical body, thus completing the Church of God, which completion will be heralded by the return of the Head Himself. We can fitly apply the word of the prophet to His desire to finish the construction of the sacred edifice of His body—"I have purposed it. I will also do it" (Isaiah 46:11). As saved men and women, we form the organ, or medium, by which others can be saved. Let us, therefore, yield ourselves anew to Him in order that His Church may be speedily completed, thus making it possible for our blessed Lord to say, in a wider sense still—"I have finished the work which Thou gavest me to do" (John 17:4).

The Church—Her Order

This aspect of our theme arises out of the last, for no matter whether you think of an organism, or an organization, there must of necessity be order, if either is to prove its utility and efficiency. And it is this question of order that causes one to think, especially when they compare the present-day Church with the Early Church. In the outward, or organized Church, no one regular order is followed; different denominations adhere to their own particular order; and moreover, in the main, it is the question of exact order and form that has rent the visible Church asunder.

But God is not the Author of confusion, but order, and as "Order is Heaven's first law," then surely the New Testament, which is the Church's Charta, holds some guidance as to the order and government of that Church. It was not His purpose that she should present such a scene of anarchy as she does, but employ the machinery of government with which He has provided her.

While it may be true that "It is remarkable that the New Testament as compared with the Old, is nearly silent as to the procedure of public worship"; and that as we seek to discover what kind of church government is mirrored in the New Testament no perfect definiteness can be gained, yet the fact remains that no one can read the epistles of Paul without formulating the order established by the apostles for the aid of the Church at its inception. For, as one writer points out—"Immediately upon the establishment of the Church it be-

came necessary to appoint officers. These were required to conduct its worship and services, to promote its efficiency and organization, and to discharge its business."

Thus, we must realize that those early assemblies, founded principally by Paul, were definitely and permanently organized bodies, and not temporary and loose aggregations of individuals.

His letters, addressed to the various churches, cannot be regarded as addressed to other than permanent and definitely organized bodies. "As there is no Church where there is no order, no ministry; so, where the same order and ministry is, there is the same Church."

Of course, it is necessary to use great care "in seeking to interpret the example of the first century into the practice of the twentieth." Cautious distinction must be drawn between details that have a spiritual significance, and those which were essentially due to local conditions and without any deeper meaning.

"The early disciples talked in Greek, their dress and furniture differed from ours; being mostly slaves they found it easier to meet in the evenings and to have a meal together; they had no hymn books, although fragments of Christian hymns seem to peep out here and there in the epistles; they greeted one another with a holy kiss, and perhaps washed one another's feet. These were all matters of local custom, and although some have attempted to revive them in part, we are not called upon to do so."

A further word might be added ere we take up the subject of *order* definitely, and it is this, that as we approach this section of our study, it is essential to read the New Testament without bias, traditional or denominational, if we are to discover how the first churches were governed or instituted. We are returning, not to the second or third century, when the Church after her expansion appointed for herself many phases of government, phases which have remained with her, but back to the Virgin Church, if we might put it that way, back to the Church of the apostles, the Church brought into being in their day by the power of the Holy Spirit.

THE ORDER RESPECTING WORSHIP

In considering the order of the Church, we naturally commence with its worship as such constitutes its greatest, highest element. The Church ceases to exert any spiritual influence whenever she forfeits the place or time which should be given to spiritual worship.

Concerning the nature of order, there are several important facts to note, all of which still constitute the right order of worship for the present Church, as the Holy Spirit has given us no new revelation since the apostolic period.

The Worshipers Themselves

As there can be no worship without worshipers, we stop to consider what the Scriptures have to say about the nature and attitude of such. In Philippians 3:3 Paul gives us the threefold description of true worshipers.

1. Worship God in the Spirit

Whenever we come together to worship God, we must recognize that the true spirit of worship can only be begotten by the Holy Spirit within our hearts. Alas! often worship, so called, is an effort of the flesh, and is often attempted by man in his natural, unregenerate state. But how can God accept the worship of any heart that is not saved or regenerate?

2. Rejoice in Christ Jesus

This is an aspect of worship we sadly neglect. Often in our worship there is the lack of consciousness of what Christ has done for us, His sacrifice, Resurrection, Ascension and intercession are not sufficiently in our minds; and yet they form the basis of our worship. At times, in our gatherings, we rejoice in many things, the splendid singing, the fellowship of kindred minds, the attractiveness of some preacher; but Christ must ever be the sole object of our heart's love and praise if our worship is to be acceptable to the Father.

3. Have no Confidence in the Flesh

How the flesh creeps in and mars even the sacred moments of spiritual worship. Paul enumerates the things that the flesh delights to glory in, circumcision, pride of birth, legal precision, zeal for God (Philippians 3:5,6), and these have their counterparts in our minds as we draw near to God, for self is so apt to plead its goodness, even as it did when the Pharisee tried to enter the presence of God.

Coming into His most holy awesome presence, we must adopt the attitude of Paul, and count even our excellent possessions as dung, so that Christ may become the all-occupying and all-satisfying object of our love, hope and worship. "One thing," sang David, "have I desired, and that will I seek after: that I may dwell in the house of the Lord all the days of my life, to behold the beauty of the Lord" (Psalm 27:4). May this dominating desire be ours!

The Form of Worship

Three phases are to be distinguished:—
Public Worship—Fellowship with the saints
Private Worship—Family altar. Circle of loved ones
Personal Worship—Individual communion —God and Soul.

Regarding the elements and principles of worship it is evident that Paul regarded the act of common worship as of "capital importance," serving, as it did, at once to express the faith of the saints and to quicken and guide their spiritual energies. He does not prescribe a model service, but he gives a general description of the service in use in Corinth, and passes some strictures upon it.

The Corinthian service included praise, prayer, preaching, but in two particulars it stands in marked contrast to the worship of modern times.

First of all we are impressed with the share the worshipers had in the service and the variety of their contributions. "When ye come together each one hath a psalm, hath a teaching, hath a revelation, hath a tongue, hath an interpretation" (I Corinthians 14: 26). To this principle the apostle does not object, but only requires that it be so organized as to prevent confusion, and to make for edification (v. 40).

The second feature was the association with the service of a common meal elsewhere described as the love-feast (II Peter 2:13; Jude 12). This practice he condemned in I Corinthians 11:22. It was more for edification that the Lord's Supper should be disassociated from the satisfaction of hunger and thirst, and should be made a part of a purely spiritual service. This, however, we shall consider further under the subject of "Ordinances."

It would seem from I Corinthians that Paul presents to us two kinds of worship, each of which we still recognize and follow.

1. The Public Order of Service

In chapter 14 he describes a meeting whose chief aim is mutual edification, and where a public order of service was recognized, and which was open to non-Christians as well as Christians. In this respect such gatherings had a missionary aspect and were of great usefulness in spreading the knowledge of Christ.

2. The Private Order of Service

In chapter 11:17-34, however, we have a service of a private character, limited to baptized Christians, a service which was ceremonial, the purpose of which was to partake of the Lord's Supper.

The Substance of Worship

In the more public aspect of worship there are one or two prominent and essential elements to be observed. Our first glimpse of a worshiping Church is in Acts 2:42—"They continued stedfastly in the apostle's doctrine, and fellowship, and in breaking of bread, and in prayers" (2:46). Continuing daily, etc.

1. Teaching

Under this would be included the reading of the Scriptures, a practice followed from the Jewish synagogue (Luke 4:16-27; Acts 13:15), and one which we still adhere to. See Colossians 4:16; James 1:22; I Thessalonians 5:27; I Timothy 4:13, for reference to this aspect of teaching.

Again, a discourse or sermon came after the reading of the Scriptures in the synagogue and this was also followed in Christian assemblies, as can be proven by Acts 20:7.

Then, as we shall see later on, there were certain men like Aquila and Appollos, who had the gift of teaching, and who gave themselves to the much needed work of instructing the new converts regarding the great truths of the Old Testament and of Christian doctrines.

2. Prayer

The following facts emerge as we piece the several aspects of the Early Church's prayer life together. And how worthy they are of our emulation!

Prayer was made standing or kneeling with uplifted hands (Mark 11:25; Acts 20:36; 21:5; I Timothy 2:8).

The prayer of one person was often accepted as the prayer of all, the congregation assenting to it (Acts 4:24-30).

There were special objects of prayer. Prayer lists were in operation then.

They prayed for persecuted Christians (Acts 12:5).

They interceded for the advance of the Gospel (Romans 15:30; Ephesians 6:18; Colossians 4:3).

They included civil rulers in their prayers (I Timothy 2:1).

They carried their erring brethren in the arms of prayer (James 5:16; I John 5:16).

There were no formulated set of prayers unless the Lord's prayer as it is termed, in Matthew 6:9-13, was used.

Certain benedictions there are which were constantly quoted (Romans 15:33; 16:20).

3. Praise

Hymns and ascriptions of praise are frequently found in the New Testament and the early Christian writers. It is this aspect of praise that causes the Christian religion to differ from all false religions. Take Mohammedanism. It has no songs, and never sings, but Christianity is essentially joyful, and always has expressed itself in bursting song. The passages regarding the praise-aspect of worship are too numerous to quote at length but Ephesians 5:19,20; Philippians 4:4 can serve as examples.

4. The Occasion

When and where did these early believers meet together for mutual worship is the next question facing us. It is taken for granted that the services in those days were of a purely voluntary character. No one allied himself with any branch of the Church who did not desire to do so, and because of his conviction of—and acceptance of—the truth in Jesus Christ. Hence, the organization consisted of those who were profoundly impressed with the preaching of the new way—and walked in it (Acts 2:41).

A Stated Place

That those who embraced the faith came together for worship into one stated place is evident from one or two phrases in I Corinthians 14, e.g. "If therefore the whole Church be come together into one place" (v. 23), and also in v. 26—"How is it then, brethren? when ye come together." The same thought can be traced in I Corinthians 11:18—"When ye come together in the Church,"—and then in verse 20—"When ye come together into one place."

A Stated Day

That they came together on a certain day or days for worship and ministry, is evident from many sources. The stated day on which Pliny says the Christians of Bithynia met together was doubtless the Lord's day, which was kept from the beginning in commemoration of the resurrection of our Lord. Even during the early part of the second century, at least in the west, it was the only feast of the Church. Every day there were morning meetings for prayer, but the Sunday services were marked by special solemnities (See Acts 20:7; I Corinthians 16:2; Acts 2:46,47; 6:1; 16:5; 17:11). Besides the facts that one can gather together from the writings of the apostles regarding the nature and occasions of the worship of the Early Church, we here append two striking descriptions. One is by a Christian, and the other by a heathen writer.

Justin Martyr, an early Church Father (A.D. 105-165) wrote:

> And on the day called Sunday all who live in the city or in the country gather together to one place and the memoirs of the apostles or the writings of the prophets are read, as long as time permits; then, when the reader has ceased, the president verbally instructs and exhorts to the imitation of these good things. Then we all rise together and pray, and as we before said when our prayer is ended, bread and wine and water are brought, and the president in like manner offers prayers and thanksgivings according to his ability and the people assent saying Amen. And there is a distribution to each and a participation of that over which thanks have been given, and to those who are absent a portion is sent by the deacons. And they who are well to do and willing, give what each thinks fit, and what is collected is deposited with the president who succours the orphans and widows and those in sickness or want, the prisoners and the strangers among us.

Pliny, the governor of Bithynia in Asia Minor, in A.D. 112 wrote a letter to the Emperor Trajan in which he says—after a careful official examination of many Christians in regard to their worship with a view of finding charges against them—

> They affirmed that they were wont to meet together on a stated day before it was light and sing among themselves a hymn to Christ as a God, and to bind themselves with an oath not to the commission of any wickedness, but that they would not be guilty of theft or robbery, or adultery: would not falsify their word or refuse to return a pledge committed to them, when called upon to do so. When these things were performed, it was their custom to separate and then come together for a meal which they ate in common but without disorder.

THE ORDER RESPECTING MINISTRY

We have now reached a point in our study that calls for careful thought and handling, as it is one which contradicts the present order of ministry, revealing how definite and direct was the ministry of the Holy Spirit through channels in contrast to the present method of man-ministry. The earliest evidence of anything like distinction in respect to ministry is found in the distinction drawn by the Twelve themselves between the ministry of the Word and the ministry of tables (Acts 6:2-4), a distinction which was fully recognized by Paul (Romans 12:6-8; I Corinthians 1:17; 9:14; 12:28), though he enlarged the latter type of ministry so as to include much more than the care of the poor and destitute.

There were, then, broadly speaking, two kinds of ministry exercised in the early days of the Church's career, and it is our present endeavor to classify all the offices mentioned under these two respective sections, namely, the general and prophetic on one hand, the local and practical on the other.

1. *The General and Prophetic*

Under this heading we may place the following offices noting at the same time the significance of each, not in respect to present usage, but just what they meant in that first epoch of Christian history.

APOSTLES (I Corinthians 12:28; Ephesians 4:11). The "apostle" heads the list of titles used to describe those who ministered to the Church. His official relation to the churches was general. He did not necessarily belong to the group of the original eleven, as Matthias, Paul and Barnabas, James, the Lord's brother, Andronicus and Junia, are reckoned as "apostles" (Acts 1:26; I Corinthians 9:5,6; Galatians 1:19; Romans 16:7).

The one invariable and necessary qualification of an apostle was that he should have seen the Lord after His Resurrection (Acts 1:22; I Corinthians 9:1).

Another qualification was to have wrought "the signs of an apostle" (I Corinthians 9:2; II Corinthians 12:12). He was to bear witness to what he had seen and heard, to preach the Gospel (Acts 1:8; I Corinthians 1:17). He also founded churches, having also the general care of such (II Corinthians 11:28).

This office was temporary, having ceased when all who had seen our Lord after

His Resurrection, had passed away. Therefore, it is contrary to Scripture to speak about apostolic succession, for as *apostles* they were not succeeded. As W. Townsend points out—"Equally unscriptural is the theory of apostolic succession which is urged by Romish and Anglican writers. This teaches that no ordinations to the ministry of the Church are valid, save those which come through bishops, and by bishops only who can claim unbroken descent from the bishops of Rome since the days of the apostles. This claim is grounded upon the commission given by Christ to His disciples (John 20:21,22; Matthew 28:19,20). But the office of an apostle was not a permanent one, and ceased with the apostles. In their writings there is not a trace of evidence that they ordained successors to themselves, nor is there any proof that an order of bishops was appointed in the Apostolic Churches, with an exclusive right to ordain."

PROPHET (Ephesians 3:5; 4:11). The relation of the "prophet" was also general. It was not necessary that he should have seen the Lord, but it appertained to his spiritual function that he should have revelations. It would seem as if the prophet was directly inspired with knowledge of the future (Acts 11:28), and with truth of spiritual doctrine (Ephesians 3:5; I Corinthians 14): being specially commissioned to preach and teach such things revealed. There is every indication that this inspired superior ministry gradually passed away, when the men endued with the prophetic gift of that generation died—

> The harp of prophecy, so long
> By sacred impulse fired,
> Had breathed its last entrancing song,
> And with the seer expired.

The Apostle John might be looked upon as the last one of such a prophetic order.

EVANGELIST (Ephesians 4:11). The evangelist was a traveling preacher, one whose work it was to publish the Gospel, or Evangel, as the name implies. He pointed the people to the open door of God's grace, inviting them to enter and be saved.

TEACHER (Ephesians 4:11). It will be noticed that Paul combines two offices together—"Pastors and teachers," inferring that one who has a special aptitude for giving instruction combined both within his ministry. At Ephesus Paul appears to have acted as a "pastor-teacher" (Acts 20),

where indeed he had also acted as an "evangelist" or missionary.

These pastor-teachers were a direct gift to the Church, and not the production of any system. "In a true sense, such a one cannot be ordained by any set of men, or called, or elected by any assembly; he is such by divine ordination, altogether superior to any human planning; and any church which has a pastor-teacher, has him by the Providence and 'call of God,' exclusively." In those early days nothing was left to mere human judgment or self-choosing, for even an apostle was not permitted to choose his place of service (Acts 16:7,8). Were that this was still so!

Special Offices. Paul gives us in I Corinthians 12:9,10,28 a few special offices, such as the gift of healing, working of miracles, discerning of spirits, speaking with and the interpretation of tongues, all of which appear to have been temporary gifts bestowed to impress men with the reality and power of the new message, but which after the Church was established, ceased to operate.

2. The Local and Practical.

The work of the last list of ministers was general, that is, these men exercised their ministry among all the churches, we now turn to the consideration of those offices more limited in character, which were exercised in a local church or assembly wherever such was found.

1. Elders
2. Bishops
3. Deacons

We group these three offices together because they are practically the same. In Acts 20:17-28 it is clear that the office of elder, bishop and even pastor, was one; for there the apostle charges the elders of the church to feed (pastor) the church in which the Holy Spirit has made them bishops—see Titus 1:5-7; I Peter 5:12.

However, it may be best to take them separately, noting the significance of each.

Elders. The office of elder or presbyter was adopted into the Church from the Jewish synagogue; and the function of such was, in general, spiritual, but involved an oversight of all the affairs of the Church (I Timothy 3:2-5; 5:17; Acts 20:17-28). The word "elder" comes from *presbuteros*, an aged person, and therefore signifies that a person ordained to this office was elderly and therefore experienced. "As a rule the apostles never appointed persons as elders directly after they were converted. A certain time was needed for the Spirit of God to work in the soul, and discipline them in the midst of their brethren. They would then and thus manifest certain capabilities and moral qualities, and acquire weight, which would make them respected and valued." "Not a novice" (I Timothy 3:6).

Bishops. This word is *episcopus*, meaning "superintendent," and is equivalent to "elder" or "overseer," being used interchangeably by the apostles. If, however, there is any distinction between the two, it can be found in this—"Elder" signifies the character of the person bearing office, that is, an elderly man. "Bishop" sets forth on the other hand, the character of the office borne by the elder.

That there should be the exercise of oversight in the assemblies of God's people is of course clearly recognized, therefore the office of an elder or bishop with its attachment of authority, the guardianship of its truth, and the general superintendence of the flock, coupled with the gift of teaching is still necessary. But what we affirm is that anyone filling such an office today, does so not by any human ordination, but by recognition and appointment.

Although we have our elders in the Presbyterian Church, and our bishops in other churches, the fact remains, dispute it as we may, that such offices, as ordained offices, ceased with the apostolic age. Elders or bishops were ordained by apostles or apostolic delegates, but as we have neither of these, ordination such as is common today in respect to these two offices is not scriptural.

As one writer has ably put it, "When you provide apostles to choose elders for us, we shall be exceedingly obliged for both. How can we have elders appointed according to Scripture unless we have apostles or their delegates?"

Elders and bishops are not mentioned among the gifts to the Church, but were selected by the churches and approved or ordained by the apostles (Acts 14:23; Titus 1:5-7); and as the power to ordain was not exercised apart from the apostles or apostolic men like Timothy and Titus, it is only logical to conclude that with the cessation of the ordaining authorities there was also the cessation of the offices in respect to ordination.

It was not until the second century that a distinction is found between the bishop and the elder, the former being applied to those chosen to preside in church meetings or assemblies, the latter to those holding some inferior office in the same assembly. And, as it has been put, "From thence the office of bishop advanced its claims until from this divergence from apostolic usage there has been developed the whole system of modern episcopacy, from the Pope downwards, with its assumption and arrogance and worldly estate."

Jerome states:"Among the ancients, presbyters were the same as bishops; but by degrees, that the plants of dissension might be rooted up, all responsibility was transferred to one person."

Distinctive dress and designations came into being about the second or third century.

Ere leaving this point we might add one word regarding the common distinction made between the clergy and laity. It is the custom to speak of the minister of a church as a clergyman, but such is contrary to the New Testament where the whole Church is called the clergy of God. In I Peter 5:3 we have the word "heritage"—neither as being lords over God's heritage—the word rendered heritage is *kleros*, from which we get our word, "clergy." It is therefore unscriptural for anyone to call himself a clergyman in distinction to, and as indicating an official superiority over, the rest of the Church.

And yet how ministerial pride can drive people away from the place of worship. Moule affirms that the deepest principles of Christianity preclude the idea of an ultimately indispensable ministry.

The primary and ruling idea of the Church is that of a body whose every member, by the Spirit, lives directly by his Head; and a ministerial theory which really crosses that idea is untenable. It is remarkable that the Christian minister as such is never in the New Testament called *sacerdos*. As one of the true Israel, he is "a king and a priest to God," but on a footing precisely that of his lay brethren.

Deacons. The twelve apostles were at the first, the sole administrators of the Church affairs, but speedily the work became too great for them, and provision had to be made for the discharge of duties of a secular or inferior nature. This led to the appointment of deacons (Acts 6:2). The word "deacon" really means a servant, and the qualifications of such are specified by Paul in I Timothy 3:8-13.

Deacons were not ordained, and were not regarded as being in office, (the phrase, "the office of a deacon" I Timothy 3:10, is one word, meaning "to serve") but as exercising the God-given grace-gifts in subjection to their Lord. The exercise of any gift is deaconing.

In closing this section, it is necessary to observe two important facts or principles applicable alike to the Early Church, and our own day:

1. The fundamental principle is that in all gifts it is the duty of every member to place his powers, of whatsoever sort they may be, at the service of the community (Romans 12:5). The Church is a Body, and the members, which are many, have each their peculiar service which they are able and which they are therefore bound to render to the whole (I Corinthians 12:21).
2. The second rule is that the gifts should be esteemed and coveted in the Church in proportion to the utility which they have for such.

In connection with "Spiritual Gifts," as outlined in I Corinthians 12, Dr. A. T. Pierson points out that several lessons of great importance are taught:

1. Everyone has a gift, therefore all should be encouraged.
2. No one has all the gifts, therefore all should be humble.
3. All gifts are for the one body, therefore all should be harmonious.
4. All gifts are from the Lord, therefore all should be contented.
5. All gifts are mutually helpful and needful, therefore all should be studiously faithful.
6. All gifts promote the health and strength of the whole body, therefore none can be safely dispensed with.
7. All gifts depend on His fulness for power, therefore all should keep in close touch with Him.

THE ORDER RESPECTING DISCIPLINE

There was laid upon the authorities in the Early Church a special duty of meting out discipline to unworthy members. The offenses which they are exhorted to deal with are chiefly breaches of morality, and the first case of discipline forced upon

the Church by a flagrant instance of deliberate lying (Acts 5:1-11), shows how evil began very early to mar church life.

The Scripture Text-Book summarizes the discipline of the Church under the following convenient heads:

Ministers authorized to establish, Matthew 16:19; 18:18.

Consists in—
  Maintaining sound doctrine, I Timothy 1:3; Titus 1:13.
  Ordering its affairs, I Corinthians 11:34; Titus 1:5.
  Rebuking offenders, I Timothy 5:20; II Timothy 4:2.
  Removing obstinate offenders, I Timothy 1:20; I Corinthians 5:3-5,13.
  Should be submitted to, Hebrews 13:17.
  As for edification, II Corinthians 10:8; 13:10.
  Decency and order, the object of, I Corinthians 14:40.
  Exercise, in a spirit of charity, II Corinthians 2:6-8.
  Prohibits women preaching, I Corinthians 14:34; I Timothy 2:12.

1. *Internal Management*

Each church was left to manage its own business, and deal with its own offenders. The comprehensive injunction given by Paul to the church at Corinth,—"Let all things be done decently and in order" (I Corinthians 14:10), implies the control of its own affairs. No directions are given about taking matters to a higher court.

Each church was an independent organization. There is no warrant in Scripture for the ecclesiastical grades in the ministry of the churches, and also for the ascending series of courts which may review a case of disorder arising in a local church. Each church or assembly was reckoned competent to perform every function necessary without reference to any other source. The inclusion, exclusion and restoration of members were effected by each church.

2. *External Authority*

As the churches were not to be dominated by any external authority, so they were not to be interfered with, in their church life, by civil government. This at once proves the untenable position of the so-called State Church. It is only where the life of the church touches the civic life of the community that the civil authorities have any right to interfere.

Both our Lord and the apostles taught that believers should be good citizens (Matthew 22:15-22; Romans 13:1-7; I Peter 2:13-16), but such is another thing altogether from that of state or civic patronage or authority.

3. *Fraternal Relationship*

While each local church, according to the New Testament is independent of every other in the sense that no other has jurisdiction over it, yet co-operative relations were entered into, as can be proven by the witness of such passages as Romans 15: 1-27; II Corinthians 8:9; Galatians 2:10; III John 8. The principle of co-operation effective in those cases is susceptible to indefinite expansion. Churches may properly co-operate in matters of discipline, by seeking and giving counsel, and by respecting each other's disciplinary measures. In the great paramount business of evangelizing and teaching the nations, they may co-operate in a multitude of ways. There is no sphere of general Christian activity in which they may not voluntarily and freely co-operate for the betterment of the world, the salvation of humanity.

4. *Exclusions*

The early Christian society would not suffer the presence of those immoral persons referred to in I Corinthians 5:11, nor of the heretics mentioned frequently in the epistles, e.g., Titus 3:10. The Church would not tolerate those who denied any important part of the faith Gospel. Alas! willing toleration is the order of our day.

THE ORDER RESPECTING MONEY

In these days when the Church engages in unworthy, questionable and dishonoring methods in order to secure the necessary finance to carry on different aspects of her work, methods not only foreign to her holy calling, but alien to the mind of the Lord, as revealed in the practices of the first century, it is well to have before us the methods of the Early Church and thus learn how its ministry was supported so that we may be able to detect the weakness of the present day system of maintenance.

Dr. A. T. Pierson tells us that Dr. Mackay, of Formosa, quaintly characterized the changes he met with in his visits to Canada, since he went out to the East, in the following way. "Twenty-three years ago it was the ice age in the Church, and he was treated as a hot enthusiast. Thirteen years ago it was the water age, and the Church was floating bazaars. Now it is the steam age, and the Church is full of her machin-ery; but there is too much of the treadmill about it all. We are at the same place at night as in the morning." He also says that present methods of raising money for missions are anti-scriptural, anti-historical and anti-spiritual; and that not until the era of unselfish and self-denying giving is inaugurated once more, can there be much progress in reaching men with the Gospel.

1. *The First Essential*

With the Apostle Paul, the question of giving was of vital importance, so much so that after writing to the Corinthian believers about such a lofty, cardinal truth of the Christian faith as the Resurrection, he does not deem it to be out of place to close his great message in I Corinthians 15 by linking on to it the question of money and in closing this wonderful epistle speaks about the "collection" (16:1).

And why should he not class them together? Is not our giving a part of the Gospel? Can we divorce our possessions from our persons when we offer ourselves to God?

Paul's great classical treatise, however, in which he deals fully and clearly with the matter of the consecration of our substance is to be found in II Corinthians 8,9; two chapters which all of us should read, carefully and prayerfully, if we desire to experience the true joy in ministering unto the Lord with our possessions, whether they be meager or many. In turning to these chapters we discover the first essential, or basis of all faithful stewardship definitely emphasized by the apostle in the words— "They first gave their own selves unto the Lord"—then follows the streams from this fountain—"and unto us (that is, in their contributions) by the will of God" (II Corinthians 8:5).

This wonderful expression is nowhere else found in Scripture, its nearest approach is in Romans 12:1, where Paul beseeches the Roman believers to present their bodies as a living sacrifice unto the Lord, for at the least, such was their reasonable service.

And this is ever the right attitude, for the giving of our money will have no value except we first give ourselves. Many a man is lured into a false security by thinking that his giving can atone for the sin of his soul, and merit acceptance with heaven. But God requires our souls before our substance; our selves before our silver; our lives before our liberality; and when He fully and truly possesses us, then He possesses all that we have, just as in having Him, we ourselves have all connected with Him. In fact, our giving after we have given ourselves to the Lord, is just the renewal and carrying out of the first great act of self-surrender: each new gift of money may be a renewal of the blessedness of entire consecration.

Moreover, it is only the grace of God within the heart that enables us to understand this "grace" as Paul calls "giving" in the second epistle. "In the course of the two chapters the word 'grace' occurs eight times. Once of 'the grace of our Lord Jesus Christ, who for our sakes became poor.' Once of 'the grace which God is able to make abound to us.' The other six times of the special grace of giving. So the grace we get from God, finds expression in the grace we give to others."

Thus, the word means not only the gracious disposition of God toward us, but also that gracious disposition which God bestows and works in us. Grace is the force, the power, the energy of the Christian life, as it is wrought in us by the Holy Spirit, and which finds expression in the entire consecration of what we have, as well as what we are. And the lesson we have yet to learn is that the use of our money for others is one of the ways by which grace can be expressed and strengthened. The grace of God is His compassion on the unworthy, it is wondrously free, it is given without regard to merit. Therefore as He finds His life and His delight in giving thus, so our grace in respect to giving should follow the divine pattern. In learning, then, this opening thought, let us make sure of this first essential, namely, the surrender of ourselves to the Lord. It is because He is more concerned about our persons than our purses that this is urged, for He knows that converted hearts lead to converted pockets, and that as one has put it, "a converted hand in its own pocket is the *Biblical* way of 'raising' money for the Lord's work."

2. The Manner of Giving

It is clearly evident that the modern forms of securing money were not necessary among the Early Christians, and yet the Church suffered no retrenchment, but on the other hand spread like a wild prairie fire, thus causing us to confess that had the Church continued such forms of sustaining and extending her ministry, the na-

tions would have been evangelized long ago.

Another noticeable feature about those first days is that the majority of the believers were poor people, slaves in many cases, and yet what remarkable giving characterized their lives, and how wonderfully the Apostle Paul could bear the Gospel abroad through their sacrificial contributions. These early givers had no rich sources to tap, no reserves to fall back upon, and yet there is the entire absence of the solicitation of means from other sources. "Little is much if God is in it"—such is the secret of II Corinthians 8,9.

In seeking to analyze the manner in which the Early Church gave of her substance to the Lord and His work and workers, the following salient features can be named. Her money was given—

Voluntarily. Turning to II Corinthians 8, we catch several glimpses of the willingness of these Macedonian believers to further the cause of Christ by their gifts— "They were willing of themselves" (v. 3). "There was a readiness to will" (v. 11). "If there be first a willing mind" (v. 12).

The offerings or collections were not exacted from the people and given by them grudgingly, nor were they prescribed in any shape or form, but were called forth as the free-will offerings of grateful hearts. And in this they resembled the Israelites in the building of the Tabernacle, who with "willing hearts" we are told, brought the necessary materials for its erection (Exodus 35:5).

Individually. What great words these are in II Corinthians 8:13,14, where Paul describes the equality of the saints in respect to their giving—"I mean not that other men be eased, and ye burdened. But . . . an equality."

The support of the work that the Church undertook in those days was not left to a few individuals favored by God with greater possessions than others, but every believer realized his or her responsibility and gave their quota. The same thought is emphasized in I Corinthians 16:2, where the churches of Galatia as well as this Corinthian Church were taught the principle of personal giving—"Let every one of you lay by him in store," etc. And how much has the present Church to learn here, especially when one realizes that the vast majority of professing Christians forget their individual responsibility to the

Lord. In the wilderness the Israelites long ago were left to gather the manna, the feeble and the strong alike bringing in their store: and thus like them we deal as individuals with what God has given us. True it is that there is not an equality in possessions, some have more than others, but God allows riches and poverty and apparent inequality in His gifts that our love may have the high privilege of restoring the equality. And this is only done when "every one of you" is enforced among believers.

Proportionately. That God sees the heart, and judges each gift by the ability to give is evident from these striking words in verse 12—"For if the readiness is there, it is acceptable according as a man hath, not according as he hath not." It is here that the question arises of how much one should set aside for the Lord's work. In the Old Testament a tithe was imposed, like Jacob's tenth of Genesis 28:22, or other aspects like 14:20; Leviticus 7:30, but in the New Testament no tithe is imposed, the giving is to be proportioned to the income, and given as we have seen, voluntarily, and as a test of sincerity and love. Still, it is helpful to impose some sort of a tithe upon ourselves, keeping in mind the injunction of Paul in I Corinthians 16:2, that our tithing must increase as God prospers us. But tithing may have its dangers, for alas! there are those who give their tenth and then use the rest just how they please, without any reference to God regarding the use of it. We must never forget that it is all His—"The silver is mine, and the gold is mine, saith the Lord of Hosts" (Haggai 2:8)—therefore every penny must be treated as His, and used as He directs.

Systematically. The importance of a systematic course of saving was not overlooked by Paul, for he speaks about the Macedonians making up beforehand their bounty, that the same might be ready for him when he visits them (II Corinthians 9:5). To this we can add the passage from I Corinthians 16, that reveals the system enforced and adopted—"Upon the first day of the week let every one of you lay by him in store, as God hath prospered him, that there be no gatherings (collections?) when I come" (v. 2).

It is the lack of system in our giving that often robs us of true joy in service for the Lord, and also makes many of the schemes necessary for raising money, schemes which would be obsolutely unnecessary if every believer gave systematically to the Lord's work, both at home and abroad.

Sacrificially. There is no greater example of heroism than that depicted by the apostle in II Corinthians 8:2,3, where he shows that the giving of those Macedonians was woven with sacrifice,—"In a great trial of affliction the abundance of their joy and their deep poverty abounded unto the riches of their liberality. . . . Beyond their power, they were willing." What an example to the whole Christian world! How ashamed we are before such blood-stained giving. What contrasts this portion affords. Affliction and poverty on the one hand, and the riches of liberality on the other.

Affliction and deep poverty, then, are no excuse for not giving after this, because after all it is not our giving but the motive behind such that the Lord watches. And what is the use of our giving if it costs us nothing? We talk about giving what we can afford but these believers in Macedonia gave what they could ill afford, hence the apostle's refusal to take their gift, implied by the fact that they had to entreat him to receive it.

"Far beyond their power"—and strange though it may seem, yet as Dr. Murray has said—"It is remarkable how much more liberality there is among the poor than the rich. It is as if they do not hold so fast what they have: they more easily part with all; the deceitfulness of riches has not hardened them; they have learned to trust God for tomorrow." A penny, therefore, from a poor struggling widow may be of more value to the Lord than five or five hundred dollars from a wealthy source, at least such is the deduction we draw from the widow's mite in Luke 21:3,4.

And this element of sacrifice in giving appears to be characteristic of those early days, for in other passages, like Philippians 4:18,19, where Paul refers to the gifts of the Church at Philippi as "an odour of a sweet smell, a sacrifice acceptable, well-pleasing to God." The same thought is expressed in Hebrews 13:16—"With such sacrifices God is well pleased."

Cheerfully. Gold given with groans achieves nothing, such is the interpretation of II Corinthians 9:7-9, where Paul speaks about giving not grudgingly, or of necessity, that is because we have to give it as our own hearts prompt us to give, "For God loveth a cheerful giver," which, connected with verse 15, means that God loves people who give as He does. We must never give the impression that our giving is a hardship, or that we are giving it under some constraint, for with such giving God is not well-pleased. As we give joyfully, it becomes itself a new fountain of joy to us, as a participation in the joy of Him who said, "It is more blessed to give than to receive."

The blessedness of giving? Would that men believed how sure this way to unceasing joy is, to be ever giving as God loves to give.

Of the day when Israel brought its gifts for the Temple, it is said, "then the people rejoiced, because with a perfect heart they offered willingly to the Lord; and David the King also rejoiced with great joy." That is a joy we may carry with us through life and through each day, unceasingly dispensing our gifts of money, our lives or service all around.

Promptly. Those early Christians did not content themselves with good resolutions about giving but performed the act itself —"You were the first to make a beginning a year ago, not only to do, but also to will" (II Corinthians 8:10,11). "To will" and "to do," these are two arrestive phrases. "We all know," says Andrew Murray, "what a gulf in the Christian there often is between the willing and the doing. This prevails in the matter of giving, too . . . . How many count themselves really liberal, because of what they *will*, while what they *do*, even up to their present means, is not what God would love to see . . . . 'It is God which worketh in us both to will and to do': let us beware, in any sphere, of hindering Him by unbelief or disobedience, and resting in the *to will*, without going on to the *to do*."

Simply. If we would add one word more it is this, let there be no parade about our giving—"He that giveth, let him do it with simplicity" (Romans 12:8). Some contribute their money for the sake of notoriety, their names are seen in balance sheets, and because of the attention paid to them on account of their giving, they become purse proud.

It is here that one recognizes the charm of anonymous gifts to the Lord's work for such reveal the humility, sincerity and simplicity of the giver. Other features there are that one could add, but sufficient has been said to prove that the collections or contributions of the Early Church were valued because they were voluntary and sacrificial.

If a man chose to give all he had or a certain proportion, then that was a matter to be settled between the soul and God. No universal, compulsory act or method was enforced, but all were urged to give to the full extent of their ability; and the principles regulating the giving of those days are still applicable to modern believers.

3. *The Motive in Giving*

No one can read the New Testament without realizing that there were certain deep spiritual motives actuating the believers of the first century, motives that carried them along like strong currents, thus making their giving so easy and liberal. And possibly there is something for us to learn here. Are we actuated by spiritual motives, or do we give irrespective of motives? Let us look at three of these impelling forces.

4. *The Example of Christ in Giving*

A close study of Paul's epistles reveals the fact that, in every matter concerning Christian life and service, he sets the background of Christ's life and example (Romans 15:1-3). Having a burning passion to know Him, and the power of His Resurrection, and the fellowship of His sufferings, he could do nothing else but color his appeals for morality and money with the rich, royal blood of his Lord.

This is one reason why Paul presents the giving *of* Christ as the actuating motive of all our giving *to* Christ. Listen to the music of his appeal—"Ye know the grace of our Lord Jesus Christ; that, though He was rich, yet for your sakes He became poor, that ye through His poverty might be rich" (II Corinthians 8:9). Such a message, presenting as it did, the example of Christ, must have caused those Macedonian Christians to see in a new light the motives in their own sacrificial giving. They would see in it the reflection of Calvary, the poured-out sacrifice for them.

These believers had made the apostle rich through their deep poverty, and in thanking them for their blood-tinted gifts, he bids them remember the poverty of Another, poverty self-imposed that had made them rich, a sacrifice the reception of which had impelled them to give to the Lord's work as they had.

Who among us can refuse Christ anything when we repeat over and over again to our hearts the words of Paul—"Though He was rich, yet for our sakes He became poor,"—and then take them and stretch them right across the glory He had with the Father before the foundation of the world, and then across the manger with its poverty and shame, and then across His earthly life with its hardship and renunciations, and then at last His cross of ignominy and anguish.

"His poverty"—how real it was! He was born in another's abode; dined at another's table; depended upon the sustenance of others; was buried in another's tomb, and left nothing but His dear mother, and the crown of thorns encircling His brow. Ah! but through His poverty we are rich—rich whether it be in gold or grace, possessions or pardon, for everything we have, and are, we owe to the grace of our Lord Jesus Christ, who gave His all.

What a motive for giving! Friend, if your hand is tight upon the purse-strings go home and bow in silence before the God who created every penny the world owns, and seek to see Him condescending to live and die as a Pauper for you, as rich yet possessing nothing, and then before rising from your knees sing with a Spirit-filled heart the words of Isaac Watts—

Were the whole realm of nature mine,
That were an offering far too small;
Love so amazing, so divine,
Shall have my soul, my life, my all.

And then give Him, not what you have not got and will never have, namely, the whole realm of nature, but what you have and are, and let such bear the marks of His ownership.

5. *The Estimate of Christ Respecting Money*

In seeking to train His disciples in the school of humility, our Lord declared that "the servant is not greater than his lord" (John 13:16), therefore, with the question of money we should regard it as Christ did, and be ready to treat it as He did. Says Andrew Murray,—"In all our religion and our Bible study, it is of the greatest consequence to find out what the mind of Christ is, to think as He thought, and to feel as He felt. There is not a question that concerns us, not a single matter that ever comes before us, but we find in the words of Christ something for our guidance and help. We want to get at the mind of Christ about money; to know exactly what He thought and act just as He would do."

He judges the motive in giving. We have already referred to the Saviour's commendation of the widow for the mite she gave. But let us pause to mark the position of Christ in that portion Mark gives us about this incident—"Jesus sat over against the treasury and beheld how the people cast money into the treasury" (12:41). What a piercing thought! Jesus sits and watches the collection plate; and "as He does so He weighs each gift in the balance of God, and puts His value upon it. In heaven He does this still. Not a gift for any part of God's work, great or small, but He notices it, and puts its value on it for the blessing, if any, that it is to bring in time or eternity. And He is willing, even here on earth, in the waiting heart to let us know what He thinks of our giving."

But how different is our standard. We ask how much a man gives, Christ asks how much he keeps. We look at the gift, Christ asks whether the gift was a sacrifice. Shall we then say to our hearts—My Lord sees all, knows all, nothing is hid from His loving glance, therefore willingly I lay everything at His feet, and trust Him to lead me in the right use of what I possess.

He taught its spiritual value. The spiritual value of money is emphasized by our Lord in the Parable of the Talents, as well as elsewhere. Notice in passing the phrase we are apt to forget when we read this parable in Matthew 25—"Thou oughtest therefore to have put my money to the exchangers, and then at my coming I should have received mine own with usury" (v. 27). My money! Mine own!—And yet our handling of money suggests that it is ours. But it is His, all His, and no one else's, not even yours. Therefore, we should allow Him to trade with it, and use it for spiritual purposes. It has been said that all men adopt as their motto—"Win gold," but men are distinguished from each other by the practical ending of that motto.

The vain man adds, "and wear it."
The generous man adds, "and share it."
The miser adds, "and spare it."
The prodigal adds, "and spend it."
The usurer adds, "and lend it."
The fool adds, "and end it."
The gambler adds, "and lose it."
But the wise man adds, "and use it."—

And if we would be wise then let us use our means, not as our own, but His.

If, on the other hand, we are denied this world's goods, and feel the pinch of things in these hard days, let us surrender our poverty to Him, and trust Him to deal with it, because as all money is His, He will meet our needs, even as He made the fish produce the necessary tax money both for Himself and His followers, who had left all to be with Him.

He taught its dangers. Again and again He warned His disciples about the alluring power of money by bringing before them, and before the rich who were attracted to Him, several danger signals like Matthew 6:19-21; Luke 18:25.

Doubtless there are other aspects of Christ's teaching regarding money that one can adduce, but enough has been shown to prove that "the Christ who sat over against the treasury, is my Christ, He watches my gifts. What is given in the spirit of whole-hearted devotion and love He accepts. He teaches His disciples to judge as He judges. He will teach us how to give, how much, how lovingly, how truthfully."

6. The Experience of the Apostles Regarding Money

In conclusion, let us glance through the Acts and see how these men who were with Christ and had imbibed His Spirit, especially in regard to money, acted. And how, in their attitude toward it, the churches they founded were guided and inspired in their use and treatment of it.

They consecrated their possessions. It is apparent to the most casual reader of the Acts that with the descent of the Holy Spirit, the apostles allowed Him to assume the charge and control of their whole life; and that in respect to money matters they recognized the claim of the Spirit to guide and judge them in the use and disposal of what they had.

In Acts 2:44,45; 4:34, we have not only ideal Christian socialism, but the utter abandonment of all possessions to the Lord —possessions yielded to Him for His work, without any express command or instructions to surrender them, but yielded spontaneously to Him as the result of the filling of the Holy Spirit. And let it be said, nothing will help a believer to treat this question of money as he should unless he is responsive to the Spirit in allowing Him to rule and govern the life in every particular.

Today the Church is languishing for the want of money, retrenchment is her Gospel, and her only remedy lies in the pouring forth of God's Spirit upon her, for with revivals there is always an outburst of liberality in respect to His work.

But along with such an entrancing story of dedication there is placed the sad account of deception, a story proving to the whole Church of God that, like our Lord, the Holy Spirit has the power to test the value of our giving and gifts. Ananias and Sapphira we are told kept back part of the price and brought but a certain portion to the apostles, an action that resulted in sudden death for them both. Andrew Murray asks—"What can have made the gift such a crime? He was a deceitful giver. He kept back part of the price. He professed to give all and did not. He gave with half a heart and unwillingly, and yet would have the credit of having given all" (Acts 5:1-11).

This sin of Ananias is spoken of as a sin against God the Holy Ghost. "And what was the sin? Simply this: he did not give all he professed. This sin, not in its greatest form, but in its spirit and more subtle manifestations, is far more common than we think. Are there not many who say they have given their all to God, and yet prove false to it in the use of their money?" Do we not need to pray that we may be kept from deceptive as well as defective consecration? O, the peril of false appearances in our Christian life and service! There is nothing that "can save us from this danger, but the holy fear of ourselves, the very full and honest surrender of all our opinions and arguments, about how much we possess, and how much we may give, to the testing and the searching of the Holy Spirit. Our giving must be in the light, if it is to be in the joy of the Holy Ghost."

They had power, although they were poor. There is a wonderful contrast between this thought and the last. The Church of Pentecost needs money for the work, and the Spirit of Pentecost provided it by constraining those who formed the Church to give their all. But in Acts 3:6, we find that the apostles had evidently dispensed with money, proving that the Holy Ghost can work without it, as well as with it, and that poverty is no hindrance to a life of usefulness. To the man begging for alms at the gate of the Temple, Peter answered his request for money thus: "Silver and gold have

I none; but such as I have give I thee." "Silver and gold have I none"—this points us back to the poverty enjoined and exemplified by Christ, and also to the fact that the inner circle of His disciples had caught His Spirit and were following in the footsteps of His poverty, and like Him proving to the outside world that the possession of power and of heavenly riches is independent of earthly goods.

And further, can we not trace the rapid increase of the Early Church to its poverty? Was it not its poverty that drove her back upon God, thus bringing to Him the opportunity of displaying His power? "The history of the Church tells us a sad story of the increase of wealth and worldly power, and the proportionate loss of the heavenly gift with which she had been entrusted, and which could alone bless the nations. The contrast to the apostolic state is set in the clearest light by a story that is told of one of the Popes.

When Thomas Aquinas first visited Rome, and expressed his amazement at all the wealth he saw, the Pope said, "We can no longer say, 'Silver and gold have I none.'" "No, indeed," was the answer, "nor can we say, 'What I have that give I thee. In the name of Jesus Christ of Nazareth rise up and walk.'" The earthly poverty and the heavenly power had been closely allied, with the one the other had gone.

Poverty and power are often closely allied, and what God joins together let no man put asunder. The great sin-sick world has many needs, and its greatest is not the possession of material things, but the consecrated lives of men and women through whom God can say to the multitudes—"Rise up and walk." And this, after all, is the most blessed gift we can bestow upon crippled souls. Had Peter thrown that beggar a penny, and left him there, he would have required another gift when the apostle came that way to pray; but by healing him, Peter made it possible for the man to walk and worship and work, and thus earn his own bread, and be independent of all. While charitable institutions are necessary and worthy of our support, let us realize that the deeper need of this life is not for loaves and fishes, but the power to walk for God, and it is our imperative duty to meet this need first of all.

They deliberately refused money. There is yet another lesson to learn from Peter regarding money. In Acts 8:9 we find the Holy Ghost using him for the spiritual quickening of the Samaritans, and how Simon, the sorcerer, who witnessed the display of the power of the Spirit through Peter desired the Apostle to sell him the same. "Simon offered them money saying, Give me also this power . . . . But Peter said unto him, Thy money perish with thee, because thou has thought to obtain the gift of God with money (Acts 8:19,20).

Peter had no love of money in his soul; he loved his Lord too much to allow gold to capture his affections. He knew that his Master would meet his every need without condescension to a dishonorable way of obtaining such as Simon suggested, for was it not he who had caught the fish with its silver piece. "Get the fish," said Jesus and, "you'll find the money," and Peter believed this especially in dealing with souls. Ah! but is it not true that many like Simon think that power or influence in the Church can be gained by money; that the rich can acquire the place or position denied to a poorer man? Are there not others who think that they can merit heaven by the use of their check-books? To all such the Spirit says—"Thy heart is not right with God."

So, as we take this last glimpse of Peter, let us seek like him to hate money as bribery for any blessing, and not to love it for itself, but only regard it as something that can be used for the glory of God. It is said that the Pope's ambassador came to Martin Luther offering him bribes for his return to the bosom of a corrupt Church, but upon the Reformer's refusal, he exclaimed with disappointment—"That German beast does not care for gold!" And Luther's example is surely worth following in this respect. Thus we have seen that the actuating motives of the Early Church regarding money were the witness of its apostles and the words and ways of its Founder, and such are still sufficient to guide and shape our attitude toward money and its uses.

7. The Objects Subscribed to

While it is true that all the apostles gave was given to the Lord, nevertheless money was designated for specific purposes; and as our money is His we have no right to use it for anything that has not His sanction. It will be seen that these early believers gave:

1. For the support of the ministry (I Corinthians 9:4-14; Galatians 6:6; I

Timothy 5:18; Philippians 4:15,16).
2. For missionary purposes (Acts 24:17; I Corinthians 16:1).
3. For the poor among believers (Acts 20:35; 11:29; 6:1; 4:35; 2:45; Romans 15:25,26; Galatians 2:10).
4. For other expenses of maintaining the church organization, and gifts for special objects. But as now, so then, many church members shirked their responsibility for Paul is found speaking about "no church communicating with me as concerning giving and receiving" (Philippians 4:15).

8. *The Reward of True Giving*

Although the true Christian does not give to get, yet Scripture is not silent regarding the rewards of blessings attached to right giving. There is truth and instruction in the inscription on the Italian tombstone—

What I gave away I saved,
What I spent I used,
What I kept I lost.

1. Bountiful giving brings a bountiful reward (II Corinthians 9:6).
2. It brings glory to God, by the thanksgiving of those we bless (II Corinthians 9:11-13).
3. Our giving reminds of God's giving and calls to thanks for His gift (II Corinthians 9:15).
4. Treasures in heaven will be ours (Matthew 6:20). "Giving to the Lord," says one, "is but transporting our goods to a higher floor."
5. Liberality occasions the love and good pleasure of God (II Corinthians 9:7), "God loveth." "God is well pleased" (Hebrews 13:16). "I will pour you out a blessing" (Malachi 3:10).

Bunyan declared, in that couplet of his, that by giving we get—

A man there was, some called him mad,
The more he gave, the more he had.

Says Dr. Barrow—"The liberal man will ever be rich, for God's providence is his estate, God's wisdom and power his defense, God's love and favor his reward, and God's word his security."

The Church—Her Ordinances

It is a natural sequence that, being a spiritual organism, the Church of God should have some outward signs or seals of its invisible life, signs or seals distinguishing those who form it from the rest of man-

kind. So we come to examine its ordinances, or as they are generally termed—"The Sacraments of the Church."

THE TERM

The word "sacrament" comes from the Latin word *sacramentum*, a word which, in the classical period of the Latin language, was used in a twofold way—
1. As a legal term to denote the sum of money deposited by two parties to a suit, which was forfeited by the loser and appropriated to sacred uses.
2. As a military term to designate the oath of obedience taken by newly enlisted soldiers in the Roman army.

Among Latin Christian writers the word was long used in a loose way to include anything sacred. It was first applied to Christians by Pliny, who in his famous letter speaks of them, as we have already seen, "binding themselves with an oath (*sacramentum*) not to the commission of any wickedness." Tertullian next uses the word, and speaks of baptism as being a sacrament, or vow, to serve Christ faithfully. Thus, referring as it did, to something set apart for a sacred purpose, or as an oath of obedience, the term stole into circulation and is now used to describe the two ordinances or sacraments of the Church. "By a large consent of the Christian Church," says Handley Moule, "the word is restricted to denote such Christian rites as have an immediate divine institution and a revealed connection with the conveyance of spiritual blessings.

"Baptism, and the Supper of the Lord, alone answer this description. They thus stand in a sacred position of their own."

These then, Baptism and the Supper of the Lord, are the Church's "sacramentum"; and as we have been commanded by the Head of the Church to observe these two ordinances it is well to be sure of their scriptural significance.

THEIR NUMBER

Although we have observed that the number of the Church's ordinances is two, yet it may surprise one to know that the number has varied from two to twelve. Hugo of St. Victor, who lived in the twelfth century, enumerated as many as 30 sacraments that had been recognized in the Church. During the period of 1562, however, it was determined at the Council of Trent that the number should be limited to seven because of the idea of perfection being connected with such a number. The seven sacraments instituted being—Baptism, confession, the Lord's Supper, penance, extreme unction, orders, marriage—all of which are still upheld by the Romish Church as valid sacraments.

But to think of all these as sacraments in the sense in which baptism and the Lord's Supper are received, is contrary to the New Testament. Nor were these seven acknowledged as such by the early churches, or by the Fathers. Justin Martyr, Tertullian, Augustine, Chrysostum, and the Fathers generally, speak of two sacraments.

THEIR INSTITUTION

As it is always profitable to trace the great doctrines, and all the important features of our Christian life, back to their original source or institution, just as one would trace a river back to its spring or beginning, so here in respect to the sacraments fresh light upon their meaning may be seen by tracing them back to their original inception.

Their Old Testament Foundation

It is apparent to all Bible readers that the ordinances of the Church have their roots in, and grew out of, the ordinances or rites of the old dispensation. Says H. C. G. Moule, "The sacramentalism of the New Testament will not be viewed aright in isolation from that of the Old. The gospel sacraments are most sacred parts of a sacred whole, the sacramental idea pervading Scripture. From the beginning onward, the convenanted idea appears, and everywhere, at its side, the sacramental institution. . . . Perhaps the tree of life to Adam, certainly the rainbow to Noah, federal sacrifice (Genesis 15) and circumcision (Genesis 17; Romans 4:10,11) to Abraham, the Passover Sacrifice and Feast to Israel; are all instances of one idea, the giving of an external, and usually lasting or recurring, divine sign along with a divine promise. It is the same thing, in its last and noblest development, when at length the eternal Covenant appears fully revealed, and brings with it its laver, its bread, its cup."

In the Old Testament the two ceremonies of circumcision and the Passover Feast were the most distinctive rites of the Old Covenant. "These ceremonies were to the Jews what baptism and the Supper are to Christians. Circumcision and baptism repre-

sent a Covenant relation which the Passover and the Supper were intended to commemorate and deepen."

Circumcision was the rite of initiation, whereby a male Israelite was henceforth included in the covenant of Israel, and made an heir to all the blessings thereof (Deuteronomy 10:16; 30:6).

Baptism, on the other hand, speaks of the included in the covenant of Israel, and is the sign that he or she is a child of God and an inheritor of the kingdom of heaven (Galatians 3:27-29; Colossians 2:10-12).

The Passover Feast commemorated a great national deliverance from a bondage worse than death, but the Lord's Supper declares an experience of sins forgiven, of salvation enjoyed, and the divine fullness realized by the believer (Matthew 26:26-29; John 6:53,54; I Corinthians 5:7).

That we are justified in treating these two Old Testament rites as the roots of the New Testament ordinances can be proved by "the way in which they are associated by the New Testament (Acts 2:41-42; I Corinthians 10:1-4) and also in the analogy which Paul traces between baptism and the Lord's Supper on the one hand, the circumcision and the Passover—the two most distinctive rites of the Old Covenant—on the other (Colossians 2:11; I Corinthians 5:7; 11:26)." This analogy, however, is limited, especially in the matter of circumcision and the corresponding initiatory rite of baptism. Some affirm that infant baptism has taken the place of circumcision, but this is not so, as the two dispensations being different require different ordinances. As a Jewish male, Christ was circumcised the eighth day, but as the Representative of sinners, He was baptized at the age of 30.

Their New Testament Institution

Although there is a similarity between the sacraments of the Church and the rites of Israel, yet we must not forget that the former bear a distinct and separate relationship from the latter, in that both baptism and the Supper owe their origin as the two ordinances of the Church to the definite appointment by Christ Himself, and then to the practice of the apostles.

BAPTISM

In regard to the institution of baptism we can summarize the truth regarding such in the following way:

John the Baptist was divinely commissioned to baptize (John 1:33; 3:28).

Jesus submitted Himself to the ordinance (Matthew 3:13-17; Mark 1:9-11), not as a babe, but as a young man of 30.

With the aid of His disciples He practiced baptism (John 4:1-3).

The Master included baptism in His last commission (Matthew 28:16-20; Mark 16:15).

The apostles enjoined it upon the converts of the Early Church (Acts 2:38-47; 8:13-40; 9:18; 10; 16:14; 15:32-34; 18:8-15; 19:17; I Corinthians 1:14-16).

It is incorporated in the teaching of the epistles (Romans 6:3,4; Galatians 3:2-7; Ephesians 4:5; Colossians 2:12; I Corinthians 10:1,2).

It is also vitally connected with the cardinal doctrines of our Gospel—see Matthew 3:15; 28:19; 16:16, and passages above.

THE LORD'S SUPPER

In spite of the fact that some modern critics challenge the assumption that the Lord's Supper along with baptism owe their definite appointment to Christ Himself, yet there are four distinct accounts given in Scripture regarding the institution of the Supper that no critic can gainsay (cf. Matthew 26:26-30; Mark 14:22-25; Luke 22:17-20; I Corinthians 11:21-35).

"These narratives agree in every essential feature of the event, and only differ in such small details as might be expected from independent witnesses." It will be noticed that the observance of both of these institutions is not voluntary but obligatory, for they are given to us in the nature of commands—"Repent and be baptized"—"This do ye." And, as a divine law must continue obligatory until it is repealed by divine authority, it is only logical to conclude that these two commanded ordinances require continual observance as they have not been repealed by the Master's authority. And, says the prophet—"To obey is better than sacrifice, and to hearken than the fat of rams" (I Samuel 15:20).

THEIR SIGNIFICANCE

Perhaps Hodge's definition of what the real significance of the sacraments is, may be received as one of the clearest and most concise—"Sacraments are holy signs and seals of the Covenant of Grace (Romans 4:11; Genesis 17:7-10). Immediately instituted by God (I Corinthians 11:23), to represent Christ and His benefits, and to confirm our interest in Him (I Corinthians 10:16; 11:25-28; Galatians 3:17-27), and

also to put a visible difference between those who belong unto the Church, and the rest of the world (Romans 15:8; Exodus 12:48; Genesis 34:14), and solemnly engage them to the service of God in Christ, according to His word (Romans 6:3,4; I Corinthians 16:21)."

1. *The General Significance of both Ordinances.*

It will be recognized that a sacrament possesses a twofold part, the one an outward and visible sign used according to Christ's own appointment, the other an inward and spiritual grace signified by the sacrament (Matthew 3:11; Romans 2:28,29; I Peter 3:21). Such a twofold aspect has been observed from the days of the Early Fathers down to our own.

Augustine defines a sacrament as "the visible form of an invisible grace."

The *Shorter Catechism* says that—"A sacrament is an holy ordinance instituted by Christ wherein by sensible signs, Christ and the benefits of the New Covenant are represented, sealed and applied to the believer."

The *Church Catechism* puts it thus—"An outward and visible sign of an inward and spiritual grace given unto us, ordained by Christ Himself, as a means whereby we receive the same, and a pledge to assure us thereof."

Other definitions could be quoted, but as it will be seen, Augustine's phrase is the foundation of the two above mentioned. Suffice it to say, that "The sacraments are both signs and seals of grace, and when observed in faith become the channels of grace to the soul. As outward acts they symbolize the impartation of grace to the soul, and are a testimony on the part of the believer to the reception of the grace given."

Noting this fact, let us now deal separately with the two sacraments of the Church.

Baptism. The *Free Church Catechism* asks—What is the visible sign in the sacrament of baptism? And the answer is given —Water: wherein the person is baptized into the name of the Father, and of the Son, and of the Holy Ghost. What inward benefits does this signify? *Answer*—The washing away of sin and the new birth wrought by the Holy Spirit in all who repent and believe. Hodge's definition is equally as clear—"In Baptism the sign is water, applied in the name of the Triune

God to the one baptized. The inward spiritual grace is the spiritual purification by the work of the Holy Ghost in the soul, water being the symbol of His cleansing power."

The Lord's Supper. Turning again to the *Free Church Catechism* we find these further questions—What are the outward signs in the Lord's Supper? *Answer*—Bread and wine, which the Lord has commanded to be given and received for a perpetual memorial of His death. What is signified by the bread and wine? *Answer*—By the bread is signified the Body of our Lord Jesus Christ in which He lived and died; by the wine is signified His Blood, shed once for all upon the cross for the remission of sins.

Here again we find Hodge in his "Confessions of Faith" reiterating the same thoughts—"In the Lord's Supper the outward signs are bread broken and wine poured out and distributed to, and appropriated by, the partakers of same. The inward spiritual grace is that the crucified Christ with His torn flesh and shed blood has been spiritually received as the substitute for the soul, followed by the consciousness of regeneration, justification and sanctification, all of which are benefits secured by our Lord's sacrificial death."

Such a consideration of the general significance of the sacraments, leads us to make two further important remarks, which, if comprehended, will safeguard us from all error surrounding the Church's ordinances.

1. The Sacraments Are Only Symbolical

It is necessary to note that the sacraments are only symbolical and representative. Take the ordinance of baptism, which from its institution has only acted as a sign or symbol of a spiritual grace, but which has been treated not only as the symbol of that grace but the grace itself. From the Third Century, or so, many have held that fatal doctrine of baptismal regeneration, which term implies two things.

First, that at the baptism of a child new life is imparted and the babe becomes by the act of baptism, a member of Christ's Church.

The other aspect is that a soul can only be regenerated if the act of baptism is engaged in, and that consequently the soul unbaptized is unregenerate.

But both of these implications are contrary to the revealed Word, for regeneration, whether in a child or adult, is the direct work of the Holy Ghost apart from any ordinance, the only necessary condition being that true submissive faith which makes the impartation of the new life possible.

The same is true in respect to the Lord's Supper. It is only symbolical and representative. The bread and wine is not actually His body and blood, but only representing such, sacramentally. Yet from the time of Luther down to the present day the Romish and Lutheran Churches understand the Supper to be a literal identity, as is known as "transubstantiation," or "Exchange of Essences," implying that in the partaking of these two sacred elements, the real body and blood of our Lord are conveyed to the partaker. But such a pernicious doctrine as "Transubstantiation (or the change of the substance of bread and wine) in the Supper of the Lord, cannot be proved by Holy Writ; but it is repugnant to the plain words of Scripture, overthroweth the nature of a sacrament, and hath given occasion to many superstitions," says the Church's Creed.

These errors have arisen, then, from the substitution of the grace for the sign, for mistaking the sacrament for that which it symbolized. Why, it is possible "to receive the sign without the thing, and the thing without the Sign (as Cornelius did, Acts 10)." This means it is possible to observe the rites of baptism and the Supper and yet be destitute of the regeneration and redemption they signify: and on the other hand, one may be born again and certain of eternal life without ever partaking of either baptism or the Supper, as to wit, the dying thief, and many another dying sinner.

As Ambrose of Milan put it—"Many press upon Christ in outward ordinances, but believers touch Him. It is by faith that He is touched so as to have virtue from Him" (Luke 8:45,46).

2. The Sacraments Are Only Instrumental

Although the sacraments are only symbolical, they are yet the instruments of divine appointment whereby spiritual influence and power are communicated unto us as we engage in them, their efficacy being not in themselves but in the sovereign and ever-present personal agency of the Holy Ghost, who uses the sacraments as His instruments and medium of operation.

For instance, the public confession of one's regeneration by the act of baptism is a means of spiritual stimulus to the believer, and at the same time a means of forcible witness to the unconverted who witness the performance of the ordinance, a witness more forcible among the heathen than ourselves.

And then, in the participation of the Lord's Supper the same thought of communicated blessing is present, for as the bread is eaten and wine drunk, the mind is centered on the blood, so red, spilt on our behalf, and the soul looks up in adoring worship to Him who paid the price and set us free. Then silently, as Calvary is brought to our remembrance, we seek to give ourselves to Him in a fuller measure, that some reward might be His for the travail of His soul.

> We see Thee at Thy table, Lord,
> By faith, with great delight;
> Oh, how refined these joys will be
> When faith is turn'd to sight!

2. *The New Testament Teaching, Regarding Each Sacrament*

So far, we have doubtless been agreed upon the significance of the sacraments, but entering a particular study of each, one fully expects to encounter criticism regarding their exact mode and manner of observance. But if our foundation is the New Testament, then we have nothing to fear. Therefore, let us seek to listen, not to the voice of tradition, but of truth.

Baptism

We commence with baptism seeing it is the initial rite of our Christian faith, which once administered is not repeated.

The Lord's Supper, on the other hand, is the continuous ordinance of the Church. Baptism is a figure of our union with the Lord by the work of the Spirit. The Supper is a figure of our communion with the same Lord through the work of His cross.

The former signifies *regeneration;* the latter, *redemption.*

1. *Its Institution*

We have already seen that baptism was instituted by our Lord and practiced by His disciples. To what we have already said we might add these words of H. C. G. Moule—"In the epistles, eight or nine places deal with baptism, teaching that in it we are baptized into our Lord (Galatians 3:27), into His death, into His grave (Romans 6:3,4; Colossians 2:12), raised with Him (Colossians 2:13), clothed with Christ (Galatians 3:27), saved, that is, saved by the answer of a good conscience in it (I Peter 3:21), all knit into one body (I Corinthians 12:13). The Church is (Ephesians 5:26) 'sanctified and cleansed by the laver of the water, attended, or conditioned, by an utterance' (of the divine name and promise). Baptism is the 'laver of new birth' (Titus 3:5). On the other hand, baptizing appears as a work secondary to preaching the Gospel (I Corinthians 1:17).'"

Possibly some of the passages quoted may be open to other interpretations than those given by Moule, but the quotation as it stands gives one an idea of the significance of baptism to the apostles who received the commission to baptize directly from the Lord.

2. *Its Subjects*

The question that has divided the Church regarding baptism is whether infants or only those who comprehend and accept the truths of the Gospel are fit subjects for baptism.

Infant Baptism. If one uses the words of those who adhere to, and practice this form of baptism, which is better known as sprinkling, they cannot be guilty of treating the subject with biased minds if adult baptism by immersion is held. Take H. C. G. Moule who declared, although a non-immersionist, that—"in the New Testament we have not indeed any mention of infant baptism," but who, when seeking a justification of such a practice, says—"But we find not the least explicit caution against it, and no injunction to Christian parents to prepare their children for baptism." Or, think of the view that Dr. Paterson of the Church of Scotland expresses in his article on "The Church and its Ordinances" under the section of baptism—"Whether he sanctioned the baptism of infants does not clearly appear . . . . The case for infant baptism must be made out on other grounds. What is here perhaps more important to bear in mind is that, when he addresses baptized persons, he is addressing persons, who, from the nature of the case, had been received in mature life by the rite of baptism into the Church."

What are the true facts of the case, however, but these, that "we have no hint or record anywhere in the New Testament nor in early church history, that baptism was ever allowed to those who were not already professed believers. . . . About A.D. 200 Tertullian of Carthage strongly denounced infant baptism, which was just beginning to come into fashion, for the sensible reason that the child may afterward give up all his faith when he develops views of his own. The custom did not become general until the fifth century. Neither Chrysostom, Basil, Augustine, Jerome, nor Ambrose, who all lived at the end of the fourth century, were baptized until they became believers, although one or both of their parents were Christians."

Adult Baptism. The words of the *Prayer Book Catechism* regarding the baptism of infants reads thus—"at my baptism wherein I was made a child of God, a member of Christ, and an inheritor of the kingdom of Heaven," but such a time and method of inclusion in the Church is contrary to New Testament faith and doctrine.

The dominant note of the New Testament is the soul's personal relation to Christ apart from any ordinance, but how can there be a personal relationship if such is not conscious and voluntary? The non-immersionists within the Church say that infants through baptism become eligible members of the Church, even though they are unconscious and involuntary—The witness of the New Testament is that we must enter the Kingdom by our own responsibility, and to adopt any other method of entrance nullifies the need of conversion and personal faith in the risen Lord.

"Ye must be born again"—is the pivot around which our glorious Evangel revolves and any denial or whittling down of such a personal, voluntary entrance into Christ's Church, symbolized as it is by the waters of baptism, destroys the whole fabric of Christianity and contradicts the revelation of the New Testament.

The unassailable testimony of the gospels and the epistles is that baptism was the rite by which the convert was formally admitted to the Church, and was to such the outward sign of inward blessing or cleansing, being administered to Christians only (Acts 19:1-5; Romans 6:3; Colossians 2:11-13; John 3:5; I Peter 3:20,21).

> Saviour, we seek the watery tomb,
>   Illumed by love divine:
> Far from the deep tremendous gloom,
>   Of that which once was thine.
>
> Down to the hallow'd grave we go,
>   Obedient to Thy word:

> 'Tis thus the world around shall know,
>   We're buried with the Lord.
>
> 'Tis thus we bid its pomp adieu,
>   And boldly venture in:
> Oh may we rise to live anew,
>   And only die to sin.

3. *Its Mode*

The whole organized Church is united upon this fact, that water is necessary for the administration of the rite of baptism, but great division has been caused over the question of the quantity and mode to be employed. Is it a few drops as in sprinkling? Or is it immersion in water? Well, to show that we are not treating the subject with bias, let us look at what scholarly men who upheld the view of infant baptism have to say regarding the exact New Testament mode of baptism, and by doing so we shall find that such scholars range themselves on the side of immersion without partiality or force.

Martin Luther. The words of this reformer are remarkable—"I could wish that such as are to be baptized should be completely immersed into water, according to the meaning of the word and the significance of the ordinance."

Dean Stanley. This famous scholar and writer said—"There can be no question that the original form of baptism—the very meaning of the word—was complete immersion in the deep baptismal waters."

Sanday and Headlan. In their powerful work on Romans, these two gifted expositors express this interpretation of Romans 6:4—"It (baptism) expresses symbolically a series of acts corresponding to the redeeming acts of Christ. Immersion—Death. Submersion—Burial (ratification of death). Emergence—Resurrection."

Dr. Marcus Dods. This notable Presbyterian, adding to a quotation of Bishop Lightfoot's, where he also argues for immersion—"To use the Pauline language, his old man is dead and buried in the water and he rises from this cleansing grave a new man. The full significance of the rite would have been lost had immersion not been practiced."

Professor Lindsay. As another outstanding scholar and a non-immersionist, he adds a striking quota to the New Testament mode of immersion—"It may be admitted at once that immersion, where the whole body including the head is plunged into a pool of

pure water, gives a more vivid picture of
the cleansing of the soul from sin: and that
complete surrounding with water suits better the metaphors of burial in Romans 6:4,
and Colossians 2:12, and being surrounded
by the cloud in I Corinthians 10:2."

If one desired to go further they could
show that the circumstances attending its
observance warrant immersion (Matthew
3:6; Mark 1:5; Acts 8:38), and that the
word "baptize" both in the New Testament
and in Greek literature signifies "dip" or
"immerse," but possibly the above quotations from non-immersionists, as well as the
practice of non-immersionists of immersion
in heathen lands, is sufficient evidence for
the scripturalness of such a mode.

4. Its Meaning

There is no need to tarry over this aspect of the ordinance as we have already
indicated its significance under the general
treatment of the ordinances. Baptism, the
outward sign of an inward cleansing, was
—and still is—a badge of discipleship, and
an act of obedience on the part of the
disciple in response to the direct command
of our Lord.

The Lord's Supper

In seeking to analyze the New Testament
significance of this most sweet and blessed
ordinance of the Church, one realizes that
there is not so much adverse opinion regarding its observance, as there is in respect
to the ordinance of baptism, although different interpretations are held in connection with minor details.

1. Why Taken

Christians everywhere partake of the
Supper because it is not only a part of
their worship, but a cardinal point in it,
being instituted by our Lord Himself, as
we have had occasion to show. H. C. G.
Moule shows, apart from the fourfold record of the institution (Matthew 26; Mark
14; Luke 22; I Corinthians 11), that "we
have in the Acts five mentions, without
comment, of the breaking of bread—2:42-
46; 10:7-11; 27:25. We have in the epistles
two great didactic passages, only two, but
fuller than any baptismal passage, I Corinthians 10:16-21; 11:17-34—there is a possible further reference to the rite in I Corinthians 12:13, we were all made to drink
into one Spirit . . . . Such is the special
New Testament material for this sacramental doctrine."

Therefore believers observe this sacred
Feast because our Lord instituted it, and
commanded the observance of it by His
professed followers—"This do, in remembrance of Me."

But not only are we to partake of the
Supper as a commanded ordinance; its
chief substance is commemorative, thus it
is observed as a memorial of the sufferings
and death of Christ (I Corinthians 11:25,
26).

"The Passover Feast was a monument of
the nation's deliverance and was celebrated
with solemn sacrifice and thanksgiving. So
the Supper is to be a standing monument
of the expiatory work of Jesus as the procuring cause of His people's salvation (John
6:54,55)."

The Supper, then, is a remembrance of
Him, not merely His work, but Himself.
Knowing that our memories are so weak,
He would constantly bring to our minds
the great truths of our peace and deliver-
ance, and of Himself, in the emblems He
Himself has sanctioned.

There are other features that one can
mention:

It is a proclamation. The Supper not
only commemorates but proclaims the
Lord's death. The words, "shew forth," in
I Corinthians 11:26 mean to "proclaim,"
that is, telling news to human hearers. Believers, therefore, in observing this simple
ordinance proclaim to themselves and to
each other and the world, that the death
of Christ is the foundation of their salvation and life. "A solemnly 'acted word'
about the Lord's death."

It is an anticipation. The Supper presents us with a threefold view of Christ
and the believer. *Past*—Calvary, the Lord's
death. *Present*—As often as ye eat this
bread, and drink this cup, ye do show the
Lord's death, that is, the continuous spiritual efficacy of the Feast. *Prospective*—
Till He come. The Supper is the table
spread in the presence of our foes (Psalm
23:5). It bids us remember with joyful
anticipation the day of union awaiting the
members of the Head of the mystical body.

*It is a sign or symbol of the saving truth
of the Gospel.* Hodge terms it, "A badge
of Christian profession—a mark of allegiance of a citizen of the kingdom of
Heaven." It is by this rite that believers
demonstrate the reality of salvation and
bear witness to the power of Christ to deliver them from all iniquity.

It is a seal to the believer's privileges in Christ. The Lord's Supper is the seal of the covenant of grace, for, said our Lord in Luke 22:20: "This cup is the new testament (covenant) in My blood, which is shed for you." Thus it is that "God's assurances to man, and man's obligations to God, are certified by this special signature. It is the sign of man's admission to the fellowship of the Father and His Son Jesus Christ."

It is the bond of union and communion among believers. Participation in the Supper is a token and sign to faith of the union existing between Christ and all the members of His body—"fellowship in His blood and in His body." This is the thought emphasized by Paul in I Corinthians 10:16,17.

Unworthy participation is condemned by the apostle in I Corinthians 11:29, and if partaken by either the unregenerated or by believers having unjudged sin upon their conscience, enmity in their hearts against others gathered at the Table, carelessness in respect to the spiritual state necessary to discern the Lord's body, then the Supper only communicates condemnation instead of blessing.

Considered, then, in these aspects the Lord's Supper "becomes invested with a solemnity, an importance, and a richness of experience which belong to no other institution of the Church." In the early days the true significance of this ordinance was deepened and intensified in the minds and hearts of the Christians as its great spiritual meaning was more and more clearly perceived; and such is still the case, for the oftener the sacred elements are taken in our hands and appropriated, the more do our trustful hearts come to know the infinite cost of our redemption, and the preciousness of Him who redeemed us.

> According to Thy gracious word,
> In meek humility,
> This will I do, my dying Lord,
> I will remember Thee.
>
> Remember Thee, and all Thy pains;
> And all Thy love to me:
> Yea, while a breath, a pulse remains,
> Will I remember Thee.

2. *When Taken*

Difference of opinion exists among the several sections of the Church regarding the mode and time of observing the Supper.

In the Early Church the service was of a much more private character than the public one of worship (I Corinthians 11:17-34) and restricted to baptized Christians. From Acts 20:7 we learn that it was the practice of the disciples to meet on the first day of the week and break bread, while in Acts 2:46 there appears to have been a daily administration of this ordinance. The first Supper was celebrated at eventide, and the disciples following the example of Christ, held it in the evening at the close of a meal eaten in common, called the *Agape*—or love feast, but was afterward separated from the *Agape* by Paul on account of the abuses connected with it, and observed in the morning while the Agape, or common meal, was eaten at night.

Thus in respect to the mode and time Scripture offers no explicit command—"This do ye, as *oft* as ye drink" allowing latitude regarding both. "Our Lord and His followers took it in the prevailing fashion of reclining upon couches. It is now received kneeling, sitting or standing, according to the conviction or the opportunity of the recipient. The first Supper was celebrated at evening, but now at all hours of the day as best suits the convenience of Church or individual believers."

Doubtless we derive most profit from the ordinance, when, like the apostles, we observe it each Lord's day morning as that is the morning that reminds, not only of His death, but His victory over it. Still, the "posture of the body, or the hour of the clock, are unimportant compared with the spirit of faith and devotion in which the elements should be received."

The Church—Her Obligations

The consideration of the manifold obligations of the Church of God brings us to a most vital section of our study, a section, which, as we compare the ideal church with the actual, reveals how the present day mode of church life and influence has traveled far from the explicit orders and obligations of the New Testament. Like Samson of old, the Church is trying to shake herself again and manifest something of her old-time strength and glory, but the Delilah of apostasy has shorn her of her power, and the tragedy is that many church leaders wist not that the Lord has departed.

By way of introduction we might observe

that the Church is a distinctively spiritual institution, existing mainly for two purposes, namely, the maintenance of spiritual worship, and the out-gathering of souls. God placed the Church in the world for such purposes, but we fear that the devil has succeeded in placing the world in the Church for the perversion of such purposes.

The position of the Church is akin to Israel's position in that the Jews had been called out and separated from the surrounding nations, and yet left in the world that they might testify for God among the nations. Like Israel, the members of the Church are called "peculiar"—a word signifying, a people for God's possession, and not the acquired meaning of the word, that is, a people who are odd, or beset with idiosyncrasies, strange and uncommon in their ways and manners. True it is that among the Lord's professed people there are those who love to be odd, peculiar, different from others, and who are deluded by the devil into believing that crankyism or unconventional methods of service are a certain proof of inspiration. But the word —"peculiar"—in its Biblical sense, never means oddity, it springs from a Latin term, *Peculium* meaning "private property," and is used especially of that which is given by a father to a son. In Scripture the word conveys three meanings, all of which declare the obligations of the Church, and the character of its members.

1. *Separation*

This word occurs five times in the Old Testament, being used four times out of the five, of Israel. For instance, take Psalm 135:4—"The Lord hath chosen Jacob unto himself, and Israel for his peculiar treasure." In this, as well as in the other Old Testament references (Exodus 19:5; Deuteronomy 14:2; 26:18; see Ecclesiastes 2:8), there is the idea of separation.

Israel had been separated from the surrounding nations, and as a pilgrim people lived in tents, and as an holy nation worshiped God in the ways appointed by Him in the service of the Tabernacle and Temple.

The inner meaning of the word "peculiar" in the Old Testament is that of an enclosure, something excluded and kept distinct or separate from other things. Thus it is, that the Church, like Israel, is a peculiar body, that is, marked off, separated from the rest of mankind, or God's sacred enclosure, so to speak.

The Church, however, is a greater treasure of the Lord than Israel, peculiar and precious as she was, and is, to Him, for the formation of Israel as a nation cost God nothing but the display of His favor and choice, whereas the Church has been purchased with His own blood, and is therefore, of all His creations, the greatest, grandest, most glorious and costliest.

2. *Character*

Coming to the New Testament we discover that Paul uses the word in one instance only. In Titus 2:14 he refers to the Saviour as, "the One who gave Himself for us, that He might redeem us from all iniquity and purify unto Himself a peculiar people (R.V. a people for His own possession), zealous of good works."

Here the word signifies, "beyond the ordinary," and is connected with the character of those who form Christ's mystical body, as the context fully shows. As believers we are His possession and must therefore live lives beyond the ordinary. In verse 12 Paul outlines what such a life is—"We should live soberly (inward), righteously (outward), and godly (upward)."

"Beyond the ordinary." What a solemn obligation that is to face! And we should constantly remind our hearts that the Lord expects us to live lives beyond the ordinary standards of religious profession, and beyond the ordinary ways and habits of the world.

3. *Ownership*

The word is used once again in the New Testament with another significance. Peter, in his first epistle, describes the Church as, "a chosen generation (R.V. an elect race), a royal priesthood, an holy nation, a peculiar people" (R.V. a people for God's own possession). In his use of the word "peculiar," he emphasizes the thought of divine ownership, as the Revised Version fully shows (I Peter 2:9).

With Peter it means "acquisition," that is, something acquired, and the Church is thus greatly prized by God for He has acquired her, called her into being, gave Himself for her birth, and now fills her continually with His blessed Spirit, making her His holy habitation.

Because the Church belongs to the Lord, having been acquired with the purchase price of Calvary, it is her solemn obligation to obey, please and serve her Lord. Turning now more definitely to the thought of the Church's obligations, we recognize that such can be classed as—general and personal.

General Obligations

Under this heading we naturally think of the obligations of the Church as a whole to her Lord, to the Truth and to the world.

1. To Her Lord

Because the Church is God's own possession, and He is her Lord, then first and foremost she is obliged to obey and honor His injunctions regarding her life, service, worship and government.

She must follow the dictates of her Lord. In His parting words to the first representatives of the Church, our Lord said that they must teach men and women to observe all the things that He had commanded them (Matthew 28:20). And such a word must still be observed if the Church is to wield any spiritual influence upon the world. Her commands must be received, not from kings, governments, or even church leaders, but from the divine Head Himself. She must be subservient to Him in all things, and endeavor to know and do His will in all things. And, moreover, He has no more new orders to issue or fresh obligations to impose. When He called His Church into being He saw her end from the beginning, and recorded for her guidance all that she needs to know and do until she is united to Him in glory. Therefore, the paramount obligation of the Church is to discover the explicit commands of her Lord, obey them, and then proclaim them fearlessly, urging the nations to duly observe the same.

She must wait for His return. As we hope to say more about this obligation a word or two will suffice at this point. Paul, in seeking to establish the Church at Thessalonica, refers to the threefold aspect of the life of his converts there—"Ye turned to God from idols to serve the living and true God; And to wait for His Son from heaven." The epistles are full of injunctions imposed upon the Church by the Holy Ghost, in which she is enjoined to wait in readiness for her returning Lord, and those who fail to see this glorious hope of the Church, whether they be ministers or laymen, are suffering from spiritual catarrh. Those within the Church who discredit such a cardinal truth may scoff at us as we proclaim it, but let us daily fulfill this blessed obligation and "wait for His Son from heaven."

We are to be "like unto men that wait for their Lord" (Luke 12:36).

2. To the Truth

It is here that we seem to hear the divine voice re-echoing the words—"I have somewhat against thee," for if there is one thing the Lord has had against His Church during the last fifty years or so, it is the fact that she has been false to her obligations regarding His Truth, or revealed Word. There are two phases connected with this particular obligation that emerge as we study the New Testament, namely, that of guardianship and proclamation.

Loyal Guardianship. Paul has a wonderful way of describing the Church in I Timothy 3:15. He calls it—"the Church of the living God, the pillar and ground (margin 'stay,' that is, basis) of truth." The apostle here describes the Church as a massive pillar, holding up and displaying before men and angels *the Truth*—the saving truth of the Gospel.

But is the Church, generally speaking, still the pillar and ground of truth? Our hearts answer—No! The Scriptures form the sole pillar and ground of truth, and such have been committed into the guardianship of the Church, but if she destroys this basis or foundation as she certainly is, through the medium of the so-called higher criticism, then does she not stand condemned with disloyalty?

Because of this contemptible disloyalty from those who profess to be the Church's leaders and teachers, we hail with prayerful sympathy any who expose Modernism and restore the Scriptures to their unique position as the infallible Word of God. We must guard jealously its precious contents from its foes, cloaked as friends, as they try to mutilate the truth, and disown it as the complete and final revelation of the divine will.

Universal Proclamation. The Church's obligation is to receive the truth, believe and obey it, and then publish it abroad among the nations. This can be gathered from our Lord's marching orders given to His disciples ere He returned to glory— "Go ye into all the world and preach the gospel to every creature" (Matthew 28:19, 20; Mark 16:15).

The constant obligation, then, of Christ's Body, regarding the Truth, is to preach and teach it. Not to criticize or question its veracity, but accept it and proclaim it everywhere.

And yet one wonders how it is that ministers are content to preach anything else but the Gospel. Current topics—latest sensations—catchy themes—cinema films—morals—ethics—politics—in fact anything and everything to tickle itching ears is served up for many congregations on the Lord's Day, while the Gospel which never fails to attract and satisfy the people if preached with the Holy Ghost sent down from heaven, is sadly neglected and despised.

Preach the Word! said Paul, in writing to Timothy, the young preacher (II Timothy 4:2), and the multitude in our churches throughout the land are dying of spiritual starvation for the want of such wholesome food as the Word supplies. And, moreover, if souls have a real hunger for the truth then they will go where they can get it, even to those who endeavor to realize their solemn obligation of preaching and teaching the Word of Truth.

3. To the World

In His high-priestly prayer of John 17 our Lord tells the Father that we have been given to Him as the Father's special love-gift, and that although He is about to leave the world, yet He is going to leave His Church in the world—"These are in the world and I come to Thee" (17:11). Why has Christ left His Church in this wilderness? What are her obligations regarding the world in which she sojourns?

Service for its salvation. The first obligation toward the world is that of faithful service in respect to its salvation—"Ye shall be witnesses unto Me both in Jerusalem, and in all Judea, and in Samaria, and unto the uttermost parts of the earth" (Acts 1:8). Such a parting message reveals that the desire of the Lord regarding His Church, is that she must preach the Gospel in every part of the world so that His redemptive work might be fully known among all men, so that at the Judgment Bar all nations will be without excuse. "Go ye into all the world and preach the gospel to every creature" (Mark 16:15).

But the Church has failed in this most sacred obligation, for in spite of the fact that she has now existed for over 1900 years, there are still unreached millions in the regions beyond who have never had the Gospel preached unto them. There are vast untouched interiors of great countries, where Satan holds unchallenged sway, and which although still open in many cases to missionary effort, are not being entered by the Church because of the lack of funds, and the scarcity of laborers who are willing to go.

Ere passing from this aspect of the Church's obligation, let us pause to reaffirm that it is the duty, as well as the privilege, of the Church, to labor for the salvation of all those outside the *organism,* and that such a salvation can only be produced by the proclamation of the saving truth of the Gospel. The explicit injunctions of our Lord regarding the Church He was about to leave in the world, were, that she should preach and teach the divine message and baptize those who believed. This leads us to say that the work of the Church is not educative, ameliorative, or instructive, primarily, but first and foremost evangelistic. She was not instituted to provide entertainments, amusements and social pleasures to keep the young within her borders, nor was she enjoined to use all her strength to grapple with great social problems like poverty and drink, although her influence should be felt in these directions, neither does she reach her highest vocation in training the young along the line of Scouts, Guildries and Brigades.

Her primary obligation is to work for the salvation of men and women through one medium, namely, the preaching of the Gospel, and that without any attractive additions. When this saving message is embraced, preached and truly believed, and exemplified by the lives of those who receive it, then there is no need for the hundred and one things that sap up the energies of many Church workers, energies that would produce greater results if concentrated upon the definite salvation of souls.

Separation from its ways. The united witness of the New Testament writers is that the Church, as a called-out body, must draw the sharp line of demarcation and live a life totally reverse to that of the world. Take our Lord's word of John 17:16, "They are not of the world, even as I am not of the world." Or, think of Paul's strong message of II Corinthians 6:17-7:1, "Come out from among them and be ye separate." Or, his word to Titus, "Teaching us that, denying ungodliness and worldly lusts, we should live soberly, righteously and godly in this present world" (2:12). Or, the test that

James emphasizes—"Pure religion and undefiled before God and the Father, is this. To visit the fatherless and widows in their affliction, and to keep himself unspotted from the world" (1:27).

But the tragedy is that in many quarters the Church has accommodated itself to the spirit, methods and ways of this worldly age, and is consequently crippled in its spiritual influence and power. No particular church can expect to influence the world, if, like the world, it has its social clubs, dramatic societies, cricket and football teams, cinema shows and concert displays. Were our Lord to enter some churches as He did the Temple long ago, we feel sure that He would re-echo His stern message of condemnation—"Take these things hence; make not my Father's house an house of merchandise" (John 2:16).

The weapons of the Church are not carnal, but spiritual. By prayer, holiness, faith and consecrated service, she is to win the world. And, needless to say, the clearer and cleaner the mark of separation from those pursuits and ways that characterize the world, the greater is the influence and power she exerts. Nothing is gained but all is lost by compromise, as many have proved to their sad cost.

Individual and Personal Obligations

The rise or fall of the Church depends upon individual responsibility. Each member of the Body can either help or hinder the other. Our own personal life either furthers or frustrates the most solemn obligations of the Church of God. Criticism for the Church is cheap, and to advertise its faults to those outside its borders is mean and unworthy, therefore the Bible insists upon, not our endeavors to put others right, but to keep ourselves right—"Take heed unto thyself," "Let him that thinketh he standeth take heed lest he fall." Let us examine one or two personal obligations imposed upon us by the inspired Record:

1. Personal Loyalty to the Word.

The epistles to Timothy and Titus are full of exhortations to hold fast, and to stand fast in the faith. Believing that example is better than precept, the apostle, with the axman's block in sight, declared that he had kept the faith. To every one of us in these apostate days there comes the clarion call from Paul of loyalty to the Scriptures and to the faith once delivered unto the saints.

Some of our theological seminaries and colleges are hotbeds of destructive, diabolical criticism. Many of our pulpits are manned by those who, in their hearts, discredit many of the cardinal truths of Scripture, but who dare not preach all that they believe and discuss in their ministerial fraternals in case the outcry against them is greater than it is at present.

A certain minister who attended one of these fraternals for a number of years eventually became so grieved with the unsound doctrines advocated by the rest of the ministers, that he at last withdrew. On leaving he addressed them as follows: "Gentlemen, why don't you teach what you believe? You are waiting until the old members of your churches die, and then you will let it be known what you hold. Good-day, Gentlemen"—and he then departed never to return. Let us, likewise, if we believe and receive the Scriptures as the whole Word of God, not surrender one inch of ground but earnestly contend for the faith, and if needs be, disassociate ourselves from the people and the organization permeated with unbelief, as a manifest indication of our loyalty to the Word. "If any man teach otherwise, and consent not to wholesome words, even the words of our Lord Jesus Christ . . . from such withdraw thyself" (I Timothy 6:3-5).

The late C. H. Spurgeon separated himself from the London Baptist Association on account of serious doctrinal errors that such held, and speaking of those who continued in the Association, he said:

> Numbers of good brethren remain in fellowship with those who are undermining the Gospel, and they talk of their conduct as if it were a loving course which the Lord will approve of in the day of His appearing. We cannot understand them. The bounden duty of a true believer towards men who profess to be Christians, and yet deny the word of the Lord and reject the fundamentals of the Gospel, is to come out from among them. Complicity with error will take from the best of men the power to enter any successful protest against it.

Upon withdrawing from the Baptist Association, Mr. Spurgeon asked the question: "When will Christians learn that separation from evil is not only our privilege, but our duty?" Doubtless sentiment and long association with those who are now apostate may keep many from going all the way with Spurgeon, but the time has come to pocket our sentiments and range ourselves on the side of those who are loyal to the Word.

2. Personal Holiness of Life

While it is imperative to hold fast the faithful word, we must never forget that before protest, there is purity. Personally, one is more afraid of an unholy life than of accepting unwholesome doctrine.

Thus it is that Paul is careful to put personal holiness before loyalty to the truth —"Take heed unto thyself, and unto the doctrine" (I Timothy 4:16), or as he puts it in the next chapter—"Keep thyself pure" (I Timothy 5:22). If I desire to help the Church of which I am part, then let me know that the unanswerable argument to all adverse criticism of the Bible, and the most silent yet effective condemnation of all worldly methods, is the witness of a holy life.

Holy lives! These are the Church's greatest assets, and when every believer aspires after personal holiness then the Church will be found on a higher, holier level.

3. Personal Home-Influence

Paul has a striking word in I Timothy 3:5 applicable to all believers irrespective of position—"If any man know not how to rule his own house how shall he take care of the church of God?" Many men are public successes but private failures, that is, they are well thought of by those who hear and meet them publicly, but who only make the religion of Jesus Christ obnoxious to those within their own inner circle by their crooked, inconsistent, un-Christlike ways and conduct. A notable writer of fiction makes one of her characters to say—"Never follow a reformer beyond the threshold of his own home." But surely this is not what the Lord expects from His redeemed? If any part of our life is to become fragrant with the holiness of Christ, then should not our homes above all places be filled with such a pleasant odor? What the land and Church needs is a revival of true home-religion, when, within the borders of our own homes, we shall live and act, no matter what our relationship is, as those who really claim to be the Lord's. "Here will I sit best!" was a motto found in an old country house. Let us make it our own.

4. Personal Reverence

There are two portions of Scripture that show to us our individual obligation regarding our right and reverent demeanor within any place of worship. For instance, how solemn are the words of Solomon in Ecclesiastes 5:1,2—"Keep thy foot when thou goest to the house of God, and be more ready to hear, than to give the sacrifice of fools: for they consider not to do evil. Be not rash with thy mouth, and let not thy heart be hasty to utter any thing before God: for God is in heaven, and thou upon earth: therefore let thy words be few." Our feet, ears, lips and heart are all mentioned here, and our worship will become more sweet and blessed if we but heed the instructions regarding such.

How pointed is the advice of Paul to Timothy—"That thou mayest know how thou oughtest to behave thyself in the house of God" (I Timothy 3:15). One fears that many Christians are not as careful as they ought to be regarding personal behavior within the place of worship. It is not the market place for gossip, neither is it the place for levity, irreverence or unworthy behavior, but the hallowed spot, where as a body we meet with God, and therefore the place that should witness our best conduct and most prayerful, reverent attention. When Jacob came to the place he named Bethel, we are told that he was afraid, and said—"How dreadful is this place! this is none other but the house of God, and this is the gate of heaven" (Genesis 28:17). Let these be our feelings as we gather together in His name. May God enable His Church, both collectively and individually, to realize her solemn obligations, and to rise anew and live for Him who bought her with His own precious blood, that the whole world may realize indeed that she is His holy habitation; and likewise the most potent force that sin and Satan have to contend against, and that when fulfilling all her divine obligations, the gates of hell cannot prevail against her.

The Church—Her Outlook

The outlook of the Church of the living God—or should we say her *uplook*—is glorious! Her Head, who died to give her birth, is returning as the Bridegroom to claim Her as His Bride. Christ's sole purpose in tarrying for awhile "in the air," on His way to inaugurate His reign on the earth, is to gather His completed Church unto Himself. The *Church Triumphant* in heaven will be joined to the *Church Militant* on earth, and together will be caught up to meet the Lord (I Thessalonians 4:16,17). What a blessed consummation that will be!

In our last chapter on "The Doctrine of Last Things" there can be found a more detailed study of our Lord's return. Thus, in the present consideration of "the blissful hope" of the Church, a brief reference to His glorious appearing will suffice. We cannot understand or interpret aright Christ's parabolic teaching, as we have shown in *All the Parables of the Bible*, if we fail to accept His explicit teaching about His return. As Dr. W. Graham Scroggie expresses it—

> The message of some of these parables gathers around *the period of His absence*, with its necessary boundaries, His *departure* and His *return*, so that if there is no Second Advent these parables lose their significance.

The triple fact associated with the parables of the Bridegroom and the Virgins, the Talents, the Master of the House, the Good Samaritan, the Pounds, The Lord and His Servants (Matthew 24:45-51; 25:1-13,14-30; Mark 13: 34-37; Luke 10:30-35; 19:12-27), is that He who *was* here, went away, is now *absent* and is pledged to *return*. Over 20 times, in one way or another Christ spoke of His Second Advent.

After Christ's Ascension, the truth of His return possessed the minds of the first Christians and acted as a powerful stimulus as they served and suffered for the Master. The watchword of the Early Church was—*Maranatha!*—"Our Lord cometh" (I Corinthians 16:22). Those saints did not limit His promised coming to His spiritual presence with His Church. They expected His personal, visible appearance. They believed that when He said, "I will come again" (John 14:3) that He meant what He said, and so anticipated sharing in the glory of His appearance (Colossians 3:4; I Peter 5:4).

Our position is that Christ will appear "the second time"—that His *First* Advent is to be followed by His *Second* Advent. Christ *testified* to His return (Matthew 24:30; 25: 19; 26:64; John 14:3). Heaven *confirmed* Christ's promise to return (Acts 1:10,11). The apostles *proclaimed* His return (Philippians 3:20; I Thessalonians 4:13-18; II Thessalonians 1:7,10; Titus 2:13; Hebrews 9:28; Revelation 22).

XXXI

The Doctrine of Last Things

We have reached the last and the most awesome and absorbing section of our study, namely, *death and the vast beyond*. Endeavoring to understand what the Bible teaches regarding the Hereafter, we commence with the premise that the Bible alone supplies us with the only authentic revelation of the future of saint and sinner alike. We may feel that the curtain on the unseen has not been raised high enough, yet sufficient has been revealed of God's purposes concerning the destiny of this present world and of the world beyond, to form a satisfying eschatological plan.

It is to be regretted that *eschatology* or "the Doctrine of Last Things," does not occupy the large place it ought to in the minds of men, as well as in the modern pulpit. A generation or so ago, *eschatology* was a somewhat favorite topic, stressed it may be, at the expense of other aspects of the divine revelation. Today, many recoil from extremes and treat the subject with undeserved neglect. The social gospel tends to concentrate upon the practical, and not the prophetical implications of New Testament truth. Generally speaking, preachers are more at home in the sphere of Christian ethics than in apocalyptic visions. They are more anxious to bring Christ down to earth, than to urge the saints to be ready to be caught up to meet Him in the heavenlies. Why be concerned with ages to come and worlds unknown, when there are so many urgent moral and social problems to settle in the present?

Our answer to this comparative reticence on the part of many as to the larger questions of the Hereafter is that the few years we spend on earth pale into insignificance alongside the unending eternity of the human race. Certainly we should not be negligent as to our present obligations as Christians and as citizens, but the main emphasis in the Bible is condensed for us in the exhortation, "Prepare to meet thy God" (Amos 4:12). We have a feeling that too many are silent as to "The Doctrine of Last Things" because they have either not studied them or thought of them to no purpose.

Because man was created to live forever there is in his heart an insatiable curiosity about the Hereafter that cannot be silenced or quenched; and ministers of the Word fail in their solemn task if they do not make available for anxious hearts the Biblical light on the future. Contrary to what we are told about discussion of the future having no practical application, we affirm that Christians who have the strongest hope and most joyous certainty of a life beyond are those who do the most for the world they live in. They are not so heavenly-minded as to be of no earthly use. *The Last Things* we are now to consider have an immediate and most practical bearing on the present life to the intensity of conviction with which they are held. *Eschatology* is a powerful factor in shaping conduct, quickening conscience and enforcing the obligations of service for God and man.

As it is our purpose to dwell upon *Christian eschatology* we are not giving space to the eschatology of non-Christian religions, profitable though such a subject is. Examination of the future, as taught by the ancient Egyptians, Assyrians, Babylonians, Persians and Greeks, proves that their dim light was evidence of a Hereafter in the human heart. Buddhism, Hinduism and Mohammedanism have their coarser and ruder forms of the eternal hope the Bible presents.

In the realm of eschatology, more possibly than in any other realm, we have witness of a progressive revelation. Old Testament saints were not without their hope of future bliss. They looked for a city whose Builder and Maker is God (Hebrews 11:10). It is only when we come to the teaching of Christ and His apostles, however, that we have all we can know of the Great Beyond until we reach it. Life and immortality have been brought to light through the Christian Gospel. Under the guidance of the Holy Spirit, then, whose province it is to lead us into *all* truth, let us consider what the coming years and the eternity beyond hold for the Christians and non-Christian alike.

Of Death

The ancient Jews had a saying that, "In this life, death never suffers a man to be glad." Death is a fact all of us have to face. Every moment of the day, death is a tragedy to someone. The Christian has the hope that he may not die, but like Enoch and Elijah be raptured at Christ's return, and thus not taste death (I Thessalonians 4:17; I Corinthians 15:12-19). Millions alive today may never die.

"O joy, O delight,
Should we go without dying"—and we may!

Ordinarily, however, no corner is safe from the dripping rain of earth's tears. Death is the skeleton at every feast, the bitterness in every cup; the discord in our music; the nameless dread that has haunted man from the time sorrow had its first birthplace in a mother's broken heart, as she knelt by the side of her boy, murdered through the passionate violence of his own brother.

For the majority of millions thronging the earth, death has not lost its fearful countenance. It is still a tremendous and terrible fact that must be faced. It cannot be ignored for continually it intrudes into the circle of our loved ones and friends. Many may feel that *death* is not a pleasant subject to think about, yet because of its certainty it is incumbent upon us to consider its reality and issues.

Death Is Inevitable

The fact of death, or physical dissolution, is the inescapable lot of all mankind, with the exception of those who are alive at Christ's return. "Certain things," says a writer, "may be done by proxy; other things may be bought off and evaded; but we cannot evade death. Each man and woman, saint and scoundrel alike, passes through the portal of death . . . when death comes— the great leveller—all men are equal in the solemn stillness of the sepulchre."

Death Is Uncertain

Although the fact is certain, the time is uncertain. The "lifting of the curtain upon the unseen" is hidden. And because it is the one experience overtaking all mankind, it behooves us to set our house in order and to pray—

Teach me to live that I may dread
The grave as little as my bed;
Teach me to die, that so I may
Rise glorious at the awful day.

Death Is Termination

Death is not the termination of our existence. It is an *act*, not a *state*. If Christ's, then death is but a gate through which we pass into a richer, fuller life. "The substance of the soul is indissoluble," says Bishop Moule, "and therefore indestructible. The mysterious 'I' can never terminate. Moral personality is mysteriously permanent as God has constituted things." Death, however, is the end of many things we cherish, such as physical beauty, material riches and earthly honors.

Death Is Necessary

Death is a necessary law of nature to which we must submit. If people never died, the world would not be habitable, for according to the natural law of increase, the number would be absolutely appalling. "People speak of death," says Frederick C. Spurr, "as if it were something horrible and to be afraid of, but life should be regarded socially as a banquet to which many guests are invited, and where there are many sittings. The first take their place, and, having finished, make room for other relays, until all are served. If we were here forever, the firstcomers to the banquet would gain all; the lastcomers, nothing."

Death Is Unmagical

Some there are, who, when they come to die, seek out the ministrations of preacher or priest, as if he had the power to enable them to die sinners and wake up saints. The mere act of removing from one house to another, in no way changes the person removing. Thus we continue on the other side, as we depart from this. Life *here* determines *that*. Death works no magic, produces no miracle for the dying one. If we are Christ's, then, when we come to pull up the tent-pegs, death will be gain. Paul could say, "To die is gain," and the gains through dying are immeasurable. To depart and be with Christ is far better than anything earth can offer.

Dust, then, to dust must go. "Ashes to ashes, dust to dust," announces man's physical dissolution. "His body belongs to nature; every particle of which it was composed had been drawn from her stores, and back to nature every particle returns. It was borrowed only; it is repaid; no part is lost. Hence the euphemism by which we seek to soften the word 'death,' by saying such or such a one has 'paid the debt of nature.'

Once the spirit has departed, nature and we are quits; we cannot defraud her; she will receive her own to the exacted title." As Von Stolberg expresses it:

Mother Earth, she gathers all
Unto her bosom, great and small;
Oh, could we look into her face,
We should not shrink from her embrace.

Death, however, holds no dread for those who have received the Lord Jesus as a personal Saviour. Redeemed souls can sing:

The fear of death has gone forever,
No more to cause my heart to grieve;
There is a place, I do believe,
In heaven for me beyond the river.

In extreme old age Mrs. Barbauld wrote the following stanza which the poet, Samuel Rogers, regarded as one of the finest things in English literature. Henry Crabbe Robinson says that he repeated it to Wordsworth twice, and then heard him say: "I am not in the habit of grudging people their good things; but I wish that I had written those lines."

Life! We have been long together
Through pleasant and through cloudy
    weather;
'Tis hard to part when friends are dear,
Perhaps 'twill cost a sigh, a tear;
Then steal away, give little warning,
Choose thine own time;
Say not 'Good night,' but in some brighter
    clime
Bid me 'Good morning.'

It is said that in his last moments, Dr. Fuller said to his nephew, Dr. Cuthbert, on taking leave of him: "Good night, James, but it will soon be morning." Perhaps the echo of the beautiful lines above were in the mind of the dying preacher.

Death means "separation" and, in the Scriptures, is of a threefold kind.

1. Physical or Natural Death

Physical death occurs when the inmates—spirit and soul—leave the house or body in which they lived. And this cessation of man to function as a living human being can be summarized thus—

It is by Adam, Genesis 3:19; I Corinthians 15:21,22.

It is the consequence of sin, Genesis 2:17; Romans 5:12.

It is the lot of all, Ecclesiastes 8:8; Hebrews 9:27.

It is ordered by God, Deuteronomy 32:39; Job 14:5.

It is the end of earthly projects and possessions, Ecclesiastes 9:10; I Timothy 6:6.

It is the leveler of all ranks, Job 3:17-19.

It was conquered by Christ, Romans 6:9; Revelation 1:8; II Timothy 1:10.

It is to be finally destroyed, Hosea 13:14; I Corinthians 15:26.

It holds no fear for the believer, Hebrews 2:15.

It is to be regarded as at hand, Job 14:1, 2; Psalm 90:9; I Peter 1:24.

It is to be prepared for, Psalm 39:4,13; 90:12.

It inspires diligence and devotion, John 9:4; Isaiah 38:18,20.

It illustrates conversion, Romans 6:2; Colossians 2:20.

It never enters heaven, Luke 20:36; Revelation 21:4.

It is described as a sleep, John 11:11; fleeing as a shadow, Job 14:2; as the putting off the tabernacle, II Corinthians 5:1; II Peter 1:14.

2. *Spiritual Death*

To be spiritually dead means to be separated from life in God. As in material death there is the separation of the spirit from the body, so in spiritual death there is the separation of the spirit from God.

This aspect of death is outlined for us as follows—

It is alienation from God, Ephesians 4:18.

It is carnal-mindedness, Romans 8:6.

It is a walk in trespass and sin, Ephesians 2:1; Colossians 2:13.

It is spiritual ignorance, Isaiah 9:2; Ephesians 4:18.

It is unbelief, John 3:36; I John 5:12.

It is living in worldly pleasure, I Timothy 5:6.

It is hypocrisy, Revelation 3:1,2.

It is the consequences of the fall, Romans 5:15.

It is the state of all men by nature, Romans 6:13; 8:6.

Its fruits are dead works, Hebrews 6:1; 9:14.

It can be banished by Christ, Ephesians 5:14; 2:5; John 5:24,25; Romans 6:13.

Its banishment is proved by love, I John 3:14.

It is illustrated in Ezekiel 37:2,3; Luke 15:24.

3. *Eternal Death*

Eternal separation from the presence of God is implied in John's terrible phrase,

"the second death" (Revelation 21:8). "Eternal" or "everlasting" means "perpetual" or "forever." There is an everlasting, perpetual life to be lived forever away from God, and this is eternal death. There is an everlasting, perpetual life to be lived with God and this is eternal life. And to gather together what the Scriptures have to say regarding eternal death is to find fresh cause for gratitude that we have been saved from everlasting woe through Him who came to the place of death for lost, guilty sinners.

It is the necessary consequence of sin, Romans 6:16,21; 8:13; James 1:15.

It is the wages of sin, Romans 6:23.

It is the portion of the wicked, Matthew 24:41,46; Romans 1:32.

It is the fruit of self-righteousness, Proverbs 14:12.

It is divine punishment, Matthew 10:28; James 4:12; Matthew 25:31,41; II Thessalonians 1:7,8.

Its only avenue of escape is Christ, John 3:16; 8:51; Acts 4:12.

It has no hold upon saints, Revelation 2:11; 20:6.

It is something from which saints should strive to save sinners, James 5:20.

It is described as banishment from God, II Thessalonians 1:9; society with the devil, Matthew 25:41; a lake of fire, Revelation 19:20; 21:8; unrelieved darkness, Matthew 25:30; II Peter 2:17; a resurrection to eternal condemnation, Daniel 12:2; John 5:29; Matthew 25:46; eternal torment, Luke 16:23-26.

After death there is destiny, and God's Word sets down this destiny as being one of two alternatives known as heaven or hell. There is a state of unbroken peace and pure joy in the presence of the Lord for all the redeemed; or there is banishment from God's presence to a state of misery and dread.

Moreover, these two states of being are declared to be absolute, fixed, eternal. At death, the soul, after life's probation, passes into a destiny, absolutely fixed and final. The broad proofs of such an affirmation are threefold.

1. *There Is the Teaching of Christ*

With unmistakable clarity the Master spoke of heaven and hell. But while certainties are set down so that no man can miss them, yet details are treated with divine reserve.

Unspeakable anguish and woe are indicated by the explicit parables of judgment. For example: We have the great gulf fixed —the door shut which cannot be opened— the outer darkness with its weeping and gnashing of teeth.

The other destiny carrying with it a state of close fellowship with Christ can be gleaned from the following—"Where I am, there shall also my servant be"—"Abraham's bosom"—"The Father's house."

Doubtless there is a sharp, emphatic division in Christ's teaching somewhat repugnant to the modern mind. He speaks not only of heaven where "ancient dreams as substance are," but of hell, that dreary abode, where "the worm dieth not and the fire is not quenched." There are wheat and tares; good fish and bad; sheep and goats; loyal and disloyal; saved and lost; those who do His will and those who do it not; children of God and children of the devil. Each soul goes to its place.

2. *There Is the Inevitable Contrast*

Another reason for the two alternatives of heaven and hell lies in the contrast between those who are holy and those who are sinful. Our sins are set in the awful light of God's countenance, not in the partial discernment of man. Evil cannot stand in God's presence, so we have those awful sentences —"I never knew you"—"Depart from me"— "The wrath of the Lamb."

3. *There Are the Facts of Life*

Beyond the explicit teaching of Jesus and the irreconcilable nature of good and evil, there is the conclusion to be drawn from the facts of life. Habit makes character, and character fixes destiny.

> Sow a thought, and reap an act;
> Sow an act, and reap a character;
> Sow a character, and reap a destiny.

The young are impressionable and plastic. The old find it almost impossible to change. The repentance of an old man is one of the rarest of spiritual experiences, as any preacher will tell you. Thus it is not difficult to realize that when a soul passes out into eternity, it continues to be what it was in time, only more fixed in an inevitable destiny (Revelation 22:11). May you and I have the assurance that, when the day breaks and the shadows flee away, the realms of the blest will be our everlasting abode.

Of Immortality

While all men agree that *all* must die in some way or another, for "What man is he that liveth, and shall not see death"? (Psalm 89:48), not all are agreed that dying we live again. The unbelief and despair of the cry of those who believe that death ends all, offers no solace for those whose hearts are torn by grief.

> To thy dark chamber, Mother Earth, I
>   come:
> Prepare my dreamless bed for my last
>   home;
>   Shut down the marble door,
>   And leave me: let me sleep;
>   But deep, deep;
>   Never to waken more.

If "Mother Earth" is our last home then surely man's innate desire for immortality is hollow and false. Emerson, in one of his sunny-hearted letters to Carlyle remarked—

"What have we to do with old age? Our existence looks to me, more than ever, initial. We have come to see the ground and look at the materials and tools."

What a noble expression! It is certainly true that life provides us materials and tools whereby character can be shaped for eternity.

Apart from the Biblical revelation, history and archeology indicate belief in some sort of existence after death. In his *Christian View of God and the World,* Professor James Orr says that "nearly every tribe and people on the face of the earth, savage and civilized, has held in some form this belief in a future state of existence." While no two nations or cultures may agree as to the exact nature of *immortality,* nevertheless, the light is there. Dr. Salmond, in what he calls the "ethnic preparation" in connection with the universal belief of an after life, states that three things attest this faith in man's survival beyond the tomb, to have the *monuments* like the mysterious "Pyramids" built with chambers because of the belief that the dead still lived and revisited their tombs. *Rites* and *incantations,* with food being placed at the graves for the sustenance of those who had died. In the Egyptian *Book of the Dead* there are prayers and formulae for the guidance and protection of the deceased in the After-World.

The *Hindu* yearns for "long life among the gods"—The *Buddhist* for his four-and-twenty heavens—The *Babylonian* for the "Merciful One among the gods . . . who restores the dead to life"—The *Persian* for the naked body to be "clothed only with the light of Heaven"—The *Grecian* for survival. Socrates, who believed in immortality, said as he died, "Bury me, if you can catch me" —The *African* for a new abode out west, in the way of the setting sun. Taylor, in *Primitive Culture* dealing with this universal belief that the dead do not wholly die, but live elsewhere, says—

"Looking at the religion of the lower races as a whole we shall at least not be ill-advised in taking as one of its general and principle elements the doctrine of the soul's future life."

The question might be asked, How did this wide-spread belief in a future life originate? Atheism and agnosticism offer puerile answers. The only true answer is that God set eternity in the heart of man (Ecclesiastes 3:11 R.V. margin). This hope of immortality, resident with the breast of savage and saint, was planted there by Him who has no beginning or end. This brings us to the Biblical answer to the question, "If a man die, shall he live again?" (Job 14:14).

We could dwell upon the *analogical argument* for "Immortality" from nature and science. The law of nature is life out of death, production out of destruction. The annual miracle of spring, the caterpillar from a tiny egg, the marvelous transformation of the hard, unsightly chrysalis into the gorgeous butterfly are natural emblems of life's continuance.

From dearth to plenty, from death to life,
Is Nature's progress.

Then the scientific tenet of the conservation of energy teaches us that nothing ever perishes, it only changes its condition and combination. But while nature and science show that "immortality" is possible, it is the Bible alone which offers conclusive proof. Divine revelation supplies what human speculation lacks, and turns guesses into an absolute certainty (Isaiah 25:8). Max Muller says that—

"Without a belief in personal immortality, religion is like an arch resting on one pillar, or a bridge ending in an abyss."

First of all, let us briefly glance at the Old Testament evidences of life after death.

As God is eternal, man made in His image shares His everlastingness. "The breath of the Almighty have given him life"—life here and hereafter (Genesis 1:27; 2:7; Job 32:8 R.V.; 33:4; Ecclesiastes 12:7). These Biblical expressions stating that man shares the immortality of his Creator are reflected in the Apocrypha—

"God created man to be immortal, and made him to be an image of His own Eternity" (Wisdom 2:23).

It is interesting to gather together the Old Testament expressions of death.

He was gathered to his people, is a repeated phrase indicating Jewish belief in an after life. Used alike of saints and sinners, it goes to disprove the theory of conditional immortality (Genesis 25:8,17; 35:29; 49:33).

Giving up the ghost is employed both in the Old and New Testaments of death, and implies the return of the spirit to God (Genesis 49:33; Matthew 27:50).

In the New Testament, where we have the fullest revelation of life beyond the grave, we expect to find more expressive declarations of such a hope. From our Lord we learn that—

"God is not the God of the dead, but of the living, for all live unto Him" (Luke 20:37,38 R.V.; Exodus 3:6).

This is why God is the God of Abraham, Isaac and Jacob who are alive forevermore. Paul reminds us that our Saviour—

"Brought life and *immortality* to light through the gospel" (II Timothy 1:10). His further teaching is unfolded in other passages which were expanded by Paul (John 5:28,29; 11:25, 26; I Corinthians 15:20,22, 51-54; I Thessalonians 4:13-18; 5:9,10). John likewise speaks of *eternal life* as a blessing bestowed upon all who believe (John 5:24; 6:53; I John 3:14; Revelation 3:1). Thus, as John Ellerton reminds us in his beautiful funeral hymn our God is—

God of the living, in whose eyes
Unveiled Thy whole creation lies,
All souls are Thine: we must not say
That those are dead who pass away;
Not spilt like water on the ground,
Not wrapped in dreamless sleep profound.
Nor left to die like fallen tree;
Not dead, but living unto Thee.

Other expressions describing the present condition of those who died with hope of a continued existence are—

In Abraham's Bosom, speaking of rest,

refreshment and fellowship with other departed believers (Luke 16:22).

In Paradise (Luke 23:43; cf. II Corinthians 12:4; Revelation 2:7). This phrase represents the immediate presence of God.

Under the Altar (Revelation 6:9-11; 16:7). Here we have complete security but suspended perfection (Hebrews 11:39,40).

Sleep is the usual designation for the death of believers and applies only to the body (Matthew 9:24; John 11:11; Acts 7:60; 13:36). This expression signifies rest, but not unconsciousness (Luke 23:42; II Corinthians 5:6-8 R.V.; Philippians 1:21,23 R.V.; Revelation 14:13). The Apocrypha says—

"The righteous live for evermore, their reward is also with the Lord, and the care of them is with the Most High" (Wisdom 3:1-3; 5:15).

'Tis Immortality deciphers man,
And opens all the mysteries of his make;
Without it, half his instincts are a riddle;
Without it, all his virtues are a dream.

From the inscriptions on the graves in the *Catacombs* we have evidence of the hope of immortality which burned so brightly in the hearts of those early martyrs.

"The soul lives, unknowing of death, and consciously rejoices in the vision of Christ."

"Received into the light of the Lord."

"Thou dost repose forever, free from care."

Of Resurrection

As we have seen, the doctrine of immortality is common to almost all cultures and religions. The resurrection of the body, however, is peculiar to Christianity, which is not to be numbered among comparative religions. Man is not perfect without a body. This is why the New Testament teaches the immortality of human nature as well as the immortality of the soul. Ancient philosophers believed the latter, but denied the former. The Jews themselves were bitterly divided upon the question of bodily resurrection (Acts 4:1,2; 17:18,32; 23:6-8; 26:8).

At the outset it must be stated that the Bible does not teach a general resurrection, that is, all the dead whether saved or lost rising at the same time. Under the inspiration of the Holy Spirit, Paul distinctly taught that "the dead in Christ shall rise first" (I Thessalonians 4:15, 16). Daniel also hinted at two resurrections when he said that—

"Many of them that sleep in the dust of the earth shall awake, some to everlasting life and some to shame and everlasting contempt" (Daniel 12:2,13; cf. Job 19:25; I Corinthians 15:52).

When Christ returns all who died in Him are to be raised, but the rest of the dead, the wicked dead remain in their graves until the setting up of the Great White Throne when they are raised for the ratification of their condemnation (Revelation 20:11-15). How blessed we are if ours is the prospect of the first resurrection.

That there were clear anticipations of resurrection among Old Testament saints can be gathered from their expressed desire. Job knew that his Redeemer was alive forever more and that even after worms destroyed his original body, that in another he would see God (14:13-15; 19:25-27). Psalmists and prophets alike declared their belief in a resurrection from among the dead. They loved to speak of it as an awakening from sleep, and as the completion of the work of God's hands (Psalms 16:9,10; 17:15; 119:73; 138:8; 139:13-16; Isaiah 26:19; Hosea 13:14).

The Apocrypha likewise contains definite statements as to the doctrine of resurrection—

"Those that be dead will I raise up again from their places, and bring them out of their graves" (II Esdras 2:16; 7:32).

"The earth shall give back that which has been entrusted to it, and sheol also shall give back that which it has received" (Book of Enoch 51:1; cf. II Maccabees 7).

It is in the New Testament, however, that we have the clearest doctrinal statements of our resurrection, and the distinction drawn between "the resurrection *of* the dead," and "the resurrection *from* the dead" or *out from among the dead.* Our Lord is explicit upon this point that although there will be a resurrection for all, that it will not be the *same* resurrection for all (John 5:28, 29), as Daniel foreshadowed. "The resurrection of the just" will be "to everlasting life" and is called "the resurrection of life." The second resurrection is referred to as "the resurrection of the unjust" . . . "to shame and everlasting contempt," which is also described as "the resurrection of damnation" (Luke 14:14; Hebrews 11:35—"A better resurrection" is meaningless if there is to be only one general resurrection).

Dr. W. J. Townsend reminds us that— "A reconstruction of the whole man, body, soul and spirit, is in the plan and purpose of Redemption. Sin and Death are not to triumph over man even to the extent of retaining possessions of the material of the body, but *it* shall be restored and man shall stand complete in his nature before the Judgment Seat . . . The word *Resurrection* means, 'a standing up' and when the trumpet sounds we shall stand up complete in one threefold personality once more."

The resurrections recorded in the Old Testament and the gospels were foregleams of "the resurrection of the just." In His Resurrection, our Lord became "the First-fruits" which implies and involves the similar resurrection of all who died in Him (John 6:39,40,44,54; 11:25; 14:19; Romans 6:5,8; 8:11; I Corinthians 6:14; 15; II Corinthians 4:14; 13:4). But what must not be forgotten is the fact that "the Firstfruits" are not merely a pledge of the glorious harvest, they are also *a part of it*. The expression, "resurrection from the dead," is used 34 times of Christ's Resurrection, and 15 times of that of His redeemed people. How apt are the lines of Bishop Wordsworth—

Christ is risen, Christ the Firstfruits of the holy harvest field,
Which will all its full abundance at His Second Coming yield;
Then the golden ears of harvest will their heads before Him wave,
Ripen'd by His glorious sunshine from the furrows of the grave.

Christ's glorious Resurrection, the greatest of Bible miracles (see *All the Miracles of the Bible*) was at once the pledge and pattern of the resurrection of believers. As Christ, as the Head and Representative of the race, arose from the dead according to His expressed prophecy and purpose (Matthew 28:6; John 2:19-21; 10:18), so in Him all saved by His grace will share His triumph over the grave.

The book of the Acts testifies to the power of Christ's Resurrection. It was "the choral peal of triumph over the final defeat of man's last enemy" that made the early Church so dynamic in her witness (Acts 4:2; 17:18,32; 23:6-8; 24:15,21; I Thessalonians 4:6; Hebrews 6:2; 11:35; I Co-

rinthians 15—which has been called "The Magna Charta of the Resurrection") Christ's defeat of death will be consummated on the morning of our resurrection (I Corinthians 15:57).

When loving friends buried the body of Jesus in Joseph's tomb, it was the natural body subject to earthly limitations He received at His birth that the grave received. But the body He rose with was "a spiritual body" endowed with supernatural powers (Mark 16:12; Luke 24:31; John 20:19,20). Yet it was a real body of "flesh and bones," which could be seen and "handled" and which, although it required no food, could yet "eat" (Luke 24:36-43; John 20:20,27; Acts 1:3, margin; 10:40,41). Christ's present glorified body bears the likeness of the transformed body of the believer (Philippians 3:20,21 R.V.). Such a body, like unto His own, will be one "fitted to us, suitable for us and a perfect medium of sensation and action in the higher sphere."

While the Bible declares the resurrection of the Christless, it gives us no information as to the nature of the resurrection bodies of those who die in their sins. Whatever its form or nature, it will be fitted to endure the quenchless fire of judgment. If ours is the assurance of life forever more, we shall never cease to bless God for the fact that when the trumpet sounds, we shall rise in the likeness of Him who died that we might live.

Of Judgment

The inescapable judgments presented in the Bible open up the study of God's justice. These varied judgments bear eloquent testimony to the truth that as the Judge of all the earth, He must do right. If there is no judgment upon men and nations for their sins, then God is not a just God, as the Bible claims Him to be, and therefore not perfect in His Being. But we are to see that this shining attribute, like all others, is identical with His essence.

Concerning the justice of God, the Scriptures speak in no uncertain tones:

"Just and right is He" (Deuteronomy 32:4).

"He is excellent . . . in plenty of justice" (Job 37:23).

"Justice and judgment are the habitations ᴼ ˚ thy throne" (Psalm 89:14).

"A just ᴵd and a Saviour . . ." (Isaiah 45:2.

In God, power and justice kiss each other. His power holds the scepter—His justice holds the balance.

What, exactly, is this attribute of divine justice? Is it not God's ability to render to every man according to his works? (Deuteronomy 2:7). Justice means that all men, whether good or bad, will receive their due. "God's justice is the rectitude of His nature, whereby He is carried to the doing of that which is righteous and equal."

In all His judgments, God is ever impartial. He judges the cause. Man often judges the person, not the cause of his sin—which is not justice but malice. "I will go down now, and see whether they have done altogether according to the cry of it, which is come unto me; and if not, I will know" (Genesis 18:21). When engaged in His punitive work, God weighs all circumstances in the balance. He never punishes rashly nor indiscriminately. There are at least six principles governing divine justice—

1. Because of who and what God is, He cannot but be just. His august holiness is the cause of His justice, and His unflecked holiness will not suffer Him to do anything but what is righteous. God can no more be unjust than He can be unholy.

2. God's will is the supreme rule of justice; it is the standard of equity. His will is perfect, wise and good. He, therefore, wills nothing but what is just.

3. God does justice voluntarily. He loves righteousness (Hebrews 1:9). As a part of His Being, it flows from his nature. He is just out of love for His justice. Earthly judges may judge unjustly, because they are bribed or forced. But because God represents perfect justice, He cannot be bribed; and because of His power, He cannot be forced.

4. Justice is the perfection of His nature. Aristotle says, "Justice comprehends in it all virtues." God is not only just, but justice itself. All perfections meet in Him.

5. God does not judge according to the rigor of the law.

It is ever true of His dealings with men. "Thou hast punished us less than our iniquities deserve" (Ezra 9:13). Mercies received are more than we deserve—punishments less than we should endure. God abates something of His severity. If He rewarded according to our iniquity, we would not be able to stand before Him. While man continually wrongs the justice of God, He Himself cannot wrong anyone.

6. Because of the perfection of His justice we can never demand a reason for His judicial actions, even when they seem to be against our reason. God has not only authority on His side, but equity. He lays judgment to the line and righteousness to the plummet (Isaiah 28:17). The plumb line of our reason is too short to fathom the depths of divine justice. How unsearchable are His judgments (Romans 11:33)! And all of God's judgments, as we are to see, run in two channels, namely, the distribution of rewards to the deserving and of punishments to the wicked.

The Reward of Saints

God is not unrighteous to forget all Spirit-inspired labor on His behalf (Hebrews 6:10). Though we may be losers *for* Him, we are never losers *by* Him. "There is a reward for the righteous" (Psalm 58:11). Often God's people suffer great afflictions which seem to contradict His justice. Yet He never permits injury and persecution to overtake His own without a cause. The true rule of John Austin, English jurist, was "God's ways of judgment are sometimes secret but never unjust." Why does present judgment fall upon so many who appear to be upright in heart? What the full answer is we do not know. Many of the trials and sufferings of the godly are designed to refine and purify them.

The best among God's children have their blemishes. "Are there not with you, even with you, sins against the Lord?" (II Chronicles 28:10). Even spiritual diamonds have their flaws. Pride, jealousy, self-will, passion, are among some of the iniquities we deserve to be punished for (Amos 3:2). Surely God is not unjust when He puts His gold in the furnace to purify it! "In thy faithfulness . . . thou hast corrected me" (Psalm 119:75). God is not unjust to inflict a lesser punishment and prevent a greater. Is the father unjust if he only corrects his child, who deserves to be disinherited? No matter what we may endure—what judgment our sin merits, God only puts wormwood in our cup, whereas He might fill it up with fire and brimstone.

The Retribution of the Sinner

God is ever just in punishing offenders. He has given them His laws, and their disobedience and transgression testify against them. "Where there is no law, there is no transgression" (Romans 4:15). But sinners have God's law and His Gospel, and the rejection of both merits divine judgment.

It would seem as if God permits sinners to continue in their sin and prosper. But seeming indulgence on God's part is that the sinners might become more inexcusable. "I gave her space to repent of her fornication" (Revelation 2:21). God is always just *when* He judges (Psalm 51:4). He lengthens out His mercy toward sinners, then if they repent not, His patience witnesses against them and His justice is cleared when condemnation falls. It must never be forgotten that if God does allow men to prosper while in their sin, His vial of wrath is all the while falling. The longer God is in taking His blow, the heavier it will be at last. As long as eternity lasts, God has time enough to reckon with His enemies. Justice may be as a lion asleep, but at last the lion will awake and roar upon the sinner. And when judgment does overtake the sinner, his sin will be the cause of his eternal despair. Willfully opposing the offer of grace, punishment will come because of his rejection, rather than because of God's justice.

Often courts of judicature pervert justice. Isaiah speaks of those who "decree unrighteous decrees" (10:1). Good laws are useless when we do not have good judges to enforce them. The injustice of corrupt judges lies in two things—either not to punish where there is a fault, or to punish where there is no fault. God, however, because of His perfection, can never pervert justice. It is because He is perfectly just that a day of judgment awaits those who reject His mercy. He has appointed that day when He will condemn the wicked and crown the righteous (Acts 17:31). The sinful must drink of the sea of His righteous wrath, but not one will sip a drop of injustice. He will judge the world in righteousness. All coming judgments will fully vindicate God's justice. His judgments are ever righteous in operation (II Thessalonians 1:5). When meted out upon the godless, then their punishment will only be what their sins truly deserve.

One of God's acts of judgment, as given by Jeremiah, outlines the scope of many of His judicial acts (chapter 25)—

1. The *channel* of judgment—"I will send" (v. 9).
2. The *nature* of judgment—"I will destroy" (v. 9).
3. The *misery* of judgment—"I will take from them the mirth" (v. 10).
4. The *stroke* of judgment—"I will punish" (v. 12).
5. The *desolation* of judgment—"I will make it desolate (v. 12).
6. The *certainty* of judgment—"I will bring to pass all the words which I have promised" (v. 13).
7. The *righteousness* of judgment—"I will recompense them according to their deeds" (v. 14).
8. The *effect* of judgment—"Be mad because of the sword" (v. 16).
9. The *crushing* of judgment—"Drink ye and be drunken" . . . "rise no more" (v. 27).
10. The *terror* of judgment—"He will mightily roar" (v. 30).
11. The *sphere* of judgment—"Jehovah will roar from on high" (v. 30).
12. The *shout* of judgment—"He will give a shout" (v. 30).
13. The *universality* of judgment—"He will plead with all flesh" (v. 31).
14. The *subjects* of judgment—"As for the wicked, He will give them the sword" (v. 31).

Two observations are necessary as we approach a study of the judgments of God. The first is that the Bible nowhere teaches a "general judgment." Judgments differ as to subjects, places, time and results. Those who are ignorant of God's blueprint of the future lose sight of specific judgments. Scripture nowhere affirms that at some future time all mankind will simultaneously appear before the Lord to be judged and be parted right and left. The Pre-millennial position is that judgment is general *only* in the sense that all are to be judged but *not* all at *the same time*.

The saints and the sinners are not to be parted at the one assize. Saints are to be dealt with at one judgment, as saints—sinners, at another judgment, as sinners.

The next matter is that the Old Testament Scriptures are heavy with the judgments of God. While this aspect is not within the realm of our present study, yet severe judgments fell upon individuals from Adam and Cain on. Terrible and deserved judgments also overtook sinful cities like Sodom, and likewise fell upon God-defying nations like Assyria. When God's judgments, as a great deep, were abroad in the land, the inhabitants learned righteousness (Psalm 36:6).

Among clearly defined judgments, the

following seven are worthy of our prayerful meditation:

Judgment of Sin Upon the Cross

This fearful judgment took place in the year A.D. 30 at Calvary. There on the cross, the Lord Jesus Christ, who knew no sin, was made sin for us. Once and for all He dealt with *sin*, and now sins must be put away daily by confession (I John 1:9). When He cried, "It is finished," He implied that through the act of dying as the Sin-bearer, He secured a perfect salvation for a sinning race. What was death for Christ, is life and justification for the believing sinner. Now our judgment as sinners is past (John 5:24; Romans 8:1,3; 10:4).

> Bearing shame and scoffing rude,
> In my place, condemned, He stood;
> Sealed my pardon with His blood,
> Hallelujah! What a Saviour!

Judgment of Sins in the Believer

Dr. C. I. Scofield remarks that this "self-judgment is not so much the believer's moral condemnation of his own ways or habits, as of *himself* for allowing such ways. Self-judgment avoids chastisement. If neglected, the Lord judges and the result is chastisement but never condemnation (I Corinthians 11:31,32; I Timothy 1:20)."

The believer's judgment of himself takes place any time and anywhere, and results in confession and forgiveness. The more we walk in the light, as He is in the light, the more we discern those things worthy of judgment. The flesh hates this self-examination and self-condemnation. "If we are judged, we shall not be judged." Too much introspection and self-judgment can become morbid and harmful to one's peace of mind. The divine examination of self, however, never operates in this way. The Lord's present judgment of His children is beneficial. "When we are judged, we are chastened of the Lord" (I Corinthians 11:32). When He searches the soul, we have nothing to fear, for what the light reveals the blood can cleanse.

Under this aspect of judgment, we can include the Church's judgment in discipline which Paul so clearly taught the Church in Corinth (I Corinthians 5:3-5). We have too little of this form of judgment today, hence so much moral laxity in church circles. This phase of judgment must ever be undertaken in true humility and in all love. As a church judges one of its members for wrong committed, there must be the absence of all harsh and acrimonious feelings.

The Lord's judgment of His house as a whole is implied by Peter: "The time is come that judgment must begin at the house of God" (I Peter 4:17). The corporate body of professed believers, Christendom as such, because of its Modernism, worldliness and practices alien to the mind of the Lord, is under His condemnation. The result of the cleansing judgment is the liberation of the reviving grace and power of the Holy Spirit, and the restoration of the voice of spiritual authority to the Church.

Judgment Seat of Christ for Believers

When Paul declared, "*We* shall all stand before the Judgment Seat of Christ," he had in mind a particular group, even those he describes as "*We* are the Lord's" (Romans 14:8,10). Comparing the apostle here, and in similar passages, like I Corinthians 3:12-15; 4:5; II Corinthians 5:9,10; II Timothy 4:8, we come to the truth of the judgment of believers only, for the service and deeds done in the body. Conduct toward fellow-believers will be scrutinized, labor in the name of the Lord will be tested, motives examined and rewards given for faithfulness.

This judgment, taking place in the air, after the true Church has been caught up to meet the Lord, while bringing reward to some, will bring loss to others. Many will stand before the Lord at the *Bema* with a saved soul, but a lost life. "Saved, yet so as by fire." How solemn a truth this is! Surely there is no other truth that is able to revolutionize the life and labors of all believers, like that of the Judgment Seat of Christ.

Rewards in the shape of crowns await all those who have been true to the Lord and His infallible Word. There is—

The Crown of Life, of loyalty unto death (Revelation 2:10; James 1:12).

The Crown of Glory, for true shepherding (I Peter 5:4).

The Crown of Rejoicing for soul-winning (I Thessalonians 2:19,20).

The Crown of Righteousness for living in the light of the blessed hope (II Timothy 4:8).

The Crown Incorruptible for victorious living (I Corinthians 9:25).

Judgment of Angels and World by Believers

It is to be feared that the majority of God's children do not realize what a privilege is to be theirs. Presently many of them are despised by the world, and treated as dirt and rubbish and offscouring of the earth, as Paul expresses it. But the day is coming when the Church Jesus purchased with His own blood will assist Him in His judicial capacity. "The saints shall judge the world . . . we shall judge angels" (I Corinthians 6:2,3). They are to be identified with Him in His judgeship. The all-important question to face is this: Are we permitting the Lord to prepare us in every way for coming, judicial responsibilities?

Judgment of the Jews

During the great tribulation, in Jerusalem and its vicinity, the Messiah will deal with His own ancient people. The basis of this judgment will be Israel's rejection of the Godhead. As a nation, Israel has been guilty of rejecting—

God the Father   I Samuel 8:7
God the Son   John 1:11; Luke 23:18
God the Spirit   Acts 7:51,54-56

While the Church is being judged in the air by Christ, the Jews will be judged under the Anti-christ, and they are to suffer much under his rule (Revelation 12). Scattered among the nations because of their sin, the Jews are to be regathered. As an earthly people receiving earthly promises, their judgment will be of an earthly nature. The result of this judgment, known as "the time of Jacob's trouble," will be the conversion of the Jews and their reception of Christ as their Messiah (Zechariah 12:10). Then the godly remnant will go to the ends of the earth as heralds of the coming kingdom. The converted Jews will function as forerunners of the coming of their Messiah as the King of Kings.

Judgment of the Living Nations

The judgment of the Gentile nations by Christ when He returns to earth as the Son of Man will take place in the Valley of Jehoshaphat. What fearful carnage will be witnessed at this "Day of Judgment," as Christ ascends His "throne of glory" (Isaiah 2:4; Joel 3:1,2). The basis of this national judgment will be the treatment of the Jews, "His brethren," not reckoned among the nations (Numbers 23:7,9).

The result of this judgment will be the separation of the Gentile nations. Those nations treating the Jews kindly are called "sheep" nations, and will pass into the Millennium. The other nations, despising the Jews, and known as "goat" nations, are to be destroyed by the Judge. With His keen, penetrating wisdom, He will gather out and punish "all that doth offend" (Matthew 13:41,42). Present-day nations fostering anti-Semitism might do well to pause in their Jew-bating policy and meditate upon the dread consequences of cursing a people God has so signally blessed. It is in this judgment that the saints are to be associated with Christ (I Corinthians 6:2).

Judgment of the Great White Throne

This most terrible of all divine judgments following, as it does, the fiery judgment of heaven upon the rebellious of earth at the conclusion of Christ's millennial reign (Revelation 20:7-9), and God's final judgment upon the devil (Revelation 20:10), is the last of all the judgments (Revelation 20:11-15). It is called "The Day of Judgment" (Matthew 10:15), and "The Great Day" (Acts 2:20), and is described by Peter and Jude in vivid terms (II Peter 2:3,4,7; Jude 6).

The basis of this dread assize can be simply stated. The justice of God makes it necessary. It is at this judgment that He will ratify His condemnation of the unrepentant wicked (Luke 17:26; II Thessalonians 1:6,7).

The accusation of natural conscience likewise testifies in favor of this just judgment (Daniel 5:5,6; Acts 24:25; Romans 2:15).

The Great White Throne also proves that man is a creature and must face his Creator. Such a relationship involves punishment for disobedience. God gave His creatures laws to live by, and they are to be held accountable for the breach of same (Romans 14:12). Many Scriptures predict this fearful judgment and because the Word of God is true, it must take place as described by John (Matthew 25; Romans 14:10,11; II Thessalonians 1:7-10; Jude 14,15). The Resurrection of Christ is also a certain proof of this last judgment (Acts 17:31; Romans 14:9).

As to the august Judge Himself, the consistent testimony of Scripture is that God will judge the lost by His Son, Jesus Christ (John 5:23; Acts 17:31). While the

Triune God will judge as to original authority, power, and right of judgment, yet according to divine plan settled upon by the Father, Son and Spirit, the work of executing judgment will be assigned to the Son. Appearing in great power and glory and naked to every eye, His searching glance will penetrate every heart, and in strict justice He will pronounce the doom of the wicked (Romans 2:16; I Corinthians 4:5).

All the wicked dead of all ages and the host of demons will be arraigned before this glistening throne to receive their final sentences (Ecclesiastes 12:14; Jude 6; Revelation 20:11). As the books are opened and the condemned stand silent and accused, what solemnity will characterize such a judgment at the end of time and of the world. For a fuller treatment of *The Great White Throne*, the reader is referred to the writer's book by this name.

What are the damning records to be presented at this sad, awe-inspiring judgment? The books are to be opened. What books? Scripture reminds us of a few condemning volumes—

1. The Book of Remembrance (Malachi 3:16).
2. The Book of Conscience (Romans 1:19).
3. The Book of Providence (Romans 11:14,15).
4. The Book of God—(The Law and The Gospel, Romans 2:12-16).
5. The Book of Life—(Revelation 3:5; 20:12-15; Luke 10:20).

Our last word on the judgments is that *fire*—expressive of divine holiness and divine hatred of sin—is connected with them all. If, as believers, we stand up at the Judgment Seat of Christ, the fire is to try our work for Him, of what sort it is. For all those, however, who live and die in their sin, the verdict of the Judge at the Last Judgment will be eternal remorse in the Lake of Fire. May yours be the assurance, dear reader, of life forevermore with Christ!

Of the Second Coming of Christ

While *prophecy* in general is not before us in this chapter, it may be deemed fitting to have a word about this most fascinating aspect of Bible study. It has been computed that over one-fourth of Scripture is taken up with *prophecy*, and if any of the prophecies can be proven false, the claims of the Bible as a divine revelation are seriously impaired. If, however, the prophecies can be shown to have been literally fulfilled down the long avenue of history, then such claims are greatly strengthened.

Bible prophecies "form a regular chain or system, which may be reduced to four classes," Bishop Horne tells us—

"1. Prophecies relating to the Jewish nation in particular.
2. Prophecies relating to the neighboring nations or empires.
3. Prophecies directly announcing the Messiah.
4. Prophecies delivered by Jesus Christ and His apostles."

It is the last section we are now to deal with, especially the prediction of Christ and His apostles as to our Lord's return as the Bridegroom for His Church, and as the Prince of the kings of the earth.

The Rapture

While the term "rapture," as well as the word "trinity," does not appear in the Bible, their exclusion is no argument for their unreality. Unassailable proofs of both truths are clearly evident to the lover of the Word. When Paul used the phrase, "caught up" (I Thessalonians 4:17), he was describing the rare joy, the ecstasy of being transferred from the dusty lanes of earth to the realms of bliss above. Robert Barbour writes in one of his letters: "We are Jacobites to the Lord Jesus. To us, too, as to our fathers, 'the King is over the water,' and we keep our heart's best place for an absent One." And there is a perpetual song in our hearts and on our lips if we believe that the absent King will soon return.

It was said of Corot, the renowned artist, that he never began the painting of his immortal landscapes except with the skies. If the skies, soon to be purpled with Christ's glory, influence our life and labors, then earth with its tarnished and rusting gold, will not hold us prisoner. Let us therefore gather anew comfort from the words Christ and His apostles have left us as to the Church's most glorious prospect.

If we had no other evidence of Christ's return than His own promise in John 14:3, the same would be sufficient. He assured His disciples that He would come again, and He was not a man that He should lie. Language has no meaning if Christ is not returning as He said. Such a declaration was confirmed as soon as Jesus ascended on high. The two heavenly messengers of Acts 1:10, came with the express message that the same Jesus who had just left His own, would come again in like manner as He went away.

When He returns to the air, we are to see Him and be like Him (I John 3:2). Our resurrection will be assured (II Corinthians 5:8; Philippians 1:23,24). A blissful reunion with all our dear ones who died in Christ will also be consummated (I Thessalonians 4:16,17). The Lord will not be slack concerning the realization of these Advent promises. The last promise and the last prayer of the Bible form a fitting close to the Bible, God's great Promise Box. "Surely, I come quickly." Do we love and long for His appearing as we pray with John, "Even so, come Lord Jesus?" (Revelation 22:20,21).

The fact that Christ rose from the dead as He said He would should be ample proof that His promise of our resurrection at His coming will be fulfilled. In the great resurrection chapter (I Corinthians 15), Paul bases the resurrection of the believer upon Christ's victory over the grave. In Him, we are to be made alive (I Corinthians 15: 22).

Our obligation in this period of grace is to be fully prepared for the Rapture. Its *promise* is plain—its *proof* is positive—its *preparation* is personal. Every person, whether saved or lost, should pause and examine life in the light of "the blessed hope." The very uncertainty of such an event calls for earnest thought. Just when Jesus will appear is one of God's secrets. No one has any knowledge of the day marked off on His calendar for His Son to come again, in fulfillment of His promise. The solemn question is, Are we ready for His appearing? Are we being sanctified wholly as we await His return? (I Thessalonians 5:23). Every phase of life is influenced, when life as a whole bears the impact of this prominent truth of the New Testament (Titus 2:13; I John 2:28). We cannot live just any kind of a life if we believe that Christ may appear at any moment and rapture His own to Glory. Such a hope purifies life and living (I John 3:1-3).

While the term, "The Second Coming," is not used in the Bible, it is nevertheless implied by the writer of the Hebrews in the phrase—

"Unto them that look for Him shall He appear *the second time*" (Hebrews 9:28). But when we use the above time it is essential to bear in mind that it covers a series of events. We are apt to apply it to the return of the Lord for His own. The *First* Advent of our Lord "covered" over 33 years and included many events and crises such as His birth, flight into Egypt, upbringing in Nazareth, temptation in the wilderness, three years service, Gethsemane, Calvary, Resurrection and Ascension. So the *Second* Advent covers further events and crises including the return of Christ for His own, the Great Tribulation, the Millennial reign, the Great White Throne, all of which come within the range of Christ's next appearance.

There are two events that must be distinguished, and we shall be hopelessly confused if we do not preserve the distinction between them. When the day comes on God's calendar for His Beloved Son to return, He is not coming all the way to earth at once, without a break. Paul definitely states that He is to tarry *in the air* (I Thessalonians 4:16,17), and that at that moment all His saints are to be caught up to meet Him. This is the "Rapture" and is spoken of as "The Day of Christ," and as the time of our gathering unto Him. Then, after a period of seven years, the period known as "The Great Tribulation" symbolized by Daniel's seventieth week, our Lord will continue His return and journey from the *air* to the earth (Zechariah 14:4,5), in order to usher in His Millenial reign. The first aspect of His Coming will be a *private* manifestation—the second aspect, His *public* manifestation. He comes as *The Morning Star* for His Church—as *The Sun of Righteousness* for the world.

There are various *Advent attitudes* to be distinguished as we trace the theme of Christ's return through the New Testament. Occupied with Him as a present Saviour, there must be the constant expectation of Him as the Coming Master and King. We should—

1. *Believe His Coming* (I Thessalonians 4:14).
   This is not a fad or theory, but a definite part of our faith.
2. *Pray for His Coming* (Matthew 6: 10; Revelation 22:20).
   Prevailing intercession inspires us to fruitful service and holiness of life.
3. *Love His Coming* (II Timothy 4:8).

"All who have loved and longed for His appearing." Have we, are we, loving and longing?

4. *Preach His Coming* (II Timothy 4: 1,2).

   The Second Advent is a vital part of the message we have to declare.

5. *Watch for His Coming* (I Thessalonians 5:6).

   We must keep alive the flame of hope as well as exercise faith and love.

6. *Expect His Coming* (Romans 8:19, 23).

   Here Paul urges us eagerly to anticipate the coming and welcome the first indication of it.

7. *Look for His Coming* (Mark 13:35; Titus 2:13).

   "Looking carries the double meaning of separation and expectation (Acts 3: 12; Hebrews 12:2).

8. *Wait for His Coming* (I Thessalonians 1:10; II Thessalonians 3:5).

   The margin reads, "The patience of Christ." Patiently He awaits the Rapture, and we are to manifest His patience.

9. *Do not Despise His Coming* (II Peter 3:3,4).

   Scoffers abound today, who reject any approach to prophecy.

10. *Hasten His Coming* (II Peter 3:12).

    Weymouth translates the phrase, "Expecting and hastening."

11. *Power of His Coming* (II Peter 1:16).

    Christ's return is not a spiritual luxury, but a source of power for daily life.

12. *Live His Coming* (Philippians 3:20).

    It is not sufficient to grasp the truth—
    —it must grasp us.

13. *Unashamed at His Coming* (I John 2:28).

    As saints we must never be ashamed of this truth, or be a shame to it. Alas, too many of us will meet Christ at that day with a saved soul, but a lost life, and will feel like shrinking away in shame!

A point of deep interest concerning many sincere seekers after truth is that of silence regarding the exact time of Christ's Coming. Teaching His imminent return, Jesus yet withheld any reference to the precise hour of His appearing. Other aspects are dealt with, but the *time* is omitted. While in the flesh enduring the limitations of our humanity, He Himself knew not the time (Mark 13:32). The absence of information as to the date serves as a stimulus to expectancy. Our obligation is so to live this very moment that if He should come the next, we should not be ashamed before Him at His Coming. Because there is no fixed date, each succeeding generation of believers can derive comfort from the truth of Christ's glorious appearing. Archbishop Trench has it—

It is not that He desires each succeeding generation to believe that He will certainly return in their time; for He does not desire one faith and one practice to be founded on an error, as, in that case, the faith and practice of all generations except the last would be. But it is a necessary element of the doctrine concerning the Second Coming of Christ, that it should be possible at any time, that no generation should consider it improbable in theirs.

The Great Tribulation

We now come to the period between the return of Christ to the air for His true Church, and then His appearance on the earth to assume the governmental control of its affairs. This darkest period of human history represents the seventieth week of Daniel, and covers about seven years. With the translation of the saints, the Jew and the Jewish question are taken up governmentally by God, and the course of the seventy weeks is resumed at the point where they were broken off (Daniel 9:27).

This last week of seven years starts with the Roman Prince making a league or covenant with the restored Jewish nation (Isaiah 18), then apostate from God and truth. The Jews, returning to their land, proceed to build the Temple, and offer sacrifices, accepting the Antichrist as their king (Daniel 11:36), and "*the* prophet" in his false ministry among them. It would seem as if "the false prophet" and the "king" are one and the same person (Deuteronomy 18:15).

Daniel's seventieth week is divided into two equal parts. Not much is revealed of the activities of the first half. The covenant is broken in the midst of the week (Daniel 9:27) and the beast out of the bottomless pit forces idolatry upon the nation (Revelation 17:8), sets up an image on the Temple as an object of general or national worship, which God-fearing Jews refuse. This second half of the Tribulation, spoken of as time, times, and half a time; 42 months; 1,260 days; 3½ years, is referred to as "the time of Jacob's trouble," seeing its horrors are felt and endured chiefly in Judea, in Jerusalem especially. Its effect, of course, extend to the limits of a rejected Christendom.

The Tribulation Era is to be a judgment period, when the vials of divine wrath are to be emptied out upon Jews and Gentiles alike. Judgments upon an apostate Church; upon a rebuilt Babylon; upon apostate Israel; upon the Beast and the false prophets; upon apostate nations. This is one reason why the born-again ones must be raptured ere such judgment breaks loose, for there is, for them, therefore now no condemnation (Romans 8:1).

The Book of Revelation from chapter 4 through chapter 19, should be carefully studied for an unfolding of heaven's dealings with earth. The following outline may serve to help the student—

The Manifestation of the Divine Glory, chapter 4.
1. The Throne (1-3) The Splendor of Jehovah
2. The Elders (4) Representatives of the Redeemed
3. The Lamps (5) The Fullness of the Spirit
4. The Living Creatures (6,8) Symbols of Creation
5. The Hymn of Praise (9-11)

The Book of the Seven Seals, chapter 5.
1. The Book Closed (1-4)
2. The Book Opened (5-8)
3. The Lamb Adored (9-14)

The Opening of the Seven Seals, Chapters 6-11.
1. The Great Scene (6)
2. The Saved during the Tribulation (7)
3. The Opening of the Seventh Seal (8, 9)
4. The Angel and the Book (10)
5. The Times of the Gentiles (11:1-14)
6. The Seventh Trumpet Sounded (11: 14-19)
   (What follows is given in 15. From 12-14 is a parenthesis.)

The Seven Mystic Signs, chapters 12-14.
1. The Woman clothed with the Sun (12:1,2)
2. The Great Dragon (12:3,4)
3. The Man Child (12:5-17)
4. The Beast out of the Sea (13:1-10)

5. The Beast out of the Earth (13:11-18)
6. The Lamb on Mount Sion (14:1-13)
7. The Son of Man in the Cloud (14: 14-20).

The Seven Vials, chapters 15,16.
1. Preparation in Heaven (15)
2. Devastation on Earth (16)

The Doom of Babylon, chapters 17 and 18.
1. Babylon the Great (17:1-7)
2. The Leader of the Revolt (17:8-18)
3. Babylon's glory, sin and doom (18)

The Marriage Supper of the Lamb, chapter 19.
1. Rejoicing in Heaven (1-6)
2. The Bride and the Marriage (7-10)
3. The Second Coming of Christ (11-16)
4. The Battle of Armageddon (17-21)

Of the Millennium

How impossible it is to condense all that is associated with "Earth's last day-week" into a few pages! Here we have the world's most glorious era—its Sabbath Rest. Some argue that the term *Millennium* is not in the Bible. Neither is the word "Grandfather," yet there are grandfathers in abundance. As is well-known, *Millennium* is from "mille" meaning *thousand* and "annum" signifying *year*. The phrase, "A thousand years," occurs six times (Revelation 20:2-7). *Three* out of the number are connected with Satan; *two* of them assert the reigns of the saints with Christ; the *sixth* intimates the period between the resurrection of the saints and that of the wicked. All these *six* occurrences of a definite period refer to the same time, although used in different connections.

While John alone states the actual duration of Christ's millennial reign, the fact of the Millennium permeates the Bible, and is spoken of as a time of peace and of unmistakable blessing (Psalm 72:7-11; Isaiah 2:2-4; 11:10; 65;66). Those who reject the Millennium as a specific period argue that as the language of the *Revelation* is symbolic its numerals must be treated as such. Therefore, "one thousand years" is not to be taken literally but figuratively. It is a poetic way of describing an undetermined period of Christ's sway. But the sixfold repetition proves that the writer was describing an exact and literal denomination of time.

Dr. David Cooper, writing on principles of correct Bible exposition, wisely says—

"When the plain sense of Scripture makes common sense, seek no other sense: therefore take every word at its primary, ordinary, usual, literary meaning unless the facts of the context indicate otherwise."

In this case the doctrine of the Millennium makes sense when viewed in the light of the context. Further, proof of it is altogether independent of John's statement as to its precise length. The *Millennium*, then, is a designation related to the period of our Lord's reign—public and personal with His saints, as we gather from Revelation 19. Walter Scott reminds us that—

"According to Jewish reasoning the six millenniums drawing to a close answer to the six days in which the heavens and earth were made, the seventh sabbatic day of rest looking forward to that long and blessed Sabbath of a thousand years. 'There remaineth therefore a Sabbath rest for the people of God' (Hebrews 4:9 R.V.).

Fausset speaks of this era as—

"The period of Christ's coming reign with His saints over the earth delivered from Satan's possession. As Satan and his kingdom sink, Christ and His Kingdom rise."

The Millennium is equivalent to the *Stone Kingdom* of Daniel 2, and is the converging point of prophecy. Our responsibility is to accept the prophecies as they are, and not whittle down their significance, nor distort their meaning. But the *Millennium* is approached in diverse ways. Among the schools of thought we have—

1. *Pre-Millennialism*

Pre-Millennialists are those who believe that Christ will return for His Church *before* the Millennium. *Pre* simply means "before." Pre-Millennialists are divided into two groups, namely, those who believe that Christ will return before the great Tribulation takes place—then those who hold that He will come half-way through the Tribulation. The latter are known as "Mid-Tribulationists."

2. *Post-Millennialism*

Post, meaning "after," represents those who affirm that Christ will not appear until *after* the Millennium—which is to be brought about through preaching of the Gospel. The morals of the world are to gradually improve, men are to become brothers all over the earth, wickedness is to

disappear, then the Golden Age will dawn. The terrible condition of the world in our time, however, indicates that such a Utopia is millenniums away. The Millennium is not to come about through man's effort but as the result of the appearance of the King of Kings to inaugurate His beneficent reign.

3. *A-Millennialism*

A signifies "no," hence the "A-Millennialist" is one who declares that there is *no* Millennium. All the prophecies of the Old Testament, relative to Christ's reign, are being realized in this present Church period. Through the Gospel, He is reigning in grace, and will continue to do so. Sects like *Jehovah's Witness, Seventh Day Adventists, Mormons and Roman Catholics* are to be found in this camp. The mystery is that a few evangelicals have been deluded into accepting this erroneous interpretation of millennial truth. Here is our outline of the Biblical presentation of the period—

The Millennium and Prophecy

Our Lord's coming Kingdom is woven into the fabric of both Old and New Testaments (Psalm 72:19; Isaiah 11; Daniel 7; Matthew 6:10). The Early Fathers accepted these, and other Scriptures, as prophetical of Christ's coming reign. Fisher in his *Church History* says that "the belief in a Millennium Kingdom on earth to follow the Second Advent was widely diffused."

The Millennium and the Lord Jesus Christ

The King Himself will be the chief Figure during this predicted era. It will be the day of His reign when He will be revered as—

1. *The sole Object of worship.* Then He will combine in harmony His kingly and priestly functions (Zechariah 6:13).

2. *The Lamb, Son of God, Son of Man, Son of David.* Combining all that He was and is, He will reign without a rival, with the entire earth-planet as His domain, with His center or seat in Jerusalem (Psalm 96:10; Psalm 2:6-8; Psalm 22:29).

3. *As the One whose knowledge and glory fill the earth.* Then, *all* about Him will be known to *all*. None will be able to say they do not know Him. From the least to the greatest He will be revealed in all His glory (Isaiah 11:9). He will command universal recognition (Philippians 2:9-11).

4. *As the Exalted One to whom a yearly pilgrimage will be made.* While His scepter

will be a universal one, His dominion will be, not only *terrestrial,* covering the entire earth, but *celestial,* including all forces above, and *infernal* including the control of all evil powers. All human, heavenly and hellish spheres come under His control. On earth, however, the multitudes are to journey to adore and worship Him (Zechariah 14:16; II Thessalonians 1:10; See Psalm 18:44; Micah 5:8-10; Hebrews 10:13).

The Millennium and the Jews

A-Millennialists say that there is no future for the Jew—that all the Old Testament promises and prophecies given to them have been taken over by the Church. What robbers! If we take Jewish blessings we should also take Jewish curses. When it comes to prophecy, the Jew is ever God's index finger, and all belonging to the Jew will yet be realized.

1. Israel is to be the nation around which the Lord is to group the nations of the earth (Deuteronomy 32:8).

2. Israel's promises of blessedness will be literally fulfilled. God will not forget her. As in her early history, so in the Millennium she will function as the channel of revelation to surrounding nations (Matthew 5:18).

3. Israel's blindness is to be removed, and all Israel saved (Romans 11:25,26; Revelation 7:1-7).

4. Israel, under Christ's rule, will be a world blessing. She will be used to gather the multitudes to the King (Isaiah 27:6; Acts 3:19-21).

5. Israel will rule over her former oppressors who possessed the land which has ever been hers by divine right and gift (Genesis 12:1-3; Amos 9:15).

6. Israel is to have Palestine equally divided among her twelve tribes (Ezekiel 47-48, See particularly 47:14).

7. One third of Israel will come through the great Tribulation into the Millennium (Zechariah 13:8,9).

The Millennium and the Gentiles

Because Christ's kingdom is to stretch from shore to shore all Gentiles are to recognize His sovereignty.

1. All Gentiles are to be judged and brought under His dominion, and made His footstool (Zephaniah 3:8).

2. Gentile government will be theocratic. The Lord will personally rule. Forced to obey Him, many will only yield Him feigned obedience. They will have no other course but to obey (Psalm 17:1; Jeremiah 3:10; Zechariah 14:9; Revelation 2:27; 12:5; 19:5,15).

3. Gentile nations will learn war no more. They will be freed from Satan, instigator of wars, Christ's reign is one of peace (Isaiah 2:4; Micah 4).

The Millennium and the Church

The three streams forming the broad river of humanity—the Jew, the Gentile, the Church of God—are all seen in the Millennium. *The Church,* composed of regenerated Jews and Gentiles, to share in the glories of Christ's kingdom.

1. As the Head, He will be united to the members, and together share the blessedness of this millennial age (II Timothy 2:12; John 17:24).

2. The Church is to hold and exercise judicial authority (I Corinthians 6:2-4; Revelation 20:4). Do we presently realize that we should be preparing ourselves for coming responsibilities?

3. The Church's honor will be to reign with Christ, assisting Him in His governmental control of all things. Then she will be a channel of grace to the peoples of the earth (Revelation 5:10; 20:4; Hebrews 12:22; Zechariah 6:13).

The Millennium and Satan

What a relief for the world it will be to know that its satanic god and prince is no longer active in its affairs! The Lion of Judah will have no interference from the roaring lion.

1. Satan, the deceiver, is to be bound and imprisoned for 1,000 years (Revelation 20:1-3).

2. The earth and the air are to be relieved of Satan's polluting presence and influence (Ephesians 2:2; Revelation 20:3). Christ broke the seal on His grave. Satan will not be able to break his seal.

3. Although Satan is removed, his influence remains in the hearts of many, hence, the universal revolt when he is freed. The *root* of sin is removed for a 1,000 years, but the *fruit* remains (Revelation 20:7-9).

The Millennium and the Creation

What wonderful changes await God's universe, sin has marred through the past millenniums!

1. The Mount of Olives is to be cleft in the midst, making more effective a more

rapid progress through the land (Zechariah 14:4).

2. All nations are to be restored and blessed (Isaiah 35:1,2; Romans 8:19-21).

3. Perpetual water is to flow from Jerusalem (Zechariah 14:8).

4. Animal creation is to be transformed. Christ, presenting in Himself the unity between the Lion and the Lamb is to eliminate all that is furious among beasts (Isaiah 11:6,8; 65:25).

5. Great rapidity of growth in nature (Amos 9:13; Isaiah 30:26).

6. Moonlight is to equal Sunlight, and the Sunlight will be sevenfold (Isaiah 30:26).

The Millennium and Its Subjects

Blessings are to abound for all who throng the earth when Christ, in person, is its rightful Lord and King.

1. The age of child life is to be extended. Children will not die as such. There will be death, but only for those who reject the King's authority (Isaiah 65:20,22). Methuselah died 31 years short of a millennium, at 969 years. The honor of living for a millennium is reserved for millennium saints. "The days of a tree" is an emblem of longevity.

2. Petitions are to be answered immediately. None who call upon the King will experience delay (Isaiah 65:24).

3. Injustice will be removed, and individual sin dealt with by death (Isaiah 65:20,23).

4. Physical ailments are to cease. The leaves of the tree are to be for the *healing* not health, of the nations (Isaiah 35:5,6; Revelation 22:2).

5. It will be a period of joyful thanksgiving, peace and righteousness (Isaiah 12:1-6; 25:9).

6. From the seat of government in Jerusalem, Christ will rule over all His enemies (Psalm 18:44; Micah 5:8-10; Hebrews 10:13).

After the presence and reign of Christ for a thousand years we would expect the earth to be so blissfully satisfied that men everywhere would urge Him to continue His control of things for ever and ever. Outwardly loyal subjects of the King, multitudes of earth-dwellers, will be inwardly rebellious for with the end of the Millennium when Satan is loosed from his prison, and goes out to deceive the nations, they immediately rally to him who has ever been the deceiver. This will be earth's last revolt against Christ, and the last act of Satan against Him. Immediately fire from heaven destroys the rebels. How long this *little season* is we are not told. Suffice it to say, that following such rebellion, Satan is banished to his eternal doom, as well as the impenitent wicked. The perfect kingdom is created. Paradise is restored. At long last God becomes all in all (I Corinthians 15:24,28). God takes back his own sole sovereignty with all things subjugated unto Himself. Eternity begins and bursts of praise rend the eternal skies as God has a total universe in which there is not one unbended knee. Then, as Pollock expresses it—

> New discoveries are made
> Of God's unbounded wisdom, power and
> love
> Which give the understanding room,
> And swell the hymn with evergrowing
> praise.

Of Heaven

An honest study of Scripture reveals as much proof for heaven as for hell. Dr. Joseph Parker once said, "The same logic which closes hell annihilates heaven." There are those who like to feel that beyond this vale of sin and sobs there is a blest abode for all mankind. Any thought, however, of a place of unrelieved anguish and torment is repugnant to those who hold only to the beneficence of God. They accept the reality of heaven, but reject the certainty of hell. But in unmistakable language, the Bible declares the actuality of both places, and man can choose one or the other. Such a choice is a magnificent possibility but a tremendous issue. Hell is the final abode of all those who live and die in their sin. Heaven is the final abode of all those redeemed by the blood of Christ, and regenerated by the Holy Spirit.

Some people do not go to heaven because they lived good lives, nor do others go to hell because they were bad in character. Relationship to Jesus Christ determines one's eternal destiny and abode. "No man cometh unto the Father *but by Me*" (John 14:6). Whether it be salvation, worship or ultimately heaven, the same principle is true, there is no access to God apart from the mediation of Jesus Christ.

The alternatives of Scripture must be faced. After *death* there is *destiny*. This destiny has been set down as one of two alternatives known as *heaven* and *hell*. There is a state of unbroken peace and un-flawed joy in the presence of God for the redeemed; or there is a sentence of ban-ishment from God's presence to a state of misery and dread.

Moreover, these two states of being are declared to be absolute, fixed, eternal. At death, the soul, after life's probation, passes into a destiny absolutely fixed and eternal. We have the clear and authoritative teach-ing of our Lord Himself regarding this twofold, fixed destiny. Yet the reticence of Christ is a great marvel.

> As the tree falls, so the tree lies.
> As man lives, so a man dies,
> As a man dies, so shall he be
> Through all the years of Eternity.

Details are omitted. The certainties are set down so that no man can miss them. The details are treated with a divine reserve.

Take, first of all, the explicit parables of judgment:

"The great gulf fixed, so that no one can pass from one state to the other";
"The door shut which cannot be opened";
"The outer darkness where there is weeping and gnashing of teeth."

These set forth the one destiny, namely that of unspeakable anguish and woe.

The other destiny declared to be a state of close fellowship with Christ can be gleaned from the following:

"Where I am, there shall also My serv-ant be" (John 12:26). It is described as the entry into a life with the angels of God—It is affirmed that reward is to be consummated and that we shall be forever with the Lord (I Thessalonians 4:17). Jesus spoke of "Abraham's bosom" with its close and tender fellowship of "My Fath-er's House" with its many rooms of shelter and rest; of "Paradise" in whose garden men may walk with God in the cool of the day (John 14:1-3).

These clear pronouncements are rein-forced by the twofold classification in all Christ's messages. There is a sharp, em-phatic division in His teaching somewhat repugnant to the modern mind. He speaks not only of heaven where "ancient dreams as substance are," but of hell, that dreary abode, where "the worm dieth not and the fire is not quenched." There are wheat and tares; good fish and bad fish; sheep and goats; loyal and disloyal; saved and lost;

those who do His will and those who do it not; children of God and children of the devil. Each soul goes to its own place.

"It has sometimes been said that a wise discernment does not see all men to be either black or white, but observes many to be gray. As an earlier writer puts it, there are not only sheep and goats but alpacas, which are in some regards like sheep, in other regards like goats. But the highest authorities both in natural science and in religious distinctions have only a two-fold classification. Jesus distrib-utes the gray either among the black or among the white." "For Me . . . Against Me!" So we have truth and falsehood, heaven and hell. They are with us now, and they are ahead of us; and some people, as they look over the world find it easier to believe in hell, than in heaven. As Brown-ing says in *Time's Revenges*:

> There may be heaven;
> There must be hell.

Another reason for the two alternatives of heaven and hell lies in the contrast be-tween those who are holy, and those who are sinful. Our sins are set in the awful light of His countenance, not in the par-tial discernment of man. Evil cannot stand in His presence, so we have those awful sentences: "I never knew you; depart from Me"; "The Wrath of the Lord." And not only so, but as the result of sin God has, through the propitiation of Christ, come into a new relationship with a guilty and sin-smitten humanity. And now the ulti-mate question both in time and in eternity is man's relationship to that Father who has redeemed him by the sacrifice of His Son. Man's works, attainments in character, amends in some intermediate state, can never pass the bar of divine judgment. Ev-ery man's destiny is shaped by his attitude and disposition toward Christ, as can be found in all His parables (Matthew 25: 12,24,40; John 3:16). Everywhere, apart from works which may be mentioned with approval or denounced with moral indig-nation, the count in the indictment at the last judgment, the count in the indictment now, is a man's relationship to God through our Lord Jesus Christ.

Many who protest against the orthodox heaven and hell speak with contradictory voices. For instance, there are those who speculate on

Universal restoration

This theory, most widely accepted, teaches that all men shall at length be saved. It does not deny evil is evil and that it merits and shall receive due punishment. What the Universalist affirms is that through discipline and purgation all souls shall at last turn to God, and then Christ's love and redemption shall achieve a complete victory in the end of ends. Universalism believes that the power of God has infinite resources, and that the love of God has unwearying persistence and that no soul can ultimately resist such resources and love. A great arsenal of tests are quoted in support of this theory, such as I Timothy 2:4; II Peter 3:9; Hebrews 6:7; John 12: 31,32; Luke 3:6; Titus 2:11; I Timothy 4:10; I John 2:2,3,8; Acts 3:21; I Corinthians 15:22-29; Ephesians 1:10-12; Romans 8:20,21.

But the advocates of universal salvation ignore or explain away much of the sterner side of the Bible. For amidst all its seeming hopefulness there is a steady, persistent note in Scripture, stern, awful, sorrowful, which is impossible to reconcile with Universalism. There are clear assertions that some men will not be saved, (Matthew 26: 24; II Thessalonians 1:9; Philippians 3:19).

The Universalist forgets that if man be a free agent there must be the possibility of his continuing in a state of alienation until the end. God cannot do contradictory things. He cannot make a door to open and shut at the same time. And so, as one states it, "Can God make a man's will free to choose good or evil, and yet secure that he shall certainly choose good at last?" No! of course He cannot.

All forms of "The Larger Hope" theory, then, are to be rejected even though they may be expressed with the poet's vagueness:

At last I heard a voice upon the slope,
Cry to the summit, "Is there any hope?"
To which an answer pealed from the high land,
But in a tongue no man could understand.
And on the glimmering summit far withdrawn
God made Himself an awful rose of dawn.

But Jesus spoke in a tongue all men can understand when He described the great gulf between those who are bad and good.

Conditional Immortality

This theory holds that the evildoer must receive the reward of the deeds done in the body. After death he goes to judgment and he will be justly condemned. But he will not pass into a hell of torment. The sinner and his sin will both be annihilated, thereby losing God and heaven for ever and ever.

But this doctrine of conditional immortality is involved in even greater difficulties than Universalism. The assumption that the soul is immortal enough to live after death but not immortal enough to live forever, is condemned both by reason and conscience. Science speaks of a great law which it terms, "The Law of the Conservation of Energy." No energy or force, it declares, is ever destroyed. It may change its form, but it is never lost. And it is with personality as it is with nature's forces. Personality is persistent, continuous, indestructible. In "Man and the Universe," Sir Oliver Lodge, the eminent scientist, says, "I want to make the distinct assertion that a really existing thing never perishes, but only changes its form." The theory of conditional immortality, however, contradicts this belief in the immortality of personality and cannot, therefore, claim authority as a theory of future punishment. And not only so, but the idea that God will finally extinguish any soul which has not yielded to Him is more repellent to the conception of God's wisdom and justice than even that of a life and state of unalterable defiance.

The Intermediate State.

The best-known form of this position is the doctrine of Purgatory as taught by the Romish Church. In Purgatory, which can only be entered by those whose final destiny is heaven, men are made fit to be with the saints through purification by suffering. But as Article XXII of "the Church of England" says: "The Romish doctrine concerning Purgatory is a fond thing vainly invented and grounded upon no warranty of Scripture, but rather repugnant to the Word of God." Doubtless this system is a source of much wealth to a corrupt church, seeing that the prayers along with the pounds (or dollars) of course, of the living can hasten the exit of the suffering from their purgatorial flames. Thus Tetzel's cry: "When money clinks at the bottom of my box a soul is released from Purgatory." The Romish Church, however, accepts the stern doctrine of hell. It remains a state of burning torture, for all those who have been disobedient, unless they have had their penalty remitted on the ground of "invincible ignorance."

But a modern theory of the intermediate state which we deem to be a false hope is finding acceptance. Many have lived and died in error and darkness. There are those who through an evil inheritance or a hindering environment have had no adequate opportunity. When we think of the grossly ignorant heathen man, or the gutter child of a profligate, surely it is not just to say that they are beyond the pale of God's mercy, but that there must be some condition of life and being, where they shall abide, and in which they shall be judged and purified.

Exponents of this theory affirm that the Holy Spirit operates in such a state doing a work of conviction and conversion. Much is made of that passage in I Peter about our Lord preaching to the spirits in prison. Consequently, there are men who fervently believe in this state of "the spirits in prison," and are assured that after a long time of tears and pain, they shall pass to Christ.

But as Professor Clow points out, "The theory of the intermediate state contradicts every conception of good as good, and evil as evil, and is entirely without support in the New Testament. Jesus is entirely silent upon the matter."

The Reality of Heaven

The Jews of old recognized three heavens—

1. The aerial or atmospheric heaven, where the birds fly, the winds blow, and the showers, mists, vapors and clouds are formed (Acts 1:11).

2. The firmament, or the region of the sun, moon and starry host (Genesis 1:1; Psalm 19:1; Job 38:31-33).

3. The heaven of heavens. This is where God dwells, and is the region spoken of as the immediate presence of God, the region of divine glory, also the dwelling place of angels and saints (I Kings 8:30; Psalm 11:4; 15:1; Matthew 6:9). This is the Temple of the divine Majesty, where His excellent glory is revealed in the most conspicuous manner. "It is the habitation of His holiness, the place where His honor dwelleth." This sacred mansion of light, joy and glory is the *third heaven* to which Paul was caught up (II Corinthians 12:2).

Summarizing the location and character of heaven, we have ample Scriptural proof that it is—

An Abode. Heaven is expressly spoken of as a definite place, as well as a state (John 14:2,3). The existence of the body of Christ, and those of Enoch and Elijah, affords further proof. If heaven is not a place, where can these bodies be? Where are the bodies of believers to exist after their resurrection? Where heaven is definitely located, God alone knows. Evidently it is above, just as hell is beneath, seeing Jesus lifted *up* His eyes to heaven. Heaven must be recognized for the country it is.

A Prepared Abode. Jesus assured His own that He was going to "prepare a place" for them. While all the saints of God from the beginning of time are to be in heaven, it would seem as if within such there is to be a prepared place for the true Church. Writing to the redeemed, Peter speaks of their incorruptible inheritance as being "reserved in heaven" for them (I Peter 1:4). Thus, in heaven, there is a prepared place for a prepared people, and to be heaven-bound, we must be heaven-born!

A Peopled Abode. What glorious company can be found in heaven! God has ever lived there (Matthew 6:9). Christ is there as the Center of glory (Hebrews 9:24). Heaven has ever been the habitation of the vast angelic host (Matthew 18:10). The godly of all ages are also there. Of His own, Jesus said: "Where I am, there ye may be also" (John 14:3).

A Paternal Abode. Jesus referred to heaven as "My *Father's* house" (John 14:2), and as its Creator, it is His in a real sense. But there as the *Father*, conveys the meaning that His abode has a warmth, love and joy about it. What kind and true earthly fathers mean to their homes, our heavenly Father and the Father of our Lord Jesus Christ means to His Home, which we are to share.

A Palatial Abode. Heaven must possess a blaze of glory, a radiant, magnificent celestial splendor overwhelming to all who enter it. Old Thomas Watson says: "If we could but look a while through the chinks of heaven's door and see the beauty and bliss of paradise, could we but lay an ear to heaven and hear the ravishing music of the seraphic spirits and the anthems of praise which they sing, how would the soul be exhilarated and transported with joy!" Once we reach the realm of eternal bliss we shall discover that its glories far outstrip the most magnificent descriptions ever given by man below. Like the Queen of Sheba, who had no more spirit in her after she beheld the glory of Solomon's palace, we shall confess, "Behold, the half was not told me."

The palace of God is transparent, it is adorned with illustrious beams of glory. Hell is a dark dungeon where there is nothing but the blackness of darkness for ever, but heaven is bespangled with light (Colossians 1:12). The heavenly palace is also "well situated for good air and a pleasant prospect," says Watson. "There is the best air, which is perfumed with the odors of Christ's ointments, and a most pleasant prospect for the Bright Morning Star. The palace is rich and sumptuous. It has gates of pearl (Revelation 21:21). It is enriched with white robes and crowns of glory: it never falls to decay and the dwellers in it never die (Revelation 22:5)."

A Pleasurable Abode. "By heaven," says Frankling, "we understand a state of happiness infinite in degree and endless in duration." Another writer, "The joys of heaven are without example, above experience and beyond imagination: for which the whole creation wants a comparison, we an apprehension, and ever the Word of God a revelation." Hannah Moore wrote of heaven as a place of "Perfect purity, fullness of joy, everlasting freedom, health and fruition, complete security and eternal good."

Reunion with loved ones, fellowship with renowned Bible saints, the absence of all sin, sorrow, pain and death, the conscious presence of God and the sight of Christ combine to make heaven the sphere of inexpressible felicity. Christ Himself will ever be the source of our unending joy (Revelation 21:23). How privileged to bask in His radiance! Oft-quoted are the lines—

The Light of Heaven is the face of Jesus;
The Joy of Heaven is the presence of Jesus;
The Melody of Heaven is the name of Jesus;
The Harmony of Heaven is the praise of Jesus;
The Theme of Heaven is the work of Jesus;
The Employment of Heaven is the service of Jesus;
The Fullness of Heaven is Jesus Himself.

A Peaceful Abode. Undisturbed calm and tranquility reign in heaven above. God, whose home it is, is the God of peace, and can therefore allow nothing to enter His presence alien to His own being. Wars, destroying countries below; wranglings, destroying peace in earthly homes, are excluded from heaven where peace, perfect peace, possesses its chambers.

A Perfect Abode. "My idea of heaven," says Wilberforce, "is perfect love"; "And mine," replied Robert Hall, "is perfect rest." Heaven is entirely separated from the impurities and imperfections, the alterations and changes we are familiar with below. Holy, eternal joy fills the hearts of all because of freedom from all evil, both of soul and body (Revelation 7:17). Nothing that defiles can enter there. There we are to be perfectly holy—as holy as Christ Himself (I John 3:2). Now we yearn for holiness of life, but sin abides. With our entrance into heaven, however, we shall gain a writ of ease from all our sins and iniquities. Heaven is a state of impeccability.

Think of it—in heaven, the saints never have a sinful thought! "Let none be so vain as to talk of purgatory," says Watson. "A soul purged by Christ's blood needs no fire of purgatory, but goes immediately from a deathbed into a glorified state."

Joyful and perfect service is also to be ours in heaven. There is no idleness there. We are to be like "angels and with the angels sing." God's children serve Him day and night forever. Then we shall labor for Him as we cannot now because of the trammeling influence of the flesh.

A Permanent Abode. Heaven, which is likewise referred to as a kingdom with a King (Matthew 18:1), is also mentioned as a city, with its citizens (Hebrews 11:10, 16; Philippians 3:30 R.V.); a country with its dwellers (Hebrews 11:16); a building and mansion of God (II Corinthians 15:1; John 14:2), is eternal in duration. As a "Home" it will never crumble and decay because of the ravages of time, storm or war. It is as eternal as God Himself.

A Prescribed Abode. Only "the godly in Christ Jesus" have the right of entrance into heaven. All the wicked and Christ rejectors are disqualified for citizenship in this city without foundations (Galatians 5: 21; Ephesians 5:5; Revelation 22:14, 15). To engage in the employments and enjoyments of heaven, one must have a heavenly nature, which is what the Holy Spirit supplies when He makes the believing sinner a partaker of the divine nature.

The Bible pictures all true believers as groaning after heaven, on a stretch for and living for heaven. Is this our attitude? That seraphic soul, Samuel Rutherford exclaimed: "Love heaven. Let your heart be in it. Up, up and visit the new land and view the fair city, and the white throne of the Lamb—run fast, for it is late."

In the deepening twilight of a summer evening, a pastor called at the home of one of his parishioners and found, seated in the doorway, a little boy with both hands extended upward, holding a line. "What are you doing here, my little friend?" enquired the minister.

"Flying my kite, sir," was the prompt reply.

"Flying your kite! I can see no kite, nor can you," said the pastor.

"I know it, sir," said the lad. "I cannot see it; but I know it is there for I feel the tug."

Are our affections set upon things above so that we can feel the tug? Possibly the tug is in the other direction—downward. We are of the earth, earthy. If the things of earth, however, are growing strangely dim, and earthly circles are being depleted, then the heavenly tug grows stronger with the passing days. May grace be ours to foster homesickness for heaven!

Because the bliss of heaven largely consists in the absence of those things which hinder happiness here below, Biblical descriptions of heaven are chiefly negative (Isaiah 25:8; 33:24; 35:10; 46:4; 50:1; 57:20; 65:10; Jeremiah 49:23 margin). John cites seven "no mores"—

"No sickness, nor pain" (Revelation 22:2).

"No hunger, nor thirst" (Revelation 7:16, 17; cf. Psalms 36:8; 46:4).

"No sorrow, nor crying, nor tears." All cause of these forever removed.

"No sea" (Ecclesiastes 1:7). The emblem of unrest and dissatisfaction.

"No death" (Hosea 13:14; I Corinthians 15:26; Revelation 20:14).

"No night." All weariness is to vanish.

"No sin." This is the primary cause of the foregoing (Romans 5:12; 8:20-23; Revelation 7:16, 17; 21:1, 4, 25, 27; 22:3, 5).

While human language cannot depict heavenly glories, there are seven positive descriptions of heaven to feast upon (Isaiah 64:4; II Corinthians 12:4 margin).

"Fulness of joy—pleasures forevermore"

(Psalms 16:11; 21:6 R.V.; 36:8; Matthew 25:21,23).

"Rest from weary labor" (Hebrews 4:9; Revelation 14:13).

"Unceasing service" (Revelation 7:15; 22:3).

"Perfect knowledge" (I Corinthians 13:9-12).

"Perfect beauty and safety" (Revelation 21:19-21).

"Happy reunion with loved ones" (II Samuel 12:23; I Thessalonians 4:13-18).

"The bliss of being with, and being like, Jesus" (Psalm 17:15; John 12:26; 14:3; 17:24; I Thessalonians 4:17; 5:10; I John 3:2; Revelation 22:4).

> Christ is the heart of Heaven,
> Its fullness and its bliss;
> The center of the heavenly throng,
> The Object of the ransomed's song
> Is Jesus in the midst.

Of Hell

Death in sin carries with it dismal effects. The wages of sin is death even "the second death" (Revelation 21:8). Sin has shame for its companion in life, and hell for its wages thereafter. Yet there is a negligence of witness to this sterner side of the Gospel. We fear that too many dwell exclusively upon the goodness of God, forgetting that goodness and severity are His twin attributes (Romans 11:22). These two virtues are exhibited in their fullness at the cross. Hell presents no darker picture than the cross, heaven has nothing more glorious than the cross. Those who are eternally lost will suffer no more for their sins than Christ endured when He died for sin.

Henry Ward Beecher spoke of the change overtaking the Church in his day. "Future retribution is only alluded to: eternal punishment almost never taught in the pulpit today—to the honor of the pulpit and the honor of God, be it said." As hell is still in the Bible, is it not to the dishonor of pulpits if they deny such a truth? Silence as to "the weeping and gnashing of teeth" Jesus spoke of (Matthew 25:30) does more to populate hell than the blasphemies of Tom Paine and Robert Ingersoll combined. Jesus possessed the tenderest heart that ever throbbed in a human breast, yet He constantly alluded to the certain, terrible and unending suffering of those who died lost. He taught eternal punishment with a boldness, plainness and awful significance no human preacher dare imitate unless he has a Calvary heart for the unsaved.

In the study of the basic doctrine of hell, we are not going to dwell too much upon the fact of eternal torment. Accepting the Bible as an inspired revelation, we take for granted the clear evidence it presents of hell. It is a fact so personal and solemn that God has not hidden it, nor is He silent concerning it. God has written it large upon the sacred page so that the wayfaring man, though a fool, may read it. In unmistakable language, the Bible speaks of unending felicity of the saved, and of unending torment for the lost, urging the latter to flee from the wrath to come.

Hell is described as being "beneath" (Proverbs 15:24). "Hell is as far under the earth as heaven is above it." Luke tells us that the devils besought Christ to command them to go into the deep (Luke 8:31). Hell, then, is in the deep. But the wise Chrysostom warns us, "Let me not so labor to know where hell is, as how to escape it."

Dwelling upon the fact and nature of hell, we use the phrase, "eternal punishment," in its natural and obvious meaning—*eternal*, which implies "unending." The continuity of hell must be the same as that of heaven, for the same words are used to describe both (Matthew 25:46). *Punishment* represents "conscious suffering." Let us try to condense Biblical material on this solemn subject—

1. The soul of man neither dies nor falls into unconsciousness when the body dies. Sinners do not cease to be, and saints do not go to sleep until the resurrection of the just. Personality is indestructible. Conscious survival after death is clearly taught in Scripture (Luke 16:19-31; II Corinthians 5:8; Philippians 1:23; Hebrews 12:22, 23; Revelation 6:9,10).

2. All who die out of Christ go to hell. The Old Testament word for hell is *Sheol*, and is used in the double sense. First of all, it represents the grave to which the bodies of both the righteous and the wicked go (Genesis 37:35; I Kings 2:6, 9; Psalm 6:5; Hosea 13:14). Then *Sheol* stands for the place of future punishment (Psalms 9:17; 55:15; 116:3; Proverbs 7:27; Isaiah 28:15-18).

The New Testament word for hell is *Hades*, and corresponds to *Sheol*. Whether *Hades* represents the grave or a definite place of conscious punishment must be

determined by the context (Luke 16:23-25; Revelation 1:18; 6:8; 20:13-15; I Corinthians 15:55).

Other designations for the place of eternal torment prepared for the devil and his angels (Matthew 25:41) are—

Gehenna (Matthew 5:22; Mark 9:43-48; James 3:6).

Eternal damnation (Mark 3:29).

Outer darkness (Matthew 8:12).

Resurrection of damnation (John 5:29).

Second death (Revelation 2:11; 21:8).

Everlasting destruction (Psalm 9:27; II Thessalonians 1:9).

Blackness of darkness (II Peter 2:4; Jude 13).

The curse of God (Deuteronomy 27:26; Galatians 3:10).

The wrath of God (John 3:36; Romans 1:18).

The Lake of Fire (Revelation 19:20; 20:15).

Eternal punishment (Matthew 25:46).

Bonds and chains (II Peter 2:4).

Worm of conscience (Mark 9:44).

Company of demons (Matthew 25:41).

Unending torments (Revelation 14:11).

These and other designations describe the dreadfulness of hell. What plurality of torments are the portion of the lost! If only there could be heard by them the groans and shrieks of the damned for one hour, how they would flee to Christ for mercy! Old Anselm says: "I had rather endure all torments, than see the devil with bodily eyes." What a hell it must be to be shut up with the raging lion forever, and have him as the old red dragon forever hiss and spit in one's face!

3. Hell is a place of conscious suffering. Time can never end hell's torment, and tears never quench it (Luke 3:23-25, 28; II Peter 2:9 R.V.). Thomas Watson, the Puritan divine, graphically describes the sorrows of hell thus: "If all the earth and sea were sand and every thousandth year a bird should come and take away one grain, it would be a long time before that heap would be removed: yet if after all that time the damned could come out of Hell, there would be some hope; but the words *forever* and *ever* break the heart."

Those rejecting the Biblical revelation of hell try to show that "eternal" or "everlasting" do not mean *eternal* or *everlasting*. Our answer to this assertion can be brief. Precisely the same word is used to define the duration of the life which believers in

Christ possess (John 3:15, 16, 36); the duration of salvation (Hebrews 5:9); the duration of heaven (II Corinthians 5:1); the duration of Christ's redemption (Hebrews 9:12); the duration of the Spirit's existence (Hebrews 9:14); the duration of the inheritance of the saints (Hebrews 9:15); the duration of divine glory (I Peter 5:10); the duration of Christ's kingdom (II Peter 1:11). How foolish then to try and dodge the plain, obvious and natural meaning of the term used for the sinner's woe—*eternal* or *everlasting!*

"Everlasting" and "eternal" are used 14 times of the duration of the righteous and seven times of the retribution of the wicked (Matthew 18:8; 25:41, 46; Mark 3:29; II Thessalonians 1:9; Hebrews 6:2; Jude 7). "Forever and ever" occurs in 17 places concerning God and His people; three times regarding the devil and his servants (Revelation 14:11; 19:3; 20:10).

4. The lake of fire is to consume hell. With the judgment of the Great White Throne, hell and all its occupants are to be cast into the Lake of Fire (Revelation 20:14, 15; 21:8). Thus in one sense hell itself, the present abode of the lost, is not eternal but its torment is. The lake of fire and the second death appear to be identical (Revelation 20:14; 21:8 R.V.).

5. The lake of fire is a place of conscious suffering. What doom awaits those who die out of Christ and also the devil and his angels! (Revelation 2:11; 19:20; 20:10; Matthew 25:41, 46). It would seem as if the conscious, unending torment of the lake of fire consists of two aspects—

The Punishment of Separation—"Depart from Me" (Matthew 7:23).

What doom! Chrysostom says that the word "depart" is worse than fire. Sin must be the greater evil when it eternally separates the sinner from the greatest good. It was hard for Absalom not to see the king's face. How tragic to be eternally banished from God's smile and presence!

The Punishment of Loss—"Ye cursed" (Matthew 25:41).

Sinners dying in their sin have to depart, not with God's blessing, but His curse, and to have as companions the occupants of eternal darkness. The present anguish of the sinner is a kind of sport to the awful torments of the lake of fire. How terrible is "the wrath of the Almighty" (Revelation 19:15)! The divine stroke is heavy

and intolerable. Sinning together, body and soul must suffer together in unending misery (Revelation 9:6; 14:11).

Hell is a definite place, as well as a moral condition. John Milton makes the devil say—

> Myself an Hell;
> And, in the lowest deep, a lower deep,
> Still threat'ning to devour me, opens wide,
> To which the Hell I suffer seems a
>   Heaven.

6. The conscious suffering of the lake of fire is unending. Already we have dealt with the fact that the word *aionios,* meaning "eternal" or "of unending duration," is used of the blessedness of the saved *and* of the suffering of the lost. Contrasted passages to study are these: Jude 7 with John 3:15; Matthew 18:8 with Romans 6:23; Matthew 25:41 with Hebrews 5:9; I Timothy 1:17 with Matthew 25:46; Revelation 10:6 with 20:10.

7. The only escape from everlasting torment is now. Acceptance of the finished work of Christ for sinners alone guarantees deliverance from the terrible doom depicted by Christ as awaiting those who die lost. Once in Him, all condemnation is removed (Romans 8:1). Hell fire can never singe the garment of divine righteousness. Pliny observes that nothing quenches fire as quickly as salt and blood. The salt tears of repentance, and the blood of Christ are efficacious to quench the hell of sin now, and the hell of torment hereafter.

If we truly believe that men and women who die in their sin are to be eternally banished from the presence of God forever, our solemn task here and now is to warn them to "flee from the wrath to come." We dare not remain indifferent to their terrible doom (Ezekiel 3:17-21).

> O God, to think the countless souls that
>   pass away
>   Through each short moment that we
>   live,
> Destined to dwell in Heaven, or groan
>   in Hell for aye.
> O stir me up, and new strength give,
> And let not one pass out through death
>   in shame and sin,
> That I through Thee might seek and win.

When one comes to enumerate the multitudinous books taken up with the manifold doctrines of the Bible he finds himself embarrassed with spiritual riches. The unknown total must run into countless thousands. Writing in 1943 Sherwood Eddy said, "Literally *a hundred thousand volumes* have been written about Jesus, or have attempted to explain Him." Since then, hundreds more have been written. If that vast number of books is true of the doctrine of Christ, the total for all the other doctrines must be astronomical.

One of the most remarkable guides in the selection of the enormous literature associated with many aspects of Bible study is Dr. A. T. Robertson's *Syllabus for New Testament Study*. The research of this renowned Greek scholar must have been prodigious. In this great volume of his, he not only gives a summary of Inter-Biblical history and New Testament history but also lists under each section the most outstanding theological works he consulted and commends. Here the reader will find expert advice on handbooks dealing with the *Intertestament Period, Bible Dictionaries, Concordances, Important Editions of the Bible*, and likewise the most profitable works to secure on every New Testament book and on Christ and His apostles. For instance, on the doctrine of Christ alone Dr. Robertson cites some 700 books dealing with every phase of our Lord's life and work.

Another profitable summary of the best study books to secure on doctrinal subjects is the bibliography Dr. W. Graham Scroggie supplies in his monumental work, *A Guide to the Gospels*. To the student who has access to a large theological library, copies should be made of the lists that scholars like Drs. Robertson and Scroggie provide, and then advantage taken of the perusal of same. If permanent possession of many\ of these listed books is required, it will be found that the majority of them can be secured at small cost from a secondhand theological book store. The most outstanding store of this kind is *Kregel's Book Store, 525 Eastern Ave., S.E., Grand Rapids, Mich., U.S.A.* A postcard will bring you the periodical catalogue of thousands of books in stock. Kregel's is unique in its scope for the Bible student. For readers in Great Britain, *The Lamp Press, Old Town, London* can supply catalogues of secondhand theological works.

Attention can be drawn to the world's greatest *Evangelical Loan Library*, with 150 branches covering five continents. All necessary information can be had from *The Evangelical Library, 78a Chiltern Street, London, W.1.* as to the 100,000 volumes at the student's disposal. A nominal annual fee is all that is asked for the loan of any books required. Ministers, students and general readers all over the world are members of this unique loan library. Why not write for a copy of its free illustrated booklet?

One of the most helpful methods adopted in research material for this present volume of mine on doctrines was to closely study the summary on any given doctrine in a standard *Bible Dictionary* or *Encyclopedia*, and then consult the list of books mentioned at the conclusion of the article. Taking the doctrine of Christ as given in *The International Standard Bible Encyclopedia*, as an example, we have not only the excellent coverage of the salient features of our Lord's life and mission by Dr. James Orr, but also his recommended books out of a vast voluminous literature on such a doctrine. In fact, no matter what phase of Bible knowledge is required, this encyclopedia concludes with a list of selected works on that particular theme.

On all of the doctrines, the literature is enormous. For instance, my shelves contain over 150 volumes dealing with *prophecy*. Kregel lists almost 300 on *The Doctrine of Last Things*—400 on *Christ*—150 on *God*—200 on *Prayer*—100 on *the Church*—160 on *the Atonement*—250 on *the Second Advent*, etc., etc. One gets lost amid a wealth of material. Our practical advice to the preacher and student, once a doctrine has been decided upon, is to turn to a treatise on it in a reliable encyclopedia or dictionary, note the writer's summary of the doctrine, and secure the reference volumes he commends from a theological library or secondhand bookstore. The latter can save the diligent student a good deal of money, if desired books are retained. If memory serves me aright, there are helpful lists on a working library any pastor should have by Dr. W. Graham Scroggie, and by that renowned bibliographer, Dr. Wilbur Smith.

A final word of caution is necessary, even though Solomon says that "in the multitude of counsellors there is safety" (Proverbs 11:14; 15:22; 24:6). Do not clutter your study table with too many books on a given theme. It is far more profitable to master one or two of the best, than get lost among the many. If you take a doctrine such as *sin*, use your Bible Concordance first of all, noting the words used to describe it, as well as its origin and consequences. Then, no matter how crude it may appear, work out your own outlines, and seeking divine guidance, set down your own thoughts. This done, turning to the exposition of more mature and scholarly teachers, you can enrich your own efforts and thus function as a worthy minister of the Word of Life. We pray that this volume in your hands will serve as a guide in this direction.

BIBLIOGRAPHY

Alleman, S. Austin, *The Union Bible Companion,* Sunday School Union, Philadelphia.

Angus, Joseph, *The Bible Handbook,* Religious Tract Society, London, 1862, 660 pages.

Banks, John S., *A Manual of Christian Doctrine,* C. H. Kelly, London, 1899, 283 pages.

Berkhof, Louis, *Summary of Christian Doctrine,* Wm. B. Eerdmans, Grand Rapids, 1938, 198 pages.

Bishop Ripon, *An Introduction to the Study of Scripture,* J. M. Dent, London.

Bromall, Wick, *Biblical Criticism,* Zondervan Publishing House, Grand Rapids.

Bube, Richard H., *A Textbook of Christian Doctrine,* Moody Press, Chicago, 1955, 510 pages.

Cana, H. E., *The Authority of the Holy Scriptures,* Southern Baptist Convention, Nashville.

Chafer, L. Sperry, *Systematic Theology,* Dunham Press, Finlay, Ohio, 1922.

Christianity Today, "Basic Christian Doctrines," Dr. Carl Henry, Editor, 1961.

Clifford, John, *The Inspiration and Authority of the Bible,* James Clarke, Edinburgh.

Collett, Sydney, *The Scripture of Truth All About the Bible* 1912, 323 pages. Fleming H. Revell, New York.

Corner, *System of Christian Ethics.*

Cumming, Dr. Elder, *The Eternal Spirit.*

Dale, R. W., *Christian Doctrine,* Hodder and Stoughton, London, 1896, 329 pages.

Fausset, A. R., *Bible Encyclopedia and Dictionary,* Zondervan, Grand Rapids, n.d., 740 pages.

Fisher, G. P., *History of Christian Doctrine,* T. and T. Clark, Edinburgh.

Frith, Wm., *The Infallible Book,* S. W. Partridge, London.

Gerdlestone, R. B., *The Foundation of the Bible,* Eyre and Spottiswoode, London.

Graebuer, Theo., *A Dictionary of Bible Topics,* Zondervan, Grand Rapids.

Griffith Thomas, W. H., *The Principles of Theology,* Church Book Room, London.

Halley, H. H., *Pocket Bible Handbook,* Zondervan, Grand Rapids, 1957, 960 pages.

Hastings, James, *Dictionary of Christ and the Gospels,*
  Dictionary of the Bible, T. and T. Clark, London, 1909, 990 pages.

Henry Carl C., *Revelation and the Bible,* Tyndale Press, London.

Henry Carl F. H., *Christian Personal Ethics*

Hodge, C. H., *Systematic Theology,* James Clarke, Edinburgh.

Hogg, C. F., *Gospel Facts and Doctrines,* Pickering and Inglis, London, 1951, 104 pages.

Ingram, Winnington, *The Love of the Trinity.*

International Standard Bible Encyclopedia, Eerdmans, Grand Rapids, 1929, 2820 pages.

Johnson, D., *The Christian and His Bible,* I.V.F., Bedford Square, London, 1960, 70 pages.

Kant, *History of Ethics.*

Kelly, Wm. *God's Inspiration of Scripture,* T. Weston, London.

Lewis, George, *Doctrines of the Bible Developed,* Thomas Constable, London, 1854, 628 pages.

Lillie, William, Oliver and Boyd, *Studies in New Testament Ethics.*

Linton, E. A., *An Introduction to Dogmatic Theology,* James Clarke, Edinburgh.

Martineau, *Christian Ethics.*

Pope, W. B., *A Compendium of Christian Theology,* Methodist Book Room, London.

Robertson, Dr. A. T., *Syllabus for New Testament Study.*

Robson, John, *The Revelation and Inspiration of the Bible,* Hodder and Stoughton, London.

Ryie, Charles C., *Biblical Theology of the New Testament,* Moody Press, Chicago.

Salvation Army, *Handbook of Doctrine,* International Headquarters, London, 1927, 200 pages.

Scroggie, Dr. W. Graham, *A Guide to the Gospels.*

Sedgwick, *Methods of Ethics.*

Shedd, T., *History of Christian Doctrine,* T. and T. Clark, Edinburgh.

Spenser, *Data of Ethics.*

Steele, Daniel, *The Gospel of the Comforter.*

Strong, A. H. *Systematic Theology,* Pickering and Inglis, London.

Stuart, Wm., *History of the Christian Church.*

Tatford, F. A., (edited) *A Symposium of Bible Doctrine,* Pickering and Inglis, London, 1955, 200 pages.

Tidwell, Josiah, B., *Christian Teachings,* Wm. B. Eerdmans, Grand Rapids, 1942.

Torrey, R. A., *What the Bible Teaches,* Fleming Revell, New York, 1898, 539 pages.

Townsend, W. J., *A Handbook of Christian Doctrine,* Burroughs, London, n.d., 153 pages.

Warfield, B. B. *Biblical Foundations,* Tyndale Press, London.
  The Inspiration and Authority of the Bible, Marshall, Morgan and Scott, London.

INDEXES

SUBJECT INDEX

Adoption, 146, 153, 199-203
  Price of, 202-3
  Purpose of, 203
  Results of, 201-2
Agassiz, Professor Louis, 16
Agnosticism, 16
a Kempis, Thomas, 92, 127
Alford, Dean, 193
All the Miracles of the Bible, 50, 274
All the Parables of the Bible, 49, 267
All the Prayers of the Bible, 225
All the Promises of the Bible, 34
Ambrose, Bishop, 34, 257
A-Millennialism, 283
Analytical Concordance, 187
An Essay on Man, 142
Angel of the Lord, 129
Angelic-Beings—Their Nature and Ministry, 132
Angels, 41, 127-32
  Appearances of, 129
  Names of, 131
  Work of, 130-31
Angus, Joseph, 2, 232
Anselm, 291
A Portrait of Jesus, 49
Apostasy, 239
Apostles, 243
Apostles Creed, 2
Aquinas, Thomas, 253
Aristotle, 33, 163
Arminianism, 223
Arnold, Rev. Thomas, 235
Arthur, William, 61
Assurance, 204-7
  Source of, 205
  Scope of, 206-7
Athanasian Creed, 123
Atheism, 14-16
Atonement, 184, 192
Auber, Harriet, 73
Augustine, 20, 122, 256

B

Bachner, 16
Barbauld, Mrs., 269
Baptism, 255-56, 258-60
  Mode, 259-60
  Of Children, 257-58
  Subjects of, 258-59

Baptism unto Repentance, 175
Barrow, Dr., 254
Beck, Professor, 79
Beecher, Henry Ward, 290
Bell, Canon C., 132
Berkhof, Louis, 25, 32, 45
Bible Call, 10
Bible Handbook, 2, 232
Bishop Horne, 9, 279
Bishop Lightfoot, 44
Bishops, 245
Bickersteth, 119
Book of Common Prayer, 166
Boswell, James, 141
Boyle, 36
Brainerd, David, 226
Brookes, Dr. James H., 9
Browning, Robert, 59, 286
Bunyan, John, 52, 156, 210, 229, 254
Burke, Edmund, 141
Burns, Robert, 226

C

Calvin, John, 205, 223
Carlyle, Thomas, 271
Carnality, 113
Carson, Herbert M., 147
Cato, Porcius, 175
Chalmers, Thomas, 170
Christ, 39-59
  And the church, 233, 236
  And the Holy Spirit, 88-100, 106
  Ascension, 54-56
  As King, 58
  As Redeemer, 188-89
  As Saviour, 161
  As Substitute, 183
  Baptism of, 46, 175
  Crucifixion of, 50, 98, 157, 192, 234
  Deity of, 45
  Dual Natures, 45
  Example to Believers, 222
  Humanity, 44-45
  Incarnation, 39, 192
  Kingdom of, 283
  Ministries of, 48
  Miracles, 49
  Preincarnation, 37
  Present ministry, 57
  Prophecies of, 37, 40

Resurrection, 53, 99, 234
Revelation of, 13
Second coming, 267, 279
Sinless nature, 47
Teaching of, 1, 49
Temptation of, 47, 97
Theophanies, 38
Titles of, 46
Virgin Birth, 39, 41
Christian Doctrine, 35
Christine Doctrines, 60
Christian ethics, 221-23
Christianity Today, 121, 147
Christian View of God and the World, 271
Christian Worker's Manual, 170, 180, 189
Chrysostom, 291, 292
Church, 67, 229-67
  And the Holy Spirit, 106, 234
  And the Millennium, 284
  Christ as Head of, 233
  Definition of, 230-31
  Discipline of, 246-47
  Finances of, 247-54
  Membership, 237
  Mission of, 261-66
  Officers, 243-46
  Ordinances, 254-61
  Organism, 235-37
  Organization of, 135-37
  Origin of, 100-1, 232-34
  Rapture of, 279
  Separation from world, 262, 264-65
  Titles of, 231-32
  Triumphant, 266-67
  Unity of, 238
  Use of *ekklesia*, 230-31
  Visible and Invisible, 239
  Worship of, 240-42
Church's One Foundation, 5
Churches, unity of, 238
Circumcision, 255
Clow, Professor, 288
Commentary on Matthew, 47
Confessions, 20
Conscience, 144
Cooper, Dr. David, 282
Corot, Jean Baptiste, 279
Cosmology, 21
Covenant with death and hell, 150-51
Covenants, 146-51
  Adamic, 147
  Abrahamic, 148
  Davidic, 149
  Mosaic, 148
  New, 150
  Palestinian, 149
Conversion, 176

Conviction, 91
Cowper, William, 80
Creation, 80, 140
Cruden, Alexander, 74, 235
Cumming, Dr. Elder, 87, 98
Cuthbert, Dr. James, 269

D

Dake, Finis, J., 132
Dale, Dr. R. W., 60, 61, 127
Davidson, Prof. A.G., 11, 24, 25, 26, 124, 147, 217
Davis, Dr. William Hersey, 44
Deacons, 245-46
Death, 268-71
  Eternal, 270
  Penalty for sin, 185
  Physical, 269-70
  Saint's, 7
  Spiritual, 270
Death of Christ, 51
Death of the Desert, 59
Deism, 19
Demons, 137-39
  Bound and Free, 137
  Nature of, 138
  Work of, 138
Demon-possession, 138
Denny, Dr. James, 51
Depravity of man, 145
Diogenes, 140
Discipline, 246-47
Dispensation of Grace, 164
Doctrine, Apostles, 1
  Definition of, 1, 3
  Study of, 2
Doddridge, 86
Dods, Dr. Marcus, 259
Downer, Dr., 64, 73
Dryden, John, 174
Dualism, 19
Duncan, Rabbi, 67

E

Eddy, Sherwood, 49, 293
Edersheim, Alfred, 176
Elders, 244
Election, 152
Ellerton, John, 272
Ellicott, Charles J., 62
Emblems of the Spirit, 82
Emerson, Ralph Waldo, 271
Eradication of old nature, 218
Erdman, Prof. Charles, 60

Eternal Security, 168, 223-25
  Scripture proofs, 224
Eternal Spirit, 99
Eternity, 27, 79
Ethics, 221-23
Evangelical Free Church Catechism, 235
Evangelism, 264
Evangelists, 244
Evolution, 140

F

Faith, 181, 193-99
  And Prayer, 196
  And Reason, 197
  Basis of, 195
  Elements of, 194
  Necessity of, 194
  Power of, 196
  Quality of, 197-99
  Source of, 195
  Work of, 196
Fausset, A. R., 8, 109, 231, 283
Fisher, 283
Fletcher, John, 169
Foreknowledge, 80, 152
Freedom, God's, 30
Fuller, Dr., 269

G

Gibbs, Albert, 177, 179, 180
Gibson, Dr. Munro, 12
Gifts, Spiritual, 246
God, 24-35
  Attributes, 27-35
  Existence of, 11, 12, 20, 24
  Goodness of, 30
  Infinity of, 25
  Justice of, 274-75
  Knowledge of, 12
  Nature of, 24
  Personality of, 25
  Revelation of, 24
  Sovereignty, 20, 28
  Spirit, 24
  Titles of, 25-26, 123
Goethe, Johann, 168
Gordon, Dr. A. J., 62
Gospel, 52
Grace, 163-168
  Attribute, 164
  Contrasted with Law, 164
  Dispensation of, 164
  Growth in, 168
  Recipients of, 167
  Riches of, 165-66

  Scope of, 167-68
  Source of, 164-65
Graham, Dr. Billy, 212
Great White Throne, 278
Great White Throne, 279
Grider, Professor J. Kenneth, 121, 124
Guide to the Gospels, 49

H

Hall, Robert, 288
Hamlet, 175
Handbook of Christian Truth, 179
Handbook of Christian Doctrines, 126
Harrison, Dr. Norman B., 108
Heaven, 285-90
  Description, 288-90
  Inhabitants of, 179
Heavens, 288
Hegel, Georg, 17
Heidelberg Catechism, 55
Hell, 290-294
Henry, Matthew, 66, 147, 174
Herbert, Edward, 19
His in the Life of Prayer, 108
History of the Christian Church, 231
History, reveals God, 13
Hodge, C. H., 256, 260
Holden, Dr. J. Stuart, 227
Holiness, 31, 80, 168, 266, 217-21
  See Sanctification
Holy Spirit
  And the church, 100, 106, 234
  Annointing of, 96, 108
  Attributes of, 79-80
  Baptism of, 106
  Blasphemy of, 111
  Conviction of, 91
  Deity of, 79
  Earnest of, 107
  Filling of, 101-4, 108
  Fruit of, 117-19
  Gifts of, 101, 114
  Grieving of, 110, 112
  In Creation, 65-68, 80
  Indwelling, 102-3, 107
  Inspiration, 80
  Insulting, 111
  New Testament teaching, 7, 87-88
  Old Testament teaching, 7, 64, 68, 72
  Pentecost, 94
  Personality of, 72-79
  Place in Trinity, 75, 81
  Quenching, 112
  Regeneration of, 80, 180-81
  Relates to Christ, 88-100
  Resisting, 111

Sealing of, 107
Symbols of, 82-87, 181
Tempting the, 112
Titles of, 77-78, 92-94
Virgin Birth, 95
Witness of, 182, 205
Work in the Believer, 165
Work in Resurrection, 81
Holy Spirit and Christian Doctrine, 60
Holy Spirit, The, 59
"Holy Trinity", 121
Hugo of St. Victor, 254
Huxley, Professor Thomas, 14, 16

I

Illumination, 4
Imitation of Christ, 92
Immensity, 27
Immersion, 259
Immortality, 271-73
    Conditional Theory of, 287
Immutability, 28
Imputation, 209
Ingersoll, Robert G., 17, 290
Ingram, Dr. Winnington, 126
Inspiration, 4, 7, 67
    Extent of, 8
    Mode of, 8
    Plenary theory, 9
    Verbal theory, 9-10
International Standard Bible Encyclopedia,
    49, 124, 293
Irenaeus, 122

J

Jerome, 245
Jowett, Dr., 73
Judgment
    Cross, 277
    Great White Throne, 278
    Of Angels, 278
    Of Jews, 278, 281-82
    Of Saints, 275
    Of the sinners, 275-76
    Of the Nations, 278
    Of the world, 278
    Self-judgment, 277
Judgments, 274-79
Judgment Seat of Christ, 277
jjulius Caesar, 141
Justice, 32, 274-75
Justification, 150, 208-9
    Results of, 211

K

Kelly, W., 42
Kenosis theory, 43-44
Keswick Convention, 238
Kingsley, Charles, 14
Kinsman-Redeemer, 188-89
Knowing the Scriptures, 6
Knox, John, 230
Kuyper, Abraham, 59

L

Lamb, Charles, 141
Lange, John P., 47
Langland, William, 167
Larkin, Clarence, 4
Latimer, Hugh, 206
Lee, Robert, 201
Lidgett, Dr. Scott, 15
Lightfoot, Bishop, 259
Lindsay, Professor, 259
Lindsell and Woodbridge, 179
Lodge, Sir Oliver, 287
Lord Avebury, 22
Lord Byron, 166, 174
Lord Kelvin, 16
Lord's Supper, 256-57, 260-61
Love, 117-21
Love, God's, 32
Love of the Trinity, 126
Lowry, Chrles W., 124
Luther, Martin, 5, 108, 205, 253, 259
Lyttleton, George, 169

M

Macartney, Dr. Clarence E., 36
MacGregor, C. H., 77, 78
Maclaren, Alexander, 168
Major Covenants of Scripture, 150
Man, 139-146
    Body of, 143
    Carnal, 113
    Conscience of, 23-24, 144
    Conscious of God, 23
    Creation of, 140, 142, 144
    Fall, 145
    Freedom of the will, 23
    Image of God, 142-43
    Natural, 113
    Nature of, 143
    Personality of, 144
    Soul, 22, 143
    Spirit of, 144
    Spiritual, 113-17
    Trichotomy, 143

Will of, 144
Manicheism, 20
Marsh, Dr. F. E., 77, 82, 226
Martyr, Justin, 143, 209, 243
Mary, Queen of Scots, 230
Materialism, 16
Matheson, Dr. George, 65, 66, 117
McIntyre, Dr. D. M., 5, 6
Meldau, Dr. F. J., 150
Mercy, 33
Meyer, Dr. F. B., 140, 145, 215
Millennium, 282-285
    And Christ, 283
    And the church, 284
    And Gentiles, 284
    And Jews, 284
    Effect upon creation, 284-85
    Subjects of, 285
Miller, H. S., 170, 176, 180, 189, 196
Milton, John, 7, 35, 139, 145, 292
Ministry, 243-46
Miracles, 49
Mission and Ministration of the Holy Spirit, 73
Monod, Theodore, 8
Monotheism, 18
Montgomery, James, 225
Moody, D. L., 82, 96
Moore, Hannah, 289
Moorehead, Professor E., 44
Morality, 222
Morgan, G. Campbell, 39, 61, 139
Moule, Dr. Handley, 13, 19, 64, 74, 75, 77,
    90, 231, 237, 245, 254, 255, 258, 260, 269
Muller, George, 226
Muller, Max, 272
Mullins, Professor E., 69
Murray, Andrew, 121, 249
Mystery and Ministry of Angels, 127, 137

N

Napoleon, 36
Nature, reveals God, 12
Nicene Creed, 123
Nicol, W. Robertson, 5
Notes on Psalms, 132
Noyes, Alfred, 193

O

Omnipotence, 28, 79, 196
Omnipresence, 29, 79
Omniscience, 29, 79, 152
Ontology, 23
Orr, James, 4, 39, 43, 45, 47, 49, 271, 293
Oxenham, John, 29

P

Paine, Tom, 290
Pantheism, 17
Parables, 49
Paraclete, The, 59
Paradise Lost, 145
Parker, Dr. Joseph, 59, 285
Pascal, Blaise, 94, 163
Passover, 255
Pastors, 244
Paterson, Dr., 258
Peace, 212-16
    Elements of, 215-16
    Results of, 215
    With God, 212-16
Peace with God, 212
Pearce-Higgins, Rev. John, 133
Pentecost, 94, 234
Perseverance of the saints, 223
Philopatris, 122
Pierson, Dr. A. T., 5, 6, 7, 8, 13, 14, 15, 40,
    63, 65, 246, 247
Pilgrim's Progress, 156, 229
Plato, 140
Plenary, Theory of Inspiration, 9
Pliny, 242, 243, 254
Pollock, 285
Polytheism, 18
Pope, Alexander, 29, 142, 169
Pope, W. P., 123
Post-Millennialism, 283
Prayer, 108, 110, 225-29, 242
    Christ and prayer, 227
    Examples of, 226-27
    Scriptural basis, 225-26
    Unanswered, 228-29
Predestination, 151-53
Pre-Millennialism, 283
Primitive Culture, 272
Progress of Doctrine, 6
Prophets, 244
Propitiation, 184, 191
Providence, 35
Psyche, definition of, 23
Purgatory, 287

Q

Quarles, Francis, 139

R

Ramsey, Archbishop, 133
Rapture, 279
Rationalism, 16
Reconciliation, 191-92, 212-14

In death of Christ, 191
Of all things, 192
Redemption, 186-90
  Accomplished by Christ, 188-89
  Results of, 189-90
  Tenses of, 190
  Terms used, 187-88
Redemption of the body, 190
Regeneration, 67, 80, 146, 176-83
  Agents of, 180-81
  And Conversion, 176-77
  Evidences of, 182
  Necessity of, 177-78
  Results of, 181-82
  Terms used, 178
Relapse, The,
Repentance, 169-76, 181, 193
  And Faith, 174
  Characteristics, 172-73
  Condition of salvation, 173
  God Repenting, 176
  Greek Forms, 171
  Necessity of, 169, 170
  Scope of, 174-75
  Source of, 173-74
Resurrection, 81, 273-74
Revelation, 3-7
  Biblical, 13
  Finality of, 10
  Progressive, 6
Ridley, Nicholas, 2
Righteousness, 207-12
  Attributes of God, 208-10
  Imputation of, 209
  Practical, 211, 221
  Received by faith, 210
Robertson, Dr. A. T., 293
Robinson, Henry Crabbe, 269
Rob Roy, 172
Rock versus Sand, 12
Rogers, Samuel, 269
Rutherford, Samuel, 290
Ryle, Bishop J. C., 236

S

Sacraments, 254
Salmond, Dr., 271
Salvation, 159-63
  Agent of, 160
  And Repentance, 173
  Assurance of, 204-7
  Decreed by God, 159
  Duration of, 161
  Price of, 160
  Results of, 157-59
  Saviour, 161

Tenses of, 161-62
  Universality of, 160
  Universal Theory of, 287
Sanctification, 217-21
  Evidences of, 220
  Methods of, 219-20
  Positional, 218
  Progressive, 218-19
  Work of Holy Spirit, 218
Sanday and Headlam, 259
Satan, 217-221
  Bound, 284
  Character of, 135-36
  History of, 135
  Origin, 133
  Personality of, 135
  Titles of, 135
  Work of, 136
Scofield, Dr. C. I,, 8, 10, 30, 40, 81, 108, 134,
    151, 152, 154, 165, 191, 203, 211, 225, 232,
    277
Scott, Walter, 152, 153, 172, 178, 192, 208,
    283
Scroggie, Dr. Graham, 11, 49, 106, 233, 267,
    293
Second Coming, 279-80
Seed Thoughts for Public Speakers, 6
Seneca, 141, 172
Shakespeare, William, 7, 35, 175
Sheldon, Charles, 92
Sin, 153-56
  Origin of, 154
  Remedy, 157-59
  Universality of, 178, 184
Slessor, Mary, 120
Smellie, Alexander, 194, 195, 215
Smith, Dr. Wilbur, 293
Soul, 22, 143-44
  Ontological Argument, 23
  Psychological Argument, 23
Sovereignty, 80
Spenser, Edmund, 164
Spinoza, B., 17
Spurgeon, Charles H., 183, 265
Spurr, Frederick C., 269
Stalker, Dr. James, 44
Stanley, Dean, 259
Steele, Dr. Daniel, 120
Stevenson, Robert Louis, 155
Stewart, William, 231
Strauss, 17
Strong, Dr. A. H., 139
Structure of Scripture, 77
Style of Scripture, The, 36
Substitution, 183-86
  Apostolic teaching of, 185-86
  Examples of, 184

Results of, 185
Sweet, Professor, 41
Syllabus for New Testament Study, 293
Systematic Theology (Strong's), 139

T

Taylor, J. Hudson, 10, 154, 226, 272
Teachers, 244
Teleological Argument, 22
Temptation, 136
Tennyson, Alfred, 141, 144
Tertullian of Carthage, 254, 259
Theology of the Old Testament, 11, 25
Theophanies, 38
Theophilus, Bishop of Antioch, 122
Through the Eternal Spirit, 87
Tidwell, Dr. J. B., 33
Time's Revenges, 286
Tirocinium Fori, 200
Tithing, 249
Torrey, Dr. R. A., 64, 73, 107, 118, 145, 193,
    205
Townsend, Dr. W. J., 35, 45, 126, 221, 244,
    274
Transubstantiation, 257
Trench, Archbishop, 230, 281
Tribulation, 278, 281-82
Trinity, 75, 121-27
Trinity in Christian Devotion, 124
Truth, 34

U

Unity, God's, 28
Universe, Cause, 21
    Order of, 21
Unpardonable Sin, 111

V

Vanbrugh, Sir John, 172
Virgin Birth, 95
Virgin Birth of Our Lord, 39
Vision Splendid, 29
Von Stolberg, 269

W

Ward, Professor Wayne E., 44
Warfield, Professor B., 59, 124, 125
Watson, R., 123
Watson, Thomas, 201, 217, 288, 289, 291
Watts, Isaac, 139, 251
Way, Arthur, 193
Webster, Daniel, 121, 146
Wesley, Charles, 85, 119
Wesley, John, 205, 223
Westminster Catechism, 201
Westminster Confession, 210, 211
Weymouth, Dr., 62, 118
What Jesus Really Taught, 36
What the Bible Teaches, 193
What Would Jesus Do?, 92
Whitefield, George, 223
Whitelaw, Dr. T., 14
Wilberforce, William, 289
Wisdom, God's, 29
Wordsworth, Bishop, 274
Wordsworth, William, 269
Worship, 241-42

Y

Young *(Analytical Concordance)*, 187

Z

Zoroastrianism, 19-20

BIBLICAL INDEX

Genesis
1:1 25
1:2 65
1:21,24,25 142
1:26 . . . . 65, 140
1:28-30 147
2:1 239
2:4,7,15,16 26
2:7 . . . . . 65, 143, 144
3:15 . . . . 38, 39
3:24 129
6:12 156
6:18 148
9:8-17 148
12:1-3 148
13:2 26
14:13 154
14:18 25
15 255
15:1-7 148
15:2 200
16:1-3 200
16:7-14 38
16:10 129
17 255
17:1 26
18:1 38
18:21 275
21:33 . . . . 26, 27
22:13 184
22:14 26
28:3 230
28:17 266
28:22 249
32:24-32 38
41:39 68
48:4 200
48:16 187

Exodus
2:10 200
3:2,6,14 38
3:14,15 25
4:10-12 9
6:6 187
8:19 87
8:23 187
12:13 213
15:11 . . . . 18, 25, 218
15:26 26
17:8-15 26
18:11 18
19:20 148

20:22,23 151
27:1 184
31:18 86
34:10,27 148
40:33 239

Leviticus
1:4 183
2:4,5 84
2:13 151
7:30 249
14:4 184
21:8 218
23:39 87
25:48 188
26:1-13 149
26:9 148
26:41 172

Numbers
18:19 151
23:7,9 278
24:2 69

Deuteronomy
2:7 275
4:15,16,19 24
5:2 148
5:9 119
7:8 188
7:11-25 148
8:1,19,20 148
9:10 86
10:16 255
10:17 18
18:15 281
21:8 187
28:29,30 149
30:1-10 149
30:6 255
32:4 32,34
32:5 102
32:8 . . . . 25, 284
32:20 197

Joshua
5:13-15 38

Judges
6:24 26
6:34 71
8:18 200
10:15,16 173

14:6,19 71
14:15-23 38

I Samuel
1:3 26
10:6,10 71
15:20 256
15:29 34
15:30 155
16:13 71
29:4 191

II Samuel
7:8-17 149
12:13 174
14:14 177

I Kings
8:47 170
8:56 34
14:26,27 217
21:27 172

I Chronicles
12:18 71
16:25 18

II Chronicles
6:18 27
7:11 239
13:5 151
24:20 71
28:10 275

Ezra
9:3 172
9:13 . . . . 33, 275

Nehemiah
1:10 188
9:20 77
13:1 230

Esther
2:7 200

Job
14:4 . . . . 67, 219
14:14 272
19:25 . . . . 17, 187
20:22 155
22:21 213
23:8,9 197

26:13 65
32:8 7
33:4 65
34:32 4
38:6 134
38:7 129
42:5 197

Psalms
5:12 211
6:6 172
8:3 87
9:10 .... 26, 28
9:17 156
14:1 14
19 .... 21, 66
19:1 12
19:7 3
19:7-11 24
23:1 26
23:5 260
25:5 162
27:1 161
27:4 241
32:3 156
33:5 139
34:19 211
34:22 187
35:3 162
36:6 276
48:1 159
49:7,8 188
50:12 28
51:3,4 ...... 175, 276
58:11 275
62:2 161
66:18 155
72:6 83
77:6 215
78:40 111
82:6,7 143
86:8 17
89:3,20-27 149
89:34 146
89:48 271
90:2 27
95:3 18
97:9 18
101:3 155
103:4 187
104:24 139
104:30 .... 65, 66
110:3 218
119:18 5
119:59,60 171
119:68 34
119:75 275
119:165 216

135:4 262
136:24 187
139:7-10 79
139:24 155
147:5 .... 24, 29
148:2,5 129
150:1 139

Proverbs
3:19 30
6:13 87
6:34 119
10:12 13
13:15 155
13:20 219
14:9 156
15:24 291
15:26 156
18:10 26
23:7 62
25:25 52

Ecclesiastes
3:11 15
3:14 224
5:1,2 266

Song of Solomon
8:6-8 32

Isaiah
1:6 156
1:16-18 174
1:18 161
2:4 278
3:10 211
4:4 83
9:6 106
10:1 276
11:2 106
12:2 .... 161, 206
14:12-14 135
25:8 272
26:3 216
28:15 155
28:17 .... 33, 275
32:17 211
34:11 43
40:25,26 25
44:3 83
45:15 24
45:22 194
46:11 240
48:18 216
49:24 189
53 186
53:6 156
54:9 148

54:13 216
54:14 221
55:3 194
57:21 ...... 206, 212
59:1,2 28
59:20 187
61:1,2 106
63:10 111
64:6 155
65:24 284
66:2,5 5

Jeremiah
1:4-10 69
4:3 169
10:12 30
15:21 187
17:9 155
23:6 26
31:18,19 172
32:17,18 28
33:20-25 148
33:21 149

Ezekiel
3:17-21 292
14:6 170
18:4 185
18:20 156
18:30 170
28:11-19 134
36:26 221
48:35 26

Daniel
4:27 173
4:35 16
5:5 87
9:27 281
11:36 281
12:3 209

Hosea
6:7 154
7:13 187
8:12 11
9:7 115
12:10 82
13.4 187
14:5 83

Joel
3:1,2 278

Amos
3:2 275
4:12 268

Jonah
3 169

Micah
6:8 221
7:18 221

Zephaniah
3:8 284

Haggai
2:8 249

Zechariah
1:8-13 38
6:13 283
12:10 . . . . . . 108, 278

Malachi
3:1 151
3:6 . . . . 25, 176

Matthew
1:1 39
1:16 42
1:18 94
1:21 159
2:11 42
2:13 42
3:6 46
3:15 176
3:16 119
4:1-11 47
4:11 130
5:13 83
5:24 191
6:6 227
6:14, 15 228
6:19-21 252
6:33 221
7:23 292
8:26 198
10:24 88
12:28 . . . . 86, 92
12:31 111
13:41, 42 278
14:31 198
15:9 1
16:12 1
16:18 . . . . . . 230, 233
18:17 230
19:28 178
21:21, 22 227
25:27 251
25:30 290
25:41 292
25:46 291
28:16-20 81

28:19 125
28:20 262

Mark
4:40 198
7:7 1
9:1 237
12:36, 37 209
12:41 251
13:32 281
16:15 263

Luke
1 41
1:13 41
1:27-33 149
1:35 41
1:35-37 125
1:68, 69 162
2:14 213
2:40-51 44
3:23 41
4:18 92
6:13 232
7:9 198
8:5 84
8:31 291
8:45, 46 257
9:28-36 54
11:9 228
11:13 92
11:20 86
14:14 273
14:29, 30 239
18:9-14 228
18:13 . . . . . . 172, 175
18:25 252
19:9 162
19:10 158
22:20 261
22:32 176
22:43 130
24:21 50
24:45 5
24:47 169

John
1:12 . . . . 194, 200
1:13 . . . . 179, 180
1:14, 18 . . . . . . 36, 45
1:29 157
2:16 265
3:4 180
3:5, 6, 8 . . 92, 178, 180
3:7 237
3:8 82
3:16 32
4:14 83

4:24 24
5:28, 29 273
7:17 8
7:37-39 . . 83, 89, 104
8:44 189
12:26 286
12:27, 28 50
13:13 209
13:16 251
14:1-3 . . . . . . 286, 288
14:6 285
14:7-9 14
14:10 49
14:16, 17 . . 7, 92, 119
14:22 215
14:26 . . . . . 77, 89, 92
15:3 219
15:13 32
15:19 232
15:26, 27 . . . . . 77, 89
16:7 55
16:9 91
16:10 91
16:11 91
16:12, 15 5
16:13 . . . 62, 89, 227
17:4 240
17:12 223
17:17-19 217
19:30 239
20:22 89
21:24, 25 36

Acts
1:8 264
2:3 83
2:4, 33 103
2:38 . . . . 107, 238
2:41 242
2:42 1
3:19 238
4:12 . . . . 159, 238
5:1-11 . . . . . 246, 252
5:3, 4 112
5:9 112
6:2 246
6:6 227
7:51 111
8:9 253
8:15 . . . . 104, 227
9:15 232
9:31 101
11:24 198
12:5 227
13:3 227
14:23 245
16:6,7 . . . . 77, 94
17:18 217

17:28 21
17:29, 30 174
17:31 276
19:2 112
19:32 ......230, 231
20:7 261
20:21 173
20:28 ......67, 234
20:36 227
28:31 207

Romans
1:4 74
1:11 114
1:16 162
1:19, 20 ......21, 139
1:25 15
1:31 151
2:12-15 13
2:14, 15 21
3:23 154
4:10, 11 255
4:15 275
4:25 ....184, 210
5:1 86
5:5 119
5:10 ......162, 191
5:12 ......145, 153
6:4 259
6:12 218
8:1 ....201, 282, 292
8:6 117
8:8 179
8:9 ......94, 102, 107
8:14 ....77, 86
8:16 ....86, 181
8:26 ..77, 86, 108, 111
8:27 76
8:28 ....19, 152
8:29 152
8:34 110
9:4 ....150, 200
10:8, 9 ......53, 162
10:17 194
11:22 290
11:33 275
12:5 246
12:8 250
12:19 220
13:11 162
14:1 198
14:8, 10 277
14:12 177
15:1-3 250
15:27 114
15:30 76
16:5, 23 231

I Corinthians
1:20 30
1:27, 28 232
1:30 210
2:2 51
2:9-14 10
2:10 ....77, 79
2:11, 14 5
2:13 ....3, 9
2:14 113
2:15 116
3:1 ....113, 116
3:9 233
5:11 246
6:2, 3 278
6:11 221
6:17 102
6:19, 20 160
10:3, 4 114
10:16, 17 261
11:25, 26 260
11:29 261
11:32 277
12:11 76
12:13 .....107, 234
12:21 246
13:9-12 3
14:10 246
14:19, 28, 35 ...231
14:37 116
15:12-19 268
15:14, 17 ...53, 198
15:44 115
15:45 143
16:1 247
16:22 267

II Corinthians
1:22 ....85, 107
3:6 150
3:8 61
5:6-8 182
5:17 181
5:18, 19 191
5:20 213
6:2 162
6:6 118
6:10 206
8:5 247
8:9 247
9:5 249
9:7-9 249
11:2 119
11:4 61
13:5 206
13:14 ....120, 126

Galatians
1:7-9 62
1:13 233
3 148
3:10 185
3:13 .....185, 187
3:16 84
3:17-24 148
3:22 184
3:26 ......181, 202
3:27, 28 100
4:1-5 200
4:4 ....39, 187
4:6 ....77, 201
4:7 201
4:19 94
5:1 168
5:22 ......118, 206
6:1 117
6:15 181
6:16 215

Ephesians
1:3 ....114, 126
1:4 221
1:4-6 233
1:5 152
1:6, 7 ..163, 166, 182
1:13, 14 85
1:22, 23 236
2:5-8 166
2:10 ......166, 181
2:12 182
2:13, 14 206
2:18 12
3:5 244
3:16 103
3:19 103
4:3, 4 100
4:3-6 ......106, 238
4:11 244
4:19 204
4:24 ......178, 181
4:29 166
4:30 ....80, 112, 118
5:15-17 220
5:16 187
5:18 108
5:19 115
5:19, 20 242
6:11 220
6:12 115
6:24 166

Philippians
1:6 182
1:19 94
1:23 182

2:5 182
2:7 44
3:5, 6 240
3:10 53
4:4 242
4:7 . . . . .215, 216

Colossians
1:6 129
1:8 118
1:12 289
1:15-18 134
1:18 236
1:20 . . . . . . .191, 213
2:2 206
2:5 198
2:6 193
2:19 236
3:1 220
3:4 203
3:10 . . . . . .146, 182
4:12 227

I Thessalonians
1:4, 5 . . . . . .151, 206
4:7 221
4:16, 17 . . . .182, 266,
    268, 273, 279, 286
5:19 112
5:23 227

II Thessalonians
1:5 276
1:9 159
2:4 79

I Timothy
1:5 198
1:9 154
1:15 159
2:1-7 152
2:5 57
3:5 266
3:6 244
3:8-13 246
3:15 263
4:1 77
4:16 266
5:22 266
6:3-5 265

II Timothy
1:5 198
1:12 206
2:19 107
3:5 217
3:16 . . . . .3, 7, 24, 39
4:2 264

Titus
1:5-7 244
2:14 262
3:4, 5 . .163, 178, 180,
    258
3:10 247

Philemon
17, 18 209

Hebrews
1:1 36
1:9 . . . . .33, 275
1:12 28
2:3 159
2:9-15 189
2:14-18 189
2:17 191
3:7 111
4:9 283
4:15 204
6:11 206
6:13-20 150
7:24 110
7:25 . . . . . .161, 162
7:26 158
9:14 . . . . .79, 111
9:27 177
9:28 280
10:5-10 184
10:12-28 150
10:22 . . . . .110, 206
10:29 111
10:37 34
11:1 193
11:3 15
11:6 174
11:10 268
11:35 273
12:14 221
12:23 234
12:24 213
13:5 206
13:16 249

James
1:17 32
2:5 198
2:17 198
2:23 209
4:4 220
5:17, 18 226

I Peter
1:1 210
1:2 218
1:4 288
1:16 220

1:18 . . . . . . .187, 188
2:5 115
2:9 262
2:21 88
3:4 . . . . .218, 220
4:17 277
5:3 245
5:12 244

II Peter
1:1 199
1:4 182
1:20 5
1:21 . . . . .4, 9
3:11 203

I John
1:9 277
2:23 207
3:1, 2 . . . . . .163, 206
3:4 154
3:7 210
3:9 . . . . .84, 182
3:14 . . . . . .182, 206
3:17 207
4:13 86
4:16 32
5:2 207
5:4, 18 . .182, 193, 206
5:6 221
5:7, 8 81
5:12 181
5:13 204
5:14 207

Jude
3 161
6 137
19 . . . . .113, 179
20 . . . . .109, 199

Revelation
1:3, 4 85
1:18 . . . . .56, 181
2:4, 5 175
2:7 . . . . .77, 111
2:16 175
2:21, 22 . . . .175, 276
3:3 175
3:16-22 237
3:19 175
4:5 105
5:6 105
5:9 188
12:11 182
14:3, 4 188
17:1-6 238
17:8 281

18:3, 11-20 238   20:11-15 273   22:18, 19 10
19:6 80   21:8. ....270, 290   21:21 289
19:15 292   22:20, 21 280
20:2-7 282   22:11 271